HOLY BIBLE

Berean Literal Bible

New Testament

Contents

Matthew.............. 4	Ephesians 232	Hebrews 259
Mark.................. 45	Philippians 237	James................271
Luke 71	Colossians..........241	1 Peter 275
John 115	1 Thessalonians..244	2 Peter 279
Acts 146	2 Thessalonians..247	1 John 282
Romans 186	1 Timothy 249	2 John 286
1 Corinthians 202	2 Timothy 253	3 John 287
2 Corinthians 217	Titus..................256	Jude..................287
Galatians............227	Philemon............258	Revelation..........289

Preface

*Now the Bereans were more noble-minded than the Thessalonians,
for they received the message with great eagerness
and examined the Scriptures every day
to see if these teachings were true.*
− Acts 17:11

The Berean Literal Bible (BLB) is a word for word translation that takes the reader to the core of the Greek and Hebrew meanings:

1. Parts of speech match as closely as possible in translation from Greek to English.
2. Tense, mood, and voice of verbs are maintained as closely as possible.
3. All tags from the interlinear are maintained so that the word for word translation can be connected back to each element of the original text.
4. Gender is translated to be consistent with the Greek sources.
5. Pronouns that represent Deity are capitalized for clearer study of difficult passages.
6. Sentence structure is maintained so that, in general, the flow of the longer Greek sentences is not interrupted in the translation to the literal version.

The Berean Bible Translation Committee has employed an open process where translation tables are freely available and all comments are welcomed and considered. Please see the Berean Bible website for a full description of the translation committee and process.

We pray that this text will enable readers to connect with God's Word to study it, memorize it, share it, and proclaim it. We are inspired by the model of the early Christian church:

*After this letter has been read among you,
make sure that it is also read in the church of the Laodiceans,
and that you in turn read the letter from Laodicea.*
− Colossians 4:16

The Scriptures belonged to the churches. Just as Paul encouraged the churches to pass on his letters, the Berean Bible is intended to be offered freely in websites, apps, software, and various text and audio formats.

The Holy Bible, Berean Standard Bible (BSB) and Berean Literal Bible (BLB) is produced in cooperation with Bible Hub, Discovery Bible, unfoldingWord, Bible Aquifer, OpenBible.com, and the Berean Bible Translation Committee.

This text of God's Word has been dedicated to the public domain. Free resources and databases are available at BereanBible.com.

Feedback about the text should be made at BereanBible.com. Feedback about this printing may be provided at Innovativeeggz.com.

Licensing of the text is not necessary, but it is available if you wish to receive updates as new materials are released. See any of these Berean Bible websites for further information:

www.Berean.Bible	Berean Bible Homepage
www.InterlinearBible.com	Berean Interlinear Bible (BIB)
www.LiteralBible.com	Berean Literal Bible (BLB)
www.BereanBible.com	Berean Standard Bible (BSB)
www.MajorityBible.com	Majority Standard Bible (MSB)
www.ReadersBible.com	Reader's Bible
www.EmphasizedBible.com	Emphasized Bible
www.AnnotatedBible.com	Annotated Bible
www.AudioBible.org	Audio Bible

~ ※ ~

Greek, Hebrew, and Aramaic Sources and Abbreviations

NA	Nestle Aland, Novum Testamentum Graece
SBL	Society of Biblical Literature, Greek New Testament
ECM	Editio Critica Maior, Novum Testamentum Graecum
NE	Eberhard Nestle Novum Testamentum Graece
WH	Westcott and Hort, New Testament in the Original Greek
BYZ	The New Testament in the Original Greek: Byzantine Textform
GOC	Greek Orthodox Church, New Testament
TR	Scrivener's Textus Receptus; Stephanus Textus Receptus
DSS	Dead Sea Scrolls
MT	Hebrew Masoretic Text: Westminster Leningrad Codex
	Hebrew Masoretic Text: Biblia Hebraica Stuttgartensia
LXX	Greek OT Septuagint: Rahlfs-Hanhart Septuaginta
	Greek OT Septuagint: Swete's Septuagint
SP	Samaritan Pentateuch

Matthew

Matthew 1
The Genealogy of Jesus
(Ruth 4:18-22; Luke 3:23-38)

¹ *The* book of *the* genealogy of Jesus Christ, son of David, son of Abraham:
²Abraham begat Isaac,
and Isaac begat Jacob,
and Jacob begat Judah and his brothers.
³And Judah begat Perez and Zerah out of Tamar,
and Perez begat Hezron,
and Hezron begat Ram.
⁴And Ram begat Amminadab,
and Amminadab begat Nahshon,
and Nahshon begat Salmon.
⁵And Salmon begat Boaz out of Rahab,
and Boaz begat Obed out of Ruth,
and Obed begat Jesse,
⁶and Jesse begat David the king.

Next:
David begat Solomon, out of the *wife* of Uriah,
⁷and Solomon begat Rehoboam,
and Rehoboam begat Abijah,
and Abijah begat Asa.
⁸And Asa begat Jehoshaphat,
and Jehoshaphat begat Joram,
and Joram begat Uzziah.
⁹And Uzziah begat Jotham,
and Jotham begat Ahaz,
and Ahaz begat Hezekiah.
¹⁰And Hezekiah begat Manasseh,
and Manasseh begat Amos,
and Amos begat Josiah,
¹¹and Josiah begat Jechoniah and his brothers
at *the time* of the carrying away to Babylon.
¹²And after the carrying away to Babylon:
Jechoniah begat Shealtiel,
and Shealtiel begat Zerubbabel,
¹³and Zerubbabel begat Abiud,
and Abiud begat Eliakim,
and Eliakim begat Azor.
¹⁴And Azor begat Zadok,
and Zadok begat Achim,
and Achim begat Eliud.
¹⁵And Eliud begat Eleazar,
and Eleazar begat Matthan,
and Matthan begat Jacob,
¹⁶And Jacob begat Joseph, the husband of Mary,
of whom was born Jesus, the *One* being called Christ.

¹⁷So all the generations from Abraham to David *were* fourteen generations, and from David until the carrying away to Babylon fourteen generations, and from the carrying away to Babylon to the Christ fourteen generations.

The Birth of Jesus
(Isaiah 7:10-16; Micah 5:1-6; Luke 2:1-7)

¹⁸Now the birth of Jesus Christ came about in this way: His mother Mary, having been pledged to Joseph, before their coming together, was found holding in womb through *the* Holy Spirit. ¹⁹Then Joseph her husband, being righteous and not willing to shame her publicly, resolved to divorce her quietly.

²⁰But on his having pondered these things, behold, an angel of *the* Lord appeared to him in a dream, saying, "Joseph, son of David, you should not be afraid to receive Mary *as* your wife, for that having been conceived in her is from *the* Holy Spirit. ²¹And she will bring forth a son, and you shall call His name Jesus, for He will save His people from their sins."

²²And all this has come to pass, so that it may be fulfilled that having been spoken by the Lord through the prophet, saying,
²³"Behold, the virgin will hold in womb,
and will bring forth a son,
and they will call His name Immanuel"[a]
which is, being translated, "God with us."

²⁴And Joseph, having been awoken from sleep, did as the angel of *the* Lord had commanded him and received his wife.

²⁵But he did not know her until she had brought forth a Son, and he called His name Jesus.

a 23 Isaiah 7:14

Matthew 2
The Pilgrimage of the Magi

¹Now Jesus having been born in Bethlehem of Judea in *the* days of Herod the king, behold, Magi from *the* east arrived in Jerusalem, ²saying, "Where is the *One* having been born King of the Jews? For we saw His star in the east and have come to worship Him."
³And King Herod having heard *this*, was disturbed, and all Jerusalem with him. ⁴And having assembled all the chief priests and scribes of the people, he was inquiring of them where the Christ was to be born.
⁵And they said to him, "In Bethlehem of Judea, for thus has it been written through the prophet:

⁶'And you, Bethlehem, land of Judah,
    are by no means least among the rulers of Judah,
for out of you will come forth *One* leading,
    who will shepherd My people Israel.'*ᵃ*"

⁷Then Herod, having called the Magi secretly, inquired of them the exact time of the star appearing. ⁸And having sent them to Bethlehem, he said, "Having gone, search carefully for the Child; and when You shall have found *Him*, bring word back to me, so that I also having come, may worship Him."
⁹And having heard the king, they departed. And behold, the star they had seen in the east went before them until, having arrived, it stood over the place where the Child was. ¹⁰And having seen the star, they rejoiced *with* exceedingly great joy. ¹¹And having come into the house, they found the Child with His mother Mary, and having fallen down, they worshiped Him. And having opened their treasures, they offered to Him gifts, gold and frankincense and myrrh.
¹²And having been divinely warned in a dream not to return to Herod, they withdrew into their own country by another route.

The Flight to Egypt
(Hosea 11:1-7)

¹³And of them having withdrawn, behold, an angel of *the* Lord appears to Joseph in a dream saying, "Having arisen, take the Child and His mother, and flee into Egypt, and remain there until I should tell you, for Herod is about to seek the Child to destroy Him."
¹⁴And having arisen, he took the Child and His mother by night and withdrew into Egypt, ¹⁵and there he remained until the death of Herod, so that it might be fulfilled what had been spoken by *the* Lord through the prophet, saying, "Out of Egypt I have called my Son."*ᵇ*

The Slaughter of Infants
(Jeremiah 31:1-30)

¹⁶Then Herod, having seen that he had been outwitted by the Magi, was intensely enraged. And having sent forth, he put to death all the boys in Bethlehem and in all its vicinity from two years old and under, according to the time he had ascertained from the Magi. ¹⁷Then was fulfilled what was spoken through the prophet Jeremiah, saying:

¹⁸"A voice was heard in Ramah,
    weeping and great mourning,
Rachel weeping *for* her children;
    and she would not be comforted,
because they are not."*ᶜ*

The Return to Nazareth
(Isaiah 61:1-11; Matthew 13:53-58; Mark 6:1-6; Luke 2:39-40; Luke 4:16-30)

¹⁹But of Herod having died, behold, an angel of *the* Lord appears in a dream to Joseph in Egypt, ²⁰saying, "Having arisen, take the Child and His mother and go into *the* land of Israel; for those seeking the life of the Child have died."

²¹And having arisen, he took the Child and His mother and came into *the* land of Israel. ²²And having heard that Archelaus reigns over Judea in place of his father Herod, he was afraid to go there. And having been divinely warned in a dream, he withdrew into the district of Galilee. ²³And having come, he dwelt in a city being called Nazareth, so that it should be fulfilled that having been spoken through the prophets, that "He will be called a Nazarene."

a 6 Micah 5:2,4
b 15 Hosea 11:1
c 18 Jeremiah 31:15

Matthew 3
The Mission of John the Baptist
(Isaiah 40:1-5; Mark 1:1-8; Luke 3:1-20; John 1:19-28)

¹Now in those days John the Baptist comes, preaching in the wilderness of Judea, ²and saying, "Repent, for the kingdom of the heavens has drawn near." ³For this is the *one* having been spoken of through the prophet Isaiah, saying,

"*A* voice of one crying in the wilderness:

'Prepare the way of *the* Lord; make straight His paths.'"ᵃ

⁴And John himself had his garment of camel's hair, and a leather belt around his waist, and his food was locusts and wild honey. ⁵At that time were going out to him Jerusalem, and all Judea, and all the region around the Jordan, ⁶and confessing their sins, were being baptized by him in the Jordan River.

⁷But having seen many of the Pharisees and Sadducees coming to his baptism, he said to them, "Brood of vipers, who warned you to flee from the coming wrath? ⁸Therefore produce fruit worthy of repentance. ⁹And do not presume to say within yourselves, 'We have Abraham *as* father.' For I say to you that out of these stones God is able to raise up children unto Abraham. ¹⁰Already now the ax is applied to the root of the trees. Therefore every tree not producing good fruit is cut down and thrown into *the* fire. ¹¹I indeed baptize you withᵇ water unto repentance, but after me is coming He *who* is mightier than I, of whom I am not worthy to carry the sandals. He will baptize you with *the* Holy Spirit and with fire, ¹²whose winnowing fork *is* in His hand, and He will clear His threshing floor and will gather His wheat into the barn; but He will burn up the chaff with unquenchable fire."

The Baptism of Jesus
(Mark 1:9-11; Luke 3:21-22; John 1:29-34)

¹³Then Jesus comes from Galilee to the Jordan, unto John, to be baptized by him. ¹⁴But John was hindering Him, saying, "I have need to be baptized by You, and do You come to me?"

¹⁵But Jesus answering, said unto him, "Permit *it* presently; for thus it is fitting to us to fulfill all righteousness." Then he permits Him.

¹⁶And immediately, having been baptized, Jesus went up from the water; and behold, the heavens were openedᶜ and he saw the Spirit of God descending as a dove, and alighting upon Him. ¹⁷And behold, a voice out of the heavens, saying, "This is my Son, the beloved, in whom I was well pleased."

a 3 Isaiah 40:3
b 11 Or *in water ... in the Holy Spirit*
c 16 NA, BYZ, and TR include *to Him*

Matthew 4
The Temptation of Jesus
(Mark 1:12-13; Luke 4:1-13)

¹Then Jesus was led up into the wilderness by the Spirit to be tempted by the devil. ²And having fasted forty days and forty nights, afterward He was hungry.

³And the *one* tempting, having come to Him, said "If You are Son of God, speak, that these stones may become loaves of bread."

⁴But answering He said, "It has been written:

'The man shall live not by bread alone,
> but by every word coming out of *the* mouth of God.'*ᵃ*"

⁵Then the devil takes Him to the holy city and sets Him upon the pinnacle of the temple, ⁶and says to him, "If You are Son of God, throw Yourself down. For it has been written:
> 'He will give orders to His angels concerning You,
>> and will they bear You up in *their* hands,
> lest ever You strike Your foot against a stone.'*ᵇ*"

⁷Jesus said to him, "Again it has been written: 'You shall not test *the* Lord your God.'*ᶜ*"

⁸Again the devil takes Him to a mountain exceedingly high and shows to Him all the kingdoms of the world and their glory. ⁹And he says to Him, "All these things I will give to You, if falling down, You will worship me."

¹⁰Then Jesus says to him, "Get you away, Satan! For it has been written: 'You shall worship *the* Lord your God, and Him alone shall you serve.'*ᵈ*"

¹¹Then the devil leaves Him, and behold, angels came and were ministering to Him.

Jesus Begins His Ministry
(Isaiah 9:1-7; Mark 1:14-15; Luke 4:14-15)

¹²And having heard that John had been arrested, He withdrew into Galilee. ¹³And having left Nazareth, having come, he dwelt at Capernaum, on the sea-side in *the* region of Zebulun and Naphtali, ¹⁴that it might be fulfilled that having been spoken through the prophet Isaiah, saying:
> ¹⁵"Land of Zebulun and land of Naphtali,
>> way of *the* sea, beyond the Jordan,
> Galilee of the Gentiles—
> ¹⁶the people sitting in darkness have seen a great light,
>> and to those sitting in *the* land and shadow of death,
> a light has dawned on them."*ᵉ*

¹⁷From that time Jesus began to proclaim and to say, "Repent, for the kingdom of the heavens has drawn near!"

The First Disciples
(Matthew 13:47-52; Mark 1:16-20; Luke 5:1-11; John 1:35-42)

¹⁸Now walking beside the Sea of Galilee, He saw two brothers, Simon called Peter, and his brother Andrew, casting a net into the sea, for they were fishermen. ¹⁹And He says to them, "Come follow after Me, and I will make you fishers of men." ²⁰And immediately having left the nets, they followed Him.

²¹And having gone on from there, He saw two other brothers, James the *son* of Zebedee and his brother John, in the boat with their father Zebedee, mending their nets. And He called them, ²²and immediately having left the boat and their father they followed Him.

Jesus Heals the Multitudes
(Luke 6:17-19)

²³And He was going throughout all Galilee, teaching in their synagogues, and proclaiming the gospel of the kingdom, and healing every disease and every sickness among the people. ²⁴And the news of Him went out into all Syria. And they brought to Him all the sick having various diseases and oppressing pains, and being possessed by demons, and having seizures, and paralytics—and He healed them.

²⁵And there followed Him great crowds from Galilee, and *the* Decapolis,*ᶠ* and Jerusalem, and Judea, and beyond the Jordan.

a 4 Deuteronomy 8:3
b 6 Psalm 91:11,12
c 7 Deuteronomy 6:16
d 10 Deuteronomy 6:13
e 15-16 Isaiah 9:1,2
f 25 That is, the Ten Cities

Matthew 5
The Sermon on the Mount

¹And having seen the crowds, He went up on the mountain. And He having sat down, His disciples came to Him, ²and

opening His mouth, He was teaching them, saying:

The Beatitudes
(Psalm 1:1-6; Luke 6:20-23)

³"Blessed *are* the poor in the spirit,
   for theirs is the kingdom of the heavens.
⁴Blessed *are* those mourning,
   for they will be comforted.
⁵Blessed *are* the meek,
   for they will inherit the earth.
⁶Blessed *are* those hungering and thirsting for righteousness,
   for they will be filled.
⁷Blessed *are* the merciful,
   for they will receive mercy.
⁸Blessed *are* the pure in heart,
   for they will see God.
⁹Blessed *are* the peacemakers,
   for they will be called sons of God.
¹⁰Blessed *are* those having been persecuted on account of righteousness,
   for theirs is the kingdom of the heavens.

¹¹Blessed are you when they shall insult you and shall persecute *you*, and lying shall say all kinds of evil against you on account of Me. ¹²Rejoice and exult, because great *is* your reward in the heavens; for thus they persecuted the prophets before you.

Salt and Light
(Philippians 2:12-18)

¹³You are the salt of the earth, but if the salt becomes tasteless, with what will it be salted. For nothing is it potent any longer except, having been cast out, to be trampled upon by men.
¹⁴You are the light of the world. A city lying on a hill is unable to be hidden.
¹⁵Nor do they light a lamp and put it under a basket, but upon the lampstand, and it gives light to all those in the house.
¹⁶Thus let your light shine before men, so that they may see your good works and they should glorify your Father in the heavens.

The Fulfillment of the Law

¹⁷Do not think that I have come to abolish the law or the Prophets. I have not come to abolish, but to fulfill. ¹⁸For truly I say to you, until heaven and earth shall pass away, not even one iota, nor one stroke of a letter, shall pass away from the law, until everything should happen.
¹⁹Whoever then shall break one of the least of these commandments and shall teach others the same, he will be called least in the kingdom of the heavens; but whoever shall keep and shall teach *them*, he will be called great in the kingdom of the heavens. ²⁰For I say to you that unless your righteousness shall abound above *that* of the scribes and Pharisees, you shall never enter into the kingdom of the heavens.

Anger and Reconciliation
(Luke 12:57-59)

²¹You have heard that it was said to the ancients, 'You shall not murder' and 'Whoever shall murder will be liable to the judgment.'ᵃ ²²But I say to you that everyone being angry with his brotherᵇ will be liable to the judgment, and whoever shall say to his brother 'Raca,'ᶜ will be liable to the Sanhedrin. But whoever shall say, 'Fool!' will be liable to the Gehenna of fire.
²³Therefore, if you shall offer your gift at the altar, and there shall remember that your brother has something against you, ²⁴leave your gift there before the altar and first go away, be reconciled to your brother; and then having come, offer your gift.
²⁵Be agreeing quickly with your accuser while you are on the way with him, lest ever the accuser deliver you to the judge, and the judge to the officer, and you will be cast into prison. ²⁶Truly I say to you, you shall not come out from there until you should pay the last kodranten!ᵈ

Adultery
(Leviticus 18:1-30)

²⁷You have heard that it was said, 'You shall not commit adultery.'*ᵉ* ²⁸But I say to you that everyone looking upon a woman in order to lust after her already has committed adultery with her in his heart. ²⁹And if your right eye causes you to stumble, pluck it out and cast *it* from you. For it is better for you that one of your members should perish and not *that* your whole body should be cast into Gehenna. ³⁰And if your right hand causes you to stumble, cut it off and cast *it* from you, for it is better for you that one of your members should perish and not *that* your whole body should depart into Gehenna.

Divorce
(Deuteronomy 24:1-5; Luke 16:18-18)

³¹It was also said, 'Whoever shall divorce his wife, let him give her a letter of divorce.'*ᶠ* ³²But I say to you that everyone divorcing his wife, except on account of sexual immorality, causes her to commit adultery. And whoever shall marry her who has been divorced commits adultery.

Oaths and Vows
(Numbers 30:1-16)

³³Again, you have heard that it was said to the ancients, 'You shall not swear falsely, but you shall keep your oaths to the Lord.' ³⁴But I say to you not to swear at all: neither by heaven, because it is *the* throne of God; ³⁵nor by the earth, because it is *the* footstool of His feet; nor by Jerusalem, because it is *the* city of the great King. ³⁶Neither shall you swear by your head, because you are not able to make one hair white or black. ³⁷But let your statement 'Yes' be 'Yes,' *and* 'No,' 'No.' Anything more than these comes from evil.*ᵍ*

Love Your Enemies
(Leviticus 24:17-23; Luke 6:27-36)

³⁸You have heard that it was said, 'Eye for eye and tooth for tooth.'*ʰ* ³⁹But I tell you not to resist the evil *person*. Instead, whoever shall strike you on your right cheek, turn to him the other also. ⁴⁰And to the one willing to sue you and to take your tunic, yield to him the cloak as well. ⁴¹And whoever shall compel you to go one mile, go with him two. ⁴²Give to the *one* asking of you, and you shall not turn away from the *one* desiring to borrow from you.

⁴³You have heard that it was said, 'You shall love your neighbor and hate your enemy.'*ⁱ* ⁴⁴But I say to you, love your enemies and pray for those persecuting you,*ʲ* ⁴⁵so that you may be sons of your Father in *the* heavens. For He makes His sun rise on evil and good, and He sends rain on righteous and unrighteous. ⁴⁶For if you love those loving you, what reward do you have? Do not even the tax collectors do the same? ⁴⁷And if you greet only your brothers, what extraordinary are you doing? Do not even the Gentiles do the same? ⁴⁸You shall be perfect, therefore, as your Heavenly Father is perfect.

a 21 Exodus 20:13; Deuteronomy 5:17
b 22 BYZ and TR include *without cause*
c 22 An Aramaic expression of contempt
d 26 A roman copper coin worth about 1/64 of a denarius
e 27 Exodus 20:14; Deuteronomy 5:18
f 31 Deuteronomy 24:1
g 37 Or *from evil*
h 38 Exodus 21:24; Leviticus 24:20; Deuteronomy 19:21
i 43 Leviticus 19:18
j 44 BYZ and TR *bless those who curse you, do good to those who hate you, and pray for those who despitefully accuse you, and persecute you*

Matthew 6
Giving to the Needy
(Deuteronomy 15:7-11)

¹And beware not to do your righteousness before men in order to be seen by them. Otherwise you have no reward in the presence of your Father in the heavens.

²Therefore when you perform acts of charity, do not sound a trumpet before you as the hypocrites do in the synagogues and in the streets, so that they may have glory from men. Truly I say to you, they have their recompense. ³But you, doing acts of charity, do not let your left *hand* know what your right hand is doing, ⁴so that your giving may be in

secret. And your Father, the *One* seeing in secret, will reward you.

The Lord's Prayer
(Luke 11:1-4)

⁵And when you pray, you shall not be like the hypocrites, for they love to pray standing in the synagogues and on the corners of the streets so that they might be seen by men. Truly I say to you, they have their recompense. ⁶But you when you pray, enter into your inner room, and having shut your door, pray to your Father, the *One* in secret. And your Father, the *One* seeing in secret, will reward you.
⁷And praying, do not use vain repetitions like the pagans, for they think that in their many words they will be heard. ⁸Therefore do not be like to them, for your Father knows of what things you have need before your asking Him.
⁹Therefore pray you like this:

    'Our Father in the heavens,
        hallowed be Your name!
    ¹⁰Your kingdom come.
        Your will be done
          as in heaven, *so* also upon earth.
    ¹¹Our daily bread, grant us today.
    ¹²And forgive us our debts,
        as we also have forgiven our debtors.
    ¹³And lead us not into temptation,
        but deliver us from evil.'ᵃ

¹⁴For if you forgive men their trespasses, your Heavenly Father will also forgive you. ¹⁵But if you do not forgive men their trespasses, neither will your Father forgive your trespasses.

Proper Fasting

¹⁶And whenever you fast, do not be downcast in countenance like the hypocrites, for they disfigure their faces so that they might appear to men *as* fasting. Truly I say to you, they have their recompense. ¹⁷But you fasting, anoint your head and wash your face, ¹⁸so that you might not appear to men *as* fasting, but to your Father, the *One* in secret. And your Father, the *One* seeing in secret, will reward you.

Treasures in Heaven
(Matthew 13:44-46)

¹⁹Do not store up for yourselves treasures upon the earth, where moth and rustᵇ destroy, and where thieves break in and steal. ²⁰But store up for yourselves treasures in heaven, where neither moth nor rust destroy, and where thieves do not break in nor steal. ²¹For where your treasure is, there your heart will be also.

The Lamp of the Body
(Luke 11:33-36)

²²The eye is the lamp of the body. So if your eye is clear, your whole body will be full of light. ²³But if your eye is evil, your whole body will be full of darkness. If then the light within you is darkness, how great *is* that darkness!
²⁴No one is able to serve two masters, for either he will hate the one and he will love the other, or he will be devoted to *the* one and he will despise the other. You are not able to serve God and mammon.

Do Not Worry
(Luke 12:22-34)

²⁵Because of this I say to you, do not worry about your life, what you should eat or what you should drink; nor your body, what you should put on. Is not life more than food, and the body *more* than clothing? ²⁶Look at the birds of the air. They do not sow nor do they reap, nor do they gather into barns, and your Heavenly Father feeds them. Are you not much more valuable than they? ²⁷And who of you by worrying is able to add one cubit to his stature?ᶜ
²⁸And why do you worry about clothing? Consider carefully how the lilies of the field grow: They do not labor nor do they spin. ²⁹Yet I say to you that not even Solomon in all his glory was adorned like one of these. ³⁰But if God thus clothes the grass of the field, existing today and tomorrow being thrown into the furnace,

will *He* not much more *clothe* you, O *you* of little faith? ³¹Therefore do not be anxious, saying, 'What shall we eat?' Or 'What shall we drink?' Or 'What shall we wear?' ³²For the Gentiles seek after all these things. For your Heavenly Father knows that you have need of them all. ³³But seek first the kingdom of God and His righteousness, and all these things will be added unto you.
³⁴Therefore do not worry about tomorrow, for tomorrow will worry about itself. Sufficient to the day *is* its own trouble.

a 13 Or *from the evil one*; BYZ and TR include *For yours is the kingdom and the power and the glory, to the ages. Amen*
b 19 Or *worm*; also in verse 20
c 27 A cubit was about 18 inches or 45 centimeters.

Matthew 7
Do Not Judge
(Luke 6:37-42; Romans 14:1-12)

¹Do not judge, lest you should be judged. ²For with that verdict you pronounce, you will be judged; and with that measure you measure, it will be measured to you.
³And why do you look at the splinter in your brother's eye, but not notice *the* beam in your *own* eye? ⁴Or how shall you say to your brother, 'Permit that I might cast out the splinter from your eye,' and behold, the beam *is* in your eye? ⁵Hypocrite! First cast out the beam from your eye, and then you will see clearly to cast out the splinter from the eye of your brother.
⁶Do not give that which *is* holy to the dogs, nor cast your pearls before the pigs, lest they shall trample upon them with their feet, and having turned, tear you to pieces.

Ask, Seek, Knock
(Luke 11:5-13)

⁷Ask and it will be given to you; seek and you will find; knock and it will be opened unto you. ⁸For everyone asking receives; and the *one* seeking finds; and to the *one* knocking, it will be opened.

⁹Or which man is among you who, *if* his son will ask for bread, will give him a stone? ¹⁰Or also, *if* he will ask for a fish, will give him a serpent? ¹¹Therefore, if you, being evil, know how to give good gifts to your children, how much more will your Father in the heavens give good things to those asking Him!
¹²All things therefore, as many as you might desire that men should do to you, so also you do to them, for this is the law and the prophets.

The Narrow Gate
(Luke 13:22-30)

¹³Enter through the narrow gate for wide *is* the gate and broad the way leading to destruction, and many are those entering through it. ¹⁴For small *is* the gate and narrow the way leading to life, and few are those finding it.

A Tree and its Fruit
(Matthew 12:33-37; Luke 6:43-45)

¹⁵Beware of the false prophets, who come to you in sheep's clothing, but inwardly are ravenous wolves. ¹⁶By their fruits you will recognize them. Are grapes gathered from thornbushes, or figs from thistles? ¹⁷So every good tree bears good fruits, but *the* rotten tree bears bad fruits. ¹⁸*A* good tree is not able to bear bad fruits, nor a bad tree to bear good fruits. ¹⁹Every tree not bearing good fruit is cut down and is thrown into fire. ²⁰Then surely by their fruits you will recognize them.
²¹Not everyone saying to Me, 'Lord, Lord,' will enter into the kingdom of the heavens, but the *one* doing the will of My Father in the heavens. ²²Many will say to Me in that day, 'Lord, Lord, did we not prophesy in Your name, and *in* Your name cast out demons and *in* your name perform many miracles?' ²³And then I will declare unto them, 'I never knew you; depart you from Me, those working lawlessness.'

The House on the Rock
(Luke 6:46-49)

²⁴Therefore everyone who hears these words of Mine and does them will be like a wise man who built his house upon the rock. ²⁵And the rain came down, and the torrents came, and the winds blew and beat upon that house; and it did not fall, for its foundation had been lain upon the rock. ²⁶And everyone hearing these words of Mine and not acting on them, he will be likened to a foolish man who built his house upon the sand. ²⁷And the rain came down, and the torrents came, and the winds blew and beat upon that house; and it fell—and great was its collapse!"

The Authority of Jesus
²⁸And it came to pass, when Jesus had finished these words, the crowds were astonished at His teaching. ²⁹for He was teaching them as *one* having authority, and not as their scribes.

Matthew 8
The Leper's Prayer
(Leviticus 14:1-32; Mark 1:40-45; Luke 5:12-16)

¹And He having come down from the mountain, great crowds followed Him. ²And behold a leper[a] having come, was worshipping Him, saying, "Lord, if You are willing, You are able to cleanse me." ³And having stretched out the hand, He touched him saying, "I am willing; be you cleansed!" And immediately his leprosy was cleansed. ⁴And Jesus says to him, "See that you tell no one. But go, show yourself to the priest and offer the gift that Moses commanded, for a testimony to them."

The Faith of the Centurion
(Luke 7:1-10; John 4:43-54)

⁵And He having entered into Capernaum, a centurion came to Him, imploring Him, ⁶and saying, "Lord, my servant is lying in the house paralyzed, grievously tormented." ⁷And He says to him, "I having come, will heal him." ⁸But the centurion answering, said, "Lord, I am not worthy that You should come under my roof; but just say the word, and my servant will be healed. ⁹For I also am a man under authority, having soldiers under me. And I say to this *one*, 'Go,' and he goes; and to another, 'Come,' and he comes; and to my servant, 'Do this,' and he does *it*." ¹⁰And Jesus having heard, marveled and said to those following, "Truly I say to you, no one in Israel *with* faith so great have I found. ¹¹And I say to you that many will come from east and west, and will recline with Abraham and Isaac and Jacob in the kingdom of the heavens. ¹²But the sons of the kingdom will be cast out into the outer darkness; there will be weeping and gnashing of the teeth." ¹³And Jesus said to the centurion, "Go! As you have believed, be it to you." And his servant was healed in that very hour.

Jesus Heals at Peter's House
(Mark 1:29-34; Luke 4:38-41)

¹⁴And Jesus having come to the house of Peter, He saw his mother-in-law lying sick and fevering. ¹⁵And He touched her hand and the fever left her; and she arose and was ministering unto them. ¹⁶And evening having come, they brought to Him many being possessed with demons, and He cast out the spirits with a word and He healed all those being sick, ¹⁷so that it might be fulfilled that having been spoken through the prophet Isaiah, saying,

"He Himself took our infirmities,
and bore our diseases."[b]

The Cost of Discipleship
(Luke 9:57-62; Luke 14:25-33; John 6:60-65)

¹⁸And Jesus, having seen a great crowd around Him, gave orders to depart to the other side. ¹⁹And one scribe, having approached Him, said "Teacher, I will follow You wherever that You should go." ²⁰And Jesus says to him, "Foxes have holes, and the birds of the air nests, but *the* Son of Man has nowhere He might lay the head."

²¹And another of His disciples said to Him, "Lord, allow me first to go and to bury my father."
²²But Jesus said to him, "Follow Me, and leave the dead to bury their own dead."

Jesus Calms the Storm
(Mark 4:35-41; Luke 8:22-25)

²³And He having entered into the boat, His disciples followed Him. ²⁴And behold, a great storm arose in the sea so that the boat was being swamped by the waves; but He Himself was sleeping. ²⁵And having approached, they awoke Him, saying, "Lord, save us, we are perishing!"
²⁶And He says to them, "O *you* of little faith, Why are you afraid?" Then having arisen, He rebuked the winds and the sea, and there was a great calm.
²⁷And *the* men marveled, saying, "What kind *of man* is this, that even the winds and the sea obey Him?"

The Demons and the Pigs
(Mark 5:1-20; Luke 8:26-39)

²⁸And He having come to the other side, to the region of the Gadarenes,ᶜ two being possessed by demons met Him, coming forth out of the tombs, extremely violent, so that no one was able to pass by that way.
²⁹And behold, they cried out saying, "What to us and to you Son of God? Have You come here to torment us before *the* time?"
³⁰Now there was far off from them a herd of many pigs feeding. ³¹And *the* demons were begging Him, saying, "If You cast us out, send us away into the herd of pigs."
³²And He said to them, "Go!" And having gone out, they went away into the pigs, and behold, all the herd rushed down the steep bank into the sea and perished in the waters.
³³And those feeding *them* fled, and having gone away into the city, they related everything, including the *matter* of those being possessed by demons.
³⁴And behold, all the city went out to meet Jesus. And having seen Him, they begged *Him* that He would depart from their region.

a 2 Leprosy was a term for several skin diseases. See Leviticus 13.
b 17 Isaiah 53:4
c 28 BYZ and TR *Gergesenes*

Matthew 9
Jesus Heals a Paralytic
(Mark 2:1-12; Luke 5:17-26)

¹And having entered into a boat, He passed over and came to the own city.
²And behold, they were bringing to Him a paralytic lying on a bed. And Jesus, having seen their faith, said to the paralytic, "Take courage, son; your sins have been forgiven."
³And behold, some of the scribes said to themselves, "This one blasphemes!"
⁴And Jesus, having known their thoughts, said, "Why do you think evil in your hearts? ⁵For which is easier, to say, 'Your sins are forgiven,' or to say, 'Arise and walk?' ⁶But so that you may know that the Son of Man has authority on earth to forgive sins..." Then He says to the paralytic, "Having arisen, take up your mat and go to your house." ⁷And having arisen, he went away to his house.
⁸And the crowds having seen, marveled and glorified God, the *One* having given such authority to men.

The Calling of Matthew
(Mark 2:13-17; Luke 5:27-32)

⁹And Jesus passing on from there saw a man called Matthew sitting at the tax booth. And He says to him, "Follow Me." And having arisen, he followed Him.
¹⁰And it came to pass, of Him reclining in the house, that behold, many tax collectors and sinners having come, were reclining with Jesus and His disciples.
¹¹And having seen *it*, the Pharisees said to His disciples, "Why does your Teacher eat with the tax collectors and sinners?"
¹²And having heard, He said, "Not those being strong have need of a physician, but those being sick. ¹³But having gone, learn what is, 'I desire mercy and not

sacrifice.'[a] For I came not to call *the* righteous, but sinners."

Questions about Fasting
(Mark 2:18-20; Luke 5:33-35)

[14] Then the disciples of John come to Him saying, "Why do we and the Pharisees often fast, but Your disciples do not fast?" [15] And Jesus said to them, "Can the sons of the bridechamber mourn as long as the bridegroom is with them? But days will come when the bridegroom shall have been taken away from them, and then they will fast.

The Patches and the Wineskins
(Mark 2:21-22; Luke 5:36-39)

[16] But no one puts a patch of unshrunk cloth on old clothing, for the filling up of it tears away from the garment, and a worse tear emerges.
[17] Nor do they pour new wine into old wineskins. Otherwise the wineskins are burst, and the wine is poured out, and the wineskins are destroyed. But they pour new wine into new wineskins, and both are preserved."

The Healing Touch of Jesus
(Mark 5:21-43; Luke 8:40-56)

[18] Of Him speaking these things to them, behold, a certain ruler having come, was kneeling down to Him, saying, "My daughter presently has died; but having come, lay Your hand upon her, and she will live."
[19] And having arisen, Jesus followed him, also His disciples. [20] And behold a woman having had a flux of blood twelve years, having come up behind *Him*, touched the fringe of His garment. [21] For she was saying within herself, "If only I shall touch His garment, I will be healed."
[22] And Jesus, having turned and having seen her said, "Take courage, daughter. Your faith has cured you." And the woman was cured from that very hour.
[23] And Jesus having come into the ruler's house and having seen the flute players and the crowd making a commotion, [24] He says, "Go away, for the girl is not dead, but sleeps." And they began to laugh at Him.
[25] And when the crowd had been put outside, having entered, He took hold of her hand, and the girl arose. [26] And this report went out into all that land.

Jesus Heals the Blind and Mute
(Isaiah 35:1-10; Mark 7:31-37)

[27] And Jesus passing on from there, two blind *men* followed Him, crying out and saying, "Have mercy on us, Son of David." [28] And having come into the house, the blind *men* came to Him, and Jesus says to them, "Do you believe that I am able to do this?"
They say to him, "Yes, Lord."
[29] Then He touched their eyes, saying, "According to your faith be it to you."
[30] And their eyes were opened. And Jesus strictly instructed them, saying, "See that no one knows!" [31] But having gone out, they made Him known in all that land.
[32] And *as* they were going out, behold, they brought to Him a mute man, possessed by a demon. [33] And the demon having been cast out, the mute *man* spoke. And the crowds marveled, saying, "Never thus was it seen in Israel."
[34] But the Pharisees were saying, "By the prince of the demons He casts out demons."

The Lord of the Harvest

[35] And Jesus was going throughout all the cities and the villages, teaching in their synagogues, and proclaiming the gospel of the kingdom, and healing every disease and every sickness. [36] And having seen the crowds, He was moved with compassion for them, because they were wearied and cast away, as sheep not having a shepherd.
[37] Then He says to His disciples, "The harvest indeed *is* plentiful, but the workmen *are* few. [38] Beseech the Lord of the harvest, therefore, that He might send out workmen into His harvest."

a 13 Hosea 6:6

Matthew 10
The Twelve Apostles
(Mark 3:13-19; Luke 6:12-16)

¹And having summoned His twelve disciples, He gave to them authority over unclean spirits, so as to cast them out and to heal every disease and every sickness. ²And these are the names of the twelve apostles: first Simon called Peter, and his brother Andrew; and James the *son* of Zebedee, and his brother John; ³Philip and Bartholomew; Thomas and Matthew the tax collector; James the *son* of Alphaeus, and Thaddaeus; ⁴Simon the Zealot, and Judas Iscariot, the *one* also having betrayed Him.

The Ministry of the Twelve
(Mark 6:7-13; Luke 9:1-6)

⁵These twelve, Jesus sent forth, having instructed them, saying: "Do not go into *the* way of the Gentiles and do not enter into any city of *the* Samaritans. ⁶But go rather to those being the lost sheep of *the* house of Israel. ⁷And going on, proclaim, saying, 'The kingdom of the heavens has drawn near!' ⁸Heal *the* ailing, raise *the* dead, cleanse *the* lepers,ᵃ cast out demons! Freely you received; freely give. ⁹Take along neither gold nor silver nor copper in your belts, ¹⁰nor provision-bag for *the* way, nor two tunics, nor sandals, nor a staff; for the workman *is* worthy of his provisions.

¹¹And into whatever city or village you enter, inquire who is worthy in it. Remain there until you go forth. ¹²And entering into the house, greet it. ¹³And if indeed the house is worthy, let your peace come upon it; but if it is not worthy, let your peace return to you. ¹⁴And whoever will not receive you nor will hear your words, shake off the dust of your feet going forth out of *that* house or that city! ¹⁵Truly I say to you, on *the* day of judgment, it will be more tolerable for *the* land of Sodom and of Gomorrah than for that city.

Sheep among Wolves
(2 Timothy 1:6-12)

¹⁶Behold, I send you forth as sheep in *the* midst of wolves; therefore be shrewd as serpents and innocent as doves. ¹⁷But beware of men; for they will deliver you into *the* courts and they will flog you in their synagogues. ¹⁸And you will be brought also before governors and kings on account of Me, as a testimony to them and to the Gentiles. ¹⁹And when they deliver you up, do not be anxious how or what you should speak; for in that hour you will be given what you should say, ²⁰for you are not those speaking, but the Spirit of your Father speaking through you.

²¹And brother will deliver up brother to death, and father, child; and children will rise up against parents and will put them to death. ²²And you will be hated by all on account of My name; but the *one* having endured to *the* end, he will be saved.

²³And whenever they persecute you in one city, flee to the next. For truly I say to you, you shall not have completed the cities of Israel until the Son of Man comes.

²⁴A disciple is not above the teacher, nor a servant above his master. ²⁵*It is* sufficient for the disciple that he become like his teacher, and the servant like his master. If the master of the house they called Beelzebul, how much more those of his household!

Fear God Alone
(Luke 12:4-7)

²⁶Therefore you should not fear them! For nothing is concealed that will not be revealed, or hidden that will not be known. ²⁷What I tell you in the darkness, speak in the light; and what you hear in the ear, proclaim upon the housetops! ²⁸And you should not be afraid of those killing the body but not being able to kill the soul. Indeed rather you should fear the *One* being able to destroy both soul and body in Gehenna.

29Are not two sparrows sold for an assarion?^b And not one of them will fall to the ground apart from your Father. 30And even the hairs of your head are all numbered. 31Therefore you should not fear; you are worth more than many sparrows.

Confessing Christ
(Luke 12:8-12)

32Therefore everyone who will confess in Me before men, I also will confess in him before My Father in the heavens. 33And whoever shall deny Me before men, I also will deny him before My Father in the heavens.

The Sword of the Gospel
(Luke 12:49-53)

34Do not think that I came to bring peace to the earth; I came not to bring peace, but a sword. 35For I came to set at variance

'A man against his father,
    and a daughter against her mother,
    and a daughter-in-law against her mother-in-law,
36and *the* enemies of the man *are* his own household.'^c

Take up Your Cross
(Matthew 16:24-28; Mark 8:34-38; Luke 9:23-27)

37The *one* loving father or mother above Me is not worthy of Me, and the *one* loving son or daughter above Me is not worthy of Me. 38And he who does not take his cross and follow after Me is not worthy of Me. 39The *one* having found his life will lose it, and the *one* having lost his life on account of Me will find it.

The Reward of Service
(2 Kings 4:8-17)

40The *One* receiving you receives Me, and the *one* receiving Me receives the *One* having sent Me. 41The *one* receiving a prophet in *the* name of a prophet will receive *the* reward of a prophet, and the *one* receiving a righteous *man* in *the* name of a righteous *man* will receive the reward of a righteous *man*. 42And whoever shall give to drink to one of these little ones only a cup of cold *water* in *the* name of a disciple, truly I say to you, he shall certainly not lose his reward."

a 8 Leprosy was a term for several skin diseases. See Leviticus 13.
b 29 A Roman copper coin worth about 1/16 of a denarius
c 35-36 Micah 7:6

Matthew 11
John's Inquiry
(Luke 7:18-23)

1And it came to pass when Jesus had finished commanding His twelve disciples, He departed from there to teach and to preach in their cities.
2And John, having heard in prison the works of the Christ, having sent two of his disciples, 3said to Him, "Are You the coming *One*, or are we to look for another?"
4And Jesus answering, said to them, "Having gone, relate to John what you hear and see: 5*The* blind receive sight, and *the* lame walk, *the* lepers^a are cleansed, and *the* deaf hear, and *the* dead are raised, and *the* poor are gospelized. 6And blessed is he who shall not fall away in Me."

Jesus Testifies about John
(Luke 1:5-25; Luke 7:24-35; Luke 16:14-17)

7And as these were going away, Jesus began to speak to the crowds concerning John: "What did you go out into the wilderness to see? A reed shaken by *the* wind? 8But what did you go out to see? A man having been dressed in delicate *clothing*? Behold, those wearing delicate *clothing* are in kings' houses. 9But what did you go out to see? A prophet? Yes, I say to you, and *one* more excellent than a prophet. 10For this is *he* about whom it has been written:

'Behold, I send My messenger before Your face,
    who will prepare Your way before You.'^b

11Truly I say to you, among *those* born of women there has not risen one greater than John the Baptist. Yet *the* least in the kingdom of the heavens is greater than he! ¹²And from the days of John the Baptist until now, the kingdom of the heavens is taken by violence[c] and *the* violent seize it. ¹³For all the prophets and the law prophesied until John. ¹⁴And if you are willing to receive *it*, he is Elijah, the one being about to come.

¹⁵The *one* having ears,[d] let him hear!

¹⁶But to what will I compare this generation? It is like little children sitting in the markets and calling out to others, ¹⁷saying:

> 'We piped for you,
>> and you did not dance;
> we sang a dirge
>> and you did not wail.'

¹⁸For John came neither eating nor drinking, and they say, 'He has a demon!' ¹⁹The Son of Man came eating and drinking, and they say, 'Behold a man, a glutton and a drunkard, a friend of tax collectors and of sinners!' But wisdom is justified by her deeds."

Woe to the Unrepentant
(Luke 10:13-16)

²⁰Then He began to denounce the cities in which most of His miracles had taken place, because they did not repent. ²¹"Woe to you Chorazin! Woe to you Bethsaida! For if the miracles having taken place in you had taken place in Tyre and Sidon, then they would have repented long ago in sackcloth and ashes. ²²But I say to you, in *the* day of judgment it will be more tolerable for Tyre and Sidon than for you. ²³And you, Capernaum, will not be exalted to heaven, *but* will be brought down to Hades! For if the miracles having taken place in you had taken place in Sodom, it would have remained until this day. ²⁴But I say to you that in day of judgment it will be more tolerable for *the* land of Sodom than for you."

Rest for the Weary
(Luke 10:21-24)

²⁵At that time, Jesus answering said, "I fully consent to You, Father, Lord of the heaven and the earth, that You did hide these things from *the* wise and learned, and did reveal them to little children. ²⁶Yes, Father, for this was well-pleasing before You. ²⁷All things have been delivered to Me by My Father. And no one knows the Son, except the Father; nor does anyone know the Father, except the Son, and to whom the Son might choose to reveal *Him*. ²⁸Come to Me, all those toiling and being burdened, and I will give you rest. ²⁹Take My yoke upon you and learn from Me, for I am gentle and humble *in* heart, and you will find rest *for* your souls. ³⁰For My yoke *is* easy and My burden is light."

a 5 Leprosy was a term for several skin diseases. See Leviticus 13.
b 10 Malachi 3:1
c 12 Or *has been forcefully advancing*
d 15 BYZ and TR *ears to hear*

Matthew 12
The Lord of the Sabbath
(1 Samuel 21:1-9; Mark 2:23-28; Luke 6:1-5)

¹At that time Jesus went through the grainfields on the Sabbaths, and His disciples were hungry, and they began to pluck *the* heads of grain and to eat *them*. ²And the Pharisees, having seen, said to Him, "Behold, Your disciples are doing what it is not lawful to do on Sabbath." ³And He said to them, "Have you not read what David did when he was hungry, and those with him— ⁴how he entered into the house of God, and they ate the loaves of the presentation, which it was not lawful for him nor for those with him to eat, but only for the priests? ⁵Or have you not read in the law that on the Sabbath the priests in the temple profane the Sabbath, and are guiltless? ⁶But I say to you that a greater than the temple is here. ⁷But if you had known what this is, 'I desire mercy and not sacrifice,'[a] then you would not have condemned the guiltless.

⁸For the Son of Man is Lord of the Sabbath."

Jesus Heals on the Sabbath
(Mark 3:1-6; Luke 6:6-11)

⁹And having departed from there, He went into their synagogue. ¹⁰And behold, a man having a withered hand, and they asked Him saying, "Is it lawful to heal on the Sabbaths?"—so that they might accuse Him.

¹¹And He said to them, "What man will there be among you, who will have one sheep, and if it falls into a pit on the Sabbaths, will not take hold of it and will raise *it* up? ¹²How much more valuable therefore *is* a man than a sheep! Therefore it is lawful to do good on the Sabbaths."

¹³Then He says to *the* man, "Stretch out your hand." And he stretched *it* out, and it was restored, as sound as the other. ¹⁴And the Pharisees having gone out, held a counsel against Him, how they might destroy Him.

God's Chosen Servant
(Isaiah 42:1-9)

¹⁵And Jesus having known, withdrew from there. And great multitudes followed Him, and He healed them all, ¹⁶and He warned them that they should not make Him known— ¹⁷so that it might be fulfilled that having been spoken by the prophet Isaiah, saying:

¹⁸"Behold My servant,
   whom I have chosen,
My beloved,
   in whom My soul has found delight.
I will put My Spirit upon Him,
   and He will proclaim justice to the Gentiles.
¹⁹He will not quarrel nor will he cry out;
   nor will anyone hear His voice in the streets.
²⁰A bruised reed He will not break,
   and a smoldering wick He will not quench,
until He leads justice to victory.
²¹And in His name *the* Gentiles will hope."ᵇ

A House Divided
(Mark 3:20-27; Luke 11:14-23)

²²Then was brought to Him *one* possessed by a demon, blind and mute, and He healed him, in order for the mute *man* to speak and to see. ²³And all the crowds were amazed, and were saying, "Could this be the Son of David?"

²⁴And *the* Pharisees having heard, said, "This *man* casts out the demons only by Beelzebul, *the* prince of the demons."

²⁵And having known their thoughts, He said to them, "Every kingdom having been divided against itself is brought to desolation, and every city or house having been divided against itself will not stand. ²⁶And if Satan casts out Satan, he is divided against himself. How then will his kingdom stand?

²⁷And if I cast out demons by Beelzebul, by whom do your sons cast them out? On account of this, they will be your judges. ²⁸But if I cast out demons by *the* Spirit of God, then the kingdom of God has come upon you.

²⁹Or how is anyone able to enter into the house of the strong *man*, and to plunder his goods, unless first he binds the strong *man*? And then he will plunder his house. ³⁰The *one* not being with Me is against Me, and the *one* not gathering with Me scatters.

The Unpardonable Sin
(Mark 3:28-30)

³¹Because of this I say to you, every sin and blasphemy will be forgiven men; but blasphemy against *the* Spirit will not be forgiven. ³²And if anyone speaks a word against the Son of Man, it will be forgiven him; but if anyone speaks against the Holy Spirit, it will not be forgiven him, neither in this age nor in the coming *one*.

Good and Bad Fruit
(Matthew 7:15-23; Luke 6:43-45)

³³Either make the tree good and its fruit good, or make the tree bad and its fruit bad. For the tree is known by the fruit.

34Offspring of vipers, how are you able to speak good things, being evil? For out of the abundance of the heart, the mouth speaks. 35The good man out of his good treasure puts forth good things, and the evil man out of his evil treasure puts forth evil things. 36And I say to you that every careless word that they will speak, men will give an account of it in day of judgment. 37For by your words you will be justified, and by your words you will be condemned."

The Sign of Jonah
(Luke 11:29-32)

38Then some of the scribes and Pharisees answered him, saying "Teacher, we wish to see a sign from You."
39And answering He said to them, "An evil and adulterous generation seeks for a sign, and no sign will be given to it, except the sign of Jonah the prophet. 40For just as Jonah was in the belly of the great fish three days and three nights, so the Son of Man will be in the heart of the earth three days and three nights.
41The men of Nineveh will stand up in the judgment with this generation and will condemn it. For they repented at the preaching of Jonah, and behold, a greater than Jonah *is* here. 42The queen of *the* south will rise up in the judgment with this the generation and will condemn it. For she came from the ends of the earth to hear the wisdom of Solomon, and behold, a greater than Solomon is here.

An Unclean Spirit Returns
(Luke 11:24-26)

43Now when the unclean spirit is gone out from the man, it passes through waterless places seeking rest, and does not find *it*. 44Then it says, 'I will return to my house from where I came out.' And having come, it finds *it* being unoccupied, and swept, and put in order. 45Then it goes and takes with itself seven other spirits more evil than itself; and having entered in, they dwell there, and the last of that the man becomes worse than the first. So also will it be unto this evil generation."

Jesus' Mother and Brothers
(Mark 3:31-35; Luke 8:19-21)

46Now while He was speaking to the crowds, behold, His mother and brothers were standing outside, seeking to speak to Him.c 47Then someone said to Him, "Behold, Your mother and Your brothers are standing outside, seeking to speak to You."
48And answering, He said to the *one* telling Him, "Who is My mother, and who are My brothers?" 49And having stretched out His hand to His disciples, He said, "Behold, My mother and My brothers. 50For whoever shall do the will of My Father who *is* in *the* heavens, he is My brother and sister and mother."

a 7 Hosea 6:6
b 18-21 Isaiah 42:1-4
c 46 WH and some manuscripts do not include verse 47

Matthew 13
The Parable of the Sower
(Mark 4:1-9; Luke 8:4-15)

1In that *same* day, Jesus, having gone forth *from* the house, was sitting by the sea. 2And great crowds were gathered together to Him, so that He having entered into a boat, sat down, and all the crowd stood on the shore.
3And He spoke to them many things in parables, saying, "Behold, the *one* sowing went out to sow. 4And in his sowing, indeed some fell along the road, and the birds having come, devoured them.
5And other fell upon the rocky places where it did not have much soil. And it sprang up immediately, through having no depth of soil. 6And *the* sun having risen, they were scorched, and through not having root, were dried up.
7And other fell upon the thorns, and the thorns grew up and choked them.
8And other fell upon the good soil and were yielding fruit—indeed some a hundredfold, and some sixty, and some thirty.
9The *one* having ears,a let him hear!"

The Purpose of Jesus' Parables
(Mark 4:10-12)

10 And the disciples having approached, said to Him, "Why do You speak to them in parables?"

11 And answering He said to them, "Because it has been granted to you to know the mysteries of the kingdom of the heavens, but to them it has not been granted. **12** For whoever has, to him will be given, and he will be in abundance. And whoever *does* not have, even what he has will be taken away from him. **13** Because of this I speak to them in parables:

'Because seeing they do not see,
 and hearing they do not hear,
  nor do they understand.'

14 And in them is fulfilled the prophecy of Isaiah, saying:

'In hearing you will hear and never understand;
 and in seeing you will see and never perceive.
15 For the heart of this people has grown dull,
 and they barely hear with the ears,
 and they have closed their eyes,
lest ever they should see with the eyes,
 and they should hear with the ears,
 and they should understand with the heart,
and should turn,
 and I will heal them.'[b]

16 But blessed *are* your eyes because they see, and your ears because they hear. **17** For truly I say to you that many prophets and righteous *men* longed to see what you see, and did not see; and to hear what you hear, and did not hear.

The Parable of the Sower Explained
(Mark 4:13-20)

18 You, therefore, hear the parable of the *one* having sown: **19** Everyone hearing the word of the kingdom and not understanding, the evil one comes and snatches away that having been sown in his heart. This is the *one* having been sown on the path.

20 And the *one* having been sown upon the rocky places, this is the *one* hearing the word and immediately receiving it with joy. **21** And he has in himself no root, but is temporary. And having come tribulation or persecution on account of the word, immediately he falls away.

22 And the *one* having been sown among the thorns, this is the *one* hearing the word, but the care of this present age and the deceit of riches choke the word, and it becomes unfruitful.

23 But the *one* having been sown on the good soil, this is the *one* hearing the word and understanding, who indeed brings forth fruit and produces—indeed, some a hundredfold, and some sixty, and some thirty."

The Parable of the Weeds
(Ezekiel 17:1-10)

24 He put before them another parable, saying, "The kingdom of the heavens has become like a man having sown good seed in his field. **25** And while the men are sleeping, his enemy came and sowed weeds in *the* midst of the wheat, and went away. **26** And when the plants sprouted and produced fruit, then the weeds also appeared.

27 And the servants, having approached the master of the house, said to him, 'Sir, did you not sow good seed in your field? How then does it have weeds?'

28 And he said to them, 'An enemy did this.'

And *the* servants said to him, 'Then do you desire *that* having gone forth, we should gather them?'

29 And he said, 'No, lest gathering the weeds, you would uproot the wheat with them. **30** Allow both to grow together until the harvest; and in the time of the harvest I will say to the harvesters, "First gather the weeds, and bind them into bundles in order to burn them; then gather together *the* wheat into my barn.""'"

The Parable of the Mustard Seed
(Mark 4:30-34; Luke 13:18-19)

31He put before them another parable, saying: "The kingdom of the heavens is like a grain of mustard *seed*, which a man having taken, sowed in his field, **32**which indeed is smallest of all the seeds; but when it is grown, it is greater than the garden plants, and becomes a tree, so that the birds of the air come and encamp in its branches."

The Parable of the Leaven
(Judges 20:18-23; 2 Samuel 2:12-32; 2 Chronicles 13:4-19; Luke 13:20-21)

33He spoke to them another parable: "The kingdom of the heavens is like leaven, which a woman having taken, hid in three measures of flour until all of it was leavened."

I will Open My Mouth in Parables
(Psalm 78:1-72)

34Jesus spoke all these things to the crowds in parables, and He was not speaking to them without a parable, **35**so that it might be fulfilled that having been spoken by the prophet, saying:

"I will open My mouth in parables;
I will utter things hidden from *the* foundation *of the* world."[c]

The Parable of the Weeds Explained
(Zephaniah 1:1-6)

36Then having dismissed the crowds, He went into the house. And His disciples came to Him, saying, "Explain to us the parable of the weeds of the field."

37And answering He said, "The *One* sowing the good seed is the Son of Man; **38**and *the* field is the world; and *the* good seed, these are the sons of the kingdom; and *the* weeds are the sons of the evil *one*; **39**and the enemy having sown them is the devil; and the harvest is *the* consummation of the age; and *the* harvesters are angels.

40Therefore, as the weeds are gathered and consumed in fire, so will it be in the consummation of the age. **41**The Son of Man will send forth His angels, and they will gather out of His kingdom all the stumbling blocks and those practicing lawlessness, **42**and they will cast them into the furnace of fire, *where* there will be weeping and gnashing of teeth. **43**Then the righteous will shine forth as the sun in the kingdom of their Father. The *one* having ears,[d] let him hear!

The Parables of the Treasure and Pearl
(Matthew 6:19-21)

44The kingdom of the heavens is like treasure having been hidden in the field, which a man having found, hid. And for joy over it, he goes and he sells all that he has, and buys that field.

45Again, the kingdom of the heavens is like a merchant seeking fine pearls. **46**And having found one very precious pearl, having gone away, he has sold all things as many as he had, and bought it.

The Parable of the Net
(Matthew 4:18-22; Mark 1:16-20; Luke 5:1-11; John 1:35-42)

47Again, the kingdom of the heavens is like a dragnet having been cast into the sea, and having gathered together of every kind, **48**which when it was filled, they having drawn *it* up on the shore and having sat down, collected the good into vessels, and they cast out the bad.

49Thus will it be in the consummation of the age: The angels will go out and will separate the evil from *the* midst of the righteous, **50**and will cast them into the furnace of fire, *where* there will be weeping and gnashing of the teeth.

51Have you understood all these things?"

"Yes," they say to Him.

52And He said to them, "Because of this, every scribe having been discipled into the kingdom of the heavens is like a man, a master of a house, who puts forth out of his treasure new and old."

The Rejection at Nazareth
(Isaiah 61:1-11; Matthew 2:19-23; Mark 6:1-6; Luke 2:39-40; Luke 4:16-30)

⁵³And it came to pass, when Jesus had finished these parables, He withdrew from there. ⁵⁴And having come into His *own* region, He was teaching them in their synagogue, so that they are astonished and are saying, "From where came to this *One* this wisdom and these miraculous powers? ⁵⁵Is this not the son of the carpenter? *Is* not His mother called Mary, and His brothers James and Joseph and Simon and Judas? ⁵⁶And are not all His sisters with us? Then from where came to this *One* all these things?" ⁵⁷And they were offended at Him.

But Jesus said to them, "A prophet is not without honor, except in the hometown and in his own household." ⁵⁸And He did not do many mighty works there, because of their unbelief.

a 9 BYZ and TR *ears to hear*
b 14-15 Isaiah 6:9,10
c 35 Psalm 78:2
d 43 BYZ and TR *ears to hear*

Matthew 14
The Beheading of John
(Mark 6:14-29; Luke 9:7-9)

¹At that time Herod the tetrarch heard the news of Jesus, ²and he said to his servants, "This is John the Baptist; he is risen from the dead, and because of this, the miraculous powers are working in him."
³For Herod, having seized John, bound him and put *him* in prison, on account of Herodias, the wife of his brother Philip. ⁴For John had been saying to him, "It is not lawful for you to have her." ⁵Although wishing to kill him, he feared the multitude, because they were holding him as a prophet.
⁶But *on the* birthday of Herod having been celebrated, the daughter of Herodias danced in the midst, and pleased Herod, ⁷whereupon he promised with an oath to give to her whatever she should ask.
⁸And having been urged on by her mother she says, "Give me here upon a platter the head of John the Baptist."
⁹And the king having been grieved, on account of the oaths and those reclining with *him*, he commanded *it* to be given. ¹⁰And having sent, he beheaded John in the prison.
¹¹And his head was brought on a platter and was given to the girl, and she brought *it* to her mother. ¹²And his disciples having come, took the body and buried it, and having come, they told Jesus.

The Feeding of the Five Thousand
(Mark 6:30-44; Luke 9:10-17; John 6:1-15)

¹³And Jesus having heard, withdrew from there by boat to a secluded place by Himself. And the crowds having heard *of it*, followed Him on foot from the towns. ¹⁴And having gone out, He saw a great crowd and was moved with compassion toward them, and He healed their sick.
¹⁵And evening having come, the disciples came to Him saying, "This place is desolate, and the time already is gone by. Therefore dismiss the crowds, that having gone into the villages, they might buy food for themselves."
¹⁶And Jesus said to them, "They have no need to go away. You give to them *something* to eat."
¹⁷And they say to Him, "We have here only five loaves and two fish."
¹⁸And He said, "Bring them here to Me."
¹⁹And having commanded the crowds to sit down on the grass, having taken the five loaves and the two fish, having looked up to heaven, He spoke a blessing. And having broken, He gave the loaves to the disciples, and the disciples to the crowds.
²⁰And all ate and were satisfied, and they took up that being over and above of the fragments, twelve hand-baskets full. ²¹And those eating were about five thousand men, besides women and children.

Jesus Walks on Water
(Mark 6:45-52; John 6:16-25)

²²And immediately He compelled the disciples to enter into the boat and to go before Him to the other side, until He would have dismissed the crowds. ²³And having dismissed the crowds, He went up on the mountain by Himself to pray. And evening having arrived, He was there alone, ²⁴and the boat being now many stadia^a from the land, tossed by the waves, for the wind was contrary.

²⁵And in *the* fourth watch of the night, He went to them, walking on the sea. ²⁶And the disciples having seen Him walking on the sea, were troubled saying, "It is a ghost!" And they cried out in fear.

²⁷But immediately Jesus spoke to them saying, "Take courage! It is I. Fear not."

²⁸And Peter answering said to Him, "Lord, if *it* is You, command me to come to You upon the waters."

²⁹And He said, "Come."

And Peter having descended from the boat, walked upon the water and came to Jesus. ³⁰And seeing the charging wind, he was afraid, and having begun to sink, he cried out saying, "Lord, save me!"

³¹And immediately Jesus having stretched out the hand, took hold of him and says to him, "O Little faith, why did you waver?"

³²And they having entered into the boat, the wind ceased. ³³And those in the boat worshiped Him, saying, "Truly You are Son of God."

Jesus Heals at Gennesaret
(Mark 6:53-56)

³⁴And having crossed over, they came to the land of Gennesaret. ³⁵And the men of that place having recognized Him, sent to all that surrounding region, and brought to Him all those being sick, ³⁶and were begging Him that only they might touch the fringe of His garment, and as many as touched were cured.

---
a 24 A stadion was about 607 feet or 185 meters

Matthew 15
Tradition and Worship
(Mark 7:1-13)

¹Then Pharisees and scribes come to Jesus from Jerusalem, saying, ²"Why do Your disciples break the tradition of the elders? For they do not wash their hands when they shall eat bread."

³And answering He said to them, "Why also do you break the commandment of God on account of your tradition? ⁴For God commanded, 'Honor the Father and mother'^a and, 'The *one* speaking evil of father or mother, in death must end!'^b ⁵But you say, 'Whoever shall say to the father or mother, "Whatever you might be profited by me *is* a gift," ⁶he shall not honor his father or his mother.' And you made void the commandment of God on account of your tradition! ⁷Hypocrites! Isaiah prophesied rightly concerning you, saying,

> ⁸'This people honors Me with the lips,
>> but their heart is kept far away from Me.
>
> ⁹And in vain they worship Me,
>> teaching *as* doctrines *the* precepts of men.'^c

What Defiles a Man
(Mark 7:14-23)

¹⁰And having summoned the crowd, He said to them, "Hear and understand! ¹¹*It is* not what is entering into the mouth *that* defiles the man; but that going forth out of the mouth, this defiles the man."

¹²Then the disciples having approached, said to Him, "Do You know that the Pharisees, having heard this saying, were offended?"

¹³And answering He said, "Every plant that My Heavenly Father has not planted will be rooted up. ¹⁴Leave them! They are blind guides of the blind.^d And if *the* blind lead *the* blind, both will fall into a pit."

¹⁵And Peter answering said to Him, "Explain this parable to us."

¹⁶And He said, "Are you also still without understanding? ¹⁷Do you not yet

understand that everything entering into the mouth goes into the stomach, and is cast out into *the* sewer? ¹⁸But the things going forth out of the mouth come forth out of the heart, and these defile the man. ¹⁹For out of the heart come forth evil thoughts, murders, adulteries, sexual immorality, thefts, false testimonies, slanders. ²⁰These are the things defiling the man, but to eat with unwashed hands does not defile the man."

The Faith of the Canaanite Woman
(Mark 7:24-30)

²¹And having gone forth from there, Jesus withdrew to the district of Tyre and Sidon. ²²And behold, a Canaanite woman from the same region having approached, was crying out saying, "Have mercy on me, Lord, Son of David! My daughter is miserably possessed by a demon."
²³But He did not answer her a word. And His disciples having approached, were imploring Him, saying, "Dismiss her, for she cries out after us!"
²⁴And answering He said, "I was sent only to those being lost sheep of *the* house of Israel."
²⁵And having come, she was worshiping Him saying, "Lord, help me!"
²⁶And answering He said, "It is not right to take the children's bread and to cast *it* to the dogs."
²⁷And she said, "Yes Lord, but even the dogs eat the crumbs falling from their masters' table."
²⁸Then Jesus answering said to her, "O woman, great *is* your faith. It shall be to you as you desire." And her daughter was healed from that very hour.

The Feeding of the Four Thousand
(Mark 8:1-10)

²⁹And having departed from there, Jesus went along the Sea of Galilee, and having gone up on the mountain, He was sitting there. ³⁰And great crowds came to Him, having with them *the* lame, crippled, blind, mute, and many others. And they placed them at His feet, and He healed them, ³¹so that the crowd marveled, seeing *the* mute speaking, *the* crippled restored, and *the* lame walking, and *the* blind seeing. And they glorified the God of Israel.
³²And Jesus, having called His disciples *to Him*, said, "I am moved with compassion toward the crowd, because they continue with Me three days already and have nothing that they might eat. And I am not willing to send them away hungry, lest they faint on the way."
³³And the disciples say to Him, "From where *will be* to us in a secluded place so many loaves, as so great a crowd to satisfy?"
³⁴And Jesus says to them, "How many loaves do you have?"
And they said, "Seven, and a few small fish."
³⁵And having commanded the crowds to sit down on the ground, ³⁶having taken the seven loaves and the fish, and having given thanks, He broke *them* and kept giving *them* to *the* disciples, and the disciples to the crowd.
³⁷And all ate and were satisfied, and they took up that being over and above of the fragments, seven baskets full. ³⁸And those eating were four thousand men, besides women and children.
³⁹And having dismissed the crowds, He entered into the boat and came to the region of Magadan.

a 4 Exodus 20:12; Deuteronomy 5:16
b 4 Exodus 21:17; Leviticus 20:9
c 8-9 Isaiah 29:13
d 14 Or *blind guides*

Matthew 16
The Demand for a Sign
(Mark 8:11-13; Luke 12:54-56)

¹And the Pharisees and Sadducees having approached testing *Him*, asked Him to show them a sign out of heaven.
²And answering He said to them, "Evening having come, you say, 'Fair weather, for the sky is red,' ³and in the morning, 'Today a storm, for the sky is red, being overcast.' Indeed you know *how* to discern the appearance of the sky,

but the signs of the times[a] you are not able! ⁴*An* evil and adulterous generation seeks a sign, but no sign will be given to it except the sign of Jonah." And having left them, He went away.

The Leaven to Beware
(Mark 8:14-21)

⁵And the disciples, having come to the other side, forgot to take bread. ⁶And Jesus said to them, "Watch and beware of the leaven of the Pharisees and Sadducees."
⁷And they were reasoning among themselves, saying, "*It is* because we did not take bread."
⁸But having known *this*, Jesus said, "Why do you reason among yourselves, *you* of little faith, because you did not take bread? ⁹Do you not yet understand, nor remember the five loaves for the five thousand, and how many hand-baskets you gathered? ¹⁰Nor the seven loaves for the four thousand, and how many baskets you gathered? ¹¹How do you not understand that I did not speak to you concerning bread, but to beware of the leaven of the Pharisees and Sadducees?"
¹²Then they understood that He did not say to beware of the leaven of bread, but of the teaching of the Pharisees and Sadducees.

Peter's Confession of Christ
(Mark 8:27-30; Luke 9:18-20; John 6:66-71)

¹³And Jesus having come into the district of Caesarea Philippi, He was questioning His disciples saying, "Whom do men pronounce the Son of Man to be?"
¹⁴And they said, "Some indeed, John the Baptist; and others, Elijah; and others, Jeremiah or one of the prophets."
¹⁵He says to them, "But whom do you pronounce Me to be?"
¹⁶And Simon Peter answering said, "You are the Christ, the Son of the living God."
¹⁷And Jesus answering, said to him, "Blessed are you, Simon Barjona! For flesh and blood did not reveal *it* to you, but My Father in the heavens. ¹⁸And I also say to you that you are Peter, and on this rock I will build My church, and *the* gates of Hades not will prevail against it. ¹⁹I will give to you the keys of the kingdom of the heavens, and whatever you might bind on the earth shall have been bound in the heavens, and whatever you might loose on the earth shall have been loosed in the heavens."
²⁰Then He instructed the disciples that they should tell no one that He is the Christ.

Christ's Passion Foretold
(Mark 8:31-33; Luke 9:21-22)

²¹From that time Jesus[b] began to show to His disciples that it is necessary for Him to go away to Jerusalem, and to suffer many things from the elders and chief priests and scribes, and to be killed, and to be raised on the third day.
²²And Peter having taken Him aside, began to rebuke Him, saying, "Far be it from You, Lord! This never will be to You!"
²³And having turned, He said to Peter, "Get behind Me, Satan! You are a stumbling block to Me. For your thoughts are not of the things of God, but the things of men."

Take Up Your Cross
(Matthew 10:37-39; Mark 8:34-38; Luke 9:23-27)

²⁴Then Jesus said His to disciples, "If anyone desires to come after Me, let him deny himself, and take up his cross, and follow Me. ²⁵For whoever might desire to save his life will lose it; but whoever might lose his life on account of Me will find it. ²⁶For what will it profit a man if he gains the whole world, but loses his soul? Or what will a man give *as* an exchange for his soul? ²⁷For the Son of Man is about to come in the glory His Father, with His angels, and then He will give to each according to his deeds.
²⁸Truly I say to you, there are some of those standing here who shall not taste of death until they have seen the Son of Man coming in His kingdom."

a 2-3 Several manuscripts do not include *When evening comes . . . of the times.* from verses 2 and 3.
b 21 NE and WH *Jesus Christ*

Matthew 17
The Transfiguration

(Mark 9:1-13; Luke 9:28-36; 2 Peter 1:16-21)

¹And after six days, Jesus takes with *Him* Peter, and James, and John his brother, and brings them up into a high mountain by themselves. ²And He was transfigured before them, and His face shone like the sun, and His clothes became white as the light.
³And behold, Moses and Elijah appeared to them, talking with Him. ⁴And Peter answering said to Jesus, "Lord, it is good for us to be here. If You wish, I will make here three tabernacles: one for You, and one for Moses, and one for Elijah."
⁵While yet he was speaking, behold, a bright cloud overshadowed them; and behold, a voice out of the cloud saying, "This is My Son, the beloved, in whom I am well pleased. Listen to Him!" ⁶And the disciples having heard *it*, fell upon their face and were greatly terrified.
⁷And Jesus having come to *them* and having touched them, said, "Rise up, and do not be afraid." ⁸And having lifted up their eyes, they saw no one except Jesus Himself alone.
⁹And *as* they were descending from the mountain, Jesus instructed them, saying, "Tell to no one the vision, until the Son of Man is risen out from *the* dead."
¹⁰And the disciples asked Him, saying, "Why then do the scribes say that it behooves Elijah to come first?"
¹¹And answering He said, "Elijah indeed comes and will restore all things. ¹²But I say to you that Elijah already is come, and they did not know him, but did to him whatever they desired. Thus also, the Son of Man is about to suffer from them."
¹³Then the disciples understood that He spoke to them concerning John the Baptist.

The Boy with a Demon

(Mark 9:14-29; Luke 9:37-42; Luke 17:5-10)

¹⁴And they having come to the crowd, a man came to Him kneeling down to Him ¹⁵and saying, "Lord, have mercy on my son, for he is epileptic and suffers miserably; for often he falls into the fire, and often into the water. ¹⁶And I brought him Your to disciples, and they were not able to heal him."
¹⁷And Jesus answering said, "O unbelieving and perverted generation, how long will I be with you? How long will I bear with you? Bring him here to Me."
¹⁸And Jesus rebuked him, and the demon went out from him, and the boy was healed from that hour.
¹⁹Then the disciples, having come to Jesus in private, said, "Why were we not able to cast it out?"
²⁰And He said to them, "Because of your little faith. For truly I say to you, if you have faith as of a mustard seed, you will say to this mountain, 'Move from here to there,' and it will move. And nothing will be impossible for you."ᵃ

The Second Prediction of the Passion

(Mark 9:30-32; Luke 9:43-45)

²²And *while* they were abiding in Galilee, Jesus said to them, "The Son of Man is about to be betrayed into *the* hands of men, ²³and they will kill Him, and on the third day He will be raised up." And they were deeply grieved.

The Temple Tax

²⁴And they having come to Capernaum, those collecting the didrachmas came to Peter and said, "Does your Teacher pay the didrachmas?"
²⁵He says, "Yes."
And he having entered into the house, Jesus anticipated him, saying, "What do you think, Simon? From whom do the kings of the earth receive custom or tribute? From their sons, or from strangers?"
²⁶And he having said, "From the strangers," Jesus said to him, "Then the

sons are free. ²⁷But that we might not offend them, having gone to the sea, cast a hook and take the first fish having come up, and having opened its mouth, you will find a stater.ᵇ Having taken that, give *it* to them for Me and yourself."

a 20 See Mark 9:29. BYZ and TR include *21 But this kind does not come out except by prayer and fasting.*
b 27 A silver coin worth four drachmas or approximately one shekel

Matthew 18
The Greatest in the Kingdom
(Mark 9:33-37; Luke 9:46-50)

¹In that hour the disciples came to Jesus, saying, "Who then is *the* greatest in the kingdom of the heavens?"
²And having summoned a child, He set it in their midst, ³and said, "Truly I say to you, if you are not converted and become as the little children, you shall never enter into the kingdom of the heavens. ⁴Therefore whoever will humble himself as this little child, he is the greatest in the kingdom of the heavens. ⁵And whoever shall receive one such little child in My name, receives Me.
⁶And whoever shall cause to stumble one of these of the little ones believing in Me, it is better for him that a heavy millstone should be hung around his neck, and he be sunk in the depth of the sea.

Temptations and Trespasses
(Mark 9:42-50; Luke 17:1-4)

⁷Woe to the world because of the causes of sin. For the stumbling blocks *are* necessary to come, but woe to the man by whom the offense comes!
⁸Now if your hand or your foot causes you to sin, cut it off and cast *it* from you; it is better for you to enter into life crippled or lame, than having two hands or two feet, to be cast into the eternal fire. ⁹And if your eye causes you to sin, gouge it out and cast *it* from you; it is better for you to enter into life one-eyed, than having two eyes to be cast into the Gehenna of fire.

The Parable of the Lost Sheep
(Luke 15:1-7)

¹⁰See *that* you do not despise one of these little ones. For I say to you that their angels in *the* heavens continually behold the face of my Father, who *is* in *the* heavens.ᵃ
¹²What do you think? If to any man there should be a hundred sheep, and one of them has gone astray, will he not leave the ninety nine on the mountains and, having gone, seek the *one* going astray? ¹³And if he should find it, truly I say to you that he rejoices over it more than over the ninety nine not having gone astray. ¹⁴Thus it is not *the* will of your Father who *is* in *the* heavens that one of these little ones should perish.

A Brother who Sins
(Deuteronomy 19:15-21)

¹⁵And if your brother sins against you,ᵇ go reprove him, between you and him alone. If he will hear you, you have gained your brother. ¹⁶But if he will not hear, take with you one or two more, that 'every word may be strengthened upon *the* testimony of two or three witnesses.'ᶜ
¹⁷And if he fails to listen to them, tell *it* to the church. And if he fails to listen to even to the church, let him be to you as the pagan and the tax collector.
¹⁸Truly I say to you, whatever you shall bind on earth shall have been bound in heaven, and whatever you shall loose on the earth shall have been loosed in heaven.
¹⁹Again truly I say to you that if two of you on the earth might agree concerning any matter that they shall ask, it will be done for them by My Father who *is* in *the* heavens. ²⁰For where two or three are gathered together unto My name, there am I in their midst."

The Unforgiving Servant
(Romans 12:14-21)

²¹Then Peter having come, said to Him, "Lord, how often will my brother sin against me, and I will forgive him? Up to seven times?"

²²Jesus says to him, "I say to you not up to seven times, but up to seventy times seven!ᵈ
²³Because of this, the kingdom of the heavens has become like to a man, a king, who desired to settle accounts with his servants. ²⁴And he having begun to settle, one was brought to him, a debtor of ten thousand talents.ᵉ ²⁵And of him having nothing to pay, the master commanded him to be sold, and the wife and children, and everything that he had, and payment to be made.
²⁶Therefore the servant, having fallen down, was bowing on his knees to him, saying, 'Have patience with me, and I will pay everything to you.'
²⁷And the master of that servant having been moved with compassion, released him and forgave him the debt.
²⁸But the same servant having gone out, found one of his fellow servants who was owing him a hundred denarii,ᶠ and having seized him, he was throttling *him*, saying, 'Pay what you owe.'
²⁹Therefore his fellow servant having fallen down, was begging him, saying, 'Have patience with me, and I will pay you.'
³⁰But he was not willing. Rather, having gone, he cast him into prison until he should pay what was owed.
³¹Therefore his fellow servants having seen the things having taken place, were deeply grieved, and having gone, narrated to their master everything having taken place.
³²Then his master having called him, says to him, 'Evil servant, I forgave you all that debt because you begged me. ³³Did it not behoove you also to have pitied your fellow servant, as I also had pitied you?'
³⁴And having been angry, his master delivered him to the jailers, until that he should pay all being owed to him.
³⁵Thus also My Heavenly Father will do to you, unless each of you forgives his brother from your heart."

a 10 See Luke 19:10. BYZ and TR include *11 For the Son of Man came to save the lost.*
b 15 NE and WH do not include *against you*
c 16 Deuteronomy 19:15
d 22 Or *seventy-seven times*
e 24 A talent was worth about twenty years' wages for a laborer
f 28 A denarius was customarily a day's wage for a laborer (see Matthew 20:2)

Matthew 19
Teachings about Divorce
(Mark 10:1-12)

¹And it came to pass, when Jesus had finished these words, He withdrew from Galilee and came to the region of Judea, beyond the Jordan. ²And great crowds followed Him, and He healed them there. ³And Pharisees came to Him, testing Him and saying, "Is it lawful for a man to divorce his wife for every cause?"
⁴And answering He said, "Have you not read that the *One* having created from *the* beginning 'made them male and female,'ᵃ ⁵and said, 'On account of this a man will leave the father and mother and be joined with his wife, and the two will become into one flesh'ᵇ?— ⁶so that they are no longer two, but one flesh. Therefore what God united together, *let* man not separate."
⁷They say to Him, "Why then did Moses command to give a roll of divorce and to send her away?"
⁸He says to them, "In view of your hardness of heart, Moses allowed you to divorce your wives; but *it* was not this way from *the* beginning. ⁹And I say to you that whoever shall divorce his wife except for sexual immorality, and shall marry another, commits adultery."ᶜ
¹⁰His disciples say to Him, "If this is the case of the man with the wife, it is better not to marry."
¹¹And He said to them, "Not all receive this word, but only *those* to whom it has been given. ¹²For there are eunuchs who were born thus from their mother's womb, and there are eunuchs who were made eunuchs by men, and there are eunuchs who made themselves eunuchs for the sake of the kingdom of the

heavens. The *one* being able to receive *it*, let him receive *it*."

Jesus Blesses the Children
(Mark 10:13-16; Luke 18:15-17)

¹³Then little children were brought to Him, that He might lay the hands on them, and might pray. But the disciples rebuked them. ¹⁴But Jesus said, "Permit the little children, and do not forbid them to come to Me, for of such is the kingdom of the heavens." ¹⁵And having laid the hands upon them, He departed from there.

The Rich Young Man
(Mark 10:17-31; Luke 18:18-30)

¹⁶And behold, one having come to Him said, "Teacher, what good *thing* shall I do that I might have eternal life?"
¹⁷And He said to him, "Why do you ask Me about what is good? Only One is good. But if you desire to enter into life, keep the commandments."
¹⁸He says to Him, "Which?"
And Jesus said, "'You shall not murder, you shall not commit adultery, you shall not steal, you shall not bear false witness, ¹⁹you shall honor the father and mother, and you shall love your neighbor as yourself.'*ᵈ*
²⁰The young man says to him, "All these things I have kept. What do I still lack?"
²¹Jesus was saying to him, "If you desire to be perfect, go, sell what you are possessing, and give to the poor, and you will have treasure in *the* heavens; and come, follow Me."
²²And having heard this statement, the young man went away grieving; for he was *one* having many possessions.
²³And Jesus said His to disciples, "Truly I say to you that with difficulty a rich man will enter into the kingdom of the heavens. ²⁴And again I say to you, *it* is easier for a camel to go through *the* eye of a needle, than a rich man to enter into the kingdom of God."
²⁵And the disciples having heard were exceedingly astonished, saying, "Who then is able to be saved?"

²⁶And Jesus having looked on *them*, said to them, "With men this is impossible, but with God all things *are* possible."
²⁷Then Peter answering said to Him, "Behold, we left all things and followed You; what then will be to us?"
²⁸And Jesus said to them, "Truly I say to you that in the regeneration, when the Son of Man shall sit down upon His throne of glory, you having followed Me, you also will sit on twelve thrones, judging the twelve tribes of Israel. ²⁹And everyone who has left houses, or brothers, or sisters, or father, or mother, or wife,*ᵉ* or children, or lands, for the sake of My name, will receive a hundredfold, and will inherit eternal life. ³⁰But many *who are* first will be last, and *the* last first.

a 4 Genesis 1:27
b 5 Genesis 2:24
c 9 SBL and BYZ include *And whoever marries a divorced woman commits adultery*
d 18-19 Exodus 20:12-16; Deuteronomy 5:16-20; Leviticus 19:18
e 29 NE, WH, and NA do not include *or wife*

Matthew 20
The Parable of the Workers

¹For the kingdom of the heavens is like to a man, a master of a house, who went out in *the* morning to hire workmen for his vineyard. ²And having agreed with the workmen on a denarius*ᵃ* for the day, he sent them into his vineyard.
³And having gone out about the third hour, he saw others standing idle in the marketplace, ⁴and to them he said, 'You also go into the vineyard, and I will give you whatever might be right.' ⁵And they went.
And having gone out again about *the* sixth and ninth hour, he did likewise.
⁶And about the eleventh having gone out, he found others standing, and says to them, 'Why do you stand here all the day idle?'
⁷They say to him, 'Because no one has hired us.'
He says to them, 'You go also into the vineyard.'*ᵇ*

8And evening having arrived, the master of the vineyard says to his foreman, 'Call the workmen and pay them the wages, having begun from the last, up to the first.'
9And those *hired* about the eleventh hour having come, they received a denarius each. 10And the first having come, they thought that they will receive more, but they themselves also received a denarius each.
11And having received *it*, they were grumbling against the master of the house, 12saying, 'These the last have worked one hour, and you have made them equal to us, the *ones* having borne the burden of the day and the scorching heat.'
13And answering one of them, he said, 'Friend, I am doing you no wrong. Did you not agree with me for a denarius? 14Take what *is* yours and go; and I desire to give to this last, as to you also. 15Or is it not lawful for me to do what I will with that which *is* mine? Or is your eye envious because I am generous?'
16Thus the last will be first, and the first, last."c

The Third Prediction of the Passion
(Mark 10:32-34; Luke 18:31-34)

17And Jesus going up to Jerusalem, He took the twelve disciples aside themselves on the way, and said to them, 18"Behold, we go up to Jerusalem, and the Son of Man will be betrayed to the chief priests and scribes, and they will condemn Him to death. 19And they will betray Him to the Gentiles to mock and to flog and to crucify; and the third day He will rise again."

A Mother's Request
(Mark 10:35-45)

20Then the mother of the sons of Zebedee came to Him with her sons, kneeling down and asking something from Him.
21And He said to her, "What do you desire?"
She says to Him, "Say that these two sons of mine might sit, one on Your right hand and one on Your left hand, in Your kingdom."
22And Jesus answering, said, "You do not know what you ask for. Are you able to drink the cup which I am about to drink?"d
They say to Him, "We are able."
23He says to them, "Indeed you will drink My cup,e but to sit on My right hand and on *My* left, this is not Mine to give, but for whom it has been prepared by My Father."
24And the ten having heard *this*, were indignant about the two brothers. 25And Jesus having summoned them, said, "You know that the rulers of the Gentiles exercise lordship over them, and the great ones exercise authority over them. 26Thus will it not be among you. But whoever wishes to become great among you, he will be your servant; 27and whoever wishes to be first among you, he will be your slave— 28even as the Son of Man did not come to be served, but to serve, and to give His life *as* a ransom for many."

The Blind Men by the Road
(Mark 10:46-52; Luke 18:35-43)

29And *as* they were going out from Jericho, a great crowd followed Him. 30And behold, two blind *men* sitting beside the road, having heard that Jesus is passing by, cried out saying, "Lord, have mercy on us, Son of David!"
31And the crowd rebuked them that they should be silent. But they cried out all the more, saying, "Lord, have mercy on us, Son of David!"
32And Jesus having stopped, called them and said, "What do you desire I should do unto you?"
33They say to Him, "Lord, that our eyes might be opened."
34And having been moved with compassion, Jesus touched their eyes; and immediately they received sight, and they followed Him.

a 2 A denarius was customarily a day's wage for a laborer
b 7 BYZ and TR include *and whatever is right, you shall receive.*
c 16 BYZ and TR include *For many are called, but few are chosen.*
d 22 BYZ includes *or be baptized with the baptism that I am baptized with.* TR is similar.
e 23 BYZ and TR include *and be baptized with the baptism that I am baptized with*

Matthew 21
The Triumphal Entry
(Zechariah 9:9-13; Mark 11:1-11; Luke 19:28-40; John 12:12-19)

¹And when they drew near to Jerusalem and came to Bethphage on the Mount of Olives, then Jesus sent two disciples, ²saying to them, "Go into the village in front of you, and immediately you will find a donkey having been tied, and a colt with her. Having untied *them*, bring *them* to Me, ³and if anyone says anything to you, you will say that the Lord has need of them, and he will send them immediately."
⁴And this came to pass, that it might be fulfilled that having been spoken by the prophet, saying,
 ⁵"Say to the daughter of Zion,
  'Behold, your King comes to you,
 gentle and mounted on a donkey,
  even upon a colt, *the* foal of a beast of burden.'"ᵃ
⁶And the disciples having gone and having done as Jesus commanded them, ⁷brought the donkey and the colt and put their cloaks upon them, and He sat on them.
⁸And the very great crowd spread their the cloaks on the road, and others were cutting down branches from the trees and were spreading *them* on the road.
⁹And the crowds going before Him and those following were crying out, saying:
 "Hosanna to the Son of David!"ᵇ
 "Blessed is the *One* coming in *the* name of *the* Lord!"ᶜ
 "Hosanna in the highest!"ᵈ
¹⁰And of Him having entered into Jerusalem, all the city was stirred, saying, "Who is this?"
¹¹And the crowds were saying, "This is the prophet, Jesus, the *One* from Nazareth of Galilee."

Jesus Cleanses the Temple
(Mark 11:15-19; Luke 19:45-48; John 2:12-25)

¹²And Jesus entered into the templeᵉ and cast out all those selling and buying in the temple, and He overturned the tables of the money changers and the seats of those selling the doves. ¹³And He says to them, "It has been written: 'My house will be called a house of prayer.'ᶠ But you have made it 'a den of robbers.'ᵍ"
¹⁴And *the* blind and *the* lame came to Him in the temple, and He healed them. ¹⁵And the chief priests and the scribes, having seen the wonders that He did and the children crying out in the temple and saying, "Hosanna to the Son of David," were indignant ¹⁶and said to Him, "Do you hear what these say?"
And Jesus says to them, "Yes, have you never read:
 'Out of *the* mouth of babes and sucklings
  You have prepared for yourself praise'ʰ?"
¹⁷And having left them, He went out of the city to Bethany, and He passed the night there.

The Barren Fig Tree
(Mark 11:12-14; Mark 11:20-26)

¹⁸And in the morning, having come back into the city, He became hungry. ¹⁹And having seen one fig tree along the road, He came to it and found nothing on it except only leaves. And He says to it, "Never let there be *any* more fruit from you, to the age." And the fig tree withered immediately.
²⁰And having seen *it*, the disciples marveled, saying, "How did the fig tree wither so quickly?"
²¹And Jesus answering said to them, "Truly I say to you, if you have faith and not do doubt, you will do not only *this* of the fig tree, but even if you should say to this mountain, 'Be you taken away and be

you cast into the sea,' it will come to pass. ²²And all things, as many as you might ask in prayer, believing, you will receive."

Jesus' Authority Challenged
(Mark 11:27-33; Luke 20:1-8)

²³And of Him having come into the temple, teaching, the chief priests and the elders of the people came to Him, saying, "By what authority are You doing these things? And who gave to You this authority?"
²⁴And Jesus answering, said to them, "I also will ask you one thing, which if you tell Me, I also will say to you by what authority I do these things. ²⁵From where was the baptism of John? From heaven, or from men?"
And they were reasoning with themselves, saying, "If we should say, 'from heaven,' He will say to us, 'Why then did you not believe him?' ²⁶But if we should say, 'from men,' we fear the multitude; for all hold John as a prophet."
²⁷And answering Jesus, they said "We do not know."
And He said to them, "Neither do I tell you by what authority I do these things.

The Parable of the Two Sons

²⁸But what do you think? A man had two sons, and having come to the first he said, 'Son, go work in the vineyard today.' ²⁹And answering he said, 'I will not.' But afterward, having repented,ⁱ he went.
³⁰And having come to the second, he said likewise.
And answering he said, 'I *will* sir,' and he did not go.
³¹Which of the two did the will of the father?"
They say, "The first."
Jesus says to them, "Truly I say to you that the tax collectors and the prostitutes go before you into the kingdom of God. ³²For John came to you in *the* way of righteousness, and you did not believe him, but the tax collectors and the prostitutes believed him; and you having seen, did not even repent afterward to believe him.

The Parable of the Wicked Tenants
(Mark 12:1-12; Luke 20:9-18)

³³Hear another parable: There was a man, a master of a house, who planted a vineyard, and placed around it a fence, and dug a winepress in it, and built a tower; and he rented it out to farmers and traveled abroad.
³⁴And when the season of the fruits drew near, he sent his servants to the farmers, to receive his fruits. ³⁵And the farmers having taken his servants, one they beat, and one they killed, and one they stoned. ³⁶Again he sent other servants, more than the first, and they did likewise to them.
³⁷And afterward he sent his son to them, saying, 'They will respect my son.'
³⁸But the farmers having seen the son, said among themselves, 'This is the heir; come, let us kill him and gain possession of his inheritance.' ³⁹And having taking him, they cast *him* out of the vineyard and killed *him*.
⁴⁰Therefore when the master of the vineyard shall come, what will he do to those farmers?"
⁴¹They say to him, "He will destroy them, *the* wretches, grievously, and he will rent out the vineyard to other farmers who will give to him the fruits in their seasons."
⁴²Jesus says to them, "Did you never read in the Scriptures:

> '*The* stone that those building rejected,
>> this has become the chief corner.
>
> This was from *the* Lord,
>> and it is marvelous in our eyes'ʲ?

⁴³Because of this I say to you that the kingdom of God will be taken away from you, and will be given to a people producing its fruits.ᵏ ⁴⁴And the *one* having fallen on this stone will be broken; but on whomever it shall fall, it will grind him to powder."
⁴⁵And the chief priests and the Pharisees, having heard His parables, knew that He

speaks about them. ⁴⁶And seeking to lay hold of Him, they feared the crowds, because they were holding Him as a prophet.

a 5 Zechariah 9:9
b 9 Psalm 118:25
c 9 Psalm 118:26
d 9 Psalm 148:1
e 12 BYZ *temple of God*
f 13 Isaiah 56:7
g 13 Jeremiah 7:11
h 16 Psalm 8:2
i 29 NE and WH do not include *having repented*
j 42 Psalm 118:22,23
k 43 Tischendorf and some manuscripts do not include verse 44.

Matthew 22
The Parable of the Banquet
(Luke 14:15-24)

¹And answering, Jesus spoke to them again in parables, saying, ²"The kingdom of the heavens has become like a man, a king, who made a wedding feast for his son. ³And he sent his servants to call those having been invited to the wedding feast—and they were not willing to come. ⁴Again he sent other servants, saying, 'Say to those having been invited, "Behold, I have prepared my dinner. My oxen and the fatlings have been killed, and all things *are* ready; come to the wedding feast."'
⁵And having paid no attention they went away, one to the own field, and one to his business. ⁶And the rest, having laid hold of his servants, mistreated and killed *them*.
⁷And the king was angry, and having sent his armies, he destroyed those murderers and burned their city. ⁸Then he says to his servants, 'Indeed the wedding feast is ready, but those having been invited were not worthy. ⁹Therefore go into the thoroughfares of the highways, and invite to the wedding feast as many as you shall find.'
¹⁰And those servants, having gone out into the highways, brought together all, as many as they found, both evil and good; and the wedding hall became full of those reclining.

¹¹And the king having entered in to see those reclining, he beheld a man there not being dressed in wedding clothes. ¹²And he says to him, 'Friend, how did you enter here not having a wedding garment?'
And he was speechless.
¹³Then the king said to the servants, 'Having bound his hands and feet, cast him out into the outer darkness, *where* there will be weeping and gnashing of the teeth.'
¹⁴For many are called, but few chosen."

Paying Taxes to Caesar
(Mark 12:13-17; Luke 20:19-26)

¹⁵Then the Pharisees having gone out, took counsel how they might trap Him in His words. ¹⁶And they send their disciples to Him, with the Herodians, saying, "Teacher, we know that You are true, and You teach the way of God in *the* truth, and to You there is care about no one, for You do not look on *the* appearance of men. ¹⁷Therefore tell us, what do You think? Is it lawful to give tribute to Caesar, or not?"
¹⁸But having known their malice, Jesus said, "Hypocrites, why do you test Me? ¹⁹Show Me the coin of the tribute."
And they presented to Him a denarius.ᵃ
²⁰And He says to them, "Whose likeness and whose inscription *is* this?"
²¹They say to Him, "Caesar's."
Then He says to them, "Therefore give back to Caesar the things of Caesar, and to God the things of God."
²²And having heard, they marveled. And having left Him, they went away.

The Sadducees and the Resurrection
(Mark 12:18-27; Luke 20:27-40)

²³On that day Sadducees, those saying there is no resurrection, came to Him, and they questioned Him, ²⁴saying, "Teacher, Moses said, 'If anyone should die not having children, his brother will marry his wife and will raise up offspring for his brother.' ²⁵Now there were seven brothers among us; and the first died,

and having married not having seed, he left his wife to his brother. ²⁶Likewise also the second, and the third, unto the seventh. ²⁷And last of all, the woman died. ²⁸In the resurrection, therefore, of which of the seven will she be wife? For all had her."

²⁹And, Jesus answering said to them, "You err, not knowing the Scriptures, nor the power of God. ³⁰For in the resurrection, neither do they marry, nor are given in marriage, but they are like angels[b] in heaven. ³¹And concerning the resurrection of the dead, have you not read that which has been spoken to you by God, saying, ³²'I am the God of Abraham and the God of Isaac and the God of Jacob?'[c] He is not the God of *the* dead, but of *the* living."

³³And the crowds having heard, were astonished at His teaching.

The Greatest Commandment
(Deuteronomy 6:1-19; Mark 12:28-34)

³⁴And the Pharisees, having heard that He had silenced the Sadducees, were gathered together the same. ³⁵And one of them, a lawyer, questioned *Him*, testing Him, ³⁶"Teacher, which commandment *is the* greatest in the Law?"

³⁷And He said to him, "'You shall love *the* Lord your God with all your heart, and with all your soul, and with all your mind.'[d] ³⁸This is the great and first commandment. ³⁹And *the* second *is* like it: 'You shall love your neighbor as yourself.'[e] ⁴⁰On these two commandments hang all the Law and the Prophets."

Whose Son is the Christ?
(Mark 12:35-37; Luke 20:41-44)

⁴¹And the Pharisees having been assembled together, Jesus questioned them, ⁴²saying, "What do you think concerning the Christ? Of whom is He son?"

They say to Him, "Of David."

⁴³He says to them, "How then does David in spirit call Him Lord, saying:

⁴⁴'The Lord said to my Lord,
"Sit at My right hand,
until I place Your enemies
as a footstool for Your feet."'[f]

⁴⁵If therefore David calls Him Lord, how is He his son?"

⁴⁶And no one was able to answer Him a word, nor did anyone dare from that day to question Him *any* longer.

a 19 A denarius was customarily a day's wage for a laborer (see Matthew 20:2)
b 30 SBL, BYZ and TR *the angels of God*
c 32 Exodus 3:6
d 37 Deuteronomy 6:5
e 39 Leviticus 19:18
f 44 Psalm 110:1

Matthew 23
Woes to Scribes and Pharisees
(Luke 11:37-54)

¹Then Jesus spoke to the crowds and to His disciples, ²saying, "The scribes and the Pharisees have sat down on Moses' seat; ³therefore keep and observe all things whatsoever they might tell you. But do not do according to their works, for they preach and do not act. ⁴And they tie up burdens heavy and hard to bear[a] and lay *them* on the shoulders of men; but they themselves are not willing to move them with their finger.

⁵And they do all their deeds in order to be seen by men. For they broaden their phylacteries and enlarge their tassels, ⁶and they love the chief place at the banquets, and the first seats in the synagogues, ⁷and the greetings in the marketplaces, and to be called 'Rabbi' by men.

⁸But you shall not be called 'Rabbi,' for your Teacher is One, and you are all brothers. ⁹And call no *one* your father on the earth; for One is your Father, who *is* in heaven. ¹⁰Neither be called instructors; since One is your instructor, the Christ. ¹¹But the greatest among you will be your servant. ¹²And whoever shall exalt himself will be humbled, and whoever shall humble himself will be exalted.

¹³But woe to you, scribes and Pharisees, hypocrites! For you shut up the kingdom

of the heavens before men. For you neither enter, nor even do you allow those who are entering to go in.[b]

15 Woe to you, scribes and Pharisees, hypocrites! For you traverse the sea and the dry *land* to make one convert, and whenever it may happen, you make him twofold more a son of Gehenna than yourselves.

16 Woe to you, blind guides, those saying, 'Whoever shall swear by the temple, it is nothing; but whoever shall swear by the gold of the temple is bound by his oath.' 17 Foolish and blind! For which is greater, the gold, or the temple having sanctified the gold? 18 And *you say*, 'Whoever shall swear by the altar, it is nothing; but whoever shall swear by the gift that *is* upon it is bound by his oath.' 19 Blind! For which *is* greater, the gift, or the altar sanctifying the gift? 20 Therefore the *one* having sworn by the altar swears by it and by all things that *are* upon it. 21 And the *one* having sworn by the temple swears by it and by the *One* dwelling in it. 22 And the *one* having sworn by heaven swears by the throne of God and by the *One* sitting upon it.

23 Woe to you, scribes and Pharisees, hypocrites! For you pay tithes of mint and dill and cummin, and you have neglected the weightier *things* of the Law: justice and mercy and faithfulness. It behooved you to do these, and not to be leaving aside those. 24 Blind guides—those straining out the gnat and swallowing the camel!

25 Woe to you, scribes and Pharisees, hypocrites! For you cleanse the outside of the cup and of the dish, but inside they are full of greed and intemperance. 26 Blind Pharisee! First cleanse the inside of the cup and of the dish, that their outside might become clean also.

27 Woe to you, scribes and Pharisees, hypocrites! For you are like tombs having been whitewashed, which indeed outwardly appear beautiful, but inside they are full of bones of *the* dead, and of all impurity. 28 Thus indeed outwardly you also appear righteous to men, but inwardly you are full of hypocrisy and lawlessness.

29 Woe to you, scribes and Pharisees, hypocrites! For you build the tombs of the prophets and adorn the monuments of the righteous; 30 and you say, 'If we had been in the days of our fathers, we would not have been partakers with them in the blood of the prophets.' 31 Thus you bear witness to yourselves that you are sons of those having murdered the prophets. 32 You, then, fill up the measure of your fathers. 33 Serpents! Offspring of vipers! How shall you escape from the sentence of Gehenna?

34 Because of this, behold, I send to you prophets and wise *men* and scribes. Some of them you will kill and will crucify, and *some* of them you will flog in your synagogues, and will persecute from town to town; 35 so that upon you shall come all *the* righteous blood being poured out upon the earth, from the blood of the righteous Abel to the blood of Zechariah son of Berekiah, whom you murdered between the temple and the altar. 36 Truly I say to you, all these things will come upon this generation.

Lament over Jerusalem
(Luke 13:31-35)

37 Jerusalem, Jerusalem, killing the prophets and stoning those having been sent to her! How often would I have gathered together your children, the way in which a hen gathers together her chicks under the wings, and you were not willing! 38 Behold, your house is left to you desolate! 39 For I say to you, you shall not see Me from now until you say, 'Blessed *is* the *One* coming in *the* name of *the* Lord.'[c]

a 4 SBL, NE, and WH do not include *and hard to bear*
b 13 See Mark 12:40 and Luke 20:47. BYZ and TR *14 Woe to you, scribes and Pharisees, you hypocrites! You swindle widows out of their houses, and for a show make lengthy prayers. Therefore you will receive greater condemnation.*
c 39 Psalm 118:26

Matthew 24
Temple Destruction Foretold
(Mark 13:1-9; Luke 21:5-9)

¹And having gone forth from the temple, Jesus was going away, and His disciples came to *Him* to point out to Him the buildings of the temple. ²And answering, He said to them, "Do you not see all these things? Truly I say to you, no not even a stone shall be left here upon a stone, which will not be thrown down."

Signs of the End of the Age

³And *as* He was sitting upon the Mount of Olives, the disciples came to Him in private, saying, "Tell us, when these things will be? And what *is* the sign of Your coming, and the consummation of the age?"

⁴And Jesus answering, said to them, "Take heed, lest anyone mislead you. ⁵For many will come in My name, saying, 'I am the Christ,' and they will mislead many. ⁶And you will begin to hear of wars and rumors of wars. Behold, do not be alarmed; for it is necessary to take place, but the end is not yet. ⁷For nation will rise up against nation, and kingdom against kingdom, and there will be famines and earthquakes in *various* places. ⁸And all these *are the* beginning of birth pains.

Witnessing to All Nations
(Mark 13:10-13; Luke 21:10-19)

⁹Then will they deliver you to tribulation, and will kill you, and you will be hated by all the nations on account of My name. ¹⁰And then many will fall away, and they will betray one another, and will hate one another; ¹¹and many false prophets will arise, and will lead many astray.

¹²And because lawlessness is to be multiplied, the love of the many will grow cold. ¹³But the *one* having endured to *the* end, he will be saved.

¹⁴And this gospel of the kingdom will be proclaimed in the whole earth, for a testimony to all the nations; and then the end will come.

The Abomination of Desolation
(Mark 13:14-23; Luke 21:20-24)

¹⁵Therefore when you shall see 'the abomination of desolation,'[a] having been spoken of by the prophet Daniel, standing in *the* holy place—the *one* reading, let him understand— ¹⁶then those in Judea, let them flee to the mountains; ¹⁷the *one* on the housetop, do not let him come down to take anything out of his house; ¹⁸and the *one* in the field, do not let him return back to take his cloak.

¹⁹And woe to those having in womb, and to the *ones* nursing infants in those days! ²⁰But pray that your flight might not be in winter, nor on a Sabbath. ²¹For then there will be great tribulation, such as has not been from *the* beginning of *the* world until now, *and* never shall be. ²²And unless those days had been shortened, no flesh would have been saved; but because of the elect, those days will be shortened.

²³Then if anyone says to you, 'Behold, here *is* the Christ,' or 'Here,' do not believe *it*. ²⁴For false Christs and false prophets will arise and will give great signs and wonders, so as to mislead, if possible, even the elect. ²⁵Behold, I have foretold you.

The Return of the Son of Man
(Mark 13:24-27; Luke 21:25-28)

²⁶Therefore if they say to you, 'Behold, He is in the wilderness,' do not go forth; *or* 'Behold, in the inner rooms,' do not believe. ²⁷For just as the lightning comes forth from *the* east and shines as far as *the* west, so will be the coming of the Son of Man. ²⁸For wherever the carcass may be, there the vultures will be gathered.

²⁹And immediately after the tribulation of those days:

> 'The sun will be darkened,
>> and the moon will not give its light,
>
> and the stars will fall from the sky,
>> and the powers of the heavens will be shaken.'[b]

30 And then the sign of the Son of Man will appear in heaven, and then all the tribes of the earth will mourn. And they will see the Son of Man coming on the clouds of heaven, with power and great glory.[c] 31 And He will send His angels with a great trumpet call, and they will gather together His elect from the four winds, from *the* ends of the heavens to the ends thereof.

The Lesson of the Fig Tree
(Mark 13:28-31; Luke 21:29-33)

32 Now learn the parable of the fig tree: When its branch already may have become tender and it puts forth leaves, you know that the summer *is* near. 33 So also you, when you see all these things, know that He is[d] near, at *the* doors. 34 Truly I say to you that this generation will not have passed away until all these things shall have taken place. 35 The heaven and the earth will pass away, but My words shall not pass away.

Readiness at Any Hour
(Genesis 6:1-7; Mark 13:32-37; Luke 12:35-48)

36 But concerning that day and hour, no one knows, not even the angels of the heavens, nor the Son,[e] except the Father only. 37 For as *were* the days of Noah, so will be the coming of the Son of Man. 38 For as in those days before the flood, they were eating and drinking, marrying and giving in marriage, until that day Noah entered into the ark, 39 and they were unaware until the flood came and took away all; so also will be the coming of the Son of Man. 40 Then two will be in the field: one is taken, and one is left. 41 Two *women* will be grinding at the mill: one is taken, and one is left.
42 Therefore keep watch, for you do not know on what day your Lord comes. 43 And know this, that if the master of the house had known in what time of night the thief comes, he would have watched and not have allowed his house to be broken into. 44 Because of this, you also be ready, for the Son of Man comes in that hour you do not expect.
45 Who then is the faithful and wise servant, whom the master has set over his household, to give to them the food in season? 46 Blessed *is* that servant whom his master, having come, will find thus doing. 47 Truly I say to you that he will set him over all of his possessing.
48 But if that evil servant should say in his heart, 'My master delays,' 49 and should begin to beat his fellow servants, and to eat and to drink with those being drunkards, 50 the master of that servant will come in a day in which he does not expect, and in an hour which he is unaware, 51 and will cut him in pieces, and will appoint his place with the hypocrites, *where* there will be weeping and gnashing of teeth.

a 15 Daniel 9:27; 11:31; 12:11
b 29 Isaiah 13:10; 34:4; Joel 2:10
c 30 See Daniel 7:13-14
d 33 Or *it is*
e 36 BYZ and TR do not include *nor the Son.*

Matthew 25
The Parable of the Ten Virgins

1 Then the kingdom of the heavens will be likened to ten virgins, who, having taken their lamps, went forth to meet the bridegroom. 2 And five of them were foolish, and five wise. 3 For the foolish, having taken their lamps, took no oil with them; 4 but the wise took oil in vessels with their lamps. 5 And the bridegroom tarrying, they all became drowsy and were sleeping.
6 And at *the* middle of *the* night, there was a cry: 'Behold, the bridegroom! Go forth to meet him!'
7 Then all those virgins arose and trimmed their lamps. 8 And the foolish said to the wise, 'Give us of your oil, for our lamps are going out.'
9 And the wise answered, saying, 'No, lest it might not suffice for us and you. Go rather to those selling, and buy for yourselves.'

¹⁰And *while* they are going away to buy, the bridegroom came, and those ready went in with him to the wedding feast. And the door was shut.
¹¹And afterward, the other virgins come also, saying, 'Lord, Lord, open to us!'
¹²And answering he said, 'Truly I say to you, I do not know you.'
¹³Therefore watch, for you do not know the day, nor the hour.[a]

The Parable of the Talents
(Luke 19:11-27)

¹⁴For *it is* like a man going on a journey *who* called his own servants and delivered his possessing to them. ¹⁵And indeed to one he gave five talents;[b] and to one, two; and to one, one; to each according to his own ability. And he left the region immediately.
¹⁶The *one* having received the five talents, having gone, traded with them, and made five more. ¹⁷Likewise, the *one* with the two gained two more. ¹⁸But the *one* having received the one *talent*, having gone away, dug in the ground and hid his master's money.
¹⁹And after much time, the master of those servants comes and takes account with them. ²⁰And the *one* having received the five talents, having come, brought to *him* five other talents, saying, 'Master, you did deliver to me five talents. Behold, I have gained five talents more.'
²¹His master said to him, 'Well done, good and faithful servant! You were faithful over a few things; I will set you over many things. Enter into the joy of your master!'
²²And the *one* with the two talents, also having come said, 'Master, you did deliver to me two talents. Behold, I have gained two talents more.'
²³His master said to him, 'Well done, good and faithful servant! You were faithful over a few things; I will set you over many things. Enter into the joy of your master!'
²⁴And the *one* having received the one talent, having come, also said, 'Master, I knew you, that you are a hard man, reaping where you did not sow, and gathering from where you did not scatter. ²⁵And having been afraid, having gone away, I hid your talent in the ground. Behold, you have what *is* yours.'
²⁶And his master answering, said to him, 'Wicked and lazy servant! You knew that I reap where I did not sow and gather from where I did not scatter. ²⁷Therefore it behooved you to put my money to the bankers, and having come, I would have received my own with interest.
²⁸Therefore take the talent from him, and give *it* to the *one* having the ten talents. ²⁹For to everyone having will be given, and he will have in abundance. But the *one* not having, even that which he has will be taken away from him. ³⁰And cast out the worthless servant, into the outer darkness, *where* there will be weeping and gnashing of teeth.'

The Sheep and the Goats

³¹And when the Son of Man comes in His glory, and all the angels with Him, then He will sit upon His throne of glory. ³²And all the nations will be gathered before Him, and He will separate them one from another, as the shepherd separates the sheep from the goats. ³³And indeed He will set the sheep on His right hand, and the goats on *His* left.
³⁴Then the King will say to those on His right hand, 'Come, those being blessed of my Father, inherit the kingdom having been prepared for you from *the* foundation of *the* world. ³⁵For I hungered, and you gave Me to eat; I thirsted, and you gave Me to drink; I was a stranger, and you took Me in; ³⁶naked, and you clothed Me; I was sick, and you visited Me; I was in prison, and you came to Me.'
³⁷Then the righteous will answer Him, saying, 'Lord, when did we see You hungering, and fed *You*? Or thirsting, and gave *You* to drink? ³⁸And when did we see You a stranger, and took *You* in? Or naked, and clothed *You*? ³⁹And when did

we see You ailing or in prison, and came to You?'
⁴⁰And the King answering, will say to them, 'Truly I say to you, to the extent that you did *it* to one of the least of these brothers of Mine, you did *it* to Me.'
⁴¹Then also He will say to those on *the* left, 'Depart from Me, those being cursed, into the eternal fire, having been prepared for the devil and his angels. ⁴²For I hungered, and you gave to Me nothing to eat; and I thirsted, and You gave Me nothing to drink; ⁴³I was a stranger, and You did not take Me in; naked, and you did not clothe Me; sick and in prison, and you did not visit Me.'
⁴⁴Then they also will answer, saying, 'Lord, when did we see You hungering, or thirsting, or a stranger, or naked, or sick, or in prison, and did not minister to You?' ⁴⁵Then He will answer them, saying, 'Truly I say to you, to the extent that you did not do *it* to one of the least of these, neither did you to Me.'
⁴⁶And these will go away into eternal punishment; but the righteous into eternal life."

a 13 BYZ and TR include *when the Son of man comes*
b 15 A talent was worth about twenty years' wages for a laborer

Matthew 26
The Plot to Kill Jesus
(Mark 14:1-2; Luke 22:1-6; John 11:45-57)

¹And it came to pass, when Jesus had finished all these words, He said to His disciples, ²"You know that after two days the Passover takes place, and the Son of Man is delivered over to be crucified."
³Then the chief priests and the elders of the people were gathered together in the courtyard of the high priest, who is called Caiaphas, ⁴and they plotted together, in order that they might seize Jesus by guile and kill *Him*. ⁵But they were saying, "Not during the feast, lest there be a riot among the people."

Jesus Anointed at Bethany
(Mark 14:3-9; John 12:1-8)

⁶And of Jesus having been in Bethany in *the* house of Simon the leper,ᵃ ⁷a woman came to Him, having an alabaster flask of very costly fragrant oil, and poured *it* on His head *as* He is reclining.
⁸And the disciples having seen, became indignant, saying, "For what purpose *is* this waste? ⁹For this could have been sold for much, and have been given to *the* poor."
¹⁰And Jesus having known, said to them, "Why do you cause trouble to the woman? For she did a beautiful work to Me. ¹¹For the poor you always have with you,ᵇ but not always do you have Me. ¹²For this *woman*, in pouring this fragrant oil on My body, did *it* for My burial. ¹³Truly I say to you, wherever this gospel shall be proclaimed in the whole world, that which this *woman* did also will be spoken of, for a memorial of her."

Judas Agrees to Betray Jesus
(Zechariah 11:10-17; Matthew 27:3-10; Mark 14:10-11)

¹⁴Then one of the Twelve, the *one* being called Judas Iscariot, having gone to the chief priests, ¹⁵said, "What are you willing to give me, and I will betray Him to you?" And they appointed to him thirty pieces of silver. ¹⁶And from that time, he was seeking an opportunity that he might betray Him.

Preparing the Passover
(Psalm 41:1-13; Mark 14:12-21; Luke 22:7-13; John 13:18-30)

¹⁷And on the first *day* of the unleavened *bread*, the disciples came to Jesus, saying, "Where do you desire we should prepare for You to eat the Passover?"
¹⁸And He said, "Go into the city unto a certain man and tell him the Teacher says, 'My time is near; I will keep the Passover with you with My disciples.'"
¹⁹And the disciples did as Jesus directed them, and prepared the Passover.
²⁰And evening having arrived, He was reclining with the twelve disciples.ᶜ ²¹And

as they were eating, He said to them, "Truly I say to you that one of you will betray Me."
²²And being grieved exceedingly, they began, each one, to say to Him, "Is it I, Lord?"
²³And answering He said, "The *one* having dipped the hand in the dish with Me, he will betray Me. ²⁴Indeed the Son of Man goes as it has been written about Him; but woe to that man by whom the Son of Man is betrayed. It would be better for him if that man had not been born."
²⁵And Judas who was betraying Him, answering, said, "Is it I, Rabbi?" He says to him, "You have said."

The Last Supper
(Mark 14:22-26; Luke 22:14-23; 1 Corinthians 11:17-34)

²⁶Now *as* they were eating, Jesus, having taken bread and having blessed *it*, broke *it*, and having given *it* to the disciples, He said, "Take, eat; this is My body."
²⁷And having taken *the* cup and having given thanks, He gave *it* to them, saying, "Drink of it, all of you. ²⁸For this is My blood of the covenant,ᵈ being poured out for many, for forgiveness of sins. ²⁹And I say to you, I will not drink of this fruit of the vine from now until that the day when I drink it anew with you in the kingdom of My Father."
³⁰And having sung a hymn, they went out to the Mount of Olives.

Jesus Predicts Peter's Denial
(Mark 14:27-31; Luke 22:31-38; John 13:36-38)

³¹Then Jesus says to them, "You all will fall away because of Me during this night. For it has been written:
   'I will strike the shepherd,
      and the sheep of the flock will be scattered.'ᵉ
³²But I, after being raised, will go before you into Galilee."
³³And Peter answering, said to Him, "If all will fall away because of You, I never will fall away."
³⁴Jesus said to him, "Truly I say to you, during this night, before *the* rooster crowing, you will deny Me three times."
³⁵Peter says to Him, "Even if it were necessary for me to die with You, I will never deny You." And all the disciples said likewise.

Jesus Prays at Gethsemane
(Mark 14:32-42; Luke 22:39-46)

³⁶Then Jesus comes with them to a place called Gethsemane, and He says to the disciples, "Sit here until that having gone away over there, I shall pray."
³⁷And having taken with *Him* Peter and the two sons of Zebedee, He began to be sorrowful and deeply distressed. ³⁸Then He says to them, "My soul is very sorrowful, even to death. Remain here and watch with Me."
³⁹And having gone forward a little, He fell upon His face, praying, and saying, "My Father, if it is possible, let this cup pass from Me. Nevertheless not as I will, but as You."
⁴⁰And He comes to the disciples and finds them sleeping. And He says to Peter, "So, were you not able to watch with Me one hour? ⁴¹Watch and pray, that you do not enter into temptation. For the spirit *is* willing, but the flesh weak."
⁴²Again for a second time having gone away, He prayed, saying, "My Father, if this is not possible to pass unless I drink it, Your will be done." ⁴³And having come again, He finds them sleeping, for their eyes were heavy.
⁴⁴And having left them again, having gone away, He prayed for *the* third time, having said the same thing again. ⁴⁵Then He comes to the disciples and says to them, "Sleep and take your rest later on. Behold, the hour has drawn near, and the Son of Man is betrayed into *the* hands of sinners. ⁴⁶Rise up, let us go! Behold, he who is betraying Me has drawn near!"

The Betrayal of Jesus
(Mark 14:43-52; Luke 22:47-53; John 18:1-14)

⁴⁷And as He is still speaking, behold, Judas, one of the Twelve, came, and with him great a crowd with swords and clubs, from the chief priests and elders of the people. ⁴⁸And the *one* betraying Him gave them a sign, saying, "Whomever I shall kiss, it is He; seize Him." ⁴⁹And having come up to Jesus immediately, he said, "Greetings, Rabbi," and kissed Him. ⁵⁰And Jesus said to him, "Friend, for what are you come?"*f* Then having approached, they laid hands on Jesus and seized Him. ⁵¹And behold, one of those with Jesus, having stretched out the hand, drew his sword, and having struck the servant of the high priest, cut off his ear. ⁵²Then Jesus says to him, "Return your sword into its place; for all those having taken *the* sword, will perish by *the* sword. ⁵³Or do you think that I am not able to call upon My Father, and He will furnish to Me presently more than twelve legions of angels? ⁵⁴How then should the Scriptures be fulfilled, that it must be so?" ⁵⁵In that hour, Jesus said to the crowds, "Did you come out with swords and clubs, as against a robber, to capture Me? Every day in the temple I was sitting, teaching, and you did not seize Me. ⁵⁶And all this is come to pass, that the Scriptures of the prophets might be fulfilled." Then the disciples all, having forsaken Him, fled.

Jesus Faces the Sanhedrin
(Isaiah 53:1-8; Mark 14:53-65; John 18:19-24; 1 Peter 2:21-25)

⁵⁷And those having seized Jesus led *Him* away to Caiaphas the high priest, where the scribes and the elders were assembled. ⁵⁸And Peter was following Him from afar, even to the court of the high priest. And having entered within, he was sitting with the guards to see the outcome. ⁵⁹And the chief priests and the whole Council were seeking false evidence against Jesus, so that they might put Him to death. ⁶⁰But they did not find any, of many false witnesses having come forward. And at last, two having come forward, ⁶¹they said, "This *man* has been saying, 'I am able to destroy the temple of God and to rebuild it in three days.'" ⁶²And the high priest having stood up, said to Him, "Answer you nothing? What do these witness against you?" ⁶³But Jesus was silent. And the high priest said to Him, "I adjure you by the living God, that You tell us if You are the Christ, the Son of God." ⁶⁴Jesus says to him, "You have said. But I say to you, from now on you will see the Son of Man sitting at *the* right hand of Power and coming upon the clouds of heaven."*g* ⁶⁵Then the high priest tears his garments, saying, "He has blasphemed; why do we have any more need of witnesses? Behold now, you have heard the blasphemy. ⁶⁶What do you think?" And answering they said, "He is deserving of death." ⁶⁷Then they spat in His face and struck Him. And others slapped *Him*, ⁶⁸saying, "Prophesy to us, Christ, who is the *one* having struck You?"

Peter Denies Jesus
(Mark 14:66-72; Luke 22:54-62; John 18:15-18)

⁶⁹And Peter was sitting outside in the court, and one servant girl came to him, saying, "You also were with Jesus the Galilean." ⁷⁰And he denied *it* before all, saying, "I do not know what you say." ⁷¹And having gone out to the porch, another saw him, and says to those there, "This *man* was with Jesus of Nazareth." ⁷²And again he denied *it* with an oath, "I do not know the man." ⁷³And after a little while those standing by having approached, said to Peter,

"Surely you are of them also, for even your speech gives you away."
⁷⁴Then he began to curse and to swear, "I do not know the man!"
And immediately a rooster crowed.
⁷⁵And Peter remembered the word of Jesus, He having said, "Before the rooster crowing, you will deny Me three times."
And having gone out, he wept bitterly.

a 6 Leprosy was a term for several skin diseases. See Leviticus 13.
b 11 See Deuteronomy 15:11.
c 20 BYZ and TR *the Twelve*
d 28 BYZ and TR *the new covenant*
e 31 Zechariah 13:7
f 50 Or *Friend, why have you come?*
g 64 See Psalm 110:1; Daniel 7:13.

Matthew 27
Jesus Delivered to Pilate
(Mark 15:1-5)

¹And morning having arrived, all the chief priests and the elders of the people took counsel against Jesus, so that they might put Him to death. ²And having bound Him, they led *Him* away and delivered *Him* to Pilate the governor.

Judas Hangs Himself
(Zechariah 11:10-17; Matthew 26:14-16; Mark 14:10-11)

³Then Judas, the *one* having delivered Him up, having seen that He was condemned, having regretted *it*, he returned the thirty pieces of silver to the chief priests and elders, ⁴saying, "I sinned, having betrayed innocent blood." And they said, "What *is that* to us? You will see."
⁵And having cast down the pieces of silver into the temple, he withdrew, and having gone away, hanged himself.
⁶And the chief priests, having taken the pieces of silver, said, "It is not lawful to put them into the treasury, since it is *the* price of blood." ⁷And having taken counsel, they bought with them the potter's field, for a burial place for strangers. ⁸Therefore that field was called Field of Blood, to this day. ⁹Then was fulfilled that having been spoken by the prophet Jeremiah, saying,

"And they took the thirty pieces of silver,
> the price of the *One* having been priced,
> whom they set a price on by *the* sons of Israel,

¹⁰and they gave them for the potter's field,
> as *the* Lord directed me."[a]

Jesus Before Pilate
(Luke 23:1-6; John 18:28-40)

¹¹Now Jesus stood before the governor, and the governor questioned Him, saying, "Are You the King of the Jews?"
And Jesus said, "You say."
¹²And in His being accused by the chief priests and elders, He answered nothing.
¹³Then Pilate says to Him, "Do You not hear how many things they witness against You?"
¹⁴And He did not answer him, not even to one word, so as to amaze the governor exceedingly.

The Crowd Chooses Barabbas
(Mark 15:6-11; Luke 23:13-25)

¹⁵And at *the* feast, the governor was accustomed to release one prisoner to the multitude, whom they were wishing. ¹⁶And at that time they were holding a notable prisoner called Barabbas.[b] ¹⁷Therefore of them being gathered together, Pilate said to them, "Whom want you *that* I shall release to you? Barabbas, or Jesus, who is called Christ?" ¹⁸For he knew that they had delivered Him up through envy.
¹⁹And as he was sitting on the judgment seat, his wife sent to him, saying, "Nothing to you and that righteous *man*; for I suffered many things in a dream today because of Him."
²⁰But the chief priests and the elders persuaded the crowds that they should ask for Barabbas, and should destroy Jesus.
²¹And the governor answering said to them, "Which of the two do you desire *that* I release to you?"
And they said, "Barabbas."

⁲²Pilate says to them, "What then should I do with Jesus, who is called Christ?" They all say, "Let *Him* be crucified." ²³And he said, "For what evil did He commit?" And they kept crying out all the more, saying, "Let *Him* be crucified."

Pilate Washes his Hands
(Mark 15:12-15)

²⁴And Pilate having seen that it availed nothing, but rather a riot is arising, having taken water, washed the hands before the crowd, saying, "I am guiltless of the blood of this *man*. For yourselves you will see."ᶜ
²⁵And all the people answering said, "His blood *be* on us, and on our children."
²⁶Then he released Barabbas to them; and having flogged Jesus, He delivered *Him* up that He might be crucified.

The Soldiers Mock Jesus
(Isaiah 50:4-11; Mark 15:16-20; Luke 22:63-65; John 19:1-15)

²⁷Then the soldiers of the governor, having taken Jesus into the Praetorium, gathered the whole cohort before Him. ²⁸And having stripped Him, they put a scarlet robe around Him. ²⁹And having twisted together a crown of thorns, they put *it* on His head, and a reed in His right hand; and having bowed the knees before Him, they mocked Him, saying, "Hail, King of the Jews!" ³⁰And having spit upon Him, they took the reed and kept striking *Him* on His head.
³¹And when they had mocked Him, they took off Him the robe, and they put His garments on Him and led away Him to crucify *Him*.

The Crucifixion
(Psalms 22:1-31; 69:1-36; Mark 15:21-32; Luke 23:26-43; John 19:16-27)

³²And going forth, they found a man of Cyrene, named Simon. They compelled him that he might carry His cross.
³³And having come to a place called Golgotha, which is called Place of a Skull, ³⁴they gave Him wine to drink, mingled with gall; and having tasted, He was not willing to drink *it*.
³⁵And having crucified Him, they divided His garments, casting lots.ᵈ ³⁶And sitting down, they were guarding Him there.
³⁷And they put up over His head the written accusation against Him:
THIS IS JESUS,
THE KING OF THE JEWS.
³⁸At the same time two robbers are crucified with Him, one at *the* right hand, and one at *the* left.
³⁹And those passing by kept railing at Him, wagging their heads ⁴⁰and saying, "The *One* destroying the temple and building *it* in three days, save Yourself! If You are *the* Son of God, also descend from the cross!"
⁴¹Likewise also, the chief priests with the scribes and elders, mocking, were saying, ⁴²"He saved others. He is not able to save Himself. He is King of Israel! Let Him descend now from the cross, and we will believe in Him. ⁴³He trusted on God. Let Him deliver Him now if He wants. For He said, 'I am *the* Son of God.'"
⁴⁴And likewise even the robbers, those having been crucified with Him, were upbraiding Him.

The Death of Jesus
(Psalm 22:1-31; Mark 15:33-41; Luke 23:44-49; John 19:28-30)

⁴⁵And from *the* sixth hour, darkness was over all the land, until *the* ninth hour. ⁴⁶And about the ninth hour, Jesus cried out in a loud voice, saying, "Eli, Eli,ᵉ lama sabachthani?" That is, "My God, My God, why have you forsaken Me?"ᶠ
⁴⁷And some of those who were standing there, having heard, began saying, "This *man* calls Elijah." ⁴⁸And immediately one of them, having run and having taken a sponge, and having filled *it* with vinegar and having put *it* on a reed, gave Him to drink.
⁴⁹And the rest were saying, "Let *it* be. Let us see whether Elijah comes to save Him."

⁵⁰And Jesus, having cried again in a loud voice, yielded up *His* spirit. ⁵¹And behold, the veil of the temple was torn into two from top to bottom. And the earth was shaken, and the rocks were split. ⁵²And the tombs were opened, and many bodies of the saints having fallen asleep arose. ⁵³And having gone forth out of the tombs after His resurrection, they entered into the holy city and appeared to many.

⁵⁴And the centurion and those with him keeping guard over Jesus, having seen the earthquake and the things taking place, feared greatly, saying, "Truly this was God's Son."

⁵⁵And many women were there, looking on from afar off, who had followed Jesus from Galilee, ministering to Him— ⁵⁶among whom was Mary Magdalene, and Mary the mother of James and Joseph, and the mother of the sons of Zebedee.

The Burial of Jesus
(Isaiah 53:9-12; Mark 15:42-47; Luke 23:50-56; John 19:38-42)

⁵⁷And evening having arrived, a rich man from Arimathea named Joseph came, who himself also was discipled to Jesus. ⁵⁸Having gone to Pilate, he asked for the body of Jesus. Then Pilate commanded it to be given up. ⁵⁹And Joseph having taken the body, wrapped it in a clean linen cloth ⁶⁰and placed it in his new tomb, which he had cut in the rock. And having rolled a great stone to the door of the tomb, he went away. ⁶¹And Mary Magdalene was there, and the other Mary, sitting opposite the tomb.

The Guards at the Tomb

⁶²And the next day, which is after the Preparation, the chief priests and the Pharisees were gathered together before Pilate, ⁶³saying, "Sir, we have remembered how that deceiver, while living, said, 'After three days I arise.' ⁶⁴Therefore command the tomb to be secured until the third day, lest ever His disciples having come, steal Him away and say to the people, 'He is risen from the dead.' And the last deception will be worse than the first."

⁶⁵Pilate said to them, "You have a guard. Go make *it as* secure as you know *how*." ⁶⁶And having gone with the guard, they made the tomb secure, having sealed the stone.

a 9-10 See Zechariah 11:12,13; Jeremiah 19:1-13; 32:6-9.
b 16 SBL and NA *Jesus Barabbas*; also in verse 17.
c 24 BYZ and TR *for this righteous blood*
d 35 TR includes *to fulfill what was said through the prophet, They divided my garments among them, and cast lots for my clothing.*
e 46 NE and WH *Eloi, Eloi*
f 46 Psalm 22:1

Matthew 28
The Resurrection
(Psalm 16:1-11; Psalm 49:1-20; Mark 16:1-8; Luke 24:1-12; John 20:1-9)

¹And after *the* Sabbaths, it being dawn toward *the* first *day* of *the* week, Mary Magdalene and the other Mary came to see the tomb.

²And behold, there was a great earthquake; for an angel of *the* Lord, having descended out of heaven and having come, rolled away the stone and was sitting upon it. ³And his appearance was like lightning, and his clothing white as snow. ⁴And those keeping guard trembled from fear of him, and they became as dead *men*.

⁵And the angel answering said to the women, "Fear not; for I know that you seek Jesus, the *One* having been crucified. ⁶He is not here, for He is risen as He said! Come, see the place where He was lying.ᵃ ⁷And having gone quickly, say to His disciples that He is risen from the dead and behold, He goes before you into Galilee; you will see Him there. Behold, I have told you."

⁸And having gone out quickly from the tomb with fear and great joy, they ran to tell His disciples. ⁹Andᵇ behold, Jesus met them, saying, "Greetings!" And having approached, they took hold of His feet and worshiped Him. ¹⁰Then Jesus says to them, "Do not fear. Go, tell My brothers,

so that they should go into Galilee, and there will they see Me."

The Report of the Guards

¹¹And *while* they were going, behold, some of the guard, having gone into the city, reported to the chief priests all the things having been done. ¹²And having been gathered together with the elders, and having taken counsel, they gave many silver pieces to the soldiers, ¹³saying, "Say that His disciples, having come by night, stole Him—we being asleep. ¹⁴And if this is heard by the governor, we will persuade him and will keep you out of trouble."

¹⁵And having taken the money, they did as they were instructed. And this report is spread abroad among *the* Jews until the present day.

The Great Commission
(Mark 16:14-18)

¹⁶And the eleven disciples went into Galilee, to the mountain where Jesus assigned them. ¹⁷And having seen Him they worshiped; but some doubted.

¹⁸And having come to *them*, Jesus spoke to them, saying, "All authority in heaven and on the earth has been given to Me. ¹⁹Therefore having gone, disciple all the nations, baptizing them in the name of the Father, and of the Son, and of the Holy Spirit, ²⁰teaching them to observe all things, whatever I commanded you. And behold, I am with you all the days, until the completion of the age."

a 6 BYZ and TR *where the Lord lay*
b 9 BYZ and TR include *as they were going to tell to his disciples*

Mark

Mark 1
The Mission of John the Baptist
(Isaiah 40:1-5; Matthew 3:1-12; Luke 3:1-20; John 1:19-28)

¹*The* beginning of the gospel of Jesus Christ, Son of God.ᵃ ²As it has been written in the prophet Isaiah:

"Behold, I send My messenger before Your face,
    who will prepare Your way."ᵇ
³"*The* voice of one crying in the wilderness,
    'Prepare the way of *the* Lord,
    make straight His paths.'"ᶜ

⁴John came baptizing in the wilderness and proclaiming a baptism of repentance for forgiveness of sins. ⁵And all the region of Judea and all of Jerusalem were going out to him and were being baptized by him in the Jordan river, confessing their sins.

⁶And John was clothed in camel's hair and a belt of leather around his waist; and he is eating locusts and wild honey. ⁷And he was preaching, saying, "He who comes after me *is* mightier than I, of whom I am not sufficient, having stooped down, to untie the strap of His sandals. ⁸I baptized you with water,ᵈ but He will baptize you with *the* Holy Spirit."

The Baptism of Jesus
(Matthew 3:13-17; Luke 3:21-22; John 1:29-34)

⁹And it came to pass in those days *that* Jesus came from Nazareth of Galilee and was baptized in the Jordan by John. ¹⁰And immediately going up from the water, he saw the heavens tearing open and the Spirit descending as a dove upon Him. ¹¹And a voice came out of the heavens: "You are My Son, the beloved; in You I am well pleased."

The Temptation of Jesus
(Matthew 4:1-11; Luke 4:1-13)

¹²And immediately the Spirit drives Him out into the wilderness. ¹³And He was in the wilderness forty days, being tempted by Satan. And He was with the wild animals, and the angels were ministering to Him.

Jesus Preaches in Galilee
(Isaiah 9:1-7; Matthew 4:12-17; Luke 4:14-15)

¹⁴And after the delivering up of John, Jesus came into Galilee, proclaiming the gospel of God ¹⁵and saying, "The time

has been fulfilled, and the kingdom of God has drawn near; repent and believe in the gospel."

The First Disciples
(Matthew 4:18-22; Matthew 13:47-52; Luke 5:1-11; John 1:35-42)

16And passing by the Sea of Galilee, He saw Simon and Andrew, the brother of Simon, casting a net into the sea; for they were fishermen. 17And Jesus said to them, "Come after Me, and I will make you to become fishers of men." 18And immediately, having left the nets, they followed Him.

19And having gone on a little, He saw James the *son* of Zebedee and his brother John, and they *were* in the boat mending the nets. 20And immediately He called them, and having left their father Zebedee in the boat with the hired servants, they went away after Him.

Jesus Expels an Unclean Spirit
(Luke 4:31-37)

21And they go into Capernaum; and immediately on the Sabbaths, having entered into the synagogue, He was teaching. 22And they were astonished at His teaching, for He was teaching them as having authority, and not as the scribes.

23And immediately there was a man in their synagogue with an unclean spirit, and he cried out, 24saying, "What to us and to You, Jesus of Nazareth? Did You come to destroy us? I know who You are, the Holy *One* of God!"

25And Jesus rebuked him, saying, "Be silent, and come forth out of him!" 26And having thrown him into convulsions, and having cried in a loud voice, the unclean spirit came forth out of him.

27And all were astonished, so as to question among themselves, saying, "What is this new teaching? With authority He commands even the unclean spirits, and they obey Him!" 28And news of Him immediately went out everywhere into all the surrounding region of Galilee.

Jesus Heals at Peter's House
(Matthew 8:14-17; Luke 4:38-41)

29And immediately having gone forth out of the synagogue, they came into the house of Simon and Andrew, with James and John. 30And the mother-in-law of Simon was laying sick fevering. And immediately they speak to Him about her. 31And having come to *her*, He raised her up, having taken hold of the hand. And the fever left her, and she began to minister to them.

32And evening having come, when the sun went down, they began bringing to Him all those being sick and those being possessed by demons. 33And all the city was gathered together at the door. 34And He healed many being sick of various diseases, and He cast out many demons. And He would not allow the demons to speak, because they knew Him.

Jesus Prays and Preaches
(Luke 4:42-44)

35And having risen up very early, still much in night, He went out and departed into a solitary place, and there He was praying. 36And Simon and those with him went after Him. 37And having found Him, also they say to Him, "Everyone seeks You!"

38And He says to them, "Let us go another way into the neighboring towns, so that I might preach there also; for I have come forth for this." 39And He was going in all Galilee, preaching in their synagogues and casting out demons.

The Leper's Prayer
(Leviticus 14:1-32; Matthew 8:1-4; Luke 5:12-16)

40And a leper^e comes to Him, imploring Him and kneeling down to Him, and saying to Him, "If You are willing, You are able to cleanse me."

41And having been moved with compassion,^f having stretched out His hand, He touched him and says to him, "I am willing, be cleansed."

42And immediately the leprosy departed from him, and he was cleansed.

⁴³And having sternly warned him, He sent him away immediately. ⁴⁴And He says to him, "See *that* you speak nothing to *anyone*. But go, show yourself to the priest, and offer for your cleansing what Moses commanded, for a testimony to them."
⁴⁵But having gone out, he began to proclaim much and to spread abroad the matter, so that He was no longer able to enter openly into *the* city, but He was out in solitary places. And they were coming to Him from every quarter.

a 1 SBL and WH do not include *the Son of God*.
b 2 Malachi 3:1
c 3 Isaiah 40:3
d 8 Or *in water*
e 40 Leprosy was a term for several skin diseases. See Leviticus 13.
f 41 SBL *indignant*

Mark 2
Jesus Heals a Paralytic
(Matthew 9:1-8; Luke 5:17-26)

¹And He having entered again into Capernaum after *some* days, it was heard that He is in *the* house. ²And many were gathered together, so as to have no more space, not even at the door. And He was speaking the word to them.
³And they come, bringing to Him a paralytic, being carried by four. ⁴And not being able to come near to Him on account of the crowd, they removed the roof where He was, and having broken *it* up, they let down the pallet on which the paralytic was lying.
⁵And Jesus, having seen their faith, says to the paralytic, "Son, your sins are forgiven."
⁶And some of the scribes were sitting there and reasoning in their hearts, ⁷"Why does this *man* speak thus? He blasphemes! Who is able to forgive sins, except God alone?"
⁸And immediately Jesus, having known in His spirit that they are reasoning thus within themselves, says to them, "Why do you reason these things in your hearts? ⁹Which is easier, to say to the paralytic, 'Your sins are forgiven,' or to say, 'Arise, and take up your mat, and walk'? ¹⁰But that you might know that the Son of Man has authority to forgive sins on the earth…" He says to the paralytic, ¹¹"I say to you, arise, take up your mat, and go to your home."
¹²And he arose, and immediately, having taken up the mat, he went forth before all, so as for all to be amazed and to glorify God, saying, "Never did we see thus."

The Calling of Levi
(Matthew 9:9-13; Luke 5:27-32)

¹³And He went forth again beside the sea, and all the crowd was coming to Him, and He taught them.
¹⁴And passing on, He saw Levi the *son* of Alphaeus sitting at the tax booth, and says to him, "Follow Me." And having arisen, he followed Him.
¹⁵And it came to pass in His reclining in his house, that many tax collectors and sinners were reclining with Jesus and His disciples; for there were many, and they were following Him. ¹⁶And the scribes of the Pharisees, having seen Him eating with the sinners and tax collectors, were saying to His disciples, "Why does He eat[a] with the tax collectors and sinners?"
¹⁷And Jesus having heard, says to them, "Those being strong have no need of a physician, but those being sick. I did not come to call *the* righteous, but sinners."

Questions about Fasting
(Matthew 9:14-15; Luke 5:33-35)

¹⁸And the disciples of John and the Pharisees were fasting. And they come and say to Him, "Why do the disciples of John and the disciples of the Pharisees fast, but Your disciples do not fast?"
¹⁹And Jesus said to them, "Are the sons of the bridechamber able to fast while the bridegroom is with them? As long a time *as* they have the bridegroom with them, they are not able to fast. ²⁰But *the* days will come when the bridegroom will have been taken away from them, and then they will fast in those days.

The Patches and the Wineskins
(Matthew 9:16-17; Luke 5:36-39)

21 No one sews a patch of unshrunk cloth on old clothing. Otherwise the patch tears away from it, the new from the old, and a worse tear takes place. 22 And no one puts new wine into old wineskins; otherwise the wine will burst the wineskins, and the wine will be destroyed—and the wineskins. Instead, new wine *is poured* into new wineskins."[b]

The Lord of the Sabbath
(1 Samuel 21:1-9; Matthew 12:1-8; Luke 6:1-5)

23 And it came to pass, He is passing through the grainfields on the Sabbaths, and His disciples began to make *their* way, plucking the heads of grain. 24 And the Pharisees were saying to Him, "Behold, why do they that which is unlawful on the Sabbaths?" 25 And He said to them, "Did you never read what David did when he had need, and he and those with him hungered— 26 how he entered into the house of God in *the days of* Abiathar the high priest, and ate the loaves of the presentation, which is not lawful to eat except for the priests—and he even gave to those being with him?" 27 And He said to them, "The Sabbath was made on account of the man, and not the man on account of the Sabbath. 28 So then, the Son of Man is Lord even of the Sabbath."

a 16 **BYZ and TR include** *and drink*
b 22 Tischendorf and some other texts do not include *Instead, new wine is poured into new wineskins*

Mark 3
Jesus Heals on the Sabbath
(Matthew 12:9-14; Luke 6:6-11)

1 And He entered into the synagogue again, and a man having a withered hand was there. 2 And they were watching Him, whether He will heal him on the Sabbaths, in order that they might accuse Him. 3 And He says to the man having the withered hand, "Arise into the midst." 4 And He says to them, "Is it lawful on the Sabbaths to do good, or to do evil, to save life, or to kill?"

But they were silent. 5 And having looked around on them with anger, being grieved at the hardness of their heart, He says to the man, "Stretch out your hand." And he stretched *it* out, and his hand was restored. 6 And the Pharisees having gone out, immediately began to take counsel with the Herodians against Him, how they might destroy Him.

Multitudes Follow Jesus

7 And Jesus withdrew with His disciples to the sea, and a great multitude from Galilee followed, and from Judea, 8 and from Jerusalem, and from Idumea, and beyond the Jordan, and around Tyre and Sidon. A great multitude came to Him, having heard how much He was doing. 9 And He spoke to His disciples, that a boat might wait upon Him, on account of the crowd, that they might not press upon Him. 10 For He healed many, so as for as many as had diseases to press upon Him, that they might touch Him. 11 And the unclean spirits, whenever they beheld Him, were falling down before Him and crying out, saying, "You are the Son of God." 12 And He would rebuke them much, so that they should not make Him known.

The Twelve Apostles
(Matthew 10:1-4; Luke 6:12-16)

13 And He goes up on the mountain and calls near those whom He Himself wanted, and they went to Him. 14 And He appointed twelve ones, and He called *them* apostles, that they might be with Him, and that He might send them to preach, 15 and to have authority to cast out demons.

16 And He appointed the Twelve; and to Simon He added *the* name Peter; 17 and James the *son* of Zebedee, and John the brother of James, and He added to them *the* name Boanerges, which is, Sons of Thunder; 18 and Andrew, and Philip, and

Bartholomew, and Matthew, and Thomas, and James the *son* of Alphaeus, and Thaddaeus, and Simon the Zealot, [19]and Judas Iscariot, who also betrayed Him.

A House Divided
(Matthew 12:22-30; Luke 11:14-23)

[20]And He comes to a house, and a crowd comes together again, so that not even are they able to eat bread. [21]And those belonging to Him having heard, went out to seize Him; for they were saying, "He is out of His mind." [22]And the scribes, those having come down from Jerusalem, were saying, "He has Beelzebul," and "By the prince of the demons He casts out the demons." [23]And having called them to *Him*, He began speaking to them in parables: "How is Satan able to cast out Satan? [24]And if a kingdom is divided against itself, that kingdom is not able to stand. [25]And if a house is divided against itself, that house will not be able to stand. [26]And if Satan has risen up against himself and has been divided, he is not able to stand, but is coming to an end. [27]But no one is able, having entered into the house of the strong man, to plunder his goods, unless first he binds the strong man. And then he will plunder his house.

The Unpardonable Sin
(Matthew 12:31-32)

[28]Truly I say to you that all sins and blasphemies will be forgiven the sons of men, as many as they shall have blasphemed. [29]But whoever shall blaspheme against the Holy Spirit does not have forgiveness, to the age, but is guilty *of* eternal sin." [30]For they were saying, "He has an unclean spirit."

Jesus' Mother and Brothers
(Matthew 12:46-50; Luke 8:19-21)

[31]And His mother and His brothers arrive, and standing outside, sent to Him, calling Him. [32]And a crowd was sitting around Him, and they said to Him, "Behold, Your mother and Your brothers[a] outside are seeking You." [33]And He answering them says, "Who are My mother and My brothers?" [34]And having looked around on those who were sitting around Him in a circle, He says, "Behold, My mother and My brothers! [35]For whoever shall do the will of God, he is My brother and sister and mother."

a 32 NE and NA include *and your sisters*

Mark 4
The Parable of the Sower
(Matthew 13:1-9; Luke 8:4-15)

[1]And again He began to teach beside the sea. And a great crowd was gathered together to Him, so that He, having entered into a boat, sat in the sea, and all the crowd was on the land, close to the sea.

[2]And He began teaching them many things in parables, and in His teaching He was saying to them, [3]"Listen! Behold, the *one* sowing went out to sow. [4]And it came to pass as he sowed, some fell along the road, and the birds came and devoured it.

[5]And other fell upon the rocky place where it had not much soil, and it sprang up immediately, because of not having depth of soil. [6]And after the sun rose, it was scorched, and because of not having root, it withered away.

[7]And other fell among the thorns, and the thorns grew up and choked it, and it yielded no fruit.

[8]And other fell into the good soil and began yielding fruit, growing up and increasing, and one bearing thirtyfold, and one sixty, and one a hundred."

[9]And He was saying, "He who has ears to hear, let him hear."

The Purpose of Jesus' Parables
(Matthew 13:10-17)

[10]And when He was alone, those around Him with the Twelve began asking Him about the parable.

[11]And He was saying to them, "To you has been given the mystery of the

kingdom of God, but to those who are outside, everything is done in parables, ¹²so that,

> 'Seeing, they might see and not perceive;
>> and hearing, they might hear and not understand;
>
> lest ever they should turn,
>> and they should be forgiven.'ᵃ"

The Parable of the Sower Explained
(Matthew 13:18-23)

¹³And He says to them, "Do you not understand this parable? Then how will you understand all the parables? ¹⁴The *one* sowing sows the word. ¹⁵And these are those along the road, where the word is sown; and when they hear, immediately Satan comes and takes away the word having been sown in them.
¹⁶And these are likewise those sown upon the rocky places, who when they hear the word, immediately receive it with joy, ¹⁷and they have no root in themselves, but are temporary. Then tribulation or persecution having arisen on account of the word, immediately they fall away.
¹⁸And these are those sown among the thorns. These are those having heard the word, ¹⁹and the cares of this age and the deceit of riches, and the desires of the other things entering in, choke the word, and it becomes unfruitful.
²⁰And these are those having been sown upon the good soil, such as hear the word and receive *it*, and bring forth fruit: one thirtyfold, and one sixty, and one a hundred."

The Lesson of the Lamp
(Luke 8:16-18)

²¹And He was saying to them, "The lamp is not brought in so that it might be put under the basket, or under the bed. *Is it* not that it might be put upon the lampstand? ²²For there is nothing which *is* hidden except that it should be made manifest; nor has taken place a secret thing, but that it should come to light. ²³If anyone has ears to hear, let him hear."

²⁴And He was saying to them, "Take heed what you hear. With what measure you measure it will be measured to you, and more will be added to you. ²⁵For whoever may have, it will be given to him; and he who does not have, even that which he has will be taken away from him."

The Seed Growing Secretly

²⁶And He was saying, "The kingdom of God is thus, as a man should cast the seed upon the earth, ²⁷and should sleep and rise night and day, and the seed should sprout and grow—he not knows how. ²⁸Of itself, the earth brings forth fruit—first a plant, then an ear, then full grain in the ear. ²⁹And when the fruit offers itself, he sends the sickle immediately, for the harvest has come."

The Parable of the Mustard Seed
(Matthew 13:31-32; Luke 13:18-19)

³⁰And He was saying, "To what shall we liken the kingdom of God? Or with what parable shall we present it? ³¹As a grain of mustard, which, when it has been sown upon the earth, is smallest of all the seeds that *are* upon the earth, ³²and when it has been sown, it grows up, and becomes greater than all the garden plants, and produces great branches, so that the birds of the air are able to encamp under its shadow."

³³And with many such parables He kept speaking the word to them, as they were able to hear, ³⁴and He would not speak to them without parables; but privately He would explain all things to His own disciples.

Jesus Calms the Storm
(Matthew 8:23-27; Luke 8:22-25)

³⁵And on that day, evening having come, He says to them, "Let us pass over to the other side." ³⁶And having dismissed the crowd, they take Him with *them* since He was in the boat; and other boats were with Him.
³⁷And a violent storm of wind comes, and the waves were breaking over the boat, so that the boat already is being filled up. ³⁸And He was in the stern, sleeping on

the cushion. And they awaken Him and say to Him, "Teacher, is it no concern to You that we perish?"

³⁹And having been awoken, He rebuked the wind and said to the sea, "Silence, be still!" And the wind abated, and there was a great calm.

⁴⁰And He said to them, "Why are you fearful? Have you still no faith?"

⁴¹And they feared *with* great fear and were saying to each other, "Who then is this, that even the wind and the sea obey Him?"

a 12 Isaiah 6:9,10

Mark 5
The Demons and the Pigs
(Matthew 8:28-34; Luke 8:26-39)

¹And they came to the other side of the sea, to the region of the Gerasenes.ᵃ ²And of Him having gone forth out of the boat, immediately out of the tombs a man with an unclean spirit met Him, ³who had the dwelling in the tombs. And no longer was anyone able to bind him, not even with chains, ⁴because he often had been bound with shackles and chains, and the chains had been torn in two by him, and the shackles had been shattered, and no one was able to subdue him. ⁵And constantly all night and day in the tombs and in the mountains, he was crying out and cutting himself with stones.

⁶And having seen Jesus from afar, he ran and fell on his knees before Him. ⁷And having cried in a loud voice, he said, "What to me and to You, Jesus, Son of the Most High God? I adjure You by God, do not torment me." ⁸For He was saying to him, "You come forth out of the man, unclean spirit!"

⁹And He was asking him, "What *is* your name?"

And he answered saying, "My name *is* Legion, because we are many." ¹⁰And he begged Him numerous times that He would not send them out of the country.

¹¹Now there was a great herd of pigs there near the mountain, feeding. ¹²And they begged Him, saying, "Send us into the pigs, so that we may enter into them."

¹³And He allowed them. And the unclean spirits having gone out, entered into the pigs, and the herd—about two thousand—rushed down the steep bank into the sea, and they were drowned in the sea.

¹⁴And those feeding them fled and proclaimed *it* to the city and to the country. And they went out to see what it is that has been done. ¹⁵And they come to Jesus and see the *man* possessed by demons sitting, clothed and sound minded—the *one* having had the legion—and they were afraid. ¹⁶And those having seen *it* related to them how it happened to the *one* being possessed by demons, and concerning the pigs. ¹⁷And they began to implore Him to depart from their region.

¹⁸And He having entered into the boat, the *one* having been possessed by demons was begging Him that he might be with Him. ¹⁹And He did not permit him, but He says to him, "Go to your home, to your own, and preach to them how much the Lord did for you and had mercy on you."

²⁰And he departed and began to proclaim in the Decapolisᵇ how much Jesus had done for him; and all were marveling.

The Healing Touch of Jesus
(Matthew 9:18-26; Luke 8:40-56)

²¹And Jesus having passed over again in the boat to the other side, a great crowd was gathered to Him, and He was beside the sea. ²²And one of the synagogue rulers comes, named Jairus, and having seen Him, falls at His feet, ²³and he begs Him much, saying, "My little daughter is holding at the end, that having come, You would lay the hands on her, so that she might be cured, and she shall live."

²⁴And He departed with him. And a great crowd was following Him and pressing in on Him. ²⁵And a woman, being with a flux of blood twelve years, ²⁶and having suffered much under many physicians

and having spent everything of hers, and having benefited in no way, but rather to the worse having come, ²⁷having heard concerning Jesus, having come up in the crowd behind, she touched His clothing. ²⁸For she was saying, "If I shall touch even His garments, I will be healed." ²⁹And immediately her flow of blood was dried up, and she knew in the body that she was healed from the affliction.
³⁰And immediately Jesus, having known in Himself the power having gone forth out of Him, having turned in the crowd, said, "Who touched My garments?"
³¹And His disciples were saying to Him, "You see the crowd pressing in on You, and You say, 'Who touched Me?'"
³²And He was looking around to see the *one* having done this. ³³And the woman, having been frightened and trembling, knowing what had been done to her, came and fell down before Him, and told Him the whole truth.
³⁴And He said to her, "Daughter, your faith has healed you; go in peace and be sound from your affliction."
³⁵*While* yet He is speaking, they come from the ruler of the synagogue's *house*, saying, "Your daughter is dead; why do you trouble the Teacher still?"
³⁶But Jesus, having heard the word spoken, says to the ruler of the synagogue, "Do not fear; only believe."
³⁷And He did not allow *anyone* to follow with Him, except Peter, and James, and John the brother of James.
³⁸And they come to the house of the ruler of the synagogue, and He beholds a commotion, and much weeping and wailing. ³⁹And having entered, He says to them, "Why do you make a commotion and weep? The child is not dead, but sleeps." ⁴⁰And they were laughing at Him.
And He, having put all outside, takes with *Him* the father and the mother of the child, and those with Him, and enters in where the child was. ⁴¹And having taken the hand of the child, He says to her, "Talitha, koum!" which is translated, "Little girl, I say to you, arise!" ⁴²And immediately the girl arose and began walking, for she was twelve of years. And immediately they were overcome with great amazement. ⁴³And He instructed them strictly that no one should know this; and He commanded to be given to her to eat.

a 1 BYZ and TR *Gadarenes*
b 20 That is, the Ten Cities

Mark 6
The Rejection at Nazareth
(Isaiah 61:1-11; Matthew 2:19-23; Matthew 13:53-58; Luke 2:39-40; Luke 4:16-30)

¹And He went out from there and came into His hometown; and His disciples follow Him. ²And *the* Sabbath having come, He began to teach in the synagogue; and many hearing were astonished, saying, "From where to this *man are* these things, and what *is* the wisdom having been given to Him, even the miracles such as are done by His hands? ³Is not this the carpenter, the son of Mary, and brother of James and Joseph and Judas and Simon? And are not His sisters here with us?" And they took offense at Him.
⁴And Jesus said to them, "A prophet is not without honor, except in his hometown, and among his relatives, and in his household." ⁵And He was not able to do *any* work of power there, except having laid the hands on a few sick, He healed *them*. ⁶And He was amazed because of their unbelief. And He was going around the villages, teaching.

The Ministry of the Twelve
(Matthew 10:5-15; Luke 9:1-6)

⁷And He calls to *Him* the Twelve, and He began to send them forth two *by* two, and He gave to them authority over the unclean spirits. ⁸And He instructed them that they should take nothing for *the* journey, except only a staff—no bread, nor bag, nor money in the belt— ⁹but wearing sandals, and do not put on two tunics.

¹⁰And He would say to them, "Wherever you enter into a house, remain there until you go out from there. ¹¹And if any place will not receive you nor hear you, departing from there, shake off the dust which *is* under your feet, for a testimony against them."ᵃ

¹²And having gone out, they preached that they should repent. ¹³And they were casting out many demons, and were anointing many sick with oil, and healing *them*.

The Beheading of John
(Matthew 14:1-12; Luke 9:7-9)

¹⁴And King Herod heard; for His name became well known. And *people* were saying, "John, the *one* baptizing, is risen out from *the* dead, and because of this the miraculous powers operate in him." ¹⁵But others were saying, "He is Elijah," and others were saying, "A prophet, like one of the prophets."

¹⁶And Herod having heard, was saying, "John, whom I beheaded—he is risen!" ¹⁷For Herod himself, having sent, seized John, and bound him in prison, on account of Herodias, the wife of Philip his brother, because he had married her. ¹⁸For John had been saying to Herod, "It is not lawful for you to have your brother's wife."

¹⁹And Herodias held it against him, and wished to kill him, and was not able. ²⁰For Herod was afraid of John, knowing him a righteous and holy man; and he kept him safe. And having heard him, he was greatly perplexed, and heard him gladly.

²¹And an opportune day having come, when Herod on his birthday made a banquet to his great men, and to the chief captains, and to the leading *men* of Galilee, ²²and the daughter of Herodias herself having come in, and having danced, pleased Herod and those reclining with *him*. And *the* king said the to the girl, "Ask me whatever you wish, and I will give to you." ²³And he swore to her, "Whatever you might ask me, I will give you, up to half of my kingdom."

²⁴And she having gone out, said to her mother, "What shall I ask?"

And she said, "The head of John the *one* baptizing."

²⁵And having entered immediately with haste to the king, she asked, saying, "I desire that you give to me the head of John the Baptist upon a platter at once." ²⁶And the king, having been made very sorrowful, on account of the oaths and those reclining with *him*, did not want to refuse her. ²⁷And immediately the king, having sent an executioner, commanded to be brought his head. And having gone, he beheaded him in the prison, ²⁸and brought his head upon a platter, and gave it to the girl, and the girl gave it to her mother. ²⁹And his disciples having heard *it*, came and took up his body, and laid it in a tomb.

The Feeding of the Five Thousand
(Matthew 14:13-21; Luke 9:10-17; John 6:1-15)

³⁰And the apostles are gathered together to Jesus, and they related to him all things, what they had done and what they had taught. ³¹And He said to them, "You yourselves come apart to a solitary place, and rest a little." For those coming and those going were many, and not even did they have opportunity to eat.

³²And they went away by the boat into a solitary place by themselves. ³³And many saw them going, and recognized, and ran together there on foot from all the cities, and went before them. ³⁴And having gone out, He saw a great crowd and was moved with compassion toward them, because they were like sheep not having a shepherd. And He began to teach them many things.

³⁵And the hour already being late, having come to Him, his disciples were saying, "The place is desolate, and the hour already *is* late. ³⁶Dismiss them, that having gone to the surrounding region

and villages, they might buy for themselves something to eat."

³⁷But answering, He said to them, "You give to them to eat."

And they say to Him, "Having gone, shall we buy two hundred denarii[b] of bread and give them to eat?"

³⁸And He says to them, "How many loaves do you have? Go, see."

And having known, they say, "Five, and two fish."

³⁹And He commanded them to make them all recline, groups *by* groups, on the green grass. ⁴⁰And they sat down groups *by* groups, by hundreds and by fifties.

⁴¹And having taken the five loaves and the two fish, having looked up to the heaven, He blessed and broke the loaves, and He kept giving *them* to His disciples, that they might set before them. And He divided the two fish among all.

⁴²And all ate and were satisfied. ⁴³And they took up twelve hand-baskets full of fragments, and also of the fish. ⁴⁴And those having eaten of the loaves were five thousand men.

Jesus Walks on Water
(Matthew 14:22-33; John 6:16-25)

⁴⁵And immediately He compelled His disciples to enter into the boat and to go before *Him* to the other side, to Bethsaida, until He should dismiss the crowd. ⁴⁶And having taken leave of them, He departed into the mountain to pray.

⁴⁷And evening having come, the boat was in the midst of the sea, and He alone upon the land. ⁴⁸And He having seen them straining in the rowing—for the wind was contrary to them—about *the* fourth watch of the night, He comes to them, walking on the sea, and He was wishing to pass by them. ⁴⁹And having seen Him walking on the sea, they thought that *it* is a ghost, and cried out. ⁵⁰For all saw Him and were troubled.

And immediately He spoke with them, and says to them, "Take courage; I am *He*; fear not." ⁵¹And He went up to them into the boat, and the wind ceased. And exceedingly in abundance they were amazed in themselves, ⁵²for they had not understood about the loaves, but their heart had been hardened.

Jesus Heals at Gennesaret
(Matthew 14:34-36)

⁵³And having passed over, they came to the land, to Gennesaret, and drew to shore. ⁵⁴And of them having come out of the boat, having recognized Him immediately, ⁵⁵they ran through all that country, and they began to carry about on mats those being sick to wherever they were hearing that He is. ⁵⁶And wherever He entered into villages or into cities or into fields, they were laying the ailing in the marketplaces and were begging Him that only they might touch the fringe His clothing; and as many as touched Him were being healed.

a 11 BYZ and TR include *Truly I tell you, It will be more tolerable for Sodom and Gomorrah in the day of judgment, than for that town.*
b 37 A denarius was customarily a day's wage for a laborer (see Matthew 20:2)

Mark 7
Tradition and Worship
(Matthew 15:1-9)

¹And the Pharisees and some of the scribes, having come from Jerusalem, are gathered together to Him. ²And they had seen that some of His disciples are eating the bread with defiled, that is, unwashed hands.

³For the Pharisees and all the Jews do not eat unless they wash the hands carefully, holding the tradition of the elders; ⁴and *on coming* from the market, they do not eat unless they wash; and there are many other things which they received, *for them* to hold to—washings of cups and vessels and utensils and couches for dining.[a]

⁵And the Pharisees and the scribes questioned Him, "Why do Your disciples not walk according to the tradition of the elders, but eat the bread with unwashed hands?"

⁶And He said to them, "Isaiah prophesied rightly concerning you hypocrites, as it has been written:

> 'This people honors Me with the lips,
>   but their heart is kept far away from Me;
> ⁷and they worship Me in vain,
>   teaching *as* doctrines the precepts of men.'*b*

⁸Having neglected the commandment of God, you hold to the tradition of men."*c*
⁹And He was saying to them, "Neatly do you set aside the commandment of God, that you might keep*d* your tradition. ¹⁰For Moses said, 'Honor your Father and your mother,'*e* and, 'The *one* speaking evil of father or mother must surely die.'*f* ¹¹But you say *that* if a man says to the father or the mother, 'Whatever you might be profited from me, *it is* Corban,' that is, a gift, ¹²no longer do you permit him to do anything for the father or the mother, ¹³making void the word of God for your tradition, which you have handed down. And you do many *things* like such."

What Defiles a Man
(Matthew 15:10-20)

¹⁴And having summoned the crowd again, He was saying to them, "Listen to Me, all, and understand: ¹⁵There is nothing from outside the man entering into him which is able to defile him; but the things proceeding out of the man are the things defiling the man."*g*
¹⁷And when He went into *the* house from the crowd, His disciples were asking Him the parable.
¹⁸And He says to them, "Thus are you also without understanding? Do you not understand that everything entering into the man from outside is not able to defile him, ¹⁹because it does not enter into his heart, but into the belly, and goes out into the sewer?" (*Thus* purifying all foods.)
²⁰And He was saying, "That going forth out of the man, that defiles the man. ²¹For from within the heart of men go forth evil thoughts, sexual immorality, thefts, murders, adulteries,*h* ²²covetous desires, wickednesses, deceit, sensuality, an evil eye, slander, pride, foolishness. ²³All these evils go forth from within, and they defile the man."

The Faith of the Gentile Woman
(Matthew 15:21-28)

²⁴And from there having risen up, He went away into the region of Tyre.*i* And having entered into a house, He was wishing no one to know *it*, but He was not able to be hidden. ²⁵But immediately, having heard about Him, a woman whose little daughter had *an* unclean spirit, having come, fell at His feet. ²⁶Now the woman was Gentile, Syrophoenician by race, and kept asking Him that He should cast forth the demon out of her daughter.
²⁷And He was saying to her, "Permit the children to be satisfied first; for it is not good to take the children's bread and to cast *it* to the dogs."
²⁸But she answered and says to Him, "Yes, Lord, even the dogs under the table eat of the children's crumbs."
²⁹And He said to her, "Because of this word, go; the demon has gone forth out of your daughter." ³⁰And having gone away to her home, she found the child lying on the bed, and the demon having gone out.

The Deaf and Mute Man
(Isaiah 35:1-10; Matthew 9:32-34)

³¹And again having departed from the region of Tyre, He came through Sidon, to the Sea of Galilee, through *the* midst of the region of *the* Decapolis.*j* ³²And they bring to Him a man *who was* deaf and who spoke with difficulty, and they implore Him that He might lay the hand on him.
³³And having taken him away from the crowd privately, He put His fingers to his ears, and having spit, He touched his tongue, ³⁴and having looked up to heaven He sighed deeply, and He says to him, "Ephphatha!" (that is, "Be opened!"). ³⁵And immediately his ears were opened, and the band of his tongue

was loosed, and he began speaking plainly.

³⁶And He instructed them that they should tell no one. But as much as He kept instructing them, they were proclaiming *it* more abundantly. ³⁷And they were astonished above measure, saying, "He has done all things well. He makes both the deaf to hear and the mute to speak."

a 4 NE and WH do not include *couches for dining*
b 7 Isaiah 29:13
c 8 BYZ and TR include *washings of cups and pots and many such things like these*
d 9 NA *establish*
e 10 Exodus 20:12; Deuteronomy 5:16
f 10 Exodus 21:17; Leviticus 20:9
g 15 BYZ and TR include *16 If anyone has ears to hear, let him hear.*
h 21 Many Sources move *adulteries* to verse 22
i 24 WH, BYZ and TR include *and Sidon*
j 31 That is, the Ten Cities

Mark 8
The Feeding of the Four Thousand
(Matthew 15:29-39)

¹In those days, *of the* crowd again being great and not having what they might eat, having summoned the disciples, He says to them, ²"I am moved with compassion upon the crowd, because they continue with Me three days already, and have nothing that they might eat. ³And if I shall send them away hungry to their homes, they will faint on the way. For some of them are come from afar."

⁴And His disciples answered Him, "From where will anyone be able to satisfy these with bread, here in this desolate place?"

⁵And He was asking them, "How many loaves do you have?"

And they said, "Seven."

⁶And He directs the crowd to recline on the ground. And having taken the seven loaves, having given thanks, He broke *them* and kept giving *them* to His disciples, that they might set before *them*. And they set *it* before the crowd.

⁷And they had a few small fish. And having blessed them, He ordered these also to be set before *them*.

⁸And they ate and were satisfied. And they took up seven baskets of fragments over and above. ⁹And there were about four thousand. And He sent them away. ¹⁰And immediately having entered into the boat with His disciples, He came into the district of Dalmanutha.

The Demand for a Sign
(Matthew 16:1-4; Luke 12:54-56)

¹¹And the Pharisees went out and began to dispute with Him, seeking from Him a sign from heaven, testing Him.

¹²And having sighed deeply in His spirit, He says, "Why does this generation seek a sign? Truly I say to you, no sign will be given to this generation." ¹³And having left them, having embarked again, He went away to the other side.

The Leaven to Beware
(Matthew 16:5-12)

¹⁴And they forgot to take loaves, and except one loaf, they did not have *any* with them in the boat. ¹⁵And He was instructing them, saying, "Watch out! Take heed of the leaven of the Pharisees and the leaven of Herod." ¹⁶And they were reasoning with one another because they had no loaves.

¹⁷And having known, He says to them, "Why do you reason because you have no loaves? Do you not yet perceive nor understand? Do you have your heart hardened? ¹⁸'Having eyes, do you not see? And having ears, do you not hear?' And do you not remember? ¹⁹When I broke the five loaves for the five thousand, how many hand-baskets full of fragments did you take up?"

They say to Him, "Twelve."

²⁰"And when the seven *were* to the four thousand, how many baskets full of fragments did you take up?"

And they said, "Seven."

²¹And He was saying to them, "Do you not yet understand?"

The Blind Man at Bethsaida

²²And they come to Bethsaida. And they bring to Him a blind *man* and implore Him that He might touch him. ²³And having taken hold of the hand of the blind *man*, He led him forth out of the village, and

having spit upon his eyes, having laid the hands upon him, He was asking him if you see anything.

²⁴And having looked up, he was saying, "I see the men, for I see *them* as trees walking."

²⁵Then He laid the hands upon his eyes again, and he opened his eyes and was restored, and he began to see everything clearly. ²⁶And He sent him to his home, saying, "You may not enter into the village."ᵃ

Peter's Confession of Christ
(Matthew 16:13-20; Luke 9:18-20; John 6:66-71)

²⁷And Jesus and His disciples went forth into the villages of Caesarea Philippi. And on the way, He was questioning His disciples, saying to them, "Whom do men pronounce Me to be?"

²⁸And they answered Him, saying, "John the Baptist; and others, Elijah; and others, one of the prophets."

²⁹And He was questioning them, "But whom do you pronounce Me to be?" Peter answering, says to Him, "You are the Christ."

³⁰And He warned them that they should tell no one concerning Him.

Christ's Passion Foretold
(Matthew 16:21-23; Luke 9:21-22)

³¹And He began to teach them that it is necessary for the Son of Man to suffer many things, and to be rejected by the elders and the chief priests and the scribes, and to be killed, and after three days to rise *again*. ³²And He was speaking openly the word. And Peter having taken Him to him, began to rebuke Him.

³³And having turned and having looked upon His disciples, He rebuked Peter, and said, "Get behind Me, Satan, for your thoughts are not of the things of God, but the things of men."

Take up Your Cross
(Matthew 10:37-39; Matthew 16:24-28; Luke 9:23-27)

³⁴And having summoned the crowd with His disciples, He said to them, "If anyone desires to come after Me, let him deny himself, and let him take up his cross, and let him follow Me. ³⁵For whoever might desire to save his life will lose it, and whoever will lose his life on account of Me and of the gospel, he will save it.

³⁶For what does it profit a man to gain the whole world and to lose his soul? ³⁷For what shall a man give *as* an exchange for his soul? ³⁸For whoever may be ashamed of Me and My words in this adulterous and sinful generation, the Son of Man also will be ashamed of him when He shall come in the glory of His Father, with the holy angels."

a 26 **BYZ** and **TR** *Do not go and tell anyone in the village*

Mark 9
The Transfiguration
(Matthew 17:1-13; Luke 9:28-36; 2 Peter 1:16-21)

¹And He was saying to them, "Truly I say to you that there are some of those standing here who shall not taste of death until they see the kingdom of God having come with power."

²And after six days, Jesus takes with *Him* Peter and James and John, and brings them up into a high mountain by themselves alone. And He was transfigured before them, ³and His garments became exceedingly shining white, such as no launderer on the earth is able thus to whiten. ⁴And Elijah appeared to them with Moses, and they were talking with Jesus.

⁵And Peter answering, says to Jesus, "Rabbi, it is good for us to be here. And let us make three tabernacles: one for You, and one for Moses, and one for Elijah." ⁶For he did not know what he should say; for they were terrified.

⁷And there came a cloud overshadowing them, and there came a voice out of the cloud: "This is My Son, the beloved; listen

to Him." ⁸And suddenly, having looked around, no longer did they see *anyone* with them, except Jesus alone.

⁹And *as* they were descending from the mountain, He instructed them that they should tell to no one what they had seen, except until the Son of Man had risen out from *the* dead. ¹⁰And they kept that saying among themselves, questioning what it is to rise out from *the* dead. ¹¹And they were asking Him, saying, "The scribes say that it behooves Elijah to come first."

¹²And He was saying to them, "Elijah indeed, having come first, restores all things; and how has it been written of the Son of Man, that He should suffer many things and be set at naught? ¹³But I say to you, that also Elijah has come, and they did to him whatever they desired, as it has been written of him."

The Boy with an Evil Spirit
(Matthew 17:14-21; Luke 9:37-42; Luke 17:5-10)

¹⁴And having come to the disciples, they saw a great crowd around them, and scribes arguing with them. ¹⁵And immediately the whole crowd, having seen Him, were greatly amazed, and running to *Him*, were greeting Him. ¹⁶And He asked them, "What are you disputing with them?"

¹⁷And one out of the crowd answered Him, "Teacher, I brought to You my son, having a mute spirit; ¹⁸and whenever it seizes him, it throws him down; and he foams and gnashes his teeth, and is withering away. And I spoke to Your disciples, that they might cast it out, and they had no power."

¹⁹And answering him He says, "O unbelieving generation! Until when will I be with you? Until when will I bear with you? Bring him to Me."

²⁰And they brought him to Him. And having seen Him, the spirit immediately threw him into convulsions, and having fallen upon the ground, he began rolling around, foaming.

²¹And He asked his father, "How long a time is it that this has been with him?"

And he said, "From childhood. ²²And often it casts him both into fire and into waters, that it might destroy him. But if You are able *to do* anything, having compassion on us, help us."

²³And Jesus said to him, "If You are able? All things are possible to the *one* believing."

²⁴Immediately the father of the child, having cried out,ᵃ was saying, "I believe; help my unbelief!"

²⁵And Jesus, having seen that a crowd was running together, rebuked the unclean spirit, saying to it, "Mute and deaf spirit, I command you, come out of him, and you may enter into him no more."

²⁶And it came out, having cried out and having thrown him into many convulsions; and he became as if dead, in order for many to say that he was dead. ²⁷And Jesus, having taken him by the hand, raised him up, and he arose.

²⁸And He having entered into *the* house, His disciples were asking Him in private, "Why were we not able to cast it out?"

²⁹And He said to them, "This kind is able to go out by nothing except by prayer."ᵇ

The Second Prediction of the Passion
(Matthew 17:22-23; Luke 9:43-45)

³⁰Having gone forth from there, they were passing through Galilee; and He did not want that anyone should know, ³¹for He was teaching His disciples. And He was saying to them, "The Son of Man is delivered into *the* hands of men, and they will kill Him; and having been killed, on the third day He will arise." ³²And they did not understand the saying, and they were afraid to ask Him.

The Greatest in the Kingdom
(Matthew 18:1-6; Luke 9:46-50)

³³And they came to Capernaum. And having been in the house, He was asking them, "What were you discussing on the way?" ³⁴And they were silent, for along

the road they had been discussing with one another which *was* greatest.

³⁵And having sat down, He called the Twelve, and He says to them, "If anyone desires to be first, he will be last of all and servant of all."

³⁶And having taken a child, He set it in *the* midst of them; and having taken it in *His* arms, He said to them, ³⁷"Whoever shall receive one of such little children in My name, receives Me; and whoever shall receive Me, does not receive Me, but the *One* having sent Me."

Miracles in Jesus' Name

³⁸John answered Him, "Teacher, we saw someone who does not follow us casting out demons in Your name, and we were forbidding him, because he was not following us."

³⁹And Jesus said, "Do not forbid him. For there is no one who will do a work of power in My name, and will be able readily to speak evil of Me. ⁴⁰For whoever is not against us is for us. ⁴¹For whoever might give you to drink a cup of water because you are Christ's in name, truly I say to you, that he shall certainly not lose his reward.

Temptations and Trespasses
(Matthew 18:7-9; Luke 17:1-4)

⁴²And whoever might cause to stumble one of these little ones believing in Me, it is better for him rather if a heavy millstone is put around his neck, and he has been cast into the sea.

⁴³And if your hand should cause you to stumble, cut it off; it is better for you to enter into life crippled, than having two hands to go away into Gehenna, into the unquenchable fire.ᶜ ⁴⁵And if your foot should cause you to stumble, cut it off; it is better for you to enter into life lame, than having the two feet, to be cast into Gehenna.ᵈ ⁴⁷And if your eye should cause you to stumble, cast it out; it is better for you to enter into the kingdom of God with one eye, than having two eyes, to be cast into Gehenna, ⁴⁸where 'their worm does not die, and the fire is not quenched.'ᵉ

⁴⁹For everyone will be salted with fire.ᶠ ⁵⁰The salt *is* good, but if the salt becomes unsalty, with what will you season it? Have salt in yourselves, and be at peace with one another."

a 24 BYZ and TR include *with tears*
b 29 BYZ and TR *prayer and fasting*
c 43 See Isaiah 66:24, Mark 9:48. BYZ and TR *44 where 'their worm never dies, and the fire is never quenched.'*
d 45 See Isaiah 66:24, Mark 9:48. BYZ and TR *46 where 'their worm never dies, and the fire is never quenched.'*
e 48 Isaiah 66:24
f 49 BYZ and TR include *and every sacrifice will be salted with salt*

Mark 10
Teachings about Divorce
(Matthew 19:1-12)

¹And from there having risen up, He comes into the region of Judea, and beyond the Jordan. And again crowds come together to Him, and again, as He had been accustomed, He was teaching them.

²And the Pharisees, having approached, were demanding of Him if it is lawful for a husband to divorce a wife, testing Him. ³And He answering said to them, "What did Moses command you?"

⁴And they said, "Moses permitted to write a roll of divorce, and to send *her* away."

⁵But Jesus said to them, "He wrote this commandment for you because of your hardness of heart; ⁶but from *the* beginning of creation, 'He made them male and female.'ᵃ ⁷On account of this, a man will leave his father and mother and be joined to his wife,ᵇ ⁸and the two will be for one flesh.'ᶜ Therefore they are no longer two, but one flesh. ⁹Therefore what God has joined together, let man not separate."

¹⁰And in the house again, the disciples were asking Him concerning this. ¹¹And He says to them, "Whoever shall divorce his wife, and shall marry another, commits adultery against her. ¹²And if a woman, having divorced her husband, should marry another, she commits adultery."

Jesus Blesses the Children
(Matthew 19:13-15; Luke 18:15-17)

¹³And they were bringing little children to Him, that He might touch them. But the disciples rebuked them.
¹⁴And having seen, Jesus was indignant and said to them, "Permit the little children to come to Me; do not hinder them! For to such belongs the kingdom of God. ¹⁵Truly I say to you, whoever shall not receive the kingdom of God as a child shall never enter into it." ¹⁶And having taken *them* in arms, He was blessing them, having laid the hands on them.

The Rich Young Man
(Matthew 19:16-30; Luke 18:18-30)

¹⁷And going forth on His journey, one having run up and having knelt down to Him, was asking Him, "Good Teacher, what shall I do that I might inherit eternal life?"
¹⁸And Jesus said to him, "Why do you call Me good? No one *is* good, except God alone. ¹⁹You know the commandments: 'You shall not murder, you shall not commit adultery, you shall not steal, you shall not bear false witness, you shall not defraud, you shall honor your father and mother.'ᵈ"
²⁰And he was saying to Him, "Teacher, all these I have kept from my youth."
²¹And Jesus, having looked upon him, loved him and said to him, "One thing to you is lacking: Go, sell as much as you have, and give to the poor, and you will have treasure in heaven; and come, follow Me."
²²And having been sad at the word, he went away grieving; for he was *one* having many possessions.
²³And Jesus having looked around, says to His disciples, "How difficultly those having riches will enter into the kingdom of God!" ²⁴And the disciples were astonished at His words. But Jesus answering says to them again, "Children, how difficult it is to enterᵉ into the kingdom of God! ²⁵It is easier *for* a camel to pass through the eye of the needle, than *for* a rich man to enter into the kingdom of God."
²⁶And they were exceedingly astonished, saying among themselves, "Then who is able to be saved?"
²⁷Having looked on them, Jesus says, "With men *it is* impossible, but not with God; for all things *are* possible with God."
²⁸Peter began to say to Him, "Behold, we have left all and followed You."
²⁹Jesus was saying, "Truly I say to you, there is no one who has left house, or brothers, or sisters, or mother, or father, or children, or lands for My sake and because of the gospel, ³⁰who shall not receive a hundredfold now in this time—houses and brothers and sisters and mothers and children and lands, with persecutions—and in the age which is coming, eternal life. ³¹But many first will be last; and the last, first."

The Third Prediction of the Passion
(Matthew 20:17-19; Luke 18:31-34)

³²And they were on the way, going up to Jerusalem, and Jesus was going on before them. And they were astonished, and those following were afraid. And having taken to *Him* the Twelve again, He began to tell them the things being about to happen to Him: ³³"Behold, we go up to Jerusalem, and the Son of Man will be betrayed to the chief priests and to the scribes, and they will condemn Him to death, and will betray Him to the Gentiles. ³⁴And they will mock Him, and will spit upon Him, and will flog and will kill Him, and on the third day He will rise again."

The Request of James and John
(Matthew 20:20-28)

³⁵And James and John, the sons of Zebedee, come up to Him saying to Him, "Teacher, we desire that You would do for us whatever we might ask you."
³⁶And He said to them, "What do you desire Me to do for you?"
³⁷And they said to Him, "Grant to us that we might sit, one of *us* at *Your* right hand and one at *Your* left hand, in Your glory."

38 And Jesus said to them, "You do not know what you ask. Are you able to drink the cup that I drink, and to be baptized *with* the baptism *with* which I am baptized?"
39 And they said to Him, "We are able." And Jesus said to them, "You will drink the cup that I drink, and you will be baptized *with* the baptism *with* which I am baptized, 40 but to sit at My right hand or at *My* left hand, is not Mine to give, but *to those* for whom it has been prepared."
41 And having heard *this*, the ten began to be indignant about James and John.
42 And Jesus having called them near, says to them, "You know that those being accounted to rule over the Gentiles exercise lordship over them, and their great ones exercise authority over them. 43 But it shall not be thus among you. Instead, whoever desires to become great among you will be your servant, 44 and whoever desires to become first among you will be slave of all. 45 For even the Son of Man came not to be served, but to serve, and to give His life *as* a ransom for many."

Jesus Heals Bartimaeus
(Matthew 20:29-34; Luke 18:35-43)

46 And they come to Jericho. And as He was going out from Jericho—and His disciples, and a large crowd—a blind beggar, Bartimaeus, son of Timaeus, was sitting beside the road. 47 And having heard that it is Jesus of Nazareth, he began to cry out and to say, "Jesus, Son of David, have mercy on me."
48 And many were rebuking him, that he should be silent; but he kept crying out much more, "Son of David, have mercy on me."
49 And Jesus, having stopped, commanded him to be called.
And they call the blind *man*, saying to him, "Take courage! Rise up! He calls you."
50 And having cast away his cloak, having risen up, he came to Jesus.
51 And Jesus answering him says, "What do you desire I should do to you?"
And the blind *man* said to Him, "Rabboni, that I may receive sight."
52 And Jesus said to him, "Go, your faith has healed you." And immediately he received sight and began following Him on the way.

a 6 Genesis 1:27
b 7-8 NE and WH do not include *and be united to his wife*.
c 8 Genesis 2:24
d 19 Exodus 20:12-16; Deuteronomy 5:16-20
e 24 BYZ and TR *how hard it is for those who trust in riches to enter*

Mark 11
The Triumphal Entry
(Zechariah 9:9-13; Matthew 21:1-11; Luke 19:28-40; John 12:12-19)

1 And when they drew near to Jerusalem, to Bethphage and Bethany near the Mount of Olives, He sends two of His disciples 2 and says to them, "Go into the village before you, and immediately entering into it, you will find a colt having been tied, upon which no one of men has ever sat; having untied it, also bring *it*. 3 And if anyone says to you, 'Why are you doing this?' say, 'Because the Lord has need of it, and He will send it back here soon.'"
4 And they departed and found the colt having been tied at the door outside, by the street. And they untied it, 5 and some of those standing there were saying to them, "What are you doing, untying the colt?"
6 And they spoke to them as Jesus had commanded, and they allowed them. 7 And they led the colt to Jesus, and they cast upon it their cloaks, and He sat on it. 8 And many spread their cloaks on the road, and others, branches having been cut down from the fields. 9 And those going before and those following were crying out:
"Hosanna!"[a]
"Blessed is the *One* coming in *the* name of *the* Lord!"[b]

¹⁰"Blessed *is* the coming kingdom of our father, David!"

"Hosanna in the highest!"ᶜ

¹¹And He entered into Jerusalem, into the temple; and having looked around on all things, the hour being already late, He went out to Bethany with the Twelve.

Jesus Curses the Fig Tree
(Matthew 21:18-22; Mark 11:20-26)

¹²And on the next day, they having gone out from Bethany, He was hungry. ¹³And having seen a fig tree from afar, having leaves, He went *to see* if perhaps He will find anything on it. And having come to it, He found nothing except leaves; for it was not the season of figs. ¹⁴And answering He said to it, "May no one eat *the* fruit of you, no more to the age." And His disciples were listening.

Jesus Cleanses the Temple
(Matthew 21:12-17; Luke 19:45-48; John 2:12-25)

¹⁵And they come to Jerusalem. And having entered into the temple, He began to cast out those selling and those buying in the temple. And He overturned the tables of the money changers, and the seats of those selling doves. ¹⁶And He would not permit that anyone should carry a vessel through the temple. ¹⁷And He began teaching, and was saying to them, "Has it not been written: 'My house will be called a house of prayer for all the nations'ᵈ? But you have made it 'a den of robbers.'ᵉ"

¹⁸And the chief priests and the scribes heard *it*, and they were seeking how they might destroy Him. For they were afraid of Him, for the whole crowd was astonished at His teaching.

¹⁹And when evening came, they were going forth out of the city.

The Withered Fig Tree
(Matthew 21:18-22; Mark 11:12-14)

²⁰And passing by in the morning, they saw the fig tree having been dried up from *the* roots. ²¹And Peter having remembered, says to Him, "Rabbi, look, the fig tree that You cursed is dried up."

²²And Jesus answering, says to them, "Have faith from God. ²³Truly I say to you that whoever shall say to this mountain, 'Be you taken away and be you cast into the sea,' and shall not doubt in his heart, but shall believe that what he says takes place, it will be done for him. ²⁴Because of this I say to you, all things whatever praying, you also ask, believe that you receive, and it will be to you.

²⁵And when you may stand praying, if you have anything against anyone, forgive *it*, so that your Father in the heavens also might forgive you your trespasses."ᶠ

Jesus' Authority Challenged
(Matthew 21:23-27; Luke 20:1-8)

²⁷And they come again to Jerusalem. And as He is walking in the temple, the chief priests and the scribes and the elders come to Him. ²⁸And they were saying to Him, "By what authority are You doing these things? Or who gave You this authority, that You should do these things?"

²⁹And Jesus said to them, "I will ask you one thing, and you answer Me, and I will tell you by what authority I do these things. ³⁰The baptism of John, was it from heaven, or from men? Answer Me."

³¹And they began reasoning with themselves, saying, "What should we say? If we should say, 'From heaven,' He will say, 'Why then did you not believe him?' ³²But should we say, 'From men'..." They were afraid of the people, for all were holding that John truly was a prophet. ³³And answering to Jesus, they say, "We do not know."

And Jesus says to them, "Neither do I tell you by what authority I do these things."

a 9 Psalm 118:25
b 9 Psalm 118:26
c 10 Psalm 148:1
d 17 Isaiah 56:7
e 17 Jeremiah 7:11
f 25 See Matthew 6:15. BYZ and TR *26 But if you do not forgive, neither will your Father in heaven forgive your trespasses.*

Mark 12
The Parable of the Wicked Tenants
(Matthew 21:33-46; Luke 20:9-18)

¹And He began to speak to them in parables: "A man planted a vineyard, and placed around *it* a fence, and dug a wine vat, and built a tower, and rented it out to farmers, and traveled abroad.
²And he sent a servant to the farmers at the due time, that he might receive from the farmers from the fruit of the vineyard.
³But having taken him, they beat *him*, and sent *him* away empty-handed.
⁴And again he sent to them another servant, and him they struck on the head, and treated shamefully. ⁵And He sent another, and him they killed; also many others, indeed some beating, and some killing.
⁶Yet having one beloved son, he sent him to them last, saying, 'They will have respect for my son.'
⁷But those farmers said to themselves, 'This is the heir; come, let us kill him, and the inheritance will be ours.' ⁸And having taken *him*, they killed him, and cast him forth outside the vineyard.
⁹What therefore will the master of the vineyard do? He will come and will destroy the farmers, and will give the vineyard to others. ¹⁰Have you not even read this Scripture:

'*The* stone which those building rejected,
 this has become the chief corner;
¹¹this was from *the* Lord,
 and it is marvelous in our eyes'[a]?"

¹²And they were seeking to lay hold of Him, and yet they feared the crowd; for they knew that He had spoken the parable against them. And having left Him, they went away.

Paying Taxes to Caesar
(Matthew 22:15-22; Luke 20:19-26)

¹³And they send some of the Pharisees and Herodians to Him, that they might catch Him in discourse. ¹⁴And having come, they say to Him, "Teacher, we know that You are true, and to You there is no care about *any* one; for You do not look on *the* appearance of men, but teach the way of God on the basis of *the* truth. Is it lawful to give tribute to Caesar or not? Should we pay or not pay?"
¹⁵And knowing their hypocrisy, He said to them, "Why do you test Me? Bring Me a denarius,[b] that I might see *it*." ¹⁶And they brought *it*, and He says to them, "Whose likeness and inscription *is* this?"
And they said to Him, "Caesar's."
¹⁷And Jesus said to them, "Give back to Caesar the things of Caesar, and to God the things of God."
And they were amazed at Him.

The Sadducees and the Resurrection
(Matthew 22:23-33; Luke 20:27-40)

¹⁸And Sadducees, who say there is not a resurrection, come to Him. And they began questioning Him, saying, ¹⁹"Teacher, Moses wrote for us, that if anyone's brother should die and leave behind a wife and not leave children, that his brother should take the wife and raise up seed for his brother. ²⁰There were seven brothers; and the first took a wife, and dying, left no seed. ²¹And the second took her, and died, not having left seed. And the third likewise. ²²And the seven left no seed. Last of all, the woman also died. ²³In the resurrection, when they rise,[c] of which of them will she be wife? For the seven had her as wife."
²⁴Jesus was saying to them, "Do you not err because of this, not knowing the Scriptures nor the power of God? ²⁵For when they rise out from *the* dead, neither do they marry, nor are given in marriage; but they are like angels in the heavens.
²⁶And concerning the dead, that they rise, have you not read in the book of Moses on the bush, how God spoke to him, saying, 'I *am* the God of Abraham, and the God of Isaac, and the God of Jacob'[d]? ²⁷He is not God of *the* dead, but of *the* living. You err greatly."

The Greatest Commandment
(Deuteronomy 6:1-19; Matthew 22:34-40)

²⁸And one of the scribes having come up, having heard them reasoning together, having seen that He answered them well, questioned Him, "Which commandment is *the* first of all?"

²⁹Jesus answered, "The foremost is, 'Hear this O Israel: *The* Lord our God is One Lord, ³⁰and you shall love *the* Lord your God with all your heart, and with all your soul, and with all your mind, and with all your strength.'[e] ³¹*The* second *is* this: 'You shall love your neighbor as yourself.'[f] There is not another commandment greater than these."

³²And the scribe said to Him, "Right, Teacher. You have spoken according to truth that He is One, and there is not another besides Him, ³³and to love Him with all the heart and with all the understanding and with all the strength, and to love the neighbor as oneself is more important than all the burnt offerings and sacrifices."

³⁴And Jesus, having seen him that he answered wisely, said to him, "You are not far from the kingdom of God." And no one dared to question Him *any* longer.

Whose Son is the Christ?
(Matthew 22:41-46; Luke 20:41-44)

³⁵And answering, Jesus was saying, teaching in the temple, "How do the scribes say that the Christ is *the* son of David? ³⁶David himself said by the Holy Spirit:

'*The* Lord said to my Lord,
"Sit at My right hand,
until I place Your enemies
as a footstool of Your feet."'[g]

³⁷David himself calls Him Lord. And from where is He his son?"

And the great crowd was listening to Him gladly.

Warning against the Scribes
(Luke 20:45-47)

³⁸And in His teaching He was saying, "Beware of the scribes, desiring to walk about in robes, and greetings in the marketplaces, ³⁹and first seats in the synagogues, and first places at the feasts; ⁴⁰those devouring the houses of widows, and praying at great length as a pretext. These will receive greater judgment."

The Widow's Offering
(Luke 21:1-4)

⁴¹And having sat down opposite the treasury, He was watching how the crowd cast money into the treasury; and many rich were casting *in* much. ⁴²And one poor widow having come, cast *in* two lepta,[h] which is a kodrantes.

⁴³And having summoned His disciples, He says to them, "Truly I say to you that this poor widow has cast *in* more than all of those casting into the treasury. ⁴⁴For all cast *in* out of that which was abounding to them, but she out of her poverty cast *in* all, as much as she had of her whole livelihood."

a 10-11 Psalm 118:22,23
b 15 A denarius was customarily a day's wage for a laborer (see Matthew 20:2)
c 23 WH does not include *when they rise*
d 26 Exodus 3:6
e 29-30 Deuteronomy 6:4,5
f 31 Leviticus 19:18
g 36 Psalm 110:1
h 42 A lepton was a Jewish copper coin worth about 1/128 of a denarius

Mark 13
Temple Destruction Foretold
(Matthew 24:1-4; Luke 21:5-9)

¹And of Him going forth out of the temple, one of His disciples says to Him, "Teacher, behold what stones and what buildings!"

²And Jesus said to him, "Do you see these great buildings? Not *one* stone shall be left here upon a stone, which shall not be thrown down."

³And of Him sitting upon the Mount of Olives, opposite the temple, Peter and James and John and Andrew asked Him in private, ⁴"Tell us when these things will be, and what *will be* the sign when all these things are going to be accomplished?"

⁵And Jesus began to say to them, "Take heed, lest anyone mislead you. ⁶Many will come in My name, saying, 'I am *He*,' and they will mislead many. ⁷And when you shall hear of wars and rumors of wars, do not be disturbed. It must come to pass, but the end *is* not yet. ⁸For nation will rise up against nation, and kingdom against kingdom. There will be earthquakes in various places; there will be famines. These *are the* beginning of birth pains.

Witnessing to All Nations
(Matthew 24:9-14; Luke 21:10-19)

⁹But you take heed to yourselves. They will betray you to courts, and you will be beaten in synagogues; and you will stand before governors and kings because of Me, for a testimony to them. ¹⁰And the gospel it behooves first to proclaim to all the nations. ¹¹But when they might lead you away, delivering *you* up, do not be anxious beforehand what you should say; but whatever might be given to you in that hour, speak that. For you are not those speaking, but the Holy Spirit. ¹²And brother will deliver up brother to death, and father, child; and children will rise up against parents, and will put them to death. ¹³And you will be hated by all on account of My name; but the *one* having endured to *the* end, he will be saved.

The Abomination of Desolation
(Matthew 24:15-25; Luke 21:20-24)

¹⁴And when you see the abomination of the desolation,[a] standing where it should not[b] (the *one* reading, let him understand), then those in Judea, let them flee to the mountains; ¹⁵and the *one* upon the housetop, let him not come down nor go in to take anything out of his house; ¹⁶and the *one* in the field, let him not return to the things behind to take his clothing. ¹⁷And woe to those having in womb and to the *ones* nursing infants in those days! ¹⁸And pray that it might not be in winter, ¹⁹for *in* those days will be tribulation, the like such as never has been from *the* beginning of creation which God created until now—and never shall be. ²⁰And if *the* Lord had not shortened the days, not any flesh would have been saved; but on account of the elect whom He chose, He has shortened the days. ²¹And then if anyone says to you, 'Behold, here *is* the Christ! Behold, there!' you shall not believe *it*. ²²For false Christs and false prophets will arise and will give signs and wonders so as to deceive, if possible, the elect. ²³But you take heed; I have foretold to you all things.

The Return of the Son of Man
(Matthew 24:26-31; Luke 21:25-28)

²⁴But in those days, those after the tribulation,
   'The sun will be darkened,
      and the moon will not give its light;
   ²⁵and the stars will be falling out of the heaven,
      and the powers that *are* in the heavens will be shaken.'[c]

²⁶And then will they see the Son of Man coming in *the* clouds with great power and glory. ²⁷And then He will send the angels and will gather together His elect from the four winds, from *the* end of earth to *the* end of heaven.

The Lesson of the Fig Tree
(Matthew 24:32-35; Luke 21:29-33)

²⁸And learn the parable of the fig tree: When its branch already has become tender, and it puts forth leaves, you know that summer is near. ²⁹So also you, when you see these things coming to pass, know that He is near,[d] at *the* doors. ³⁰Truly I say to you that this generation will not have passed away until all these things shall have taken place. ³¹The heaven and the earth will pass away, but My words will certainly not pass away.

Readiness at Any Hour
(Genesis 6:1-7; Matthew 24:36-51; Luke 12:35-48)

³²And concerning that day or hour no one knows, not even the angels in heaven, nor the Son, but only the Father. ³³Take

heed; watch;[e] for you do not know when the time is. ³⁴*It is* like a man going on a journey, having left his house, and having given his servants authority, to each one his work. And he commanded the doorkeeper that he should keep watch. ³⁵Therefore watch—for you do not know when the master of the house comes: either at evening, or at midnight, or when the rooster crows, or morning— ³⁶lest having come suddenly, he should find you sleeping. ³⁷And what I say to you, I say to all: Watch!"

a 14 Daniel 9:27; 11:31; 12:11. BYZ and TR include *spoken of by Daniel the prophet*
b 14 Or *he should not be*
c 24-25 Isaiah 13:10; 34:4
d 29 Or *it is near*
e 33 BYZ and TR include *and pray*

Mark 14
The Plot to Kill Jesus
(Matthew 26:1-5; Luke 22:1-6; John 11:45-57)

¹And after two days it would be the Passover and the *Feast of* Unleavened Bread. And the chief priests and the scribes were seeking how, having taken Him by stealth, they might kill *Him*. ²For they were saying, "Not during the feast, lest there will be an uproar of the people."

Jesus Anointed at Bethany
(Matthew 26:6-13; John 12:1-8)

³And of Him being in Bethany in the house of Simon the leper,[a] of Him having reclined, a woman came having an alabaster flask of fragrant oil of pure nard, of great price. Having broken the alabaster flask, she poured *it* on His head. ⁴And some were indignant within themselves: "Why has this the waste of the fragrant oil been made? ⁵For this fragrant oil could have been sold for above three hundred denarii,[b] and have been given to the poor." And they were grumbling at her.
⁶And Jesus said, "Leave her alone; why do you cause trouble to her? She did a good work toward Me. ⁷For the poor you always have with you,[c] and you are able to do them good whenever you desire; but not always do you have Me. ⁸She did what she could. She came beforehand to anoint My body for the burial. ⁹And truly I say to you, wherever the gospel shall be proclaimed in the whole world, what this *woman* has done also will be spoken of, for a memorial of her."

Judas Agrees to Betray Jesus
(Zechariah 11:10-17; Matthew 26:14-16; Matthew 27:3-10)

¹⁰And Judas Iscariot, one of the Twelve, went away to the chief priests, that he might betray Him to them. ¹¹And having heard, they rejoiced and promised to give him money. And he was seeking how he might deliver Him up conveniently.

Preparing the Passover
(Psalm 41:1-13; Matthew 26:17-25; Luke 22:7-13; John 13:18-30)

¹²And on the first day of unleavened *bread*, when they were to sacrifice the Passover lamb, His disciples say to Him, "Where do You desire *that*, having gone, we should prepare that You may eat the Passover?"
¹³And He sends forth two of His disciples and says to them, "Go into the city, and a man carrying a pitcher of water will meet you. Follow him. ¹⁴And wherever he might enter, say to the master of the house that the Teacher says, 'Where is My guest room, where I may eat the Passover with My disciples?' ¹⁵And he will show you a large upper room, having been furnished *and* ready. And prepare for us there."
¹⁶And his disciples went away, and came into the city, and found as He had said to them, and they prepared the Passover. ¹⁷And evening having arrived, He comes with the Twelve.
¹⁸And *as* they were reclining and were eating, Jesus said, "Truly I say to you that one of you who is eating with Me will betray Me."
¹⁹They began to be grieved and to say to Him one by one, "Surely not I?"

20 And He said to them, "*It is* one of the Twelve, the *one* dipping in the bowl with Me. 21 For indeed the Son of Man goes as it has been written concerning Him; but woe to that man by whom the Son of Man is betrayed; *it were* better for him if that man had not been born."

The Last Supper
(Matthew 26:26-30; Luke 22:14-23; 1 Corinthians 11:17-34)

22 And as they were eating, having taken bread, having spoken a blessing, He broke *it* and gave *it* to them and said, "Take *it*; this is My body."
23 And having taken the cup, having given thanks, He gave *it* to them, and they all drank of it. 24 And He said to them, "This is My blood of the covenant,[d] which is being poured out for many. 25 Truly I say to you that never will I drink of the fruit of the vine *again*, until that day when I drink it anew in the kingdom of God."
26 And having sung a hymn, they went out to the Mount of Olives.

Jesus Predicts Peter's Denial
(Matthew 26:31-35; Luke 22:31-38; John 13:36-38)

27 And Jesus says to them, "You will all fall away,[e] for it has been written:
 'I will strike the shepherd,
  and the sheep will be scattered.'[f]
28 But after having arisen, I will go before you into Galilee."
29 And Peter was saying to Him, "Even if all will fall away, yet I *will* not."
30 And Jesus says to him, "Truly I say to you that now this night, before that *the* rooster crows twice, you yourself will deny Me three times."
31 And he kept saying emphatically, "If it is needful of me to die with You, never will I deny You." And all of them were saying likewise also.

Jesus Prays at Gethsemane
(Matthew 26:36-46; Luke 22:39-46)

32 And they come to a place, the name of which *is* Gethsemane; and He says to His disciples, "Sit here, while I shall pray."
33 And He takes Peter and James and John with Him; and He began to be greatly awe-struck and deeply distressed.
34 And He says to them, "My soul is very sorrowful, even to death; remain here and watch."
35 And having gone forward a little, He fell upon the ground, and was praying that if it is possible, the hour might pass from Him. 36 And He was saying, "Abba, Father, all things *are* possible to You; take away this cup from Me; but not what I will, but what You *will*."
37 And He comes and finds them sleeping. And He says to Peter, "Simon are you asleep? Were you not able to watch one hour? 38 Watch and pray, so that you may not enter into temptation. For the spirit *is* willing, but the flesh *is* weak."
39 And again having gone away, He prayed, having said the same thing.
40 And again having returned, he found them sleeping. For their the eyes were heavy, and they did not know what they should answer Him.
41 And He comes the third time and says to them, "Are you still sleeping and taking your rest? It is enough; the hour has come. Behold, the Son of Man is delivered up into the hands of the sinful. 42 Rise, let us go. Behold, the *one* betraying Me has drawn near!"

The Betrayal of Jesus
(Matthew 26:47-56; Luke 22:47-53; John 18:1-14)

43 And immediately while yet He is speaking, Judas, one of the Twelve, comes up, and with Him a crowd with swords and clubs, from the chief priests and the scribes and the elders.
44 And the *one* delivering Him up had given to them a sign, saying: "Whomever I shall kiss is He; seize Him and lead *Him* away securely." 45 And having arrived, having come up to Him immediately, he says, "Rabbi!" And he kissed Him.
46 And they laid hands on Him and seized Him. 47 And a certain one of those standing by, having drawn the sword,

struck the servant of the high priest and cut off his ear. ⁴⁸And Jesus answering said to them, "Are you come out with swords and clubs as against a robber, to capture Me? ⁴⁹Every day I was with you in the temple teaching, and you did not seize Me. But *it is* that the Scriptures may be fulfilled." ⁵⁰And all having left Him, fled. ⁵¹And a certain young man was following Him, having cast a linen cloth about *his* naked *body*. And they seize him, ⁵²and having left behind the linen cloth, he fled naked.

Jesus Faces the Sanhedrin
(Isaiah 53:1-8; Matthew 26:57-68; John 18:19-24; 1 Peter 2:21-25)

⁵³And they led away Jesus to the high priest. And all the chief priests, and the elders, and the scribes come together. ⁵⁴And Peter followed Him from afar off, as far as to within the court of the high priest; and he was sitting with the officers and warming himself at the fire. ⁵⁵And the chief priests and all the Council were seeking testimony against Jesus to put Him to death, but they were not finding *any*. ⁵⁶For many were bearing false testimony against Him, but their testimonies were not alike. ⁵⁷And some having risen up, were bearing false testimony against Him, saying, ⁵⁸"We heard Him saying, 'I will destroy this temple, the *one* made with hands, and in three days I will build another, not made with hands.'" ⁵⁹And their testimony was thus not alike. ⁶⁰And the high priest having stood up in the midst, questioned Jesus, saying, "Do You not answer? What *is it* these testify against You?" ⁶¹But He was silent, and did not answer. Again the high priest was questioning Him, and says to Him, "Are You the Christ, the Son of the Blessed *One*?" ⁶²And Jesus said, "I am. And you will see the Son of Man sitting at *the* right hand of Power and coming with the clouds of heaven."

⁶³And the high priest, having torn his garments, says, "Why have we need of witnesses? ⁶⁴You heard the blasphemy. What does it appear to you?" And all condemned Him to be deserving of death. ⁶⁵And some began to spit upon Him, and to cover up His face, and to strike Him and to say to Him, "Prophesy!" And the officers struck Him with the palms.

Peter Denies Jesus
(Matthew 26:69-75; Luke 22:54-62; John 18:15-18)

⁶⁶And Peter being below in the courtyard, one of the servant girls of the high priest comes, ⁶⁷and having seen Peter warming himself, having looked at him, she says, "You also were with the Nazarene, Jesus." ⁶⁸But he denied *it*, saying, "I neither know nor even understand what you say." And he went forth out into the porch; and the rooster crowed.[g] ⁶⁹And the servant girl, having seen him, began to say again to those standing by, "This is *one* of them." ⁷⁰But he denied *it* again. And after a little, again those standing by were saying to Peter, "Truly you are of them, for you also are a Galilean."[h] ⁷¹But he began to curse and to swear, "I do not know this man whom you speak of!" ⁷²And immediately a rooster crowed for the second time. And Peter remembered the word that Jesus had said to him, "Before *the* rooster crows twice, you will deny Me three times." And having broken down, he began to weep.

a 3 Leprosy was a term for several skin diseases. See Leviticus 13.
b 5 A denarius was customarily a day's wage for a laborer (see Matthew 20:2)
c 7 See Deuteronomy 15:11
d 24 BYZ and TR *new covenant*
e 27 BYZ and TR include *because of me this night*
f 27 Zechariah 13:7
g 68 NE and WH do not include *and the rooster crowed*
h 70 BYZ and TR include *and your speech is similar*

Mark 15
Jesus Delivered to Pilate
(Matthew 27:1-2)

¹And early in the morning, having formed a counsel, the chief priests, with the elders and scribes and the whole Council, having bound Jesus, led *Him* away and delivered *Him* to Pilate.
²And Pilate questioned Him, "Are You the King of the Jews?"
And answering, He says to him, "You have said."
³And the chief priests were accusing Him harshly.
⁴And Pilate began to question Him again, saying, "Do You not answer? See how many things they testify against You!"
⁵But Jesus answered no further, so as to amaze Pilate.

The Crowd Chooses Barabbas
(Matthew 27:15-23; Luke 23:13-25)

⁶And at *the* feast, he used to release to them one prisoner, whom they requested. ⁷And the *one* called Barabbas was there, having been bound with the rebels who had committed murder in the insurrection. ⁸And the crowd having cried out, began to beg *him to do* as usually he did for them.
⁹But Pilate answered them, saying, "Do you wish *that* I should release to you the King of the Jews?" ¹⁰For he was aware that the chief priests had delivered Him up because of envy.
¹¹But the chief priests stirred up the crowd, that he might release to them Barabbas instead.

Pilate Delivers up Jesus
(Matthew 27:24-26)

¹²And Pilate answering was saying to them again, "Then what do you wish *that* I should do to Him whom you call the King of the Jews?"
¹³And they cried out again, "Crucify Him!"
¹⁴And Pilate was saying to them, "Why? What evil did He commit?"
But they shouted much more, "Crucify Him!"
¹⁵And Pilate, desiring to do that which *was* satisfactory to the crowd, released Barabbas to them. And having flogged *Him*, he delivered Jesus that He might be crucified.

The Soldiers Mock Jesus
(Isaiah 50:4-11; Matthew 27:27-31; Luke 22:63-65; John 19:1-15)

¹⁶And the soldiers led Him away into the palace, that is *the* Praetorium, and they call together the whole cohort. ¹⁷And they put on Him purple, and having twisted together a crown of thorns, they placed *it* on Him, ¹⁸and they began to salute Him, "Hail, King of the Jews!"
¹⁹And they kept striking His head with a reed and spitting on Him; and bending the knees, they were kneeling down to Him. ²⁰And when they had mocked Him, they took off Him the purple and put on Him His own garments. And they are leading Him out, that they might crucify Him.

The Crucifixion
(Psalms 22:1-31; 69:1-36; Matthew 27:32-44; Luke 23:26-43; John 19:16-27)

²¹And they compel one passing by, Simon of Cyrene, the father of Alexander and Rufus, coming from the country, that he might carry His cross.
²²And they bring Him to a place, Golgotha, which is translated, Place of a Skull. ²³And they were offering Him wine, having been mixed with gall; but He did not take *it*.
²⁴And having crucified Him, they also divided His garments, casting lots for them, who should take what.
²⁵And it was *the* third hour, and they crucified Him. ²⁶And there was the inscription of the accusation against Him, having been written:
THE KING OF THE JEWS.
²⁷And with Him they crucify two robbers, one at *the* right hand, and one at His left.[a]
²⁹And those passing by were railing at Him, shaking their heads and saying, "Aha! The *One* destroying the temple and

building *it* in three days, ³⁰save Yourself, having descended from the cross!" ³¹Likewise also the chief priests, with the scribes, mocking among one another, were saying, "He saved others; He is not able to save Himself. ³²The Christ, the King of Israel, let Him descend now from the cross, that we might see and believe!" And those being crucified with Him were upbraiding Him.

The Death of Jesus
(Psalm 22:1-31; Matthew 27:45-56; Luke 23:44-49; John 19:28-30)

³³And *the* sixth hour having arrived, darkness came over the whole land, until *the* ninth hour. ³⁴And at the ninth hour Jesus cried out in a loud voice, "Eloi, Eloi, lama sabachthani?" Which is translated, "My God, My God, why have You forsaken Me?"ᵇ

³⁵And some of those standing by, having heard, were saying, "Behold, He calls Elijah."

³⁶And one having run and having filled a sponge with vinegar, having put *it* on a reed, gave Him to drink, saying, "Let be; let us see if Elijah comes to take Him down."

³⁷But Jesus, having uttered a loud cry, breathed His last. ³⁸And the veil of the temple was torn into two from top to bottom.

³⁹And the centurion standing opposite of Him, having seen that He breathed His last,ᶜ thus said, "Truly this man was *the* Son of God!"

⁴⁰And there were also women looking on from afar off, among whom also *were* Mary Magdalene, and Mary the mother of James the least and of Joseph, and Salome, ⁴¹who had been following Him and had been ministering to Him when He was in Galilee, and many other *ones* having come up with Him to Jerusalem.

The Burial of Jesus
(Isaiah 53:9-12; Matthew 27:57-61; Luke 23:50-56; John 19:38-42)

⁴²And evening having arrived already, since it was *the* Preparation, that is, the day before Sabbath, ⁴³having come, Joseph from Arimathea, a prominent Council member, who was also himself waiting for the kingdom of God, having boldness, went in to Pilate and asked for the body of Jesus.

⁴⁴And Pilate wondered if already He were dead. And having summoned the centurion, he questioned him whether He had died already. ⁴⁵And having known *it* from the centurion, He granted the body to Joseph.

⁴⁶And having bought a linen cloth, having taken Him down, he wrapped *Him* in the linen cloth and laid Him in a tomb which was cut out of a rock. And he rolled a stone to the door of the tomb. ⁴⁷And Mary Magdalene and Mary the *mother* of Josephᵈ were watching where He was laid.

a 27 BYZ and TR include *28 So the Scripture was fulfilled that says, "And He was numbered with the transgressors."*
b 34 Psalm 22:1
c 39 BYZ and TR *having cried out, He had breathed His last*
d 47 Or *Joses*

Mark 16
The Resurrection
(Psalm 16:1-11; Psalm 49:1-20; Matthew 28:1-10; Luke 24:1-12; John 20:1-9)

¹And the Sabbath having passed, Mary Magdalene, and Mary the *mother* of James, and Salome bought spices, that having come, they might anoint Him. ²And very early on the first *day* of the week, they come to the tomb, the sun having arisen. ³And they were saying among themselves, "Who will roll away the stone for us from the door of the tomb?" ⁴And having looked up, they see that the stone has been rolled away; for it was extremely large.

⁵And having entered into the tomb, they saw a young man clothed in a white robe, sitting on the right; and they were greatly amazed. ⁶And he says to them, "Do not be amazed. You seek Jesus, the Nazarene, the *One* having been crucified. He is risen! He is not here! Behold the place where they laid Him. ⁷But go, say

to His disciples and to Peter that He goes before you into Galilee; there you will see Him, as He said to you."
⁸And having gone out, they fled from the tomb, for trembling and amazement had seized them. And they spoke nothing to *anyone*, for they were afraid.ᵃ

Jesus Appears to Mary Magdalene
(John 20:10-18)

⁹And having risen early *the* first *day* of the week, He appeared first to Mary Magdalene, from whom He had cast out seven demons. ¹⁰She having gone, told *it* to those having been with Him, mourning and weeping. ¹¹And they having heard that He is alive and has been seen by her, disbelieved.

Jesus Appears to Two Disciples
(Luke 24:13-24)

¹²And after these things, He appeared in another form to two of them as they are walking, going into *the* country. ¹³And they having gone, told *it* to the rest; neither did they believe them.

The Great Commission
(Matthew 28:16-20)

¹⁴And afterward, *as* they were reclining, He appeared to the eleven and rebuked their unbelief and hardness of heart, because they did not believe those having seen Him arisen.

¹⁵And He said to them, "Having gone into all the world, proclaim the gospel to all the creation. ¹⁶The *one* having believed and having been baptized will be saved, but the *one* having disbelieved will be condemned. ¹⁷And these signs will accompany those having believed: In My name they will cast out demons; they will speak with new tongues; ¹⁸and with their hands they will take up serpents; and if they drink anything deadly, it shall never hurt them; they will lay hands upon *the* sick, and they will be well."

The Ascension
(Luke 24:50-53; Acts 1:6-11)

¹⁹Therefore indeed the Lord Jesus, after speaking to them, was taken up into the heaven and sat at *the* right hand of God. ²⁰And having gone forth, they preached everywhere, the Lord working with *them* and confirming the word by the accompanying signs.

a 8 Some manuscripts end the Gospel of Mark after verse 8 or 9. Some of these include a version of the following after verse 8: *But they quickly reported all these instructions to Peter's companions. Afterward, Jesus himself, through them, sent out from east to west the sacred and imperishable proclamation of eternal salvation. Amen.*

Luke

Luke 1
Dedication to Theophilus
(Acts 1:1-3)

¹Inasmuch as many have undertaken to draw up a narration concerning the things having been accomplished among us, ²just as those from *the* beginning having been eyewitnesses and servants of the word delivered *them* to us, ³it seemed good also to me, having been acquainted with all things carefully from the first, to write with method to you, most excellent Theophilus, ⁴so that you may know the certainty concerning *the* things which you were instructed.

Gabriel Foretells John's Birth
(Matthew 11:7-19; Luke 7:24-35; Luke 16:14-17)

⁵There was in the days of Herod king of Judea a certain priest named Zacharias, of *the* division of Abijah, and his wife of the daughters of Aaron, and her name Elizabeth. ⁶And they were both righteous before God, walking blameless in all the commandments and ordinances of the Lord. ⁷And to them there was no child, inasmuch as Elizabeth was barren, and both were advanced in their years.

⁸Now it came to pass, in his fulfilling the priestly service before God in the order of his division, ⁹according to the custom of the priesthood, it fell to him by lot to burn incense, having entered into the temple of the Lord. ¹⁰And the whole multitude of

the people were praying outside at the hour of the incense.
¹¹And an angel of *the* Lord appeared to him, standing at *the* right of the altar of the incense. ¹²And having seen *him*, Zechariah was troubled, and fear fell upon him.
¹³And the angel said to him, "Fear not, Zechariah, because your prayer has been heard, and Your wife Elizabeth will bear to you a son, and you shall call his name John. ¹⁴And he will be joy and gladness to you, and many will rejoice at his birth. ¹⁵For he will be great before the Lord. And he shall never drink wine and strong drink, and he will be full of *the* Holy Spirit even from his mother's womb. ¹⁶And he will turn many of the sons of Israel to *the* Lord their God. ¹⁷And he will go forth before Him in *the* spirit and power of Elijah, to turn *the* hearts of *the* fathers to *the* children, and *the* disobedient to *the* wisdom of *the* righteous—to make ready a people prepared for *the* Lord."
¹⁸And Zechariah said to the angel, "By what will I know this? For I am an old man, and my wife is advanced in her years."
¹⁹And the angel answering, said to him, "I am Gabriel, the *one* standing before God; and I was sent to speak to you, and to bring these glad tidings to you. ²⁰And behold, you will be silent, and not able to speak until that day these things shall take place, because you did not believe my words, which will be fulfilled in their season."
²¹And the people were expecting Zechariah, and they were wondering at his delaying in temple. ²²And having come out, he was not able to speak to them, and they recognized that he had seen a vision in the temple. And he was making signs to them, and remained mute. ²³And it came to pass, when the days of his service were fulfilled, he departed to his home.
²⁴And after these days, his wife Elizabeth conceived, and she hid herself five months, saying, ²⁵"Thus the Lord has done to me, in *the* days in which He looked upon *me* to take away my disgrace among men."

Gabriel Foretells Jesus' Birth

²⁶And in the sixth month, the angel Gabriel was sent by God to a city of Galilee whose name *was* Nazareth, ²⁷to a virgin betrothed to a man whose name *was* Joseph, of *the* house of David. And the name of the virgin *was* Mary. ²⁸And having come to her, he said, "Greetings, *you* favored with grace! The Lord *is* with you."[a]
²⁹And she was troubled at the statement and was pondering what kind this salutation might be. ³⁰And the angel said to her, "Fear not, Mary; for you have found favor with God. ³¹And behold, you will conceive in womb, and will bring forth a son, and you shall call His name Jesus. ³²He will be great, and He will be called Son of *the* Most High. And the Lord God will give Him the throne of His father David, ³³and He will reign over the house of Jacob to the ages. And of His kingdom there will be no end!"
³⁴And Mary said to the angel, "How will this be, since I do not know a man?"
³⁵And the angel answering, said to her, "*The* Holy Spirit will come upon you, and *the* power of *the* Most High will overshadow you; therefore also the Holy One being born[b] will be called *the* Son of God. ³⁶And behold your relative Elizabeth, she also has conceived a son in her old age, and this is *the* sixth month to her who *was* called barren. ³⁷For nothing will be impossible with God."
³⁸And Mary said, "Behold, the Lord's handmaid. May it happen to me according to your word." And the angel departed from her.

Mary Visits Elizabeth

³⁹And in those days Mary, having risen up, went with haste into the hill country, to a town of Judah, ⁴⁰and she entered into the house of Zechariah and greeted Elizabeth. ⁴¹And it came to pass, as

Elizabeth heard the greeting of Mary, the baby in her womb leaped. And Elizabeth was filled with *the* Holy Spirit, ⁴²and she cried out in a loud voice and said, "Blessed are you among women, and blessed is the fruit your of womb. ⁴³And from where *is* this to me, that the mother of my Lord should come to me? ⁴⁴For behold, as the voice of your greeting came into my ears, the baby in my womb leaped in exultation. ⁴⁵And blessed *is* the *one* having believed that there will be a fulfillment to the things spoken to her from *the* Lord."

Mary's Song
(1 Samuel 2:1-11)

⁴⁶And Mary said:
"My soul magnifies the Lord,
 ⁴⁷and my spirit rejoices in God my Savior.
⁴⁸For He has looked upon the humiliation of His handmaiden.
 For behold, from henceforth all the generations will count me blessed.
⁴⁹For the mighty One has done great things to me.
 And holy *is* His name.
⁵⁰And His mercy *is* to generations and generations,
 to those fearing Him.
⁵¹He has shown strength with His arm,
 He has scattered *the* proud in *the* thought of their heart.
⁵²He has brought down rulers from thrones,
 and exalted *the* humble.
⁵³He has filled *those* hungering with good things,
 and *those* being rich He has sent away empty.
⁵⁴He has helped Israel His servant,
 remembering mercy,
⁵⁵as He spoke to our fathers,
 to Abraham and his to descendants to the age."

⁵⁶And Mary dwelt with her about three months, and returned to her home.

The Birth of John the Baptist

⁵⁷Now the time was fulfilled to Elizabeth for her to give birth, and she bore a son. ⁵⁸And her neighbors and relatives heard that *the* Lord was magnifying His mercy with her, and they were rejoicing with her.

⁵⁹And it came to pass on the eighth day, they came to circumcise the child, and were calling it after the name of his father, Zechariah. ⁶⁰And his mother answering said, "No, but he will be called John."

⁶¹And they said to her, "There is no one among your relatives who is called by this name." ⁶²And they were making signs to his father, what he might wish him to be called.

⁶³And having asked for a writing tablet, he wrote, saying, "John is his name." And they all marveled. ⁶⁴And his mouth was opened immediately, and his tongue, and he was speaking, blessing God.

⁶⁵And fear came upon all those dwelling around them. And in all the hill country of Judea all these words were being talked about. ⁶⁶And all those having heard laid *them* up in their heart, saying, "What then will this child be?" And indeed, *the* hand of *the* Lord was with him.

Zechariah's Song

⁶⁷And his father Zechariah was filled with *the* Holy Spirit and prophesied, saying,
 ⁶⁸"Blessed be *the* Lord, the God of Israel,
  because He has visited and has performed redemption *on* His people,
⁶⁹and has raised up a horn of salvation for us,
  in *the* house of His servant David;
⁷⁰as He spoke by *the* mouth
  of His holy prophets of old,
⁷¹salvation from our enemies,
  and from *the* hand of all those hating us,
⁷²to fulfill mercy toward our fathers,

and to remember His holy covenant,
⁷³the oath that He swore to Abraham our father,
to grant us, ⁷⁴having been saved from *the* hand of our enemies,
to serve Him without fear,
⁷⁵in holiness and righteousness before Him,
all the days of our life.
⁷⁶And you, child, will be called prophet of *the* Most High;
for you will go before the Lord to prepare His ways,
⁷⁷to give knowledge of salvation to His people,
in forgiveness of their sins,
⁷⁸through *the* affections of compassion of our God,
in which *the* Sunrise will visit us from on high,
⁷⁹to shine upon those sitting in darkness
and in *the* shadow of death,
to direct our feet into *the* way of peace."
⁸⁰And the child continued to grow and was strengthened in spirit;ᶜ and he was in the deserted places until *the* day of his appearance to Israel.

a 28 BYZ and TR include *Blessed are you among women!*
b 35 TR *born of you*
c 80 Or *in the Spirit*

Luke 2
The Birth of Jesus
(Isaiah 7:10-16; Micah 5:1-6; Matthew 1:18-25)

¹And it came to pass in those days, a decree went out from Caesar Augustus to register all the world. ²This registration first took place whenᵃ Quirinius was governing Syria. ³And all were going to be registered, each to his own city.
⁴And Joseph also went up from Galilee out of *the* town of Nazareth, to Judea, to *the* City of David, which is called Bethlehem, because of his being of *the* house and family of David, ⁵to register with Mary the *one* being betrothed to him, she being with child.
⁶And it came to pass, in their being there, the days of her giving birth were fulfilled. ⁷And she brought forth her firstborn son, and she wrapped Him in swaddling cloths and laid Him in a manger, because there was no place for them in the inn.

The Shepherds and the Angels

⁸And there were shepherds in the same region, lodging in the fields and keeping watch over their flock by night. ⁹And an angel of *the* Lord stood by them, and *the* glory of *the* Lord shone around them, and they feared *with* great fear. ¹⁰And the angel said to them, "Fear not, for behold, I bring good news to you *of* great joy, which will be to all the people. ¹¹For today in *the* City of David a Savior has been born to you, who is Christ *the* Lord. ¹²And this *is* the sign to you: You will find a baby wrapped in swaddling cloths, and lying in a manger."
¹³And suddenly there came with the angel a multitude of *the* heavenly host, praising God and saying:
¹⁴"Glory to God in *the* highest,
and on earth peace among men with whom He is pleased!"
¹⁵And it came to pass, as the angels were departing from them into the heaven, the shepherds were saying to one another, "Let us go through indeed as far as Bethlehem, and let us see this word that has come to pass, which the Lord has made known to us."
¹⁶And having hurried, they came and found both Mary and Joseph, and the baby, lying in the manger. ¹⁷And having seen, they proclaimed abroad concerning the saying having been told them concerning this Child. ¹⁸And all those having heard marveled concerning the things having been spoken to them by the shepherds. ¹⁹But Mary was treasuring up all these matters, pondering *them* in her heart.
²⁰And the shepherds returned, glorifying and praising God for all things which they

had heard and seen, as it was said to them.

Jesus Presented at the Temple

²¹And when eight days to circumcise Him were fulfilled, then His name was called Jesus, which He had been called by the angel before He was conceived in the womb. ²²And when the days of their purification were fulfilled according to the Law of Moses, they brought Him to Jerusalem to present to the Lord ²³(as it has been written in *the* Law of *the* Lord: "Every male opening a womb shall be called holy to the Lord"*ᵇ*), ²⁴and to offer a sacrifice, according to that having been said in the Law of *the* Lord, "A pair of turtle doves or two young pigeons."*ᶜ*

The Prophecy of Simeon

²⁵And behold, there was a man in Jerusalem whose name *was* Simeon. And this man *was* righteous and devout, waiting for *the* consolation of Israel; and *the* Holy Spirit was upon him. ²⁶And it was divinely revealed to him by the Holy Spirit not to see death before that he should see the Lord's Christ. ²⁷And he came in the Spirit into the temple. And in the *time when* the parents were bringing in the child Jesus, the *thing* they were doing for Him according to that having become customary by the Law, ²⁸then he received Him into the arms, and blessed God, and said:

> ²⁹"Now Lord, You dismiss Your servant in peace,
> according to Your word.
> ³⁰For my eyes have seen Your salvation,
> ³¹which You have prepared before *the* face of all the peoples,
> ³²a light for revelation of *the* Gentiles,
> and glory of Your people Israel."

³³And His father and mother were marveling at the things having been spoken concerning Him. ³⁴And Simeon blessed them and said to His mother Mary:

> "Behold, this *Child* is appointed
> for *the* falling and rising up of many in Israel,
> and for a sign spoken against—
> ³⁵and a sword also will go through your *own* soul—
> so that *the* thoughts of many hearts may be revealed."

The Prophecy of Anna

³⁶And there was a prophetess, Anna, daughter of Phanuel, of *the* tribe of Asher. She, being advanced greatly in years, had lived with a husband seven years from her marriage, ³⁷and she *was* a widow of about eighty-four years,*ᵈ* who did not depart the temple, serving with fastings and prayers night and day. ³⁸And having come up at that hour, she was giving praise to the Lord and was speaking concerning Him to all those waiting for *the* redemption of Jerusalem.

The Return to Nazareth

(Isaiah 61:1-11; Matthew 2:19-23; Matthew 13:53-58; Mark 6:1-6; Luke 4:16-30)

³⁹And when they had performed everything according to the Law of *the* Lord, they returned to Galilee, to their town, Nazareth. ⁴⁰And the Child continued to grow and become strong, being filled with wisdom. And *the* grace of God was upon Him.

The Boy Jesus at the Temple

⁴¹And His parents were going to Jerusalem every year at the feast of the Passover. ⁴²And when He was twelve years *old*, they having gone up according to the custom of the Feast, ⁴³and having completed the days, in their returning, the boy Jesus remained behind in Jerusalem. But His parents did not know. ⁴⁴And having supposed Him to be in their company, they went a day's journey, and began seeking Him among the relatives and the acquaintances; ⁴⁵and not having found *Him*, they returned to Jerusalem, seeking Him.

⁴⁶And it came to pass after three days, they found Him in the temple, sitting in *the* midst of the teachers, both hearing them and questioning them. ⁴⁷And all those hearing Him were amazed at His understanding and answers.

⁴⁸And having seen Him, they were astonished, and His mother said to Him, "Child why have You done thus to us? Behold, Your father and I were seeking You, distressing."

⁴⁹And He said to them, "Why *is it* that you were seeking Me? Did you not know that it behooves Me to be in the *house* of My Father?"ᵉ ⁵⁰And they did not understand the word that He spoke to them.

⁵¹And He went down with them and came to Nazareth, and He was subject to them. And His mother was treasuring up all these matters in her heart.

⁵²And Jesus continued to advance in wisdom and stature, and in favor with God and men.

a 2 Or *This was the census before*
b 23 Exodus 13:2,12
c 24 Leviticus 12:8
d 37 Or *was a widow for eighty-four years*
e 49 Or *be about my Father's business*

Luke 3
The Mission of John the Baptist
(Isaiah 40:1-5; Matthew 3:1-12; Mark 1:1-8; John 1:19-28)

¹And in *the* fifteenth year of the reign of Tiberius Caesar, Pontius Pilate being governor of Judea, and Herod being tetrarch of Galilee, and his brother Philip being tetrarch of the region of Ituraea and of Trachonitis, and Lysanias being tetrarch of Abilene, ²during *the* high priesthood of Annas and Caiaphas, *the* word of God came upon John son of Zechariah in the wilderness.

³And he went into all the region surrounding the Jordan, proclaiming a baptism of repentance for forgiveness of sins, ⁴as it has been written in *the* book of *the* words of Isaiah the prophet:

"*The* voice of one crying in the wilderness,
'Prepare the way of *the* Lord;
make His paths straight.'
⁵Every valley will be filled,
and every mountain and hill will be made low;
and the crooked will become into straight,
and the rough ways into smooth.
⁶And all flesh will see the salvation of God."ᵃ

⁷So he was saying to the crowds coming out to be baptized by him, "Offspring of vipers, who forewarned you to flee from the coming wrath? ⁸Therefore produce fruits worthy of repentance. And do not begin to say in yourselves, 'We have Abraham *as* father.' For I say to you that God is able to raise up children to Abraham from these stones. ⁹And already also the ax is applied to the root of the trees; therefore every tree not producing good fruit is cut down and is thrown into *the* fire."

¹⁰And the crowds were asking him, saying, "What then shall we do?"

¹¹And answering, he was saying to them, "The *one* having two tunics, let him impart to the *one* having none; and the *one* having food, let him do likewise."

¹²And tax collectors also came to be baptized, and they said to him, "Teacher, what shall we do?"

¹³And he said to them, "Collect nothing more beyond that having been appointed to you."

¹⁴And those being soldiers also were asking him, saying, "And what shall we do?"

And he said to them, "Extort no one, nor accuse falsely, and be content with your wages."

¹⁵And the people are expecting and all wondering in their hearts concerning John, whether he might be the Christ. ¹⁶John answered all saying, "I indeed baptize you with water,ᵇ but the *One* mightier than I comes, of whom I am not worthy to untie the strap of His sandals; He will baptize you with *the* Holy Spirit

and with fire,[c] [17]of whom the winnowing fork *is* in His hand to clear His threshing floor, and to gather the wheat into His barn. But He will burn up the chaff with unquenchable fire."
[18]Therefore indeed exhorting many other things, he was preaching the good news to the people. [19]But Herod the tetrarch, being reproved by him concerning Herodias the wife of his brother, and concerning all *the* evils that Herod had done, [20]added this yet to all: He also locked up John in prison.

The Baptism of Jesus
(Matthew 3:13-17; Mark 1:9-11; John 1:29-34)

[21]Now it came to pass, in all the people having been baptized, Jesus also having been baptized and having prayed, the heaven was opened, [22]and the Holy Spirit descended upon Him in a bodily form as a dove, and a voice came out of heaven: "You are My Son, the beloved; in You I am well pleased."

The Genealogy of Jesus
(Ruth 4:18-22; Matthew 1:1-17)

[23]And Jesus beginning, was Himself about thirty years *old*,
being son as was supposed, of Joseph,
of Heli,
[24]of Matthat, of Levi, of Melchi,
of Jannai, of Joseph,
[25]of Mattathias, of Amos, of Nahum,
of Esli, of Naggai,
[26]of Maath, of Mattathias, of Semein,
of Josech, of Joda,
[27]of Joannen, of Rhesa, of Zerubbabel,
of Shealtiel, of Neri,
[28]of Melchi, of Addi, of Cosam,
of Elmadam, of Er,
[29]of Joshua, of Eliezer, of Jorim,
of Matthat, of Levi,
[30]of Simeon, of Judah, of Joseph,
of Jonam, of Eliakim,
[31]of Melea, of Menna, of Mattatha,
of Nathan, of David,
[32]of Jesse, of Obed, of Boaz,
of Sala,[d] of Nahshon,
[33]of Amminadab, of Admin,[e] of Arni,[f]
of Hezron, of Perez, of Judah,
[34]of Jacob, of Isaac, of Abraham,
of Terah, of Nahor,
[35]of Serug, of Reu, of Peleg,
of Eber, of Shelah,
[36]of Cainan, of Arphaxad, of Shem,
of Noah, of Lamech,
[37]of Methuselah, of Enoch, of Jared,
of Mahalalel, of Cainan,
[38]of Enosh, of Seth, of Adam,
of God.

a 4-6 Isaiah 40:3-5
b 16 Or *in water*
c 16 Or *in the Holy Spirit and in fire*
d 32 BYZ and TR *Salmon*
e 33 BYZ and TR *Aram*, others *Ram*
f 33 WH, BYZ, and TR do not include *the son of Arni*

Luke 4
The Temptation of Jesus
(Matthew 4:1-11; Mark 1:12-13)

[1]And Jesus, full of *the* Holy Spirit, returned from the Jordan and was led by the Spirit into the wilderness, [2]being tempted forty days by the devil. And He ate nothing in those days, and they having ended, He was hungry.
[3]And the devil said to Him, "If You are *the* Son of God, speak to this stone, that it should become bread."
[4]And Jesus answered to him, "It has been written: 'Man shall not live on bread alone.'[a]"
[5]And having led Him up, he showed Him all the kingdoms of the world in a moment of time. [6]And the devil said to Him, "I will give to You all this authority, and its glory; for it has been delivered to me, and I give it to whom I wish. [7]Therefore if You will worship before me, all will be Yours."
[8]And Jesus answering, said to him, "It has been written: 'You shall worship *the* Lord your God, and you shall serve Him only.'[b]"
[9]And he led Him to Jerusalem and set *Him* upon the pinnacle of the temple, and said to Him, "If You are *the* Son of God,

cast Yourself down from here. ¹⁰For it has been written:

> 'He will give orders to His angels concerning You,
> to guard You;
> ¹¹and in *their* hands will they bear You *up*,
> lest ever You strike Your foot against a stone.'*ᶜ*"

¹²And Jesus answering, said to him, "It has been said, 'You shall not test *the* Lord your God.'*ᵈ*"
¹³And the devil, having finished every temptation, departed from Him until an opportune time.

Jesus Begins His Ministry
(Isaiah 9:1-7; Matthew 4:12-17; Mark 1:14-15)

¹⁴And Jesus returned in the power of the Spirit to Galilee, and a report concerning Him went out into all the surrounding region. ¹⁵And He was teaching in their synagogues, being glorified by all.

The Rejection at Nazareth
(Isaiah 61:1-11; Matthew 2:19-23; Matthew 13:53-58; Mark 6:1-6; Luke 2:39-40)

¹⁶And He came to Nazareth, where He had been brought up; and according to His custom, He entered into the synagogue on the day of the Sabbaths, and stood up to read. ¹⁷And *the* scroll of the prophet Isaiah was given to Him, and having unrolled the scroll, He found the place where it was written:

> ¹⁸"*The* Spirit of *the* Lord *is* upon Me, because of which He has anointed Me
> to preach good news to *the* poor.
> He has sent Me*ᵉ* to proclaim deliverance to *the* captives,
> and recovery of sight to *the* blind,
> to send forth in deliverance *the* oppressed,
> ¹⁹to proclaim *the* year of *the* Lord's favor."*ᶠ*

²⁰And having rolled up the scroll, having delivered *it* to the attendant, He sat down, and the eyes of all in the synagogue were fixed upon Him. ²¹And He began to say to them, "Today this Scripture is fulfilled in your hearing."
²²And all were bearing witness to Him and marveling at the grace of the words that are proceeding out of His mouth. And they were saying, "Is this not the son of Joseph?"
²³And He said to them, "Surely you will say to Me this proverb, 'Physician heal yourself! Whatsoever we have heard has been done in Capernaum, do here in Your hometown also.'"
²⁴And He said, "Truly I say to you that no prophet is acceptable in his hometown. ²⁵And in truth I say to you, there were many widows in Israel in the days of Elijah, when the heaven was shut up for three years and six months, when there was a great famine upon all the land; ²⁶and Elijah was sent to none of them, except to Zarephath of Sidon, to a woman, a widow. ²⁷And many lepers*ᵍ* were in Israel in the time of Elisha the prophet, and none of them was cleansed, except Naaman the Syrian."
²⁸And all in the synagogue were filled with anger, hearing these things, ²⁹and having risen up, they cast Him out of *the* city, and led Him unto *the* brow of the hill upon which their town had been built, in order to throw Him over. ³⁰But He, having passed through their midst, went away.

Jesus Expels an Unclean Spirit
(Mark 1:21-28)

³¹And He went down to Capernaum, a city of Galilee. And He was teaching them on the Sabbaths; ³²and they were astonished at His teaching, for His message was with authority.
³³And in the synagogue was a man having a spirit of an unclean demon; and he cried out in a loud voice, ³⁴"Ha! What to us and to You, Jesus of Nazareth? Are You come to destroy us? I know who You are, the Holy *One* of God!"

35 And Jesus rebuked him, saying, "Be silent and come forth out of him!" And having thrown him into the midst, the demon came out from him, in nothing having hurt him.

36 And astonishment came upon all, and they were speaking to one another, saying, "What word *is* this, that He commands the unclean spirits with authority and power, and they come out?" 37 And the report concerning Him was spreading into every place of the surrounding region.

Jesus Heals at Peter's House
(Matthew 8:14-17; Mark 1:29-34)

38 And having risen up out of the synagogue, He entered into the house of Simon. And Simon's mother-in-law was oppressed with a great fever, and they appealed to Him for her. 39 And having stood over her, He rebuked the fever, and it left her; and immediately having arisen, she began to serve them.

40 And at the setting of the sun, all, as many as had *any* ailing with various diseases, brought them to Him, and having laid the hands on each one of them, He would heal them. 41 And demons also were going out from many, crying out and saying, "You are the Son of God." And rebuking *them*, He did not allow them to speak, because they knew Him to be the Christ.

Jesus Preaches in Judea
(Mark 1:35-39)

42 And daybreak having arrived, having gone out, He went into a solitary place, and the crowds were seeking Him, and came up to Him and were detaining Him, not to go from them. 43 But He said to them, "It behooves Me to preach *the* good news of the kingdom of God to the other towns also, because for this I have been sent forth."

44 And He was preaching in the synagogues of Judea.[h]

a 4 Deuteronomy 8:3. BYZ and TR include *but on every word of God*
b 8 Deuteronomy 6:13
c 10-11 Psalm 91:11,12
d 12 Deuteronomy 6:16

e 18 BYZ and TR include *to heal the brokenhearted*,
f 18-19 Isaiah 61:1,2
g 27 Leprosy was a term for several skin diseases. See Leviticus 13.
h 44 BYZ and TR *Galilee*

Luke 5
The First Disciples
(Matthew 4:18-22; Matthew 13:47-52; Mark 1:16-20; John 1:35-42)

1 And it came to pass, in the crowd pressing on Him also to hear the word of God, and He was standing by the lake of Gennesaret,[a] 2 and He saw two boats lying by the lake, but the fishermen, having gone out from them, were washing the nets. 3 And having entered into one of the boats which was Simon's, He asked him to put off a little from the land. And having sat down, He was teaching the crowds from the boat.

4 And when He left off speaking, He said to Simon, "Put off into the deep and let down your nets for a catch."

5 And Simon answering, said, "Master, having toiled through whole night, we have taken nothing; but at Your word, I will let down the nets." 6 And having done this, they enclosed a great multitude of fishes; and their nets were breaking. 7 And they beckoned to the partners in the other boat, having come, to help them, and they came and filled both boats, so that they were sinking.

8 And having seen, Simon Peter fell at Jesus' knees, saying, "Depart from me, Lord. For I am a sinful man." 9 For amazement laid hold on him, and on all those with him, at the catch of the fish which they had taken, 10 and likewise also James and John, *the* sons of Zebedee, who were partners with Simon.

And Jesus said to Simon, "Fear not; from now on you will be catching men." 11 And having brought the boats to the land, having left all, they followed Him.

The Leper's Prayer
(Leviticus 14:1-32; Matthew 8:1-4; Mark 1:40-45)

12 And it came to pass in His being in one of the cities, that behold, a man full of

leprosy,[b] and having seen Jesus, having fallen upon *his* face, begged Him, saying, "Lord, if You would be willing, You are able to cleanse me."

¹³And having stretched out the hand, He touched him, saying, "I am willing; be you cleansed!" And immediately the leprosy departed from him.

¹⁴And He ordered him to tell no one: "But having gone, show yourself to the priest, and offer for your cleansing, as Moses commanded, for a testimony to them."

¹⁵And the report concerning Him was spread abroad still more; and great crowds were coming to hear and to be healed from their sicknesses. ¹⁶And He Himself was withdrawing into the wilderness and praying.

Jesus Heals a Paralytic
(Matthew 9:1-8; Mark 2:1-12)

¹⁷And it came to pass on one of the days that He was teaching, and Pharisees and teachers of the law were there sitting by, who were come out of every village of Galilee, and of Judea, and of Jerusalem. And *the* power of *the* Lord was *there* for Him to heal.

¹⁸And behold, men carrying upon a mat a man who was paralyzed, and they were seeking to bring him in and to place him before Him. ¹⁹And not having found what way they should bring him in, on account of the crowd, having gone up on the housetop, they let him down with the mat through the tiles, into the midst before Jesus.

²⁰And having seen their faith, He said, "Man, your sins have been forgiven you."

²¹And the scribes and the Pharisees began to reason, saying, "Who is this who speaks blasphemies? Who is able to forgive sins, except God alone?"

²²And Jesus, having known their reasonings, answering, said to them, "Why do you reason in your hearts? ²³Which is easier, to say, 'Your sins have been forgiven you,' or to say, 'Arise and walk?' ²⁴But that you may know that the Son of Man has authority on the earth to forgive sins..." He said to the *one* having been paralyzed, "I say to you, arise, and having taken up your mat, go to your house."

²⁵And immediately having stood up before them, having taken up *that* on which he was lying, he departed to his home, glorifying God. ²⁶And amazement seized all, and they were glorifying God, and were filled with fear, saying, "We have seen remarkable things today."

The Calling of Levi
(Matthew 9:9-13; Mark 2:13-17)

²⁷And after these things He went forth and saw a tax collector named Levi sitting at the tax booth. And He said to him, "Follow Me." ²⁸And having left all, having arisen, he began to follow Him.

²⁹And Levi made a great banquet for Him in his house, and there was a great multitude of tax collectors and others, who were reclining with them. ³⁰And the Pharisees and their scribes were grumbling at His disciples, saying, "Why do you eat and drink with the tax collectors and sinners?"

³¹And Jesus answering, said to them, "Those being well have no need of a physician, but those being sick. ³²I have not come to call righteous *ones*, but sinners, to repentance."

Questions about Fasting
(Matthew 9:14-15; Mark 2:18-20)

³³And they said to Him, "The disciples of John fast often and make prayers; likewise also those of the Pharisees; but Yours eat and drink."

³⁴And Jesus said to them, "Are you able to make the sons of the bridechamber to fast while the bridegroom is with them? ³⁵But days will come also when the bridegroom shall be taken away from them; then they will fast in those days."

The Patches and the Wineskins
(Matthew 9:16-17; Mark 2:21-22)

³⁶And He was speaking also a parable to them: "No one having torn a piece of new a garment, puts *it* on an old garment; but if otherwise, he will tear the new also, and

the old will not match *the* piece which *is* of the new. ³⁷And no one puts new wine into old wineskins; if now otherwise, the new wine will burst the wineskins, and it will be spilled out, and the wineskins will be destroyed. ³⁸But new wine must be put into fresh wineskins. ³⁹And no one having drunk old *wine* desires new; for he says, 'The old is better.'"

a 1 That is, the Sea of Galilee
b 12 Leprosy was a term for several skin diseases. See Leviticus 13.

Luke 6
The Lord of the Sabbath
(1 Samuel 21:1-9; Matthew 12:1-8; Mark 2:23-28)

¹And it came to pass on a Sabbath,ᵃ He is passing along through grainfields; and His disciples were plucking and were eating the heads of grain, rubbing *them* in the hands. ²But some of the Pharisees said, "Why are you doing that which is not lawful *on* the Sabbaths?" ³And Jesus answering, said to them, "Not even have you read this, that which David did when he himself was hungry, and those who were with him: ⁴how he entered into the house of God, and having taken the loaves of the presentation, ate and gave to those with him, which it is not lawful to eat, except to the priests only?" ⁵And He was saying to them, "The Son of Man is Lord of the Sabbath."

Jesus Heals on the Sabbath
(Matthew 12:9-14; Mark 3:1-6)

⁶And it came to pass on another Sabbath, He entered into the synagogue and taught; and there was a man there, and his right hand was withered. ⁷And the scribes and the Pharisees were closely watching Him, whether He will heal on the Sabbath, that they might find *reason* to accuse Him.
⁸And He knew their thoughts, and He said to the man having the withered hand, "Arise and stand in the midst." And having risen up, he stood. ⁹Then Jesus said to them, "I ask you whether it is lawful on the Sabbath to do good or to do evil, to save life or to destroy?" ¹⁰And having looked around on them all, He said to him, "Stretch out your hand." And he did, and his hand was restored. ¹¹And they themselves were filled with rage, and were discussing with one another what they might do to Jesus.

The Twelve Apostles
(Matthew 10:1-4; Mark 3:13-19)

¹²And it came to pass in those days, He went out to the mountain to pray, and He was spending the night in prayer to God. ¹³And when it became day, He summoned His disciples, also having chosen out from them twelve, whom also He named apostles: ¹⁴Simon whom He also named Peter, and his brother Andrew; and James and John; and Philip and Bartholomew; ¹⁵and Matthew and Thomas; and James *son of* Alphaeus; and Simon the *one* called Zealot; ¹⁶and Judas *son* of James; and Judas Iscariot, who became *the* betrayer.

Jesus Ministers to a Great Crowd
(Matthew 4:23-25)

¹⁷And having descended with them, He stood on a level place, and a large crowd of His disciples, and a great multitude of the people from all Judea, and Jerusalem, and the sea coast of Tyre and Sidon, ¹⁸who came to hear Him and to be healed of their diseases. And those troubled with unclean spirits were healed. ¹⁹And the whole multitude were seeking to touch Him, because power was going out from Him and healing all.

The Beatitudes
(Psalm 1:1-6; Matthew 5:3-12)

²⁰And He, having lifted up His gaze upon His disciples, was saying:
"Blessed *are* the poor,
   for yours is the kingdom of God.
²¹Blessed *are* those hungering now,
   for you will be filled.
Blessed *are* those weeping now,
   for you will laugh.

²²Blessed are you when men shall hate you, and when they shall exclude you, and shall insult *you*, and shall cast out your name as evil, on account of the Son of Man. ²³Rejoice in that day, and leap for joy; for behold, your reward *is* great in heaven. For their fathers according to these things used to treat the prophets likewise.

Woes
(Amos 6:1-7)

²⁴But woe to you who are rich,
  for you are receiving your comfort.
²⁵Woe to you having been filled now,
  for you will hunger.
Woe to those laughing now,
  for you will mourn and weep.
²⁶Woe to you when all men speak well of you,
  for according to these things their fathers used to treat the false prophets likewise.

Love Your Enemies
(Leviticus 24:17-23; Matthew 5:38-48)

²⁷But to you hearing I say: Love your enemies, do good to those hating you, ²⁸bless those cursing you, pray for those mistreating you. ²⁹To the *one* striking you on the cheek, offer the other also; and from the *one* taking away your cloak, do not withhold the tunic also. ³⁰Give to everyone asking you, and from the *one* taking away what *is* yours, do not ask *it* back. ³¹And as you desire that men should do to you, do likewise to them.

³²And if you love those loving you, what credit is it to you? For even sinners love those loving them. ³³And indeed, if you do good to those doing good to you, what credit is it to you? For even sinners do the same. ³⁴And if you lend *to those* from whom you expect to receive back, what credit is it to you? Even sinners lend to sinners, that they might receive the same amount.

³⁵But love your enemies, and do good, and lend, expecting nothing in return, and your reward will be great, and you will be sons of the Most High; for He is kind to the ungrateful and evil. ³⁶Be you merciful, as your Father also is merciful.

Do Not Judge
(Matthew 7:1-6; Romans 14:1-12)

³⁷And do not judge that you should not be judged; and do not condemn that you should not be condemned; forgive and you will be forgiven. ³⁸Give, and it will be given to you. A good measure pressed down, shaken together, running over will they put into your lap. For with that measure you measure, it will be measured again to you."

³⁹And He spoke a parable also to them. "Is a blind *man* able to lead a blind *man*? Will they not both fall into a pit? ⁴⁰A disciple is not above the teacher, and everyone fully trained will be like his teacher.

⁴¹And why do you look at the splinter that *is* in your brother's eye and not notice *the* beam that *is* in the own eye? ⁴²How are you able to say to your brother, 'Brother let *that* I might cast out the splinter that *is* in your eye,' yourself not seeing *the* beam in your eye? Hypocrite! First cast out the beam from your eye, and then you will see clearly to cast out the splinter in the eye of your brother.

A Tree and its Fruit
(Matthew 7:15-23; Matthew 12:33-37)

⁴³For there is no good tree producing bad fruit, nor again a bad tree producing good fruit. ⁴⁴For each tree is known by its own fruit. For they do not gather figs from thorns, nor do they gather grapes from a bramble bush. ⁴⁵The good man out of the good treasure of his heart brings forth that which *is* good; and the evil out of the evil brings forth that which *is* evil. For out of the abundance of his heart, his mouth speaks.

The House on the Rock
(Matthew 7:24-27)

⁴⁶And why do you call Me 'Lord, Lord,' and not do what I say? ⁴⁷Everyone who is coming to Me, and hearing My words,

and doing them, I will show you whom he is like. ⁴⁸He is like to a man building a house, who dug and deepened, and laid a foundation on the rock. And a flood having come, the stream burst upon that house, and was not able to shake it, because it had been built well.ᵇ ⁴⁹But the *one* having heard and not having done is like to a man having built a house on the ground without a foundation, on which the stream burst, and immediately it fell, and the ruin of that house was great."

a 1 BYZ and TR *On the second Sabbath after the first*
b 48 BYZ and TR *founded upon the rock*

Luke 7
The Faith of the Centurion
(Matthew 8:5-13; John 4:43-54)

¹And when He had completed all His words in the hearing of the people, He entered into Capernaum. ²And a certain servant of a centurion, who was valued highly to him, being sick, was about to die. ³And having heard about Jesus, he sent elders of the Jews to Him, begging Him that having come, He might save his servant. ⁴And having come to Jesus, they were begging Him earnestly, saying, "He is worthy to whom You will grant this, ⁵for he loves our nation, and he built the synagogue for us."
⁶And Jesus was going with them. And already, He being not far distant from the house, the centurion sent friends, saying to Him, "Lord, do not trouble Yourself, for I am not worthy that You should come under my roof. ⁷Therefore neither did I count myself worthy to come to You; but say in a word, and my servant shall be healed. ⁸For I also am a man appointed under authority, having soldiers under me; and I say to this *one*, 'Go,' and he goes; and to another, 'Come,' and he comes; and to my servant, 'Do this,' and he does *it*."
⁹And Jesus having heard these things, marveled at him; and having turned to the crowd following Him, He said, "I say to you, not even in Israel did I find such great faith." ¹⁰And having returned to the house, those having been sent found the servant in good health.

Jesus Raises a Widow's Son

¹¹And it came to pass on the next *day*, He went into a town called Nain, and His disciples were going with Him, and a great crowd. ¹²And as He drew near to the gate of the town, also behold, *one* having died was being carried out, *the* only begotten son of his mother; and she was a widow. And a considerable crowd of the town was with her. ¹³And the Lord having seen her, was moved with compassion on her and said to her, "Do not weep."
¹⁴And having come up, He touched the bier; and those bearing *it* stopped. And He said, "Young man, I say to you, Arise!" ¹⁵And the dead *man* sat up and began to speak, and He gave him to his mother.
¹⁶And fear seized all, and they began glorifying God, saying, "A great prophet has risen up among us!" and, "God has visited His people!" ¹⁷And this report concerning Him went out in all Judea and all the surrounding region.

John's Inquiry
(Matthew 11:1-6)

¹⁸And his disciples brought word to John concerning all these things. ¹⁹And having summoned a certain two his disciples, John sent *them* to the Lord saying, "Are You the coming *One*, or are we to look for another?"
²⁰And the men having come to Him said, "John the Baptist has sent us to you, saying, 'Are You the coming *One*, or are we to look for another?'"
²¹At that very hour, He healed many of diseases and afflictions and evil spirits, and He granted many blind to see. ²²And answering, He said to them, "Having gone, relate to John what you have seen and heard: Blind receive sight, lame walk, lepersᵃ are cleansed and deaf hear, dead are raised, poor are gospelized. ²³And blessed is whoever shall not be offended in Me."

Jesus Testifies about John

(Matthew 11:7-19; Luke 1:5-25; Luke 16:14-17)

²⁴And the messengers of John having departed, He began to speak to the crowds concerning John: "What have you gone out into the wilderness to see? A reed shaken by *the* wind? ²⁵But what have you gone out to see? A man arrayed in fine clothing? Behold, those in splendid clothing and living in luxury are in palaces.
²⁶But what have you gone out to see? A prophet? Yes, I say to you, and *one* more excellent than a prophet. ²⁷This is he concerning whom it has been written:

'Behold, I send My messenger before your face,
   who will prepare Your way before You.'[b]

²⁸I say to you, no one among *those* born of women is greater than John; yet the least in the kingdom of God is greater than he."
²⁹And all the people having heard, even the tax collectors, declared God righteous, having been baptized *with* the baptism of John. ³⁰But the Pharisees and the lawyers rejected the counsel of God as to themselves, not having been baptized by him.
³¹"To what therefore will I liken the men of this generation? And to what are they like? ³²They are like to little children sitting in *the* marketplace and calling to one another, saying:

'We piped to you, and you did not dance;
   we sang a dirge, and you did not weep.'

³³For John the Baptist has come neither eating bread nor drinking wine, and you say, 'He has a demon!' ³⁴The Son of Man has come eating and drinking, and you say, 'Behold, a man, a glutton and a drunkard, a friend of tax collectors and of sinners!' ³⁵And wisdom was justified by all her children."

A Sinful Woman Anoints Jesus

³⁶And one of the Pharisees was asking Him that He should eat with him, and having entered into the house of the Pharisee, He reclined. ³⁷And behold, a woman in the city who was a sinner. And she having known that He had reclined in the Pharisee's house, having taken an alabaster flask of fragrant oil, ³⁸and having stood behind Him at His feet weeping, she began to wet His feet with the tears, and she was wiping *them* with the hairs of her head, and was kissing His feet, and was anointing *them* with the fragrant oil.
³⁹And the Pharisee, the *one* having invited Him, having seen, spoke within himself, saying, "If this were a prophet, He would have known who and what the woman *is* who touches Him; for she is a sinner."
⁴⁰And answering, Jesus said to him, "Simon, I have something to say to you." And he says, "Teacher, say *it*."
⁴¹"There were two debtors to a certain creditor. The one owed five hundred denarii,[c] and the other fifty. ⁴²They having nothing to pay, he forgave both. Therefore which of them will love him more?"
⁴³Simon answering, said, "I take it that *he* to whom he forgave the most."
And He said to him, "You have judged rightly."
⁴⁴And having turned to the woman, He was saying to Simon, "Do you see this woman? I entered into your house; you did not give water for My feet, but she wet My feet with her tears and wiped *them* with her hair. ⁴⁵You did not give to Me a kiss, but from which *time* I came in, she herself has not ceased kissing My feet. ⁴⁶You did not anoint My head with oil, but she herself anointed My feet with fragrant oil. ⁴⁷Therefore I say to you this: Her many sins have been forgiven, for she loved much; but to whom little is forgiven, he loves little."

⁴⁸And He said to her, "Your sins have been forgiven."
⁴⁹And those reclining began to say within themselves, "Who is this who even forgives sins?"
⁵⁰And He said to the woman, "Your faith has saved you; go in peace."

a 22 Leprosy was a term for several skin diseases. See Leviticus 13.
b 27 Malachi 3:1
c 41 A denarius was customarily a day's wage for a laborer (see Matthew 20:2)

Luke 8
Women Minister to Jesus

¹And it came to pass soon afterward that He was traveling throughout city and village, preaching and proclaiming the good news of the kingdom of God. And the Twelve were with Him, ²and certain women who had been cured from evil spirits and infirmities: Mary who is called Magdalene, from whom seven demons had gone out, ³and Joanna wife of Chuza, a steward of Herod, and Susanna, and many others, who were ministering to them ᵃ out of their own means.

The Parable of the Sower
(Matthew 13:1-9; Mark 4:1-9)

⁴And as a great crowd is assembling, and those from each town are coming to Him, He spoke by a parable: ⁵"The one sowing went out to sow his seed. And in his sowing, some indeed fell along the road, and it was trampled upon, and the birds of the air devoured it.
⁶And other fell upon the rock, and having sprung up it withered through having no moisture.
⁷And other fell in the midst of the thorns, and the thorns having sprung up with it, choked it.
⁸And other fell upon the good soil, and having sprung up, it produced fruit—a hundredfold."
Saying these things, He was calling out, "The one having ears to hear, let him hear."
⁹And His disciples were asking Him, "What does this parable mean?"

¹⁰And He said, "To you it has been given to know the mysteries of the kingdom of God, but to the rest, it is in parables, so that,

'Seeing, they may not see;
and hearing, they may not understand.'ᵇ

¹¹And the parable is this: The seed is the word of God. ¹²And those along the road are those having heard; then the devil comes and takes away the word from their heart, lest having believed, they should be saved.
¹³And those upon the rock are those who receive the word with joy when they hear; and these have no root, who believe for a time, and in time of testing fall away.
¹⁴And that having fallen into the thorns, these are those having heard, and moving along are choked under the cares and riches and pleasures of life, and do not mature.
¹⁵And that in the good soil, these are those who, having heard the word, keep it in a worthy and good heart and bring forth fruit by perseverance.

The Lesson of the Lamp
(Mark 4:21-25)

¹⁶And no one having lighted a lamp, covers it with a vessel, or puts it under a bed. But he puts it on a lampstand, so that those entering in may see the light.
¹⁷For nothing is hidden which will not become manifest, nor secret which shall not be known and come to light.
¹⁸Therefore take heed how you hear; for whoever might have, to him will be given; and whoever might not have, even what he seems to have will be taken away from him."

Jesus' Mother and Brothers
(Matthew 12:46-50; Mark 3:31-35)

¹⁹And His mother and brothers came to Him, and they were not able to get to Him, because of the crowd. ²⁰And it was told Him, "Your mother and Your brothers are standing outside, wishing to see You."

²¹But answering, He said to them, "My mother and my brothers are those who are hearing and doing the word of God."

Jesus Calms the Storm
(Matthew 8:23-27; Mark 4:35-41)

²²And it came to pass, on one of the days also, He with His disciples entered into a boat, and He said to them, "Let us pass over to the other side of the lake." And they launched out. ²³And of them sailing, He fell asleep. And a storm of wind came down on the lake, and they were being swamped, and were in danger. ²⁴And having approached, they awoke Him, saying, "Master, Master, we are perishing!"

And having arisen, He rebuked the wind and the raging of the water, and they ceased, and there was a calm. ²⁵And He said to them, "Where is your faith?"

And having been afraid, they marveled, saying to one another, "Who then is this, that He commands even the winds and the water, and they obey Him?"

The Demons and the Pigs
(Matthew 8:28-34; Mark 5:1-20)

²⁶And they sailed down to the region of the Gerasenes,ᶜ which is opposite Galilee. ²⁷And He having gone forth upon the land, a certain man out of the city met Him, having demons, and a long time he was not wearing clothing and did not abide in a house, but in the tombs. ²⁸And having seen Jesus, having cried out, he fell down before Him and said in a loud voice, "What to me and to You, Jesus, Son of the Most High God? I implore of You *that* You might not torment me!" ²⁹For He was commanding the unclean spirit to come out from the man. For it had seized him many times, and he was bound, being kept with chains and shackles. And breaking the chains, he was driven by the demon into the deserts. ³⁰And Jesus asked him, "What is your name?"

And he said, "Legion," because many demons were entered into him. ³¹And they were begging Him not to command them to depart into the abyss. ³²And there was a herd of many pigs feeding there in the mountain, and they begged Him that He would allow them to enter into them; and He allowed them. ³³And the demons having gone out from the man, entered into the pigs, and the herd rushed down the steep bank into the lake, and was drowned. ³⁴And those feeding *them*, having seen that having taken place, fled and reported *it* to the city and to the country. ³⁵And they went out to see that having taken place, and they came to Jesus and found the man from whom the demons had gone out sitting, clothed, and being of sound mind, at the feet of Jesus. And they were afraid. ³⁶And those having seen *it* related to them how the *one* having been possessed by demons was healed. ³⁷And all the multitude of the surrounding region of the Gerasenes asked Him to depart from them, because they were seized with great fear. And He, having entered into the boat, turned back. ³⁸But the man from whom the demons had gone was begging Him to be *taken* with Him. But He sent him away saying, ³⁹"Return to your house, and relate all that God has done for you." And he departed, proclaiming through the whole city all that Jesus had done for him.

The Healing Touch of Jesus
(Matthew 9:18-26; Mark 5:21-43)

⁴⁰And when Jesus returned, the crowd received Him, for they were all looking for Him. ⁴¹And behold, a man whose name *was* Jairus came, and he was a ruler of the synagogue, and having fallen at the feet of Jesus, he began begging Him to come to his house, ⁴²because he had an only daughter, about twelve years *old*, and she was dying.

And as He went, the crowds were pressing around Him. ⁴³And a woman being with a flux of blood for twelve years, who, having spent all her living on physicians,*d* was not able to be healed by *anyone*. ⁴⁴Having come behind *Him*, she touched the fringe of His cloak, and immediately her flux of blood stopped.

⁴⁵And Jesus said, "Who *is* the *one* having touched Me?"

But all were denying *it*. Peter*e* said, "Master, the people surround You and press in."

⁴⁶But Jesus said, "Someone touched Me, for I know power has gone out from Me."

⁴⁷And the woman, having seen that she was not hidden, came trembling, and having fallen down before Him before all the people, she declared for what cause she touched Him, and how she was healed immediately.

⁴⁸And He said to her, "Daughter, your faith has healed you; go in peace."

⁴⁹Of Him still speaking, one comes from the synagogue ruler, saying, "Your daughter has died; trouble the Teacher no longer."

⁵⁰But Jesus having heard, answered him, "Fear not; only believe, and she will be saved."

⁵¹And having entered into the house, He did not allow anyone to go in with Him, except Peter and John and James and the father and the mother of the child. ⁵²And all were weeping and mourning for her. But He said, "Do not weep; for she is not dead, but sleeps."

⁵³And they were laughing at Him, knowing that she was dead.

⁵⁴And He having taken hold her of hand, called out, saying, "Child, arise!" ⁵⁵And her spirit returned, and she arose immediately; and He directed to be given to her to eat. ⁵⁶And her parents were amazed; and He instructed them to tell no one what had happened.

a 3 TR *to Him*
b 10 Isaiah 6:9
c 26 BYZ and TR *Gadarenes*; also in verse 37
d 43 NE and WH do not include *She had spent all her money on physicians*
e 45 BYZ and TR include *and those who were with him*

Luke 9
The Ministry of the Twelve
(Matthew 10:5-15; Mark 6:7-13)

¹And having called together the Twelve, He gave to them power and authority over all the demons, and to heal diseases, ²and He sent them to proclaim the kingdom of God and to heal the sick. ³And He said to them, "Take nothing for the journey, neither staff, nor bag, nor bread, nor money, nor two tunics apiece to have. ⁴And into whatever house you might enter, remain there, and go forth from there. ⁵And as many as might not receive you, going forth from that city, shake off the dust from your feet, as a testimony against them."

⁶And going forth, they were passing through the villages, proclaiming the gospel and healing everywhere.

Herod Desires to See Jesus
(Matthew 14:1-12; Mark 6:14-29)

⁷And Herod the Tetrarch heard of all the things being done, and was perplexed, because it was said by some that John has been raised out from *the* dead, ⁸and by some that Elijah had appeared, and by others that a prophet of the ancients had arisen.

⁹And Herod said, "John I beheaded, but who is this concerning whom I hear such things?" And he was seeking to see Him.

The Feeding of the Five Thousand
(Matthew 14:13-21; Mark 6:30-44; John 6:1-15)

¹⁰And having returned, the apostles related to Him whatever they had done. And having taken them, He withdrew by Himself into a town called Bethsaida. ¹¹And the crowds having known *it*, followed Him; and having received them, He was speaking to them concerning the kingdom of God, and He was healing those having need of healing.

¹²And the day began to decline, and the Twelve having come, said to Him, "Dismiss the crowd, that having gone into the surrounding villages and countryside, they might lodge and might find

provisions; for we are in a desolate place here."

¹³And He said to them, "You give to them to eat."

But they said, "There are no more than five loaves to us, and two fish, unless we, having gone, should buy food for all this people." ¹⁴For they were about five thousand men.

And He said to His disciples, "Make them sit down in groups of about fifty." ¹⁵And they did so and made all sit down.

¹⁶And having taken the five loaves and the two fish, having looked up to the heaven, He blessed and broke them, and He kept giving *them* to the disciples to set before the crowd.

¹⁷And they all ate and were satisfied; and that having been a surplus to them was taken up, twelve hand-baskets of fragments.

Peter's Confession of Christ
(Matthew 16:13-20; Mark 8:27-30; John 6:66-71)

¹⁸And it came to pass as He was praying in solitary, the disciples were with Him, and He questioned them, saying, "Whom do the crowds pronounce Me to be?"

¹⁹And answering, they said, "John the Baptist; and others, Elijah; and others, that a prophet, one of the ancients, has arisen."

²⁰And He said to them, "But whom do you pronounce Me to be?"

And Peter answering said, "The Christ of God."

Christ's Passion Foretold
(Matthew 16:21-23; Mark 8:31-33)

²¹And having strictly warned *them*, He instructed them to tell this to no one, ²²having said, "It is necessary for the Son of Man to suffer many things, and to be rejected by the elders and chief priests and scribes, and to be killed, and on the third day to be raised."

Take Up Your Cross
(Matthew 10:37-39; Matthew 16:24-28; Mark 8:34-38)

²³And He was saying to all, "If anyone desires to come after Me, let him deny himself, and let him take up his cross every day, and let him follow Me. ²⁴For whoever might desire to save his life will lose it; but whoever might lose his life on account of me, he will save it.

²⁵For what is a man profited, having gained the whole world, and having destroyed or having suffered the loss of himself? ²⁶For whoever may have been ashamed of Me and My words, the Son of Man will be ashamed of him when He shall come in His glory, and *that* of the Father and of the holy angels. ²⁷And I say to you truthfully, there are some of those standing here who shall not taste of death until they shall have seen the kingdom of God."

The Transfiguration
(Matthew 17:1-13; Mark 9:1-13; 2 Peter 1:16-21)

²⁸And it came to pass, about eight days after these sayings, and having taken Peter and John and James, He went up on the mountain to pray. ²⁹And it came to pass in His praying, the appearance of His face *was* altered, and His clothing became dazzling white. ³⁰And behold, two men began talking with Him, who were Moses and Elijah. ³¹Those having appeared in glory were speaking of His going out, which He was about to accomplish in Jerusalem.

³²And Peter and those with him were heavy with sleep; and having awoken fully, they saw His glory, and the two men standing with Him. ³³And it came to pass in their departing from Him, Peter said to Jesus, "Master, it is good for us to be here; let us make also three tabernacles, one for You, and one for Moses, and one for Elijah," not knowing what he is saying.

³⁴And as he is saying these things, a cloud came and was overshadowing them; and they feared in their entering

into the cloud. ³⁵And a voice came out of the cloud, saying, "This is My Son,ᵃ whom I have chosen; listen to Him!" ³⁶And as the voice occurred, Jesus was found alone. And they were silent, and they told to no one in those days anything of what they had seen.

The Boy with an Evil Spirit
(Matthew 17:14-21; Mark 9:14-29; Luke 17:5-10)

³⁷And it came to pass the next day, on their having come down from the mountain, a great crowd met Him. ³⁸And behold, a man from the crowd cried out, saying, "Teacher, I implore You to look upon my son, for he is an only child to me. ³⁹And behold, a spirit takes him, and suddenly he cries out, and it throws him into convulsions with foaming, and with difficulty it departs from him, crushing him. ⁴⁰And I begged Your disciples that they might cast it out, and they were not able."
⁴¹And Jesus answering said, "O unbelieving and perverted generation, until when will I be with you and bear with you? Bring your son here."
⁴²And while he was coming near, the demon threw him down, and threw *him* into convulsions. And Jesus rebuked the unclean spirit and healed the boy, and gave him back to his father.

The Second Prediction of the Passion
(Matthew 17:22-23; Mark 9:30-32)

⁴³And all were astonished at the majesty of God.
But of all wondering at all that He did, He said to His disciples, ⁴⁴"You let these words sink into your ears; for the Son of Man is about to be betrayed into *the* hands of men." ⁴⁵But they did not understand this saying, and it was veiled from them, that they should not understand it. And they were afraid to ask Him concerning this saying.

The Greatest in the Kingdom
(Matthew 18:1-6; Mark 9:33-37)

⁴⁶And an argument came up among them, which of them might be greatest. ⁴⁷But Jesus, having known the reasoning of their heart, having taken hold of a child, set it by Him, ⁴⁸and He said to them, "Whoever shall receive this child in My name, receives Me; and whoever shall receive Me, receives the *One* having sent Me. For the *one* being least among you all, he shall be great."
⁴⁹And John answering said, "Master, we saw someone casting out demons in Your name, and we were forbidding him, because he does not follow with us."
⁵⁰And Jesus said to him, "Do not forbid *it*; for whoever is not against us is for us."

The Samaritans Reject Jesus
⁵¹And it came to pass in the completing of the days of His ascension, that He steadfastly set the face to go to Jerusalem. ⁵²And He sent messengers before His face. And having gone, they entered into a village of the Samaritans, so as to make ready for Him. ⁵³And they did not receive Him, because His face was going toward Jerusalem.
⁵⁴And the disciples James and John having seen *it*, said, "Lord, will You *that* we should call fire to come down from heaven and to consume them?"ᵇ
⁵⁵And having turned, He rebuked them,ᶜ ⁵⁶and they went to another village.

The Cost of Discipleship
(Matthew 8:18-22; Luke 14:25-33; John 6:60-65)

⁵⁷And as they were going along the road, someone said to Him, "I will follow You wherever You may go."
⁵⁸And Jesus said to him, "The foxes have holes, and the birds of the air nests; but the Son of Man has nowhere He might lay the head."
⁵⁹And He said to another, "Follow Me."
But he said, "Lord, allow me first, having gone away, to bury my father."

⁶⁰And He said to him, "Leave the dead to bury their own dead; but you, having gone forth, declare the kingdom of God."
⁶¹And another also said, "I will follow You, Lord; but first allow me to bid farewell to those at my home."
⁶²And Jesus said to him, "No one having laid the hand upon *the* plow, and looking on the things behind, is fit for the kingdom of God."

a 35 BYZ and TR *This is my Beloved Son*
b 54 BYZ and TR include *as Elijah did*
c 55 BYZ and TR include *and he said, 'You do not know what manner of spirit you are of. 56 For the Son of Man did not come to destroy the lives of men, but to save them'*

Luke 10
Jesus Sends Out the Disciples

¹Now after these things, the Lord also appointed seventy-two[a] others and sent them in two *by* two before His face, into every city and place where He Himself was about to go. ²And He was saying to them, "The harvest *is* indeed plentiful, but the workmen *are* few. Therefore pray earnestly to the Lord of the harvest, that He may send out workmen into His harvest.
³Go; behold, I send you forth as lambs in *the* midst of wolves. ⁴Carry no purse, nor bag, nor sandals; and greet no one on the road.
⁵And into whatever house you might enter, first say, 'Peace to this house.'
⁶And if a son of peace is there, your peace will rest upon it; but if not so, it will return to you. ⁷And remain in the same house, eating and drinking the things *supplied* by them; for the workman *is* worthy of his wages.[b] Do not move from house to house.
⁸And into whatever city you might enter and they receive you, eat the things set before you. ⁹And heal the sick in it, and say to them, 'The kingdom of God has drawn near to you.'
¹⁰And into whatever city you might enter and they do not receive you, having gone out into its streets, say, ¹¹'Even the dust from your city having clung to our feet, we wipe off against you; yet know this, that the kingdom of God has drawn near.'
¹²I say to you that it will be more tolerable in that day for Sodom than for that city.

Woe to the Unrepentant
(Matthew 11:20-24)

¹³Woe to you, Chorazin! Woe to you, Bethsaida! For if the miracles having taken place in you had taken place in Tyre and Sidon, they would have repented long ago, sitting in sackcloth and ashes.
¹⁴But it will be more tolerable for Tyre and Sidon in the judgment than for you.
¹⁵And you, Capernaum, will you be lifted up to heaven? No, you will be brought down to Hades.
¹⁶The *one* hearing you hears Me; and the *one* rejecting you rejects Me; and the *one* rejecting Me rejects the *One* having sent Me."

The Joyful Return

¹⁷And the seventy-two returned with joy, saying, "Lord, even the demons are subject to us through Your name."
¹⁸And He said to them, "I beheld Satan having fallen as lightning out of heaven.
¹⁹Behold, I give you the authority to tread upon serpents and scorpions, and upon all the power of the enemy, and nothing will injure you. ²⁰Yet do not rejoice in this, that the spirits are subjected to you; but rejoice that your names are written in the heavens."

Jesus' Prayer of Thanksgiving
(Matthew 11:25-30)

²¹In the same hour, He rejoiced in the Holy Spirit and said, "I fully consent to You, Father, Lord of the heaven and of the earth, that You have hidden these things from *the* wise and intelligent, and have revealed them to little children; yes, Father, for thus was it well-pleasing before You.
²²All things have been delivered to Me by My Father. And no one knows who the Son is, except the Father; and who the Father is, except the Son, and those to

whom the Son might resolve to reveal *Him*."

²³And having turned to the disciples, He said in private, "Blessed *are* the eyes seeing what you see! ²⁴For I say to you that many prophets and kings desired to see what you see, and did not see; and to hear what you hear, and did not hear."

The Parable of the Good Samaritan

²⁵And behold, a certain lawyer stood up, testing Him, saying, "Teacher, what having done, will I inherit eternal life?" ²⁶And He said to him, "What has been written in the Law? How do you read *it*?" ²⁷And answering, he said, "'You shall love *the* Lord your God with all your heart, and with all your soul, and with all your strength, and with all your mind'*c* and 'Your neighbor as yourself.'*d*" ²⁸And He said to him, "You have answered correctly. Do this and you will live."

²⁹But desiring to justify himself, he said to Jesus, "And who is my neighbor?" ³⁰Jesus having taken *it* up, then said, "A certain man was going down from Jerusalem to Jericho, and fell among robbers, who both having stripped him and having inflicted wounds, went away having left *him* half dead. ³¹Now by chance a certain priest was going down on that road, and having seen him, he passed by on the opposite side. ³²And likewise also a Levite having come to the spot, and having seen *him*, passed by on the opposite side. ³³But a certain Samaritan journeying came to him, and having seen *him* was moved with compassion, ³⁴and having approached *Him*, he bound up his wounds, pouring on oil and wine; and having put him on his own beast, he brought him to an inn and took care of him. ³⁵And on the next day, having taken out two denarii,*e* he gave *them* to the innkeeper and said, 'Take care of him, and whatever more you might expend, I will repay you on my returning.' ³⁶Which of these three seems to you to have been a neighbor of the *one* having fallen among the robbers?" ³⁷And he said, "The *one* having shown compassion toward him."

Then Jesus said to him, "You go and do likewise."

Martha and Mary

³⁸Now in their proceeding, He entered into a certain village; and a certain woman named Martha received Him into the home. ³⁹And she had a sister called Mary, who also, having sat down at the feet of the Lord, was listening to His word. ⁴⁰But Martha was distracted about much service; and having come up, she said, "Lord, is it not concerning to You that my sister has left me alone to serve? Therefore speak to her, that she might help me!" ⁴¹And the Lord answering said to her, "Martha, Martha, you are anxious and troubled about many things; ⁴²but one thing is necessary, only one; for Mary has chosen the good portion, which will not be taken away from her."

a 1 NE, BYZ, and TR *seventy*; also in verse 17
b 7 Leviticus 19:13; Deuteronomy 24:14,15
c 27 Deuteronomy 6:5
d 27 Leviticus 19:18
e 35 A denarius was customarily a day's wage for a laborer (see Matthew 20:2)

Luke 11
The Lord's Prayer
(Matthew 6:5-15)

¹And it came to pass in His being in a certain place praying, when He ceased, one of His disciples said to Him, "Lord, teach us to pray, as John also taught his disciples."

²And He said to them, "When you pray say:

'Father,*a* hallowed be Your name.
Your kingdom come.*b*
³Give us each day our daily bread.
⁴And forgive us our sins,
   for also we ourselves forgive
   everyone indebted to us;

and lead us not into temptation.'"ᶜ

Ask, Seek, Knock
(Matthew 7:7-12)

⁵And He said to them, "Who among you will have a friend, and will go to him at midnight and say to him, 'Friend, lend me three loaves, ⁶since a friend of mine is come to me off a journey, and I have nothing that I will set before him.'

⁷And he answering from within will say, 'Do not cause me trouble; the door already has been shut, and my children are with me in bed; I am not able, having risen up, to give to you.'

⁸I say to you, even though he will not give to him, having risen up because of being his friend; yet because of his persistence, having risen, he will give him as much as he needs.

⁹And I say to you: Ask and it will be given to you; seek and you will find; knock and it will be opened to you. ¹⁰For everyone asking receives; and the *one* seeking finds; and to the *one* knocking, it will be opened.

¹¹And which father among you, *if* the son*ᵈ* will ask for a fish, and instead of a fish, will give to him a serpent? ¹²Or also *if* he will ask for an egg, will he give to him a scorpion? ¹³Therefore if you, being evil, know to give good gifts to your children, how much more will the Father who *is* in heaven give *the* Holy Spirit to those asking Him!"

A House Divided
(Matthew 12:22-30; Mark 3:20-27)

¹⁴And He was casting out a demon, and it was mute; and it came to pass, the demon having gone out, the mute *man* spoke. And the crowds marveled. ¹⁵And some of them said, "By Beelzebul the prince of the demons He casts out the demons." ¹⁶And others, testing, were seeking from Him a sign from heaven.

¹⁷And He knowing their thoughts, said to them, "Every kingdom having been divided against itself is brought to desolation; and a house against a house falls. ¹⁸And if Satan also is divided against himself, how will his kingdom stand? For you say I cast out the demons by Beelzebul. ¹⁹And if I cast out the demons by Beelzebul, by whom do your sons cast *them* out? On account of this, they will be your judges. ²⁰But if I cast out the demons by *the* finger of God, then the kingdom of God has come upon you.

²¹When the strong *man* being armed might guard his house, his possessions are in peace. ²²But when *one* stronger than he, having come upon *him*, shall overcome him, he takes away his complete armor in which he had trusted, and he divides his plunder.

²³The *one* not being with Me is against Me; and the *one* not gathering with Me scatters.

An Unclean Spirit Returns
(Matthew 12:43-45)

²⁴When the unclean spirit is gone out from the man, it passes through waterless places, seeking rest and not finding *any*. Then it says, 'I will return to my house, from where I came out.' ²⁵And having come, it finds *it* swept and put in order. ²⁶Then it goes and takes seven other spirits more evil than itself, and having entered, they dwell there; and the last of that man becomes worse than the first."

True Blessedness

²⁷And it came to pass, in His saying these things, a certain woman from the crowd, having lifted up *her* voice, said to Him, "Blessed *is* the womb having borne You, and *the* breasts at which You nursed."

²⁸And He said, "No rather, blessed *are* those hearing the word of God and keeping it."

The Sign of Jonah
(Matthew 12:38-42)

²⁹And of the crowds being pressed around together, He began to say, "This generation is an evil generation; it seeks after a sign, and no sign will be given to it, except the sign of Jonah. ³⁰For as Jonah was a sign to the Ninevites, thus

also the Son of Man will be to this generation.

³¹The Queen of *the* South will rise up in the judgment with the men of this generation and will condemn them. For she came from the ends of the earth to hear the wisdom of Solomon, and behold, greater than Solomon *is* here. ³²*The* men of Nineveh will stand up in the judgment with this generation and will condemn it. For they repented at the preaching of Jonah, and behold, greater than Jonah *is* here.

The Lamp of the Body
(Matthew 6:22-24)

³³But no one having lit a lamp, sets it in secret, nor under the basket, but upon the lampstand, that those entering in may see the light.

³⁴Your eye is the lamp of your body. When your eye is clear, your whole body is also light; but when it is evil, your body *is* also dark. ³⁵Therefore take heed, lest the light that *is* in you be darkness. ³⁶If therefore your body *is* full of light, not having any part dark, it will be all light, as when the lamp shining might light you."

Woes to Religious Leaders
(Matthew 23:1-36)

³⁷And as He was speaking, a Pharisee asked Him that He would dine with him. And having entered, He reclined. ³⁸And the Pharisee, having seen, marveled that He did not wash first before the dinner.

³⁹And the Lord said to him, "Now you Pharisees, you cleanse the outside of the cup and of the dish, but your inside is full of plundering and wickedness. ⁴⁰Fools! *Did* not the *One* having made the outside make the inside also? ⁴¹But give *as* alms the things being within, and behold, all things are clean to you.

⁴²But woe to you Pharisees, for you pay tithes of mint and rue and every herb; and you pass by justice and the love of God. But it behooved *you* to do these things, and those not to neglect.

⁴³Woe to you Pharisees, for you love the first seat in the synagogues and the greetings in the marketplaces. ⁴⁴Woe to you, for you are like unmarked graves, and the men walking above have not known *it.*"

⁴⁵And one of the lawyers answering, says to Him, "Teacher, saying these things You insult us also."

⁴⁶And He said, "Woe to you lawyers also! For you burden men *with* burdens heavy to bear, and you yourselves do not touch the burdens with one of your fingers. ⁴⁷Woe to you, for you build the tombs of the prophets, yet your fathers killed them. ⁴⁸So you are witnesses and consent to the works of your fathers; for indeed they killed them, and you build *their tombs.* ⁴⁹Because of this also, the Wisdom of God said, 'I will send to them prophets and apostles, and *some* of them they will kill and persecute,' ⁵⁰so that the blood of all the prophets having been poured out from *the* foundation of *the* world might be charged against this generation, ⁵¹from the blood of Abel to the blood of Zechariah, the *one* having perished between the altar and the house. Yes, I say to you, it will be required of this generation.

⁵²Woe to you lawyers, for you have taken away the key of knowledge. You yourselves did not enter, and you hindered those who are entering."

⁵³Of Him having gone forth from there, the scribes and the Pharisees began urgently to press upon *Him* and to make Him speak about many things, ⁵⁴watching to catch Him in something out of his mouth.

a 2 BYZ and TR *Our Father who art in the heavens*
b 2 BYZ and TR include *Your will be done on as it is in heaven*
c 4 BYZ and TR include *but deliver us from evil*
d 11 BYZ and TR include *asks for bread, will give him a stone*

Luke 12
The Leaven of the Pharisees

¹In these *times,* the myriads of the crowd having been gathered together so as to trample upon one another, He began to say to His disciples first, "Take heed to

yourselves of the leaven of the Pharisees, which is hypocrisy. ²And nothing is concealed up which will not be revealed, nor hidden which will not be known. ³Instead, whatever you have said in the darkness will be heard in the light, and what you have spoken into the ear in the inner rooms will be proclaimed upon the housetops.

Fear God Alone
(Matthew 10:26-31)

⁴And I say to you, My friends, you should not fear because of those killing the body and after these things not being able to do anything more abundantly. ⁵But I will show you whom you should fear: Fear the *One who* has authority, after the killing, to cast into Gehenna. Yes, I say to you, fear Him.

⁶Are not five sparrows sold for two assarion?ᵃ And not one of them is forgotten before God. ⁷But even the hairs of your head all have been numbered. Fear not; you are more valuable than many sparrows.

Confessing Christ
(Matthew 10:32-33)

⁸And I say to you, everyone who will confess in Me before men, the Son of Man also will confess in him before the angels of God. ⁹And the *one* having denied Me before men will be denied before the angels of God. ¹⁰And everyone who will speak a word against the Son of Man, it will be forgiven him; but the *one* having blasphemed against the Holy Spirit will not be forgiven.

¹¹And when they bring you before the synagogues and the rulers and the authorities, do not be anxious how or what you shall reply in defense, or what you should say. ¹²For the Holy Spirit will teach you in the same hour what it behooves *you* to say."

The Parable of the Rich Fool

¹³And one from the crowd said to Him, "Teacher, say to my brother to divide the inheritance with me."

¹⁴And He said to him, "Man, who appointed Me a judge or partitioner over you?" ¹⁵And He said to them, "Beware, and keep yourselves from all covetousness; for not to anyone is his life in the abundance of that which he possesses."

¹⁶And He spoke a parable to them, saying, "The ground of a certain rich man brought forth abundantly. ¹⁷And he was reasoning within himself, saying, 'What shall I do, for I have nowhere I will store up my fruits?' ¹⁸And he said, 'I will do this: I will tear down my barns, and will build greater *ones*, and will store up there all my grain and goods. ¹⁹And I will say to my soul, "Soul, you have many good things laid up for many years; take your rest; eat, drink, be merry."'

²⁰And God said to him, 'Fool! This night, your soul is required of you; and what you did prepare—to whom will *it* be?'

²¹So *is* the *one* treasuring up for himself, and not being rich toward God."

Do Not Worry
(Matthew 6:25-34)

²²And He said to His disciples, "Because of this I say to you, do not be anxious for life, what you should eat, nor for your body, what you should put on. ²³For life is more than food, and the body than clothing. ²⁴Consider the ravens, that they do not sow, nor reap; to them there is not a storehouse, nor barn—and God feeds them. How much more valuable are you than the birds! ²⁵And which of you, being anxious, is able to add one hour to his lifespan?ᵇ ²⁶If, then, you cannot even do *the* least, why are you anxious about the rest?

²⁷Consider the lilies, how they grow: They do not labor, nor do they spin.ᶜ But I say to you, not even Solomon in all his glory was arrayed as one of these. ²⁸But if God thus clothes the grass in *the* field, being *here* today and tomorrow being thrown into the furnace, how much more you, O *you* of little faith!

²⁹And you, do not seek what you might eat, and what you might drink, and do not be in suspense; ³⁰for all the nations of the world seek after these things, and your Father knows that you have need of these. ³¹But seek you His^d kingdom, and these things will be added to you.

³²Do not fear, little flock, for your Father took delight to give you the kingdom.

³³Sell your possessions and give alms; make to yourselves purses not growing old, an unfailing treasure in the heavens, where thief does not draw near, nor does moth destroy. ³⁴For where your treasure is, there your heart will be also.

Be Ready for Service
(Genesis 6:1-7; Matthew 24:36-51; Mark 13:32-37)

³⁵Let your waist be girded about, and the lamps burning. ³⁶And you, like to men waiting for their master, whenever he shall return from the wedding feasts, that having come and having knocked, they might open to him immediately. ³⁷Blessed *are* those servants whom, having come, the master will find watching. Truly I say to you that he will gird himself and will make them recline, and having come up, will serve them. ³⁸And if he comes in the second, and if in the third watch, and finds *them* thus, blessed are those! ³⁹But know this, that if the master of the house had known in what hour the thief is coming,^{e} he would not have allowed his house to be broken into. ⁴⁰You also, be ready; for the Son of Man comes in the hour you do not expect."

⁴¹And Peter said, "Lord, do You speak this parable to us, or also to all?"

⁴²And the Lord said, "Who then is the faithful, wise manager, whom the master will set over the care of his *servants*, to give *them* the measure of food in season? ⁴³Blessed *is* that servant whom, having come, his master will find thus doing. ⁴⁴Of a truth I say to you that he will set him over all his possessions.

⁴⁵But if that servant should say in his heart, 'My master delays to come,' and should begin to beat the men-servants and the maid-servants, and to eat and to drink and to get drunk, ⁴⁶the master of that servant will come in a day in which he does not expect, and in an hour that he does not know, and he will cut him in two and will appoint him a place with the unbelievers.

⁴⁷Now that servant, the *one* having known the will of his master, and not having prepared nor having done according to his will, will be beaten with many *blows*. ⁴⁸But the *one* not having known, but having done *things* worthy of stripes, will be beaten with few. And everyone to whom much has been given, much will be required; and from him to whom much has been committed, more will they ask of him.

Not Peace, But Division
(Matthew 10:34-36)

⁴⁹I came to cast fire upon the earth, and how I wish it were kindled already! ⁵⁰But I have a baptism *with which* to be baptized, and how I am distressed until it should be accomplished!

⁵¹Do you think that I came to give peace on the earth? No, I say to you, but rather division. ⁵²For from now there will be five in one house divided, three against two, and two against three. ⁵³They will be divided father against son and son against father, mother against daughter and daughter against mother, mother-in-law against her daughter-in-law and daughter-in-law against mother-in-law."

Interpreting the Present Time
(Matthew 16:1-4; Mark 8:11-13)

⁵⁴And also He was saying to the crowds, "When you see a cloud rising up from *the* west, immediately you say, 'A shower is coming,' and so it happens. ⁵⁵And when a south wind is blowing, you say, 'There will be heat,' and it happens. ⁵⁶Hypocrites! You know *how* to discern the appearance of the earth and of the

sky, but how do you not know to discern this time?

Reconcile with an Adversary
(Matthew 5:21-26)

⁵⁷And why do you not even judge for yourselves what *is* right? ⁵⁸For as you are going with your adversary before a magistrate, give earnestness to be set free from him in the way, lest he should drag you away to the judge, and the judge will deliver you to the officer, and the officer will cast you into prison. ⁵⁹I say to you, you shall never come out from there until you shall have paid even the last lepton."ᶠ

a 6 An assarion was a Roman copper coin worth about 1/16 of a denarius
b 25 Or *a single cubit to his height*; a cubit was about 18 inches or 45 centimeters.
c 27 NE and Tischendorf *Consider the lilies: they do not spin or weave*
d 31 BYZ and TR *God's*
e 39 BYZ and TR include *he would have stayed awake and*
f 59 A Jewish bronze or copper coin worth about 1/128 of a denarius

Luke 13
A Call to Repentance
(Joel 1:13-20; Amos 5:4-15; Zephaniah 2:1-3)

¹Now at the same time some were present, telling Him about the Galileans whose blood Pilate had mingled with their sacrifices. ²And answering, He said to them, "Do you think that these Galileans were sinners beyond all the Galileans, because they have suffered such things? ³No, I say to you; but unless you repent, you will all perish likewise. ⁴Or those eighteen on whom the tower in Siloam fell and killed them: Do you think that these were debtors beyond all the men dwelling in Jerusalem? ⁵No, I say to you; but unless you repent, you will all perish likewise."

The Parable of the Barren Fig Tree
(Isaiah 5:1-7)

⁶And He was speaking this parable: "A certain *man* had a fig tree planted in his vineyard; and he came seeking fruit on it, and not did find *any*. ⁷And he said to the vinedresser, 'Behold, throughout these three years I come seeking fruit on this fig tree, and do not find *any*. Therefore cut it down! Why even should it use up the ground?' ⁸And answering, he says to him, 'Sir, let it alone this year also, until I shall dig around it, and put *in* manure, ⁹and if indeed it should bear fruit in the *time*, so be it. But if not, you will cut it down.'"

Jesus Heals a Woman on the Sabbath

¹⁰And He was teaching in one of the synagogues on the Sabbaths. ¹¹And behold, a woman having a spirit of infirmity eighteen years, and she was bent over and not able to lift herself up to the full. ¹²And having seen her, Jesus called *her* near and said to her, "Woman, you have been freed from your sickness." ¹³And He laid the hands upon her, and immediately she was made straight and began to glorify God.

¹⁴And answering, the ruler of the synagogue, indignant because Jesus had healed on the Sabbath, was saying to the crowd, "There are six days in which it behooves *one* to work. Therefore coming, be healed in these, and not on the day of the Sabbath."

¹⁵Therefore the Lord answered him and said, "Hypocrites! Does not each one of you untie his ox or donkey from the stall on the Sabbath, and having led *it* away, give *it* to drink? ¹⁶And this, being a daughter of Abraham whom Satan has bound, behold, eighteen years, ought *she* not to be loosed from this bond on the day of the Sabbath?"

¹⁷And of Him saying these things, all those opposed to Him were ashamed; and the whole crowd was rejoicing at all the glorious things that were being done by Him.

The Parable of the Mustard Seed
(Matthew 13:31-32; Mark 4:30-34)

¹⁸And He was saying, "To what is the kingdom of God like? And to what shall I liken it? ¹⁹It is like a grain of mustard, which a man having taken, cast into his

garden; and it grew and came into a tree, and the birds of the air encamped in its branches."

The Parable of the Leaven
(Judges 20:18-23; 2 Samuel 2:12-32; 2 Chronicles 13:4-19; Matthew 13:33)

20 And again He said, "To what shall I liken the kingdom of God? 21 It is like to leaven, which a woman, having taken, hid in three measures of meal, until it all was leavened."

The Narrow Door
(Matthew 7:13-14)

22 And He was going through by towns and villages, teaching and making progress toward Jerusalem. 23 And someone said to Him, "Lord, if those being saved *are* few?"

And He said to them, 24 "Strive to enter in through the narrow door; for many, I say to you, will seek to enter in, and will not be able. 25 From the time the master of the house shall have risen up and shall have shut the door, then you shall begin to stand outside and to knock at the door, saying, 'Lord, open to us.'

And he answering, will say to you, 'I do not know from where you are.'

26 Then will you begin to say, 'We ate and drank in your presence, and you taught in our streets.'

27 And he will say, 'I tell you, I do not know from where you are; depart from me, all *you* workers of unrighteousness.'

28 There will be weeping and gnashing of the teeth when you see Abraham and Isaac and Jacob and all the prophets in the kingdom of God, but you are being cast out. 29 And they will come from east and west, and from north and south, and will recline in the kingdom of God. 30 And behold, there are last who will be first, and there are first who will be last."

Lament over Jerusalem
(Matthew 23:37-39)

31 In the same hour certain Pharisees came near, saying to Him, "Go out and proceed from here, for Herod desires to kill You."

32 And He said to them, "Having gone, say to that fox, 'Behold, I cast out demons and I complete cures today and tomorrow, and the third *day* I am perfected.' 33 But it behooves Me to proceed today and tomorrow and the following *day*. For it is not possible *for* a prophet to perish outside of Jerusalem.

34 Jerusalem, Jerusalem, killing the prophets, and stoning those having been sent to her, how often I have wanted to gather your children, *the* way that a hen *gathers* her brood under the wings, and you were not willing. 35 Behold, your house is left to you. And I say to you, you shall not see Me until *the time* comes when you say, 'Blessed is the *One* coming in *the* name of *the* Lord.'[a]"

a 35 Psalm 118:26

Luke 14
Jesus Heals a Man with Dropsy

1 And it came to pass, on His going into a house of one of the rulers of the Pharisees on a Sabbath, to eat bread, that they were watching Him. 2 And behold, there was a certain man with dropsy before Him. 3 And Jesus answering, spoke to the lawyers and to *the* Pharisees, saying, "Is it lawful to heal on the Sabbath or not?"

4 But they were silent.

And having taken hold *of him*, He healed him and let *him* go. 5 And He said to them, "Which of you *whose* son[a] or ox will fall into a pit on the Sabbath day, also will not immediately pull him up?"

6 And they were not able to reply to these things.

The Parable of the Guests

7 And He was speaking a parable to those having been invited, remarking how they were choosing out the first places, saying to them, 8 "When you are invited by anyone to wedding feasts, do not recline in the first place, lest *one* more honorable than you might have been invited by him. 9 And the *one* having invited you and him, having come, will say to you, 'Give *your*

place to this one,' and then with shame you should begin to take the last place.
¹⁰But when you are invited, having gone, recline in the last place, so that when the *one* having invited you might come, he will say to you, 'Friend, come up higher.' Then glory will be to you before all those reclining *with* you. ¹¹For everyone exalting himself will be humbled, and the *one* humbling himself will be exalted."
¹²And also He was saying to the *one* having invited Him, "When you make a dinner or a supper, do not call your friends, nor your brothers, nor your relatives, nor rich neighbors, lest ever they also should invite you in return, and recompense be made to you. ¹³But when you make a feast, call the poor, the crippled, the lame, the blind, ¹⁴and you will be blessed, because they have nothing to repay you. For it will be recompensed to you in the resurrection of the righteous."

The Parable of the Banquet
(Matthew 22:1-14)

¹⁵And one of those reclining with *Him*, having heard these things, said to Him, "Blessed *is he* who will eat bread in the kingdom of God."
¹⁶But He said to him, "A certain man was preparing a great supper, and invited many. ¹⁷And at the hour of the supper, he sent his servant to say to those having been invited, 'Come, for now *it* is ready.' ¹⁸And all with one *voice* began to excuse themselves. The first said to him, 'I have bought a field, and I have need, going out, to see it. I beg of you, hold me excused.'
¹⁹And another said, 'I have bought five yoke of oxen, and I am going to prove them. I beg of you, hold me excused.'
²⁰And another said, 'I have married a wife, and because of this I am not able to come.'
²¹And the servant having come, reported these things to his master. Then the master of the house, having become angry, said to his servant, 'Go out quickly into the streets and lanes of the city, and bring in here the poor and crippled and blind and lame.'
²²And the servant said, 'Sir, as you did command, it has been done, and there is still room.'
²³And the master said to the servant, 'Go out into the highways and hedges and compel *them* to come in, so that my house may be filled. ²⁴For I say to all of you that not one of those men having been invited will taste my supper.'"

The Cost of Discipleship
(Matthew 8:18-22; Luke 9:57-62; John 6:60-65)

²⁵And great crowds were going with Him, and having turned, He said to them, ²⁶"If anyone comes to Me, and does not hate his father and mother and wife and children and brothers and sisters and yes, even his life, he is not able to be My disciple. ²⁷Whoever does not carry his cross and come after Me is not able to be My disciple.
²⁸For which of you, desiring to build a tower, does not first, having sat down, count the cost, whether he has *enough* for *its* completion? ²⁹Otherwise, he having laid its foundation and not being able to finish, all seeing *it* may begin to mock him, ³⁰saying, 'This man began to build and was not able to finish.'
³¹Or what king, proceeding to engage with another king in war, will not, having sat down, first take counsel whether he is able with ten thousand to meet the *one* coming against him with twenty thousand? ³²And if not, of him being still far off, having sent an embassy, he asks for peace.
³³So therefore every one of you who does not give up all that he himself possesses, is not able to be My disciple.

Good Salt

³⁴Therefore salt *is* good, but if even the salt becomes tasteless, with what will it be seasoned? ³⁵It is fit neither for soil nor for manure; they cast it out.

The *one* having ears to hear, let him hear."

a 5 TR *donkey*

Luke 15
The Parable of the Lost Sheep
(Matthew 18:10-14)

¹Now all the tax collectors and the sinners were drawing near to Him to hear Him. ²And both the Pharisees and the scribes were grumbling saying, "This *man* receives sinners and eats with them."
³And He spoke to them this parable, saying, ⁴"What man of you, having a hundred sheep, and having lost one of them, does not leave the ninety nine in the open field, and go after the *one* having been lost, until he finds it? ⁵And having found *it*, he lays *it* on his shoulders, rejoicing. ⁶And having come to the house, he calls together the friends and the neighbors, saying to them, 'Rejoice with me, for I have found my sheep, the *one* having been lost!' ⁷I say to you that in the same way there will be joy in heaven over one sinner repenting, rather than over ninety nine righteous ones who have no need of repentance.

The Parable of the Lost Coin

⁸Or what woman having ten drachmas,ᵃ if she should lose one drachma, does not light a lamp and sweep the house, and seek carefully until she finds it? ⁹And having found *it*, she calls together the friends and neighbors, saying, 'Rejoice with me, for I have found the drachma that I lost.' ¹⁰Thus I say to you, there is joy before the angels of God over one sinner repenting."

The Parable of the Prodigal Son
(Deuteronomy 21:18-21)

¹¹And He said, "A certain man had two sons. ¹²And the younger of them said to *the* father, 'Father, give to me the portion of the property falling *to me*.' And he divided the property between them.
¹³And not many days later, the younger son having gathered together all, went away into a distant country, and there he wasted his estate, living prodigally.
¹⁴But of him having spent all, there arose a severe famine throughout that country, and he began to be in need. ¹⁵And having gone, he joined himself to one of the citizens of that country, and he sent him into his fields to feed pigs. ¹⁶And he was longing to fill his belly from the pods that the pigs were eating, and no one was giving to him.
¹⁷But having come to himself, he was saying, 'How many of my father's hired servants have abundance of bread, but here I am perishing with hunger? ¹⁸Having risen up, I will go to my father, and I will say to him, "Father, I have sinned against heaven and before you; ¹⁹no longer am I worthy to be called your son. Make me like one of your servants."'
²⁰And having risen up, he went to his father. And he still being far distant, his father saw him, and was moved with compassion, and having run, fell upon his neck and kissed him.
²¹And the son said to him, 'Father, I have sinned against heaven and before you; no longer am I worthy to be called your son.'
²²And the father said to his servants, 'Quickly bring out the best robe and clothe him, and give *him* a ring for his hand and sandals for his feet; ²³and having brought the fattened calf, kill *it*, and having eaten, let us be merry. ²⁴For this son of mine was dead and is alive again; he was lost and is found.' And they began to be merry.
²⁵And his elder son was in *the* field, and while coming *up*, he drew near to the house; he heard music and dancing. ²⁶And having called near one of the servants, he began inquiring what these things might be.
²⁷And he said to him, 'Your brother is come, and your father has killed the fattened calf, because he has received him in good health.'

²⁸But he was angry, and was not willing to go in. And his father, having gone, was begging him. ²⁹And answering, he said to his father, 'Behold, so many years I serve you, and never did I disobey a commandment of yours; and never did you give to me a young goat, that I might make merry with my friends. ³⁰But when this son of yours came, the *one* having devoured your living with prostitutes, you have killed the fattened calf for him!' ³¹And he said to him, 'Son, you are always with me, and all that *is* mine is yours. ³²But it was fitting to make merry and to rejoice, because this brother of yours was dead and is alive again; and he was lost and is found.'"

a 8 Or *ten silver coins*. Each was worth about a day's wages.

Luke 16
The Parable of the Shrewd Manager

¹Now also He was saying to the disciples, "There was a certain rich man who had a manager, and was accused unto him as he is wasting his possessions. ²And having called him, he said to him, 'What *is* this I hear concerning you? Give the account of your stewardship, for you are not able to manage any longer.' ³And the manager said within himself, 'What shall I do, for my master is taking away the management from me? I am not able to dig; I am ashamed to beg. ⁴I know what I will do, so that when I shall have been removed from the management, they might receive me into their homes.' ⁵And having summoned each one of his master's debtors, he was saying to the first, 'How much do you owe to my master?' ⁶And he said, 'A hundred baths^a of oil.' And he said to him, 'Take your bill, and having sat down quickly, write fifty.' ⁷Then he said to another, 'And how much do you owe?' And he said, 'A hundred cors^b of wheat.' He says to him, 'Take your bill and write eighty.' ⁸And the master praised the unrighteous manager because he had acted shrewdly. For the sons of this age are more shrewd than the sons of the light in their own generation. ⁹And I say to you, make friends for yourselves by the mammon of unrighteousness, that when it fails, they might receive you into the eternal dwellings. ¹⁰The *one* faithful in very little is also faithful in much, and the *one* unrighteous in very little is also unrighteous in much. ¹¹If therefore you have not been faithful in unrighteous mammon, who will entrust to you the true? ¹²And unless you have been faithful in that which *is* of another, who will give to you that which *is* yours? ¹³No servant is able to serve two masters. For either he will hate the one and he will love the other, or he will be devoted to one and he will despise the other. You are not able to serve God and mammon."

The Law and the Prophets
(Matthew 11:7-19; Luke 1:5-25; Luke 7:24-35)

¹⁴Now the Pharisees, being lovers of money, were listening to all these things, and they were ridiculing Him. ¹⁵And He said to them, "You are those justifying themselves before men, but God knows your hearts; for that which *is* exalted among men *is* an abomination before God. ¹⁶The Law and the prophets *were* until John. From that time the kingdom of God is proclaimed, and everyone forces his way into it. ¹⁷But it is easier for heaven and earth to pass away than one stroke of a letter of the Law to fail. ¹⁸Everyone putting away his wife and marrying another commits adultery. And the *one* marrying her put away from a husband commits adultery.

The Rich Man and Lazarus
(John 5:39-47)

¹⁹And there was a certain rich man, and he was clothed in purple and fine linen,

making good cheer in splendor every day. ²⁰And a certain poor man named Lazarus, being full of sores, was laid at his gate ²¹and desiring to be fed from that falling from the table of the rich man; but even the dogs, coming, were licking his sores. ²²And it came to pass that the poor man died, and he was carried away by the angels into the bosom of Abraham. And the rich man also died and was buried. ²³And in Hades, having lifted up his eyes, being in torment, he sees Abraham from afar, and Lazarus in his bosom.
²⁴And having cried out, he said, 'Father Abraham, have mercy on me and send Lazarus, that he might dip the tip of his finger in water and cool my tongue; for I am suffering in this flame.'
²⁵And Abraham said, 'Child, remember that you did fully receive your good *things* in your lifetime, and Lazarus likewise the evil *things*. But now he is comforted here, and you are suffering. ²⁶And besides all these things, a great chasm has been fixed between us and you, so that those desiring to pass from here to you are not able, nor can they pass from there to us.'
²⁷And he said, 'Then I implore you, father, that you would send him to my father's house— ²⁸for I have five brothers—so that he might warn them, that they also might not come to this place of torment.'
²⁹But Abraham says, 'They have Moses and the prophets; let them hear them.'
³⁰And he said, 'No, father Abraham, but if one from *the* dead should go to them, they will repent.'
³¹But he said to him, 'If they do not hear Moses and the prophets, not even will they be persuaded if one should rise out from *the* dead.'"

a 6 About 875 gallons or 3,200 liters
b 7 Approximately 1,100 bushels or 40,000 liters

Luke 17
Temptations and Trespasses
(Matthew 18:7-9; Mark 9:42-50)

¹And He said to His disciples, "It is impossible for the stumbling blocks not to come, but woe *to him* by whom they come! ²It is better for him if a millstone is hung around his neck and he is thrown into the sea, than that he should cause one of these little *ones* to stumble.
³Take heed to yourselves: If your brother should sin, rebuke him; and if he should repent, forgive him. ⁴And if he should sin against you seven times in the day, and seven times should return to you, saying 'I repent,' you shall forgive him."

The Power of Faith
(Matthew 17:14-21; Mark 9:14-29)

⁵And the apostles said to the Lord, "Add to us faith!"
⁶And the Lord said, "If you have faith like a grain of mustard, you would have said to this mulberry tree, 'Be uprooted and be planted in the sea,' and it would have obeyed you.
⁷And which of you having a servant plowing or shepherding, the *one* having come in out of the field, will say to him 'Having come, immediately recline?' ⁸Instead, will he not say to him, 'Prepare what I may eat, and having girded yourself about, serve me while I eat and drink; and after these things you shall eat and drink'? ⁹Is he thankful to the servant because he did the things having been commanded? ¹⁰Thus you also, when you may have done all the *things* having been commanded you, say, 'We are unworthy servants; we have done that which we were bound to do.'"

The Ten Lepers
(2 Kings 5:1-14)

¹¹And it came to pass in going up to Jerusalem, that He was passing through *the* midst of Samaria and Galilee. ¹²And on His entering into a certain village, ten leprous[a] men met Him, who stood afar off. ¹³And they lifted up *their* voice, saying, "Jesus, Master, have compassion on us."
¹⁴And having seen *them*, He said to them, "Having gone, show yourselves to the priests." And it came to pass in their going, they were cleansed.

15 And one of them, having seen that he was healed, turned back, glorifying God with a loud voice, 16 and he fell on *his* face at His feet, giving thanks to Him. And he was a Samaritan.

17 And Jesus, having answered, said, "Were not the ten cleansed? But where are the nine? 18 Was there found none having returned to give glory to God, except this foreigner?" 19 And He said to him, "Having risen up go forth; your faith has cured you!"[b]

The Coming of the Kingdom

20 And having been asked by the Pharisees when the kingdom of God is coming, He answered them and said, "The kingdom of God does not come with careful observation, 21 nor will they say, 'Behold here,' or 'There.' For behold, the kingdom of God is in your midst."[c]

22 And He said to the disciples, "*The* days will come when you will desire to see one of the days of the Son of Man, and you will not see *it*. 23 And they will say to you, 'Behold there,' or 'Behold here.' Do not go forth nor follow. 24 For as the lightning shines, flashing from the *one end* of the sky to the *other end* of the sky, thus the Son of Man will be in His day. 25 But first it behooves Him to suffer many things, and to be rejected by this generation.

26 And as it came to pass in the days of Noah, thus also will it be in the days of the Son of Man: 27 They were eating, they were drinking, they were marrying, they were being given in marriage, until that day Noah entered into the ark, and the flood came and destroyed all.

28 Likewise, as it came to pass in the days of Lot, they were eating, they were drinking, they were buying, they were selling, they were planting, they were building; 29 and in that day Lot went out from Sodom, it rained fire and brimstone from heaven and destroyed all.

30 It will be according to these in that day the Son of Man is revealed. 31 In that day, the *one who* will be on the housetop, and his goods in the house, do not let him come down to take them away; and likewise the *one* in *the* field, do not let him return to the things behind. 32 Remember Lot's wife! 33 Whoever may seek to save his life will lose it; but whoever will lose *it* will preserve it. 34 I say to you, in that night there will be two upon one bed: The one will be taken, and the other will be left. 35 There will be two *women* grinding at the same *place*: The one will be taken, and the other will be left."[d]

37 And answering, they say to Him, "Where, Lord?"

And He said to them, "Where the body *is*, there also the vultures will be gathered together."

a 12 Leprosy was a term for several skin diseases. See Leviticus 13.
b 19 Or *has saved you*
c 21 Or *within you*, or *within your grasp*
d 35 See Matthew 24:40. TR includes *36 Two men will be in the field. One will be taken and the other left.*

Luke 18
The Persistent Widow

1 And He was speaking to them a parable about the *way* it behooves them always to pray and not to lose heart, 2 saying, "In a certain city, there was a certain judge, not fearing God, and not respecting man. 3 And there was a widow in that city, and she was coming to him, saying, 'Avenge me of my adversary.'

4 And for a time he would not, but afterward he said within himself, 'Even if I do not fear God, nor respect man, 5 yet because this widow causes me trouble, I will avenge her, so that in *the* end she does not exhaust me, coming *to me.*'"

6 And the Lord said, "Hear what the unrighteous judge says. 7 And shall not God execute the avenging of His elect, the *ones* crying out to Him day and night, and be deferring in regard to them? 8 I say to you that He will execute their avenging in quickness. Nevertheless, the Son of Man having come, will He find faith on the earth?"

The Pharisee and Tax Collector

⁹And He also spoke this parable to some trusting in themselves that they are righteous, and despising others: ¹⁰"Two men went up into the temple to pray; the one a Pharisee, and the other a tax collector. ¹¹The Pharisee having stood, was praying toward himself thus: 'God, I thank You that I am not like the rest of the men—swindlers, unrighteous, adulterers—or even like this tax collector. ¹²I fast twice in the week; I tithe all things, as many as I gain.'

¹³But the tax collector, standing afar off, was not even willing to lift up the eyes to heaven, but was striking his breast, saying, 'God, be merciful to me, the sinner!' ¹⁴I say to you, this one went down to his house justified, rather than that. For everyone exalting himself will be humbled; but the *one* humbling himself will be exalted."

Jesus Blesses the Children
(Matthew 19:13-15; Mark 10:13-16)

¹⁵And they were bringing the infants also to Him, that He might touch them; but the disciples having seen, were rebuking them. ¹⁶But Jesus, having called them to *Him*, said, "Permit the little children to come to Me, and do not forbid them; for of the such is the kingdom of God. ¹⁷Truly I say to you, whoever shall not receive the kingdom of God as a child, shall not at all enter into it."

The Rich Young Ruler
(Matthew 19:16-30; Mark 10:17-31)

¹⁸And a certain ruler asked Him, saying, "Good Teacher, having done what, will I inherit eternal life?" ¹⁹And Jesus said to him, "Why do you call Me good? No one *is* good, except God alone. ²⁰You know the commandments: 'You shall not commit adultery, you shall not murder, you shall not steal, you shall not bear false witness, you shall honor your father and mother.'ᵃ"

²¹And he said, "All these have I kept from my youth."

²²And having heard, Jesus said to him, "To you, yet one thing is lacking: Sell all, as much as you have, and distribute to *the* poor, and you will have treasure in the heavens; and come, follow Me."

²³And having heard these things, he became very sorrowful; for he was extremely rich. ²⁴And having seen him, Jesus became sorrowful, saying, "How difficultly those having riches shall enter into the kingdom of God. ²⁵For it is easier for a camel to go through an eye of a needle, than a rich man to enter into the kingdom of God."

²⁶And those having heard said, "Then who is able to be saved?"

²⁷But He said, "The things impossible with men are possible with God."

²⁸And Peter said, "Behold, we having left the own, followed You."

²⁹And He said to them, "Truly I say to you that there is no one who has left house or wife or brothers or parents or children for the sake of the kingdom of God, ³⁰who shall not receive manifold more in this time—and in the age that is coming, eternal life."

The Third Prediction of the Passion
(Matthew 20:17-19; Mark 10:32-34)

³¹And having taken aside the Twelve, He said to them, "Behold, we go up to Jerusalem, and all things having been written by the prophets about the Son of Man will be accomplished. ³²For He will be betrayed to the Gentiles and will be mocked and will be insulted and will be spit upon. ³³And having flogged *Him*, they will kill Him; and on the third day He will rise again."

³⁴And they understood none of these things, and this word was hidden from them, and they did not know the things being spoken.

Jesus Heals a Blind Beggar
(Matthew 20:29-34; Mark 10:46-52)

³⁵And it came to pass in His drawing near to Jericho, a certain blind *man* was sitting beside the road, begging. ³⁶And having

heard a crowd passing along, he was asking what this might be.
³⁷And they told him, "Jesus of Nazareth is passing by."
³⁸And he called out saying, "Jesus, Son of David, have mercy on me!"
³⁹And those going before were rebuking him, that he should be silent. But he kept crying out much more, "Son of David, have mercy on me."
⁴⁰And Jesus, having stopped, commanded him to be brought to Him. And of him having drawn near, He asked him, ⁴¹"What do you desire I shall do to you?"
And he said, "Lord, that I might receive sight."
⁴²And Jesus said to him, "Receive sight! Your faith has healed you." ⁴³And immediately he received sight and began following Him, glorifying God. And all the people having seen *it* gave praise to God.
a 20 Exodus 20:12-16; Deuteronomy 5:16-20

Luke 19
Jesus and Zacchaeus
(Numbers 5:5-10)

¹And having entered, He was passing through Jericho. ²And behold, a man by name called Zacchaeus, and he was a chief tax collector, and he *was* rich. ³And he was seeking to see Jesus, who He is. And he was not able because of the crowd, for he was small in stature. ⁴And having run to the front, he went up into a sycamore-fig tree, so that he might see Him; for He was about to pass that *way*.
⁵And as He came to the place, Jesus having looked up, said to him, "Zacchaeus, having hurried, come down, for it behooves Me to stay in your house today."
⁶And having hurried, he came down and received Him, rejoicing. ⁷And having seen *it*, all were grumbling, saying, "He has entered to stay with a sinful man."
⁸And Zacchaeus having stood, said to the Lord, "Behold, half of my possessions, Lord, I give to the poor; and if I have defrauded anything of anyone, I restore *it* fourfold."
⁹And Jesus said to him, "Today salvation has come to this house, because he also is a son of Abraham. ¹⁰For the Son of Man came to seek and to save that having been lost."

The Parable of the Ten Minas
(Matthew 25:14-30)

¹¹While they were hearing these things, having proceeded, He spoke a parable because of His being near Jerusalem and of their thinking that the kingdom of God is about to appear immediately. ¹²Therefore He said, "A certain man of noble birth proceeded to a distant country, to receive for himself a kingdom and to return. ¹³And having called ten of his servants, he gave to them ten minas[a] and said to them, 'Do business until that I come back.'
¹⁴But his citizens hated him and sent a delegation after him, saying, 'We are not willing *for* this *man* to reign over us.'
¹⁵And it came to pass, on his returning, having received the kingdom, that he directed these servants to whom he had given the money to be called to him, in order that he might know what each had gained by trading.
¹⁶And the first came up, saying, 'Lord, your mina has produced ten more minas.'
¹⁷And He said to him, 'Well done, good servant! Because you were faithful in very little, you are to be having authority over ten cities.'
¹⁸And the second came, saying, 'Lord, your mina has made five minas.'
¹⁹And he said to this one also, 'And you are to be over five cities.'
²⁰And another came, saying, 'Lord, behold your mina, which I kept lying away in a handkerchief. ²¹For I was afraid of you, because you are a harsh man. You take up what you did not lay down, and you reap what you did not sow.'
²²He says to him, 'Out of your mouth I will judge you, evil servant. You knew that I am a harsh man, taking up what I

did not lay down and reaping what I did not sow? ²³Why then did you not give my money to *the* bank, and I having come, might have collected it with interest?'
²⁴And to those standing by he said, 'Take from him the mina, and give *it* to the *one* having the ten minas.'
²⁵And they said to him, 'Master, he has ten minas!'
²⁶'I say to you that to everyone having will be given, but from the *one* not having, even that which he has will be taken away. ²⁷Furthermore, these enemies of mine, those not having been willing *for* me to reign over them, bring *them* here and slay them before me.'"

The Triumphal Entry
(Zechariah 9:9-13; Matthew 21:1-11; Mark 11:1-11; John 12:12-19)

²⁸And having said these things He went on ahead, going up to Jerusalem.
²⁹And it came to pass as He drew near to Bethphage and Bethany, toward the mount called Olivet, He sent two of the disciples, ³⁰saying, "Go into the village ahead, in which entering you will find a colt having been tied, on which no one of men has ever yet sat; and having untied it, bring *it*. ³¹And if anyone asks you, 'Why do you untie *it*?' thus will you say, 'Because the Lord has need of it.'"
³²And having departed, those having been sent found *it* as He had said to them. ³³And on their untying the colt, its masters said to them, "Why do you untie the colt?"
³⁴And they said, "The Lord has need of it."
³⁵And they led it to Jesus, and having cast their garments on the colt, they put Jesus on *it*.
³⁶And as He is going, they were spreading their garments on the road.
³⁷And as He is drawing near, already at the descent of the Mount of Olives, the whole multitude of the disciples rejoicing, began to praise God in a loud voice for all *the* mighty works which they had seen, ³⁸saying:

"Blessed is the King who comes in *the* name of *the* Lord!"ᵇ
"Peace in heaven and glory in *the* highest!"
³⁹And some of the Pharisees from the crowd said to Him, "Teacher, rebuke Your disciples."
⁴⁰And answering He said, "I say to you that if these will be silent, the stones will cry out."

Jesus Weeps over Jerusalem
(Isaiah 29:1-16)

⁴¹And as He drew near, having seen the city, He wept over it, ⁴²saying, "If you had known in this day, even you, the things for peace! But now they are hidden from your eyes. ⁴³For days will come upon you that your enemies will cast around you a barricade, and will surround you and will hem you in on every side. ⁴⁴And they will level you to the ground, and your children within you, and will not leave a stone upon a stone within you, because you did not know the season of your visitation."

Jesus Cleanses the Temple
(Matthew 21:12-17; Mark 11:15-19; John 2:12-25)

⁴⁵And having entered into the temple, He began to cast out those selling, ⁴⁶saying to them, "It has been written: 'And My house will be a house of prayer.'ᶜ But you have made it 'a den of robbers.'ᵈ"
⁴⁷And He was teaching every day in the temple. But the chief priests and the scribes and the foremost of the people were seeking to destroy Him. ⁴⁸And they did not find what they might do; for all the people are listening, hanging on His *words*.

a 13 A mina was worth about three months' wages for a laborer
b 38 Psalm 118:26
c 46 Isaiah 56:7
d 46 Jeremiah 7:11

Luke 20
Jesus' Authority Challenged
(Matthew 21:23-27; Mark 11:27-33)

¹And it came to pass on one of the days He was teaching the people in the temple

and proclaiming the gospel, the chief priests and the scribes came up with the elders, ²and spoke to Him, saying, "Tell us by what authority You do these things, or who is the *one* having given to You this authority?"

³And answering, He said to them, "I also will ask you one thing, and you tell Me: ⁴The baptism of John, was it from heaven, or from men?"

⁵And they reasoned among themselves, saying, "If we should say 'From heaven,' He will say, 'Why did you not believe him?' ⁶But if we should say, 'From men,' all the people will stone us, for they are having been persuaded John to be a prophet."

⁷And they answered, they did not know from where.

⁸And Jesus said to them, "Neither do I tell you by what authority I am doing these things."

The Parable of the Wicked Tenants
(Matthew 21:33-46; Mark 12:1-12)

⁹And He began to speak to the people this parable: "A certain man planted a vineyard, and rented it to farmers, and went abroad a long time. ¹⁰And *in the* season, he sent a servant to the farmers, that they will give to him from the fruit of the vineyard. But the farmers sent him away empty-handed, having beaten *him*. ¹¹And he proceeded to send another servant; but having beaten *him* and having dishonored him, they sent *him* away empty-handed.

¹²And he proceeded to send a third; and having wounded him also, they cast *him* out.

¹³Then the master of the vineyard said, 'What shall I do? I will send my beloved son; perhaps they will respect him.'

¹⁴And having seen him, the farmers began reasoning among themselves, saying, 'This is the heir; let us kill him, so that the inheritance might become ours.'

¹⁵And having cast him forth outside the vineyard, they killed *him*.

What therefore will the master of the vineyard do to them? ¹⁶He will come and will destroy these farmers, and will give the vineyard to others."

And having heard *it*, they said, "Never may it be!"

¹⁷But having looked at them, He said, "What then is this that has been written:
'*The* stone which those building rejected,
this has become into *the* head of *the* corner'ᵃ?

¹⁸Everyone falling on that stone will be broken, but on whomever it might fall, it will grind him into powder."

Paying Taxes to Caesar
(Matthew 22:15-22; Mark 12:13-17)

¹⁹And the scribes and the chief priests sought to lay hands on Him in that hour, and they feared the people. For they perceived that He was speaking this parable against them.

²⁰And having watched *Him*, they sent spies, feigning themselves to be righteous, that they might catch *Him* in His word, in order to deliver Him to the rule and to the authority of the governor.

²¹And they questioned Him, saying, "Teacher, we know that You speak and teach rightly, and do not receive *any* person, but teach the way of God on the basis of truth. ²²Is it lawful for us to give tribute to Caesar, or not?"

²³But having perceived their craftiness, He said to them, ²⁴"Show Me a denarius.ᵇ Whose image and inscription does it have?"

And they said, "Caesar's."

²⁵And He said to them, "Therefore give back to Caesar the things of Caesar, and to God the things of God."

²⁶And they were not able to catch Him in His word before the people. And having marveled at His answer, they became silent.

The Sadducees and the Resurrection
(Matthew 22:23-33; Mark 12:18-27)

²⁷And some of the Sadducees, the ones denying there is a resurrection, having approached, questioned Him, ²⁸saying, "Teacher, Moses wrote to us if anyone's brother should die having a wife, and he is childless, that his brother should take the wife and should raise up seed to his brother. ²⁹Therefore there were seven brothers. And the first, having taken a wife, died childless; ³⁰and the second^c ³¹and the third took her; and likewise also the seven did not leave children and died. ³²Finally the woman also died. ³³Therefore in the resurrection, the woman, whose wife does she become? For the seven had her as wife."

³⁴And Jesus said to them, "The sons of this age marry and are given in marriage. ³⁵But those having been considered worthy to obtain that which *is* to the age, and the resurrection which *is* from *the* dead, neither marry nor are given in marriage. ³⁶For neither are they able to die any more, for they are like *the* angels and are sons of God, being sons of the resurrection.

³⁷But that the dead are raised, even Moses showed at the bush, when he calls *the* Lord 'the God of Abraham, and God of Isaac, and God of Jacob.'^d ³⁸Now He is not God of *the* dead, but of *the* living; for all live to Him."

³⁹And some of the scribes answering, said, "Teacher, you have spoken well." ⁴⁰And no longer did they dare to ask Him anything.

Whose Son is the Christ?
(Matthew 22:41-46; Mark 12:35-37)

⁴¹And He said to them, "How do they declare the Christ to be Son of David? ⁴²For David himself says in *the* book of Psalms:

'*The* Lord said to my Lord,
"Sit at My right hand,
⁴³until I place Your enemies,
as a footstool of Your feet."'^e

⁴⁴David therefore calls Him Lord, and how is He his son?"

Beware of the Scribes
(Mark 12:38-40)

⁴⁵While all the people were listening, He said to His disciples, ⁴⁶"Beware of the scribes, desiring to walk in long robes, and loving greetings in the marketplaces and first seats in the synagogues and first places in the banquets, ⁴⁷who devour the houses of widows, and pray at great length as a pretext. These will receive more abundant condemnation."

a 17 Psalm 118:22
b 24 A denarius was customarily a day's wage for a laborer (see Matthew 20:2)
c 30 BYZ and TR include *married the widow, and he also died*
d 37 Exodus 3:6
e 42-43 Psalm 110:1

Luke 21
The Poor Widow's Offering
(Mark 12:41-44)

¹And having looked up, He saw the rich casting their gifts into the treasury, ²and He saw a certain poor widow casting in two lepta.^a

³And He said, "Truly I say to you that this poor widow has cast in more than all *of them*. ⁴For these all cast in gifts out of that which was abounding to them; but she, out of her poverty, did cast in all the livelihood that she had."

Temple Destruction Foretold
(Matthew 24:1-4; Mark 13:1-9)

⁵And as some were speaking about the temple, that it was adorned with goodly stones and consecrated gifts, He said, ⁶"*As to* these things which you are beholding, *the* days will come in which no stone will be left upon a stone, which will not be thrown down."

⁷And they asked Him, saying, "Teacher, when will these things be, and what *will be* the sign when these things are about to take place?"

⁸And He said, "Take heed, lest you be led astray; for many will come in My name, saying, 'I am *He*,' and 'The time is drawn near.' Do not go after them. ⁹And when

you should hear of wars and commotions, do not be terrified; for it behooves these things to take place first, but the end *is* not immediately."

Witnessing to All Nations
(Matthew 24:9-14; Mark 13:10-13)

¹⁰Then He was saying to them, "Nation will rise up against nation, and kingdom against kingdom. ¹¹There will be both great earthquakes, and famines and pestilences in different places. There will also be fearful sights and great signs from heaven.

¹²But before all these things, they will lay their hands upon you, and will persecute *you*, delivering *you* to the synagogues and prisons, bringing *you* before kings and governors on account of My name. ¹³It will result to you for a testimony. ¹⁴Settle therefore in your minds not to premeditate to make a defense. ¹⁵For I will give you a mouth and wisdom, which all those opposing you will not be able to resist nor to reply to.

¹⁶And you will be betrayed even by parents and brothers and relatives and friends, and they will put to death *some* from among you. ¹⁷And you will be hated by all because of My name. ¹⁸And no, not a hair of your head should perish. ¹⁹By your patient endurance, you will gain your souls.

The Destruction of Jerusalem
(Matthew 24:15-25; Mark 13:14-23)

²⁰And when you see Jerusalem being encircled by encampments, then know that her desolation has drawn near. ²¹Then those in Judea, let them flee to the mountains; and those in her midst, let them depart out; and those in the countries, let them not enter into her. ²²For these are *the* days of avenging, to fulfill all things having been written.

²³But woe to those having in womb, and to the *ones* nursing in those days. For there will be great distress upon the land and wrath to this people. ²⁴And they will fall by *the* edge of *the* sword, and will be led captive into all the nations; and Jerusalem will be trodden down by *the* Gentiles, until *the* times of *the* Gentiles are fulfilled.

The Return of the Son of Man
(Matthew 24:26-31; Mark 13:24-27)

²⁵And there will be signs in sun and moon and stars; and upon the earth distress of nations with perplexity, sea roaring and surge rolling, ²⁶men fainting from fear and expectation of that which is coming on the earth. For the powers of the heavens will be shaken. ²⁷And then will they see the Son of Man coming in a cloud, with power and great glory. ²⁸And of these things beginning to come to pass, look up and lift up your heads, because your redemption draws near."

The Lesson of the Fig Tree
(Matthew 24:32-35; Mark 13:28-31)

²⁹And He spoke to them a parable: "Behold the fig tree and all the trees. ³⁰When they sprout already, looking for yourselves, you know that already summer is near. ³¹So also you, when you see these things coming to pass, know that the kingdom of God is near. ³²Truly I say to you that this generation will not have passed away until all shall have taken place. ³³The heaven and the earth will pass away, but My words will never pass away.

Be Watchful for the Day

³⁴And take heed to yourselves, lest your hearts ever be burdened with dissipation and drunkenness and *the* cares of life— and that day would come upon you suddenly as a snare. ³⁵For it will come upon all those sitting upon the face of all the earth. ³⁶Watch also at every season, praying that you may have strength to escape all these things that are about to come to pass and to stand before the Son of Man."

³⁷And during the day He was teaching in the temple, and in the evening going out, He was lodging on the mount called Olivet. ³⁸And all the people would come to Him early in the morning in the temple, to hear Him.

a 2 A lepton was a Jewish copper coin worth about 1/128 of a denarius

Luke 22
The Plot to Kill Jesus
(Matthew 26:1-5; Mark 14:1-2; John 11:45-57)

¹And the Feast of Unleavened *Bread*, called Passover, was drawing near. ²And the chief priests and the scribes were seeking how the they might put Him to death; for they were afraid of the people. ³And Satan entered into Judas the *one* being called Iscariot, being of the number of the Twelve. ⁴And having gone away, he spoke with the chief priests and captains, how he might betray Him to them. ⁵And they rejoiced and agreed to give him money. ⁶And he promised, and began seeking opportunity to betray Him to them apart from *a* crowd.

Preparing the Passover
(Psalm 41:1-13; Matthew 26:17-25; Mark 14:12-21; John 13:18-30)

⁷And the day of Unleavened *Bread* came, on which it was necessary for the Passover lamb to be sacrificed. ⁸And He sent Peter and John, having said, "Having gone, prepare the Passover for us, that we might eat *it*."
⁹And they said to Him, "Where do You desire we should prepare *it*?"
¹⁰And He said to them, "Behold, of you having entered into the city, a man carrying a pitcher of water will meet you. Follow him into the house into which he enters, ¹¹and you shall say to the master of the house, 'The Teacher says to you, "Where is the guest room, where I may eat the Passover with My disciples?"' ¹²And he will show you a large furnished upper room. Prepare *it* there."
¹³And having gone, they found *it* as He had said to them, and they prepared the Passover.

The Last Supper
(Matthew 26:26-30; Mark 14:22-26; 1 Corinthians 11:17-34)

¹⁴And when the hour was come, He reclined, and the apostles with Him. ¹⁵And He said to them, "With desire I have desired to eat this Passover with you before I suffer. ¹⁶For I say to you that never again will I eat thereof, until it is fulfilled in the kingdom of God."
¹⁷And having received *the* cup, having given thanks, He said, "Take this and divide *it* among yourselves. ¹⁸For I say to you that I will not drink of the fruit of the vine from now until the kingdom of God shall come."
¹⁹And having taken *the* bread, having given thanks, He broke *it* and gave to them, saying, "This is My body, which is given for you; do this in remembrance of Me," ²⁰and the cup likewise, after having supped, saying, "This cup *is* the new covenant in My blood, which is being poured out for you.ᵃ
²¹But, behold, the hand of him betraying Me *is* with Me on the table. ²²For indeed the Son of Man goes according to that having been determined. But woe to that man by whom He is betrayed."
²³And they began to question among themselves who then of them it might be who is about to do this.

Who is the Greatest?

²⁴And there was also a dispute among them which of them is thought to be *the* greatest. ²⁵And He said to them, "The kings of the Gentiles rule over them, and those exercising authority over them are called benefactors. ²⁶But you *shall* not *be* thus. Instead, the greatest among you, let him be as the younger; and the *one* leading, as the *one* serving. ²⁷For who *is* greater, the *one* reclining or the *one* serving? *Is* not the *one* reclining? But I am in your midst as the *One* serving.
²⁸Now you are those having remained with Me in My trials. ²⁹And I appoint to you a kingdom, as My Father appointed to Me, ³⁰so that you may eat and may drink at My table in My kingdom, and may sit on thrones, judging the twelve tribes of Israel.

Jesus Predicts Peter's Denial
(Matthew 26:31-35; Mark 14:27-31; John 13:36-38)

³¹Simon, Simon, behold, Satan demanded to have all of you to sift like wheat. ³²But I begged for you, that your faith may not fail. And you, when you have turned back, strengthen your brothers."
³³And he said to Him, "Lord, I am ready to go with You both to prison and to death."
³⁴And He said, "I tell you Peter, *the rooster will not crow today until you will deny three times knowing Me.*"
³⁵And He said to them, "When I sent you without purse and bag and sandals, did you lack anything?"
And they said, "Nothing."
³⁶And He said to them, "But now, the *one* having a purse, let him take *it*, and likewise a bag; and the *one* having no sword, let him sell his cloak and buy *one*. ³⁷For I say to you that this which has been written, it behooves to be accomplished in Me: 'And He was reckoned with *the* lawless.'ᵇ For also the things concerning Me have an end."
³⁸And they said, "Lord, behold, here *are* two swords."
And He said to them, "It is enough."

Jesus Prays on the Mount of Olives
(Matthew 26:36-46; Mark 14:32-42)

³⁹And having gone forth, He went according to the custom to the Mount of Olives, and the disciples also followed Him. ⁴⁰And having come to the place, He said to them, "Pray not to enter into temptation."
⁴¹And He withdrew from them about a stone's throw, and having fallen on the knees, He was praying, ⁴²saying, "Father, if You are willing, take away this cup from Me. Yet not My will, but Yours be done."
⁴³And an angel from heaven appeared to Him, strengthening Him. ⁴⁴And having been in agony, He was praying more earnestly. And His sweat became like great drops of blood falling down upon the ground.ᶜ
⁴⁵And having risen up from the prayer, having come to the disciples, He found them sleeping from the grief. ⁴⁶And He said to them, "Why are you sleeping? Having risen up, pray that you might not enter into temptation."

The Betrayal of Jesus
(Matthew 26:47-56; Mark 14:43-52; John 18:1-14)

⁴⁷While He was still speaking, behold, a crowd, and he who is called Judas, one of the Twelve, was going before them, and drew near to Jesus to kiss Him. ⁴⁸And Jesus said to him, "Judas, are you betraying the Son of Man with a kiss?"
⁴⁹And those around Him, having seen what would be, said, "Lord, should we strike with *the* sword?" ⁵⁰And a certain one of them struck the servant of the high priest and cut off his right ear.
⁵¹And Jesus answering said, "Allow you thus far!" And having touched the ear, He healed him.
⁵²And Jesus said to those having come out against Him, *the* chief priests, and captains of the temple and elders, "Have you come out with swords and clubs as against a robber? ⁵³Every day of Me being with you in the temple, you did not stretch out the hands against Me; but this is your hour, and the power of the darkness."

Peter Denies Jesus
(Matthew 26:69-75; Mark 14:66-72; John 18:15-18)

⁵⁴And having seized Him, they led *Him* away, and led *Him* into the house of the high priest. And Peter was following afar off.
⁵⁵And they having kindled a fire in *the* midst of the courtyard, and having sat down together, Peter was sitting among them. ⁵⁶And a certain servant girl, having seen him sitting by the light, and having looked intently on him, said, "This one also was with Him."

⁵⁷But he denied *it*, saying, "Woman, I do not know Him."
⁵⁸And after a little, having seen him, another was saying, "You also are of them."
But Peter was saying, "Man, I am not."
⁵⁹And about one hour having elapsed, a certain other strongly affirmed *it*, saying, "Of a truth, this one also was with Him; for he is also a Galilean."
⁶⁰But Peter said, "Man, I do not know what you say." And immediately while he was speaking, the rooster crowed. ⁶¹And having turned, the Lord looked at Peter, and Peter remembered the word of the Lord, how He had said to him, "Before *the rooster crows today, you will deny Me three times.*" ⁶²And having gone forth outside, he wept bitterly.

The Soldiers Mock Jesus
(Isaiah 50:4-11; Matthew 27:27-31; Mark 15:16-20; John 19:1-15)

⁶³And the men who are holding Him began mocking Him, beating *Him*. ⁶⁴And having blindfolded Him,*ᵈ* they were questioning *Him*, saying, "Prophesy, who is the *one* having struck You?" ⁶⁵And they were saying many other things to Him, blaspheming.

Jesus Faces the Council
⁶⁶And when it became day, the elderhood of the people were gathered together, both chief priests and scribes, and they led Him into their council, saying, ⁶⁷"If You are the Christ, tell us."
And He said to them, "If I should tell you, you would not believe, ⁶⁸and if I should ask *you*, you would not answer. ⁶⁹But from now on the Son of Man will be sitting at *the* right hand of the power of God."
⁷⁰And they all said, "Are You then the Son of God?"
And He was saying to them, "You say that I am."
⁷¹And they said, "What need do we have of any more witness? For we ourselves have heard *it* from His mouth."

a 19-20 Some manuscripts end verse 19 after *This is My body* and do not include verse 20
b 37 Isaiah 53:12
c 43-44 Some manuscripts do not include verses 43 and 44
d 64 BYZ and TR include *they were striking him on the face*

Luke 23
Jesus Before Pilate
(Matthew 27:11-14; John 18:28-40)

¹And having risen up, all the multitude of them led Him to Pilate. ²And they began to accuse Him, saying, "We found this *man* misleading our nation, and forbidding tribute to be given to Caesar, and declaring Himself to be Christ, a king."
³And Pilate questioned Him, saying, "Are You the King of the Jews?"
And answering him, He was saying, "You say."
⁴And Pilate said to the chief priests and the crowds, "I find no guilt in this man."
⁵But they kept insisting, saying, "He stirs up the people, teaching throughout all of Judea, and He has begun from Galilee even to here."

Jesus Before Herod
⁶And Pilate having heard, asked whether the man is a Galilean, ⁷and having learned that He is from the jurisdiction of Herod, he sent Him up to Herod, he himself being also in Jerusalem in those days.
⁸And Herod, having seen Jesus, was exceedingly glad; for of a long time he is wishing to see Him, because of hearing concerning Him; and he was hoping to see some sign done by Him. ⁹And He kept questioning Him in many words, but He answered him nothing.
¹⁰And the chief priests and the scribes had been standing by, vehemently accusing Him. ¹¹And Herod, with his troops, having set Him at naught and also having mocked *Him*, having put on *Him* splendid apparel, sent Him back to Pilate. ¹²And both Herod and Pilate became friends with one another on that day; for previously it had been that they were at enmity between themselves.

The Crowd Chooses Barabbas
(Matthew 27:15-23; Mark 15:6-11)

¹³And Pilate, having called together the chief priests and the rulers and the people, ¹⁴said to them, "You brought to me this man as *one* misleading the people; and behold, having examined *Him* before you, I found nothing in this man guilty of that accusation you are bringing against Him. ¹⁵No, not even Herod *did*; for he sent Him back to us. And behold, nothing worthy of death is done by Him. ¹⁶Therefore having chastised Him, I will release *Him*."ᵃ

¹⁸But they cried out all together, saying, "Away with this *man*, and release to us Barabbas," ¹⁹who was *one* having been cast into the prison on account of a certain insurrection having been made in the city, and murder.

²⁰Therefore Pilate, wishing to release Jesus, called to them again. ²¹But they were crying out, saying, "Crucify! Crucify Him!"

²²And he said to them a third *time*, "What evil indeed did this *man* commit? I found no cause of death in Him. Therefore having chastised Him, I will release *Him*."

²³But they were urgent, asking with loud voices for Him to be crucified. And their voicesᵇ were prevailing. ²⁴And Pilate sentenced their demand to be done. ²⁵And he released the *one* having been cast into prison on account of insurrection and murder, whom they had asked for; and Jesus he delivered to their will.

The Crucifixion
(Psalms 22:1-31; 69:1-36; Matthew 27:32-44; Mark 15:21-32; John 19:16-27)

²⁶And as they led Him away, having laid hold on Simon, a certain *man* of Cyrene coming from the country, they put upon him the cross, to carry *it* behind Jesus.

²⁷And a great multitude of the people were following Him, and of women, who were mourning and lamenting for Him. ²⁸And having turned to them, Jesus said, "Daughters of Jerusalem, do not weep for Me, but weep for yourselves and for your children. ²⁹For behold, *the* days are coming in which they will say, 'Blessed *are* the barren, and the wombs that never did bear, and breasts that never nursed.' ³⁰Then

'they will begin to say to the mountains, "Fall upon us,"
and to the hills, "Cover us."'ᶜ

³¹For if they do these things in the green tree, what might take place in the dry?"

³²And two other criminals also were being led away to be put to death with Him.

³³And when they came to the place called The Skull, there they crucified Him, and the criminals, one on *the* right, and one on *the* left.

³⁴And Jesus was saying, "Father, forgive them, for they do not know what they do."ᵈ And they cast lots, dividing His garments.

³⁵And the people stood beholding. And the rulers also were deriding *Him*, saying, "He saved others; let Him save Himself, if this is the Christ of God, the Chosen *One*."

³⁶And the soldiers also mocked Him, coming near, offering Him sour wine, ³⁷and saying, "If You are the King of the Jews, save Yourself!"

³⁸And there was also this inscriptionᵉ over Him:

THE KING OF THE JEWS.

³⁹And one of the criminals having been hanged was railing at Him, saying, "Are You not the Christ? Save Yourself and us!"

⁴⁰And the other answering, was rebuking him, saying, "Do you not even fear God, that you are under the same judgment, ⁴¹and we indeed justly? For we are receiving things worthy of what we did, but *this* man did nothing wrong." ⁴²And he was saying, "Jesus, remember me when You come into Your kingdom!"

⁴³And He said to him, "Truly I say to you, today you will be with Me in Paradise."

The Death of Jesus
(Psalm 22:1-31; Matthew 27:45-56; Mark 15:33-41; John 19:28-30)

⁴⁴And now it was about *the* sixth hour, and darkness came over the whole land until *the* ninth hour. ⁴⁵The sun was darkened, and the veil of the temple was torn in *the* middle.
⁴⁶And having called out in a loud voice, Jesus said, "Father, into Your hands I commit My Spirit."*ᶠ* And having said this, He breathed His last.
⁴⁷And having seen that which had taken place, the centurion began glorifying God, saying, "Certainly this man was righteous." ⁴⁸And all the crowds having come together to this spectacle, having seen the things that had taken place, were returning *home*, beating the breasts. ⁴⁹And all from those who knew Him, and women, those having followed Him from Galilee, stood afar off, beholding these things.

The Burial of Jesus
(Isaiah 53:9-12; Matthew 27:57-61; Mark 15:42-47; John 19:38-42)

⁵⁰And behold, a man named Joseph, being also a Council member, a good and righteous man— ⁵¹he was not having consented to their counsel and deed— from Arimathea, a city of the Jews, who was waiting for the kingdom of God. ⁵²He having gone to Pilate, asked *for* the body of Jesus. ⁵³And having taken it down, he wrapped it in a linen cloth and placed it in a tomb cut in a rock, in which no one yet had been laid. ⁵⁴And it was *the* Day of Preparation, and Sabbath was just beginning.
⁵⁵And the women who were come with Him out of Galilee, having followed, saw the tomb and how His body was laid. ⁵⁶And having returned, they prepared spices and anointing oils. And they rested indeed on the Sabbath according to the commandment.

a 16 See Matthew 27:15 and Mark 15:6. BYZ and TR include *17 Now Pilate was obligated to release to the people one prisoner at the feast.*
b 23 BYZ and TR include *and that of the chief priests*
c 30 Hosea 10:8
d 34 Some manuscripts do not include *Then Jesus said ... what they are doing*
e 38 BYZ and TR include *written in Greek, Latin, and Hebrew*
f 46 Psalm 31:5

Luke 24
The Resurrection
(Psalm 16:1-11; Psalm 49:1-20; Matthew 28:1-10; Mark 16:1-8; John 20:1-9)

¹But the first *day* of the week, very early morning, they came to the tomb, bringing *the* spices that they had prepared, ²and they found the stone having been rolled away from the tomb. ³But having entered, they did not find the body of the Lord Jesus. ⁴And it came to pass that while they are perplexed about this, behold, two men in dazzling garments stood by them; ⁵and of them having become terrified and bowing the faces to the ground, they said to them, "Why do you seek the living among the dead? ⁶He is not here, but He is risen! Remember how He spoke to you, being yet in Galilee, ⁷saying, 'It behooves the Son of Man to be delivered into hands of sinful men, and to be crucified, and the third day to arise.'"
⁸And they remembered His words. ⁹And having returned from the tomb, they related all these things to the eleven and to all the rest. ¹⁰Now it was Mary Magdalene, and Joanna, and Mary the *mother* of James, and the other women with them, *who* were telling these things to the apostles. ¹¹And their words appeared before them like folly, and they did not believe them.
¹²But Peter having risen up, ran to the tomb, and having stooped down, he sees only the linen strips. And he went away, wondering in himself at that having come to pass.

The Road to Emmaus
(Mark 16:12-13)

¹³And behold, on the same day, two of them were going to a village whose name *is* Emmaus, sixty stadia*ᵃ* distant from Jerusalem. ¹⁴And they were talking with one another about all these things having

taken place. ¹⁵And it came to pass, in their talking and reasoning, that Jesus Himself, having drawn near, was walking along with them. ¹⁶But their eyes were held not to know Him.

¹⁷And He said to them, "What *are* these words that you exchange with one another, walking?"

And they stood still, looking sad. ¹⁸And *the* one named Cleopas, answering, said to Him, "Are You alone visiting Jerusalem and have not known the things having come to pass in it in these days?"

¹⁹And He said to them, "What things?"

And they said to Him, "The things concerning Jesus of Nazareth, a man who was a prophet, mighty in deed and word before God and all the people, ²⁰and that our chief priests and rulers delivered Him up to *the* judgment of death, and crucified Him. ²¹But we were hoping it is He who is about to redeem Israel. But indeed also with all these things, this brings *the* third day away from which these things came to pass.

²²But also, certain women out from us astonished us. Having been to the tomb early ²³and not having found His body, they came declaring to have also seen a vision of angels, who say He is alive. ²⁴And some of those with us went to the tomb and found *it* just as the women also said. But Him they did not see."

Jesus Opens the Scriptures

²⁵And He said to them, "O foolish and slow of heart to believe in all that the prophets have spoken. ²⁶Was it not necessary for the Christ to suffer these things and to enter into His glory?" ²⁷And having begun from Moses and from all the Prophets, He interpreted to them the things concerning Himself in all the Scriptures.

²⁸And they drew near to the village where they were going, and He appeared to be going farther. ²⁹And they constrained Him, saying, "Abide with us, for it is toward evening, and now the day has declined."

And He entered in to abide with them. ³⁰And it came to pass in His reclining with them, having taken the bread, He blessed *it*; and having broken *it*, He began giving *it* to them. ³¹And their eyes were opened, and they knew Him. And He being seen, vanished from them.

³²And they said to one another, "Was not our heart burning within us as He was speaking with us on the road, as He was opening the Scriptures to us?" ³³And having risen up *that* same hour, they returned to Jerusalem, and they found the eleven and those with them gathered together, ³⁴saying, "The Lord has risen indeed, and He has appeared to Simon." ³⁵And they began relating the things on the road, and how He was known to them in the breaking of the bread.

Jesus Appears to the Disciples
(John 20:19-23; 1 John 1:1-4)

³⁶And as they were telling these things, He Himself stood in their midst, and says to them, "Peace to you." ³⁷But having been terrified, and having been filled with fear, they were thinking *themselves* to see a spirit.

³⁸And He said to them, "Why are you troubled, and why do doubts come up in your hearts? ³⁹See My hands and My feet, that I am He. Touch Me and see, for a spirit does not have flesh and bones, as you see Me having." ⁴⁰And having said this, He showed to them the hands and the feet.

⁴¹And while they still were disbelieving for joy and were wondering, He said to them, "Have you anything here to eat?" ⁴²And they gave to Him part of a broiled fish.ᵇ ⁴³And having taken *it*, He ate *it* before them.

Jesus Unveils the Scriptures

⁴⁴And He said unto to them, "These *are* my words, which I spoke to you being still with you, that all things having been written concerning Me in the Law of Moses and the Prophets and *the* Psalms, it behooves to be fulfilled." ⁴⁵Then He

opened their mind to understand the Scriptures.

⁴⁶And He said to them, "Thus it has been written: The Christ was to suffer and to rise out from *the* dead *on* the third day, ⁴⁷and repentance and forgiveness of sins to be proclaimed in His name to all nations, having begun from Jerusalem. ⁴⁸You are witnesses of these things.

⁴⁹And behold, I am sending the promise of My Father upon you. But you, remain in the city until that you should be clothed with power from on high."

The Ascension
(Mark 16:19-20; Acts 1:6-11)

⁵⁰And He led them out as far as to Bethany, and having lifted up His hands, He blessed them. ⁵¹And it came to pass in His blessing them, He was separated from them and was carried up into heaven. ⁵²And they having worshiped Him, returned to Jerusalem with great joy, ⁵³and were continually in the temple, blessing God.

a 13 Or *sixty furlongs*; about 7 miles or 11 kilometers
b 42 BYZ and TR include *and some honeycomb*

John

John 1
The Beginning
(Genesis 1:1-2)

¹In *the* beginning was the Word, and the Word was with God, and the Word was God. ²He was in *the* beginning with God. ³All things came into being through Him, and without Him not even one *thing* came into being that has come into being. ⁴In Him was life, and the life was the light of men. ⁵And the Light shines in the darkness, and the darkness has not overcome[a] it.

The Witness of John
(Malachi 3:1-5)

⁶There came a man having been sent from God. His name *was* John. ⁷He came as a witness, that he might testify concerning the Light, that all might believe through him. ⁸He was not the Light, but *came* that he might witness concerning the Light.

⁹The true Light who enlightens every man was coming into the world. ¹⁰He was in the world, and the world came into being through Him, and the world did not know Him. ¹¹He came to the own, and the own did not receive Him. ¹²But as many as received Him, He gave to them authority to be children of God—to those believing in His name, ¹³who were born not of blood, nor of will of flesh, nor of will of man, but of God.

The Word became flesh
(Psalm 84:1-12)

¹⁴And the Word became flesh and dwelt among us. And we beheld His glory, a glory as of an only begotten from *the* Father, full of grace and truth.

¹⁵John witnesses concerning Him, and he cried out, saying, "This was He of whom I was saying, 'The *One* coming after me has precedence over me, because He was before me.'"

¹⁶For from His fullness, we have all received and grace upon grace. ¹⁷For the Law was given through Moses; grace and truth came through Jesus Christ. ¹⁸No one has ever yet seen God. *The* only begotten God,[b] the *One* being in the bosom of the Father, He has made *Him* known.

The Mission of John the Baptist
(Isaiah 40:1-5; Matthew 3:1-12; Mark 1:1-8; Luke 3:1-20)

¹⁹And this is the testimony of John when the Jews sent to him priests and Levites from Jerusalem, that they might ask him, "Who are you?" ²⁰And he confessed and did not deny, but confessed, "I am not the Christ."

²¹And they asked him, "What then? Are you Elijah?"

And he says, "I am not."

"Are you the prophet?"

And he answered, "No."

²²Therefore they said to him, "Who are you, that we might give an answer to

those having sent us? What do you say about yourself?"

²³He was saying, "I *am* a voice crying in the wilderness, 'Make straight the way of *the* Lord,'"ᶜ as Isaiah the prophet said.

²⁴And *those* having been sent were of the Pharisees, ²⁵and they asked him and said to him, "Why then do you baptize, if you are not the Christ, nor Elijah, nor the prophet?"

²⁶John answered them saying, "I baptize withᵈ water, but in *the* midst of you stands *One* whom you do not know, ²⁷the *One* coming after me, of whom am I not worthy that I should untie the strap of His sandal."

²⁸These things took place in Bethany, across the Jordan, where John was baptizing.

Jesus the Lamb of God
(Matthew 3:13-17; Mark 1:9-11; Luke 3:21-22)

²⁹On the next day, he sees Jesus coming to him and says, "Behold the Lamb of God, the *One* taking away the sin of the world. ³⁰This is He concerning whom I said, 'After me comes a man who has precedence over me, because He was before me.' ³¹And I did not know Him. But so that He might be revealed to Israel, because of this, I came baptizing with water."

³²And John bore witness saying, "I have beheld the Spirit descending as a dove out of heaven, and it remained upon Him. ³³And I did not know Him; but the *One* having sent me to baptize with water, He said to me, 'Upon whom you shall see the Spirit descending and abiding on Him, He is the *One* baptizing with *the* Holy Spirit.' ³⁴And I have seen and have borne witness that this is the Sonᵉ of God."

The First Disciples
(Matthew 4:18-22; Matthew 13:47-52; Mark 1:16-20; Luke 5:1-11)

³⁵On the next day John again was standing, and two of his disciples. ³⁶And having looked at Jesus walking, he says, "Behold the Lamb of God!" ³⁷And the two disciples heard him speaking, and followed Jesus.

³⁸Then Jesus having turned and having beheld them following, says to them, "What do you seek?" And they said to Him, "Rabbi" (which being translated is to say Teacher), "where are You staying?"

³⁹He says to them, "Come, and you will see." So they went and saw where He abides, and they stayed with Him that day. It was about *the* tenth hour.

⁴⁰Andrew, the brother of Simon Peter, was one of the two having heard from John and having followed Him. ⁴¹He first finds the own brother Simon and says to him, "We have found the Messiah" (which is translated Christ).

⁴²He led him to Jesus. Having looked at him, Jesus said, "You are Simon the son of Jonah. You will be called Cephas" (which means Peter).

Jesus Calls Philip and Nathanael

⁴³On the next day He desired to go forth into Galilee. And He finds Philip. And Jesus says to him, "Follow Me." ⁴⁴Now Philip was from Bethsaida, from the city of Andrew and Peter.

⁴⁵Philip Finds Nathanael and says to him, "We have found *Him* whom Moses wrote of in the Law, also the prophets, Jesus of Nazareth, *the* son of Joseph."

⁴⁶And Nathanael said to him, "Is any good thing able to be out of Nazareth?" Philip says to him, "Come and see."

⁴⁷Jesus saw Nathanael coming to Him, and He says concerning him, "Behold, truly an Israelite, in whom there is no deceit."

⁴⁸Nathanael says to Him, "From where do You know me?" Jesus answered and said to him, "Before Philip calling you, you being under the fig tree, I saw you."

⁴⁹Nathanael answered Him, "Rabbi, You are the Son of God; You are King of Israel."

⁵⁰Jesus answered and said to him, "Because I said to you that I saw you

under the fig tree, do you believe? You will see greater things than these." ⁵¹And He says to him, "Truly, truly, I say to all of you, you will see the heaven opened, and the angels of God ascending and descending on the Son of Man."ᶠ

a 5 Or *comprehended*
b 18 BYZ and TR *the only-begotten Son*
c 23 Isaiah 40:3
d 26 Or *in*; also in verses 31 and 33
e 34 SBL *the Chosen One*
f 51 See Genesis 28:12

John 2
The Wedding at Cana

¹And on the third day a wedding took place in Cana of Galilee, and the mother of Jesus was there, ²and also Jesus was invited, and His disciples, to the wedding. ³And of *the* wine having been deficient, the mother of Jesus says to Him, "They have no wine."
⁴And Jesus says to her, "What to Me and to you, woman? My hour is not yet come."
⁵His mother says to the servants, "Whatever He may say to you, do *it*."
⁶Now there were six stone water jars standing there, according to the purification of the Jews, having space for two or three metretae.ᵃ ⁷Jesus says to them, "Fill the jars with water."
And they filled them up to *the* brim.
⁸And He says to them, "Now draw *some* out and carry *it* to the master of the feast."
And they carried *it*. ⁹And when the master of the feast had tasted the water having become wine, and did not know from where it is—but the servants having drawn the water knew—the master of the feast calls the bridegroom, ¹⁰and he says to him, "Every man first sets out the good wine, and when they might have drunk freely, the inferior; you have kept the good wine until now."
¹¹This *was the* beginning of the signs Jesus did in Cana of Galilee, and He revealed His glory. And His disciples believed in Him.

Jesus Cleanses the Temple
(Matthew 21:12-17; Mark 11:15-19; Luke 19:45-48)

¹²After this, He went down to Capernaum, He and His mother, and His brothers, and His disciples, and they stayed there not many days.
¹³And the Passover of the Jews was near, and Jesus went up to Jerusalem. ¹⁴And He found in the temple those selling oxen and sheep and doves, and the money changers sitting. ¹⁵And having made a whip of cords, He drove out all from the temple, both sheep and oxen; and He poured out the coins of the money changers and overthrew the tables. ¹⁶And to those selling doves He said, "Take these things from here! Do not make My Father's house a house of trade."
¹⁷His disciples remembered that it is written: "The zeal of Your house will consume Me."ᵇ
¹⁸So the Jews answered and said to Him, "What sign do You show to us that You do these things?"
¹⁹Jesus answered and said to them, "Destroy this temple, and in three days I will raise it up."
²⁰Therefore the Jews said, "This temple was built *in* forty and six years, and You will raise it up in three days?"
²¹But He was speaking concerning the temple of His body. ²²Therefore when He was raised up out from *the* dead, His disciples remembered that He had said this, and they believed the Scripture and the word that Jesus had spoken.
²³And when He was in Jerusalem in the Passover, in the Feast, many believed in His name, beholding His signs that He was doing. ²⁴But Jesus on His part did not did entrust Himself to them, because of His knowing all *men*, ²⁵and because He had no need that anyone should testify concerning man, for He Himself knew what was in man.

a 6 Or *twenty to thirty gallons*, or *75 to 115 liters*
b 17 Psalm 69:9

John 3
Jesus and Nicodemus

¹And there was a man of the Pharisees, named Nicodemus, a ruler of the Jews. ²He came to Him by night and said to Him, "Rabbi, we know that You have come from God *as* a teacher, for no one is able to do these signs that You do, unless God should be with him."
³Jesus answered and said to him, "Truly, truly, I say to you, except anyone be born from above,*ᵃ* he is not able to see the kingdom of God."
⁴Nicodemus says to Him, "How is a man able to be born, being old? Is he able to enter into the womb of his mother a second time, and to be born?"
⁵Jesus answered, "Truly, truly, I say to you, unless anyone be born of water and of *the* Spirit, he is not able to enter into the kingdom of God. ⁶That having been born of the flesh is flesh, and that having been born of the Spirit is spirit. ⁷Do not wonder that I said to you, 'It is necessary for you *all* to be born from above.' ⁸The wind blows where it wishes, and you hear the sound of it, but you do not know from where it comes and where it goes. Thus is everyone having been born of the Spirit."
⁹Nicodemus answered and said to Him, "How are these things able to be?"
¹⁰Jesus answered and said to him, "You are the teacher of Israel, and do you not know these things? ¹¹Truly, truly, I say to you that we speak that which we know, and we bear witness to that which we have seen, and you people do not receive our witness.
¹²If I have told you earthly things and you do not believe, how will you believe if I tell you heavenly things? ¹³And no one has gone up into heaven except the *One* having come down out of heaven, the Son of Man.*ᵇ* ¹⁴And as Moses lifted up the serpent in the wilderness, thus it behooves the Son of Man to be lifted up, ¹⁵so that everyone believing in Him may have eternal life.

For God So Loved
(Genesis 22:1-10; Romans 5:6-11)

¹⁶For God so loved the world that He gave the only begotten Son, so that everyone believing in Him should not perish, but should have eternal life. ¹⁷For God did not send His Son into the world that He might judge the world, but that the world might be saved through Him. ¹⁸The *one* believing in Him is not judged, but the *one* not believing already has been judged, because he has not believed in the name of the only begotten Son of God.
¹⁹And this is the judgement, that the Light has come into the world, and men loved the darkness rather than the Light; for their deeds were evil. ²⁰For everyone practicing evil hates the Light and does not come to the Light, so that his works may not be exposed; ²¹but the *one* practicing the truth comes to the Light, that his works may be manifest as having been done in God."*ᶜ*

John's Testimony about Jesus

²²After these things, Jesus and His disciples came into the land of Judea, and there He was staying with them, and was baptizing.
²³Now John was also baptizing in Aenon, near Salim, because *the* waters were many there, and they were coming and being baptized. ²⁴For John had not yet been cast into the prison.
²⁵Then a debate arose among the disciples of John with *a certain* Jew about purification. ²⁶And they came to John and said to him, "Rabbi, He who was with you beyond the Jordan, to whom you have borne witness, behold He baptizes, and all are coming to Him."
²⁷John answered and said, "A man is able to receive not one thing if it is not given to him from heaven. ²⁸You yourselves bear witness to me that I said, 'I am not the Christ, but I am sent before Him.' ²⁹The *one* having the bride is *the* bridegroom; and the friend of the bridegroom, the *one* standing and

listening for him, rejoices with joy because of the bridegroom's voice. Therefore, this joy of mine is fulfilled. ³⁰It behooves Him to increase, but me to decrease.

³¹The *One* coming from above is above all. The *one* being from the earth is from the earth, and speaks from the earth. The *One* coming from heaven is above all. ³²What He has seen and heard, this He testifies, but no one receives His testimony. ³³The *one* having received His testimony has set his seal that God is true. ³⁴For He whom God sent speaks the words of God, for He gives the Spirit without measure.

³⁵The Father loves the Son and has given all things into His hand. ³⁶The *one* believing in the Son has eternal life, but the *one* not obeying the Son will not see life, but the wrath of God abides on him."ᵈ

a 3 Or *born again*; also in verse 7.
b 13 BYZ and TR include *who is in heaven*
c 21 Some interpreters close the quotation after verse 15.
d 36 Some interpreters close the quotation after verse 30.

John 4
Jesus and the Samaritan Woman

¹Therefore when Jesus knew that Pharisees heard that Jesus makes and baptizes more disciples than John ²(although indeed Jesus Himself was not baptizing, but His disciples), ³He left Judea and went away again into Galilee. ⁴And it was necessary for Him to pass through Samaria. ⁵Therefore He comes to a city of Samaria called Sychar, near the plot of ground that Jacob had given to his son Joseph. ⁶And Jacob's well was there. Therefore Jesus, being wearied from the journey, thus was sitting at the well. *The* hour was about *the* sixth.

⁷A woman out of Samaria comes to draw water. Jesus says to her, "Give Me to drink." ⁸For His disciples had gone away into the city, that they might buy food.

⁹Therefore the Samaritan woman says to Him, "How do You, being a Jew, ask drink from me, being a Samaritan woman?" For Jews have no association with Samaritans.

¹⁰Jesus answered and said to her, "If you had known the gift of God and who it is saying to you, 'Give Me to drink,' you would have asked Him, and He would have given to you living water."

¹¹The woman says to Him, "Sir, You have nothing to draw with, and the well is deep; from where then do You have the living water? ¹²Are You greater than our father Jacob, who gave us the well and drank of it himself, and his sons, and his livestock?"

¹³Jesus answered and said to her, "Everyone drinking of this water will thirst again; ¹⁴but whoever may drink of the water that I will give him will never thirst, to the age. Instead, the water that I will give to him will become in him a spring of water, welling up into eternal life."

¹⁵The woman says to Him, "Sir, give me this water, that I might not thirst, nor come here to draw *water*."

¹⁶He says to her, "Go, call your husband, and come here."

¹⁷The woman answered and said to Him, "I do not have a husband."

Jesus says to her, "You have spoken correctly, 'I do not have a husband.' ¹⁸For you have had five husbands, and he whom you have now is not your husband; this you have spoken truly."

¹⁹The woman says to Him, "Sir, I understand that You are a prophet. ²⁰Our fathers worshiped on this mountain, and you say that in Jerusalem is the place where it is necessary to worship."

²¹Jesus says to her, "Believe Me, woman, that an hour is coming when neither on this mountain nor in Jerusalem will you worship the Father. ²²You worship what you do not know; we worship what we know, for salvation is of the Jews. ²³But an hour is coming and now is, when the true worshipers will worship the Father in spirit and truth; for the Father also seeks such who worship Him. ²⁴God *is* Spirit,

and it behooves those worshiping Him to worship in spirit and truth."

²⁵The woman says to Him, "I know that Messiah is coming, who is called Christ; when He comes, He will tell us all things." ²⁶Jesus says to her, "I who am speaking to you am *He*."

The Disciples Return and Marvel

²⁷And upon this, His disciples came and were amazed that He was speaking with a woman. But no one said, "What do You seek?" Or "Why do You speak with her?" ²⁸Then the woman left her water pot and went away into the city, and says to the men, ²⁹"Come, see a man who told me all things I ever did. Can it be *that* this is the Christ?" ³⁰They went forth out of the city and were coming unto Him.

³¹But in the meantime the disciples were asking Him, saying, "Rabbi, eat." ³²But He said to them, "I have food to eat that you do not know."

³³Therefore the disciples were saying to one another, "No one brought Him *anything* to eat?"

³⁴Jesus says to them, "My food is that I should do the will of the *One* having sent Me, and should finish His work. ³⁵Do you not say that it is yet four months and the harvest comes? Behold, I say to you, lift up your eyes and see the fields, because they are already white toward harvest! ³⁶The *one* reaping receives a reward and gathers fruit unto eternal life, so that the *one* sowing and the *one* reaping may rejoice together. ³⁷For in this, the saying is true, that is, 'One is sowing, and another is reaping.' ³⁸I sent you to reap what you have not toiled for; others have toiled, and you have entered into their labor."

Many Samaritans Believe

³⁹And out of that city, many of the Samaritans believed in Him, because of the word of the woman testifying, "He told me all things I ever did." ⁴⁰Therefore when the Samaritans came to Him, they were asking Him to abide with them, and He stayed there two days.

⁴¹And many more believed because of His word. ⁴²And they were saying to the woman, "No longer because of your speech do we believe; for we ourselves have heard, and we know that this is truly the Savior of the world."

Jesus Heals the Official's Son
(Matthew 8:5-13; Luke 7:1-10)

⁴³And after the two days, He went forth from there into Galilee. ⁴⁴For Jesus Himself testified that a prophet has no honor in the own hometown. ⁴⁵Therefore when He came into Galilee, the Galileans received Him, having seen the greatness of all the things He had done in Jerusalem during the feast, for they themselves also had gone to the feast.

⁴⁶Therefore He came again to Cana of Galilee, where He had made the water wine. And there was in Capernaum a certain royal official whose son was sick. ⁴⁷Having heard that Jesus had come out of Judea into Galilee, he went to Him and was asking that He would come down and heal his son; for he was about to die. ⁴⁸Therefore Jesus said to him, "Unless you people see signs and wonders, you will never believe."

⁴⁹The royal official says to Him, "Sir, come down before my child dies."

⁵⁰Jesus says to him, "Go, your son lives." The man believed the word that Jesus said to him, and he went on his way. ⁵¹And already *as* he is going down, his servants met him, saying that his son lives. ⁵²Therefore he inquired from them the hour in which he got better. Therefore they said to him, "Yesterday *at the* seventh hour the fever left him." ⁵³Therefore the father knew that *it was* in that hour at which Jesus said to him, "Your son lives." And he himself believed, and his whole household.

⁵⁴This *is* now again *the* second sign that Jesus did, having come out of Judea into Galilee.

John 5
The Pool of Bethesda

¹After these things there was a feast of the Jews, and Jesus went up to Jerusalem.
²Now there is in Jerusalem by the Sheep Gate a pool, in Hebrew called Bethesda, having five porches. ³In these were lying a multitude of those ailing, blind, lame, paralyzed.[a]
⁵And a certain man was there, himself being thirty and eight years in infirmity. ⁶Jesus, having seen him lying and having known that he has been a long time already, says to him, "Do you desire to become well?"
⁷The *one* ailing answered Him, "Sir, I do not have a man, that when the water has been stirred, he might put me into the pool; and while I am going, another descends before me."
⁸Jesus says to him, "Arise, take up your mat, and walk."
⁹And immediately the man became well, and he took up his mat and began to walk.
And it was *the* Sabbath on that day. ¹⁰Therefore the Jews were saying to the *one* having been healed, "It is *the* Sabbath, and it is not lawful for you to take up your mat."
¹¹But he answered them, "The *One* having made me well, that One said to me 'Take up your mat and walk.'"
¹²Therefore they asked him, "Who is the man having said to you, 'Take *it* up and walk'?"
¹³And the *one* having been healed did not know who it is, for Jesus had moved away, a crowd being in the place.
¹⁴After these things Jesus finds him in the temple and said to him, "Behold, you have become well. Sin no more, that something worse should not happen to you." ¹⁵The man went away and told the Jews that Jesus is the *One* having made him well.

The Father and the Son

¹⁶And because of this, the Jews were persecuting Jesus, because He was doing these things on *the* Sabbath. ¹⁷But Jesus answered them, "My Father is working until now, and I am working."
¹⁸Therefore because of this, the Jews were seeking the more to kill Him, because not only was He breaking the Sabbath, but also He was calling God His own Father, making Himself equal to God.
¹⁹Therefore Jesus answered and was saying to them, "Truly, truly, I say to you, the Son is able to do nothing of Himself, if not anything He may see the Father doing; for whatever He does, these things also the Son does likewise. ²⁰For the Father loves the Son and shows to Him all things that He does. And He will show Him greater works than these, so that you may marvel.
²¹For even as the Father raises up the dead and gives life, thus also the Son gives life to whom He will. ²²For the Father judges no one, but has given all judgment to the Son, ²³so that all may honor the Son, even as they honor the Father. He who is not honoring the Son is not honoring the Father, the *One* having sent Him.
²⁴Truly, truly, I say to you that the *one* hearing My word and believing the *One* having sent Me, he has eternal life and does not come into judgment, but has passed out of death into life.
²⁵Truly, truly, I say to you that an hour is coming, and now is, when the dead will hear the voice of the Son of God, and those having heard will live. ²⁶For as the Father has life in Himself, so also He gave to the Son to have life in Himself. ²⁷And He gave Him authority to execute judgment, because He is *the* Son of Man. ²⁸Do not marvel at this, for an hour is coming in which all those in the tombs will hear His voice, ²⁹and will come forth— those having done good to *the* resurrection of life, and those having done evil to *the* resurrection of judgment.

³⁰I am able to do nothing of Myself. As I hear, I judge; and My judgment is just, because I do not seek My will, but the will of the *One* having sent Me.

Testimonies about Jesus

³¹If I bear witness concerning Myself, My testimony is not true. ³²It is another bearing witness concerning Me, and I know that the testimony which he bears witness concerning Me is true.

³³You have sent unto John, and he has borne witness to the truth. ³⁴And I do not receive testimony from man, but I say these things that you may be saved.

³⁵He was the lamp burning and shining, and you were willing to rejoice for a season in his light. ³⁶But I have testimony greater than that of John. For the works that the Father has given Me that I should complete them, the same works which I do, bear witness concerning Me that the Father has sent Me. ³⁷And the *One* having sent Me, *the* Father Himself, has borne witness concerning Me. You have neither heard His voice at any time, nor have you seen His form. ³⁸And you do not have His word abiding in you, for you do not believe Him whom He sent.

The Witness of Scripture
(Luke 16:19-31)

³⁹You diligently search the Scriptures because you think to have eternal life in them, and these are they bearing witness concerning Me; ⁴⁰and you are not willing to come to Me, that you may have life.

⁴¹I do not take glory from men, ⁴²but I have known you, that you do not have the love of God in yourselves. ⁴³I have come in My Father's name, and you do not receive Me; if another should come in the own name, you will receive him. ⁴⁴How are you able to believe, receiving glory from one another, and you do not seek the glory that *is* from the only God? ⁴⁵Do not think that I will accuse you to the Father. There is *one* accusing you: Moses, in whom you have hoped. ⁴⁶For if you were believing Moses, you would have believed Me; for he wrote concerning Me. ⁴⁷And unless you believe his writings, how will you believe My words?"

a 3 NE, BYZ, and TR include *awaiting the moving of the waters. 4 For from time to time an angel descended into the pool and stirred the water. As soon as it was stirred, the first to enter the pool would be healed of his disease.*

John 6
The Feeding of the Five Thousand
(Matthew 14:13-21; Mark 6:30-44; Luke 9:10-17)

¹After these things Jesus went away, over the Sea of Galilee (of Tiberias), ²and a great crowd was following Him because they were seeing the signs which He was doing upon those being sick. ³Now Jesus went up on the mountain and was sitting there with His disciples.

⁴Now the Passover, the feast of the Jews, was near. ⁵Then Jesus, having lifted up the eyes and having seen that a great crowd is coming to Him, says to Philip, "From where shall we buy bread that these might eat?" ⁶Now He was saying this testing him, for He knew what He was about to do.

⁷Philip answered Him, "Two hundred denarii worth[a] of loaves are not sufficient for them, that each might receive one little *piece*."

⁸One of His disciples, Andrew, the brother of Simon Peter, says to Him, ⁹"Here is a little boy who has five barley loaves and two small fish, but what are these for so many?"

¹⁰Jesus said, "Make the men to recline." Now there was much grass in the place; therefore the men reclined, about five thousand *in* number.

¹¹And Jesus took the loaves, and having given thanks, He distributed to those reclining; likewise also of the fish, as much as they wished.

¹²Now when they were filled, He says to His disciples, "Gather together the fragments having been over and above, so that not anything may be lost." ¹³So they gathered *them* together and filled twelve hand-baskets of fragments from

the five barley loaves, which were over and above to those having eaten.

¹⁴Therefore the people, having seen what sign He had done, were saying, "This is truly the prophet who is coming into the world." ¹⁵Therefore Jesus, having known that they are about to come and to seize Him that they might make *Him* king, withdrew again to the mountain Himself alone.

Jesus Walks on Water
(Matthew 14:22-33; Mark 6:45-52)

¹⁶Now when it became evening, His disciples went down to the sea, ¹⁷and having entered into a boat, they were going over the sea to Capernaum. And already it had become dark, and Jesus had not come to them. ¹⁸The sea was agitated and a strong wind is blowing. ¹⁹Therefore, having rowed about twenty-five or thirty stadia,[b] they see Jesus walking on the sea and coming near the boat, and they were frightened. ²⁰Now He says to them, "I am *He*; do not fear." ²¹Then they were willing to receive Him into the boat, and immediately the boat was at the land to which they were going.

Jesus the Bread of Life

²²On the next day, the crowd standing on the other side of the sea, having seen that no other boat was there except one, and that Jesus did not go with His disciples into the boat, but His disciples went away alone ²³(but other boats from Tiberias came near the place where they ate the bread, the Lord having given thanks), ²⁴therefore when the crowd saw that Jesus is not there, nor His disciples, they themselves entered into the boats and came to Capernaum, seeking Jesus. ²⁵And having found Him on the other side of the sea, they said to Him, "Rabbi, when have You come here?"

²⁶Jesus answered them and said, "Truly, truly, I say to you, you seek Me not because you saw signs, but because you ate of the loaves and were satisfied. ²⁷Do not work *for* the food that is perishing, but *for* the food enduring unto eternal life, which the Son of Man will give to you; for God the Father has sealed Him."

²⁸Therefore they said to Him, "What must we do, that we may be doing the works of God?"

²⁹Jesus answered and said to them, "This is the work of God, that you should believe in Him whom He has sent."

³⁰Therefore they said to Him, "Then what sign are You doing, that we may see and may believe You? What work do You perform? ³¹Our fathers ate the manna in the wilderness, as it is written: 'He gave them bread from heaven to eat.'[c]"

³²Therefore Jesus said to them, "Truly, truly, I say to you, Moses has not given you the bread from heaven, but My Father gives you the true bread from heaven. ³³For the bread of God is the *One* coming out of heaven and giving life to the world."

³⁴Therefore they said to Him, "Sir, always give to us this bread."

³⁵Jesus said to them, "I am the bread of life; the *one* coming to Me never shall hunger, and the *one* believing in Me never shall thirst at any time. ³⁶But I said to you that you have also seen Me, and yet do not believe.

³⁷All that the Father gives Me will come to Me, and the *one* coming to Me, I shall not cast out. ³⁸For I have come down from heaven, not that I should do My will, but the will of the *One* having sent Me. ³⁹Now this is the will of the *One* having sent Me, that all that He has given Me, I should lose none of it, but will raise it up in the last day. ⁴⁰For this is the will of My Father, that everyone beholding the Son and believing in Him should have eternal life, and I will raise him up in the last day."

⁴¹Therefore the Jews were grumbling about Him because He said, "I am the bread having come down from heaven." ⁴²And they were saying, "Is this not Jesus the son of Joseph, whose father and mother we know? How then does He say, 'I have come down from heaven?'"

⁴³Jesus answered and said to them, "Do not grumble with one another. ⁴⁴No one is able to come to Me unless the Father, the *one* having sent Me, draws him, and I will raise him up in the last day. ⁴⁵It is written in the prophets: 'And they will all be taught of God.'*ᵈ* Everyone having heard from the Father and having learned, comes to Me. ⁴⁶Not that anyone has seen the Father, except the *One* being from God; He has seen the Father. ⁴⁷Truly, truly, I say to you, the *one* believing has eternal life. ⁴⁸I am the bread of life. ⁴⁹Your fathers ate the manna in the wilderness and died. ⁵⁰This is the bread coming down from heaven, that anyone may eat of it and not die. ⁵¹I am the living bread, having come down from heaven. If anyone shall have eaten of this bread, he will live to the age. And also, the bread that I will give for the life of the world is My flesh."

⁵²Therefore the Jews were arguing with one another, saying, "How is this *man* able to give us His flesh to eat?"

⁵³Therefore Jesus said to them, "Truly, truly, I say to you, unless you shall have eaten the flesh of the Son of Man, and shall have drunk His blood, you do not have life in yourselves. ⁵⁴The *one* eating My flesh and drinking My blood has eternal life, and I will raise him up in the last day. ⁵⁵For My flesh is true food, and My blood is true drink.

⁵⁶The *one* eating My flesh and drinking My blood abides in Me, and I in him. ⁵⁷As the living Father sent Me and I live because of the Father, so also the *one* feeding on Me, he also will live because of Me. ⁵⁸This is the bread having come down from heaven, not as the fathers ate and died. The *one* eating this bread will live to the age."

Many Disciples Turn Back
(Matthew 8:18-22; Luke 9:57-62; Luke 14:25-33)

⁵⁹He said these things teaching in *the* synagogue in Capernaum. ⁶⁰Therefore many of His disciples having heard, said, "This word is difficult; who is able to hear it?"

⁶¹But Jesus, knowing in Himself that His disciples are grumbling about this, said to them, "Does this offend you? ⁶²Then what if you should see the Son of Man ascending to where He was before?

⁶³It is the Spirit giving life; the flesh profits nothing. The words that I speak to you are spirit and they are life. ⁶⁴But there are some of you who do not believe." (For Jesus knew from *the* beginning who are those not believing, and who it is who will betray Him.)

⁶⁵And He was saying, "Because of this, I have said to you that no one is able to come to Me, unless it shall have been granted to him from the Father."

Peter's Confession of Faith
(Matthew 16:13-20; Mark 8:27-30; Luke 9:18-20)

⁶⁶From that *time*, many of His disciples departed to the back and no longer walked with Him. ⁶⁷Therefore Jesus said to the Twelve, "You are not wishing to go away also?"

⁶⁸Simon Peter answered Him, "Lord, to whom will we go? You have *the* words of eternal life. ⁶⁹And we have believed and have known that You are the Holy One of God."

⁷⁰Jesus answered them, "Did I not choose you, the Twelve? And one of you is a devil!" ⁷¹Now He was speaking of Judas *son* of Simon Iscariot; for he, one of the Twelve, was about to betray Him.

a 7 A denarius was customarily a day's wage for a laborer (see Matthew 20:2)
b 19 Or *twenty-five or thirty furlongs*, approximately 3 to 4 miles, or 4.5 to 5.5 kilometers
c 31 Exodus 16:4
d 45 Isaiah 54:13

John 7
Jesus Teaches at the Feast

¹And after these things, Jesus was walking in Galilee; for He did not desire to walk in Judea, because the Jews were seeking to kill Him. ²Now the feast of the Jews, that of Booths, was near. ³Therefore His brothers said to Him,

"Depart from here and go into Judea, so that Your disciples will also see Your works that You are doing. ⁴For no one does anything in secret, and himself seeks to be in public. If You do these things, show Yourself to the world." ⁵For not even His brothers were believing in Him.

⁶Therefore Jesus says to them, "My time is not yet come, but your time is always ready. ⁷The world is not able to hate you; but it hates Me, because I bear witness concerning it that its works are evil. ⁸You go up to the feast. I am not*ᵃ* going up to this feast, for My time has not yet been fulfilled."

⁹Now having said these things to them, He remained in Galilee. ¹⁰But when His brothers had gone up to the feast, then He also went up—not openly, but as in secret.

¹¹Therefore the Jews were seeking Him at the feast, and were saying, "Where is He?" ¹²And there was much murmuring about Him among the crowds. For some were saying, "He is good."

But others were saying, "No, but He deceives the people."

¹³But no one was speaking publicly about Him, because of the fear of the Jews.

¹⁴And of the feast now being in the middle, Jesus went up into the temple and was teaching. ¹⁵Then the Jews were marveling, saying, "How does this one know *such* writings, not having studied?" ¹⁶Therefore Jesus answered them and said, "My teaching is not of Myself, but of the *One* having sent Me. ¹⁷If anyone desires to do His will, he will know concerning the teaching, whether it is from God, or I speak from Myself. ¹⁸The *one* speaking from himself seeks the own glory, but the *One* seeking the glory of the *One* having sent Him, He is true, and no unrighteousness is in Him.

¹⁹Has not Moses given to you the Law, and none of you keeps the Law? Why do you seek to kill Me?"

²⁰The crowd answered, "You have a demon. Who seeks to kill You?"

²¹Jesus answered and said to them, "I did one work, and you all marvel. ²²Because of the fact that Moses has given you circumcision (not that it is of Moses, but of the fathers) also on *the* Sabbath you circumcise a man. ²³If a man receives circumcision on *the* Sabbath so that the Law of Moses might not be broken, are you angry with Me because I made a man entirely sound on the Sabbath? ²⁴Do not judge according to appearance, but judge the righteous judgment."

Is Jesus the Christ?

²⁵Therefore some of those of Jerusalem were saying, "Is this not whom they seek to kill? ²⁶And behold, He speaks publicly, and they say nothing ever to Him. Have the rulers truly recognized that this is the Christ? ²⁷But we know this *man*, where He is from. But the Christ, whenever He may come, no one knows where He is from."

²⁸Therefore Jesus cried out in the temple, teaching and saying, "You know Me and you know where I am from. And I have not come of Myself, but the *One* having sent Me is true, whom you do not know. ²⁹But I know Him, because I am from Him, and He sent Me."

³⁰Therefore they were seeking to take Him, but no one laid the hand upon Him, because His hour had not yet come. ³¹Yet many out of the crowd believed in Him and were saying, "When the Christ comes, will He do more signs than this *man* has done?"

³²The Pharisees heard the crowd murmuring these things about Him, and the chief priests and the Pharisees sent officers, that they might seize Him. ³³Therefore Jesus said, "Yet a little time I am with you, and I go to the *One* having sent Me. ³⁴You will seek Me and will not find Me; and where I am, you are not able to come."

³⁵Therefore the Jews said among themselves, "Where is He about to go

that we will not find Him? Is He about to go to the Dispersion among the Greeks and to teach the Greeks? ³⁶What is this word that He said, 'You will seek Me, and will not find Me,' and 'Where I am you are not able to come'?"

Living Water

³⁷Now in the last day of the feast, the great *day*, Jesus stood and cried out, saying, "If anyone thirsts, let him come to Me and drink. ³⁸The *one* believing in Me, as the Scripture has said: 'Out of his belly will flow rivers of living water.'" ³⁹Now He said this concerning the Spirit, whom those having believed in Him were about to receive; for *the* Spirit was not yet *given*, because Jesus was not yet glorified.

Division Regarding Jesus

⁴⁰Therefore having heard these words, *some* of the people were saying, "This is truly the Prophet."
⁴¹Others were saying, "This is the Christ." But others were saying, "Surely the Christ does not come out of Galilee? ⁴²Has not the Scripture said that Christ comes out of the seed of David, and from Bethlehem, the village where David was?" ⁴³Therefore a division occurred in the crowd because of Him. ⁴⁴Now some of them desired to seize Him, but no one laid the hands on Him.

Unbelief of the Jewish Leaders

⁴⁵Therefore the officers came to the chief priests and Pharisees, and they said to them, "Why did you not bring Him?"
⁴⁶The officers answered, "Never has a man spoken like this, as this man speaks."
⁴⁷Therefore the Pharisees answered them, "Have you also been deceived? ⁴⁸Has any of the rulers or of the Pharisees believed on Him? ⁴⁹But this crowd, not knowing the Law, are accursed."
⁵⁰Nicodemus, the *one* having come to Him, the former being one of them, says to them, ⁵¹"Does our Law judge the man unless first it has heard from him and known what he does?"

⁵²They answered and said to him, "Are you not also from Galilee? Search and see that a prophet is not raised out of Galilee."*ᵇ*
⁵³And each went to his home.

a 8 NE, WH, BYZ and TR *I am not yet*
b 52 Some early manuscripts do not include John 7:53 - 8:11

John 8
The Woman Caught in Adultery

¹But Jesus went to the Mount of Olives.
²And early in the morning again He came into the temple, and all the people were coming to Him. And having sat down, He was teaching them. ³Now the scribes and the Pharisees bring to Him a woman having been caught in adultery, and having set her in *the* midst, ⁴they say to Him, "Teacher, this woman was caught in the very act, committing adultery. ⁵Now in the Law Moses commanded us such to be stoned. You therefore, what do You say?"
⁶Now they were saying this testing Him, so that they might have *grounds* to accuse Him. But Jesus, having stooped down, began writing with *His* finger on the ground.
⁷But as they continued asking Him, having lifted Himself up, also He said to them, "The *one* sinless among you, let him cast the first stone at her." ⁸And again having stooped down, He continued to write on the ground.
⁹And having heard,*ᵃ* they began to go away one by one, having begun from the elder ones until the last, and He was left alone, Jesus and the woman being in *the* midst. ¹⁰And having lifted up,*ᵇ* Jesus said to her, "Woman where are they who accuse you?*ᶜ* Has no one condemned you?"
¹¹And she said, "No one, Sir."
And to her Jesus said, "Neither I do condemn you. Go and sin no more from now *on.*"

Jesus the Light of the World
(1 John 1:5-10)

12Therefore Jesus spoke to them again, saying, "I am the light of the world. The *one* following Me shall not walk in the darkness, but will have the light of life."
13Therefore the Pharisees said to Him, "You are bearing witness concerning Yourself; Your testimony is not true."
14Jesus answered and said to them, "Even if I am bearing witness concerning Myself, My testimony is true, because I know from where I came and where I am going. But you do not know from where I come or where I am going.
15You judge according to the flesh; I am judging no one. **16**But even if I judge, My judgment is true, because I am not alone, but I and the Father, having sent Me.
17But also in your Law it has been written that the testimony of two men is true. **18**I am *One* bearing witness concerning Myself, and the Father having sent Me bears witness concerning Me."
19Therefore they were saying to Him, "Where is Your Father?"
Jesus answered, "You know neither Me nor My Father. If you had known Me, you would have known My Father also."
20He spoke these words in the treasury, teaching in the temple; and no one seized Him, for His hour had not yet come.
21Then He said to them again, "I am going away and you will seek Me, and you will die in your sin. Where I go, you are not able to come."
22Therefore the Jews were saying, "Will He kill Himself, that He says, 'Where I go, you are not able to come'?"
23And He was saying to them, "You are from below; I am from above. You are of this world; I am not of this world. **24**Therefore I said to you that you will die in your sins; for unless you believe that I am *He*, you will die in your sins."
25Therefore they were saying to Him, "Who are You?"
Jesus said to them, "Just what I am saying to you from the beginning. **26**I have many things to say and to judge concerning you. But the *One* having sent Me is true; and I what I have heard from Him, these things I say to the world."
27They did not understand that He was speaking to them *about* the Father.
28Therefore Jesus said to them, "When you shall have lifted up the Son of Man, then you will know that I am *He*, and I do nothing from Myself; but as the Father taught Me, I speak these things. **29**And the *One* having sent Me is with Me. He has not left Me alone, because I always do the things pleasing to Him."

The Truth will Set You Free
(2 John 1:4-6)

30Of His speaking these things, many believed in Him. **31**Therefore Jesus was saying to the Jews having believed in Him, "If you abide in My word, you are truly My disciples. **32**And you will know the truth, and the truth will set free you."
33They answered unto Him, "We are Abraham's seed, and to no one ever have we been under bondage. How do You say, 'You will become free'?"
34Jesus answered them, "Truly, truly, I say to you that everyone practicing the sin is a slave of the sin. **35**Now the slave does not abide in the house to the age; the son abides to the age. **36**So if the Son shall set you free, you will be free indeed.

The Children of the Devil

37I know that you are Abraham's seed; but you seek to kill Me because My word receives no place in you. **38**I speak that which I have seen with the Father; therefore you also do what you have heard from *your* father."
39They answered and said to Him, "Abraham is our father."
Jesus says to them, "If you were children of Abraham, you would do the works of Abraham. **40**But now you seek to kill Me, a man who has spoken to you the truth that I heard from God. Abraham did not do this. **41**You are doing the works of your father."

Therefore they said to Him, "We have not been born of sexual immorality. We have one Father, God."

⁴²Jesus said to them, "If God were your Father, you would have loved Me, for I came forth from God and am here; for not even have I come of Myself, but He sent Me.

⁴³Why do you not understand My speech? Because you are not able to hear My word. ⁴⁴You are of *your* father the devil, and you desire to do the desires of your father. He was a murderer from *the* beginning, and has not stood in the truth, because there is no truth in him. Whenever he might speak falsehood, he speaks from the own; for he is a liar, and the father of it. ⁴⁵Now because I speak the truth, you do not believe Me!

⁴⁶Which of you convicts me concerning sin? If I speak *the* truth, why do you not believe Me? ⁴⁷He who is of God hears the words of God; because of this, you do not hear, because you are not of God."

Before Abraham was Born, I Am

⁴⁸The Jews answered and said to Him, "Are we not rightly saying that You are a Samaritan and have a demon?"

⁴⁹Jesus answered, "I do not have a demon, but I honor My Father, and you dishonor Me. ⁵⁰Yet I do not seek My glory; there is One seeking *it* and judging. ⁵¹Truly, truly, I say to you, if anyone keeps My word, he shall never see death, to the age."

⁵²Therefore the Jews said to Him, "Now we know that You have a demon. Abraham and the prophets died, and You say, 'If anyone keeps My word, he shall never taste of death, to the age.' ⁵³Are You greater than our father Abraham, who died? And the prophets died! Whom do You make yourself?"

⁵⁴Jesus answered, "If I glorify Myself, My glory is nothing; it is My Father glorifying Me, *of* whom you say, 'He is our*ᵈ* God.' ⁵⁵And you have not known Him, but I know Him. And if I say that I do not know Him, I will be a liar like you. But I know Him, and I keep His word. ⁵⁶Abraham your father rejoiced in that he should see My day—and he saw *it* and rejoiced."

⁵⁷Therefore the Jews said to Him, "You are not yet fifty years *old*, and You have seen Abraham?"

⁵⁸Jesus said to them, "Truly, truly, I say to you, before Abraham was, I am."

⁵⁹Therefore they took up stones, that they might cast at Him; but Jesus hid Himself, and went forth out of the temple.*ᵉ*

a 9 NE, BYZ, and TR include *and were convicted by their conscience*
b 10 NE, BYZ, and TR include *and saw no one but the woman*
c 10 WH and NA *where are they*
d 54 WH and TR *Your*
e 59 BYZ and TR include *going through the midst of them, and so he passed by*

John 9
Jesus Heals the Man Born Blind

¹And passing by, He saw a man blind from birth. ²And His disciples asked Him, saying, "Rabbi, who sinned, this *man* or his parents, that he should be born blind?"

³Jesus answered, "Neither this *man* sinned, nor his parents; but *it was* that the works of God should be displayed in him. ⁴It behooves us to work the works of the *One* having sent Me while it is day; night is coming, when no one is able to work. ⁵While I shall be in the world, I am *the* light of the world."

⁶Having said these things, He spat on *the* ground, and made clay of the spittle, and applied the clay to his eyes. ⁷And He said to him, "Go, wash in the pool of Siloam" (which means Sent). Therefore he went and washed, and came seeing.

⁸Therefore the neighbors and those having seen him before, that he was a beggar, were saying, "Is this not he who was sitting and begging?"

⁹Some were saying, "It is he," but others, were saying, "No, but he is like him."
He kept saying, "I am *he*."

¹⁰Therefore they were saying to him, "How then were your eyes opened?"

¹¹He answered, "The man called Jesus made clay, and anointed my eyes, and He said to me, 'Go to Siloam and wash.' Therefore having gone and having washed, I received sight."
¹²And they said to him, "Where is He?" He says, "I do not know."

The Pharisees Investigate the Healing

¹³They bring him who once *was* blind to the Pharisees. ¹⁴Now *the* day in which Jesus had made the clay and opened his eyes was a Sabbath. ¹⁵Therefore the Pharisees also were asking him again how he had received sight.
And he said to them, "He put clay on my eyes, and I washed, and I see."
¹⁶Therefore some of the Pharisees were saying, "This man is not from God, for He does not keep the Sabbath."
But others were saying, "How is a sinful man able to do such signs?"
And there was division among them.
¹⁷Therefore they say again to the blind *man*, "What do you say concerning Him, for He opened your eyes?"
And he said, "He is a prophet."
¹⁸Therefore the Jews did not believe concerning him that he had been blind and had received sight, until they called the parents of him having received sight. ¹⁹And they asked them, saying, "Is this your son, of whom you say that he was born blind? Then how presently does he see?"
²⁰Therefore his parents answered and said, "We know that this is our son, and that he was born blind. ²¹But how he sees presently, we do not know; or who opened his eyes, we do not know. Ask him. He has age. He will speak concerning himself."
²²His parents said these things because they were afraid of the Jews. For the Jews already had agreed together that if anyone should confess Him Christ, he would be expelled from the synagogue. ²³Because of this, his parents said, "He has age. Ask him."

²⁴Therefore they called out a second time the man who had been blind, and said to him, "Give glory to God! We know that this man is a sinner."
²⁵Then he answered, "Whether He is a sinner I do not know. One *thing* I do know, that being blind, now I see."
²⁶So they said to him, "What did He do to you? How did He open your eyes?"
²⁷He answered them, "I told you already, and you did not listen. Why do you wish to hear again? Do you wish to become His disciples also?"
²⁸And they railed at him and said, "You are a disciple of that One, but we are disciples of Moses. ²⁹We know that God has spoken to Moses, but we do not know from where this *man* is."
³⁰The man answered and said to them, "In this indeed is an amazing thing, that you do not know from where He is, and yet He opened my eyes. ³¹We know that God does not hear sinners, but if anyone is God-fearing and does His will, He hears him. ³²Never out of the age has it been heard that anyone opened *the* eyes of *one* having been born blind. ³³If this *man* were not from God, He could do nothing."
³⁴They answered and said to him, "You were born entirely in sins, and do you teach us?" And they cast him out.

Spiritual Blindness

³⁵Jesus heard that they had cast him out, and having found him, He said, "Do you believe in the Son of Man?"[a]
³⁶He answered and said, "And who is He, Lord, that I may believe in Him?"
³⁷Jesus said to him, "You have both seen Him, and He is the *One* speaking with you."
³⁸And he was saying, "I believe, Lord." And he worshiped Him.
³⁹And Jesus said, "For judgment I came into this world, that those not seeing may see, and those seeing may become blind."[b]
⁴⁰*Some* of the Pharisees who were with Him heard these things, and they said to Him, "Are we also blind?"

⁴¹Jesus said to them, "If you were blind, you would have no sin. But since you say, 'We see,' your sin remains."

a 35 BYZ and TR *the Son of God*
b 38-39 Some manuscripts do not include *38 And he was saying . . . 39 Then Jesus said,*

John 10
Jesus the Good Shepherd
(Psalm 23:1-6; Ezekiel 34:11-24)

¹"Truly, truly, I say to you, the *one* not entering in by the door to the fold of the sheep, but climbing up another way, he is a thief and a robber. ²But the *one* entering in by the door is *the* shepherd of the sheep. ³To him the doorkeeper opens, and the sheep hear his voice. And he calls the own sheep by name and leads them out.
⁴When he has brought out all the own, he goes before them, and the sheep follow him, because they know his voice. ⁵But they will never follow a stranger, but will flee from him, because they do not recognize the voice of strangers."
⁶Jesus spoke to them this allegory, but they did not know what it was that He was saying to them. ⁷Therefore Jesus again said to them, "Truly, truly, I say to you, I am the door of the sheep. ⁸All who ever came before Me are thieves and robbers, but the sheep did not hear them. ⁹I am the door. If anyone enters in by Me, he will be saved, and will go in and will go out and will find pasture. ¹⁰The thief comes only that he might steal and might kill and might destroy. I came that they may have life, and may have *it* abundantly.
¹¹I am the good shepherd. The good shepherd lays down His life for the sheep. ¹²But the hired servant, being not *the* shepherd, whose own the sheep are not, sees the wolf coming and leaves the sheep and flees—and the wolf snatches them and scatters *them*— ¹³because he is a hired servant and is not himself concerned about the sheep.
¹⁴I am the good shepherd, and I know My own, and I am known by My own. ¹⁵As the Father knows Me, I also know the Father; and I lay down My life for the sheep. ¹⁶And I have other sheep which are not of this fold. It behooves Me to bring those also, and they will hear My voice, and there will be one flock with one shepherd.
¹⁷Because of this, the Father loves Me, because I lay down My life, that I might take it again. ¹⁸No one takes it from Me, but I lay it down of Myself. I have authority to lay it down, and I have authority to take it again. This commandment I received from My Father."
¹⁹Again there was division among the Jews on account of these words. ²⁰And many of them were saying, "He has a demon and is insane. Why do you listen to Him?"
²¹Others were saying, "These are not the sayings of one possessed by a demon. Is a demon able to open *the* eyes of *the* blind?"

The Unbelief of the Jews

²²At the time the Feast of Dedication[a] took place at Jerusalem. It was winter, ²³and Jesus was walking in the temple in the porch of Solomon. ²⁴Therefore the Jews encircled Him and were saying to Him, "Until when do You hold our soul in suspense? If You are the Christ, tell us plainly."
²⁵Jesus answered them, "I told you, and you do not believe. The works that I do in the name of My Father, these bear witness concerning Me. ²⁶But you do not believe, because you are not from among My sheep. ²⁷My sheep hear My voice, and I know them, and they follow Me. ²⁸And I give them eternal life, and never shall they perish to the age, and never will anyone seize them out of My hand. ²⁹My Father who has given *them* to Me is greater than all, and no one is able to seize *them* out of the Father's hand. ³⁰I and the Father are one."
³¹Therefore the Jews took up stones again, that they might stone Him. ³²Jesus

answered them, "I have shown you many good works from the Father; because of which work of these do you stone Me?"
³³The Jews answered Him, "We do not stone You for a good work, but for blasphemy, and because You, being a man, make yourself God."
³⁴Jesus answered them, "Is it not written in your Law: 'I said you are gods'[b]? ³⁵If he called them gods to whom the word of God came, and the Scripture is not able to be broken, ³⁶do you say *of Him* whom the Father sanctified and sent into the world, 'You blaspheme,' because I said, 'I am Son of God'?
³⁷If I do not do the works of My Father, do not believe Me. ³⁸But if I do, even if you do not believe Me, believe the works, so that you may know and may understand that the Father *is* in Me, and I in the Father."
³⁹Therefore they were seeking to seize Him again, but He went forth out of their hand.

John's Testimony Confirmed

⁴⁰And He departed again beyond the Jordan, to the place where John was baptizing at first. And He stayed there. ⁴¹And many came to Him and were saying, "John indeed did no sign, but everything that John said about this *man* was true." ⁴²And many believed in Him there.

a 22 That is, Hanukkah, also called the Feast of Lights
b 34 Psalm 82:6

John 11
The Death of Lazarus

¹Now a certain *man* was ailing, Lazarus of Bethany, of the village of Mary and her sister Martha. ²And Mary was the *one* having anointed the Lord with fragrant oil and having wiped His feet with her hair, whose brother Lazarus was sick. ³Therefore the sisters sent to Him, saying, "Lord, behold, *he* whom You love is sick."
⁴And having heard, Jesus said, "This sickness is not unto death, but for the glory of God, so that the Son of God may be glorified by it."
⁵Now Jesus loved Martha and her sister and Lazarus. ⁶Therefore when He heard that he is sick, then indeed He remained two days in *the* place in which He was. ⁷Then after this, He says to the disciples, "Let us go into Judea again."
⁸The disciples say to Him, "Rabbi, just now the Jews were seeking to stone You, and You are going there again?"
⁹Jesus answered, "Are there not twelve hours in the day? If anyone walks in the day, he does not stumble, because he sees the light of this world. ¹⁰But if anyone walks in the night, he stumbles, because the light is not in him."
¹¹He said these things, and after this He says to them, "Our friend Lazarus has fallen asleep, but I go that I may awaken him."
¹²Therefore His disciples said, "Lord, if he has fallen asleep, he will get well." ¹³Now Jesus had spoken of his death, but they thought that He speaks of the rest of sleep.
¹⁴So then Jesus told them plainly, "Lazarus has died, ¹⁵and I am glad for your sake I was not there, so that you may believe. But let us go to him."
¹⁶Therefore Thomas called Didymus said to the fellow disciples, "Let us also go, that we may die with Him."

Jesus Comforts Martha and Mary

¹⁷Therefore having come, Jesus found him already having been four days in the tomb. ¹⁸Now Bethany was near Jerusalem, about fifteen stadia[a] away, ¹⁹and many of the Jews had come unto Martha and Mary, that they might console them concerning the brother. ²⁰Therefore Martha, when she heard that Jesus is coming, met Him; but Mary was sitting in the house.
²¹Then Martha said to Jesus, "Lord, if You had been here, my brother would not have died. ²²Nevertheless, even now I know that whatever You might ask God, God will give You."

²³Jesus says to her, "Your brother will rise again."
²⁴Martha says to him, "I know that he will rise again in the resurrection, in the last day."
²⁵Jesus said to her, "I am the resurrection and the life; the *one* believing in Me, even if he should die, he will live. ²⁶And everyone living and believing in Me shall never die, to the age. Do you believe this?"
²⁷She says to Him, "Yes, Lord; I have believed that You are the Christ, the Son of God, the *One* coming into the world."
²⁸And having said these things she went away and called her sister Mary secretly, having said, "The Teacher is come, and He calls you." ²⁹And she, when she heard, rose up quickly and was coming to Him.
³⁰Now Jesus had not yet come into the village, but was still in the place where Martha had met Him. ³¹Then the Jews being with her in the house and consoling her, having seen that Mary rose up quickly and went out, followed her, having supposed she is going to the tomb that she might weep there. ³²Therefore Mary, when she came to where Jesus was, having seen Him, fell at His feet, saying to Him, "Lord, if You had been here, my brother would not have died."
³³Therefore Jesus, when He saw her weeping and the Jews having come with her weeping, was deeply moved in spirit^b and Himself troubled. ³⁴And He said, "Where have you laid him?"
They say to Him, "Lord, come and see."
³⁵Jesus wept.
³⁶Therefore the Jews were saying, "Behold how He loved him!"
³⁷But some of them said, "Was not this *man* having opened the eyes of the blind able to have caused that this one also should not have died?"

Jesus Raises Lazarus
(Acts 20:7-12)

³⁸So Jesus, being deeply moved in Himself again, comes to the tomb. Now it was a cave, and a stone was lying against it. ³⁹Jesus says, "Take away the stone." Martha, the sister of the *one* having died, says to Him, "Lord, he stinks already, for it is four days."
⁴⁰Jesus says to her, "Did I not say to you that if you should believe, you will see the glory of God?"
⁴¹So they took away the stone. Now Jesus lifted His eyes upwards and said, "Father, I thank You that You have heard Me. ⁴²And I knew that always You hear Me; but I said *it* on account of the crowd standing around, that they may believe that You sent Me."
⁴³And having said these things, He cried out in a loud voice, "Lazarus, come forth!"
⁴⁴The *one* having been dead came forth, the feet and hands being bound with linen strips, and his face bound about with a soudarion.
Jesus says to them, "Unbind him and allow him to go."

The Plot to Kill Jesus
(Matthew 26:1-5; Mark 14:1-2; Luke 22:1-6)

⁴⁵Therefore many of the Jews having come to Mary, and having seen what He did, believed in Him. ⁴⁶But some of them went to the Pharisees and told them what Jesus had done.
⁴⁷Therefore the chief priests and the Pharisees gathered a council and were saying, "What are we to do? For this man does many signs. ⁴⁸If we shall let Him alone like this, all will believe in Him, and the Romans will come and will take away both our place and nation."
⁴⁹But a certain one of them, Caiaphas, being high priest the same year, said to them, "You know nothing at all, ⁵⁰nor do you consider that it is profitable for you that one man should die for the people, and the whole nation should not perish."
⁵¹Now he did not say this from himself, but being high priest that year, he prophesied that Jesus was about to die for the nation, ⁵²and not for the nation only, but also that children of God, those

having been scattered, He might gather together into one.
⁵³So from that day, they took counsel together that they might kill Him. ⁵⁴Therefore Jesus no longer walked publicly among the Jews, but went away from there into the region near the wilderness, to a city called Ephraim. And there He stayed with the disciples.
⁵⁵Now the Passover of the Jews was near, and many went up to Jerusalem out of the region before the Passover, so that they might purify themselves. ⁵⁶Therefore they were seeking Jesus and were saying among one another standing in the temple, "What does it seem to you, that He will not come to the feast?" ⁵⁷Now the chief priests and the Pharisees had given a command that if anyone should know where He is, he should show *it*, so that they might seize Him.

a 18 Or *fifteen furlongs*; about 1.7 miles or 2.75 kilometers.
b 33 Or *He was angry in His spirit*; also in verse 38

John 12
Mary Anoints Jesus
(Matthew 26:6-13; Mark 14:3-9)

¹Therefore six days before the Passover, Jesus came to Bethany, where Lazarus was, whom Jesus had raised out from *the* dead. ²Therefore they made Him a supper there, and Martha was serving, and Lazarus was one of those reclining with Him. ³Therefore Mary, having taken a litra*ᵃ* of fragrant oil of pure nard, of great price, anointed the feet of Jesus and wiped His feet with her hair; and the house was filled with the fragrance of the oil.
⁴But Judas Iscariot, one of His disciples, being about to betray Him, says, ⁵"Why was this fragrant oil not sold for three hundred denarii*ᵇ* and given to *the* poor?" ⁶But he said this, not because he was caring for the poor, but because he was a thief; and having the money bag, he used to pilfer that being put into *it*.
⁷Therefore Jesus said, "Leave her alone, so that for the day of My burial she may keep it. ⁸For you always have the poor with you,*ᶜ* but not always do you have Me."

The Plot to Kill Lazarus
⁹Therefore a great crowd of the Jews knew that He is there; and they came, not only because of Jesus, but that they might see Lazarus also, whom He had raised out from *the* dead. ¹⁰But the chief priests took counsel, that they might kill Lazarus also, ¹¹because on account of him many of the Jews were going away and were believing in Jesus.

The Triumphal Entry
(Zechariah 9:9-13; Matthew 21:1-11; Mark 11:1-11; Luke 19:28-40)

¹²On the next day the great crowd having come to the feast, having heard that Jesus is coming into Jerusalem, ¹³took the branches of the palm trees and went out to meet Him, and were shouting:
"Hosanna!"*ᵈ*
"Blessed is the *One* coming in *the* name of *the* Lord!"*ᵉ*
"And the King of Israel!"*ᶠ*
¹⁴Now Jesus, having found a young donkey, sat upon it, as it is written:
¹⁵"Fear not, daughter of Zion.
Behold, your King comes,
sitting on a colt of a donkey."*ᵍ*
¹⁶His disciples did not know these things from the first, but when Jesus was glorified, then they remembered that these things were written of Him, and these things they had done to Him.
¹⁷Therefore the crowd being with Him when He called Lazarus out of the tomb and raised him out from *the* dead, continued to bear witness. ¹⁸On account of this also the crowd met Him, because they heard of His having done this sign.
¹⁹Therefore the Pharisees said among themselves, "You see that you gain nothing. Behold, the world has gone after Him."

Jesus Predicts His Death
²⁰Now there were certain Greeks among those coming up that they might worship at the feast. ²¹Therefore these came to

Philip, who was from Bethsaida of Galilee, and they were asking him, saying, "Sir, we desire to see Jesus." ²²Philip comes and tells Andrew; Andrew and Philip come and tell Jesus.

²³And Jesus answered them, saying, "The hour has come that Son of Man should be glorified. ²⁴Truly, truly, I say to you, unless the grain of wheat, having fallen into the ground, should die, it abides alone; but if it should die, it bears much fruit. ²⁵The *one* loving his life loses it, and the *one* hating his life in this world will keep it to eternal life. ²⁶If anyone serves Me, let him follow Me; and where I am, there My servant will be also. If anyone serves Me, the Father will honor him.

²⁷Now My soul has been troubled, and what shall I say? 'Father, save Me from this hour'? But on account of this I came to this hour. ²⁸Father, glorify Your name." Therefore a voice came from heaven: "I have both glorified *it*, and I will glorify *it* again."

²⁹Therefore the crowd having stood, and having heard, was saying, "There has been thunder." Others were saying, "An angel has spoken to Him."

³⁰Jesus answered and said, "This voice has not come because of Me but because of you. ³¹Now is *the* judgment of this world; now the prince of this world will be cast out. ³²And I, if I am lifted up from the earth, will draw all to Myself." ³³Now He was saying this, signifying by what death He was about to die.

³⁴Then the crowd answered Him, "We have heard from the Law that Christ abides to the age, and how do you say that it behooves the Son of Man to be lifted up? Who is this Son of Man?"

³⁵Therefore Jesus said to them, "Yet a little while, the light is with you. Walk while you have the light, so that darkness might not overtake you. And the *one* walking in the darkness does not know where he is going. ³⁶While you have the light, believe in the light, so that you may become sons of light."

Jesus spoke these things, and having gone away, He was hidden from them.

Belief and Unbelief

³⁷Although so many of His signs had been done before them, they did not believe in Him, ³⁸so that word of Isaiah the prophet might be fulfilled, that said:

"Lord, who has believed our report?
And to whom has the arm of
the Lord been revealed?"ʰ

³⁹Because of this, they were not able to believe, for again Isaiah said:

⁴⁰"He has blinded their eyes,
and has hardened their heart,
that they should not see with the eyes,
and understand with the heart, and turn,
and I will heal them."ⁱ

⁴¹Isaiah said these things because he saw His glory and spoke concerning Him. ⁴²Nevertheless, indeed many even of the rulers believed in Him, but on account of the Pharisees they were not confessing, so that they might not be put out of the synagogue. ⁴³For they loved the glory of men more than the glory of God.

⁴⁴And Jesus cried out and said, "The *one* believing in Me, does not believe in Me, but in the *One* having sent Me. ⁴⁵And the *one* beholding Me, beholds the *One* having sent Me. ⁴⁶I have come into the world *as* a light, so that everyone believing in Me should not abide in darkness.

⁴⁷And if anyone hears My words and does not keep *them*, I do not judge him; for I did not come that I might judge the world, but that I might save the world. ⁴⁸The *one* rejecting Me and not receiving My words has *one* judging him: The word which I spoke, that will judge him in the last day.

⁴⁹For I did not speak from Myself, but the Father Himself, having sent Me, gave Me a commandment, what I should say and what I should speak. ⁵⁰And I know that His commandment is eternal life.

Therefore what I speak, as the Father has said to Me, so I speak."

a 3 About a pint, or about a half liter
b 5 A denarius was customarily a day's wage for a laborer (see Matthew 20:2)
c 8 See Deuteronomy 15:11
d 13 Psalm 118:25
e 13 Psalm 118:26
f 13 Zephaniah 3:15
g 15 Zechariah 9:9
h 38 Isaiah 53:1
i 40 Isaiah 6:10

John 13
Jesus Washes His Disciples' Feet

¹Now before the feast of the Passover, Jesus, knowing that His hour had come that He would depart out of this world to the Father, having loved the own who were in the world, He loved them to the end. ²And supper taking place, the devil already having put into the heart of Judas son of Simon Iscariot that he should betray Him, ³knowing that the Father has given Him all things into the hands, and that He came forth from God and He is going to God, ⁴He rises from the supper and lays aside the garments. And having taken a towel, He girded Himself. ⁵After that, He pours water into the basin, and He began to wash the feet of the disciples and to wipe *them* with the towel with which He was girded.
⁶Then He comes to Simon Peter, who says to Him, "Lord, do You wash my feet?"
⁷Jesus answered and said to him, "What I do, you do not know presently, but you will know after these things."
⁸Peter says to Him, "Never shall You wash my feet, to the age."
Jesus answered him, "Unless I wash you, you have no part with Me."
⁹Simon Peter says to Him, "Lord, not my feet only, but also the hands and the head."
¹⁰Jesus says to him, "The *one* having been bathed has no need to wash, except the feet, but is wholly clean. And you all are clean, but not all." ¹¹For He knew the *one who* was betraying Him; on account of this He said, "You are not all clean."

¹²Therefore when He had washed their feet and taken His garments, and having reclined again, He said to them, "Do you know what I have done to you? ¹³You call Me Teacher and Lord, and you say rightly, for *so* I am. ¹⁴Therefore if I, the Lord and the Teacher, have washed your feet, you also ought to wash the feet of one another. ¹⁵For I gave you a pattern, that as I did to you, you also should do. ¹⁶Truly, truly, I say to you, a servant is not greater than his master, nor a messenger greater than the *one* having sent him. ¹⁷If you know these things, you are blessed if you do them.

Jesus Predicts His Betrayal
(Psalm 41:1-13; Matthew 26:17-25; Mark 14:12-21; Luke 22:7-13)

¹⁸I speak not about all of you. I know whom I chose; but *it is* that the Scripture may be fulfilled: 'The *one* eating My bread has lifted up his heel against Me.'ᵃ ¹⁹I am telling you from this time, before it comes to pass, so that when it comes to pass you should believe that I am He. ²⁰Truly, truly, I say to you, the *one* receiving whomever I shall send, receives Me; and the *one* receiving Me, receives the *One* having sent Me."
²¹Having said these things, Jesus was troubled in spirit, and He testified and said, "Truly, truly, I say to you that one of you will betray Me."
²²The disciples began to look upon one another, being uncertain of whom He is speaking. ²³There was reclining one of His disciples whom Jesus loved in the bosom of Jesus. ²⁴Therefore Simon Peter motions to him, to ask who it is about whom He is speaking? ²⁵Then he thus having leaned on the breast of Jesus, says to Him, "Lord, who is it?"
²⁶Then Jesus answers, "It is he to whom I will dip the morsel and will give him." Then having dipped the morsel, He takes *it* and gives *it* to Judas, *son* of Simon Iscariot. ²⁷And after the morsel, then Satan entered into him.

Therefore Jesus says to him, "What you do, do quickly." ²⁸Now none of those reclining knew why He spoke this to him. ²⁹For some were thinking, since Judas had the money bag, that Jesus is saying to him, "Buy what things we have need of for the feast," or that he should give something to the poor. ³⁰Therefore having received the morsel, he went out immediately. And it was night.

Love one another
(Romans 12:9-13; 1 John 3:11-24)

³¹Therefore when he had gone out, Jesus says, "Now the Son of Man has been glorified, and God has been glorified in Him. ³²If God is glorified in Him, God also will glorify Him in Himself, and will glorify Him immediately. ³³Little children, yet a little while I am with you. You will seek Me, and as I said to the Jews, now I say also to you: 'Where I go, you are not able to come.' ³⁴A new commandment I give to you, that you should love one another. As I have loved you, so you also should love one another. ³⁵By this all will know that you are My disciples, if you have love among one another."

Jesus Predicts Peter's Denial
(Matthew 26:31-35; Mark 14:27-31; Luke 22:31-38)

³⁶Simon Peter says to Him, "Lord, where are You going?"
Jesus answered him, "Where I go, you are not able to follow Me now, but you will follow afterward."
³⁷Peter says to Him, "Lord, why am I not able to follow You presently? I will lay down my life for You."
³⁸Jesus answered, "Will you lay down your life for Me? Truly, truly, I say to you, *the* rooster will not crow until you will deny Me three times."

a 18 Psalm 41:9

John 14
Jesus Comforts the Disciples

¹Let not your heart be troubled. You believe in God,ᵃ believe also in Me. ²In My Father's house there are many mansions. And if not so, would I have told you that I go to prepare a place for you? ³And if I go and prepare a place for you, I am coming again and will receive you to Myself, that where I am, you may be also. ⁴And you know the way to the place I am going."ᵇ

The Way, the Truth, and the Life

⁵Thomas says to Him, "Lord, we do not know where You are going; how can we know the way?"
⁶Jesus says to him, "I am the way and the truth and the life. No one comes to the Father, if not by Me. ⁷If you had known Me, you would also have known My Father. From now you know Him, and have seen Him."
⁸Philip says to Him, "Lord, show us the Father, and it is enough for us."
⁹Jesus says to him, "Am I with you so long a time, and you have not known Me, Philip? The *one* having seen Me has seen the Father. How can you say, 'Show us the Father'? ¹⁰Do you not believe that I *am* in the Father, and the Father is in Me? The words that I speak to you, I do not speak from Myself; but the Father dwelling in Me does His works. ¹¹Believe Me that I *am* in the Father, and the Father *is* in Me; but if not, believe because of the works themselves.
¹²Truly, truly, I say to you, the *one* believing in Me, the works that I do, also he will do. And he will do greater than these, because I am going to the Father. ¹³And whatever you might ask in My name, this I will do, so that the Father may be glorified in the Son. ¹⁴If you ask Meᶜ anything in My name, I will do *it*.

Jesus Promises the Holy Spirit
(Joel 2:28-32; John 16:5-16; Acts 2:1-13; Acts 10:44-48; Acts 19:1-7)

¹⁵If you love Me, you will keep My commandments.
¹⁶And I will ask the Father, and He will give you another Helper, that He may be with you to the age— ¹⁷the Spirit of truth, whom the world is not able to receive,

because it does not see Him nor know. But you know Him, for He abides with you and He will be in you.^d

¹⁸I will not leave you as orphans; I am coming to you. ¹⁹Yet a little while, and the world sees Me no more, but you see Me. Because I live, you also will live. ²⁰In that day you will know that I *am* in My Father, and you in Me, and I in you. ²¹The *one* having My commandments and keeping them, he is the *one* loving Me. Now the *one* loving Me will be loved by My Father. And I will love him, and will show Myself to him."

²²Judas (not Iscariot) says to Him, "Lord, then what has occurred, that You are about to manifest Yourself to us, and not to the world?"

²³Jesus answered and said to him, "If anyone loves Me, he will keep My word, and My Father will love him, and we will come to him and will make a home with him. ²⁴The *one* not loving Me does not keep My words. And the word that you hear is not Mine, but *that* of the Father having sent Me.

²⁵These things I have said to you *while* abiding with you. ²⁶But the Helper, the Holy Spirit, whom the Father will send in My name, He will teach you all things and will bring to your remembrance all things that I have said to you.

Peace I Leave with You
(Romans 5:1-5)

²⁷Peace I leave with you; My peace I give to you. Not as the world gives do I give to you. Let not your heart be troubled, nor let it fear. ²⁸You heard that I said to you, 'I am going away and I am coming to you.' If you loved Me, you would have rejoiced that I am going to the Father, because the Father is greater than I. ²⁹And now I have told you before it comes to pass, that when it shall have come to pass, you might believe.

³⁰No longer will I speak much with you; for the ruler of this world comes, and in Me he has nothing. ³¹But that the world may know that I love the Father, and as the Father has commanded Me, thus I do. Rise up, let us go from here.

a 1 Or *Believe in God*
b 4 BYZ and TR *And where I go you know, and the way you know.*
c 14 TR does not include *Me*
d 17 WH *He is in you*

John 15
Jesus the True Vine

¹I am the true vine and My Father is the vinedresser. ²Every branch not bearing fruit in Me, He takes it away; and every one bearing fruit, He prunes it that it may bear more fruit. ³Already you are clean by reason of the word that I have spoken to you. ⁴Abide in Me, and I in you. As the branch is not able to bear fruit of itself unless it abides in the vine, so neither you, unless you abide in Me.

⁵I am the vine; you *are* the branches. The *one* abiding in Me and I in him, he bears much fruit. For apart from Me you are able to do nothing. ⁶If anyone does not abide in Me, he is thrown out like the branch and is dried up, and they gather them and cast *them* into the fire, and it is burned. ⁷If you abide in Me and My words abide in you, you shall ask whatever you wish, and to you it will come to pass. ⁸In this My Father is glorified, that you should bear much fruit, and you shall be My disciples.

No Greater Love

⁹As the Father has loved Me, I also have loved you. Abide in My Love. ¹⁰If you keep My commandments, you will abide in My love, as I have kept My Father's commandments and abide in His love. ¹¹These things I have spoken to you, that My joy may be in you and your joy may be full.

¹²This is My commandment, that you love one another as I loved you. ¹³Greater love has no one than this, that one should lay down his life for his friends. ¹⁴You are My friends, if you do what I command you. ¹⁵No longer do I call you servants, for the servant does not know

what his master is doing. But I have called you friends, because all things that I heard from My Father, I have made known to you. ⁱ⁶You did not chose Me, but I chose you and appointed you, that you should go and you should bear fruit, and your fruit should remain, so that whatever you might ask the Father in My name, He may give you. ¹⁷These things I command you, that you love one another.

The Hatred of the World

¹⁸If the world hates you, you know that it has hated Me before you. ¹⁹If you were of the world, the world would love *you as* its own; but because you are not of the world but I chose you out of the world, on account of this, the world hates you. ²⁰Remember the word that I said to you: 'A servant is not greater than his master.' If they persecuted Me, they will also persecute you; if they kept My word, they will keep yours also. ²¹But they will do all these things against you on account of My name, because they have not known the One having sent Me. ²²If I had not come and spoken to them, they would not have had sin; but now they have no excuse for their sin.
²³The *one* hating Me hates My Father also. ²⁴If I had not done among them the works that no other has done, they would not have had sin; but now they have both seen and hated both Me and My Father. ²⁵But *this is* that the word having been written in their Law may be fulfilled: 'They hated Me without cause.'ᵃ
²⁶When the Helper comes, whom I will send to you from the Father, the Spirit of truth who goes forth from the Father, He will bear witness concerning Me. ²⁷And you also bear witness, because you are with Me from *the* beginning.

a 25 **Psalms 35:19; 69:4**

John 16
Persecution Foretold
(Acts 23:12-22)

¹I have spoken these things to you that you might not fall away. ²They will put you out of the synagogues; but an hour is coming that everyone having killed you will think *it is* to offer a service to God. ³And they will do these things because they do not know the Father nor Me. ⁴But I have said these things to you, so that when their hour might have come, you may remember that I said them to you. Now I did not say these things to you from *the* beginning, because I was with you.

The Promise of the Holy Spirit
(Joel 2:28-32; John 14:15-26; Acts 2:1-13; Acts 10:44-48; Acts 19:1-7)

⁵But now I go to the *One* having sent Me, and none of you asks Me, 'Where are You going?' ⁶But because I have said these things to you, sorrow has filled your heart. ⁷But I tell you the truth, it is profitable for you that I should go away; for unless I go away the Helper will not come to you; but if I go, I will send Him to you.
⁸And having come, He will convict the world concerning sin, and concerning righteousness, and concerning judgment: ⁹concerning sin indeed, because they do not believe in Me; ¹⁰and concerning righteousness, because I go away to the Father and you behold Me no more; ¹¹and concerning judgment, because the ruler of this world has been judged.
¹²Yet I have many things to say to you, but you are not able to bear them now. ¹³But when He the, Spirit of truth, shall come, He will guide you into all the truth. For He will not speak from Himself, but whatever He may hear, He will speak. And He will declare to you the things coming. ¹⁴He will glorify Me, for He will take from that which *is* Mine and will disclose *it* to you. ¹⁵All things that the Father has are Mine. Because of this, I said that He will take from that which *is* Mine and will disclose *it* to you.
¹⁶A little *while* and you behold Me no longer; and again a little *while* and you will see Me."ᵃ

Grief into Joy

¹⁷Therefore *some* of his disciples said to one another, "What is this that He says to us, 'A little *while* and you do not behold Me; and again a little *while* and you will see Me' and 'Because I am going to the Father'?" ¹⁸Therefore they were saying, "What is this that He says, 'a little *while*'? We do not know what He is saying."

¹⁹Jesus knew that they were desiring to ask Him, and He said to them, "Do you inquire among one another concerning this, that I said, 'A little *while* and you do not behold Me, and again a little *while* and you will see Me'? ²⁰Truly, truly, I say to you, that you will weep and will lament, but the world will rejoice. You will be grieved, but your grief will turn to joy. ²¹The woman has pain when she is giving birth, because her hour has come; but when she brings forth the child, she remembers the tribulation no longer, on account of the joy that a man has been born into the world. ²²Therefore you also indeed have grief now; but I will see you again, and your heart will rejoice, and no one will take your joy from you.

Ask and You will Receive

²³And in that day, you will ask of Me nothing. Truly, truly, I say to you, whatever you may ask the Father in My name, He will give you. ²⁴Until now you have asked nothing in My name. Ask and you will receive, that your joy may be full. ²⁵I have spoken these things to you in allegories; an hour is coming when I will speak to you no more in allegories, but I will report to you plainly concerning the Father. ²⁶In that day you will ask in My name, and I do not say to you that I will implore the Father for you. ²⁷For the Father Himself loves you, because you have loved Me and have believed that I came forth from God.ᵇ ²⁸I came forth from the Father and have come into the world; again I leave the world and go to the Father."

²⁹His disciples say, "Behold, now You speak in openness, and You do not speak allegory. ³⁰Now we know that You know all things, and have no need that anyone should ask You. In this we believe that You came forth from God."

³¹Jesus answered them, "Now do you believe? ³²Behold, an hour is coming and has come, when you will be scattered, each to the own, and I, you shall leave alone; yet I am not alone, for the Father is with Me. ³³I have spoken these things to you so that in Me you may have peace. In the world you have tribulation. But take courage; I have overcome the world."

a 16 BYZ and TR include *because I go away to the Father*
b 27 WH *from the Father*

John 17
Prayer for the Son

¹Jesus spoke these things, and having lifted up His eyes to heaven, He said, "Father, the hour has come; glorify Your Son, that the Son may glorify You. ²As You gave Him authority over all flesh, so that all whom You have given Him, He may give to them eternal life. ³Now this is eternal life, that they may know You, the only true God, and Jesus Christ, whom You have sent. ⁴I glorified You on the earth, having completed the work that You have given Me that I should do. ⁵And now glorify Me, You Father, with Yourself, with the glory that I had with You before the world existed.

Prayer for the Disciples

⁶I revealed Your name to the men whom You have given Me out of the world. They were Yours, and to Me You gave them, and they have kept Your word. ⁷Now they have known that all things You have given Me are of You. ⁸For the words that You have given Me I have given them, and they received *them*, and knew truly that I came forth from You; and they believed that You sent Me.

⁹I am praying concerning them. I do not pray concerning the world, but concerning those whom You have given Me, for they are Yours. ¹⁰And all things of

mine are Yours, and Yours Mine. And I have been glorified in them. ¹¹And I am no longer in the world, and yet they are themselves in the world, and I am coming to You.
Holy Father, keep them in Your name, which You have given Me, that they may be one as we *are*. ¹²When I was with them, I was keeping them in Your name, which You have given Me. And I guarded *them*, and none of them has perished, except the son of destruction, that the Scripture might be fulfilled.
¹³But now I am coming to You, and I speak these things in the world, so that they may have My joy fulfilled within them. ¹⁴I have given them Your word, and the world hated them, because they are not of the world, even as I am not of the world.
¹⁵I do not ask that You should take them out of the world, but that You should keep them from evil.ᵃ ¹⁶They are not of the world, as I am not of the world. ¹⁷Sanctify them by the truth; Your word is truth. ¹⁸As You sent Me into the world, I also sent them into the world; ¹⁹and for them I sanctify Myself, that they also may be sanctified in truth.

Prayer for all Believers

²⁰But I do not ask for these only, but also for those believing in Me through their word, ²¹that all may be one, as You, Father, *are* in Me, and I in You, that they also may be in Us, that the world may believe that You sent Me.
²²And I have given them the glory which You have given Me, so that they may be one, as We *are* one— ²³I in them, and You in Me—that they may be perfected in unity, so that the world may know that You sent Me and loved them even as You loved Me.
²⁴Father, *those* whom You have given Me, I desire that they also may be with Me where I am, that they may behold My glory that You gave Me because You loved Me before *the* foundation of *the* world.

²⁵Righteous Father, although the world has not known You, yet I have known You, and these have known that You sent Me. ²⁶And I made known to them Your name, and will make *it* known, so that the love with which You loved Me may be in them, and I in them."

a 15 Or *from the evil one*

John 18
The Betrayal of Jesus
(Matthew 26:47-56; Mark 14:43-52; Luke 22:47-53)

¹Having said these things, Jesus went out with His disciples beyond the winter stream of Kidron, where there was a garden, into which He and His disciples entered. ²Now Judas, who was delivering Him up, also knew the place, because Jesus often gathered together there with His disciples. ³Therefore Judas, having procured the cohort and officers from the chief priests and from the Pharisees, comes there with lanterns and torches and weapons.
⁴Therefore Jesus, knowing all things that are coming upon Him, having gone forth, also said to them, "Whom do you seek?" ⁵They answered Him, "Jesus of Nazareth."
He says to them, "I am *He*."
Now Judas, who is delivering Him up, also had been standing with them. ⁶Therefore when He said to them, "I am *He*," they drew toward the back and fell to *the* ground.
⁷Therefore He questioned them again, "Whom do you seek?"
And they said, "Jesus of Nazareth."
⁸Jesus answered, "I have told you that I am *He*. Therefore if you seek Me, allow these to go away," ⁹so that the word that He had spoken might be fulfilled, "Those whom You have given Me, I have lost none of them, not one."
¹⁰Then Simon Peter, having a sword, drew it and struck the servant of the high priest and cut off his right ear. Now the servant's name was Malchus. ¹¹Therefore

Jesus said to Peter, "Put the sword into the sheath. The cup which the Father has given Me, shall I not drink it?"
¹²Then the cohort and the commander and the officers of the Jews took hold of Jesus and bound Him. ¹³And they led *Him* away to Annas first; for he was father-in-law of Caiaphas, who was high priest the same year. ¹⁴Now Caiaphas was the *one* having given counsel to the Jews that it is profitable for one man to perish for the people.

Peter's First Denial
(Matthew 26:69-71; Mark 14:66-67; Luke 22:54-57)

¹⁵And Simon Peter and the other disciple were following Jesus. Now since that disciple was known to the high priest, he also entered with Jesus into the court of the high priest. ¹⁶But Peter stood at the door outside. Therefore the other disciple, who was known to the high priest, went out and spoke to the doorkeeper and brought in Peter.
¹⁷Therefore the servant girl, the doorkeeper, says to Peter, "Are you not also of the disciples of this man?"
He says, "I am not."
¹⁸Now the servants and the officers were standing, having made a fire of coals, for it was cold and they were warming themselves. And Peter was also standing with them and warming himself.

Jesus Before the High Priest
(Isaiah 53:1-8; Matthew 26:57-68; Mark 14:53-65; 1 Peter 2:21-25)

¹⁹Then the high priest questioned Jesus concerning His disciples and concerning His teaching.
²⁰Jesus answered him, "I have spoken openly to the world. I always taught in *the* synagogue and in the temple, where the Jews always come together; and I spoke nothing in secret. ²¹Why do you question Me? Question those having heard what I spoke to them. Behold, they know what I said."
²²Now of His having said these things, one of the officers standing by gave a blow with the palm to Jesus, having said, "Do You answer the high priest this way?"
²³Jesus answered him, "If I spoke evil, bear witness concerning the evil; but if rightly, why do you strike Me?"
²⁴Then Annas sent Him bound to Caiaphas the high priest.

Peter's Second and Third Denials
(Matthew 26:71-75; Mark 14:68-72; Luke 22:58-62)

²⁵Now Simon Peter was standing and warming himself. Therefore they said to him, "Are you not also *one* of His disciples?"
He denied *it* and said, "I am not."
²⁶One of the servants of the high priest, being kinsman *of him* whose ear Peter had cut off, says, "Did I not see you in the garden with Him?"
²⁷Then Peter denied *it* again, and immediately a rooster crowed.

Jesus Before Pilate
(Matthew 27:11-14; Luke 23:1-6)

²⁸Then they are leading Jesus from Caiaphas into the Praetorium. Now it was early, and they did not enter into the Praetorium, so that they should not be defiled, but might eat the Passover.
²⁹Therefore Pilate went out to them and said, "What accusation do you bring against this man?"
³⁰They answered and said to him, "If He were not doing evil, we would not have delivered Him to you."
³¹Therefore Pilate said to them, "Take Him yourselves and judge Him according to your Law."
The Jews said to him, "It is not permitted to us to put anyone to death"— ³²that word of Jesus might be fulfilled, which He had spoken signifying what death He was about to die.
³³Therefore Pilate entered again into the Praetorium, and he called Jesus and said to Him, "Are You the King of the Jews?"
³⁴Jesus answered, "Do you say this of yourself, or did others say *it* to you concerning Me?"

³⁵Pilate answered, "Am I a Jew? Your nation and the chief priests delivered You to me. What have You done?"
³⁶Jesus answered, "My kingdom is not of this world; if My kingdom were of this world, My attendants would fight that I might not be betrayed to the Jews. But now My kingdom is not from here."
³⁷Therefore Pilate said to Him, "Then You are a king?"
Jesus answered, "You say that I am a king. For this I have been born, and for this I have come into the world, that I may bear witness to the truth. Everyone being of the truth hears My voice."
³⁸Pilate says to Him, "What is truth?"
And having said this, he went out again to the Jews and says to them, "I find no guilt in Him. ³⁹But it is your custom that I should release to you one at the Passover; therefore do you wish I should release to you the King of the Jews?"
⁴⁰Then they cried out again saying, "Not this one, but Barabbas!" Now Barabbas was a robber.

John 19
The Soldiers Mock Jesus
(Isaiah 50:4-11; Matthew 27:27-31; Mark 15:16-20; Luke 22:63-65)

¹So at that time Pilate took Jesus and scourged *Him*. ²And the soldiers, having twisted together a crown of thorns, put *it* on His head and cast around Him a purple robe. ³And they began coming up to Him and saying, "Hail, King of the Jews!" And they kept giving Him blows with the palm.
⁴And Pilate went forth outside again and says to them, "Behold, I bring Him out to you so that you may know that I find no guilt in Him." ⁵Therefore Jesus went forth outside, wearing the thorny crown and the purple robe. And he says to them, "Behold the man!"
⁶Therefore when the chief priests and the officers saw Him, they cried out saying, "Crucify! Crucify!"
Pilate says to them, "Take Him yourselves and crucify *Him*, for I find no guilt in Him."
⁷The Jews answered him, "We have a law, and according to the law He ought to die, because He made Himself *the* Son of God."
⁸Therefore when Pilate heard this word, he was even more afraid. ⁹And he went into the Praetorium again, and he says to Jesus, "Where are You from?"
But Jesus did not give him an answer.
¹⁰Therefore Pilate says to Him, "Do You not speak to me? Do You not know that I have authority to release You, and I have authority to crucify You?"
¹¹Jesus answered him, "You would have no authority over Me, if it were not given to you from above. Because of this, the *one* having delivered Me up to you has greater sin."
¹²Out of this, Pilate was seeking to release Him; but the Jews cried out, saying, "If you release this *man*, you are not a friend of Caesar. Everyone making himself a king speaks against Caesar."
¹³Therefore Pilate, having heard these words, brought Jesus out and sat down upon *the* judgment seat at a place called *The* Stone Pavement, and in Hebrew, Gabbatha. ¹⁴Now it was the Day of Preparation of the Passover; it was about the sixth hour. And he says to the Jews, "Behold your king!"
¹⁵So they cried out, "Away with Him, away! Crucify Him!"
Pilate says to them, "Shall I crucify your King?"
The chief priests answered, "We have no king except Caesar."

The Crucifixion
(Psalms 22:1-31; 69:1-36; Matthew 27:32-44; Mark 15:21-32; Luke 23:26-43)

¹⁶So then, he delivered Him to them, that He might be crucified. Therefore they took Jesus.
¹⁷And bearing *His* own cross, He went out to the *place* called *the* Place of the Skull, which in Hebrew is called Golgotha, ¹⁸where they crucified Him, and with Him two others, on this side and on that side, and Jesus in between.

¹⁹And Pilate also wrote a title and put *it* on the cross. And it was written,
JESUS OF NAZARETH,
THE KING OF THE JEWS.
²⁰Therefore many of the Jews read this title, for the place where Jesus was crucified was near the city, and it was written in Hebrew, in Latin, *and* in Greek. ²¹Therefore the chief priests of the Jews were saying to Pilate, "Do not write, 'The King of the Jews,' but that He said, 'I am King of the Jews.'"
²²Pilate answered, "What I have written, I have written."
²³Then the soldiers, when they crucified Jesus, took His garments and made four parts, to each soldier a part, and also the tunic. Now the tunic was seamless, woven from the top all throughout. ²⁴Therefore they said to one another, "Let us not tear it up, but let us cast lots for it, whose it will be," that Scripture might be fulfilled that said:
"They divided My garments among them,
and for My clothing they cast a lot."ᵃ
So indeed the soldiers did these things.
²⁵Now His mother, and the sister of His mother, Mary the *wife* of Clopas, and Mary Magdalene, had been standing by the cross of Jesus. ²⁶Therefore Jesus, having seen *His* mother and the disciple whom He loved standing by, says to *His* mother, "Woman, behold, your son." ²⁷Then He says to the disciple, "Behold, your mother." And from that hour the disciple took her to the own.

The Death of Jesus
(Psalm 22:1-31; Matthew 27:45-56; Mark 15:33-41; Luke 23:44-49)

²⁸After this, Jesus, knowing that now all things had been accomplished, so that Scripture might be fulfilled, says, "I thirst." ²⁹A vessel full of sour wine had been set *there*. So having put on a stalk of hyssop a sponge filled with sour wine, they brought it to the mouth. ³⁰Therefore when Jesus took the sour wine, He said "It has been finished." And having bowed the head, He yielded up the spirit.

Jesus' Side is Pierced
(Zechariah 12:10-14)

³¹Therefore the Jews, because it was *the* Preparation, so that bodies would not remain on the cross on the Sabbath—for that Sabbath was a high day—asked Pilate that their legs might be broken and they might be taken away. ³²So the soldiers came, and indeed they broke the legs of the first, and of the other having been crucified with Him. ³³But having come to Jesus, when they saw Him already having been dead, they did not break His legs. ³⁴But one of the soldiers pierced His side with a spear, and blood and water came out immediately. ³⁵And the *one* having seen has borne witness, and his testimony is true. And He knows that he is speaking truth, so that you also might believe.
³⁶For these things took place so that the Scripture might be fulfilled: "Not one bone of Him will be broken."ᵇ ³⁷And again, another Scripture says: "They will look on the *One* they have pierced."ᶜ

The Burial of Jesus
(Isaiah 53:9-12; Matthew 27:57-61; Mark 15:42-47; Luke 23:50-56)

³⁸And after these things, Joseph from Arimathea, being a disciple of Jesus, but concealed through the fear of the Jews, asked Pilate that he might take away the body of Jesus; and Pilate gave permission. So he came and took away His body. ³⁹Now Nicodemus, the *one* having come to Him by night at the first, also came bearing a mixture of myrrh and aloes, about a hundred litras.ᵈ ⁴⁰So they took the body of Jesus and bound it in linen cloths, with the spices, as is *the* custom among the Jews to prepare for burial.
⁴¹Now there was a garden in the place where He was crucified, and in the garden a new tomb, in which no one had yet been laid. ⁴²So on account of the

Preparation of the Jews, because the tomb was near, they laid Jesus there.

a 24 Psalm 22:18
b 36 Exodus 12:46; Numbers 9:12; Psalm 34:20
c 37 Zechariah 12:10
d 39 About 75 pounds, or approximately 34 kilograms

John 20
The Resurrection
(Psalm 16:1-11; Psalm 49:1-20; Matthew 28:1-10; Mark 16:1-8; Luke 24:1-12)

[1] Now *on* the first *day* of the week, Mary Magdalene comes to the tomb early, it being still dark, and she sees the stone having been removed from the tomb. [2] So she runs and comes to Simon Peter and to the other disciple, whom Jesus loved, and she says to them, "They have taken away the Lord out of the tomb, and we do not know where they have laid Him." [3] Therefore Peter and the other disciple went forth and were coming to the tomb. [4] Now the two were running together, and the other disciple ran ahead faster than Peter and came to the tomb first. [5] And having stooped down, he sees the linen cloths lying *there*; but he did not enter. [6] Then Simon Peter also comes, following him, and he entered into the tomb and sees the linen cloths lying *there*, [7] and the soudarion that was upon His head, not lying with the linen cloths, but having been folded up in a place by itself. [8] So then the other disciple, the *one* having come to the tomb first, also entered; and he saw and believed. [9] For not yet did they understand the Scripture that it behooves Him to rise out from *the* dead.

Jesus Appears to Mary Magdalene
(Mark 16:9-11)

[10] Therefore the disciples went away again to their *homes*. [11] But Mary stood outside at the tomb weeping. Then as she was weeping, she stooped down into the tomb, [12] and she sees two angels in white sitting, one at the head and one at the feet, where the body of Jesus had lain. [13] And they say to her, "Woman, why do you weep?" She says to them, "Because they have taken away my Lord, and I do not know where they have laid Him." [14] Having said these things, she turned back around, and she sees Jesus standing *there*, and she had not known that it is Jesus. [15] Jesus says to her, "Woman, why do you weep? Whom do you seek?"

Thinking that it is the gardener, she says to Him, "Sir, if you have carried Him off, tell me where you have laid Him, and I will take Him away." [16] Jesus says to her, "Mary."

Having turned around, she says to Him in Hebrew, "Rabboni," that is to say, "Teacher."

[17] Jesus says to her, "Do not touch Me, for not yet have I ascended to the Father. Now go to My brothers and say to them, 'I am ascending to My Father and your Father, and *to* My God and your God.'"

[18] Mary Magdalene comes bringing word to the disciples, "I have seen the Lord," and *that* He had said these things to her.

Jesus Appears to the Disciples
(Luke 24:36-43; 1 John 1:1-4)

[19] Therefore it being evening the same day, the first of *the* week, and the doors where the disciples were having been shut through the fear of the Jews, Jesus came and stood in the midst, and He says to them, "Peace to you." [20] And having said this, He showed them both His hands and His side.

Then the disciples rejoiced, having seen the Lord. [21] Therefore Jesus said to them again, "Peace to you. As the Father has sent Me forth, I also send you." [22] And having said this, He breathed on *them* and He says to them, "Receive *the* Holy Spirit. [23] If you might forgive the sins of any, they are forgiven them; if you might retain any, they are retained."

Jesus Appears to Thomas

[24] But Thomas, one of the Twelve, the *one* called Didymus, was not with them when Jesus came. [25] So the other

disciples were saying to him, "We have seen the Lord."
But he said to them, "Unless I see in His hands the mark of the nails, and put my finger into the mark of the nails, and put my hands into His side, I will never believe."
²⁶And after eight days His disciples were again inside, and Thomas with them, the doors having been shut. Jesus comes, and He stood in the midst and said, "Peace to you." ²⁷Then He says to Thomas, "Bring your finger here, and see My hands; and bring your hand, and put *it* into My side; and be not unbelieving, but believing."
²⁸Thomas answered and said to Him, "My Lord and my God!"
²⁹Jesus says to him, "Because you have seen Me, you have believed; blessed *are* those not having seen, yet having believed."

The Purpose of John's Book
³⁰So indeed Jesus also did many other signs in the presence of His disciples, which are not written in this book. ³¹But these have been written that you may believe that Jesus is the Christ, the Son of God, and that believing, you may have life in His name.

John 21
Jesus Appears at the Sea of Galilee
¹After these things, Jesus revealed Himself again to the disciples at the sea of Tiberias. Now He revealed *Himself* in this way: ²Simon Peter, and Thomas called Didymus, and Nathanael from Cana of Galilee, and the *sons* of Zebedee, and two others of His disciples were together. ³Simon Peter says to them, "I am going to fish."
They say to him, "We also are coming with you." They went forth and went up into the boat, and during that night they caught nothing.
⁴Now morning already having come, Jesus stood on the shore, but the disciples did not know that it is Jesus.

⁵Therefore Jesus says to them, "Children do you have any food?"
They answered Him, "No."
⁶And He said to them, "Cast the net to the right side of the boat, and you will find some." So they cast, and they were not able to haul it in from the multitude of the fish.
⁷Therefore that disciple whom Jesus loved says to Peter, "It is the Lord." So Simon Peter, having heard that it is the Lord, put on the outer garment, (for he was naked), and he cast himself into the sea. ⁸Now the other disciples came in the boat, dragging the net with the fish, for they were not far from the land, but about two hundred cubits away.ᵃ
⁹So when they got out onto the land, they see a fire of coals lying, and a fish lying on *it*, and bread.
¹⁰Jesus says to them, "Bring *some* of the fish that you have now caught."
¹¹Therefore Simon Peter went up and drew the net to the land, full of large fish, a hundred fifty-three. Although there are so many, the net was not torn.
¹²Jesus says to them, "Come, have breakfast." But none of the disciples dared to ask Him, "Who are You?" knowing that it is the Lord. ¹³Jesus comes and takes the bread and gives *it* to them, and the fish likewise.
¹⁴This *is* now the third time Jesus was revealed the disciples, having been raised out from *the* dead.

Jesus Reinstates Peter
¹⁵Therefore when they had dined, Jesus says to Simon Peter, "Simon *son* of John, do you love Me more than these?"
He says to Him, "Yes, Lord; You know that I dearly love You."
He says to him, "Feed My lambs."
¹⁶He says to him again a second time, "Simon *son* of John, do you love Me?"
He says to Him, "Yes, Lord; You know that I dearly love You."
He says to him, "Shepherd My sheep."
¹⁷He says to him the third time, "Simon *son* of John, do you dearly love Me?"

Peter was grieved because He said to him the third time, "Do you dearly love Me?" And he said to Him, "Lord, You know all things; You know that I dearly love You." Jesus says to him, "Feed My sheep. ¹⁸Truly, truly, I say to you, when you were younger, you dressed yourself and walked where you desired; but when you shall be old, you will stretch forth your hands, and another will dress you and will bring *you* where you do not desire." ¹⁹Now He said this signifying by what death he will glorify God.
And having said this, He says to him, "Follow Me."

Jesus and the Beloved Apostle

²⁰Having turned, Peter sees the disciple whom Jesus loved following, *the one* who also had reclined on His bosom at the supper and said, "Lord, who is it who is betraying You?" ²¹Therefore having seen him, Peter says to Jesus, "Lord, and what about this man?"
²²Jesus says to him, "If I desire him to remain until I come, what *is it* to you? You follow Me!" ²³Therefore this saying went out among the brothers, that this disciple does not die. But Jesus had not said to him that he does not die, but, "If I desire him to remain until I come, what *is it* to you?"
²⁴This is the disciple bearing witness concerning these things, and the *one* having written these things. And we know that his testimony is true.
²⁵Now there are also many other things that Jesus did, which if every one should be written, I suppose not even the world itself to have space for the books to be written.

a 8 About 100 yards or 90 meters

Acts

Acts 1
Prologue
(Luke 1:1-4)

¹In the first account I composed, O Theophilus, concerning all the things that Jesus began both to do and to teach, ²until the day He was taken up, having given orders by *the* Holy Spirit to the apostles whom He had chosen, ³to whom He also presented Himself alive after His suffering with many proofs, being seen by them during forty days and speaking the things concerning the kingdom of God.
⁴And being assembled together,ᵃ He instructed them not to depart from Jerusalem, but to await the promise of the Father: "That which you heard of Me; ⁵for John baptized with water, but you will be baptized withᵇ *the* Holy Spirit not many days after these."

The Ascension
(Mark 16:19-20; Luke 24:50-53)

⁶So indeed those having come together were asking Him, saying, "Lord, at this time are you restoring the kingdom to Israel?"
⁷And He said to them, "It is not yours to know times or seasons that the Father put in place by His own authority. ⁸But you will receive power, the Holy Spirit having come upon you, and you will be witnesses for Me, both in Jerusalem and in all Judea and Samaria, and to *the* uttermost part of the earth."
⁹And having said these things, they beholding, He was lifted up, and a cloud hid Him from their eyes. ¹⁰And as they were looking intently into heaven as He was going, then behold, two men in white apparel stood by them, ¹¹who also said, "Men, Galileans, why do you stand looking into heaven? This Jesus, having been taken up from you into heaven, will thus come in that manner you beheld Him going into heaven."

Matthias Replaces Judas

¹²Then they returned to Jerusalem from *the* mount called Olivet, which is near Jerusalem, holding a Sabbath day's journey.*c* ¹³And when they had entered, they went up into the upper room, where they were staying, both Peter and John, and James and Andrew, Philip and Thomas, Bartholomew and Matthew, James *son* of Alphaeus and Simon the Zealot, and Judas *son* of James. ¹⁴All these were steadfastly continuing with one accord in prayer, with *the* women, and Mary the mother of Jesus, and with His brothers.

¹⁵And in these days, Peter having stood up in *the* midst of the brothers, and *the* number of names was about a hundred twenty together, the same said, ¹⁶"Men, brothers, it was necessary for the Scripture to have been fulfilled which the Holy Spirit spoke beforehand by *the* mouth of David concerning Judas, the *one* having become guide to those having arrested Jesus. ¹⁷For he was numbered with us, and was allotted a share of this ministry."

¹⁸(Then indeed this *man* acquired a field out of *the* reward of unrighteousness, and having fallen headlong, he burst open in *the* middle and all his intestines gushed out. ¹⁹And it became known to all those dwelling in Jerusalem, so that that field was called in their own language Akeldama, that is, Field of Blood.)

²⁰"For it has been written in *the* book of Psalms:

    'Let his homestead become desolate,
        and let there be not *one* dwelling in it,'*d*

and,

    'Let another take his position.'*e*

²¹Therefore it behooves the men having accompanied us during all *the* time that the Lord Jesus came in and went out among us, ²²having begun from the baptism of John until the day in which He was taken up from us, one of these, to become a witness with us of His resurrection."

²³And they put forward two, Joseph called Barsabbas, who was called Justus, and Matthias. ²⁴And having prayed, they said, "You Lord, knower of the hearts of all, show which one of these two You have chosen ²⁵to take the place of this ministry and apostleship, from which Judas turned aside to go to the own place." ²⁶And they gave lots for them, and the lot fell on Matthias, and he was numbered with the eleven apostles.

a 4 Or *eating together*
b 5 Or *in*
c 12 That is, approximately 5/8 mile or about 1 kilometer
d 20 Psalm 69:25
e 20 Psalm 109:8

Acts 2
The Holy Spirit at Pentecost

(Joel 2:28-32; John 14:15-26; John 16:5-16; Acts 10:44-48; Acts 19:1-7)

¹And during the arriving of the day of Pentecost, they were all together in one *place*. ²And suddenly a sound like a violent rushing wind came out of heaven, and it filled the whole house where they were sitting. ³And there appeared to them dividing tongues as of fire and sat upon each one of them. ⁴And they were all filled with *the* Holy Spirit and began to speak in other tongues as the Spirit was giving to them to utter forth.

⁵Now there were Jews dwelling in Jerusalem, devout men from every nation under heaven. ⁶Now of this sound having come about, the multitude came together and was confounded, because each one was hearing them speaking the own language.

⁷And they were amazed and were marveling, saying, "Behold, are not all these who are speaking Galileans? ⁸And how do we each hear our own language in which we were born? ⁹Parthians and Medes and Elamites; and those inhabiting Mesopotamia, also Judea and Cappadocia, Pontus and Asia,*a* ¹⁰both Phrygia and Pamphylia, Egypt and the parts of Libya around Cyrene; and those

visiting from Rome, ¹¹both Jews and converts; Cretans and Arabs—we hear them speaking *in* our own tongues the great things of God!"

¹²And all were amazed, and were perplexed, saying to one another, "What wishes this to be?"

¹³But others mocking were saying, "They are full of new wine."

Peter Preaches to the Crowd

¹⁴But Peter, having stood up with the eleven, lifted up his voice and spoke forth to them: "Men of Judea and all those inhabiting Jerusalem, let this be known to you, and give heed to my words. ¹⁵For these are not drunkards as you suppose, for it is *the* third hour of the day. ¹⁶But this is that having been spoken by the prophet Joel:

¹⁷'And it will be in the last days, God says,
> I will pour out of My Spirit upon all flesh,
and your sons and your daughters will prophesy,
> and your young men will see visions,
> and your elders will dream dreams.

¹⁸And even upon My servants, and upon My handmaidens,
> I will pour out of My Spirit in those days,
and they will prophesy.

¹⁹And I will show wonders in the heaven above,
> and signs on the earth below,
> blood and fire and vapor of smoke.

²⁰The sun will be turned into darkness,
> and the moon into blood,
> before the great and glorious day of *the* Lord coming.

²¹And it shall be *that* everyone who shall call upon the name of *the* Lord will be saved.'ᵇ

²²Men of Israel, hear these words: Jesus of Nazareth, a man having been set forth by God to you by miracles and wonders and signs, which God did by Him in your the midst, as you yourselves know, ²³Him delivered up by the determinate plan and foreknowledge of God, you put to death, having crucified *Him* by lawless hands, ²⁴whom God raised up, having loosed the agony of death, inasmuch as it was not possible *for* Him to be held by it.

²⁵For David says about Him:
> 'I foresaw the Lord before me continually;
>> because He is at my right hand, I should not be shaken.

²⁶Because of this my heart was glad, and my tongue rejoiced,
>> and now also my flesh will dwell in hope,

²⁷for You will not abandon my soul into Hades,
>> nor will You allow Your Holy One to see decay.

²⁸You have made known to me *the* paths of life,
>> You will fill me with joy in Your presence.'ᶜ

²⁹Men, brothers, it is permitted *me* to speak with freedom to you concerning the patriarch David, that both he died and was buried, and his tomb is among us unto this day, ³⁰being therefore a prophet and knowing that God swore to him with an oath to set out of *the* fruit of his loins upon his throne. ³¹Having foreseen, he spoke concerning the resurrection of the Christ, that neither was He abandoned into Hades, nor did His flesh see decay. ³²This Jesus God has raised up, to which we all are witnesses. ³³Therefore having been exalted at the right hand of God, and having received the promise of the Holy Spirit from the Father, He has poured out this which you are both seeing and hearing.

³⁴For David did not ascend into the heavens, but he himself says:
> 'The Lord said to my Lord,
>> "Sit at My right hand,

35until I place Your enemies
 as a footstool of Your feet.'"ᵈ
36Therefore let all *the* house of Israel know assuredly that God has made Him both Lord and Christ—this Jesus whom you crucified."

Three Thousand Believe

37And having heard, they were pierced to the heart and said to Peter and the other apostles, "Men, brothers, what shall we do?"
38And Peter says to them, "Repent and be baptized, every one of you, in the name of Jesus Christ for the forgiveness of your sins, and you will receive the gift of the Holy Spirit. 39For the promise is to you and to your children and to all those at a distance, as many as *the* Lord our God shall call to Himself."
40And he earnestly testified many other words and was exhorting them, saying, "Be saved from this perverse generation."
41Therefore those indeed having received his word were baptized, and on that day about three thousand souls were added.

The Fellowship of Believers
(Acts 4:32-37)

42Now they were steadfastly continuing in the teaching of the apostles, and in the fellowship, in the breaking of the bread, and in the prayers. 43And aweᵉ was coming upon every soul, and both many wonders and signs were taking place through the apostles.
44And all those having believed were together the same, and having all things in common. 45And they were selling the possessions and the goods, and were dividing them to all, as anyone had need. 46And every day they were steadfastly continuing with one accord in the temple and breaking bread at each house. They were partaking of food with gladness and sincerity of heart, 47praising God, and having favor with all the people. And the Lord kept adding every day to their number those who were being saved.

a 9 That is, the Roman Province of Asia
b 17-21 Joel 2:28-32
c 25-28 Psalm 16:8-11
d 34-35 Psalm 110:1
e 43 Or *fear*

Acts 3
A Lame Man Walks

1Now Peter and John were going up into the temple at the hour of prayer, the ninth. 2And a certain man was being carried, being lame from his mother's womb, whom they placed every day at the temple gate called Beautiful to ask for alms from those going into the temple, 3who having seen Peter and John being about to enter into the temple, was asking to receive alms.
4Now Peter having looked intently upon him, with John, said, "Look unto us." 5And he began to give heed to them, expecting to receive something from them. 6But Peter said, "Silver and gold, to me there is none; but what I have, this I give to you: In the name of Jesus Christ of Nazareth, rise up and walk!"ᵃ
7And having taken him by the right hand, he raised him up, and immediately his feet and ankles were strengthened. 8And leaping up, he stood and began walking, and he entered into the temple with them, walking and leaping and praising God.
9And all the people saw him walking and praising God, 10and they recognized him, that he was the *one* sitting for alms at the Beautiful Gate of the temple. And they were filled with wonder and amazement at that having happened to him.

Peter Speaks in Solomon's Colonnade

11Now as he is clinging to Peter and John, all the people ran together to them in the porch called Solomon's, greatly amazed. 12But having seen *it*, Peter answered to the people: "Men of Israel, why do you wonder at this? Or why do you look intently on us as if by *our* own power or godliness *we* have made him to walk? 13The God of Abraham, and the God of Isaac, and the God Jacob, the God of our fathers, has glorified His servantᵇ Jesus, whom indeed you betrayed and disowned in *the* presence of Pilate, that one having adjudged to release *Him*. ¹⁴But you denied the Holy and Righteous One and requested a murderer to be granted to you. ¹⁵And you killed the Author of life, whom God has raised up out from *the* dead, whereof we are witnesses.

¹⁶And on the faith in His name, this *man* whom you see and know, His name has strengthened; and the faith which *is* through Him has given to him this complete soundness before all of you.

¹⁷And now, brothers, I know that you acted in ignorance, as *did* your rulers also. ¹⁸But what God foretold by *the* mouth of all the prophets, *that* His Christ should suffer, He has thus fulfilled. ¹⁹Repent, therefore, and turn again, for the blotting out of your sins, ²⁰so that times of refreshing may come from *the* presence of the Lord, and *that* He may send the *One* having been appointed to you, Christ Jesus, ²¹whom indeed it behooves heaven to receive until *the* times of restoration of all things, of which God spoke by *the* mouth of His holy prophets from *the* age.

²²For Moses said, 'The Lord your God will raise up to you a prophet like me out from your brothers. You will listen to Him in all things, as many as He might say to you. ²³And it will be *that* every soul who might not heed that prophet will be utterly destroyed out from the people.'ᶜ

²⁴And also all the prophets from Samuel, and those subsequently, as many as have spoken, also have proclaimed these days. ²⁵You are the sons of the prophets and of the covenant that God made with your fathers, saying to Abraham, 'And in your seed all the families of the earth will be blessed.'ᵈ ²⁶God, having raised up His servant, sent Him first to you, blessing you in turning away each *of you* from your wickednesses."

a 6 SBL, NE, and WH *In the name of Jesus Christ of Nazareth, walk*
b 13 Or *child*; also in verse 26

c 23 Deuteronomy 18:15,18,19
d 25 Genesis 22:18

Acts 4
Peter and John Before the Council

¹And of them speaking to the people, the priests and the captain of the temple and the Sadducees came upon them, ²being distressed because of their teaching the people and proclaiming in Jesus the resurrection out from *the* dead. ³And they laid hands on them and put *them* in custody until the next day; for it was already evening. ⁴But many of those having heard the word believed, and the number of the men became about five thousand.

⁵And it came to pass on the next day, their rulers and elders and scribes were gathered together in Jerusalem, ⁶and Annas the high priest, and Caiaphas, and John, and Alexander, and as many as were of high-priestly descent. ⁷And having placed them in the midst, they began to inquire, "In what power or in what name have you done this?"

⁸Then Peter, having been filled with *the* Holy Spirit, said to them, "Rulers of the people and elders, ⁹if we are being examined this day as to a good work *to the* ailing man, by what *means* he has been healed, ¹⁰let it be known to all of you, and to all the people of Israel, that in the name of Jesus Christ of Nazareth— whom you crucified, whom God raised out from *the* dead—in Him this *man* stands before you sound. ¹¹This is

'the stone having been rejected by you, the builders,
which has become *the* head of *the* corner.'ᵃ

¹²And there is salvation in no other, for there is not another name under heaven having been given among men, by which it behooves us to be saved."

The Name Forbidden

¹³Now seeing the boldness of Peter and of John, and having understood that they are unschooled and ordinary men, they

were astonished. And they recognized them, that they had been with Jesus. ¹⁴And beholding the man having been healed standing with them, they had nothing to contradict. ¹⁵But having commanded them to go outside the Council, they began to confer with one another, ¹⁶saying, "What shall we do to these men? For truly that a noteworthy sign has come to pass through them *is* evident to all those inhabiting Jerusalem, and we are not able to deny *it*. ¹⁷But that it might not spread further on among the people, let us warn them to speak no longer to *any* man in this name."
¹⁸And having called them, they commanded *them* not to speak nor to teach at all in the name of Jesus.
¹⁹But Peter and John answering, said to them, "Whether it is right before God to listen to you, rather than God, you must judge. ²⁰For we are not able to stop speaking about what we have seen and heard."
²¹And having further threatened *them*, they let them go, finding no way they might punish them, on account of the people, because all were glorifying God for that having happened. ²²For the man on whom this sign of healing had taken place was more than forty years *old*.

The Believers' Prayer
(Psalm 2:1-12)

²³Now having been let go, they came to the own and reported how much the chief priests and the elders had said to them. ²⁴And having heard, they lifted up *their* voice with one accord to God and said, "Sovereign Lord, You made the heaven and the earth and the sea and all that *is* in them, ²⁵having spoken by *the* Holy Spirit through *the* mouth of Your servant,[b] our father David:

'Why did the Gentiles rage,
   and *the* peoples devise vain things?
²⁶The kings of the earth took *their* stand,
and the rulers were gathered together
   against the Lord
   and against His Christ.'[c]

²⁷For in truth, both Herod and Pontius Pilate, with *the* Gentiles and *the* peoples of Israel, were gathered together in this city against Your holy servant Jesus whom You anointed, ²⁸to do whatever Your hand and Your purpose had determined beforehand to happen. ²⁹And now, Lord, look upon their threats, and grant to Your servants to speak Your word with all boldness, ³⁰in that You stretch out Your hand for healing and signs and wonders to take place through the name of Your holy servant Jesus."

³¹And they having prayed, the place in which they were assembled was shaken, and they were all filled with the Holy Spirit and were speaking the word of God with boldness.

Sharing among Believers
(Acts 2:42-47)

³²Now the multitude of those having believed were one *in* heart and soul, and not one claimed anything of that which he possesses to be his own, but all things were theirs in common. ³³And *with* great power, the apostles were giving testimony of the resurrection of the Lord Jesus, and abundant grace was upon them all.

³⁴For there was not even anyone in need among them, for as many as were owners of lands or houses, selling *them*, were bringing the proceeds of what is sold, ³⁵and were laying *them* at the feet of the apostles, and distribution was made to each as anyone had need.

³⁶Now Joseph having been called Barnabas by the apostles (which is translated, Son of encouragement), a Levite, a Cypriot at the birth, ³⁷having sold a field he owns, brought the money and laid *it* at the feet of the apostles.

a 11 Psalm 118:22
b 25 Or *child*; also verses 27 and 30
c 25-26 Psalm 2:1,2

Acts 5
Ananias and Sapphira

¹Now a certain man named Ananias, with his wife Sapphira, sold a property, ²and he kept back from the proceeds, also the wife being aware of *it*, and having brought a certain portion, he laid *it* at the feet of the apostles.

³But Peter said, "Ananias, because of why has Satan filled your heart *for* you to lie to the Holy Spirit and to keep back from the proceeds of the land? ⁴Remaining, did not it remain yours? And having been sold, was it *not* in the own authority? Why did you purpose this deed in your heart? You have not lied to men, but to God!"

⁵And hearing these words, Ananias, having fallen down, breathed his last. And great fear came upon all those hearing. ⁶And the younger *men* having arisen, covered him, and having carried *him* out, buried *him*.

⁷Now it came to pass about three hours afterward, his wife also came in, not knowing that having come to pass. ⁸And Peter replied to her, "Tell me if you sold the land for so much?"

And she said, "Yes, for so much."

⁹But Peter *said* to her, "Why *is it* that you have agreed together to test the Spirit of *the* Lord? Behold, the feet of those having buried your husband *are* at the door, and they will carry you out."

¹⁰And immediately she fell down at his feet and breathed her last. And the young *men* having come in, found her dead; and having carried *her* out, they buried *her* by her husband. ¹¹And great fear came upon the whole church and upon all those hearing these things.

The Apostles Heal Many

¹²Now many signs and wonders were happening among the people by the hands of the apostles. And they were all with one accord in Solomon's Colonnade. ¹³Now none of the rest dared to join them, but the people were magnifying them. ¹⁴And more believing in the Lord were added, multitudes both of men and women, ¹⁵so as even to bring out the sick into the streets, and to put *them* on cots and mats, that of Peter coming, at least the shadow might envelop some of them. ¹⁶Now the multitude from the cities surrounding Jerusalem also were coming together, bringing *the* sick and *those* being tormented by unclean spirits, who were all healed.

The Apostles Arrested and Freed

¹⁷But the high priest, having risen up, and all those with him (being *the* sect of the Sadducees) were filled with jealousy, ¹⁸and they laid hands on the apostles and put them in *the* public jail. ¹⁹But during the night an angel of *the* Lord, having opened the doors of the jail, having brought them out, also said, ²⁰"Go, and having stood in the temple, speak to the people all the words of this life."

²¹And having heard, they entered into the temple at the dawn and were teaching.

Now the high priest having come, and those with him, called together the Council, even the whole Senate of the sons of Israel, and sent to the prison house to bring them. ²²But the officers, having come, did not find them in the prison. And having returned, they reported back, ²³saying, "We found the prison house shut, with all security, and the guards standing before the doors; but having opened *them*, we found no one inside."

The Apostles Before the Council

²⁴Now when both the captain of the temple and the chief priests heard these words, they were perplexed concerning them, what this might be. ²⁵And a certain one having come, reported to them, "Behold, the men whom you put in the prison are standing in the temple and teaching the people!"

²⁶Then the captain, having gone with the officers, was bringing them, not with force, for they were afraid of the people lest they might be stoned. ²⁷And having brought them, they set *them* in the Council. And the high priest asked them,

²⁸saying, "By a charge we commanded you not to teach in this name, and behold, you have filled Jerusalem with your teaching, and you intend to bring upon us the blood of this man."
²⁹But Peter and the apostles answering said, "It is necessary to obey God rather than men. ³⁰The God of our fathers raised up Jesus, whom you killed, having hanged *Him* on a tree. ³¹God exalted Him to His right hand *as* Prince and Savior, to give repentance to Israel, and forgiveness of sins. ³²And we are witnesses of these things, and also the Holy Spirit, whom God has given to those obeying Him."

Gamaliel's Advice

³³And having heard, they were cut *to the heart* and were desiring to put them to death. ³⁴But a certain *man* having risen up in the Council, a Pharisee named Gamaliel, a teacher of the law honored by all the people, commanded *them* to put the men outside for a short while.
³⁵And he said to them, "Men of Israel, take heed to yourselves what you are about to do with these men. ³⁶For before these days, Theudas rose up, affirming himself to be somebody—to whom a number of men, about four hundred, were joined—who was put to death, and all, as many as were persuaded by him, were dispersed; and it came to nothing. ³⁷After this man, Judas the Galilean rose up in the days of the registration and drew away people after him. And he perished, and all, as many as were persuaded by him, were scattered.
³⁸And now I say to you, withdraw from these men and let them alone, for if this plan or this work is from men, it will be overthrown. ³⁹But if it is from God, you will not be able to overthrow it, lest ever also you would be found fighting against God."
⁴⁰And they were persuaded by him. And having called in the apostles, having beaten *them*, they commanded *them* not to speak in the name of Jesus, and they released *them*.
⁴¹Therefore indeed they departed from *the* presence of the Council, rejoicing that they had been counted worthy to suffer dishonor for the Name. ⁴²And every day, in the temple and in *every* house, they did not cease teaching and proclaiming the good news that Jesus *is* the Christ.

Acts 6
The Choosing of the Seven
(1 Timothy 3:8-13)

¹Now in these days *when* the disciples are multiplying, there arose a grumbling of the Hellenists against the Hebrews, because their widows were being overlooked in the daily distribution.
²So the Twelve, having called near the multitude of the disciples, said, "It is not desirable *for* us, having neglected the word of God, to attend tables. ³Therefore brothers, select out from yourselves seven men being well attested, full of *the* Spirit and wisdom, whom we will appoint over this task. ⁴And we will steadfastly continue in prayer and the ministry of the word."
⁵And the statement was pleasing before the whole multitude. And they chose Stephen, a man full of faith and *of the* Holy Spirit, and Philip, and Prochorus, and Nicanor, and Timon, and Parmenas, and Nicolas of Antioch, a convert, ⁶whom they set before the apostles. And having prayed, they laid the hands on them.
⁷And the word of God continued to increase, and the number of the disciples in Jerusalem was multiplied exceedingly, and a great multitude of the priests were becoming obedient to the faith.

The Arrest of Stephen

⁸Now Stephen, full grace and power, was performing great wonders and signs among the people. ⁹But certain of those from the synagogue called Freedmen, including Cyrenians and Alexandrians and of those from Cilicia and Asia, arose, disputing with Stephen. ¹⁰And they were

not able to withstand the wisdom and the Spirit by whom he was speaking. ¹¹Then they suborned men, saying, "We have heard him speaking blasphemous words against Moses and God." ¹²And they stirred up the people, and the elders, and the scribes; and having come upon *him*, they seized him and brought *him* to the Council.

¹³And they set false witnesses, saying, "This man does not stop speaking words against this holy place and the Law. ¹⁴For we have heard him saying that this Jesus of Nazareth will destroy this place and will change the customs that Moses delivered to us."

¹⁵And having looked intently on him, all sitting in the Council saw his face as *the* face of an angel.

Acts 7
Stephen's Address to the Sanhedrin

¹And the high priest said, "Are these things so?"

²And he began to speak: "Men, brothers, and fathers, listen! The God of glory appeared to our father Abraham, being in Mesopotamia, before his dwelling in Haran, ³and said to him, 'Go out from your country and from your kindred, and come into the land that I will show you.'[a] ⁴Then having gone out from *the* land of *the* Chaldeans, he dwelt in Haran. And from there, after his father died, He removed him into this land in which you now dwell.

⁵And He did not give to him an inheritance in it, not even *the* length of a foot; but He promised to give it to him for a possession, and his to descendants after him, there being to him no child. ⁶But God spoke thus, that his seed will be a sojourner in a strange land, and they will enslave it, and will mistreat *it* four hundred years. ⁷'And the nation to which they will be in bondage, I will judge,' God said, 'and after these things they will come forth and will serve Me in this place.'[b]

⁸And He gave to him *the* covenant of circumcision; and thus he begat Isaac and circumcised him on the eighth day, and Isaac Jacob, and Jacob the twelve patriarchs.

⁹And the patriarchs, having envied Joseph, sold *him* into Egypt. But God was with him ¹⁰and rescued him out of all his tribulations, and gave him favor and wisdom before Pharaoh king of Egypt, and he appointed him ruler over Egypt and over all his house.

¹¹And there came a famine upon all of Egypt and Canaan, and great affliction, and our fathers were not finding sustenance. ¹²Now Jacob, having heard *there* is grain in Egypt, sent forth our fathers first. ¹³And on the second time, Joseph was made known to his brothers, and the family of Joseph became known to Pharaoh. ¹⁴And Joseph, having sent, called for his father Jacob and all the kindred, seventy-five souls in all.

¹⁵And Jacob went down into Egypt and died, he and our fathers, ¹⁶and they were carried over into Shechem and placed in the tomb that Abraham had bought for a sum of silver from the sons of Hamor in Shechem.

¹⁷Now as the time of the promise that God had sworn to Abraham was drawing near, the people increased and multiplied in Egypt, ¹⁸until there arose another king over Egypt, who did not know Joseph. ¹⁹Having dealt treacherously with our race, he mistreated our fathers, making *them* abandon their infants so that they would not live.

²⁰In that time Moses was born, and he was beautiful to God,[c] who was brought up three months in *his* father's house. ²¹And he having been set outside, the daughter of Pharaoh took him up, and she brought him up as her own son. ²²And Moses was instructed in all *the* wisdom of *the* Egyptians, and he was mighty in his words and deeds.

²³Now when his period of forty years was fulfilled, it came into his mind to visit his

brothers, the sons of Israel. ²⁴And having seen a certain one being wronged, he defended *him* and did vengeance for the *one* being oppressed, having struck down the Egyptian. ²⁵And he was supposing his brothers to understand that God is giving them salvation by his hand, but they did not understand.

²⁶And on the following day, he appeared to those who were quarreling and urged them to peace, having said, 'Men, you are brothers. Why do you wrong one another?'

²⁷But the *one* mistreating the neighbor pushed him away, having said, 'Who appointed you ruler and judge over us? ²⁸Do you desire to kill me, the same way you killed the Egyptian yesterday?'ᵈ

²⁹Now at this remark, Moses fled, and became exiled in *the* land of Midian, where he begat two sons.

³⁰And forty years having been passed, an angel appeared to him in the wilderness of Mount Sinai, in a flame of fire of a bush. ³¹And Moses having seen *it*, marveled at the vision. And of him coming near to behold *it*, there was *the* voice of *the* Lord: ³²'I *am* the God of your Fathers, the God of Abraham, and of Isaac, and of Jacob.'ᵉ And Moses, having become terrified, did not dare to look.

³³And the Lord said to him, 'Take off the sandal of your feet, for the place on which you stand is holy ground. ³⁴Having seen, I saw the oppression of My people in Egypt, and I have heard their groans, and I have come down to deliver them. And now come, I will send you to Egypt.'ᶠ

³⁵This Moses whom they rejected, having said, 'Who appointed you ruler and judge?'—him whom God sent and *as* ruler and redeemer by *the* hand of *the* angel having appeared to him in the bush— ³⁶this one led them out, having done wonders and signs in *the* land of Egypt, and in *the* Red Sea, and in the wilderness forty years.

³⁷This is the Moses having said to the sons of Israel, 'God will raise up for you a prophet like me out from your brothers.'ᵍ

³⁸This is the *one* having been in the congregation in the wilderness with the angel speaking to him in Mount Sinai, and who *was with* our fathers. He received living oracles to give to us, ³⁹to whom our fathers were not willing to be obedient, but thrust away, and turned back in their hearts to Egypt, ⁴⁰having said to Aaron, 'Make us gods who will go before us. As for this Moses who brought us out from *the* land of Egypt, we do not know what has happened to him.'ʰ

⁴¹And in those days they made a calf and offered a sacrifice to the idol and were rejoicing in the works of their hands. ⁴²But God turned away and delivered them to worship the host of heaven, as it has been written in *the* book of the prophets:

'Did you offer slain beasts and sacrifices to Me
    forty years in the wilderness,
    O house of Israel?
⁴³And you took up the tabernacle of Moloch
    and the star of your god Rephan,
    the images that you made to worship them;
and I will remove you
    beyond Babylon.'ⁱ

⁴⁴The tabernacle of the testimony was with our fathers in the wilderness, just as the *One* speaking to Moses had commanded to make it according to the pattern that he had seen, ⁴⁵also which, having received by succession, our fathers brought in with Joshua in taking possession of the nations whom God drove out from *the* face of our fathers, until the days of David, ⁴⁶who found favor before God and asked to find a dwelling place for the God of Jacob.ʲ ⁴⁷But Solomon built Him *the* house.

⁴⁸Yet the Most High does not dwell in hand-made *houses*. As the prophet says:

⁴⁹'Heaven *is* My throne,

and the earth a footstool of My feet.

What kind of house will you build Me, says *the* Lord,

or what *is the* place of My rest? ⁵⁰Has not My hand made all these things?'ᵏ

⁵¹You stiff-necked and uncircumcised in heart and ears always resist the Holy Spirit; as your fathers *did*, also do you. ⁵²Which of the prophets did your fathers not persecute? And they killed those having foretold about the coming of the Righteous One, of whom you have now become betrayers and murderers, ⁵³*you* who received the Law by *the* ordination of angels, and have not kept *it*."

The Stoning of Stephen

⁵⁴Now hearing these things, they were cut to their hearts and began gnashing the teeth at him. ⁵⁵But he being full of *the* Holy Spirit, having looked intently into heaven, saw *the* glory of God and Jesus standing at the right hand of God, ⁵⁶and he said, "Behold, I see the heavens having been opened, and the Son of Man standing at the right *hand* of God."

⁵⁷And having cried out with a loud voice, they held their ears and rushed upon him with one accord, ⁵⁸and having cast *him* out of the city, began to stone *him*. And the witnesses laid aside their garments at the feet of a young man named Saul.

⁵⁹And *as* they were stoning Stephen, he was calling out and saying, "Lord Jesus, receive my spirit." ⁶⁰And having fallen on *his* knees, he cried in a loud voice, "Lord, do not place this sin to them." And having said this, he fell asleep.

a 3 Genesis 12:1
b 5-7 Genesis 15:13,14
c 20 Or *he was of great status in God's eyes*
d 28 Exodus 2:14
e 32 Exodus 3:6
f 31-34 Exodus 3:5-10
g 37 Deuteronomy 18:15
h 40 Exodus 32:1
i 42-43 Amos 5:25-27
j 46 NE, NA and Tischendorf *the house of Jacob*
k 49-50 Isaiah 66:1,2

Acts 8
Saul Persecutes the Church

¹And Saul was there consenting to his killing.

And on that day a great persecution arose against the church in Jerusalem, and all except the apostles were scattered throughout the regions of Judea and Samaria. ²Now devout men buried Stephen and made great lamentation over him. ³But Saul was destroying the church. Entering *houses* after houses and dragging off men and women, he was delivering *them* to prison.

Philip in Samaria

⁴Therefore indeed those having been scattered went about preaching the word. ⁵Now Philip, having gone down to a city of Samaria, was proclaiming the Christ to them. ⁶And the crowds with one accord were giving heed to the things being spoken by Philip in the *time* for them to hear and to see the signs that he was performing. ⁷For from many of those having unclean spirits, they were coming out, crying in a loud voice. And many having been paralyzed and lame were healed. ⁸So there was great joy in that city.

Simon the Sorcerer
(Deuteronomy 18:9-14)

⁹Now a certain man named Simon had formerly been practicing sorcery in the city and amazing the people of Samaria, declaring himself to be someone great, ¹⁰to whom all were giving heed, from small to great, saying, "This one is the power of God that *is* called Great." ¹¹Now they were giving heed to him because for a long time he had amazed them with the magic arts.

¹²But when they believed Philip, proclaiming the gospel concerning the kingdom of God and the name of Jesus Christ, they were baptized, both men and women. ¹³And Simon himself also believed, and having been baptized, was steadfastly continuing with Philip. And

beholding *the* signs and great miracles being performed, he was amazed. ¹⁴Now the apostles in Jerusalem, having heard that Samaria had received the word of God, sent to them Peter and John, ¹⁵who having come down, prayed for them that they might receive *the* Holy Spirit. ¹⁶For He was not yet fallen upon any of them, but they had only been baptized into the name of the Lord Jesus. ¹⁷Then they began laying the hands upon them, and they received *the* Holy Spirit. ¹⁸Now of Simon having seen that the Spirit was given through the laying on of the apostles' hands, he offered to them money, ¹⁹saying, "Give also to me this authority, that on whomever I may lay the hands, he may receive *the* Holy Spirit." ²⁰But Peter said to him, "Your silver, may it perish with you, because you thought the gift of God to be obtained by money! ²¹To you there is no part nor lot in this matter, for your heart is not right before God. ²²Repent, therefore, of this wickedness of yours, and pray earnestly to the Lord, if indeed the intent of your heart will be forgiven you. ²³For I see you being in *the* gall of bitterness and *the* bond of iniquity." ²⁴And Simon answering said, "You pray earnestly to the Lord on behalf of me, so that nothing of which you have spoken may come upon me." ²⁵Therefore they indeed, having earnestly testified and having spoken the word of the Lord, traveled back to Jerusalem, and they were preaching the gospel to many villages of the Samaritans.

Philip and the Ethiopian

²⁶Now an angel of *the* Lord spoke to Philip, saying, "Rise up and go toward *the* south, to the road going down from Jerusalem to Gaza." (This is *the* desert road.) ²⁷And having risen up, he went. And behold, an Ethiopian eunuch, a potentate of Candace queen of *the* Ethiopians, who was over all her treasure, who had come to Jerusalem to worship. ²⁸And he was returning and sitting in his chariot, and he was reading the prophet Isaiah. ²⁹And the Spirit said to Philip, "Go near and join yourself to this chariot." ³⁰And Philip having run up, heard him reading Isaiah the prophet and said, "Do you then understand what you are reading?" ³¹And he said, "How indeed could I be able, unless someone will guide me?" And he invited Philip, having come up, to sit with him. ³²Now the passage of Scripture that he was reading was this:

"He was led as a sheep to slaughter,
and as a lamb before the *one* shearing him *is* silent,
so He does not open His mouth.
³³In His humiliation, justice was taken away from Him.
Who will describe His generation?
For His life is removed from the earth."[a]

³⁴And the eunuch answering said to Philip, "I beseech you, concerning whom does the prophet say this? Concerning himself, or concerning some other?" ³⁵And Philip, having opened his mouth and having begun from this Scripture, proclaimed the good news to him—Jesus. ³⁶And as they were going along the road they came upon some water, and the eunuch says, "Behold, water! What prevents me to be baptized?"[b] ³⁸And he commanded the chariot to stop. And they both went down to the water, both Philip and the eunuch, and he baptized him. ³⁹Now when they came up out of the water, *the* Spirit of *the* Lord carried away Philip, and the eunuch saw him no longer. For he went his way rejoicing. ⁴⁰But Philip was found at Azotus, and passing through, he was proclaiming the gospel to all the towns until his coming to Caesarea.

a 32-33 Isaiah 53:7,8
b 36 TR includes *37 And Philip said, "If you believe with all your heart, you may be baptized." The eunuch replied, "I believe that Jesus Christ is the Son of God."*

Acts 9
The Road to Damascus
(Acts 22:1-21; Acts 26:1-23)

¹Meanwhile, Saul still breathing out threats and murder toward the disciples of the Lord, having gone to the high priest, ²requested letters from him to the synagogues in Damascus, so that if he found any being of the way, both men and women, having bound *them*, he might bring *them* to Jerusalem.

³Now in proceeding, it came to pass *as* he draws near to Damascus, suddenly also a light from heaven flashed around him. ⁴And having fallen on the ground, he heard a voice saying to him, "Saul, Saul, why do you persecute Me?"

⁵And he said, "Who are You, Lord?"
And *He said*, "I am Jesus, whom you are persecuting.ᵃ ⁶But rise up and enter into the city, and it will be told you that which it behooves you to do."

⁷And the men traveling with him stood speechless, hearing the voice indeed, but seeing no one. ⁸And Saul rose up from the ground, but of his eyes having been opened, he could see nothing. And leading him by the hand, they brought *him* to Damascus. ⁹And he was three days without seeing, and neither did he eat nor drink.

Ananias Baptizes Saul

¹⁰Now there was a certain disciple in Damascus named Ananias. And the Lord said to him in a vision, "Ananias!"
And he said, "Behold me, Lord."
¹¹And the Lord *said* to him, "Having risen up, go into the street called Straight, and seek in *the* house of Judas *the one* of Tarsus named Saul, for behold, he is praying, ¹²and he saw in a vision a man named Ananias, having come and having put the hands on him, so that he might see again."

¹³But Ananias answered, "Lord, I have heard from many concerning this man, how many evils he did to Your saints in Jerusalem. ¹⁴And here he has authority from the chief priests to bind all those calling on Your name."

¹⁵But the Lord said to him, "Go, for this *man* is My vessel of choice to carry My name before the Gentiles, and also kings, and *the* sons of Israel. ¹⁶For I will show to him how much it behooves him to suffer for My name."

¹⁷And Ananias went away and entered into the house; and having laid the hands upon him, he said, "Brother Saul, the Lord Jesus, the *One* having appeared to you on the road by which you were coming, has sent me that you may see again and be filled *of the* Holy Spirit."

¹⁸And immediately *something* like scales fell from his eyes, and he regained his sight. And having risen up, he was baptized, ¹⁹and having taken food, he was strengthened. And he was some days with the disciples in Damascus.

Saul Preaches at Damascus

²⁰And immediately he began proclaiming Jesus in the synagogues, that He is the Son of God.

²¹And all those hearing were amazed and were saying, "Is this not the *one* having ravaged those in Jerusalem calling on this name? And he had come here for this, that he might bring them, having been bound, to the chief priests."

²²But Saul was empowered all the more and kept confounding the Jews dwelling in Damascus, proving that this is the Christ.

The Escape from Damascus
(1 Samuel 19:11-24)

²³Now when many days had passed, the Jews plotted together to kill him, ²⁴but their plot became known to Saul. And now they were closely watching the gates day and also night, so that they might kill him. ²⁵But having taken *him* by night, his disciples let him down through the wall, having lowered *him* in a basket.

Saul in Jerusalem

²⁶And having arrived in Jerusalem, he was attempting to join the disciples, and all were afraid of him, not believing that he is a disciple. ²⁷But Barnabas having taken him, brought *him* to the apostles and related to them how he had seen the Lord on the road, and that He had spoken to him, and how in Damascus he had spoken boldly in the name of Jesus.

²⁸And he was coming in and going out with them in Jerusalem, speaking boldly in the name of Lord. ²⁹And he was speaking and was debating with the Hellenists. But they were seeking to kill him. ³⁰But the brothers having known *it*, brought him down to Caesarea and sent him away to Tarsus.

³¹Then indeed the churches throughout all of Judea and Galilee and Samaria had peace, being edified. And going on in the fear of the Lord and in the comfort of the Holy Spirit, they were multiplied.

The Healing of Aeneas

³²Now it came to pass that Peter, passing through all *quarters*, also went down to the saints inhabiting Lydda. ³³And he found there a certain man named Aeneas, who was paralyzed, lying on a bed for eight years. ³⁴And Peter said to him, "Aeneas, Jesus Christ heals you; rise up and make the bed for yourself." And immediately he rose up. ³⁵And all those inhabiting Lydda and Sharon saw him *and* turned to the Lord.

The Raising of Dorcas

³⁶Now in Joppa there was a certain disciple named Tabitha, which translated is called Dorcas. She was full of good works and of alms that she continually did. ³⁷But in those days it came to pass *that*, having become sick, she died. And having washed *her*, they put *her* in an upper room. ³⁸Now Lydda being near Joppa, the disciples having heard that Peter is in it, sent two men to him, imploring, "Do not to delay coming to us." ³⁹And Peter having risen up, went with them, who having arrived, brought *him* into the upper room. And all the widows stood by him, weeping and showing *the* tunics and garments that Dorcas had made, being with them.

⁴⁰And Peter having put all outside and having bowed the knees, prayed. And having turned to the body he said, "Tabitha, arise!" And she opened her eyes, and having seen Peter, she sat up. ⁴¹And having given her *his* hand, he raised her up. And having called the saints and the widows, he presented her living.

⁴²And it became known throughout all of Joppa, and many believed on the Lord. ⁴³And it came to pass, he stayed many days in Joppa with a certain Simon, a tanner.

a 5 TR includes *It is hard for you to kick against the goads.*

Acts 10
Cornelius Sends for Peter

¹Now a certain man in Caesarea named Cornelius *was* a centurion of *the* Cohort that is called Italian, ²devout and fearing God with all his household, doing many alms to the people and praying to God continually. ³About the ninth hour of the day, he saw clearly in a vision an angel of God having come to him and having said to him, "Cornelius!"

⁴And having looked intently on him, and having become afraid, he said, "What is it, Lord?"

And he said to him, "Your prayers and your alms have ascended as a memorial before God. ⁵And now send men to Joppa and summon a man *named* Simon who is called Peter. ⁶He lodges with a certain Simon, a tanner whose house is by *the* sea."ᵃ

⁷And when the angel speaking to him had departed, having called two of the servants and a devout soldier of those who are attending him, ⁸and having related all things to them, he sent them to Joppa.

Peter's Vision
(Leviticus 11:1-47; Deuteronomy 14:1-21)

⁹Now on the next day *as* these are journeying and are approaching the city, Peter went up on the housetop about the sixth hour to pray. ¹⁰And he became hungry and desired to eat, but *as* they were preparing, a trance fell upon him, ¹¹and he beholds heaven opening, and a certain vessel as a great sheet descending, being let down upon the earth by four corners, ¹²in which were all the quadrupeds and creeping things of the earth, and birds of heaven. ¹³And a voice came to him: "Having risen up, Peter, kill and eat!"

¹⁴But Peter said, "In no way, Lord! For never have I eaten anything common or unclean."

¹⁵And a voice *came* again to him for the second time: "What God has cleansed, you do not call common."

¹⁶Now this took place for three times, and immediately the vessel was taken up into heaven.

Peter Called to Caesarea

¹⁷And while Peter was perplexed in himself what the vision that he had seen might be, behold, the men having been sent from Cornelius, having inquired for the house of Simon, stood at the gate. ¹⁸And having called out, they were asking if Simon who *is* called Peter is lodged here.

¹⁹And of Peter thinking over the vision, the Spirit said to him, "Behold, three men are seeking you.[b] ²⁰But having risen, go down and proceed with them, doubting nothing, because I have sent them."

²¹And Peter, having gone down to the men,[c] said, "Behold, I am whom you seek; what *is* the cause for which you are here?"

²²And they said, "Cornelius a centurion, a righteous and God fearing man—and being well testified to by the whole nation of the Jews—was divinely instructed by a holy angel to send for you to his house and to hear a message from you."

²³Therefore having called them in, he lodged *them*. And on the next day having risen up, he went forth with them, and some of the brothers from Joppa went with him.

Peter Visits Cornelius

²⁴And on the next day, he entered into Caesarea. Now Cornelius was expecting them, having called together his relatives and close friends. ²⁵And as Peter was entering, Cornelius, having met him, having fallen at the feet, worshiped *him*. ²⁶But Peter lifted him up, saying, "Rise up, I myself am also a man."

²⁷And talking with him, he entered, and he finds many having gathered together. ²⁸And he was saying to them, "You know how unlawful it is for a Jew to unite himself or to come near to a foreigner. But God has shown me not to call *any* man common or unclean. ²⁹So also without objection I came, having been summoned. Therefore I inquire, for what reason did you summon me?"

³⁰And Cornelius was saying, "Four days ago, until this hour, the ninth hour, I was praying in my house; and behold, a man in bright apparel stood before me, ³¹and said, 'Cornelius, your prayer has been heard and your alms have been remembered before God. ³²Therefore send to Joppa and call for Simon, who is called Peter; He lodges in *the* house of Simon, a tanner by *the* sea.' ³³Therefore I sent to you at once, and you did well, having come. Now therefore, we are all present before God to hear all the things having been commanded you by the Lord."

Good News for Gentiles

³⁴And Peter, having opened the mouth, said, "Of a truth I understand that God is not One who shows partiality, ³⁵but in every nation, the *one* fearing Him and working righteousness is acceptable to Him, ³⁶the word that He sent to the sons of Israel, proclaiming the gospel, peace by Jesus Christ—He is Lord of all.

³⁷You yourselves know the declaration having come through all Judea, having begun from Galilee, after the baptism that John proclaimed: ³⁸Jesus from Nazareth, how God anointed Him with *the* Holy Spirit and with power, who went about doing good and healing all those being oppressed by the devil, because God was with Him.
³⁹And we *are* witnesses of all things that He did, both in the region of the Jews and in Jerusalem, whom they also put to death, having hanged *Him* on a tree. ⁴⁰This One God raised up on the third day, and gave Him to become manifest, ⁴¹not to all the people, but to *the* witnesses having been chosen beforehand by God, to us who did eat with and drink with Him after His rising out from *the* dead. ⁴²And He instructed us to proclaim to the people and to testify fully that He is the *One* having been appointed by God *as* judge of *the* living and *the* dead. ⁴³To Him all the prophets bear witness *that* everyone believing in Him receives forgiveness of sins through His name."

The Gentiles Receive the Holy Spirit
(Joel 2:28-32; John 14:15-26; John 16:5-16; Acts 2:1-13; Acts 19:1-7)

⁴⁴Of Peter still speaking these words, the Holy Spirit fell upon all those hearing the word. ⁴⁵And the believers from *the* circumcision, as many as had come with Peter, were amazed that the gift of the Holy Spirit has been poured out even upon the Gentiles. ⁴⁶For they were hearing them speaking in tongues and magnifying God.
Then Peter answered, ⁴⁷"Is anyone able to withhold the water to baptize these who have received the Holy Spirit, just as we also *have*?" ⁴⁸And he commanded them to be baptized in the name of Jesus Christ. Then they asked him to remain some days.

a 6 TR includes *He will tell you what you need to do*
b 19 NE and WH *Two men are looking for you*; SBL, BYZ and Tischendorf *There are men looking for you*
c 21 TR *the men sent to him by Cornelius*

Acts 11
Peter's Report at Jerusalem

¹Now the apostles and the brothers being in Judea heard that the Gentiles also had received the word of God. ²And when Peter went up to Jerusalem, those of *the* circumcision began contending with him, ³saying, "You went to men having uncircumcision, and ate with them."
⁴Now Peter having begun, set forth to them in order, saying, ⁵"I was in *the* city of Joppa praying, and in a trance I saw a vision, a certain vessel like a great sheet descending, being let down out of heaven by four corners, and it came down as far as me. ⁶Having looked intently on it, I was observing *it*, and I saw the quadrupeds of the earth and the wild beasts and the creeping things and the birds of the air. ⁷And also I heard a voice saying to me, 'Having risen up, Peter, kill and eat.'
⁸But I said, 'In no way, Lord. For nothing ever common or unclean has entered into my mouth.'
⁹But for a second *time* the voice answered out of heaven, 'What God has cleansed, you do not call unholy.'
¹⁰Now this happened on three times, and all was drawn up into heaven again.
¹¹And behold, immediately three men having been sent to me from Caesarea stood at the house in which I was. ¹²Now the Spirit told me to go with them, not having discriminated. Now these six brothers also went with me, and we entered into the man's house, ¹³and he related to us how he had seen the angel having stood in his house and having said, 'Send forth to Joppa, and send for Simon who is called Peter, ¹⁴who will speak words to you in which will be saved, you and all your household.'
¹⁵And in my beginning to speak, the Holy Spirit fell upon them, even as also upon us in *the* beginning. ¹⁶And I remembered the word of the Lord, how He had said, 'John indeed baptized with water,ᵃ but you will be baptized with *the* Holy Spirit.'

¹⁷If then God has given to them the same gift as also to us having believed on the Lord Jesus Christ, how was I able to forbid God?"

¹⁸And having heard these things, they were silent and glorified God, saying, "Then indeed God has given also to the Gentiles repentance unto life."

The Church at Antioch

¹⁹So indeed those having been scattered by the tribulation having taken place over Stephen passed through to Phoenicia and Cyprus and Antioch, speaking the word to no one except to Jews alone. ²⁰But some of them were men of Cyprus and Cyrene, who having come into Antioch, were speaking also to the Hellenists, proclaiming the gospel—the Lord Jesus. ²¹And *the* hand of *the* Lord was with them, and a great number, having believed, turned to the Lord.

²²Now the report concerning them was heard in the ears of the church being in Jerusalem, and they sent forth Barnabas to go as far as Antioch, ²³who having come and having seen the grace of God, rejoiced and was exhorting all to abide in the Lord with resolute purpose of heart. ²⁴For he was a good man, and full of *the* Holy Spirit and of faith. And a large crowd was added to the Lord.

²⁵And he went forth to Tarsus to seek Saul, ²⁶and having found *him*, he brought *him* to Antioch. Now it came to pass *that* they also gathered together an entire year in the church, and taught a large crowd. And in Antioch the disciples were first called Christians.

²⁷Now in these days, prophets came down from Jerusalem to Antioch. ²⁸And one of them named Agabus, having risen up, signified by the Spirit *that* a great famine is about to be over the whole world—which came to pass under Claudius. ²⁹And the disciples, as anyone was prospered, each of them determined to send for ministry to the brothers dwelling in Judea, ³⁰which also they did, having sent *it* to the elders by *the* hand of Barnabas and Saul.

a 16 Or *in water*

Acts 12
James Killed, Peter Imprisoned

¹Now at that time, Herod the king put forth the hands to mistreat some of those of the church. ²And he put to death James the brother of John with the sword. ³And having seen that it is pleasing to the Jews, he proceeded to take Peter also—now these were the days of the Unleavened *Bread*— ⁴whom also, having seized, he put in prison, having delivered *him* to four sets of four soldiers to guard him, intending to bring him out to the people after the Passover.

The Rescue of Peter

⁵So indeed Peter was kept in the prison, but fervent prayer was being made to God by the church concerning him.

⁶And when Herod was about to bring him forth, on that night Peter was sleeping between two soldiers, having been bound with two chains, and guards before the door were watching the prison. ⁷And behold, an angel of *the* Lord stood by, and a light shone in the cell. And having struck Peter's side, he woke him up, saying, "Rise up in haste." And his chains fell off the hands. ⁸And the angel said to him, "Gird yourself about, and put on your sandals." And He did so. And he says to him, "Wrap around *you* your cloak and follow me."

⁹And having gone forth, he was following, and he did not know that what is happening by means of the angel is real, but he was thinking he saw a vision. ¹⁰And having passed through a first and a second guard, they came to the iron gate leading into the city, which opened to them by itself. And having gone out, they went on through one street, and immediately the angel departed from him.

¹¹And having come to himself, Peter said, "Now I know truly that the Lord has sent

forth His angel and delivered me out of *the* hand of Herod and all the expectation of the people of the Jews."

¹²And having considered *it*, he came to the house of Mary the mother of John, who is called Mark, where there were many having gathered together and praying. ¹³And of him having knocked *at* the door of the gate, a girl named Rhoda came to answer. ¹⁴And having recognized Peter's voice, from joy she did not open the gate, but having run in, she reported Peter to be standing before the gate.

¹⁵But they said to her, "You are out of your mind." But she kept insisting *it* to be so. And they kept saying, "It is his angel." ¹⁶But Peter continued knocking. And having opened *it*, they saw him and were amazed. ¹⁷And having made a sign to them with the hand to be silent, he related to them how the Lord had brought him out of the prison. And he said, "Report these things to James and to the brothers." And having gone out, he went to another place.

¹⁸Now day having come, there was no small disturbance among the soldiers what then has become *of* Peter. ¹⁹And Herod having sought after him and not having found *him*, having examined the guards, commanded *them* to be led away *to death*. And having gone down from Judea to Caesarea, he stayed *there*.

The Death of Herod

²⁰Now he had been furiously angry with *the* Tyrians and Sidonians, and they came to him with one accord. And having gained Blastus, who *was* over the bedchamber of the king, they were seeking peace because of their region being nourished by the king's. ²¹Now on the appointed day Herod, having put on *the* royal apparel and having sat on the throne, was making an address to them. ²²And the people were crying out, "*This is the* voice of a god and not of a man!" ²³And immediately an angel of *the* Lord struck him in return for that he did not give the glory to God. And having been eaten by worms, he breathed his last. ²⁴But the word of God continued to grow and to multiply.

²⁵And Barnabas and Saul returned, having fulfilled the mission to Jerusalem,ᵃ having taken with *them* John the *one* having been called Mark.

a 25 NE and TR *had fulfilled their mission, they returned from Jerusalem,*

Acts 13
Paul's First Missionary Journey
(Acts 15:36-41; Acts 18:23-28)

¹Now there were prophets and teachers in Antioch in the church being *there*, both Barnabas and Simeon who was called Niger, and Lucius the Cyrenian, and Manaen brought up with Herod the tetrarch, and Saul. ²Now as they were ministering to the Lord and fasting, the Holy Spirit said, "Set apart then to Me Barnabas and Saul for the work to which I have called them." ³Then having fasted and having prayed and having laid the hands on them, they sent *them* off.

On Cyprus

⁴Therefore indeed having been sent forth by the Holy Spirit, they went down to Seleucia, and they sailed from there to Cyprus. ⁵And having come into Salamis, they began proclaiming the word of God in the synagogues of the Jews. And they also had John *as* a helper.

⁶Now having passed through the whole island as far as Paphos, they found a certain magician, a Jewish false prophet whose name *was* Bar-Jesus, ⁷who was with the proconsul Sergius Paulus, an intelligent man. He, having summoned Barnabas and Saul, desired to hear the word of God. ⁸But Elymas the magician (for his name means thus) was opposing them, seeking to turn away the proconsul from the faith.

⁹And Saul, the *one* also *called* Paul, having been filled *the* Holy Spirit, having looked intently upon him, ¹⁰said, "O full of all deceit and all craft, son of *the* devil, enemy of all righteousness, will you not

cease perverting the straight ways the of Lord? ¹¹And now behold, *the* hand of the Lord *is* upon you, and you will be blind, not seeing the sun during a season." And immediately mist and darkness fell upon him, and going about, he was seeking someone to lead *him* by the hand.

¹²Then the proconsul, having seen that having happened, believed, being astonished at the teaching of the Lord.

In Pisidian Antioch

¹³And those around Paul, having sailed from Paphos, came to Perga of Pamphylia. But John, having departed from them, returned to Jerusalem. ¹⁴Now having passed through from Perga, they came to Antioch of Pisidia, and having gone into the synagogue on the day of the Sabbaths, they sat down. ¹⁵And after the reading of the Law and of the Prophets, the rulers of the synagogue sent to them, saying, "Men, brothers, if there is any word of exhortation among you toward the people, speak."

¹⁶And Paul, having risen up and having made a sign with the hand, said, "Men *of* Israel and those fearing God, listen: ¹⁷The God of this people Israel chose our fathers and exalted the people in the sojourn in *the* land of Egypt, and with uplifted arm He brought them out of it, ¹⁸and for a period of about forty years He endured their ways in the wilderness, ¹⁹and having destroyed seven nations in *the* land of Canaan, He gave as an inheritance their land— ²⁰during four hundred and fifty years.

And after these things, He gave *them* judges until Samuel the prophet. ²¹Then they asked for a king, and God gave them Saul son of Kish, a man of *the* tribe of Benjamin, *for* forty years. ²²And having removed him, He raised up David to them as king, to whom also He said, having carried witness: 'I have found David the *son* of Jesse a man according to My heart, who will do all My will.'

²³Of the seed of this *man*, according to promise, God raised up to Israel *the* Savior, Jesus— ²⁴John having proclaimed before *the* face of His coming a baptism of repentance to all the people of Israel. ²⁵And while John was fulfilling the course, he was saying, 'Whom do you suppose me to be? I am not *He*, but behold, He comes after me, of whom I am not worthy to untie a sandal of the feet.'

²⁶Men, brothers, sons of *the* family of Abraham, and those among you fearing God, to us the message of this salvation has been sent. ²⁷For those dwelling in Jerusalem and their rulers, not having known Him and the voices of the prophets that are being read on every Sabbath, having condemned *Him*, they fulfilled *them*. ²⁸And having found no cause of death, they begged Pilate to put Him to death.

²⁹And when they had finished all the things having been written about Him, having taken *Him* down from the tree, they put *Him* in a tomb. ³⁰But God raised Him out from *the* dead, ³¹who appeared for many days to those having come up with Him from Galilee to Jerusalem, who are now His witnesses to the people.

³²And we preach the gospel to you, the promise having been made to the fathers, ³³that God has fulfilled this to us their children, having raised up Jesus, as also it has been written in the second psalm:

'You are My Son,
today I have begotten you.'[a]

³⁴And that He raised Him out from *the* dead, no more being about to return to decay, He spoke thus:

'I will give to you the holy *and* sure blessings of David.'[b]

³⁵Therefore He also says in another:

'You will not allow your Holy One to see decay.'[c]

³⁶For indeed David, having served the purpose of God in his own generation, fell asleep and was added to his fathers, and saw decay. ³⁷But the *One* God raised up did not see decay.

³⁸Therefore be it known to you, men, brothers, that through this One,

forgiveness of sins is proclaimed to you. ³⁹And in Him everyone believing is justified from all things from which you were not able to be justified in *the* Law of Moses. ⁴⁰Take heed therefore, lest that having been said in the prophets might come about:

⁴¹'Behold, scoffers,
　　and wonder and perish;
for I am working a work in your days,
　　a work that you would never believe,
　　even if one should declare it to you.'*ᵈ*"

The Gentiles Ask to Hear the Gospel

⁴²And they having departed, they were begging these words to be spoken to them on the next Sabbath. ⁴³And the synagogue having broken up, many of the Jews and worshipping converts followed Paul and Barnabas, who, speaking to them, kept persuading them to continue in the grace of God.

⁴⁴And on the coming Sabbath, almost the whole city was gathered together to hear the word of *the* Lord. ⁴⁵But the Jews, having seen the crowds, were filled with jealousy, and began contradicting the things spoken by Paul, blaspheming.

⁴⁶And Paul and Barnabas, having spoken boldly, said, "It was necessary *for* the word of God to be spoken first to you. But since you thrust it away and do not judge yourselves worthy of eternal life, behold, we are turning to the Gentiles. ⁴⁷For thus the Lord has commanded us:

'I have set you for a light of *the* Gentiles,
　　you to be for salvation to *the* uttermost part of the earth.'*ᵉ*"

⁴⁸And the Gentiles hearing *it* were rejoicing and glorifying the word of the Lord, and as many as were appointed to eternal life believed. ⁴⁹And the word of the Lord was carried through the whole region.

⁵⁰But the Jews incited the worshipping women of honorable position and the principals of the city, and they stirred up a persecution against Paul and Barnabas and expelled them from their district. ⁵¹But having shaken off the dust of the feet against them, they went to Iconium; ⁵²and the disciples were filled with joy and *the* Holy Spirit.

a 33 Psalm 2:7
b 34 Isaiah 55:3
c 35 Psalm 16:10
d 41 Habakkuk 1:5
e 47 Isaiah 49:6

Acts 14
Paul and Barnabas at Iconium

¹Now it came to pass in Iconium, according to the same, they entered into the synagogue of the Jews and spoke so that a great number of both Jewish and Greeks believed. ²But the unbelieving Jews stirred up and poisoned the minds of the Gentiles against the brothers. ³Therefore indeed they stayed a long time, speaking boldly for the Lord, bearing witness to the word of His grace, granting signs and wonders to be done through their hands.

⁴Now the multitude of the city was divided, and indeed some were with the Jews, but some with the apostles. ⁵And when there was a rush both of the Gentiles and Jews, with their rulers, to mistreat and to stone them, ⁶having become aware, they fled to the Lycaonian cities Lystra and Derbe, and the surrounding region, ⁷and there they continued preaching the gospel.

The Visit to Lystra and Derbe

⁸And in Lystra a certain man was sitting, crippled in the feet, lame from *the* womb of his mother, who had never walked. ⁹This *man* heard Paul speaking, who having looked intently at him and having seen that he has faith to be healed, ¹⁰said in a loud voice, "Stand upright on your feet!" And he sprang up and began to walk.

¹¹And the crowds having seen what Paul had done, lifted up their voice in Lycaonian saying, "The gods have come

down to us, having become like men." ¹²And Barnabas, they began calling Zeus; and Paul, Hermes, because he was the leading speaker. ¹³And the priest of Zeus, being just outside the city, having brought oxen and wreaths to the gates, was desiring with the crowds to sacrifice. ¹⁴But the apostles Barnabas and Paul having heard, having torn their garments, rushed out into the crowd, crying out ¹⁵and saying, "Men, why do you do these things? We also are men of like nature with you, proclaiming the gospel to you, to turn from these vanities to *the* living God, who made the heaven and the earth and the sea and all the things in them, ¹⁶who in the generations past allowed all the nations to go their *own* ways. ¹⁷And yet He has not left Himself without witness, doing good, giving to you rains from heaven and fruitful seasons, filling your hearts with food and gladness."

¹⁸And saying these things, they hardly stopped the crowds from sacrificing to them.

¹⁹But Jews came from Antioch and Iconium, and having persuaded the crowds, and having stoned Paul, they dragged *him* outside the city, supposing him to have died. ²⁰But the disciples having surrounded him, having risen up, he entered into the city. And on the next day he went away with Barnabas to Derbe.

The Return to Syrian Antioch

²¹And having proclaimed the gospel to that city and having discipled many, they returned to Lystra, and to Iconium, and to Antioch, ²²strengthening the souls of the disciples, exhorting *them* to continue in the faith and that "through many tribulations it behooves us to enter into the kingdom of God."

²³Now having chosen elders for them in every church, having prayed, with fasting they committed them to the Lord, in whom they had believed.

²⁴And having passed through Pisidia, they came to Pamphylia, ²⁵and having spoken the word in Perga, they went down to Attalia.

The Report to the Church at Antioch

²⁶And from there they sailed to Antioch, from where they had been committed to the grace of God for the work that they had fulfilled. ²⁷Now having arrived and having gathered together the church, they began declaring all that God had done with them, and that He had opened a door of faith to the Gentiles. ²⁸And they remained no little time with the disciples.

Acts 15
The Dispute over Circumcision

(Genesis 17:9-27; Leviticus 12:1-8; Joshua 5:1-9)

¹But certain ones having come down from Judea were teaching the brothers, "Unless you are circumcised according to the custom of Moses, you are not able to be saved." ²Having been brought about, then, no small commotion and discussion by Paul and Barnabas with them, they appointed Paul and Barnabas and certain others out from them to go up to Jerusalem, to the apostles and elders, about this question.

³Therefore indeed having been sent forward by the church, they were passing through both Phoenicia and Samaria, relating in detail the conversion of the Gentiles, and they were bringing great joy to all the brothers. ⁴And having come to Jerusalem, they were welcomed by the church and the apostles and the elders. And they declared all that God had done with them.

The Council at Jerusalem

⁵Now certain of those who believed, from the sect of the Pharisees, rose up, saying, "It is necessary to circumcise them, and to command *them* to keep the Law of Moses." ⁶And both the apostles and the elders were gathered together to see about this matter.

⁷And much discussion having taken place, Peter having risen up, said to them, "Men, brothers, you know that from *the*

early days God chose among you *for* the Gentiles to hear by my mouth the word of the gospel, and to believe. ⁸And the heart-knowing God bore witness to them, having given *them* the Holy Spirit, as also to us. ⁹And He made no distinction between both us and them, having purified their hearts by the faith.
¹⁰Now therefore, why are you testing God, to put upon the neck of the disciples a yoke that neither our fathers nor we have been able to bear? ¹¹But we believe *ourselves* to be saved by the grace of *the* Lord Jesus, in *the* same manner *as* they also *are*."
¹²Now the whole multitude kept silent and were listening to Barnabas and Paul relating what signs and wonders God had done among the Gentiles by them. ¹³And after they were silent, James answered, saying, "Men, brothers, hear me. ¹⁴Simeon*ᵃ* has related how God first visited to take out of *the* Gentiles a people for His name. ¹⁵And the words of the prophets agree with this, as it is written:
¹⁶'After these things I will return
and will rebuild the tabernacle of David which has fallen,
and its ruins I will rebuild,
and I will set it upright,
¹⁷so that the remnant of men may seek out the Lord,
and all the Gentiles, upon whom has been called My name, upon them,
says *the* Lord, doing these things,
¹⁸known from eternity.'*ᵇ*
¹⁹Therefore I judge not to trouble those from the Gentiles turning to God, ²⁰but to write to them to abstain from the pollutions of idols, and sexual immorality, and that which is strangled, and from blood. ²¹For Moses has *ones* proclaiming him in every city from generations of old, being read in the synagogues on every Sabbath."

The Letter to the Gentile Believers

²²Then it seemed good to the apostles and to the elders, with the whole church, having chosen out from them, to send men to Antioch with Paul and Barnabas: Judas called Barsabbas and Silas, leading men among the brothers, ²³having written by their hand:
"The apostles and the elders, brothers,
To those brothers among *the* Gentiles in Antioch and Syria and Cilicia:
Greetings.
²⁴Inasmuch as we have heard that some went out from us, to whom we had given no instructions,*ᶜ and* troubled you by words, upsetting your minds, ²⁵it seemed good to us, having come with one accord, having chosen men to send to you with our beloved Barnabas and Paul, ²⁶men having handed over their lives for the name of our Lord Jesus Christ. ²⁷Therefore we have sent Judas and Silas, and they are telling *you* the same things by word *of mouth*.
²⁸For it seemed good to the Holy Spirit and to us, to lay upon you no further burden, except these necessary things: ²⁹to abstain from things sacrificed to idols, and from blood, and from what is strangled, and from sexual immorality. Keeping yourselves from these, you will do well.
Farewell."

The Believers at Antioch Rejoice

³⁰Therefore indeed having been sent off, they went to Antioch, and having gathered the multitude, they delivered the letter. ³¹And having read *it*, they rejoiced at the encouragement.
³²Both Judas and Silas, also being prophets themselves, exhorted and strengthened the brothers by much talk. ³³And having continued a time, they were sent away in peace from the brothers to those having sent them.*ᵈ* ³⁵But Paul and Barnabas stayed in Antioch, teaching and proclaiming the good news, the word of the Lord, with many others also.

Paul's Second Missionary Journey

(Acts 13:1-3; Acts 18:23-28)
³⁶Now after some days, Paul said to Barnabas, "Indeed, having turned back,

let us look after the brothers, how they are, in every city in which we have announced the word of the Lord." ³⁷Now Barnabas purposed also to take along John, called Mark. ³⁸But Paul thought fit not to take him along, the *one* having withdrawn from them from Pamphylia and not having gone with them to the work.

³⁹Therefore a sharp disagreement arose, so that they separated from one another. And Barnabas having taken Mark, sailed to Cyprus. ⁴⁰But Paul, having chosen Silas, went forth, having been committed to the grace of the Lord by the brothers. ⁴¹And he was passing through Syria and Cilicia, strengthening the churches.

a 14 Greek *Simeon* is a variant of Simon
b 16-18 Amos 9:11,12. BYZ and TR *says the Lord, who does all these things. 18 Known unto God are all his works from the beginning of the world.*
c 24 BYZ and TR include *saying you must be circumcised and keep the law*
d 33 TR includes *34 Silas, however, decided to remain there.*

Acts 16
Timothy Joins Paul and Silas

¹And he came also to Derbe and to Lystra. And behold, a certain disciple was there, named Timothy, *the* son of a believing Jewish woman and a Greek father, ²who was well spoken of by the brothers in Lystra and Iconium. ³Paul wanted this one to go forth with him, and having taken *him*, he circumcised him on account of the Jews being in those parts; for they all knew that his father was a Greek.

⁴And while they were passing through the cities, they were delivering to them to keep the decrees decided on by the apostles and elders who *were* in Jerusalem. ⁵So indeed the churches were strengthened in the faith and were increasing in number every day.

Paul's Vision of the Macedonian

⁶And having passed through Phrygia and the Galatian region, having been forbidden by the Holy Spirit to speak the word in Asia, ⁷and having come down to Mysia, they were attempting to go into Bithynia, and the Spirit of Jesus did not allow them. ⁸And having passed by Mysia, they came down to Troas.

⁹And a vision appeared to Paul during the night: A certain man of Macedonia was standing and beseeching him and saying, "Having passed over into Macedonia, help us." ¹⁰Now when he had seen the vision, immediately we sought to go forth to Macedonia, concluding that God had called us to preach the gospel to them.

Lydia's Conversion in Philippi
(Revelation 2:18-29)

¹¹And having sailed from Troas, we made a straight course to Samothrace, and on the following day to Neapolis, ¹²and from there to Philippi, which is *the* leading city of the district of Macedonia, a colony. Now we were staying some days in this city.

¹³And on the day of the Sabbaths, we went forth outside the city gate, by a river, where *there* was customary to be *a place of* prayer. And having sat down, we began speaking to the women having gathered.

¹⁴And a certain woman named Lydia, a seller of purple of *the* city of Thyatira, worshiping God, was listening. The Lord opened her heart to attend to the things being spoken by Paul. ¹⁵And when she was baptized, and her house, she begged, saying, "If you have judged me to be faithful to the Lord, having entered into my house, abide." And she persuaded us.

Paul and Silas Imprisoned

¹⁶Now it happened of us going to the *place of* prayer, a certain girl, having a spirit of Python,ᵃ met us, who was bringing her masters much gain by fortune-telling. ¹⁷Having followed Paul and us, she was crying out, saying, "These men are servants of the Most High God, who proclaim to you *the* way of salvation."

¹⁸And she continued this for many days. And Paul having been distressed and

having turned, said to the spirit, "I command you in *the* name of Jesus Christ to come out from her." And it came out that hour.
¹⁹Now her masters having seen that their hope of profit was gone, having taken hold of Paul and Silas, dragged *them* into the marketplace before the rulers. ²⁰And having brought them up to the magistrates, they said, "These men, being Jews, exceedingly trouble our city ²¹and preach customs that it is not lawful for us, being Romans, to accept nor to practice."
²²And the crowd rose up together against them, and the magistrates having torn off their garments, were commanding that they be beaten with rods. ²³And having laid many blows on them, they cast *them* into prison, having charged the jailer to keep them securely, ²⁴who having received such an order, threw them into the inner prison and fastened their feet in the stocks.

The Conversion of the Jailer

²⁵Now toward midnight, Paul and Silas praying, were singing praises to God. And the prisoners were listening to them. ²⁶And suddenly there was a great earthquake, so that foundations of the prison house were shaken, and immediately all the doors were opened, and the chains of all were loosed.
²⁷And the jailer having been awoken and having seen the doors of the prison open, having drawn his sword was about to kill himself, supposing the prisoners to have escaped. ²⁸But Paul called out in a loud voice saying, "Do not harm yourself, for we are all here!"
²⁹And having called for lights, he rushed in, and having become terrified, he fell down before Paul and Silas. ³⁰And having brought them out, he was saying, "Sirs, what is necessary of me to do, that I may be saved?"
³¹And they said, "Believe on the Lord Jesus and you will be saved, you and your household." ³²And they spoke the word of the Lord to him along with all those in his house. ³³And having taken them in that hour of the night, he washed *them* from the wounds, and immediately he was baptized, and all his *household*. ³⁴And having brought them into the house, he laid a table *for them* and rejoiced with all *his* household, having believed in God.

An Official Apology

³⁵And day having come, the magistrates sent the officers, saying, "Release those men."
³⁶And the jailer reported these words to Paul: "The captains have sent that you may be let go. Now therefore having gone out, depart in peace."
³⁷But Paul was saying to them, "Having beaten us publicly, uncondemned men being Romans, they cast *us* into prison, and now do they throw us out secretly? No indeed! Instead, having come themselves, let them bring us out."
³⁸And the officers reported these words to the captains, and they were afraid, having heard that they are Romans. ³⁹And having come, they appealed to them, and having brought *them* out, they were asking *them* to go out of the city. ⁴⁰And having gone forth out of the prison, they came to Lydia, and having seen *them*, they exhorted the brothers and departed.

a 16 Greek *Python*, a spirit of divination named after the mythical serpent slain by Apollo

Acts 17
Paul Preaches at Thessalonica

¹And having passed through Amphipolis and Apollonia, they came to Thessalonica, where there was a synagogue of the Jews. ²And according to the custom with Paul, he went in to them and for three Sabbaths reasoned with them from the Scriptures, ³opening and setting forth that it behooved the Christ to have suffered and to have risen out from *the* dead, and that "this Jesus whom I preach to you is the Christ." ⁴And

some of them were obedient and joined themselves to Paul and to Silas, along with a great multitude of the worshipping Greeks, and not a few of the leading women.

The Uproar in Thessalonica

⁵Now the Jews having become jealous, and having taken to *them* certain wicked men of the market-loungers, and having collected a crowd, set the city in uproar. And having assailed the house of Jason, they were seeking them to bring out to the people. ⁶But not having found them, they dragged Jason and certain brothers before the city authorities, crying out, "These ones having upset the world come here also, ⁷whom Jason has received. And these all do contrary to the decrees of Caesar, proclaiming another to be king, Jesus."

⁸And they stirred up the crowd and the city authorities, hearing these things. ⁹And having taken security from Jason and the rest, they let go them.

The Character of the Bereans

¹⁰And the brothers sent away both Paul and Silas immediately by night to Berea, who having arrived, went into the synagogue of the Jews. ¹¹Now these, who were more noble than those in Thessalonica, received the word with all readiness, on every day examining the Scriptures, whether these things were so. ¹²Therefore many of them indeed believed, and not a few of the prominent Grecian women and men.

¹³But when the Jews from Thessalonica learned that the word of God also was proclaimed by Paul in Berea, they came there also, stirring up and agitating the crowds. ¹⁴And then immediately the brothers sent away Paul to go as to the sea. And both Silas and Timothy remained there. ¹⁵Now those escorting Paul brought *him* unto Athens, and having received a command unto Silas and Timothy that as quickly as possible they should come to him, they departed.

Paul in Athens

¹⁶Now of Paul in Athens waiting for them, his spirit was provoked in him, seeing the city to be utterly idolatrous. ¹⁷So indeed he was reasoning in the synagogue with the Jews and those worshiping, and in the marketplace on every day with those meeting *him*.

¹⁸And also some of the Epicureans and Stoics, philosophers, encountered him, and some were saying, "What may this babbler desire to say?" but others, "He seems to be a proclaimer of foreign gods," because he was proclaiming the gospel of Jesus and the resurrection.

¹⁹And having taken hold of him they brought *him* to the Areopagus, saying, "Are we able to know what *is* this new teaching which is spoken by you. ²⁰For you are bringing some strange things to our ears. We resolve therefore to know what these things wish to be." ²¹Now all *the* Athenians and the visiting strangers spent their time in nothing else than to tell something and to hear something new.

Paul Before the Areopagus

²²And Paul, having stood in *the* midst of the Areopagus, was saying, "Men, Athenians, I behold that in all things you *are* very religious. ²³For passing through and beholding your objects of worship, I even found an altar on which had been inscribed:

TO AN UNKNOWN GOD.

Therefore whom you worship not knowing, Him I proclaim to you.

²⁴The God having made the world and all things that *are* in it, He being Lord of heaven and earth, does not dwell in hand-made temples, ²⁵nor is He served by hands of men as needing anything, Himself giving to all life and breath and everything. ²⁶And He made from one *man* every nation of men, to dwell upon all the face of the earth, having determined *the* appointed times and the boundaries of their habitation, ²⁷to seek God, if perhaps indeed they might palpate

for Him, and might find Him. And indeed, He is not far from each one of us. ²⁸'For in Him we live and move and are.'ᵃ As also some of the poets among you have said, 'For we are also *His* offspring.'ᵇ ²⁹Therefore, being offspring of God, we ought not to consider the Divine Being to be like to gold or to silver or to stone, a graven thing of man's craft and imagination. ³⁰So indeed God, having overlooked the times of ignorance, now commands all men everywhere to repent, ³¹because He set a day in which He is about to judge the world in righteousness by a man whom He appointed, having provided a guarantee to all, having raised Him out from *the* dead." ³²Now having heard of a resurrection of *the* dead, some indeed began to mock *him*, but some said, "We will hear you concerning this again also." ³³Thus Paul went out from their midst. ³⁴But some men, having joined themselves to him, believed, among whom also *were* Dionysius the Areopagite, and a woman named Damaris, and others with them.

a 28 Probably a quote from the Cretan philosopher Epimenides
b 28 Probably from the poem 'Phainomena' by the Cilician philosopher Aratus

Acts 18
Paul's Ministry in Corinth

¹And after these things, having departed from Athens, he came to Corinth. ²And having found a certain Jew named Aquila, a native of Pontus, and Priscilla his wife, recently having come from Italy because of Claudius having commanded all the Jews to depart out of Rome, he came to them, ³and because of being of the same trade, he stayed with them and worked. For they were tentmakers by the trade. ⁴And he was reasoning in the synagogue on every Sabbath, persuading both Jews and Greeks. ⁵Now when both Silas and Timothy came down from Macedonia, Paul was occupied with the word, earnestly testifying to the Jews Jesus to be the Christ. ⁶But of them opposing and reviling *him*, having shaken out the garments, he said to them, "Your blood *be* upon your head; I *am* clean. From now on I will go to the Gentiles."
⁷And having departed from there, he came to *the* house of a certain one named Titius Justus, worshiping God, whose house was adjoining the synagogue. ⁸And Crispus, the ruler of the synagogue, believed in the Lord, with his all household. And many of the Corinthians hearing believed and were baptized. ⁹Now the Lord said to Paul through a vision in *the* night, "Do not fear, but continue speaking, and do not be silent, ¹⁰because I am with you, and no one will lay a hand on you to harm you, because there are many people to me in this city." ¹¹And he remained a year and six months, teaching the word of God among them.

Paul Before Gallio

¹²But Gallio being proconsul of Achaia, the Jews with one accord rose up against Paul and led him to the judgment seat, ¹³saying, "This *man* persuades men to worship God contrary to the Law." ¹⁴Now Paul being about to open the mouth, Gallio said to the Jews, "If indeed it was some unrighteousness or wicked crime, O Jews, according to reason I would have endured with you. ¹⁵But if it is a question about a word, and names, and in reference to your law, you will see *to it* yourselves. I resolve not to be a judge of these things." ¹⁶And he drove them from the judgment seat.
¹⁷Then all *of them*, having seized Sosthenes the ruler of the synagogue, began to beat *him* before the judgment seat. And it mattered nothing to Gallio about these things.

Paul Returns to Antioch

¹⁸Now Paul, having remained many days more, having taken leave of the brothers, sailed away to Syria—and with him Priscilla and Aquila—having shaved the head in Cenchrea, for he had a vow.

¹⁹Now they came to Ephesus, and left them there. And he himself having entered into the synagogue, reasoned with the Jews. ²⁰Now of them asking *him* to remain for a longer time, he did not consent, ²¹but having taken leave and having said,[a] "I will return to you again, God willing," he sailed from Ephesus, ²²and having landed at Caesarea, having gone up and having greeted the church, he went down to Antioch.

Paul's Third Missionary Journey
(Acts 13:1-3; Acts 15:36-41)

²³And having stayed some time, he went forth, passing successively through the Galatian region and Phrygia, strengthening all the disciples.

²⁴Now a certain Jew named Apollos, a native of Alexandria, came to Ephesus, being an eloquent man, mighty in the Scriptures. ²⁵He was instructed in the way of the Lord. And being fervent in spirit, he was speaking and was teaching earnestly the things concerning Jesus, knowing only the baptism of John. ²⁶And he began to speak boldly in the synagogue. But Priscilla and Aquila having heard him, took him to *them* and expounded the way of God to him more accurately.

²⁷And he resolving to pass through into Achaia, the brothers, having encouraged *him*, wrote to the disciples to welcome him, who having arrived, helped greatly those having believed through grace. ²⁸For he was powerfully refuting the Jews publicly, showing by the Scriptures Jesus to be the Christ.

a 21 BYZ and TR include *I must by all means keep this feast that comes in Jerusalem, but*

Acts 19
The Holy Spirit Received at Ephesus
(Joel 2:28-32; John 14:15-26; John 16:5-16; Acts 2:1-13; Acts 10:44-48)

¹Now it came to pass, while Apollos was in Corinth, Paul having passed through the upper parts[a] to come to Ephesus, and having found certain disciples, ²he also said to them, "Did you receive *the* Holy Spirit, having believed?"

And *they said* to him, "But not even did we hear that there is a Holy Spirit."

³And he said, "Into what then were you baptized?"

And they said, "Into the baptism of John." ⁴Then Paul said, "John baptized a baptism of repentance, telling the people that they should believe in the *One* coming after him, that is, in Jesus."

⁵And having heard, they were baptized into the name of the Lord Jesus. ⁶And of Paul having laid the hands on them, the Holy Spirit came upon them, and they were speaking in tongues and prophesying. ⁷And there were in all about twelve men.

Paul Ministers in Ephesus
(Revelation 2:1-7)

⁸And having entered into the synagogue, he was speaking boldly for three months, reasoning and persuading *them* concerning the kingdom of God. ⁹But when some were hardened and were disbelieving, speaking evil of the Way before the multitude, having departed from them, he took the disciples separately, reasoning every day in the lecture hall of Tyrannus. ¹⁰And this continued for two years, so that all those inhabiting Asia heard the word of the Lord, both Jews and Greeks.

¹¹And God was performing extraordinary miracles by the hands of Paul, ¹²so that even handkerchiefs or aprons from his skin were brought to the ailing, and the diseases departed from them, and the evil spirits left.

The Sons of Sceva

¹³Now some of the itinerant Jews, exorcists, also attempted to invoke the name of the Lord Jesus over those having evil spirits, saying, "I adjure you *by* Jesus, whom Paul proclaims." ¹⁴And seven sons of Sceva, a Jewish high priest, were doing this. ¹⁵But the evil spirit answering, said to them, "Jesus I know, and Paul I am acquainted with; but you, who are you?"

¹⁶And the man in whom was the evil spirit, having leapt on them, having overpowered them all, prevailed against them so that they fled out of that house naked and wounded.
¹⁷Now this became known to all those inhabiting Ephesus, both Jews and Greeks. And fear fell upon them all, and the name of the Lord Jesus was being magnified. ¹⁸And many of those having believed were coming, confessing and declaring their deeds, ¹⁹and many of those having practiced the magic arts, having brought the books, burned *them* before all. And they counted up the prices of them and found *it* five myriads of silverlings.[b] ²⁰Thus the word of the Lord continued to increase and prevail with might.

The Riot in Ephesus

²¹Now after these things were fulfilled, Paul purposed in the Spirit to go to Jerusalem, having passed through Macedonia and Achaia, having said, "After my having been there, it behooves me to see Rome also." ²²And having sent two of those ministering to him, Timothy and Erastus, into Macedonia, he remained for a time in Asia.
²³Now at the same time no small disturbance arose concerning the Way. ²⁴For a certain silversmith named Demetrius, making silver shrines of Artemis, was bringing no little business to the craftsmen, ²⁵whom having brought together along with the workmen in such things, he said, "Men, you know that from this business is our wealth. ²⁶And you see and hear that not only in Ephesus, but almost all of Asia, this Paul, having persuaded *them*, has turned away a great many people, saying that they are not gods which have been made by hands. ²⁷Now not only is this business to us endangered to come into disrepute, but also for the temple of the great goddess Artemis to be reckoned for nothing, and also her majesty to be deposed, whom all Asia and the world worship."

²⁸And having heard, and having become full of rage, they were crying out saying, "Great *is* Artemis of *the* Ephesians." ²⁹And the whole city was filled with confusion, and with one accord they rushed to the theatre, having dragged off Gaius and Aristarchus, Macedonians, fellow travelers of Paul. ³⁰But of Paul intending to go in to the people, the disciples would not allow him. ³¹And also some of the Asiarchs being friends to him, having sent to him, were urging him not to venture into the theatre. ³²So some indeed were crying out one thing; others *another*. For the assembly was confused, and most did not know for what cause they were assembled. ³³Now out of the crowd they put forward Alexander, the Jews having thrust him forward. And Alexander, having motioned with the hand, was wanting to make a defense to the people. ³⁴But having recognized that he is a Jew, there was one cry from all, ongoing about two hours, crying out, "Great *is* Artemis of *the* Ephesians."
³⁵Then having calmed the crowd, the town clerk says, "Men, Ephesians, what man is there indeed who does not know the city of *the* Ephesians as being temple-keeper of the great Artemis, and of that fallen from the sky? ³⁶Therefore these things being undeniable, it is necessary for you to be calm and to do nothing rash. ³⁷For you brought these men, neither temple plunderers nor blaspheming our goddess.
³⁸So if indeed Demetrius and the craftsmen with him have a matter against anyone, courts are conducted, and there are proconsuls; let them accuse one another. ³⁹But if you inquire anything beyond this, it will be solved in the lawful assembly. ⁴⁰And indeed, we are in danger of being accused of insurrection in regard to this day, there existing not one cause concerning which we will be able to give a reason for this commotion."

⁴¹And having said these things, he dismissed the assembly.

_{a 1 or} *interior*
_{b 19 Or} *fifty thousand drachmas.* _{A drachma was a silver coin worth about one day's wages.}

Acts 20
Paul in Macedonia and Greece

¹Now after the uproar had ceased, Paul, having summoned the disciples and having encouraged *them and* having said farewell, departed to go to Macedonia. ²And having passed through those districts and having exhorted them with much talk, he came to Greece. ³And having continued three months, a plot having been made against him by the Jews, he being about to sail into Syria, a purpose arose to return through Macedonia.

⁴And he was accompanied by Sopater *son of* Pyrrhus from Berea, and Aristarchus, and Secundus of the Thessalonians, and Gaius of Derbe, and Timothy, and *the* Asians Tychicus and Trophimus. ⁵But these, having gone ahead, waited for us in Troas. ⁶And we sailed away from Philippi after the days of the Unleavened Bread, and within five days we came to them at Troas, where we stayed seven days.

Eutychus Revived at Troas
(John 11:38-44)

⁷And on the first *day* of the week, of us having come together to break bread, Paul, about to depart on the next day, talked to them and continued the talk until midnight. ⁸Now there were many lamps in the upper room where we were assembled. ⁹And a certain young man named Eutychus was sitting by the window, overpowered by deep sleep as Paul talked on longer. Having been overpowered by sleep, he fell down from the third story and was picked up dead. ¹⁰But Paul having descended, fell upon him, and having embraced *him*, he said, "Do not be alarmed, for his life is in him!"

¹¹And having gone up, and having broken the bread, and having eaten, and having talked at length until daybreak, so he departed. ¹²Then they brought the boy alive, and were not just a little comforted.

From Troas to Miletus

¹³But we, having gone ahead to the ship, sailed to Assos, being about to take in Paul there. For having arranged thus, he was readying himself to go on foot. ¹⁴Now when he met with us at Assos, having taken him in, we came to Mitylene. ¹⁵And having sailed away from there, on the following *day* we arrived opposite Chios, and the next *day* we arrived at Samos,[a] and the following *day* we came to Miletus. ¹⁶For Paul had decided to sail by Ephesus, so that it might not come upon him to spend time in Asia; for he was hastened, if it was possible for him, to be in Jerusalem on the day of Pentecost.

Paul's Farewell to the Ephesians

¹⁷And from Miletus, having sent to Ephesus, he called for the elders of the church.

¹⁸And when they had come to him, he said to them, "You know from the first day on which I arrived in Asia, how I was with you the whole time, ¹⁹serving the Lord with all humility and tears, and trials having befallen me in the plots of the Jews; ²⁰how I did not shrink back from declaring to you *anything* being profitable, and teaching you publicly and from house to house, ²¹earnestly testifying both to the Jewish and to Greeks repentance in God and faith in our Lord Jesus.[b]

²²And now behold, bound in the Spirit I go to Jerusalem, not knowing what will happen to me in it, ²³except that the Holy Spirit fully testifies to me in every city, saying that chains and tribulations await me. ²⁴But I make my life *neither* dear nor any account to myself, so as to finish my course and the ministry that I received from the Lord Jesus: to testify fully the gospel of the grace of God.

25And now, behold, I know that all of you among whom I have gone about proclaiming the kingdom will see my face no more. 26Therefore I testify to you in this day that I *am* innocent of the blood of all. 27For I did not shrink back from proclaiming to you the whole counsel of God. 28Take heed to yourselves and to all the flock, among which the Holy Spirit has set you overseers, to shepherd the church of God,[c] which He purchased with the own blood.[d] 29I know that after my departure, grievous wolves will come in among you, not sparing the flock, 30and out from your own selves, men will rise up, speaking perverse things to draw away disciples after them. 31Therefore stay awake, remembering that three years night and day I never ceased admonishing each one with tears.

32And now I commit you to God and to the word of His grace, being able to build *you* up and to give you an inheritance among all those having been sanctified. 33I coveted nobody's silver or gold or clothing. 34You yourselves know that these hands ministered to my needs and to those being with me. 35In everything I showed you that by thus straining, it behooves *us* to aid those being weak, and also to remember the words of the Lord Jesus, how He Himself said, 'It is more Blessed to give than to receive.'"

36And having said these things, having bowed his knee, he prayed with them all. 37Then there was much weeping among all, and having fallen upon the neck of Paul, they were kissing him, 38sorrowing especially over the word that he had spoken, that they are about to see his face no more. Then they accompanied him to the ship.

a 15 BYZ and TR include *after remaining at Trogyllium*
b 21 TR *the Lord Jesus Christ*
c 28 BYZ and Tischendorf *of the Lord*
d 28 Or *with the blood of his own Son.*

Acts 21
Paul's Journey to Jerusalem

1And it happened that after having drawn away from them, having run directly in our sailing, we came to Cos, and the next *day* to Rhodes, and from there to Patara. 2And having found a boat passing over into Phoenicia, having gone on board, we set sail. 3And having sighted Cyprus and having left it on the left, we kept sailing to Syria and landed at Tyre, for the ship was unloading the cargo there.

4And we remained there seven days, having sought out the disciples, who kept telling Paul through the Spirit not to go up to Jerusalem. 5And it happened that when we had completed the days, having set out, we journeyed, all accompanying us with wives and children as far as outside the city. And having bowed the knees on the shore, having prayed, 6having said farewell to one another, we then went up into the boat, and they returned to the own.

7And having completed the voyage from Tyre, we came down to Ptolemais, and having greeted the brothers, we stayed one day with them.

Paul Visits Philip the Evangelist

8And having gone forth on the next day, we came to Caesarea, and having entered into the house of Philip the evangelist, being of the seven, we stayed with him. 9And with this *man* there were four daughters, virgins prophesying.

10And remaining many days, a certain prophet named Agabus came down from Judea. 11And having come to us and having taken Paul's belt, having bound his feet and hands, he said, "Thus the Holy Spirit says, 'In this way the Jews in Jerusalem will bind the man whose belt this is, and will deliver *him* into *the* hands of *the* Gentiles.'" 12And when we had heard these things, both we and those of that place began begging him not to go up to Jerusalem.

13Then Paul answered, "What are you doing, weeping and breaking my heart?

For I have readiness not only to be bound, but also to die at Jerusalem for the name of the Lord Jesus." ¹⁴And of him not being persuaded, we were silent, having said, "The will of the Lord be done."

¹⁵Now after these days, having packed the baggage, we started on our way up to Jerusalem. ¹⁶And *some* of the disciples from Caesarea also went with us, bringing a certain Mnason, a Cypriot, an early disciple with whom we would lodge.

Paul's Arrival at Jerusalem

¹⁷Now of our having arrived at Jerusalem, the brothers received us gladly. ¹⁸And on the following *day*, Paul went in with us unto James, and all the elders arrived. ¹⁹And having greeted them, he began to relate, one by each, the things God had done among the Gentiles through his ministry.

²⁰And those having heard began glorifying God, and they said to him, "You see, brother, how many myriads there are among the Jews having believed, and are all zealous ones for the Law. ²¹Now they have been informed about you, that you teach all Jews among the Gentiles apostasy from Moses, telling them not to circumcise the children nor to walk in the customs. ²²What then is it? Certainly they will hear that you have come.

²³Therefore do this that we say to you. With us there are four men, having a vow on themselves. ²⁴Having taken these *men*, be purified with them and bear expense for them, so that they will shave the head, and all will know that of which they have been informed about you is nothing, but you yourself also walk orderly, keeping the Law.

²⁵Now concerning those of the Gentiles having believed, we wrote, having adjudged them to keep from both the things offered to idols, and blood, and what is strangled, and sexual immorality."

²⁶Then Paul, having taken the men on the following day, having been purified with them, entered into the temple, declaring the fulfillment of the days of the purification until the sacrifice was offered for each one of them.

Paul Seized in the Temple

²⁷Now when the seven days were about to be completed, the Jews from Asia, having seen him in the temple, began stirring up the whole crowd and laid the hands upon him, ²⁸crying out, "Men, Israelites, help! This is the man teaching all those everywhere against the people and the Law and this place. And besides, he has also brought Greeks into the temple and defiled this holy place." ²⁹For it was they having previously seen Trophimus the Ephesian in the city with him, whom they were supposing that Paul had brought into the temple.

³⁰And the whole city was provoked, and there was a rushing together of the people. And having laid hold of Paul, they dragged him outside the temple, and immediately the doors were shut. ³¹And of them seeking to kill him, a report came to the commander of the cohort that all Jerusalem was in an uproar, ³²who at once, having taken with *him* soldiers and centurions, ran down upon them. And having seen the commander and the soldiers, they stopped beating Paul.

³³Then having drawn near, the commander laid hold of him and commanded *him* to be bound with two chains, and began inquiring who he might be and what it is he has been doing. ³⁴They were crying out in the crowd one thing, but others another. And he being unable to know the facts on account of the uproar, ordered him to be brought into the barracks. ³⁵Now when he came to the stairs, it happened that he was carried by the soldiers because of the violence of the crowd. ³⁶For the multitude of the people were following, crying out, "Away with him!"

Paul Speaks to the People

³⁷And being about to be brought into the barracks, Paul says to the commander,

"Is it permitted to me to say something to you?"

Then he was saying, "Do you know Greek? ³⁸Are you not, then, the Egyptian, the *one* before these days having led a revolt and having led out into the wilderness the four thousand men of the 'Assassins?'"

³⁹But Paul said, "I am indeed a Jew, a man of Tarsus of Cilicia, a citizen *of* no insignificant city. Now I implore you, allow me to speak to the people." ⁴⁰And he having allowed *him*, Paul, having stood on the stairs, made a sign with the hand to the people. And great silence having taken place, he spoke to *them* in the Hebrew language,ᵃ saying:

a 40 Or *Aramaic*

Acts 22
Paul's Defense to the Crowd
(Acts 9:1-9; Acts 26:1-23)

¹"Men, brothers, and fathers, hear now my defense to you." ²And having heard that he was addressing them in the Hebrew language,ᵃ they became even more quiet.

And he says, ³"I am a Jew, a man born in Tarsus of Cilicia and brought up in this city at the feet of Gamaliel, having been instructed according to *the* exactness of the Law of our Fathers, being a zealous one of God, even as you all are this day, ⁴who persecuted this Way as far as death, binding and betraying to prisons both men and women, ⁵as also the high priest and the whole elderhood bears witness to me, from whom also having received letters to the brothers, I was on my way to Damascus to bring also those being there, bound to Jerusalem, in order that they might be punished.

⁶But it happened to me, journeying and drawing near to Damascus about noon, *that* suddenly a great light out of heaven shone around me, ⁷and I fell to the ground and heard a voice saying to me, 'Saul, Saul, why do you persecute Me?'

⁸And I answered, 'Who are You, Lord?'

And He said to me, 'I am Jesus of Nazareth, whom you are persecuting.'

⁹And those being with me indeed beheld the light, but they did not hear the voice of the *One* speaking to me.

¹⁰Then I said, 'What shall I do, Lord?'

And the Lord said to me, 'Having risen up, go to Damascus, and there it will be told you concerning all things that it has been appointed you to do.'

¹¹And while I could not see from the brightness of that light, I came to Damascus, being led by the hand by those being with me. ¹²And a certain Ananias, a devout man according to the Law, borne witness to by all the Jews dwelling *there*, ¹³having come to me and having stood by *me*, said to me, 'Brother Saul, receive your sight.' And the same hour I looked up at him.

¹⁴Then he said, 'The God of our fathers has appointed you to know His will, and to see the Righteous One, and to hear *the* voice out of His mouth. ¹⁵For you will be a witness for Him to all men of what you have seen and heard. ¹⁶And now why do you delay? Having arisen, be baptized, and wash away your sins, calling on His name.'

¹⁷And it happened to me, having returned to Jerusalem and of my praying in the temple, I fell into a trance ¹⁸and saw Him saying to me, 'Make haste and go away with speed out of Jerusalem, because they will not receive your testimony about Me.'

¹⁹And I said, 'Lord, they themselves know that in each of those synagogues I was imprisoning and beating those believing on You. ²⁰And when the blood of Your witness of Stephen was poured out, I myself also was standing by and consenting and watching over the garments of those killing him.'

²¹And He said to me, 'Go, for I will send you far away to *the* Gentiles.'"

Paul the Roman Citizen

²²Now they were listening to him until this word. Then they lifted up their voice,

saying, "Away with such from the earth. For he is not fit to live!" ²³And they were crying out and casting off the garments and throwing dust into the air. ²⁴The commander ordered him to be brought into the barracks, having directed him to be examined by flogging, so that he might know for what cause they were crying out against him like this. ²⁵But as he stretched him forward with the straps, Paul said to the centurion standing by, "Is it lawful to you to flog a man *who is* a Roman and uncondemned?" ²⁶And the centurion having heard *it*, having gone to the commander, reported *it* saying, "What are you going to do? For this man is a Roman." ²⁷And having come near, the commander said to him, "Tell me, are you a Roman?" And he was saying, "Yes." ²⁸Then the commander answered, "I bought this citizenship with a great sum." But Paul was saying, "But I even was born *so*." ²⁹So immediately those being about to examine him departed from him, and the commander also was afraid, having ascertained that he is a Roman, and because he had bound him. ³⁰And on the next day, desiring to know for certain why he is accused by the Jews, he unbound him and commanded the chief priests and the whole council to assemble. And having brought down Paul, he set *him* among them.

a 2 Or *Aramaic*

Acts 23
Paul Before the Sanhedrin

¹And having looked intently at the Council, Paul said, "Men, brothers, I have lived as a citizen in all good conscience to God unto this day." ²Then the high priest Ananias commanded those standing by him to strike his mouth.
³Then Paul said to him, "God is about to strike you, whitewashed wall! And you, do you sit judging me according to the Law, and, violating law, command me to be struck?"
⁴Now those who stood by said, "Do you insult the high priest of God?"
⁵And Paul was saying, "I was not aware, brothers, that he is high priest; for it has been written: 'You shall not speak evil *of the* ruler of your people.'ᵃ"
⁶Then Paul, having known that the one part consists of Sadducees, but the other of Pharisees, began crying out in the Council, "Men, brothers, I am a Pharisee, *the* son of a Pharisee; I am judged concerning *the* hope and resurrection of *the* dead."
⁷And of him saying this, a dissension arose between the Pharisees and Sadducees, and the crowd was divided. ⁸For indeed Sadducees say there to be no resurrection, nor angel, nor spirit; but Pharisees confess both.
⁹Then a great clamor arose, and some of the scribes of the party of the Pharisees, having risen up, were contending saying, "We find nothing evil in this man. And what if a spirit or an angel has spoken to him?" ¹⁰And great dissension arising, the commander, having feared lest Paul should be torn to pieces by them, commanded the troop, having gone down, to take him by force from their midst and to bring *him* into the barracks.
¹¹But the following night the Lord, having stood by him, said, "Take courage, for as you have fully testified about Me at Jerusalem, so also it behooves you to testify in Rome."

The Plot to Kill Paul
(John 16:1-4)

¹²Then when it was day, the Jews having made a conspiracy, put themselves under an oath, declaring neither to eat nor to drink until they should kill Paul. ¹³Now there were more than forty having made this conspiracy, ¹⁴who, having come to the chief priests and the elders, said, "We have bound ourselves with an oath to eat nothing until we should kill Paul. ¹⁵Now therefore you with the Council make a

report to the commander, so that he might bring him down to you, as being about to examine more earnestly the things about him. And we are ready to kill him before his drawing near."
¹⁶But the son of Paul's sister, having heard of the ambush, having come near and having entered into the barracks, reported *it* to Paul. ¹⁷Then Paul, having summoned one of the centurions, was saying, "Take this young man to the commander, for he has something to report to him."
¹⁸So indeed the *one* having taken him brought *him* to the commander, and he says, "Paul the prisoner, having called to me, asked *me* to lead this young man to you, having something to say to you."
¹⁹Then the commander, having taken hold of his hand and having withdrawn in private, began to inquire, "What is it that you have to report to me?"
²⁰And he said, "The Jews have agreed to ask you that you might bring down Paul into the Council tomorrow, as being about to inquire something more earnestly about him. ²¹You therefore should not be persuaded by them. For more than forty of their men lie in wait for him, who have put themselves under an oath neither to eat nor to drink until they have killed him; and now they are ready, awaiting the promise from you."
²²So indeed the commander dismissed the young man, having instructed *him*, "Tell no one that you have reported these things to me."

Paul Sent to Felix

²³And having summoned certain two of the centurions, he said, "Prepare for the third hour of the night two hundred soldiers and seventy horsemen and two hundred spearmen, so that they might go as far as Caesarea, ²⁴and provide mounts, so that having set Paul *upon them*, they might bring *him* safely to Felix the governor," ²⁵having written a letter having this form:
²⁶"Claudius Lysias,

To the most excellent, governor Felix: Greetings.
²⁷This man having been seized by the Jews and being about to be killed by them, having come up with the troop, I rescued *him*, having learned that he is a Roman. ²⁸And resolving to know the charge on account of which they were accusing him, I brought *him* down to their council, ²⁹whom I found being accused concerning questions of their Law, but having no accusation worthy of death or of chains.
³⁰And it having been disclosed to me of a plot that would be against the man, I sent *him* to you at once, also having instructed the accusers to speak these things against him before you."
³¹Therefore indeed the soldiers, according to that having been ordered them, having taken Paul, brought *him* to Antipatris by night. ³²And on the next day, having allowed the horsemen to go with him, they returned to the barracks, ³³who having entered into Caesarea and having delivered the letter to the governor, also presented Paul to him.
³⁴And having read *it* and having asked what province he is from, and having learned that *he is* from Cilicia, ³⁵he was saying "I will hear you fully when your accusers may have arrived also," having commanded him to be guarded in the Praetorium of Herod.

a 5 Exodus 22:28

Acts 24
Tertullus Prosecutes Paul

¹And after five days, the high priest Ananias came down with some elders and a certain orator, Tertullus, who made a representation against Paul to the governor.
²And of him having been called, Tertullus began to accuse, saying, "We are attaining great peace through you, and excellent measures are being done to this nation through your foresight. ³Both in every way and everywhere, we gladly

accept *it*, most excellent Felix, with all thankfulness. ⁴But in order that I should not be a hindrance you to any longer, I implore you to hear us briefly, *in* your kindness.

⁵For we are having found this man a pest, and stirring insurrection among all the Jews in the world, and a leader of the sect of the Nazarenes ⁶who even attempted to profane the temple, whom also we seized.ᵃ ⁸Having examined *him* yourself, you will be able to know from him concerning all these things of which we accuse him."

⁹And the Jews also agreed, declaring these things to be so.

Paul's Defense to Felix

¹⁰And the governor having made a sign to him to speak, Paul answered: "Knowing you as being judge to this nation for many years, I make a defense cheerfully to the things concerning myself. ¹¹You are able to know that there are to me not more than twelve days since I went up to worship in Jerusalem. ¹²And neither did they find me reasoning with anyone or making a tumultuous gathering of a crowd in the temple, nor in the synagogues, nor in the city. ¹³Nor are they able to prove to you concerning *the things* of which now they accuse me.

¹⁴But I confess this to you, that according to the Way which they call a sect, so I serve the God of our fathers, believing all things throughout the Law and that have been written in the Prophets, ¹⁵having a hope in God, which they themselves also await, *that* there is about to be a resurrection, both of *the* just and of *the* unjust. ¹⁶In this also I myself strive to have a conscience without offense toward God and men through everything.

¹⁷Now after many years, I arrived to bring alms to my nation, and offerings, ¹⁸during which they found me purified in the temple, not with a crowd nor in tumult. But *there are* some Jews from Asia ¹⁹who ought to appear before you and to make accusation if they may have anything against me. ²⁰Otherwise, let them say themselves any unrighteousness they found in me, having stood before the Council, ²¹other than concerning this one voice, which I cried out standing among them: 'I am judged by you this day concerning *the* resurrection of *the* dead.'"

The Verdict Postponed

²²But Felix, more precisely having knowledge of the things concerning the Way, put them off, having said, "When Lysias the commander might have come down, I will examine the things as to you," ²³having commanded the centurion to keep him and to *let him* have ease and not to forbid his own to minister to him.

²⁴Then after some days, Felix, having arrived with the own wife Drusilla, being a Jewess, sent for Paul and heard him concerning the faith in Christ Jesus. ²⁵And of him reasoning concerning righteousness and self-control and the coming judgment, Felix, having become frightened, answered, "Go away for the present, and having found opportunity, I will call for you." ²⁶At the same time also he is hoping that riches will be given him by Paul. So also sending for him often, he was talking with him.

²⁷But two years having been completed, Felix received Porcius Festus *as* successor, and wishing to acquire for himself favor with the Jews, Felix left Paul imprisoned.

a 6 BYZ and TR include *and we would have judged him according to our law. 7 But Lysias the commander came with great force and took him out of our hands, 8 ordering his accusers to come before you.*

Acts 25
Paul's Trial Before Festus

¹Therefore Festus, having arrived in the province, after three days went up to Jerusalem from Caesarea. ²And the chief priests and the chiefs of the Jews made a presentation before him against Paul, and they were begging him, ³asking a favor against him, that he would summon him

to Jerusalem, forming an ambush to kill him on the way.
⁴So indeed Festus answered that Paul is to be kept in Caesarea, and he himself is about to set out in quickness. ⁵He says, "Therefore those among you in power, having gone down together, if there is anything wrong in the man, let them accuse him."
⁶And having spent with them not more than eight or ten days, having gone down to Caesarea, on the next day having sat on the judgment seat, he commanded Paul to be brought. ⁷And he having arrived, the Jews having come down from Jerusalem stood around him, bringing many and weighty charges, which they were not able to prove.
⁸Paul made his defense: "Neither against the law of the Jews, nor against the temple, nor against Caesar, have I sinned *in* anything."
⁹But Festus, wishing to lay a favor on the Jews, answering, said to Paul, "Are you willing, having gone up to Jerusalem, to be judged before me there concerning these things?"

The Appeal to Caesar

¹⁰And Paul said, "I am standing before the judgment seat of Caesar, where it behooves me to be judged. I have done nothing wrong to *the* Jews, as you also know very well. ¹¹Therefore if indeed I do wrong and have done anything worthy of death, I do not refuse to die. But if there is nothing of which they *can* accuse me, no one can give me up to them. I appeal to Caesar!"
¹²Then Festus, having conferred with the Council, answered, "You have appealed to Caesar; to Caesar you will go!"

Festus Consults King Agrippa

¹³Now some days having passed, Agrippa the king and Bernice came down to Caesarea, greeting Festus. ¹⁴And as they stayed there many days, Festus laid before the king the things relating to Paul, saying, "There is a certain man left by Felix *as* a prisoner, ¹⁵concerning whom, on my having been in Jerusalem, the chief priests and the elders of the Jews made a presentation, asking judgment against him, ¹⁶to whom I answered that it is not *the* custom with Romans to give up any man before that the *one* being accused may have *it* to face the accusers, and he may have *the* opportunity of defense concerning the accusation. ¹⁷Therefore of them having come together here, having made no delay, the next *day* having sat on the judgment seat, I commanded the man to be brought, ¹⁸concerning whom the accusers, having stood up, were bringing no charge of *the* crimes of which I was expecting. ¹⁹But they had certain questions against him concerning *their* own religion and concerning a certain Jesus having been dead, whom Paul was affirming to be alive.
²⁰Now I, being perplexed concerning this inquiry, was asking if he was willing to go to Jerusalem and there to be judged concerning these things. ²¹But of Paul having appealed for himself to be kept for the decision of the Emperor, I commanded him to be kept until that I might send him to Caesar."
²²Then Agrippa *said* to Festus, "I have been wanting also to hear the man myself."
He says, "Tomorrow you will hear him."

Paul Before Agrippa and Bernice

²³So on the next day Agrippa and Bernice, having come with great pomp and having entered into the audience hall with both *the* commanders and the men in prominence in the city, and Festus having commanded, Paul was brought in. ²⁴And Festus says, "King Agrippa and all men being present with us, you see this one concerning whom the whole multitude of the Jews pleaded with me, both in Jerusalem and here, crying out of him *that* he ought not to live *any* longer. ²⁵But I, having understood him to have done nothing worthy of death, of this one himself now having appealed to the

Emperor, I determined to send *him*, ²⁶concerning whom I have nothing definite to write to *my* lord. Therefore I have brought him before you all, and especially before you, King Agrippa, so that of the examination having taken place, I might have something to write. ²⁷For it seems absurd to me, sending a prisoner, not also to specify the charges against him."

Acts 26
Paul's Testimony to Agrippa
(Acts 9:1-9; Acts 22:1-21)

¹And Agrippa was saying to Paul, "It is permitted you to speak for yourself."
Then Paul, having stretched out the hand, began his defense: ²"Concerning all of which I am accused by *the* Jews, King Agrippa, I esteem myself fortunate before you, being about to defend myself today, ³you being especially acquainted with all the customs and also controversies of *the* Jews. Therefore I implore *you* to hear me patiently.
⁴Then indeed all the Jews know my manner of life which *is* from youth, having been from *its* beginning among my own nation and in Jerusalem, ⁵knowing me from the first, if they would be willing to testify, that according to the strictest sect of our religion I lived *as* a Pharisee.
⁶And now I stand being judged for *the* hope of the promise having been made by God to our fathers, ⁷to which our twelve tribes hope to attain, serving in earnestness night and day, *the* hope concerning which I am accused by the Jews, O king. ⁸Why is it judged incredible by you if God raises *the* dead?
⁹Therefore I indeed in myself thought I ought to do many things contrary to the name of Jesus of Nazareth, ¹⁰which also I did in Jerusalem. And I also locked up many of the saints in prisons, having received the authority from the chief priests; and they being put to death, I cast against *them* a vote. ¹¹And in all the synagogues, punishing them often, I was compelling *them* to blaspheme. And being exceedingly furious against them, I kept persecuting *them* even as far as to foreign cities, ¹²during which, journeying to Damascus with *the* authority and commission of the chief priests, ¹³at midday on the road, O king, I saw, a light from heaven above, the brightness of the sun, having shone around me and those journeying with me. ¹⁴And of all of us having fallen down to the ground, I heard a voice saying to me in the Hebrew language,ᵃ 'Saul, Saul, why do you persecute Me? *It is* hard for you to kick against *the* goads.'
¹⁵Then I said, 'Who are You, Lord?'
And the Lord said, 'I am Jesus, whom you are persecuting. ¹⁶But rise up and stand on your feet. For I have appeared to you for this purpose, to appoint you a servant and a witness both of that which you have seen of Me, and of the things in which I will appear to you, ¹⁷delivering you out from the people and from the Gentiles to whom I am sending you, ¹⁸to open their eyes, that they may turn from darkness to light, and from the power of Satan to God, *that* they may receive forgiveness of sins and *an* inheritance among those having been sanctified by faith in Me.'
¹⁹So then, O king Agrippa, I was not disobedient to the heavenly vision, ²⁰but both first to those in Damascus and Jerusalem, and all the region of Judea, and to the Gentiles, I kept declaring to repent and to turn to God, doing works worthy of repentance. ²¹On account of these things the Jews, having seized me being in the temple, were attempting to kill *me*.
²²Therefore having obtained help from God unto this day, I have stood bearing witness both to small and to great, saying nothing other than what both the prophets and Moses said was about to happen: ²³that Christ would suffer. As first through resurrection from *the* dead, He is about to preach light both to our people and to the Gentiles."

Festus Interrupts Paul's Defense

24Now of him saying these things in his defense, Festus said in a loud voice, "You are insane, Paul! The great learning turns you to insanity!"
25But Paul says, "I am not insane, most excellent Festus, but I speak words of truth and sobriety. 26For the king understands concerning these things, to whom also I speak using boldness. For I am persuaded none of these things are hidden from him, for none of these things is done in a corner. 27Do you believe the prophets, King Agrippa? I know that you believe."
28Then Agrippa *said* to Paul, "Within so little *time* do you persuade me to become a Christian?"
29Then Paul *said*, "I would wish anyhow to God, both in a little and in much, not only you but also all those hearing me this day to become such as I also am, except these chains."
30Then the king and the governor rose up, and Bernice and those sitting with them, 31and having withdrawn, they began speaking to one another, saying, "This man is doing nothing worthy of death or of chains."
32Then Agrippa was saying to Festus, "This man could have been released if he had not appealed to Caesar."

a 14 Or *Aramaic*

Acts 27
Paul Sails for Rome

1Now when our sailing to Italy was determined, they delivered both Paul and certain other prisoners to a centurion named Julius, of the cohort of Augustus. 2And having boarded a ship of Adramyttium being about to sail to the places along Asia, we set sail—Aristarchus, a Macedonian of Thessalonica, being with us.
3And the next *day* we landed at Sidon. And Julius, having treated Paul considerately, allowed *him*, having gone to his friends, to receive care. 4And having set sail from there, we sailed under Cyprus because of the winds being contrary. 5And having sailed across *the sea* and along Cilicia and Pamphylia, we came to Myra of Lycia. 6And there the centurion, having found a ship of Alexandria sailing to Italy, placed us into it.
7Now sailing slowly for many days, and with difficulty having arrived off Cnidus, the wind not permitting us, we sailed under Crete, off Salmone. 8And coasting along it with difficulty, we came to a certain place called Fair Havens, near to which was *the* city of Lasea.
9Now much time having passed, and the voyage being already dangerous because of even the Fast[a] already being over, Paul was admonishing *them*, 10saying to them, "Men, I understand that the voyage is about to be *filled* with disaster and much loss, not only of the cargo and of the ship, but also of our lives."
11But the centurion was persuaded by the pilot and the ship owner, rather than by the things spoken by Paul. 12And the harbor being unsuitable to winter in, the majority reached a decision to set sail from there, if somehow they might be able, having arrived at Phoenix—a harbor of Crete looking toward *the* southwest and toward *the* northwest—to winter there.

The Storm at Sea
(Jeremiah 6:10-21; Jeremiah 25:15-33; Jonah 1:4-10; Romans 1:18-32)

13Now a south wind having blown gently, having thought to have obtained the purpose, having weighed *anchor*, they began coasting along very near Crete. 14But not long after, there came down from it a tempestuous wind called the Northeaster. 15And the ship having been caught and not being able to face to the wind, having given way, we were driven along.
16And having run under a certain island called Cauda,[b] we were able with difficulty to gain control of the lifeboat,

¹⁷which having taken up, they began using supports, undergirding the ship. And fearing lest they should fall into the sandbars of Syrtis, having lowered the gear,ᶜ thus they were driven along.

¹⁸And we being storm-tossed violently, on the next *day* they began to make a jettison of cargo, ¹⁹and on the third *day* they cast away the tackle of the ship with the own hands. ²⁰And neither sun nor stars appearing for many days, and no small tempest lying on *us*, from then on all hope of our being saved was abandoned.

²¹There being also much time without food, at that time having stood up in their midst, Paul said, "It behooved *you* indeed, O men, having been obedient to me, not to have set sail from Crete and to have incurred this disaster and loss. ²²And yet now I exhort you to take heart, for there will be no loss of life from among you, only of the ship. ²³For this night an angel of God, whose I am and whom I serve, stood by me, ²⁴saying, 'Fear not, Paul. It behooves you to stand before Caesar. And behold, God has granted to you all those sailing with you.' ²⁵Therefore take heart, men, for I believe God that it will be thus, according to the way it has been said to me. ²⁶But it behooves us to fall upon a certain island."

The Shipwreck

²⁷And when the fourteenth night had come, of us being driven about in the Adriatic,ᵈ toward *the* middle of the night the sailors began sensing some land to be drawing near to them. ²⁸And having taken soundings, they found twenty fathoms.ᵉ Then having gone a little farther and having taken soundings again, they found fifteen fathoms.ᶠ ²⁹And fearing lest we might fall somewhere on rocky places, having cast four anchors out of *the* stern, they were praying for day to come.

³⁰And of the sailors seeking to flee out of the ship and having let down the lifeboat into the sea under pretense as being about to cast out anchors from *the* bow, ³¹Paul said to the centurion and to the soldiers, "Unless these remain in the ship, you are not able to be saved." ³²Then the soldiers cut away the ropes of the lifeboat, and allowed her to fall away.

³³And until that day was about to come, Paul kept urging all to partake of food, saying, "Today *is* the fourteenth day you continue watching without eating, having taken nothing. ³⁴Therefore I exhort you to take food, for this is for your preservation; for not one hair of your head will perish."

³⁵Now having said these things and having taken bread, he gave thanks to God before all; and having broken *it*, he began to eat. ³⁶And all, having been encouraged, also took food themselves. ³⁷And we were altogether two hundred seventy-sixᵍ souls in the ship. ³⁸Then having been filled with food, they began to lighten the ship, casting out the wheat into the sea.

³⁹And when it was day, they did not recognize the land, but they noticed a certain bay, having a shore on which they determined to drive the ship if they should be able. ⁴⁰And having cut away the anchors, they left *them* in the sea, at the same time having loosened the ropes of the rudders. And having hoisted the foresail to the blowing *wind*, they began making for the shore. ⁴¹But having fallen into a place between two seas, they ran the vessel aground. And indeed the bow, having stuck fast, remained immovable, and the stern was being broken up by the violence of the waves.

⁴²Now *the* plan of the soldiers was that they should kill the prisoners, lest anyone, having swum away, should escape. ⁴³But the centurion, desiring to save Paul, hindered them of *the* purpose; and he commanded those being able to swim, having cast *themselves* off first, to go out on the land, ⁴⁴and the rest, some indeed on boards, and some on things

from the ship. And thus it came to pass that all were brought safely to the land.

a 9 That is, Yom Kippur, the Day of Atonement
b 16 NE, BYZ, and TR *Clauda*
c 17 Or *the sails*
d 27 The Adriatic Sea referred to an area also extending well south of Italy.
e 28 About 120 feet or 37 meters
f 28 About 90 feet or 27 meters
g 37 WH *seventy-six*

Acts 28
Ashore on Malta

¹And having been saved, we then found out that the island is called Malta. ²And the natives were showing not *just* the ordinary kindness to us. For having kindled a fire, they received all of us, because of the rain coming on and because of the cold.

³Now of Paul having gathered a quantity of sticks and having laid *them* on the fire, a viper, having come out from the heat, fastened on his hand. ⁴And when the natives saw the beast hanging from his hand, they began to say to one another, "By all means this man is a murderer whom, having been saved from the sea, Justice[a] has not permitted to live." ⁵Then indeed, having shaken off the creature into the fire, he suffered no injury. ⁶But they were expecting him to be about to become inflamed or suddenly to fall down dead. But of them waiting a great while and seeing nothing amiss happening to him, having changed their opinion, they began declaring him to be a god.

⁷Now in the *parts* around that place were lands belonging to the chief of the island, named Publius, who having received us, entertained *us* hospitably *for* three days. ⁸And it came to pass, the father of Publius was lying, oppressed with fevers and dysentery, toward whom Paul, having entered and having prayed, having laid the hands on him, healed him. ⁹And of this having taken place, also the rest in the island having infirmities were coming and were healed, ¹⁰who also honored us with many honors, and on setting sail, they laid on *us* the things for *our* needs.

Paul Arrives in Italy

¹¹Then after three months, we sailed in an Alexandrian ship having wintered in the island, with a figurehead of the Dioscuri.[b] ¹²And having put in at Syracuse, we stayed three days, ¹³from where having gone around, we arrived at Rhegium. And after one day a south wind having come on, on the second day we came to Puteoli, ¹⁴where having found *some* brothers, we were entreated to remain with them seven days. And so we came to Rome.

¹⁵And the brothers from there, having heard the things concerning us, came out as far as *the* market of Appius and *the* Three Taverns to meet us, whom Paul having seen, having given thanks to God, took courage.

Paul Preaches at Rome

¹⁶Now when we came to Rome,[c] Paul was allowed to stay by himself, with the soldier who was guarding him.

¹⁷And it came to pass after three days, he called together those being leaders of the Jews. And of them having come together, he was saying to them, "Men, brothers, having done nothing against the people or the customs of our fathers, I was delivered from Jerusalem a prisoner into the hands of the Romans, ¹⁸who having examined me, were wanting to let *me* go, on account of not one cause of death existing in me. ¹⁹But of the Jews objecting, I was compelled to appeal to Caesar, not as having anything to lay against my nation. ²⁰Therefore for this cause I have called to see you and to speak to *you*. For because of the hope of Israel, I have around *me* this chain."

²¹Then they said to him, "We received neither letters concerning you from Judea, nor any of the brothers having arrived reported or said anything evil concerning you. ²²But we deem it worthy to hear from you what you think, for truly concerning this sect, it is known to us that it is spoken against everywhere."

²³Then having appointed him a day, many came to him to the lodging, to whom he expounded from morning to evening, fully testifying to the kingdom of God and persuading them concerning Jesus from both the Law of Moses and the Prophets.
²⁴And indeed, some were persuaded of the things he is speaking, but some refused to believe. ²⁵And being discordant with one another they began to leave, Paul having spoken one word: "The Holy Spirit spoke rightly by the prophet Isaiah to your fathers, ²⁶saying:

'Go to this people and say,
"In hearing you will hear and never understand;
and in seeing you will see and never perceive."
²⁷For the heart of this people has grown dull,
and with the ears they barely hear,
and they have closed their eyes,
lest ever they should see with the eyes,
and they should hear with the ears,
and they should understand with the heart,
and should turn,
and I will heal them.'*ᵈ*

²⁸Therefore be it known to you that this salvation of God has been sent to the Gentiles, and they will listen!"*ᵉ*
³⁰And he stayed two whole years in his own rented house, and was welcoming all coming unto him, ³¹proclaiming the kingdom of God and teaching the things concerning the Lord Jesus Christ with all boldness, unhinderedly.

a 4 Greek *Dike*, that is, the Greek goddess of justice
b 11 The Twin Brothers, that is, the Greek gods Castor and Pollux
c 16 BYZ and TR include *the centurion delivered up the prisoners to the captain of the barrack, but*
d 26-27 Isaiah 6:9,10
e 28 BYZ and TR include *29 When he had said this, the Jews went away, disputing sharply among themselves.*

Romans

Romans 1
Greeting the Saints in Rome

¹Paul, servant of Jesus Christ, a called apostle having been set apart for *the* gospel of God, ²which He promised beforehand through His prophets in *the* Holy Scriptures, ³concerning His Son, having come of *the* seed of David according to flesh, ⁴having been declared *the* Son of God in power according to *the* Spirit of holiness, by resurrection *from the* dead: Jesus Christ our Lord, ⁵through whom we have received grace and apostleship unto obedience of faith among all the Gentiles on behalf of His name, ⁶among whom are you also, called of Jesus Christ.
⁷To all those being in Rome beloved of God, called saints:
Grace to you and peace from God our Father and *the* Lord Jesus Christ.

Paul's Desire to Visit Rome
(1 Thessalonians 2:17-20)

⁸First indeed, I thank my God through Jesus Christ for all of you, because your faith is being proclaimed in all the world. ⁹For God, whom I serve in my spirit in the gospel of His Son, is my witness how unceasingly I make mention of you, ¹⁰always upon my prayers imploring, if perhaps now at last by the will of God I will make a prosperous journey to come to you. ¹¹For I long to see you, that I may impart some spiritual gift to you, to your strengthening, ¹²and, that is, to be encouraged together among you through the faith among one another, both of you and of me.
¹³Now I do not want you to be ignorant, brothers, that many times I purposed to come to you, and was hindered until the present, that I might have some fruit among you also, even as among the other Gentiles. ¹⁴I am a debtor both to Greeks and to barbarians, both to *the* wise and *the* foolish. ¹⁵Thus as to me *there is*

readiness to preach the gospel also to you who *are* in Rome.

Unashamed of the Gospel

¹⁶For I am not ashamed of the gospel, for it is *the* power of God unto salvation to everyone believing—both to Jewish first, and to Greek. ¹⁷For in it *the* righteousness of God is revealed from faith to faith, as it has been written: "And the righteous will live by faith."ᵃ

God's Wrath against Sin

(Jeremiah 6:10-21; Jeremiah 25:15-33; Jonah 1:4-10; Acts 27:13-26)

¹⁸For *the* wrath of God is revealed from heaven upon all ungodliness and unrighteousness of men, suppressing the truth by unrighteousness, ¹⁹because the known of God is manifest among them, for God has revealed *it* to them. ²⁰For from *the* creation of *the* world His invisible qualities, both His eternal power and divinity, are clearly seen, being understood by the things made, for them to be without excuse.
²¹For having known God, they glorified *Him* not as God, or were thankful; but they became futile in their thinking and their foolish heart was darkened. ²²Professing to be wise, they became fools, ²³and they changed the glory of the immortal God into a likeness of an image of mortal man and birds and quadrupeds and creeping things.
²⁴Therefore God gave them up in the desires of their hearts to impurity to dishonor their bodies between themselves, ²⁵who changed the truth of God into falsehood, and reverenced and served the created thing beyond the *One* having created *it*, who is blessed to the ages! Amen.
²⁶Because of this, God gave up them to passions of dishonor. For even their females changed the natural use into that contrary to nature. ²⁷And likewise also the males, having left the natural use of the female, were inflamed in their desire toward one another, males with males, working out shame and receiving in themselves the recompense which was fitting of their error.
²⁸And as they did not see fit to have God in *their* knowledge, God gave them up to a depraved mind, to do things not being proper; ²⁹being filled with all unrighteousness, wickedness, covetousness, malice; full of envy, murder, strife, deceit, maliciousness; gossips, ³⁰slanderers, hateful to God, insolent, arrogant, boastful; inventors of evil things, disobedient to parents; ³¹foolish, untrustworthy, heartless, unmerciful; ³²who having known the righteous judgment of God, that those doing such things are worthy of death, not only are practicing them, but are also approving of those practicing *them*.

a 17 Habakkuk 2:4

Romans 2
God's Righteous Judgment

(Genesis 4:1-7; Jude 1:3-16)

¹Therefore you are inexcusable, O man, each one who is judging. For in that which you judge the other, you are condemning yourself, for you, the *one* judging, do the same things. ²But we know that the judgment of God upon those practicing such things is according to truth. ³Now do you suppose this, O man, the *one* judging those practicing such things and doing them *yourself*, that you will escape the judgment of God? ⁴Or do you despise the riches of His kindness and forbearance and patience, not knowing that the kindness of God leads you to repentance?
⁵But because of your hardness and unrepentant heart, you are treasuring up to yourself wrath in *the* day of wrath and revelation of *the* righteous judgement of God, ⁶who "will give to each according to his works,"ᵃ ⁷to those who indeed with endurance in good work are seeking glory and honor and immortality, eternal life; ⁸but to those of self-interest and disobeying the truth, but being persuaded about unrighteousness, wrath

and anger; ⁹tribulation and distress upon every soul of man working evil, both of Jewish first, and also of Greek; ¹⁰but glory and honor and peace to everyone doing good, both to Jewish first, and to Greek. ¹¹For there is no partiality with God.

¹²For as many as have sinned without *the* Law also will perish without *the* Law; and as many as have sinned in *the* Law will be judged by *the* Law, ¹³for not the hearers of *the* Law *are* righteous with God; but the doers of *the* Law will be justified.

¹⁴For when Gentiles, not having *the* Law, do by nature the things of the Law, these not having *the* Law are a law to themselves, ¹⁵who show the work of the Law, written in their hearts, their conscience bearing witness, and the thoughts between one another accusing or also defending *them* ¹⁶on that day when God will judge the secrets of men according to my gospel, by Christ Jesus.

The Jews and the Law

¹⁷But if you are called a Jew and rely on *the* Law and boast in God, ¹⁸and you know *His* will and approve the things being superior, being instructed out of the Law, ¹⁹and you are persuaded *that* you yourself are a guide of *the* blind, a light to those in darkness, ²⁰an instructor of *the* foolish, a teacher of infants, having in the Law the embodiment of knowledge and of the truth— ²¹then *you* teaching another, do you do not teach yourself? You preaching not to steal, do you steal? ²²You saying not to commit adultery, do you commit adultery? You abhorring idols, do you rob temples? ²³You who boast in Law, do you dishonor God through the transgression of the Law? ²⁴As it has been written: "For the name of God is blasphemed among the Gentiles through you."ᵇ

²⁵For circumcision profits if you do *the* Law; but if you are a transgressor of Law, your circumcision has become uncircumcision. ²⁶Therefore if the uncircumcision keeps the requirements of the Law, will not his uncircumcision be reckoned for circumcision? ²⁷And the uncircumcision by nature, fulfilling the Law, will judge you who with *the* letter and circumcision *are* a transgressor of Law.

²⁸For the *one* on the outside a Jew is not, neither *that* on the outside in flesh *is* circumcision. ²⁹But he who *is* a Jew *is one* on the inside; and circumcision *is* of heart, in spirit, not in letter, of whom the praise *is* not of men, but of God.

a 6 Psalm 62:12
b 24 Isaiah 52:5

Romans 3
God Remains Faithful
(Psalm 147:1-20; Hebrews 10:1-18)

¹What then *is* the superiority of the Jew? Or what *is* the benefit of the circumcision? ²Much in every way. For chiefly indeed, that they were entrusted with the oracles of God.

³What if indeed some disbelieved? Will their unbelief nullify the faithfulness of God? ⁴Never may it be! But let God be true, and every man a liar, as it has been written:

> "That You may be justified in Your words,
> and will prevail in Your being judged."ᵃ

⁵But if our unrighteousness shows God's righteousness, what shall we say? God, inflicting the wrath, *is* unrighteous? I speak according to man. ⁶Never may it be! Otherwise, how will God judge the world? ⁷But if in my lie, the truth of God abounded to His glory, why am I also still judged as a sinner? ⁸And *is it* not, as we are slanderously charged, and as some affirm us to say, "Let us do evil things that good things may come?" Their condemnation is just.

There is No One Righteous
(Psalm 14:1-7)

⁹What then? Are we better? Not at all. For we have already charged both Jews and Greeks all to be under sin. ¹⁰As it has been written:

"There is none righteous,
 not even one;
¹¹there is none understanding;
 there is none seeking after God.
¹²All have turned away;
 together they have become worthless;
there is none who is practicing good,
 there is not so much as one.ᵇ
¹³Their throat *is* a grave having been opened;
 they keep practicing deceitᶜ with their tongues;
 the venom of vipers *is* under their lips,ᵈ
¹⁴of whom the mouth is full of cursing and of bitterness;ᵉ
 ¹⁵their feet *are* swift to shed blood;
¹⁶ruin and misery *are* in their paths;
 ¹⁷and *the* way of peace they have not known.ᶠ
¹⁸There is no fear of God before their eyes."ᵍ

¹⁹Now we know that whatever the Law says, it speaks to those under the Law, so that every mouth may be stopped, and the whole world may be under judgment to God. ²⁰Therefore by works of *the* Law, not any flesh will be justified before Him; for through *the* Law *is* knowledge of sin.

Righteousness through Faith

²¹But now apart from Law, *the* righteousness of God has been revealed, being borne witness to by the Law and the Prophets. ²²And *the* righteousness of God *is* through faith from Jesus Christ toward all those believing. For there is no distinction, ²³for all have sinned and fall short of the glory of God, ²⁴being justified freely by His grace through the redemption that *is* in Christ Jesus, ²⁵whom God set forth as a propitiation through faith in His blood, for a showing forth of His righteousness, because of the forbearance of the sins having taken place beforehand, ²⁶in the forbearance of God, for the showing forth of His righteousness in the present time, for Him to be just, and justifying the *one* of *the* faith of Jesus.

²⁷Where then *is* boasting? It has been excluded. Through what principle? That of works? No, but through *the* principle of faith. ²⁸Therefore we reckon a man to be justified by faith apart from works of the Law. ²⁹Or *is He* the God of Jews only, not also of Gentiles? Yes, also of Gentiles, ³⁰since indeed God *is* the One who will justify *the* circumcision by faith and *the* uncircumcision through the *same* faith. ³¹Do we, then, nullify *the* Law through faith? Never may it be! Instead, we uphold Law.

a 4 Psalm 51:4
b 10-12 Psalms 14:1-3; 53:1-3
c 13 Psalm 5:9
d 13 Psalm 140:3
e 14 Psalm 10:7
f 15-17 Isaiah 59:7,8
g 18 Psalm 36:1

Romans 4
Abraham Justified by Faith

(Genesis 15:1-7; Galatians 3:1-9; Hebrews 11:8-19; James 2:14-26)

¹What then shall we say Abraham our father discovered according to *the* flesh? ²For if Abraham was justified by works, he has ground of boasting, but not toward God. ³For what does the Scripture say? "And Abraham believed God, and it was reckoned to him for righteousness."ᵃ ⁴Now to the *one* working, the reward is not reckoned according to grace, but according to debt. ⁵However, to the *one* not working, but believing on the One justifying the ungodly, his faith is reckoned for righteousness, ⁶just as David also declares the blessedness of the man to whom God credits righteousness apart from works:

⁷"Blessed *are those* whose lawless deeds are forgiven,
 and whose sins are covered;
⁸blessed *is the* man against whom *the* Lord will never reckon sin."ᵇ

⁹*Is* this blessing then on the circumcision, or also on the uncircumcision? For we are saying faith was credited to Abraham as righteousness. ¹⁰How then was it credited? Being in circumcision, or in uncircumcision? Not in circumcision, but in uncircumcision.

¹¹And he received *the* sign of circumcision, a seal of the righteousness of the faith that *he had while* in the uncircumcision, for him to be father of all those believing *while* in uncircumcision, for the righteousness to be credited also to them, ¹²and *the* father of circumcision to those not only of circumcision, but also to those walking in the steps of the faith of our father Abraham during uncircumcision.

Abraham Receives the Promise
(Genesis 15:8-21; Numbers 34:1-15)

¹³For the promise *was* to Abraham or his descendants that he should be heir *of the* world, not through *the* Law, but through *the* righteousness of faith. ¹⁴For if those of *the* Law *are* heirs, faith has been made void and the promise made of no effect. ¹⁵For Law brings wrath; and where there is no Law, neither *is* transgression.

¹⁶Therefore it *is* of faith, that *it may be* according to grace, for the promise to be sure to all the seed, not only to that of the Law, but also to that of *the* faith of Abraham, who is *the* father of us of all— ¹⁷as it has been written: "I have made you a father of many nations."[c]—before God whom he believed, the *One* giving life to the dead and calling *into* being the things not even existing, ¹⁸who against hope, in hope believed, for him to become *the* father of many nations, according to that having been spoken, "So shall your offspring be."[d] ¹⁹And not having become weak in the faith, he considered his body already having become dead, being about a hundred years old, and the lifelessness of Sarah's womb.

²⁰Yet he did not waver through unbelief at the promise of God, but was strengthened in faith, having given glory to God, ²¹and having been fully assured that what He had promised, He is also able to do. ²²Therefore also "it was credited to him unto righteousness."[e]

²³Now it was not written on account of him alone that "it was credited to him," ²⁴but also on account of us, to whom it is about to be credited, to those believing on the *One* having raised Jesus our Lord out from *the* dead, ²⁵who was delivered over for our trespasses, and was raised for our justification.

a 3 Genesis 15:6
b 7-8 Psalm 32:1,2
c 17 Genesis 17:5
d 18 Genesis 15:5
e 22 Genesis 15:6

Romans 5
The Triumph of Faith
(John 14:27-31)

¹Therefore, having been justified by faith, we have[a] peace with God through our Lord Jesus Christ, ²through whom also we have access by faith into this grace in which we stand; and we boast in *the* hope of the glory of God.

³And not only *so*, but also we glory in *our* tribulations, knowing that tribulation produces perseverance; ⁴and perseverance, character; and character, hope. ⁵And hope does not make *us* ashamed, because the love of God has been poured out into our hearts through *the* Holy Spirit, the *One* having been given to us.

Christ's Sacrifice for the Ungodly
(Genesis 22:1-10; John 3:16-21)

⁶Yet indeed Christ, of us still being without strength, according to *the* right time, died for *the* ungodly. ⁷For rarely will anyone die for a righteous *man*, though on behalf of the good *man* perhaps someone would even dare to die. ⁸But God demonstrates His love to us, that of us being still sinners, Christ died for us. ⁹Therefore much more, having been justified now by His blood, we will be saved by Him from wrath! ¹⁰For if, being enemies, we were reconciled to God

through the death of His Son, much more, having been reconciled, shall we be saved in His life! ¹¹And not only *so*, but also we are rejoicing in God through our Lord Jesus Christ, through whom we have now received reconciliation.

Death in Adam, Life in Christ
(Genesis 3:1-7; Genesis 7:1-5; 2 Peter 3:1-9)

¹²Because of this, just as sin entered into the world through one man, and death through sin, so also death passed to all men, because all sinned. ¹³For until *the* Law, sin was in *the* world; but sin is not imputed, there being no law. ¹⁴Nevertheless death reigned from Adam until Moses, even over those not having sinned in the likeness of the transgression of Adam, who is a type of the coming One.

¹⁵But so also the gift *is* not like the trespass. For if by the trespass of the one, the many died, how much more did the grace of God and the gift in grace, which *is* of the one man Jesus Christ, abound to the many! ¹⁶And the gift *is* not as through one having sinned. For truly the judgment from one *was* unto condemnation; but the gift *is* out of many trespasses unto justification. ¹⁷For if, by the trespass of the one, death reigned through the one, how much more will those receiving the abundance of grace and of the gift of righteousness reign in life through the one, Jesus Christ!

¹⁸So then, just as through one trespass, *it is* unto condemnation to all men, so also through one act of righteousness *it is* unto justification of life to all men. ¹⁹For as indeed through the disobedience of the one man, the many were made sinners, so also through the obedience of the One, the many will be made righteous.

²⁰Now *the* Law entered so that trespass might abound; but where sin abounded, grace overabounded, ²¹so that, just as sin reigned in death, so also grace might reign through righteousness, unto eternal life through Jesus Christ our Lord.

a 1 Or *let us have*

Romans 6
Dead to Sin, Alive to God
(2 Corinthians 4:7-18)

¹What then will we say? Shall we continue in sin that grace may abound? ²Never may it be! How shall we who died to sin still live in it? ³Or are you unaware that as many as have been baptized into Christ Jesus have been baptized into His death? ⁴Therefore we were buried with Him through baptism into death, so that, just as Christ was raised up out from *the* dead by the glory of the Father, so we also should walk in newness of life.

⁵For if we have become united in the likeness of His death, certainly also we will be of the resurrection, ⁶knowing this, that our old man was crucified with *Him*, so that the body of sin might be annulled, *that* we are no longer enslaved to sin. ⁷For the *one* having died has been freed from sin.

⁸Now if we died with Christ, we believe that we will also live with Him, ⁹knowing that Christ, having been raised up out from *the* dead, dies no more. Death no longer rules over Him. ¹⁰For that which He died, He died to sin once for all; but that which He lives, He lives to God. ¹¹So also you, consider yourselves to be dead indeed to sin, but living to God in Christ Jesus.

¹²Therefore do not let sin reign in your mortal body, in order to obey its desires. ¹³Neither yield your members to sin *as* instruments of unrighteousness, but yield yourselves to God, as living out from *the* dead, and your members to God *as* instruments of righteousness. ¹⁴For sin will not rule over you, for you are not under law, but under grace.

The Wages of Sin
(1 Peter 3:14-22)

¹⁵What then? Shall we sin because we are not under law, but under grace? Never may it be! ¹⁶Do you not know that to whom you yield yourselves *as* slaves

for obedience, you are slaves to him whom you obey, whether of sin to death, or of obedience to righteousness? ¹⁷But thanks *be* to God that you *who* were slaves of sin have now become obedient from *the* heart to the pattern of teaching to which you were committed. ¹⁸And having been set free from sin, you have become slaves to righteousness.

¹⁹I speak in human terms on account of the weakness of your flesh. For just as you yielded your members in bondage to impurity and to lawlessness unto lawlessness, so now yield your members in bondage to righteousness unto sanctification.

²⁰For when you were slaves of sin, you were free from righteousness. ²¹What fruit, therefore, did you have then in the *things* of which you are now ashamed? For the end of those things *is* death. ²²But now, having been set free from sin, and having become slaves to God, you have your fruit unto sanctification, and the end *is* eternal life. ²³For the wages of sin *is* death, but the gift of God *is* eternal life in Christ Jesus our Lord.

Romans 7
Release from the Law
(Galatians 3:15-25)

¹Or are you ignorant brothers (for I speak to those knowing *the* law), that the law rules over the man for as long as *the* time he is alive? ²For the married woman is bound by law to the living husband; but if the husband should die, she is cleared from the law of the husband. ³So then, if she is to another man, the husband being alive, she will be called an adulteress; but if the husband should die, she is free from the law, *so as for* her not to be an adulteress, having been to another man. ⁴Likewise, my brothers, you also have been put to death to the Law through the body of Christ, for you to belong to another, to the *One* having been raised out from *the* dead, so that we should bear fruit to God. ⁵For while we were in the flesh, the passions of sins that *were* through the Law were at work in our members, to the bringing forth of fruit to death. ⁶But now we have been released from the Law, having died to that which we were bound, in order for us to serve in newness of *the* Spirit, and not in oldness of *the* letter.

God's Law is Holy

⁷What then shall we say? *Is* the Law sin? Never may it be! But I have not known sin, if not by Law. And indeed, I had not been conscious of covetousness if the Law had not said, "You shall not covet."ᵃ ⁸But sin, having taken an occasion by the commandment, produced in me all covetousness; for apart from *the* Law, sin *is* dead.

⁹And I once was alive apart from Law; but the commandment having come, sin revived, and I died; ¹⁰and this commandment that *was* unto life proved to be death to me. ¹¹For sin, having taken an occasion by the commandment, deceived me, and by it put *me* to death. ¹²So indeed, the Law *is* holy, and the commandment *is* holy and righteous and good.

Struggling with Sin

¹³Has that which *is* good then become death to me? Never may it be! But in order that sin might be shown to be sin, it is working out death through that which *is* good to me, so that through the commandment sin might become sinful beyond excess.

¹⁴For we know that *the* Law is spiritual; but I am fleshly, having been sold under sin. ¹⁵For what I do, I do not understand. For what I want, this I do not do; but what I hate, this I do. ¹⁶Now if that which I do not want, this I do, I consent to the Law, that *it is* good. ¹⁷And in that case I am no longer doing it, but the sin dwelling in me.

¹⁸For I know that there dwells in me nothing good, that is, in my flesh. For to will is present with me, but not to do good. ¹⁹For *the* good that I desire, I do

not do; but *the* evil that I do not want, this I practice. ²⁰Now if what I do not want, I do this, *it is* no longer I who do it, but sin dwelling in me.
²¹So I find the principle in my desiring to do good, that evil is present with me. ²²For I delight in the Law of God according to the inward man; ²³but I see another law in my members, warring against the law of my mind, and making me captive to the law of sin being in my members. ²⁴O wretched man I am! Who will deliver me out of this body of death? ²⁵Thanks *be* then to God, through Jesus Christ our Lord!
So then, I myself indeed with *my* mind serve God's Law; but *with* the flesh, *the* Law of sin.

a 7 Exodus 20:17; Deuteronomy 5:21

Romans 8
Living in the Spirit
(Galatians 5:16-26)

¹Therefore *there is* now no condemnation to those in Christ Jesus.ᵃ ²For the Law of the Spirit of life has set you freeᵇ in Christ Jesus from the Law of sin and death. ³For of the Law *being* powerless in that it was weak through the flesh, God, having sent His Son in likeness of sin of flesh and for sin, condemned sin in the flesh, ⁴so that the righteousness of the Law should be fulfilled in us not walking according to *the* flesh, but according to *the* Spirit.
⁵For those being according to flesh mind the things of the flesh; but those according to Spirit, the things of the Spirit. ⁶For the mind of the flesh *is* death; but the mind of the Spirit, life and peace, ⁷because the mind of the flesh *is* hostility toward God; for it is not subject to *the* Law of God, for not even can it *be*. ⁸And those being in *the* flesh are not able to please God.
⁹Now you are not in flesh but in Spirit, if indeed *the* Spirit of God dwells in you; but if anyone does not have *the* Spirit of Christ, he is not of Him. ¹⁰But if Christ *is* in you, the body *is* indeed dead on account of sin, but the Spirit *is* life on account of righteousness. ¹¹And if the Spirit of the *One* having raised up Jesus out from *the* dead dwells in you, the *One* having raised up Christ Jesus out from *the* deadᶜ also will give life to your mortal bodies, on account of His Spirit dwelling in you.

Heirs with Christ
(Genesis 21:1-8; Galatians 4:1-7)

¹²So then, brothers, we are debtors, not to the flesh, to live according to flesh. ¹³For if you live according to flesh, you are about to die; but if by *the* Spirit you put to death the deeds of the body, you will live. ¹⁴For as many as are led by *the* Spirit of God, these are sons of God.
¹⁵For you have not received a spirit of bondage again to fear, but you have received *the* Spirit of divine adoption as sons, by whom we cry, "Abba! Father!" ¹⁶The Spirit Himself bears witness with our spirit that we are children of God, ¹⁷and if children, also heirs: heirs indeed of God, and joint-heirs of Christ, if indeed we suffer with *Him*, so that we may also be glorified together.

Future Glory
(2 Corinthians 5:1-10)

¹⁸For I reckon that the sufferings of the present time *are* not comparable to the coming glory to be revealed to us. ¹⁹For the earnest expectation of the creation awaits the revelation of the sons of God. ²⁰For the creation was subjected to futility, not willingly, but because of the *One* having subjected *it*, in hope ²¹that the creation itself will also be set free from the bondage of decay, into the freedom of the glory of the children of God.
²²For we know that the whole creation groans together and travails together until now. ²³And not only *so*, but we ourselves, even having the firstfruit of the Spirit, also groan ourselves in ourselves, awaiting divine adoption as sons, the redemption of our body. ²⁴For in this hope we were saved; but hope being

seen is no hope; for does anyone hope for what he sees? ²⁵But if we hope for what we do not see, we await in patience. ²⁶Now likewise also, the Spirit joins to help us in weakness; for we do not know the things which we should pray for as it behooves, but the Spirit Himself makes intercession with inexpressible groanings. ²⁷And the *One* searching hearts knows what *is* the mindset of the Spirit, because He intercedes for *the* saints according to God.

God Works In All Things
(Ephesians 1:3-14)

²⁸And we know that God works together all things for good to those loving God, to those being called according to *His* purpose, ²⁹because those whom He foreknew, He also predestined *to be* conformed to the image of His Son, for Him to be firstborn among many brothers. ³⁰And those whom He predestined, these also He called; and whom He called, these also He justified; and whom He justified, these also He glorified.

³¹What then will we say to these things? If God *is* for us, who *can be* against us? ³²For He who spared not the own Son, but gave Him up for us all, how will He not also, with Him, grant us all things? ³³Who will bring an accusation against *the* elect of God? God *is* the *One* justifying. ³⁴Who *is* the *one* condemning? For it is Christ Jesus, the *one* having died, now rather having been raised up, who is also at *the* right hand of God, and who is interceding for us.

More than Conquerors
(Psalm 44:1-26)

³⁵Who will separate us from the love of Christ? Will tribulation, or distress, or persecution, or famine, or nakedness, or danger, or sword? ³⁶As it has been written:

> "For Your sake we face death all the day;
>> we were regarded as sheep of slaughter."ᵈ

³⁷But in all these things, we more than conquer through the *One* having loved us. ³⁸For I am persuaded that neither death, nor life, nor angels, nor principalities, nor things present, nor things to come, nor powers, ³⁹nor height, nor depth, nor any other created thing, will be able to separate us from the love of God in Christ Jesus our Lord.

a 1 BYZ and TR include *who do not walk according to the flesh, but according to the Spirit*
b 2 BYZ and TR *set me free*
c 11 NA, BYZ, and TR *Raised Christ out from the dead*
d 36 Psalm 44:22

Romans 9
Paul's Concern for the Jews

¹I speak *the* truth in Christ. I am not lying. My conscience testifies for me in *the* Holy Spirit ²that my grief is great, and unceasing sorrow *is* in my heart. ³For I could wish myself to be a curse, separated from Christ for my brothers, my kinsmen according to *the* flesh, ⁴who are Israelites, whose *is* the divine adoption as sons, and the glory, and the covenants, and the lawgiving, and the service, and the promises; ⁵whose *are* the patriarchs; and from whom *is* Christ according to *the* flesh, being God over all, blessed to the ages. Amen.

God's Sovereign Choice
(Genesis 25:19-28; Malachi 1:1-5)

⁶And *it is* not as that the word of God has failed. For not all who *are* of Israel, *are* these Israel. ⁷Nor because they are seed of Abraham *are* all children. Rather, "In Isaac your offspring will be named."ᵃ ⁸That is, the children of the flesh, these *are* not children of God; but the children of the promise are regarded as offspring. ⁹For this *is* the word of *the* promise: "At this time I will come, and to Sarah there will be a son."ᵇ ¹⁰And not only *so*, but also Rebecca, having conception by one, Isaac our father, ¹¹for they not yet having been born nor having done anything good or evil, so that the purpose of God according to election might stand, ¹²not of works,

but of the *One* calling, it was said to her, "The older will serve the younger."*c* ¹³As it has been written: "Jacob I loved, but Esau I hated."*d*

¹⁴What then shall we say? *Is there* injustice with God? Never may it be! ¹⁵For He says to Moses:

"I will show mercy to whom I may show mercy,
 and I will have compassion on whom I may have compassion."*e*

¹⁶So then, *it is* not of the willing, nor of the running, but of God showing mercy. ¹⁷For the Scripture says to Pharaoh: "For this very *purpose* I have raised you up, so that I might show My power in you, and that My name should be declared in all the earth."*f* ¹⁸So then, He shows mercy to whom He wants, and He hardens whom He wants.

The Calling of the Gentiles

¹⁹Then you will say to me, "Why then does He still find fault? For who is resisting His purpose?" ²⁰But rather, O man, who are you, answering against God? *Shall* the thing formed say to the *One* having formed *it*, "Why have you made me like this?"*g* ²¹Or does the potter not have authority over the clay, to make out of the same lump one vessel unto honor, but one unto dishonor?

²²And what if God, desiring to show the wrath and to make known His power, bore with much patience *the* vessels of wrath, having been fitted for destruction, ²³that He might also make known the riches of His glory upon *the* vessels of mercy, which He prepared beforehand for glory, ²⁴even us, whom He has called not only out from *the* Jews, but also out from *the* Gentiles? ²⁵As He also says in Hosea:

"I will call that which *is* not My people, My people;
 and her not having been loved, having been loved,"*h*

²⁶and,

"It will happen that in the place where it was said to them,
 'You *are* not My people,'
there they will be called
 'sons of *the* living God.'"*i*

²⁷And Isaiah cries out concerning Israel:

"Though the number of the sons of Israel shall be as the sand of the sea,
 only the remnant will be saved.
²⁸For *the* Lord will perform *the* sentence
 He *is* concluding and bringing swiftly upon the earth."*j*

²⁹And, as Isaiah foretold:

"If *the* Lord of Hosts had not left us descendants,
 we would have become like Sodom,
 and we would have been made like Gomorrah."*k*

Israel's Unbelief

³⁰What then will we say? That Gentiles, not pursuing righteousness, have attained righteousness, and righteousness that *is* by faith; ³¹but Israel, pursuing a law of righteousness, did not attain to *that* law. ³²Why? Because *it was* not by faith, but as by works. They stumbled over the stone of stumbling, ³³as it has been written:

"Behold, I lay in Zion a stone of stumbling,
 and a rock of offense;
 and the *one* believing on Him
 will never be put to shame."*l*

a 7 Genesis 21:12
b 9 Genesis 18:10,14
c 12 Genesis 25:23
d 13 Malachi 1:2,3
e 15 Exodus 33:19
f 17 Exodus 9:16
g 20 Isaiah 29:16; 45:9; Jeremiah 18:6
h 25 Hosea 2:23
i 26 Hosea 1:10
j 27-28 Isaiah 10:22,23
k 29 Isaiah 1:9
l 33 Isaiah 8:14; 28:16

Romans 10
The Word Brings Salvation

¹Brothers, indeed the desire and supplication of my heart to God on behalf of them *is* for salvation. ²For I bear

witness about them that they have zeal for God, but not according to knowledge. ³For being ignorant of the righteousness of God and seeking to establish the own righteousness, they did not submit to the righteousness of God. ⁴For *the* end of Law *is* Christ, unto righteousness to everyone believing.

⁵For Moses writes *of* the righteousness that *is* of the Law that "The man having done these things will live by them."[a] ⁶But the righteousness of faith speaks thus: "You should not say in your heart, 'Who will ascend into heaven?'[b] (that is, to bring down Christ) ⁷or, 'Who will descend into the abyss?'[c] (that is, to bring up Christ out from *the* dead)."

⁸But what does it say? "The word is near you, in your mouth, and in your heart."[d] That is, the word of faith which we proclaim, ⁹that if you confess with your mouth, "Jesus *is* Lord," and believe in your heart that God raised Him out from *the* dead, you will be saved. ¹⁰For in the heart is belief unto righteousness, and in the mouth is confession unto salvation.

¹¹For the Scripture says, "Everyone believing on Him will not be put to shame."[e] ¹²For there is no difference between Jew and Greek; for the same Lord of all is rich toward all those calling Him, ¹³for, "Whoever shall call upon the name of *the* Lord will be saved."[f]

¹⁴How then shall they call on *Him* whom they have not believed? And how shall they believe on *Him* of whom they have not heard? And how shall they hear apart from preaching? ¹⁵And how shall they preach unless they are sent? As it has been written: "How beautiful *are* the feet of those[g] proclaiming good news of good things!"[h]

¹⁶But not all heeded the good news. For Isaiah says, "Lord, who has believed our report?"[i] ¹⁷So faith *is* from hearing, and hearing through *the* word of Christ.

¹⁸But I ask, did they not hear? Indeed:
"Their voice has gone out into all the earth,
and their words to the ends of the world."[j]

¹⁹But I ask, did Israel not know? First, Moses says:
"I will provoke you to jealousy by *those* not a nation;
I will anger you by a nation without understanding."[k]

²⁰And Isaiah is very bold and says:
"I was found by those not seeking Me;
I became manifest to those not inquiring after Me."[l]

²¹But as for Israel he says:
"All the day I have stretched out My hands
to a disobeying and contradicting people."[m]

a 5 Leviticus 18:5
b 6 Deuteronomy 30:12
c 7 Deuteronomy 30:13
d 8 Deuteronomy 30:14
e 11 Isaiah 28:16
f 13 Joel 2:32
g 15 BYZ and TR include *preach the gospel of peace, who*
h 15 Isaiah 52:7
i 16 Isaiah 53:1
j 18 Psalm 19:4
k 19 Deuteronomy 32:21
l 20 Isaiah 65:1
m 21 Isaiah 65:2

Romans 11
The Remnant of Israel

¹I ask, then did God reject His people? Never may it be! For I also am an Israelite, of *the* seed of Abraham, of *the* tribe of Benjamin. ²God did not reject His people, whom He foreknew. Or do you not know what the Scripture says in Elijah, how he pleads with God against Israel: ³"Lord, they have killed Your prophets, they have torn down Your altars, and I alone have been left, and they are seeking my life"[a]?

⁴But what *was* the divine answer spoken to him? "I have left to Myself seven thousand men, who have not bowed *the* knee to Baal."[b]

⁵So then also, in the present time, there has been a remnant according to *the* election of grace. ⁶And if by grace, *it is* no

longer from works; otherwise grace no longer would be grace.*c*

⁷What then? What Israel is seeking, this it has not obtained, but the elect obtained *it*. And the rest were hardened, ⁸as it has been written:

> "God gave them a spirit of stupor,
> eyes not to see,
> and ears not to hear,
> unto this very day."*d*

⁹And David says:

> "Let their table be for a snare and for a trap,
> and for a stumbling block and for a retribution to them.
> ¹⁰Let their eyes be darkened not to see,
> and their backs bent over forever."*e*

The Ingrafting of the Gentiles

¹¹I ask then, did they stumble that they might fall? Never may it be! But in their trespass *is* salvation to the Gentiles, so as to provoke them to jealousy. ¹²But if their trespass *is the* riches of *the* world, and their failure *is the* riches of *the* Gentiles, how much more their fullness!

¹³Now I am speaking to you the Gentiles. Therefore indeed inasmuch as I am apostle of *the* Gentiles, I magnify my ministry, ¹⁴if at all I shall provoke to jealousy my *own* flesh, and shall save some of them. ¹⁵For if their rejection *is the* reconciliation of *the* world, what *will their* acceptance *be* if not life out from *the* dead? ¹⁶Now if the firstfruit *is* holy, also the lump; and if the root *is* holy, also the branches.

¹⁷But if some of the branches were broken off, and you, being a wild olive tree, were grafted in among them, and have become a fellow-partaker of the fatness of the root of the olive tree, ¹⁸do not boast over the branches. And if you boast against *them*, you do not support the root, but the root you.

¹⁹You will say, then, "Branches were broken off, that I might be grafted in."

²⁰Rightly so: They were broken off by the unbelief, but you stand by faith. Do not be high minded, but be afraid. ²¹For if God did not at all spare the natural branches, neither will He spare you.

²²Behold therefore *the* kindness and severity of God: severity indeed upon those having fallen, but kindness of God toward you, if you continue in the kindness; otherwise you also will be cut off. ²³And even they, if they do not continue in unbelief, will be grafted in, for God is able to graft them in again. ²⁴For if you were cut off out of the naturally wild olive tree, and contrary to nature were grafted into a cultivated olive tree, how much more will these, the natural, be grafted into the own olive tree!

All Israel Shall Be Saved

²⁵For I do not want you to be ignorant, brothers, of this mystery, so that you may not be wise in yourselves: A hardening in part has happened to Israel, until the fullness of the Gentiles may come in. ²⁶And so all Israel will be saved, as it has been written:

> "The *One* Delivering will come out of Zion,
> He will remove ungodliness from Jacob.
> ²⁷And this *is* the covenant from Me to them,
> when I shall take away their sins."*f*

²⁸For as regards the gospel, *they are* enemies on account of you; but as regards election, beloved on account of the patriarchs. ²⁹For the gifts and the calling of God *are* irrevocable.

³⁰For just as you once were disobedient to God, but now have been shown mercy by the disobedience of these, ³¹so these also now have been disobedient for your mercy, so that they also now may have mercy shown *them*. ³²For God has bound up all in disobedience, that He may show mercy to all.

A Hymn of Praise
(Romans 16:25-27; Jude 1:24-25)

³³O, *the* depth of riches,
    both of wisdom and knowledge of God!
How unsearchable His judgments,
    and untraceable His ways!
³⁴"For who has known *the* mind of *the* Lord,
    or who has been His counselor?"[g]
³⁵"Or who has first given to Him,
    and it will be recompensed to him?"[h]
³⁶For from Him and through Him and unto Him *are* all things.
    To Him *be* the glory to the ages! Amen.

a 3 1 Kings 19:10,14
b 4 1 Kings 19:18
c 6 BYZ and TR include *But if it is by works, then is it no more grace; otherwise work is no longer work.*
d 8 Isaiah 29:10; Deuteronomy 29:4
e 9-10 Psalm 69:22,23
f 26-27 Isaiah 59:20,21; 27:9
g 34 Isaiah 40:13
h 35 Job 41:11

Romans 12
Living Sacrifices
(1 Corinthians 3:16-18; 1 Corinthians 6:18-20)

¹Therefore I exhort you, brothers, through the compassions of God, to present your bodies *as a* living sacrifice, holy to God, well-pleasing, which is your reasonable service. ²And do not be conformed to this age, but be transformed by the renewing of the mind, for you to prove what *is* the good and well-pleasing and perfect will of God. ³For through the grace having been given to me, I say to everyone being among you, not to be high-minded above what it behooves *you* to think, but to think so as to be sober-minded, as God has allotted to each a measure of faith. ⁴For just as in one body we have many members, and not all the members have the same function, ⁵so we, the many, are one body in Christ; and individually members one of another. ⁶And we are having different gifts according to the grace having been given to us: if prophecy, according to the proportion of the faith; ⁷or service, in the service; or teaching, in the teaching; ⁸or exhorting, in the exhortation; giving, in generosity; leading, in diligence; showing mercy, in cheerfulness.

Love, Zeal, Hope, Hospitality
(John 13:31-35; 1 John 3:11-24)

⁹*Let* love *be* unfeigned: abhorring evil, cleaving to good, ¹⁰devoted to one another in brotherly love, esteeming one another in honor, ¹¹not lagging in diligence, being fervent in spirit, serving the Lord, ¹²rejoicing in hope, being patient in tribulation, being constant in prayer, ¹³contributing to the needs of the saints, pursuing hospitality.

Forgiveness
(Matthew 18:21-35)

¹⁴Bless those persecuting you. Bless and do not curse; ¹⁵to rejoice with the rejoicing, to weep with the weeping; ¹⁶minding the same thing toward one another, not minding the things haughty, but going along with the lowly. Do not be wise in yourselves, ¹⁷repaying to no one evil for evil, providing right before all men; ¹⁸if possible of you, living at peace with all men; ¹⁹never avenging yourselves, beloved; instead give place to wrath, for it has been written: "Vengeance *is* Mine, I will repay, says *the* Lord."[a]
²⁰On the contrary,
    "If your enemy should hunger, feed him;
        if he should thirst, give him to drink;
    for doing this,
        you will heap coals of fire upon his head."[b]
²¹Do not be overcome by evil, but overcome evil with good.

a 19 Deuteronomy 32:35
b 20 Proverbs 25:21,22

Romans 13
Submission to Authorities
(1 Peter 2:13-20)

¹Let every soul be subject to the authorities being above *him*. For there is no authority except by God; but those existing are having been instituted by God. ²Therefore the *one* rebelling against the authority has resisted the ordinance of God, and those having resisted will bring judgment upon themselves. ³For rulers are not a terror to good works, but to evil. Now do you desire not to fear the authority? Do the good, and you will have praise from him. ⁴For he is God's servant to you for good. But if you do evil, be afraid, for he does not bear the sword in vain. For He is God's servant, an avenger for wrath to the *one* doing evil.

⁵Therefore *it is* necessary to be subject, not only on account of wrath, but also on account of the conscience. ⁶For because of this, you also pay taxes; for they are servants of God, attending continually upon this very thing. ⁷Render to all their dues: tax to whom tax, revenue to whom revenue, respect to whom respect, honor to whom honor.

Love Fulfills the Law
(Leviticus 19:9-18)

⁸Owe nothing to *anyone*, except to love one another; for the *one* loving the other has fulfilled *the* Law. ⁹For, "You shall not commit adultery," "You shall not murder," "You shall not steal," "You shall not covet,"[a] and if *there is* any other commandment, it is summed up in this word, in, "You shall love your neighbor as yourself."[b] ¹⁰Love does not do evil to *its* neighbor; therefore love *is the* fulfillment of *the* Law.

Put On Christ

¹¹And do this knowing the time, that *it is* already *the* hour for you to awaken out of sleep; for our salvation *is* nearer now than when first we believed. ¹²The night is nearly over, and the day has drawn near; therefore we should cast off the works of darkness and should put on the armor of light. ¹³We should walk properly, as in daytime; not in reveling and drinking, not in sexual immorality and sensuality, not in dissension and jealousy. ¹⁴But put on the Lord Jesus Christ, and make no provision for *the* desires of the flesh.

a 9 Exodus 20:13-17; Deuteronomy 5:17-21
b 9 Leviticus 19:18

Romans 14
The Law of Liberty
(Matthew 7:1-6; Luke 6:37-42)

¹Now receive the *one* being weak in the faith, not for passing judgment on reasonings. ²Indeed, one believes to eat all things; but the *one* being weak eats vegetables. ³The *one* eating, let him not despise the *one* not eating; and the *one* not eating, let him not judge the *one* eating, for God has received him. ⁴Who are you, judging another's servant? To the own master he stands or falls. And he will be upheld, for the Lord is able to uphold him.

⁵For indeed one judges a day *to be* above *another* day, but one judges every day *alike*. Let each be fully assured in the own mind. ⁶The *one* regarding the day, regards *it* to *the* Lord;[a] the *one* eating, eats to *the* Lord, for he gives thanks to God; and the *one* not eating, does not eat to *the* Lord and gives thanks to God.

⁷For none of us lives to himself, and no one dies to himself. ⁸For both if we should live, we live to the Lord; and if we should die, we die to the Lord. Therefore both if we should live and if we should die, we are the Lord's. ⁹For unto this, Christ died and lived again that He might rule over both *the* dead and living.

¹⁰But why do you judge your brother, or why also do you despise your brother? For we will all stand before the judgment seat of God. ¹¹For it has been written:

"I live, says *the* Lord,
 that every knee will bow to Me,
 and every tongue will confess[b]
 to God."[c]

¹²So then, each of us will give account concerning himself to God.

The Law of Love
(Ezekiel 14:1-11; 1 Corinthians 8:1-13)

¹³No longer, therefore, should we judge one another; but rather determine this, not to put *any* stumbling block or snare before *your* brother.

¹⁴I know and I am persuaded in *the* Lord Jesus that nothing *is* unclean of itself, except to him reckoning anything to be unclean—to that one *it is* unclean. ¹⁵For if on account of food your brother is grieved, no longer are you walking according to love. Do not destroy with food that one of you for whom Christ died.

¹⁶Therefore let not your good be spoken of as evil. ¹⁷For the kingdom of God is not eating and drinking, but righteousness and peace and joy in *the* Holy Spirit. ¹⁸For the *one* serving Christ in these things *is* well-pleasing to God and approved by men.

¹⁹So then, we should pursue the things of peace, and the things for edification among each other. ²⁰Do not destroy the work of God for the sake of food. All things indeed *are* clean, but *it is* wrong to the man eating through a stumbling block. ²¹*It is* good neither to eat meat, nor to drink wine, nor *anything* in which your brother stumbles.*ᵈ*

²²*The* faith that you have, keep to yourself before God. Blessed *is* the *one* not judging himself in what he approves. ²³But the *one* doubting has been condemned if he eats, because *it is* not of faith; and anything that *is* not of faith is sin.*ᵉ*

a 6 BYZ and TR include *and he who does not regard the day, to the Lord he does not regard it*
b 11 Or *will give praise*
c 11 Isaiah 45:23
d 21 SBL, BYZ, and TR include *or to be hindered or weakened*
e 23 Some manuscripts place Romans 16:25-27 here, or after Romans 15:33.

Romans 15
Accept One Another

¹Now we who *are* strong ought to bear the weaknesses of the weak and not to please ourselves. ²Let each of us please the neighbor unto the good, for edification. ³For even Christ did not please Himself, but as it has been written: "The reproaches of those reproaching You have fallen on Me."*ᵃ* ⁴For whatever was written in the past was all written for our instruction, so that through endurance and through the encouragement of the Scriptures, we might have hope.

⁵Now may the God of endurance and encouragement give you to be of the same mind with one another, according to Christ Jesus, ⁶so that with one accord, with one mouth, you may glorify the God and Father of our Lord Jesus Christ.

Christ the Servant of Jews and Gentiles

⁷Therefore receive one another as Christ also received you, to *the* glory of God. ⁸For I declare Christ to have become a servant of *the* circumcision for *the* truth of God, in order to confirm the promises given to the fathers, ⁹and *for* the Gentiles to glorify God for mercy, as it has been written:

"Because of this I will praise You
among *the* Gentiles,
and will I sing to Your name."*ᵇ*

¹⁰And again it says:

"Rejoice you Gentiles, with His people."*ᶜ*

¹¹And again:

"Praise the Lord all the Gentiles,
and praise Him, all the peoples."*ᵈ*

¹²And again, Isaiah says:

"There will be the root of Jesse,
and the *One* arising to rule over *the* Gentiles;
in Him *the* Gentiles will hope."*ᵉ*

¹³Now may the God of hope fill you with all joy and peace in believing, for you to

abound in hope in *the* power *of the* Holy Spirit.

Paul the Minister to the Gentiles

¹⁴And I myself also am persuaded concerning you my brothers, that you yourselves are also full of goodness, being filled with all knowledge, and being able to admonish one another. ¹⁵But I have written to you more boldly in part, as reminding you, because of the grace having been given to me by God ¹⁶for me to be a minister of Christ Jesus to the Gentiles, administering the sacred service of the gospel of God, so that the offering of the Gentiles might become acceptable, having been sanctified in *the* Holy Spirit. ¹⁷Therefore I have the boasting in Christ Jesus in the things pertaining to God. ¹⁸For I will not dare to speak of anything except what Christ has accomplished through me unto *the* obedience of *the* Gentiles by word and deed, ¹⁹in *the* power of signs and wonders, in *the* power of *the* Spirit of God, so as for me, from Jerusalem and around unto Illyricum, to have fully proclaimed the gospel of Christ, ²⁰and thus being ambitious to preach the gospel where Christ had not been named, so that I might not build upon another's foundation. ²¹Rather, as it has been written:

> "They will see, to whom it was not proclaimed concerning Him;
> and those who have not heard will understand."ᶠ

²²Therefore also I have been hindered many *times* to come to you.

Paul's Travel Plans

(1 Corinthians 16:5-9)

²³But now, no longer having a place in these regions, and having had a great desire for many years to come to you, ²⁴whenever I may go to Spain, I hope indeed, going through, to see you and to be equipped there by you, if first I should be filled of you in part. ²⁵But now I am going to Jerusalem, ministering to the saints. ²⁶For Macedonia and Achaia were pleased to make a certain contribution for the poor among the saints in Jerusalem. ²⁷For they were pleased, and they are debtors of them. For if the Gentiles have shared in their spiritual things, they ought also to minister to them in the material things. ²⁸Therefore having finished this, and having sealed this fruit to them, I will set off through you into Spain. ²⁹Now I know that coming to you, I will come in *the* fullness of the blessingᵍ of Christ.

³⁰Now I exhort you, brothers, by our Lord Jesus Christ and by the love of the Spirit, to strive together with me in the prayers for me to God, ³¹so that I may be delivered from those refusing to be persuaded in Judea, and *that* my service in Jerusalem may be acceptable to the saints, ³²so that having come to you in joy, by *the* will of God I may be refreshed with you.

³³Now the God of peace *be* with all of you. Amen.

a 3 Psalm 69:9
b 9 2 Samuel 22:50; Psalm 18:49
c 10 Deuteronomy 32:43
d 11 Psalm 117:1
e 12 Isaiah 11:10
f 21 Isaiah 52:15
g 29 TR and BYZ include *of the gospel*

Romans 16
Personal Greetings and Love

¹Now I commend to you Phoebe our sister, being also a servantᵃ of the church in Cenchrea, ²that you might receive her in *the* Lord worthily of *the* saints, and you might assist her in whatever matter she may need of you. For she also has been a patroness of many, and of me myself. ³Greet Priscaᵇ and Aquila, my fellow workers in Christ Jesus— ⁴who have lain down their neck for my life, whom not only I thank, but also all the churches of the Gentiles— ⁵and the church at their house.

Greet Epenetus, my beloved, who is a firstfruit of Asia for Christ.

⁶Greet Mary, who toiled much for you.

⁷Greet Andronicus and Junias, my kinsmen and my fellow prisoners, who

are of note among the apostles, and who were in Christ before me.

⁸Greet Ampliatus, my beloved in *the* Lord.
⁹Greet Urbanus, our fellow worker in Christ, and my beloved Stachys.
¹⁰Greet Apelles, the approved in Christ. Greet those of the *household* of Aristobulus.
¹¹Greet Herodion, my kinsman. Greet those of the *household* of Narcissus being in *the* Lord.
¹²Greet Tryphena and Tryphosa, those toiling in *the* Lord. Greet Persis, the beloved, who toiled much in *the* Lord.
¹³Greet Rufus, chosen in *the* Lord, and his mother and mine.
¹⁴Greet Asyncritus, Phlegon, Hermes, Patrobas, Hermas, and the brothers with them.
¹⁵Greet Philologus and Julia, Nereus and his sister, and Olympas and all the saints with them.
¹⁶Greet one another with a holy kiss. All the churches of Christ greet you.

Avoid Divisions

¹⁷Now I exhort you, brothers, to consider those causing divisions and obstacles contrary to the teaching that you have learned, and turn away from them. ¹⁸For such do not serve our Lord Christ, but their *own* belly; and by smooth talk and flattery they deceive the hearts of the naive.
¹⁹For your obedience has reached to all. Therefore I rejoice over you. But I wish you to be wise to good, and innocent to evil.
²⁰And in a short time the God of peace will crush Satan under your feet. The grace of our Lord Jesus Christ *be* with you.

Greetings from Paul's Companions

²¹Timothy, my fellow worker, greets you; also Lucius and Jason and Sosipater, my kinsmen.
²²I Tertius, the *one* having written down this letter, greet you in *the* Lord.
²³Gaius, the host of me and of all the church, greets you. Erastus, the steward of the city, greets you, and Quartus, the brother.ᶜ

Doxology
(Romans 11:33-36; Jude 1:24-25)

²⁵Now to Him being able to strengthen you according to my gospel and the proclamation of Jesus Christ, according to *the* revelation of *the* mystery having been kept secret in times of the ages, ²⁶but now having been made manifest also through *the* prophetic Scriptures, according to *the* commandment of the Eternal God, having been made known to all the Gentiles unto *the* obedience of faith— ²⁷ *to the* only wise God *be* the glory to the ages of the ages, which *is* through Jesus Christ. Amen.

a 1 Or *deaconess*
b 3 Or *Priscilla*
c 23 SBL, BYZ, and TR include *24 May the grace of our Lord Jesus Christ be with you all. Amen.*

1 Corinthians

1 Corinthians 1
Greetings from Paul
(2 Corinthians 1:1-2)

¹Paul, a called apostle of Christ Jesus by *the* will of God, and Sosthenes, *our* brother,
²To the church of God being in Corinth, having been sanctified in Christ Jesus, called holy, together with all those in every place calling on the name of our Lord Jesus Christ, both theirs and ours:
³Grace to you and peace from God our Father and *the* Lord Jesus Christ.

Thanksgiving
(Philippians 1:3-11; Colossians 1:3-14; 2 Thessalonians 1:3-4)

⁴I thank my God always concerning you for the grace of God having been given you in Christ Jesus, ⁵that in everything you have been enriched in Him, in all speech and all knowledge, ⁶as the testimony about Christ was confirmed in you, ⁷so as for you not to be lacking in

any gift as you eagerly await the revelation of our Lord Jesus Christ, ⁸who also will sustain you to *the* end, blameless in the day of our Lord Jesus Christ. ⁹God *is* faithful, by whom you were called into fellowship with His Son Jesus Christ our Lord.

Unity in the Church
(Psalm 133:1-3; Ephesians 4:1-16)

¹⁰Now I exhort you, brothers, by the name of our Lord Jesus Christ, that you all speak the same thing, and there be no divisions among you, but you may be having been knit together in the same mind and in the same judgment. ¹¹For it was shown to me concerning you, my brothers, by those of Chloe, that there are quarrels among you. ¹²Now I mean this, that each of you says, "I indeed am of Paul," and "I of Apollos," and "I of Cephas,"ᵃ and "I of Christ."
¹³Has Christ been divided? Was Paul crucified for you? Or were you baptized into the name of Paul? ¹⁴I thank God that I baptized none of you except Crispus and Gaius, ¹⁵so that no one should say that you were baptized into my name. ¹⁶Now also I baptized the household of Stephanas; as to the rest, I do not know whether I baptized any other. ¹⁷For Christ did not send me to baptize, but to preach the gospel; not in wisdom of discourse, so that the cross of the Christ should not be emptied of *its* power.

The Message of the Cross

¹⁸For the message of the cross is foolishness to those indeed perishing, but to us being saved it is *the* power of God. ¹⁹For it has been written:
"I will destroy the wisdom of the wise;
and the intelligence of the intelligent I will frustrate."ᵇ
²⁰Where *is the* wise *man*? Where *is the* scribe? Where *is the* debater of this age? Has not God made foolish the wisdom of the world? ²¹For since in the wisdom of God, the world through *its* wisdom did not know God, God was pleased through the foolishness of the proclamation to save those believing.
²²Forasmuch as both Jews ask for signs, and Greeks seek wisdom, ²³we, however, preach Christ having been crucified, a stumbling block indeed to *the* Jewish and foolishness to Gentiles, ²⁴but those called, both Jews and Greeks, Christ *the* power of God and *the* wisdom of God.
²⁵For the foolishness of God is wiser than men, and the weakness of God stronger than men.

Wisdom from God

²⁶For consider your calling, brothers, that not many *were* wise according to *the* flesh, not many powerful, not many of noble birth. ²⁷But God has chosen the foolish things of the world that He might shame the wise; and God has chosen the weak things of the world that He might shame the strong; ²⁸and the low-born of the world, and the things being despised, God also chose—the things not being— that He might annul the things being, ²⁹so that all flesh may not boast before God.
³⁰But out of Him, you are in Christ Jesus, who has been made unto us wisdom from God, and righteousness and sanctification and redemption, ³¹in order that, as it has been written: "The *one* boasting, let him boast in *the* Lord."ᶜ

a 12 That is, Peter
b 19 Isaiah 29:14
c 31 Jeremiah 9:24

1 Corinthians 2
Paul's Message by the Spirit's Power

¹And I having come to you, brothers, did not come according to excellency of speech or wisdom, proclaiming to you the testimony of God. ²For I decided to know nothing among you except Jesus Christ and Him having been crucified. ³And I was with you in weakness, and in fear, and in much trembling. ⁴And my message and my preaching *were* not in persuasive words of wisdom, but in demonstration of *the* Spirit and of power, ⁵so that your

faith might not be in *the* wisdom of men, but in *the* power of God.

Spiritual Wisdom

⁶But we speak wisdom among the mature, but not *the* wisdom of this age, nor of the rulers of this age, who are coming to naught. ⁷But we speak in a mystery, the wisdom of God having been hidden, which God foreordained before the ages for our glory, ⁸which none of the rulers of this age has understood. For if they had understood *it*, they would not have crucified the Lord of glory. ⁹But as it has been written:

"What no eye has seen,
    and no ear has heard,
    and has not entered into heart of man,
what God has prepared for those loving Him."ᵃ

¹⁰For God has revealed *it* to us through the Spirit.

For the Spirit searches all things, even the depths of God. ¹¹For who among men knows the things of the man, except the spirit of the man within him? So also, no one knows the things of God, except the Spirit of God. ¹²Now we have not received the spirit of the world, but the Spirit from God, that we may know the things having been granted to us by God, ¹³which also we speak, not in words taught of human wisdom, but in *those* taught of *the* Spirit, communicating spiritual things by spiritual *means*.

¹⁴But *the* natural man does not accept the things of the Spirit of God; for they are foolishness to him, and he is not able to understand *them*, because spiritually they are discerned. ¹⁵But he who *is* spiritual judges all things, but he himself is judged by no one. ¹⁶"For who has known *the* mind of *the* Lord? Who will instruct Him?"ᵇ But we have *the* mind of Christ.

a 9 Isaiah 64:4
b 16 Isaiah 40:13

1 Corinthians 3
God's Fellow Workers

¹And I, brothers, was not able to speak to you as to spiritual, but as fleshly—as to infants in Christ. ²I gave you milk to drink, not solid food, for not yet were you able. In fact, now you are still not able, ³for you are still fleshly. For where jealousy and strife *are* among you, are you not fleshly, and are walking according to man? ⁴For when one might say, "I indeed am of Paul," but another, "I of Apollos," are you not fleshly?

⁵Who then is Apollos? And who is Paul? Servants through whom you believed, even as the Lord has given to each. ⁶I planted, Apollos watered, but God kept *it* growing. ⁷So neither the *one* planting nor the *one* watering is anything, but *only* God, the *One* giving growth. ⁸Now the *one* planting and the *one* watering are one, and each will receive the own reward, according to the own labor. ⁹For we are God's fellow workers; you are God's field, God's building.

Christ Our Foundation
(Isaiah 28:14-22; 1 Peter 2:4-12)

¹⁰According to the grace of God having been given to me, as a wise master builder I have laid *the* foundation, but another is building upon *it*. But let each one take heed how he builds upon *it*. ¹¹For no one is able to lay another foundation, besides the *one* being already laid, which is Jesus Christ.

¹²Now if anyone builds upon the foundation *using* gold, silver, precious stones, wood, hay, *or* straw, ¹³the work of each will become manifest, for the day will disclose *it*, because it is revealed in fire, and the fire itself will prove the work of each, what sort it is. ¹⁴If the work of anyone that he built up will remain, he will receive a reward. ¹⁵If the work of anyone will be burned up, he will suffer loss; but he himself will be saved, but so as through fire.

You are God's Temple
(Romans 12:1-8; 1 Corinthians 6:18-20)

[16] Do you not know that you yourselves are God's temple, and the Spirit of God dwells in you? [17] If anyone destroys God's temple, God will destroy him; for God's temple is holy, which you are.

Worldly Wisdom

[18] Let no one deceive himself: If anyone among you thinks *himself* to be wise in this age, let him become foolish, so that he may become wise. [19] For the wisdom of this world is foolishness with God. For it has been written: "*He is* the *One* catching the wise in their craftiness."[a] [20] and again, "*The* Lord knows the thoughts of the wise, that they are futile."[b]

[21] Therefore let no one boast in men. For all things are yours, [22] whether Paul, or Apollos, or Cephas,[c] or *the* world, or life, or death, or things present, or things to come—all *are* yours, [23] and you of Christ, and Christ of God.

a 19 Job 5:13
b 20 Psalm 94:11
c 22 That is, Peter

1 Corinthians 4
Servants of Christ

[1] So let a man regard us as servants of Christ and stewards of God's mysteries. [2] In this case, moreover, it is required in the stewards, that one shall be found faithful. [3] But to me, it is the smallest matter that I be examined by you or by a human court. In fact, neither do I examine myself. [4] For I am conscious of nothing against myself, yet I have not been justified by this; but the *One* judging me is *the* Lord.

[5] Therefore do not judge anything before *the* time, until the Lord shall have come, who both will bring to light the hidden things of darkness, and will make manifest the motives of the hearts; and then the praise will come to each from God.

Fools for Christ

[6] Now I have applied these things, brothers, to myself and Apollos, on account of you, so that in us you may learn, "not beyond what has been written," so that not one *of* you should be puffed up for one over the other. [7] For who makes you any different? And what do you have that you did not receive? And if also you did receive *it*, why do you boast as not having received *it*?

[8] Already you are satiated; already you have been enriched; apart from us you reigned; and I wish that really you did reign, so that we also might reign with you. [9] For I think God has exhibited us, the apostles, last, as appointed to death, because we have become a spectacle to the world, both to angels and to men.

[10] We *are* fools on account of Christ, but you *are* wise in Christ; we *are* weak, but you *are* strong; You *are* honored, but we *are* without honor. [11] As far as the present hour, we both hunger and thirst, and are poorly clad, and are buffeted, and wander homeless, [12] and we toil, working with *our* own hands. Being reviled, we bless; being persecuted, we endure; [13] being slandered, we entreat. We have become as *the* residue of the world, *the* refuse of all, until now.

Paul's Warns his Children

[14] I do not write these things shaming you, but admonishing *you* as my beloved children. [15] For if you should have ten thousand guardians in Christ, yet not many fathers; for in Christ Jesus I have begotten you through the gospel. [16] Therefore I exhort you, become imitators of me.

[17] On account of this I sent to you Timothy, who is my beloved and faithful child in *the* Lord, who will remind of you my ways that *are* in Christ Jesus,[a] as I teach everywhere in every church.

[18] Now some have become puffed up, as if I were not coming to you. [19] But I will come to you shortly, if the Lord wills, and I will find out not the talk of those being

puffed up, but *their* power. ²⁰For the kingdom of God *is* not in word, but in power. ²¹What do you desire? Should I come to you with a rod, or in love and a spirit of gentleness?

a 17 BYZ and TR *my way of life in Christ,*

1 Corinthians 5
Immorality Rebuked
(Leviticus 20:10-21; Proverbs 5:1-23)

¹Sexual immorality is actually reported among you, and sexual immorality such as *is* not even among the pagans, so as for one to have *the* wife of the father. ²And you are puffed up, and have not rather mourned, so that the *one* having done this deed might be taken out of your midst! ³For I, though being absent in body, now being present in spirit, have already judged the *one* having thus produced this, as being present, ⁴in the name our Lord Jesus, of you having been gathered together and of me in spirit, with the power of the Lord Jesus, ⁵to deliver such a one to Satan for destruction of the flesh, so that *his* spirit may be saved in the day of the Lord.ᵃ

⁶Your boasting *is* not good. Do you not know that a little leaven leavens the whole lump? ⁷Cleanse out the old leaven, that you may be a new lump, as you are, unleavened. For also Christ our Passover lamb has been sacrificed, ⁸so that we might celebrate the feast, not with old leaven, not with leaven of malice and wickedness, but with *the* unleavened *bread* of sincerity and of truth.

Expel the Immoral Brother

⁹I wrote to you in the letter not to associate with the sexually immoral, ¹⁰not altogether with the sexually immoral of this world, or with the covetous and swindlers, or idolaters— since then you would need to depart from the world. ¹¹But now, I wrote to you not to associate with anyone being designated a brother if he is sexually immoral or a coveter, or an idolater or verbal abuser, or a drunkard or swindler—with such a one not even to eat. ¹²For what *is it* to me to judge those outside? Do you not judge those within? ¹³But God will judge those outside. "Expel the evil out from among yourselves."ᵇ

a 5 BYZ and TR *the Lord Jesus*
b 13 Deuteronomy 17:7

1 Corinthians 6
Lawsuits among Believers

¹Anyone of you having a matter against the other, dare he go to law before the unrighteous, and not before the saints? ²Or do you not know that saints will judge the world? And if the world is to be judged by you, are you unworthy of the smallest of cases? ³Do you not know that we will judge angels? How much more the things of this life?

⁴So indeed, if you have judgment *as to* the things of this life, set you up those the *ones* being despised in the church! ⁵I say this to you for shame. Thus is there not one wise *man* among you who will be able to decide in between his brother? ⁶Instead, brother goes to law against brother, and this before unbelievers! ⁷Therefore indeed it is already altogether a defeat for you that you have lawsuits among one another. Why not rather suffer wrong? Why not rather be defrauded? ⁸But you do wrong and defraud, and these things to brothers!

Members of Christ

⁹Or do you not know that *the* unrighteous ones will not inherit *the* kingdom of God? Do not be deceived: neither the sexually immoral, nor idolaters, nor adulterers, nor effeminate, nor homosexuals, ¹⁰nor thieves, nor coveters, not drunkards, nor verbal abusers, nor swindlers, will inherit *the* kingdom of God. ¹¹And some *of* you were such. But you were washed, but you were sanctified, but you were justified, in the name of the Lord Jesus Christ and by the Spirit of our God.

¹²"All things are lawful to me," but not all things do profit. "All things are lawful to me," but I will not be mastered by anything. ¹³"Foods for the belly and the belly for foods," but God will destroy both this and these. Now the body *is* not for sexual immorality, but for the Lord, and the Lord for the body. ¹⁴And by His power God has both raised up the Lord, and will raise us out.

¹⁵Do you not know that your bodies are members of Christ? Having taken then the members of the Christ, shall I make *them* members of a prostitute? Never may it be! ¹⁶Or do you not know that the *one* being joined to the prostitute is one body? For it says, "The two will become into one flesh."ᵃ ¹⁷But the *one* being joined to the Lord is one spirit.

The Temple of the Holy Spirit
(Romans 12:1-8; 1 Corinthians 3:16-18)

¹⁸Flee sexual immorality. Every sin, whatever if a man might do, is outside the body, but the *one* sinning sexually sins against the own body. ¹⁹Or do you not know that your body is a temple of the Holy Spirit in you, whom you have from God? And you are not your own, ²⁰for you were bought with a price. Therefore glorify God in your body.ᵇ

a 16 Genesis 2:24
b 20 BYZ and TR include *and with your spirit, which belong to God*

1 Corinthians 7
Principles of Marriage

¹Now concerning the things about which you wrote: *It is* good for a man not to touch a woman. ²But because of sexual immorality, let each man have his *own* wife, and let each woman have the own husband.

³Let the husband fulfill the duty to the wife, and likewise also the wife to the husband. ⁴The wife does not have authority over the own body, but the husband; and likewise also, the husband does not have authority over the own body, but the wife.

⁵Do not deprive one another, except by mutual agreement, for a time, that you might be at leisure for prayer; and be together the same again, so that Satan may not tempt you through your lack of self-control. ⁶Now I say this by way of concession, not by way of command. ⁷And I wish all men to be even like myself. But each has his own gift from God; for one *has* this, but one that.

⁸Now I say to the unmarried and to the widows, *it is* good for them if they should remain as even I. ⁹But if they do not have self-control, let them marry; for it is better to marry than to burn with passion. ¹⁰Now to those having married I give this charge (not I, but the Lord): A wife is not to be separated from a husband. ¹¹But if indeed she is separated, let her remain unmarried, or be reconciled to the husband; and a husband is not to send away a wife.

¹²Now to the rest I say (I, not the Lord): If any brother has an unbelieving wife and she consents to dwell with him, let him not divorce her. ¹³And if any woman has an unbelieving husband, and he consents to dwell with her, let her not divorce the husband. ¹⁴For the unbelieving husband is sanctified in the wife, and the unbelieving wife is sanctified in the husband. Otherwise, your children are unclean; but now they are holy.

¹⁵But if the unbeliever separates himself, let him separate himself. The brother or the sister is not under bondage in such *cases*. But God has called youᵃ into peace. ¹⁶For how do you know, wife, if you will save the husband? Or how do you know, husband, if you will save the wife?

Live Your Calling

¹⁷Nevertheless, as the Lord has assigned to each, as God has called to each, so let him walk. And thus I prescribe in all the churches. ¹⁸Was anyone called having been circumcised? Let him not be uncircumcised. Was anyone called in uncircumcision? Let Him not be

circumcised. ¹⁹Circumcision is nothing and uncircumcision is nothing, but keeping *the* commandments of God. ²⁰Each in the calling in which he has been called, in this let him abide. ²¹Were you called *while* a slave, let it not be a care to you; but if also you are able to become free, rather take advantage. ²²For the *one* having been called in *the* Lord *while* a slave is *the* Lord's freedman; likewise the *one* having been called *while* free is a slave of Christ. ²³You were bought with a price; do not become slaves of men. ²⁴Each, wherein that he was called, brothers, in that let him abide with God.

The Unmarried and Widowed

²⁵Now concerning virgins, I do not have a commandment of *the* Lord, but I give judgment as having received mercy from *the* Lord to be trustworthy. ²⁶Therefore I think this is good, because of the present*ᵇ* necessity, that *it is* good for a man to remain in the same manner. ²⁷Have you been bound to a wife? Do not seek to be loosed. Have you been loosed from a wife? Do not seek a wife. ²⁸But if also you shall have married, you did not sin; and if the virgin shall have married, she did not sin. But such will have tribulation in the flesh, and I am sparing you. ²⁹Now I say this, brothers: The season is shortened; that from now on both those having wives, should be as having none; ³⁰and those weeping, as not weeping; and those rejoicing, as not rejoicing; and those buying, as not possessing; ³¹and those using the world, as not using *it* as their own. For the present form of this world is passing away. ³²And I desire you to be without concern. The unmarried man cares for the things of the Lord, how he should please the Lord; ³³but the *one* having been married cares for the things of the world, how he should please the wife, ³⁴and is divided. And the unmarried woman and virgin cares for the things of the Lord, that she should be holy both in body and in spirit; but the *one* having been married cares for the things of the world, how she should please the husband. ³⁵Now I say this for your own benefit, not that I might place upon you a restraint, but for what *is* seemly and devoted to the Lord, without distraction. ³⁶But if anyone supposes to be behaving improperly to his virgin, if she is beyond youth, and it ought to be so, let him do what he wills; he does not sin; let them marry. ³⁷But he who stands firm in his heart, not having necessity, but having authority over the own will, and has judged this in the own heart, to keep his virgin, he will do well. ³⁸So then also, the *one* marrying the own virgin does well, and the *one* not marrying will do better. ³⁹A wife is bound for as long a time *as* her husband may live; but if the husband shall have died, she is free to be married to whom she wills, only in *the* Lord. ⁴⁰But she is more blessed if she should remain in the same manner, according to my judgment; and I think myself also to have *the* Spirit of God.

a 15 SBL, BYZ, and TR *us*
b 26 Or *impending*

1 Corinthians 8
Food Sacrificed to Idols
(Ezekiel 14:1-11; Romans 14:13-23)

¹Now concerning the things sacrificed to idols, we know indeed we all have knowledge. Knowledge puffs up, but love builds up. ²If anyone thinks to have known anything, not yet does he know as it is necessary to know. ³But if anyone loves God, he is known by Him. ⁴Therefore concerning the eating of the things sacrificed to idols, we know that an idol *is* nothing in *the* world and that *there is* no God except one. ⁵Truly even if indeed there are *those* called gods, whether in heaven or on earth, as there are many gods and many lords, ⁶yet to us *there is* one God the Father, of whom *are* all things, and we for Him; and one Lord,

Jesus Christ, by whom *are* all things, and we through Him.
⁷But this knowledge *is* not in all. And some, by habit of the idol until now, eat as of a thing sacrificed to an idol; and their conscience being weak, it is defiled.
⁸But food will not commend us to God; neither if we should eat do we come short, nor if we should not eat, do we have an advantage.
⁹But be careful, lest somehow this right of yours becomes an occasion of stumbling to those being weak. ¹⁰For if anyone sees you, having knowledge, eating in an idol's temple, will not his conscience, being weak, be built up so as to eat the things sacrificed to idols? ¹¹For the *one* being weak is destroyed through your knowledge—the brother for whom Christ died. ¹²And thus sinning against the brothers and wounding their being weak conscience, you sin against Christ.
¹³Therefore, if food snares my brother, never shall not I eat meat to the age, so that I might not snare my brother.

1 Corinthians 9
The Rights of an Apostle
(Deuteronomy 18:1-8)

¹Am I not free? Am I not an apostle? Have I not seen Jesus our Lord? Are you not my work in *the* Lord? ²If I am not an apostle to others, yet at least I am to you; for you are the seal of my apostleship in *the* Lord.
³This is my defense to those examining me: ⁴Have we no authority to eat and to drink? ⁵Have we no authority to take about a believer *as* a wife, as also the other apostles, and the brothers of the Lord, and Cephas?ᵃ ⁶Or only I and Barnabas, have we no authority not to work?
⁷Who at any time serves as a soldier at his own expense? Who plants a vineyard and does not eat the fruit of it? Or who shepherds a flock and does not drink from the milk of the flock?

⁸Do I speak these things according to man? Or does the Law not also say these things? ⁹For in the Law of Moses it has been written: "You shall not muzzle an ox treading out grain."ᵇ Is there care for the oxen with God? ¹⁰Or is He speaking because of us entirely? For it was written for us, because in hope the *one* plowing ought to plow, and the *one* threshing, in hope to partake.
¹¹If we have sown spiritual things among you, *is it* a great thing if we will reap material things from you? ¹²If others partake of the authority over you, *should* we not more? But we did not use this right. Instead, we bear all things, so that we should not place any hindrance to the gospel of Christ.
¹³Do you not know that those working in the temple eat the things of the temple; those attending at the altar partake in the altar? ¹⁴So also, the Lord has prescribed to those proclaiming the gospel to live from the gospel. ¹⁵But I have not used *any* of these. And neither have I written these things that it should be thus with me; for *it would be* better to me to die, rather than that anyone will make void my boasting.
¹⁶For if I preach the gospel, there is no boasting to me, for necessity is laid upon me. But woe be to me if I should not preach the gospel. ¹⁷For if I do this willingly, I have a reward; but if unwillingly, I am entrusted with a stewardship. ¹⁸What then is my reward? That in preaching the gospel, I should offer the gospel free of charge, so as not to use up my right in the gospel.

Paul the Servant to All

¹⁹For being free from all, I myself became servant to all, so that I might win the more. ²⁰And to the Jews I became like a Jew, so that I might win *the* Jews. To those under *the* Law, as under *the* Law (myself not being under *the* Law) so that I might win those under *the* Law. ²¹To those outside *the* Law, as outside *the* Law (not being outside *the* law of God, but

under *the* law of Christ) so that I might win those outside *the* Law. ²²To the weak I became weak, that I might win the weak. I have become all these things to all, so that by all means I might save some.

²³Now I do all *things* on account of the gospel, that I might become a fellow partaker with it.

Run Your Race to Win

²⁴Do you not know that those running in a race course, indeed all run, but one receives the prize? Run thus, that you might obtain *it.* ²⁵Now everyone striving controls himself in all things; then indeed they, that they might receive a perishable crown; but we, an imperishable. ²⁶Therefore I run thus, not as uncertainly; I fight thus, not as beating *the* air. ²⁷But I batter my body and bring *it* into servitude, lest having preached to others, I myself might be disqualified.

a 5 That is, Peter
b 9 Deuteronomy 25:4

1 Corinthians 10
Warnings from Israel's Past
(Numbers 16:41-50; Numbers 25:1-5)

¹For I do not want you to be ignorant, brothers, that our fathers were all under the cloud, and all passed through the sea. ²And all were baptized into Moses in the cloud and in the sea, ³and all ate the same spiritual food, ⁴and all drank the same spiritual drink. For they were drinking from *the* spiritual rock accompanying *them*, and the rock was Christ. ⁵Nevertheless, God was not well pleased with most of them, for they were strewn in the wilderness.

⁶Now these things have become types to us, for us not to be desirers of evil things, as they also desired. ⁷Neither are you to be idolaters, as some of them, as it has been written: "The people sat down to eat and to drink, and rose up to play."ᵃ ⁸Neither should we commit sexual immorality, as some of them committed sexual immorality, and twenty-three thousand fell in one day. ⁹Neither should we test the Christ,ᵇ as some of them tested, and were destroyed by serpents. ¹⁰Neither are you to grumble, as some of them grumbled, and perished by the Destroyer.

¹¹Now these things happened to them *as* types and were written for our admonition, to whom the ends of the ages are arrived. ¹²Therefore the *one* thinking to stand, let him take heed, lest he fall. ¹³No temptation has seized you, except what is common to man. And God *is* faithful, who will not allow you to be tempted beyond what you are able, but will also provide with the temptation the escape, to be able to endure *it.*

Flee from Idolatry
(Exodus 20:22-23; Leviticus 19:1-8)

¹⁴Therefore my beloved, flee from idolatry. ¹⁵I speak as to sensible *ones*; judge for yourselves what I say. ¹⁶Is not the cup of blessing that we bless a participation in the blood of Christ? Is not the bread that we break a participation in the body of Christ? ¹⁷Because *there is* one loaf, we the many are one body; for we all partake of the one loaf. ¹⁸Consider Israel according to flesh: Are not those eating the sacrifices fellow partakers in the altar?

¹⁹Then what do I mean? That what is sacrificed to an idol is anything, or that an idol is anything? ²⁰Rather, that what the Gentiles sacrifice, they sacrifice to demons and not to God. And I do not want you to be fellow partakers with demons. ²¹You are not able to drink *the* cup of *the* Lord and *the* cup of demons. You are not able to partake of *the* table of *the* Lord and of *the* table of demons. ²²Or do we provoke the Lord to jealousy? Are we stronger than He?

All to God's Glory

²³"All things are lawful," but not all things are profitable; "All things are lawful," but not all edify. ²⁴Let no one seek the *good* of himself, but that of the other.

²⁵Eat everything being sold in *the* meat market, inquiring nothing on account of

conscience, ²⁶for, "The earth *is* the Lord's, and its fullness."*c*
²⁷If anyone unbelieving invites you, and you wish to go, eat everything being set before you, inquiring nothing on account of conscience. ²⁸But if anyone should say to you, "This is offered to an idol," do not eat, on account of him having shown *it*, and conscience—*d* ²⁹and I am not saying your own conscience, but that of the other; for why is my freedom judged by another's conscience? ³⁰If I partake with thankfulness, why am I denounced for that which I give thanks?
³¹Therefore whether you eat or drink or whatever you do, do all things to the glory of God. ³²Be you without offense both to Jews and Greeks, and to the church of God— ³³as I also please all in all things, not seeking my *own* profit, but that of the many, that they may be saved.

a 7 Exodus 32:6
b 9 WH, NE, and Tischendorf *test the Lord*
c 26 Psalm 24:1
d 28 BYZ and TR *and for conscience' sake, for the earth is the Lord's, and the fullness thereof*

1 Corinthians 11
Roles in Worship

¹Be imitators of me, as I also *am* of Christ. ²Now I commend you that you have remembered me in all things, and you are keeping the teachings as I delivered to you. ³But I want you to know that Christ is the head of every man, and the man *is the* head of *the* woman, and *the* head of Christ *is* God.
⁴Every man praying or prophesying having *anything* on *his* head dishonors his head. ⁵And every woman praying or prophesying with the head uncovered dishonors her head; for it is one and the same with having been shaven. ⁶For if a woman does not cover her head, also let her be shorn. And if *it is* disgraceful to a woman to be shorn or to be shaven, let her cover her head.
⁷For truly a man ought not to cover the head, being *the* image and glory of God; but the woman is *the* glory of man. ⁸For man is not of woman, but woman of man. ⁹For truly man was not created on account of the woman, but woman on account of the man. ¹⁰Because of this, the woman ought to have authority on the head, on account of the angels.
¹¹However, neither *is* woman separate from man, nor man separate from woman in *the* Lord. ¹²For just as the woman *is* of the man, so also the man *is* by the woman. And all things *are* of God.
¹³Judge for yourselves: Is it becoming for a woman to pray to God with her head uncovered? ¹⁴Does not even nature itself teach you that if a man has long hair it is a dishonor to him, ¹⁵but if a woman has long hair, it is to her glory? For the long hair instead of a covering is given to her.
¹⁶Now if anyone is inclined to be contentious, we have no such practice, nor do the churches of God.

Sharing in the Lord's Supper
(Matthew 26:26-30; Mark 14:22-26; Luke 22:14-23)

¹⁷Now in this instructing, I do not praise *you*, because you come together not for the better, but for the worse. ¹⁸For first indeed, of you coming together in an assembly, I hear there to be divisions among you, and in part I believe it. ¹⁹For also it behooves there to be factions among you, so that also the approved should become evident among you.
²⁰Therefore, of you coming together in one place, it is not to eat *the* Lord's supper. ²¹For in eating, one takes first the own supper. And indeed this *one* is hungry, but that *one* is drunken. ²²What! Have you no houses in which to eat and to drink? Or do you despise the church of God and put to shame those having nothing? What shall I say to you? Shall I praise you in this? I do not praise *you*!
²³For I received from the Lord that which also I delivered to you, that the Lord Jesus in the night in which He was betrayed, took bread, ²⁴and having given thanks, He broke *it* and said, "This is My body, which *is* for you;*a* do this in

remembrance of Me." ²⁵Likewise also the cup after having supped, saying, "This cup is the new covenant in My blood; do this, as often as you might drink *it*, in remembrance of Me." ²⁶For as often as you may eat this bread and may drink the cup, you proclaim the Lord's death until He should come.

²⁷Therefore whoever should eat the bread or should drink the cup of the Lord unworthily will be guilty of the body and of the blood of the Lord. ²⁸But let a man examine himself, and in this manner let him eat of the bread, and let him drink of the cup. ²⁹For the *one* eating and drinking not discerning the body, eats and drinks judgment on himself. ³⁰Because of this, many *are* weak and sick among you, and many are fallen asleep.

³¹For if we were judging ourselves, we would not come under judgment. ³²But being judged by the Lord, we are disciplined, so that we should not be condemned with the world.

³³So then, my brothers, coming together in order to eat, wait for one another. ³⁴If anyone is hungry, let him eat at home, so that you might not come together for judgment; and I will set in order the other things as soon as I might come.

a 24 BYZ and TR *which is broken for you*

1 Corinthians 12
Spiritual Gifts

¹Now concerning spiritual *gifts*, brothers, I do not want you to be ignorant. ²You know that when you were pagans, to mute idols you were led, as being carried away. ³Therefore I make known to you that no one speaking in *the* Spirit of God says, "Jesus *is* accursed," and no one is able to say, "Jesus *is* Lord," if not in *the* Holy Spirit.

⁴Now there are varieties of gifts, but the same Spirit; ⁵and there are varieties of services, but the same Lord; ⁶and there are varieties of workings, but the same God is working all things in everyone.

⁷Now to each is given the manifestation of the Spirit, for the common profiting. ⁸For truly, to one is given a word of wisdom by the Spirit, and to another a word of knowledge according to the same Spirit, ⁹and to a different one faith by the same Spirit, and to another gifts of healing by the one Spirit, ¹⁰and to another working of miracles, and to another prophecy, and to another distinguishing of spirits, and to a different one various kinds of tongues, and to another interpretation of tongues. ¹¹Now one and the same the Spirit works all these things, apportioning individually to each as He wills.

The Body of Christ

¹²For just as the body is one, and has many members, and all the members of the body being many are one body, so also *is* Christ. ¹³For also in one Spirit we all were baptized into one body, whether Jews or Greeks, whether slaves or free, and we were all made to drink one Spirit. ¹⁴For also the body is not one member, but many. ¹⁵If the foot should say, "Because I am not a hand, I am not of the body," not on account of this is it not of the body. ¹⁶And if the ear should say, "Because I am not an eye, I am not of the body," not on account of this is it not of the body. ¹⁷If all the body *were* an eye, where *would be* the hearing? If all *were* hearing, where *would be* the sense of smell?

¹⁸But now God has arranged the members, each one of them in the body, as He desired. ¹⁹And if all were one member, where *would be* the body? ²⁰But now indeed, *there are* many members, but one body.

²¹Now the eye is not able to say to the hand, "I have no need of you." Or again the head to the feet, "I have no need of you." ²²But much rather, those members of the body seeming to be weaker are necessary, ²³and those of the body we think to be less honorable, these we bestow more abundant honor. And our

unpresentable *parts* have more abundant decorum, ²⁴but our presentable *parts* have no need.
But God has composed the body, having given more abundant honor to the *parts* being deficient, ²⁵that there should be no division in the body, but the members should have the same concern for one another. ²⁶And if one member suffers, all the members suffer with *it*; if one member is honored, all the members rejoice with *it*.

The greater gifts

²⁷Now you are *the* body of Christ, and members in particular. ²⁸And some indeed God has appointed in the church, first apostles, secondly prophets, third teachers, then miracles, then gifts of healing, helping, administrating, various kinds of tongues. ²⁹*Are* all apostles? *Are* all prophets? *Are* all teachers? Do all *work* miracles? ³⁰Do all have gifts of healings? Do all speak in tongues? Do all interpret? ³¹But earnestly desire the greater gifts. And I show to you now a more surpassing way.

1 Corinthians 13
Love

¹If I speak in the tongues of men and of angels, but have not love, I have become a sounding brass or a clanging cymbal. ²And if I should have prophecy and understand all mysteries and all knowledge, and if I should have all faith so as to remove mountains, but have not love, I am nothing. ³And if I may give away all my possessions, and I may deliver up my body that I may boast,ᵃ but have not love, I am profited nothing.
⁴Love is patient, love is kind, love is not envious, it is not boastful, it is not puffed up. ⁵It does not act unbecomingly, it does not seek the things of its own, it is not easily provoked, it keeps no account of wrongs. ⁶It does not delight at unrighteousness, but rejoices in the truth. ⁷It bears all things, believes all things, hopes all things, endures all things.

⁸Love never fails; but if *there are* prophesies, they will be done away; if *there are* tongues, they will be ceased; if *there is* knowledge it will pass away. ⁹For we know in part and we prophesy in part; ¹⁰but when the perfect should come, the partial will be done away.
¹¹When I was a child, I was speaking like a child, I was thinking like a child, I was reasoning like a child; when I became a man, I did away with the things of the child. ¹²For presently we see through a glass in obscurity; but then, face to face. Presently, I know in part; but then I will know fully, even as I have been fully known.
¹³But now these three things abide: faith, hope, love; but *the* greatest of these *is* love.

a 3 SBL, NE, BYZ, and TR *surrender my body to be burned*

1 Corinthians 14
Prophecy and Tongues

¹Earnestly pursue love, and earnestly desire spiritual gifts, and especially that you might prophesy. ²For the *one* speaking in a tongue speaks not to men, but to God. For no one hears, but in the Spirit he utters mysteries. ³But the *one* prophesying speaks to men for edification and encouragement and consolation. ⁴The *one* speaking in a tongue edifies himself, but the *one* prophesying edifies *the* church.
⁵Now I desire you all to speak in tongues, but rather that you should prophesy. Now the *one* prophesying *is* greater than the *one* speaking in tongues, unless he should interpret, so that the church might receive edification.
⁶But now brothers, if I should come to you speaking in tongues, what will I profit you, unless I should speak to you either in revelation, or in knowledge, or in prophecy, or in teaching? ⁷Even lifeless things giving a sound, whether *the* flute or harp, unless they give distinction to the

sounds, how will it be known what *is* being piped or being harped?
⁸And indeed if *the* trumpet gives an indistinct sound, who will prepare himself for battle? ⁹So also you, unless you give intelligible speech with the tongue, how will it be known what *is* being spoken? For you will be speaking into *the* air.
¹⁰There are, if it may be, so many kinds of languages in *the* world, and none without meaning. ¹¹Therefore unless I know the power of the sound, I will be a barbarian to the *one* speaking, and the *one* speaking, a barbarian to me.
¹²So also you, since you are zealous of spiritual gifts, search for the edification of the church, that you should cause *it* to abound. ¹³Therefore he who speaks in a tongue, let him pray that he might interpret. ¹⁴For if I pray in a tongue, my spirit prays, but my mind is unfruitful.
¹⁵What then is it? I will pray with the spirit, but also I will pray with the mind. I will sing praise with the spirit, but also I will sing praise with the mind. ¹⁶Otherwise if you bless with the spirit, how will the *one* filling the place of the uninstructed say the "Amen" at your thanksgiving, since he knows not what you say? ¹⁷For truly you are giving thanks well, but the other is not edified.
¹⁸I thank God, speaking in tongues more than all of you. ¹⁹But in *the* church, I desire to speak five words with my mind, that also I might instruct others, rather than ten thousand words in a tongue.
²⁰Brothers, do not be children in the minds. Yet in the evil, be little children; but in the thinking, be full grown. ²¹In the Law it has been written:
"By other tongues,
 and by other lips,
I will speak to this people,
 and not even thus will they hear Me,
says *the* Lord."ᵃ
²²So then, tongues are for a sign, not to those believing, but to the unbelieving; but prophecy *is* not to the unbelieving, but to the believing.
²³Therefore if the whole church gathers together in *one* place and all should speak in tongues, but uninstructed ones or unbelievers come in, will not they say that you are mad? ²⁴But if all prophesy, and some unbeliever or uninstructed should come in, he is convicted by all, he is examined by all, ²⁵ *and* the secrets of his heart become manifest. And thus having fallen upon *his* face, he will worship God, declaring that God is certainly among you.

Orderly Worship

²⁶What then is it, brothers? When you may come together, each has a psalm, has a teaching, has a revelation, has a tongue, has an interpretation. Let all things be done for edification.
²⁷If anyone speaks with a tongue, *let it be* by two or the most three, and in turn; and let one interpret. ²⁸But if there is no interpreter, let him be silent in *the* church, and let him speak to himself and to God.
²⁹And let two or three prophets speak, and let the others discern. ³⁰But if a revelation should be made to another sitting by, let the first be silent. ³¹For you are all able to prophesy *one* by one, so that all may learn, and all may be exhorted. ³²And *the* spirits of prophets are subject to prophets. ³³For He is not the God of disorder, but of peace.
As in all the churches of the saints, ³⁴let the women be silent in the churches. For it is not allowed to them to speak, but to be in submission, as the Law also says. ³⁵But if they desire to learn anything, let them ask the own husbands at home; for it is shameful for a woman to speak in *the* church.
³⁶Or has the word of God gone out from you? Or has it come to you only? ³⁷If anyone considers himself to be a prophet or spiritual, let him recognize that the things I write to you are *the* commands

of *the* Lord. ³⁸But if anyone is ignorant, let him be ignored.ᵇ

³⁹So, my brothers, earnestly desire to prophesy, and do not forbid to speak in tongues. ⁴⁰But let all things be done properly and with order.

a 21 Isaiah 28:11,12
b 38 BYZ and TR *let him be ignorant*

1 Corinthians 15
The Resurrection of Christ

¹Now I make known to you, brothers, the gospel that I proclaimed to you, which also you received, in which you also stand, ²by which you are also being saved, if you hold fast to the word I proclaimed to you; otherwise you have believed in vain.

³For I delivered to you in the foremost what also I received: that Christ died for our sins according to the Scriptures, ⁴and that He was buried, and that He was raised the third day according to the Scriptures, ⁵and that He appeared to Cephas,ᵃ then to the Twelve. ⁶Thereafter He appeared to more than five hundred brothers at once, the greater part of whom remain until now, although some have fallen asleep. ⁷Then He appeared to James, then to all the apostles. ⁸And last of all, He appeared also to me, as to *one of* untimely birth.

⁹For I am the least of the apostles, who am not fit to be called an apostle, because I persecuted the church of God. ¹⁰But *by the* grace of God I am what I am, and His grace toward me has not been void. Rather, I toiled more abundantly than all of them, yet not I, but the grace of God that *was* with me. ¹¹Therefore whether *it was* I or they, thus we preach, and thus you believed.

The Resurrection of the Dead

¹²Now if Christ is preached, that He has been raised out from *the* dead, how do some among you say that there is no resurrection of *the* dead? ¹³But if there is no resurrection of *the* dead, neither has Christ been raised. ¹⁴And if Christ has not been raised, then also our preaching *is* void, and your faith *is* void. ¹⁵Then also we are found false witnesses of God, because we have witnessed concerning God that He raised up Christ, whom He has not raised if then *the* dead are not raised.

¹⁶For if *the* dead are not raised, neither has Christ been raised. ¹⁷And if Christ has not been raised, your faith is futile; you are still in your sins. ¹⁸Also then those having fallen asleep in Christ have perished. ¹⁹If only in this life we are having hope in Christ, we are more to be pitied than all men.

The Order of Resurrection

²⁰But now Christ has been raised out from *the* dead, *the* firstfruit of those having fallen asleep. ²¹For since death *came* by a man, so also by a man *has come the* resurrection of *the* dead. ²²For as indeed in Adam all die, so also in Christ all will be made alive. ²³But each in the own order: Christ *the* firstfruit, then those of Christ at His coming, ²⁴then the end, when He shall hand over the kingdom to the God and Father, when He shall have annulled all dominion, and all authority and power. ²⁵For it behooves Him to reign until He shall have put all the enemies under His feet. ²⁶*The* last enemy to be abolished *is* death. ²⁷For "He has put in subjection all things under His feet."ᵇ But when it may be said that all things have been put in subjection, *it is* evident that the *One* having put in subjection all things to Him *is* excepted. ²⁸Now when all things shall have been put in subjection to Him, then also the Son Himself will be put in subjection to the *One* having put in subjection all things to Him, so that God may be all in all.

²⁹Otherwise what will they do who are baptized for the dead? If *the* dead are not raised at all, why also are they baptized for them? ³⁰And why are we in danger every hour? ³¹I die every day, as surely as the boasting in you, brothers, which I have in Christ Jesus our Lord. ³²If

according to man I fought wild beasts in Ephesus, what *is* the profit to me? If *the* dead are not raised,

"Let us eat and let us drink,
for tomorrow we die."*c*

³³Do not be misled: "Bad companionships corrupt good morals."*d* ³⁴Sober up righteously and do not sin, for some have ignorance of God. I speak to your shame.

The Resurrection Body

³⁵But someone will say, "How are the dead raised? And with what body do they come?" ³⁶You fool! What you sow does not come to life unless it dies. ³⁷And what you sow *is* not the body that will be, but you sow a bare grain, if it may be of wheat, or of some of the rest. ³⁸But God gives it a body as He has willed, and to each of the seeds, its own body.

³⁹Not all flesh *is* the same, but indeed one flesh *is* of men, and another flesh *is* of beasts, and another flesh *is* of birds, and another *is* of fish. ⁴⁰And *there are* heavenly bodies and earthly bodies. But truly the glory of the heavenly *is* one *kind*, and that of the earthly *is* another. ⁴¹*There is* one glory of *the* sun, and another glory of *the* moon, and another glory of *the* stars; for star differs from star in glory.

⁴²So also *is* the resurrection of the dead. It is sown in decay; it is raised in immortality. ⁴³It is sown in dishonor; it is raised in glory. It is sown in weakness; it is raised in power. ⁴⁴It is sown a natural body; it is raised a spiritual body. If there is a natural body, there is also a spiritual. ⁴⁵So also it has been written: "The first man Adam became into a living soul; "*e* the last Adam into a life-giving spirit.

⁴⁶However, the spiritual *was* not first, but the natural; then the spiritual. ⁴⁷The first man *was* made of dust from *the* earth; the second man from heaven. ⁴⁸As the *one was* made of dust, so also *are* those of the earth; and as *is* the heavenly *one*, so also *are* those of heaven. ⁴⁹And as we have borne the image of the earthly, we shall also bear the image of the heavenly.

Where O Death is Your Victory?
(Isaiah 57:1-2; Hosea 13:14)

⁵⁰Now I say this, brothers, that flesh and blood is not able to inherit *the* kingdom of God, nor does decay inherit immortality. ⁵¹Behold, I tell to you a mystery: We will not all sleep, but we will all be changed— ⁵²in an instant, in *the* twinkling of an eye, at the last trumpet. For the trumpet will sound, and the dead will be raised imperishable, and we will be changed. ⁵³For it behooves this, the perishable to put on *the* imperishable; and this, the mortal to put on immortality.

⁵⁴Now when this the perishable shall have put on the imperishable, and this, the mortal, shall have put on immortality, then the word having been written will come to pass: "Death has been swallowed up in victory."*f*

⁵⁵"Where O death, *is* your victory?
Where O death *is* your sting?"*g*

⁵⁶Now the sting of death *is* sin, and the power of sin *is* the Law. ⁵⁷But thanks *be* to God, the *One* giving us the victory through our Lord Jesus Christ.

⁵⁸Therefore, my beloved brothers, be steadfast, immovable, always abounding in the work of the Lord, knowing that your toil in *the* Lord is not in vain.

a 5 That is, Peter
b 27 Psalm 8:6
c 32 Isaiah 22:13
d 33 Probably a quote from the Greek comedy 'Thais' by Menander
e 45 Genesis 2:7
f 54 Isaiah 25:8
g 55 Hosea 13:14

1 Corinthians 16
The Collection for the Saints

¹Now concerning the collection for the saints, as I have directed the churches of Galatia, so also you are to do. ²Every first of the week, let each of you put *something* aside, treasuring up whatever he may be prospered in, so that when I might come, then there should be no collections. ³And when I shall have arrived, whomever you might approve, with letters I will send these to carry your

bounty to Jerusalem. ⁴And if it is suitable for me also to go, they will go with me.

Paul's Travel Plans
(Romans 15:23-33)

⁵But I will come to you when I shall have gone through Macedonia, for I am going through Macedonia. ⁶And possibly I will stay with you, or even I will winter, so that you may equip me, wherever I may go. ⁷For I do not want to see you now in passing; for I hope to remain a certain time with you, if the Lord permits. ⁸But I will remain in Ephesus until Pentecost. ⁹For a great and productive door has opened to me, and many are opposing.

Timothy Commended

¹⁰Now if Timothy comes, see that he might be with you without fear, for he is doing the Lord's work, as I also. ¹¹Therefore no one should despise him. But equip him in peace, so that he might come to me; for I am expecting him with the brothers.

¹²Now concerning Apollos *our* brother, I exhorted him greatly that he should go to you with the brothers, and *his* will was not at all that he should come now; but he will come when he shall have opportunity.

Concluding Exhortations

¹³Watch you; stand firm in the faith; act like men; be strong. ¹⁴Let all things of you be done in love.

¹⁵Now I exhort you, brothers—you know the house of Stephanas, that it is *the* firstfruit of Achaia, and they have devoted themselves to service to the saints— ¹⁶that you also be subject to such as these, and to everyone joining in the work and laboring.

¹⁷Now I rejoice at the coming of Stephanas and Fortunatus and Achaicus, because these have filled up your deficiency. ¹⁸For they refreshed my spirit and yours. Therefore recognize such as these.

Final Greetings
(2 Thessalonians 3:16-18)

¹⁹The churches of Asia greet you. Aquila and Prisca,ᵃ with the church at their house, greet you heartily in *the* Lord.

²⁰All the brothers greet you. Greet one another with a holy kiss.

²¹The greeting *is in my* own hand—Paul.

²²If anyone does not love the Lord, let him be accursed. Maranatha!ᵇ

²³The grace of the Lord Jesus *be* with you.

²⁴My love *be* with all of you in Christ Jesus.

Amen.ᶜ

a 19 Or *Priscilla*
b 22 Greek *Maranatha* is a transliteration of Aramaic meaning *Our Lord come*
c 24 SBL, WH, and NA do not include *Amen*.

2 Corinthians

2 Corinthians 1
Paul Greets the Corinthians
(1 Corinthians 1:1-3)

¹Paul, an apostle of Christ Jesus by *the* will of God, and Timothy *our* brother,
To the church of God being in Corinth, with all the saints being in all Achaia.

²Grace to you and peace from God our Father and *the* Lord Jesus Christ.

The God of All Comfort

³Blessed *be* the God and Father of our Lord Jesus Christ, the Father of compassions, and God of all comfort, ⁴the *One* comforting us in all our tribulation, for us to be able to comfort those in every tribulation through the comfort with which we ourselves are comforted by God, ⁵because as the sufferings of the Christ abound toward us, so through Christ our comfort also abounds.

⁶But if we are constricted, *it is* for your comfort and salvation; if we are encouraged, *it is* for your comfort, operating in *the* endurance of the same sufferings that we also suffer. ⁷And our hope for you *is* sure, knowing that as you

are partners of *our* sufferings, so also of *our* comfort.

⁸For we do not want you to be ignorant brothers, as to our affliction having happened in Asia, that we were weighed against excessively, beyond *our* power, so as for us to despair even to live. ⁹Indeed we had in ourselves the sentence of death, in order that we should not be trusting in ourselves, but in God, the *One* raising the dead, ¹⁰who has delivered us from such a great death and will deliver *us*, in whom we have hope that also He will deliver *us* still, ¹¹of you also joining together for us by supplication, so that thanks may be given for us by many persons for the grace bestowed toward us through many.

Paul's Change of Plans

¹²For our boasting is this: the testimony of our conscience that we have conducted ourselves in the world, and more abundantly toward you, in *the* purity and sincerity of God, and not in fleshly wisdom but in *the* grace of God. ¹³For we write no other things to you other than what you read or even understand. And I hope that you will understand to *the* end, ¹⁴as also you have understood us in part, so that we are your boasting, even as you *are* also ours, in the day of our Lord Jesus.

¹⁵And with this confidence I was planning to come to you previously, so that you might have a second blessing of grace, ¹⁶and through you to pass through into Macedonia, and to come to you again from Macedonia, and to be set forward by you to Judea.

¹⁷Thus purposing, therefore then, did I use lightness? Or do I purpose what I purpose according to flesh, so that with me there should be "Yes, yes" and "No, no"? ¹⁸But God *is* faithful, that our word to you was not "Yes" and "No." ¹⁹For the Son of God, Jesus Christ, having been proclaimed among you by us—by me and Silvanus[a] and Timothy—was not "Yes" and "No," but it has always been "Yes" in Him. ²⁰For as many as *are the* promises of God, in Him *is* the "Yes." Therefore also in Him, the "Amen" by us *is* for glory to God.

²¹Now the *One* establishing us with you unto Christ, and having anointed us, *is* God, ²²the *One* also having sealed us and having given the pledge of the Spirit in our hearts. ²³But I call God as witness upon my soul, that sparing you, I have not yet come to Corinth. ²⁴Not that we lord it over your faith, but are fellow workers with you of joy; for in the faith you stand firm.

a 19 That is, Silas

2 Corinthians 2
Reaffirm Your Love

¹For I judged this within myself, not to come to you again in grief. ²For if I grieve you again, who is making me glad, except the *one* being grieved by me? ³And I wrote this same thing, so that having come, I might not have grief from *those* of whom it behooves me to rejoice, trusting in you all, that my joy is *shared by* all of you. ⁴For out of much affliction and anguish of heart, I wrote to you through many tears, not that you might be grieved, but that you might know the love that I have more abundantly toward you.

⁵But if anyone has caused grief, he not grieved me, but—in part, that I might not put it too severely—you all. ⁶The punishment which *is* by the majority *is* sufficient to such a one, ⁷so that on the contrary, rather for you to forgive and to comfort *him*, lest perhaps such a one should be overwhelmed by more abundant sorrow. ⁸Therefore I exhort you to confirm *your* love toward him.

⁹For this indeed also did I write, so that I might know the proof of you, whether you are obedient to everything. ¹⁰Now to whomever you forgive anything, I also do; and indeed to whom I have forgiven, if I have forgiven anything, *it is* for the sake of you, in *the* person of Christ, ¹¹so

that we should not be outwitted by Satan; for we are not ignorant of his schemes.

Triumph in Christ

¹²Now having come to Troas for the gospel of Christ, a door also having been opened to me in *the* Lord, ¹³I had no rest in my spirit, in my not finding Titus my brother. Instead, having taken leave of them, I went out to Macedonia.

¹⁴But thanks *be* to God, the *One* always leading us in triumph in Christ, and through us in every place making manifest the fragrance of *the* knowledge of Him. ¹⁵For we are a sweet perfume of Christ to God in those being saved and in those perishing: ¹⁶to one indeed an odor from death to death, and to the other a fragrance from life to life. And who *is* sufficient for these things?

¹⁷For we are not like the many, peddling the word of God, but as of sincerity, but as of God, we speak before God in Christ.

2 Corinthians 3
Ministers of a New Covenant

¹Are we beginning to commend ourselves again? Or like some, do we need commendatory letters to you or from you? ²You are our letter, having been inscribed in our hearts, being known and being read by all men, ³being revealed that you are a letter of Christ, having been ministered to by us, having been inscribed not in ink, but with *the* Spirit of *the* living God, not on tablets of stone, but on tablets of human hearts.

⁴Now we have such confidence through Christ toward God. ⁵Not that we are sufficient from ourselves to reckon anything as of ourselves, but our sufficiency *is* of God, ⁶who also has made us competent *as* ministers of a new covenant, not of *the* letter, but of *the* Spirit. For the letter kills, but the Spirit gives life.

The Glory of the New Covenant
(Exodus 34:29-35)

⁷Now if the ministry of death, having been engraved in letters on stones, was produced in glory, so as for the sons of Israel not to be able to look intently into the face of Moses, on account of the glory of his face which is fading, ⁸how will the ministry of the Spirit not be more in glory? ⁹For if glory *was* in the ministry of condemnation, much more does the ministry of righteousness abound *in* glory! ¹⁰For even that having been made glorious has not been glorified in this respect, on account of the glory surpassing *it*. ¹¹For if that which is fading away *was* through glory, much more *is* that remaining in glory!

¹²Therefore having such a hope, we use great boldness, ¹³and not as Moses would put a veil over his face for the sons of Israel not to look intently into the end of that fading away.

¹⁴But their minds were hardened; for until the present day, the same veil remains at the reading of the old covenant, not being lifted, which is being removed in Christ. ¹⁵But unto this day, when Moses shall be read, a veil lies over their heart. ¹⁶But whenever *one* shall have turned to *the* Lord, the veil is taken away.

¹⁷Now the Lord is the Spirit; and where the Spirit of *the* Lord *is, there is* freedom. ¹⁸And we all having been unveiled in face, beholding as in a mirror the glory of *the* Lord, are being transformed into the same image, from glory to glory, even as from *the* Lord, *the* Spirit.

2 Corinthians 4
The Light of the Gospel

¹Because of this, having this ministry, as we received mercy, we do not lose heart. ²But we have renounced the hidden things of shame, not walking in craftiness, nor falsifying the word of God, but by manifestation of the truth, commending ourselves to every man's conscience before God.

³But if indeed our gospel is concealed, it is concealed to those who are perishing, ⁴in whom the god of this age has blinded

the minds of the unbelieving, so as for not to beam forth the illumination of the gospel of the glory of Christ, who is *the* image of God.
⁵For we do not proclaim ourselves, but Christ Jesus *as* Lord; and ourselves *as* your servants for the sake of Jesus. ⁶For *it is* God, having said, "Light shall shine out of darkness,"ᵃ who shone in our hearts for *the* radiance of the knowledge of the glory of God in *the* face of Jesus Christ.ᵇ

Treasures in Jars of Clay
(Romans 6:1-14)

⁷Now we have this treasure in earthen vessels, that the surpassingness of the power may be from God, and not from us, ⁸being hard pressed in every *way* but not being crushed, being perplexed but not despairing, ⁹being persecuted but not being forsaken, being struck down but not being destroyed, ¹⁰always carrying around the death *of* Jesus in *our* body, so that the life of Jesus also should be manifested in our body. ¹¹For we the living are always being delivered to death on account of Jesus, so that the life of Jesus may also be manifested in our mortal flesh. ¹²So then, death works in us, but life in you.
¹³But having the same spirit of faith according to that having been written: "I believed, therefore I have spoken,"ᶜ we also believe and therefore speak, ¹⁴knowing that the *One* having raised up the Lord Jesus also will raise us up through Jesus and will present *us* with you. ¹⁵For all things *are* for your sake, so that the grace having abounded through more and more *people* may increase the thanksgiving to the glory of God.
¹⁶Therefore we do not lose heart; but indeed if our outward man is being brought to decay, yet our inner *self* is being renewed day and day. ¹⁷For the momentary lightness of our affliction is producing for us an eternal weight of glory, far surpassing to excessiveness. ¹⁸We are not looking at the things being seen, but the things not being seen. For the things being seen *are* temporary, but the things not being seen *are* eternal.

a 6 Genesis 1:3
b 6 SBL, NE, and WH *in the face of Christ*
c 13 Psalm 116:10

2 Corinthians 5
Our Eternal Dwelling
(Romans 8:18-27)

¹For we know that if the tent of our earthly house should be destroyed, we have a building from God, a house not made with hands, eternal in the heavens. ²And indeed, in this we groan, longing to be clothed with our dwelling which *is* from heaven, ³if indeed also having been clothed, we will not be found naked. ⁴And indeed, being in the tent we groan, being burdened, because we do not wish to be unclothed but to be clothed, so that the mortal may be swallowed up by life. ⁵Now the *One* having prepared us for this very *purpose is* God, having given to us the pledge of the Spirit, ⁶always being confident, then, and knowing that, being at home in the body, we are absent from the Lord. ⁷For we walk by faith, not by sight.
⁸Now we are confident and are pleased rather to be absent out of the body, and to be at home with the Lord. ⁹Therefore also we are ambitious, whether being at home or being away, to be well-pleasing to Him. ¹⁰For we must all be revealed before the judgment seat of Christ, that each may receive back the things *done* through the body according to what he did, whether good or evil.

Ambassadors for Christ

¹¹Therefore knowing the fear of the Lord, we persuade men. And we have been made manifest to God, and I hope to have been made manifest in your consciences also. ¹²We are not commending ourselves to you again, but are giving to you occasion of boasting on behalf of us, so that you may have *an answer* toward those boasting in appearance, and not in *the* heart.

¹³For if we are beside ourselves, *it is* to God; or if we are sober-minded *it is* for you. ¹⁴For the love of Christ compels us, having concluded this, that One has died for all, therefore all have died. ¹⁵And He died for all that those living no longer should live to themselves, but to the *One* having died for them and having been raised again.

¹⁶Therefore from now, we regard no one according to *the* flesh. Even though we have regarded Christ according to flesh, yet now we regard *Him thus* no longer. ¹⁷Therefore if anyone *is* in Christ, *he is* a new creation.[a] The old things have passed away; behold, *the* new has come into being.

¹⁸Now all things *are* of God, the *One* having reconciled us to Himself through Christ, and having given to us the ministry of reconciliation: ¹⁹how that God was in Christ reconciling *the* world to Himself, not reckoning their trespasses to them, and having put into us the word of reconciliation.

²⁰Therefore we are ambassadors for Christ, as though God is beseeching through us. We implore on behalf of Christ: Be reconciled to God. ²¹He made the *One* not having known sin *to be* sin[b] for us, so that in Him we might become *the* righteousness of God.

a 17 Or *creature*
b 21 Or *be a sin offering*

2 Corinthians 6
Paul's Hardships and God's Grace

¹And working together, we also urge you not to receive the grace of God in vain. ²For He says:

"In *the* acceptable time I listened to you,
 and in *the* day of salvation I helped you."[a]

Behold, now *is the* time of favor; behold, now *is the* day of salvation.

³Placing no obstacle in *anyone's way* so that *our* ministry should not be blemished, ⁴in everything, rather, we are commending ourselves as God's servants: in great endurance, in tribulations, in hardships, in distresses; ⁵in beatings, in imprisonments, in riots, in labors, in watchings, in fastings; ⁶in purity, in knowledge, in patience, in kindness; in *the* Holy Spirit, in genuine love; ⁷in *the* word of truth, in *the* power of God; with the weapons of righteousness for the right hand and for *the* left; ⁸through glory and dishonor, through bad report and good report; as imposters and yet true; ⁹as being unknown and yet being well-known; as dying and yet, behold, we live; as being punished and yet not being killed; ¹⁰as being sorrowful yet always rejoicing; as poor yet enriching many; as having nothing and yet possessing all things.

¹¹Our mouth has been opened to you, Corinthians; our heart has been expanded. ¹²You are not restrained by us, but you are restrained in your *own* affections. ¹³Now *as* the same recompense, I speak as to children, be you expanded also.

Do Not Be Unequally Yoked
(Exodus 29:45-46)

¹⁴Do not become unequally yoked together with unbelievers. For what partnership *have* righteousness and lawlessness? Or what fellowship *has* light with darkness? ¹⁵And what harmony *has* Christ with Belial? Or what part to a believer *is* with an unbeliever? ¹⁶And what agreement *has the* temple of God with idols? For we are *the* temple of *the* living God. As God has said:

"I will dwell in them,
 and will walk among *them*;
and I will be their God,
 and they will be My people."[b]
¹⁷"Therefore come out from their midst
 and be separate, says *the* Lord,
and touch nothing unclean,
 and I will receive you."[c]
¹⁸and
"I will be for a father to you,

and you will be for sons and daughters to Me,
says *the* Lord Almighty."

a 2 Isaiah 49:8
b 16 Leviticus 26:12; Ezekiel 37:27
c 17 Isaiah 52:11; Ezekiel 20:34

2 Corinthians 7
Paul's Joy in the Corinthians

¹Therefore having these promises, beloved, we should cleanse ourselves from every defilement of flesh and spirit, perfecting holiness in *the* fear of God. ²Make room for us. We have wronged no one, we have corrupted no one, we have exploited no one. ³I do not speak for condemnation; for I have before said that you are in our hearts for *us* to die together and to live together. ⁴Great *is* my boldness toward you; great my boasting on behalf of you; I have been filled with encouragement; I overabound with joy upon all our affliction.

⁵And indeed, of us having come into Macedonia, our flesh had no rest; but we are being pressed in every *way*: conflicts on the outside, fears within. ⁶But God, the *One* comforting the downcast, encouraged us by the coming of Titus, ⁷and not only by his coming, but also by the comfort with which he was comforted as to you, relating to us your earnest desire, your mourning, your zeal for me, so as for me to rejoice the more.

⁸For if also I have grieved you in the letter, I do not regret *it*. For even if I did regret *it*, I see that the letter grieved you, even if for an hour. ⁹Now I rejoice, not that you were grieved, but that you were grieved into repentance. For you were grieved according to God, so that you might suffer loss in nothing through us. ¹⁰For grief according to God produces repentance to salvation without regret; but the world's grief produces death.

¹¹For behold, how much earnestness this very same thing—to have been grieved according to God—has produced in you: but reasoned defense, but indignation, but fear, but longing, but zeal, but vindication! In everything, you have proved yourselves to be innocent in this matter. ¹²So even if I wrote to you, *it was* not for the sake of the *one* having done wrong, nor for the sake of the *one* having suffered wrong, but rather for the sake of your earnestness for us being revealed to you before God. ¹³On account of this, we have been comforted.

And besides our comfort, we have rejoiced the more abundantly rather at the joy of Titus, because his spirit has been refreshed by all of you. ¹⁴For if I have boasted anything to him about you, I was not put to shame; but as we have spoken all things to you in truth, so also our boasting to Titus became truth. ¹⁵And his affections are more abundantly toward you, remembering the obedience of all of you, how you received him with fear and trembling. ¹⁶I rejoice that in everything I am confident in you.

2 Corinthians 8
Generosity Commended

¹Now we make known to you, brothers, the grace of God having been bestowed among the churches of Macedonia, ²that in much proof of tribulation, the abundance of their joy and of their deep poverty abounded into the riches of their generosity. ³For I testify *that* according to *their* ability and beyond *their* ability, they *were* willing of themselves, ⁴imploring of us with much entreaty for the grace and the fellowship of the service among the saints. ⁵And not *only* as we had hoped, but they gave themselves first to the Lord and then to us, by *the* will of God.

⁶Accordingly, we exhorted Titus that as he had begun, so also he might complete with you this grace as well. ⁷But even as you abound in every *way*—in faith, and speech, and knowledge, and all earnestness, and in the love from us to you—that also you should abound in this grace. ⁸I do not speak as a command, but proving the genuineness of your love through the earnestness of others also.

Christ's Example

⁹For you know the grace our Lord Jesus Christ, that being rich, for the sake of you He became poor, so that you through *His* poverty might be enriched. ¹⁰And I give a judgment in this *matter*, for this is profitable for you who not only have begun from a year ago to act, but also to will. ¹¹And now also complete the doing, so that just as *there was* the readiness to will, so also *there may be* to complete, out of that which you have. ¹²For if the readiness is present, *it is* acceptable as if he might have, not as he does not have. ¹³For *this is* not that to others *there may be* ease, but for you affliction; but of equality. ¹⁴At the present time, your abundance *will be* for their need, so that their abundance also may be for your need, so that there may be equality. ¹⁵As it has been written:

"He the much did not abound,
 and he the little had no lack."ᵃ

Titus Commended
(Titus 1:1-4)

¹⁶But thanks to God, the *One* putting into the heart of Titus the same earnestness for you. ¹⁷For indeed he accepted *our* appeal, but being very earnest, of his own accord he has gone out to you.

¹⁸And we have sent with him the brother whose praise in the gospel *is* through all of the churches, ¹⁹and not only *that*, but also having been chosen by the churches, *he is* our fellow traveler with this grace that *is* being administered by us toward the glory of the Lord himself and our readiness, ²⁰avoiding this, lest anyone should blame us in this abundance being administered by us. ²¹For we are taking great care to do what is right, not only before *the* Lord, but also before men.

²²Now we sent with them our brother, whom we have proven often in many things to be earnest, but now much more earnest by *his* confidence which *is* toward you. ²³Whether as regards Titus, *he is* my partner and fellow worker for you; or our brothers, *they are* apostles of *the* churches, *the* glory of Christ. ²⁴Therefore show to them the proof of your love and of our boasting about you in *the* face of the churches.

a 15 Exodus 16:18

2 Corinthians 9
God Loves a Cheerful Giver
(Leviticus 22:17-33)

¹For it is superfluous for me to write to you now concerning the service for the saints. ²For I know your readiness, which I boast of to Macedonians concerning you, that Achaia has been prepared from a year ago, and your zeal has been provoking the greater number.

³But I have sent the brothers in order that our boasting about you in this matter should not be made void, that you may be prepared, as I have been saying. ⁴Otherwise, if Macedonians should come with me and find you unprepared, we—not that we might say you—would be put to shame in this confidence. ⁵Therefore I esteemed *it* necessary to exhort the brothers that they should go before unto you and should complete beforehand your foreannounced blessing, thus this to be ready as a blessing, and not as covetousness.

⁶Now this: The *one* sowing sparingly will also reap sparingly, and the *one* sowing upon blessings will also reap upon blessings, ⁷each as he purposes in the heart, not out of regret or of necessity. For God loves a cheerful giver. ⁸And God *is* able to make all grace abound to you, so that in every *way*, always, having all sufficiency, you may abound in every good work. ⁹As it has been written:

"He has scattered abroad,
 He has given to the poor;
 His righteousness abides to the age."ᵃ

¹⁰Now the *One* supplying seed to the *one* sowing and bread for food will supply and will multiply your seed for sowing and will increase the fruits of your righteousness, ¹¹enriching you in every *way* to all

generosity, which produces through us thanksgiving to God. ¹²For the ministry of this service is not only completely filling up the needs of the saints, but is also overflowing through many thanksgivings to God, ¹³through the proof of this service, glorifying God at your submission of confession to the gospel of Christ, and *the* generosity of the participation toward them and toward all. ¹⁴And their supplication *is* for you, longing for you on account of the surpassing grace of God upon you. ¹⁵Thanks *be* to God for His indescribable gift!

a 9 Psalm 112:9

2 Corinthians 10
Paul's Apostolic Authority

¹Now I, Paul, myself exhort you by the meekness and gentleness of Christ, *I* who indeed as to appearance *am* humble among you, but being absent am bold toward you. ²Now I implore *you* that being present, I need not to be bold with the confidence with which I reckon to be daring toward some reckoning us as walking according to flesh.
³For walking in flesh, we do not wage war according to flesh. ⁴For the weapons of our warfare *are* not fleshly, but divinely powerful toward *the* demolition of strongholds, ⁵overthrowing arguments, and every high thing lifting itself up against the knowledge of God, and taking captive every thought into the obedience of Christ, ⁶and having readiness within to avenge all disobedience, when your obedience may have been fulfilled.
⁷You are looking at things according to appearance. If anyone is persuaded in himself to be of Christ, let him reckon this within himself again, that as he *is* of Christ, so also *are* we. ⁸For even if I should boast somewhat more abundantly concerning our authority, which the Lord has given *us* for building *you* up and not for tearing you down, I will not be ashamed, ⁹so that I might not seem as if to frighten you by means of the letters. ¹⁰For they say, "The letters indeed *are* weighty and strong, but the presence of the body *is* weak, and the speech having been ignored." ¹¹Let such a one reckon this, that such as we are in word by letters being absent, also such *we are* in action being present.
¹²For we dare not to classify or to compare ourselves *with* some commending themselves. But these, measuring themselves by themselves and comparing themselves with themselves, do not understand. ¹³But we will not boast into the things beyond measure, but according to the measure of the area that God has assigned to us, a measure to reach also as far as you. ¹⁴For we are not overextending ourselves, as not reaching to you. For we came also as far as you in the gospel of Christ, ¹⁵not boasting to the things beyond measure in others' labors, but having hope *of* your faith increasing, to be enlarged to abundance among you according to our area, ¹⁶so as to preach the gospel beyond you, not to boast in things already in another's area.
¹⁷But, "The *one* boasting, let him boast in *the* Lord."ᵃ ¹⁸For the *one* commending himself, this *one* is not approved, but the one whom the Lord commends.

a 17 Jeremiah 9:24

2 Corinthians 11
Paul and the False Apostles

¹I wish you were bearing with me a little in foolishness, but indeed you do bear with me. ²For I am jealous as to you with *the* jealousy of God. For I have betrothed you to one husband, to present a pure virgin to Christ.
³But I am afraid, lest by any means, as the serpent in his craftiness deceived Eve, your minds might be corrupted from the simplicity and the purity in Christ. ⁴For if indeed the *one* coming proclaims another Jesus whom we did not proclaim, or you receive a different spirit whom you did not receive, or a different gospel which

you did not accept, you are bearing with *it* well.

⁵For I reckon in nothing to have been inferior to those "most eminent apostles." ⁶But even if *I am* unpolished in speech, yet *I am* not in knowledge; but in every *way*, we have been made manifest to you in all things.

⁷Or did I commit a sin, humbling myself, so that you might be exalted, because I preached the gospel of God to you freely? ⁸I robbed other churches, having received support for service toward you. ⁹And being present with you and having been in need, I did not burden *anyone*; for the brothers having come from Macedonia completely filled up my need, and in everything I kept and will keep myself unburdensome to you. ¹⁰ *The* truth of Christ is in me, that this boasting of mine will not be sealed up in the regions of Achaia. ¹¹Why? Because I do not love you? God knows *I do*!

¹²But what I do, I will continue doing, so that I might cut off the opportunity of those desiring an opportunity that they might be found as also we in what they are boasting. ¹³For such *are* false apostles, deceitful workers, disguising themselves as apostles of Christ. ¹⁴And no wonder, for Satan himself masquerades as an angel of light. ¹⁵Therefore *it is* not surprising if his servants also masquerade as servants of righteousness, whose end will be according to their deeds.

Paul's Suffering and Service
(Colossians 1:24-29)

¹⁶Again I say, no one should think me to be a fool; but if otherwise, receive me even as a fool, that I also may boast a little. ¹⁷What I am saying in this confidence of boasting, I am not saying according to *the* Lord, but as in foolishness. ¹⁸Since many boast according to the flesh, I also will boast. ¹⁹For being wise, you bear with fools gladly! ²⁰For you bear *it* if anyone enslaves you, if anyone devours *you*, if anyone takes *from you*, if anyone exalts himself, if anyone strikes *you* in your face. ²¹I speak as to dishonor, as that we have been weak!

But in whatever anyone might dare—I speak in foolishness—I also am daring. ²²Are they Hebrews? I also. Are they Israelites? I also. Are they descendants of Abraham? I also. ²³Are they servants of Christ? I speak as being beside myself, I *too* above *measure*: more abundantly in labors, more abundantly in imprisonments, in beatings above measure, in deaths often.

²⁴Five times I received from *the* Jews *the* forty *lashes* minus one. ²⁵Three times I was beaten with rods, once I was stoned, three times I was shipwrecked. I have passed a night and a day in the deep *sea*; ²⁶in journeyings often, in perils of rivers, in perils of robbers; in perils from *my own* race, in perils from *the* Gentiles; in perils in *the* city, in perils in *the* wilderness; in perils on *the* sea, in perils among false brothers; ²⁷in labor and toil, often in watchings; in hunger and thirst, often in fastings; in cold and nakedness.

²⁸Besides *the* external things, the pressure on me on every day *is my* care for all the churches. ²⁹Who is weak, and I am not weak? Who is led into sin, and I do not burn inwardly?

³⁰If it behooves *me* to boast, I will boast *in* the things of my weakness. ³¹The God and Father of the Lord Jesus, the *One* being blessed to the ages, knows that I am not lying. ³²In Damascus the governor under the king Aretas was guarding the city of the Damascenes to seize me. ³³But I was let down in a basket through a window through the wall, and I escaped his hands.

2 Corinthians 12
Paul's Revelation

¹It behooves *me* to boast; it is not profitable indeed, but I will go on to visions and revelations of *the* Lord. ²I know a man in Christ, fourteen years

ago—whether in *the* body, I do not know, or out of the body, I do not know; God knows—such a man, having been caught up to *the* third heaven. ³And I know such a man—whether in *the* body or out of the body, I do not know; God knows— ⁴that he was caught up into Paradise, and he heard inexpressible words, not being permitted to man to speak.

Paul's Thorn and God's Grace

⁵Concerning such a man I will boast; but concerning myself I will not boast, except in the weaknesses. ⁶For if I should desire to boast, I will not be a fool, for I will be speaking *the* truth. But I refrain, lest anyone should credit to me more than what he sees in me, or anyone hears of me, ⁷and the surpassingness of the revelations.

Therefore, that I should not become conceited, a thorn in *my* flesh was given to me, a messenger of Satan, that he might buffet me, so that I should not become conceited. ⁸Three times I begged the Lord for this, that it might depart from me. ⁹And He said to me, "My grace suffices you, for the power is perfected in weakness." Therefore will I boast rather most gladly in my weaknesses, so that the power of Christ may rest upon me. ¹⁰Therefore I take pleasure in weaknesses, in insults, in hardships, in persecutions, and difficulties for Christ; for when I might be weak, then I am strong.

Concern for the Corinthians

¹¹I have become a fool; you compelled me. For I ought to have been commended by you, for in no way was I inferior to those "most eminent apostles," even though I am nothing. ¹²For the signs of the apostle were performed among you in all perseverance, and in signs, and wonders, and miracles. ¹³For in what is it that you were inferior beyond the rest *of the* churches, except that I myself did not burden you? Forgive me this wrong!

¹⁴Behold, this third time I am ready to come to you, and I will not burden *you*. For I do not seek what *is* yours, but you. For the children ought not to treasure up for the parents, but the parents for the children. ¹⁵Now I will spend most gladly, and will be utterly spent, for your souls. If loving you more abundantly, am I loved less?

¹⁶But be it so, I did not burden you; but being crafty, I caught you by trickery. ¹⁷By any of whom I have sent to you, did I exploit you by him? ¹⁸I urged Titus *to go*, and sent with *him our* brother. Did Titus exploit you? Did we not walk in the same spirit? Not in the same steps?

¹⁹Have you been thinking all along that we have been making a defense to you? We speak in Christ before God, but all things, beloved, for your edification. ²⁰For I fear lest perhaps having come, I may not find you such as I wish, and I might be found by you such as you do not wish; lest perhaps *there may be* quarreling, jealousy, anger, contentions, slander, gossip, conceit, disorder; ²¹lest of my having come again, my God should humble me as to you, and I should mourn over many of those having before sinned and not having repented of the impurity, and sexual immorality, and sensuality that they have practiced.

2 Corinthians 13
Examine Yourselves

¹This third *time* I am coming to you. "In *the* mouth of two or three witnesses every matter will be established."ᵃ ²I have warned as being present the second time, and being absent now; and I warn those having sinned before and all the rest that, if I come to the *same* again, I will not spare *anyone*, ³since you seek proof of Christ speaking in me, who is not weak toward you but is powerful among you. ⁴For indeed He was crucified in weakness, yet He lives by God's power. For we also are weak in Him, but we will live with Him by God's power toward you.

⁵Examine yourselves whether you are in the faith; test yourselves. Or do you not recognize yourselves that Jesus Christ *is* in you, unless you are unapproved? ⁶And I hope that you will realize that we are not unapproved.

⁷Now I pray to God for you to do nothing wrong. Not that we might appear approved, but that you may do what *is* right, though we might appear as unapproved. ⁸For we have no power against the truth, but for the truth. ⁹For we rejoice when we might be weak, but you might be strong. But this also we pray: for your perfection.

¹⁰Therefore I write these things being absent, so that being present I should not treat *you* with severity according to the authority that the Lord has given me for building up and not for tearing down.

Final Greetings and Blessing

¹¹Finally, brothers, rejoice! Be perfected, be exhorted,ᵇ *be of* the same mind, be at peace. And the God of love and peace will be with you.

¹²Greet one another with a holy kiss.

¹³All the saints greet you.

¹⁴The grace of the Lord Jesus Christ, and the love of God, and the fellowship of the Holy Spirit, *be* with all of you.ᶜ

a 1 Deuteronomy 19:15
b 11 Or *listen to my appeal*
c 14 Texts vary in verse numbering for the last three verses of 2 Corinthians 13. BYZ ends with *Amen*.

Galatians

Galatians 1
Paul's Greeting to the Galatians

¹Paul, an apostle—not from men, nor through man, but through Jesus Christ, and God *the* Father, the *One* having raised Him out from *the* dead— ²and all the brothers with me,
To the churches of Galatia:

³Grace to you and peace from God our Father and the Lord Jesus Christ, ⁴the *One* having given Himself for our sins, so that He might deliver us out of the evil age having come presently, according to the will our God and Father, ⁵to whom *be* the glory to the ages of the ages. Amen.

No Other Gospel

⁶I am amazed that so quickly you are deserting from the *One* having called you in *the* grace of Christ to another gospel, ⁷which is not another, except there are some who are troubling you and are desiring to pervert the gospel of Christ.

⁸But even if we or an angel out of heaven should preach a gospel to you contrary to what we proclaimed to you, let him be accursed! ⁹As we have said before, even now I say again: If anyone is preaching a gospel *to* you contrary to what you received, let him be accursed!

Paul Preaches the Gospel

¹⁰For presently do I seek approval of men, or God? Or do I seek to please men? For if I were still pleasing men, I would not be a servant of Christ. ¹¹For I make known to you, brothers, the gospel having been preached by me, that it is not according to man. ¹²For I neither received it from man, nor was I taught *it*, but by a revelation of Jesus Christ.

¹³For you have heard of my former way of life in Judaism, that beyond exceeding measure I was persecuting the church of God and was destroying it. ¹⁴And I was advancing in Judaism beyond many contemporaries among my people, being more abundantly zealous of *the* traditions of my fathers.

¹⁵But when God, the *One* having selected me from my mother's womb and having called *me* by His grace, was pleased ¹⁶to reveal His Son in me so that I might preach Him among the Gentiles, I consulted not immediately with flesh and blood, ¹⁷nor did I go up to Jerusalem to the apostles before me, but I went away into Arabia and returned again to Damascus.

¹⁸Then after three years I went up to Jerusalem to make acquaintance with Cephas,ᵃ and I remained with him fifteen days. ¹⁹But I saw none of the other

apostles, only James, the Lord's brother. ²⁰Now in what I write to you, behold, before God, I do not lie.

²¹Then I went into the regions of Syria and Cilicia. ²²And I was by face unknown to the churches of Judea that *are* in Christ. ²³But they were only hearing that "the *one* formerly persecuting us now is preaching the faith which once he was destroying." ²⁴And they were glorifying God in me.

a 18 That is, Peter

Galatians 2
The Council at Jerusalem

¹Then after fourteen years I went up again to Jerusalem with Barnabas, having taken with *me* Titus also. ²Now I went up according to a revelation and set before them the gospel that I proclaim among the Gentiles; but apart individually to those esteemed, lest hardly I might be running or have run in vain. ³But not even Titus who *was* with me, being a Greek, was compelled to be circumcised, ⁴even because of the false brothers brought in secretly, who came in by stealth to spy out our freedom which we have in Christ Jesus that they will enslave us, ⁵to whom we did not yield in subjection for even an hour, so that truth of the gospel would be preserved with you.

⁶Now of those esteemed to be something, whatsoever they were formerly makes no difference to me. God does not accept *the* person of a man—for the esteemed added nothing to me. ⁷But on the contrary, having seen that I have been entrusted with the gospel of the uncircumcision[a] just as Peter of the circumcision[b]— ⁸for the *One* having worked in Peter for apostleship of the circumcision, did also in me toward the Gentiles— ⁹and having recognized the grace having been given to me, James and Cephas[c] and John, those esteemed to be pillars, gave to me and Barnabas *the* right hands of fellowship, that we *should go* to the Gentiles, but they to the circumcision, ¹⁰only that we should be mindful of the poor, also the same thing that I was eager to do.

Paul Confronts Cephas

¹¹But when Cephas came to Antioch, I opposed *him* to his face because he stood condemned. ¹²For before certain ones came from James, he had been eating with the Gentiles. But when they came, he was drawing back and was separating himself, being afraid of those of *the* circumcision. ¹³And also the rest of *the* Jews acted hypocritically with him, so that, by their hypocrisy, even Barnabas was carried away.

¹⁴But when I saw that they are not walking in line according to the truth of the gospel, I said to Peter before all, "If you being a Jew live like a Gentile, and not like a Jew, why do you compel the Gentiles to Judaize? ¹⁵We Jews by birth and not 'sinners' of *the* Gentiles, ¹⁶nevertheless knowing that a man is not justified by works of law, except through faith from Jesus Christ, even we have believed in Christ Jesus that we may be justified by faith from Christ, and not by works of the Law, because by works of the Law not any flesh will be justified.

¹⁷But if seeking to be justified in Christ, we ourselves also have been found sinners, *is* Christ then a minister of sin? Never may it be! ¹⁸For if I build again these things that I had torn down, I prove myself a transgressor. ¹⁹For through *the* Law I died to *the* Law that I might live to God. ²⁰I have been crucified with Christ, and I no longer live, but Christ lives in me. And that which I now live in *the* flesh, I live through faith from the Son of God, the *One* having loved me and having given up Himself for me. ²¹I do not set aside the grace of God. For if righteousness *is* through *the* Law, then Christ died for naught."[d]

a 7 That is, the Gentiles
b 7 That is, the Jews
c 9 That is, Peter; also in verses 11 and 14
d 21 Some interpreters close the quotation after verse 14 or 16.

Galatians 3
Faith and Belief
(Genesis 15:1-7; Romans 4:1-12; Hebrews 11:8-19; James 2:14-26)

¹O foolish Galatians! Who has bewitched you, before whose eyes Jesus Christ was publicly portrayed *as* having been crucified? ²I wish only to learn this from you: Did you receive the Spirit by works of *the* Law or by hearing of faith?
³Are you so foolish? Having begun in *the* Spirit, are you now being perfected in *the* flesh? ⁴Did you suffer so many things in vain, if indeed also in vain? ⁵Therefore, the *One* supplying to you the Spirit and working miracles among you, *is it* out of works of the Law, or out of hearing of faith?
⁶So also, "Abraham believed God and it was reckoned to him as righteousness."*ᵃ*
⁷Know then that those of faith, these are sons of Abraham. ⁸And the Scripture, having foreseen that God justifies the Gentiles by faith, foretold the gospel to Abraham: "All the nations will be blessed in you."*ᵇ* ⁹So then, those of faith are blessed along with the believing Abraham.

Christ Redeemed Us
(Deuteronomy 21:22-23)

¹⁰For as many as are of works of *the* Law are under a curse, for it has been written: "Cursed *is* everyone who does not continue all things having been written in the book of the Law, to do them."*ᶜ* ¹¹Now *it is* evident that no one is justified before God by *the* law, because "The righteous will live by faith."*ᵈ* ¹²But the Law is not of faith. Rather, "The *one* having done these things will live by them."*ᵉ*
¹³Christ redeemed us from the curse of the Law, having become a curse for us— for it has been written: "Cursed *is* everyone hanging on a tree"*ᶠ*— ¹⁴so that the blessing of Abraham might come to the Gentiles in Christ Jesus, so that through faith we might receive the promise of the Spirit.

The Purpose of the Law
(Romans 7:1-6)

¹⁵Brothers, I am speaking according to man. No one sets aside or adds thereto a covenant even of man, having been ratified. ¹⁶Now the promises were spoken to Abraham and to his seed. It does not say "and to seeds" as of many but "and to your seed"*ᵍ* as of One, who is Christ.
¹⁷Now I say this: *The* Law, having come four hundred and thirty years afterward, does not annul *the* covenant having been confirmed beforehand by God, so as to nullify the promise. ¹⁸For if the inheritance *is* by *the* Law, *it is* no longer by a promise. But God has granted *it* to Abraham through a promise.
¹⁹Why then the Law? It was added on account of transgressions, until the seed to whom promise has been made should have come, having been ordained through angels in *the* hand of a mediator. ²⁰However, a mediator is not of one; but God is one.
²¹*Is* the Law therefore contrary to the promises of God? Never may it be! For if a law had been given being able to impart life, then righteousness indeed would have emerged from out of *the* Law. ²²But the Scripture imprisoned all things under sin, so that by faith from Jesus Christ, the promise might be given to those believing.
²³Now before faith came, we were held in custody under the Law, having been locked up until the faith being about to be revealed, ²⁴so that the Law has become our trainer unto Christ, so that we might be justified by faith. ²⁵And faith having come, we are no longer under a trainer.

Sons Through Faith in Christ
²⁶For you are all sons of God through faith in Christ Jesus. ²⁷For as many of you as were baptized into Christ have put on Christ. ²⁸There is neither Jew nor Greek, there is neither slave nor free, there is neither male and female; for you are all one in Christ Jesus. ²⁹Now if you *are* of

Christ, then you are Abraham's seed, heirs according to *the* promise.

a 6 Genesis 15:6
b 8 Genesis 12:3; 18:18; 22:18
c 10 Deuteronomy 27:26
d 11 Habakkuk 2:4
e 12 Leviticus 18:5
f 13 Deuteronomy 21:23
g 16 Genesis 12:7; 13:15

Galatians 4
Sons and Heirs
(Genesis 21:1-8; Romans 8:12-17)

¹Now I say, for as long a time as the heir is a child, he differs not from a slave, *though* being owner of everything. ²Instead, he is under guardians and trustees until the time appointed by *his* father. ³So also, we when we were children, were held in bondage under the principles[a] of the world.
⁴But when the fullness of the time had come, God sent forth His Son, having been born of a woman, having been born under *the* Law, ⁵that He might redeem those under *the* Law, so that we might receive the divine adoption as sons. ⁶And because you are sons, God sent forth the Spirit of His Son into our hearts, crying out, "Abba, Father!" ⁷So you are no longer a slave but a son; and if a son, also an heir through God.

Paul's Fears for the Galatians

⁸But at that time indeed, not knowing God, you were enslaved to those by nature not being gods. ⁹But now, having known God, but rather having been known by God, how do you turn again to the weak and destitute principles, to which you desire to be enslaved again anew? ¹⁰You observe days and months and seasons and years. ¹¹I fear for you, lest perhaps I have toiled for you in vain. ¹²I implore you, brothers, become as I *am*, because I also *have become* as you. You have wronged me in nothing.
¹³Now you know that in weakness of the flesh I proclaimed the gospel the first time to you. ¹⁴And of your test in my flesh, you did not despise *me* nor reject *me* with contempt, but you received me as an angel of God, even as Christ Jesus. ¹⁵What *has become* then of your blessedness? For I bear witness to you that, if possible, having gouged out your eyes, you would have given *them* to me. ¹⁶So have I become your enemy speaking truth to you?
¹⁷They zealously seek you, not rightly. But they desire to isolate you *from us*, so that you might be zealous after them. ¹⁸Now *it is* good to be zealous in a right *thing*, at all times and not only in my being present with you.
¹⁹My children, of whom I travail again until that Christ shall have been formed in you, ²⁰I was wishing indeed to be present with you presently and to change my tone, because I am perplexed as to you.

Hagar and Sarah

²¹Tell me, those wishing to be under *the* Law, do you do not listen to the Law? ²²For it has been written that Abraham had two sons, one of the slave woman and one of the free. ²³But indeed, the *one* of the slave woman has been born according to flesh, but the *one* of the free, through the promise, ²⁴which things are allegorized, for these are two covenants: one indeed from Mount Sinai, begetting unto slavery, which is Hagar. ²⁵Now Hagar is Mount Sinai in Arabia and corresponds to the present Jerusalem, for she is in slavery with her children. ²⁶But the Jerusalem above is free, who is our mother. ²⁷For it has been written:

"Rejoice O barren woman,
    the *one* not bearing;
break forth and call aloud,
    the *one* not travailing;
because many more *are* the children of the desolate woman
    than of her having the husband."[b]

²⁸Now you,[c] brothers, like Isaac, are children of promise. ²⁹But just as at that time the *one* having been born according to flesh was persecuting the *one born* according to Spirit, so also *it is* now.

³⁰But what does the Scripture say? "Cast out the slave woman and her son, for the son of the slave woman will never inherit along with the son of the free."ᵈ ³¹So then, brothers, we are not children of *the* slave woman, but of the free.

a 3 Or *forces; also in verse 9*
b 27 Isaiah 54:1
c 28 WH, BYZ, and TR *we*
d 30 Genesis 21:10

Galatians 5
Freedom in Christ

¹In freedom Christ has set us free. Stand firm, therefore and do not be entangled again in a yoke of slavery!
²Behold, I Paul say to you that if you shall become circumcised, Christ will profit you nothing. ³Now again I testify to every man receiving circumcision that he is a debtor to keep the whole Law. ⁴Whoever are being justified in *the* Law, you are severed from Christ; you have fallen away from grace.
⁵For through *the* Spirit, by faith, we eagerly await *the* hope of righteousness.
⁶For in Christ Jesus neither circumcision nor uncircumcision has any power, but only faith working through love.
⁷You were running well. Who hindered you, not to obey the truth? ⁸*This* persuasion *is* not of the *One* calling you.
⁹A little leaven leavens the whole lump.
¹⁰I am confident as to you in *the* Lord that you will have no other mind. But the *one* troubling you will bear the judgment, whoever he might be.
¹¹Now brothers, if I still proclaim circumcision, why still am I persecuted? In that case the offense of the cross has been abolished. ¹²I wish those upsetting you also will emasculate themselves!
¹³For you brothers were called to freedom, but not the freedom for an opportunity to the flesh. Rather, serve one another through love. ¹⁴For the entire Law is fulfilled in in this one word: "You shall love your neighbor as yourself."ᵃ ¹⁵But if you bite and devour one another, take heed, lest you might be consumed by one another.

Living by the Spirit
(Romans 8:9-11)

¹⁶Now I say, walk by *the* Spirit, and you should not gratify *the* desires *of the* flesh.
¹⁷For the flesh desires against the Spirit, and the Spirit against the flesh. For these are opposed to one another in order that you should not do those things you might wish. ¹⁸But if you are led by *the* Spirit, you are not under *the* Law.
¹⁹Now the works of the flesh are evident, which are sexual immorality, impurity, sensuality, ²⁰idolatry, sorcery, enmities, strife, jealousy, outbursts of anger, contentions, dissensions, factions, ²¹envyings, drunkennesses, carousing, and things like these, as to which I forewarn you, even as I warned before, that those doing such things will not inherit God's kingdom.
²²But the fruit of the Spirit is love, joy, peace, patience, kindness, goodness, faithfulness, ²³gentleness, self-control. Against such things there is no law.
²⁴Now those of Christ Jesus have crucified the flesh with *its* passions and desires. ²⁵If we live by *the* Spirit, we should also walk by *the* Spirit. ²⁶We should not become boastful, provoking one another, envying one another.

a 14 Leviticus 19:18

Galatians 6
Carry One Another's Burdens

¹Brothers, even if a man should be caught in some trespass, you the spiritual *ones* restore such a one in a spirit of gentleness, considering yourself, lest you also be tempted. ²Bear one another's burdens and thus you will fulfill the law of Christ. ³For if anyone thinks *himself* to be something being nothing, he deceives himself.
⁴But let each test his own work, and then he will have the ground of boasting in himself alone, and not in another. ⁵For each shall bear his own load. ⁶Now let the

one being taught in the word share in all good things with the *one* teaching.
⁷Do not be misled: God is not mocked. For whatever a man might sow, that also he will reap. ⁸For the *one* sowing to his *own* flesh, from the flesh will reap decay. But the *one* sowing to the Spirit, from the Spirit will reap eternal life.
⁹And we should not grow weary *in* well doing. For in due time we will reap a harvest, not giving up. ¹⁰So then, as we have occasion, we should work good toward all, and especially toward those of the household of the faith.

Paul's Final Warning

¹¹See *the* large letters I have written to you with my own hand!
¹²As many as desire to have a fair appearance in *the* flesh, these compel you to be circumcised, only that they might not be persecuted for the cross of Christ. ¹³For not even those being circumcised keep *the* Law themselves, but they desire you to be circumcised so that they may boast in your flesh.
¹⁴But for me, may it be never to boast, except in the cross of our Lord Jesus Christ, through which^a *the* world has been crucified to me and I *to the* world. ¹⁵For neither circumcision nor uncircumcision is anything; instead, a new creation.

Benediction

¹⁶And as many as those who will walk by this rule, peace and mercy *be* upon them, and upon the Israel of God.
¹⁷Henceforth, let no one give to me troubles, for I bear on my body the marks of Jesus.
¹⁸The grace of our Lord Jesus Christ *be* with your spirit, brothers.
Amen.

a 14 Or *through whom*

Ephesians

Ephesians 1
Paul's Greeting to the Ephesians

¹Paul, an apostle of Christ Jesus by *the* will of God,
To the saints being in Ephesus,^a and faithful in Christ Jesus:
²Grace to you and peace from God our Father and *the* Lord Jesus Christ.

Spiritual Blessings
(Romans 8:28-34)

³Blessed *be* the God and Father of our Lord Jesus Christ, the *One* having blessed us in Christ with every spiritual blessing in the heavenly realms, ⁴just as He chose us in Him before *the* foundation of *the* world for us to be holy and blameless before Him, in love ⁵having predestined us for divine adoption as sons to Himself through Jesus Christ, according to the good pleasure of His will, ⁶to *the* praise of *the* glory of His grace, which He has freely given us in the Beloved *One*, ⁷in whom we have redemption through His blood, the forgiveness of trespasses, according to the riches of His grace ⁸which He lavished upon us in all wisdom and understanding, ⁹having made known to us the mystery of His will according to His pleasure, which He purposed in Him ¹⁰for *the* administration of the fullness of the times, to bring together all things in Christ—the things in the heavens and the things upon the earth— ¹¹in Him, in whom also we have obtained an inheritance, having been predestined according to *the* purpose of the *One* working all things according to the counsel of His will ¹²for us, the *ones* having first trusted in Christ, to be to *the* praise of His glory, ¹³in whom you also, having heard the word of truth, the gospel your of salvation, in whom also having believed you were sealed with the Holy Spirit of promise, ¹⁴who is *the* guarantee of our inheritance to *the*

redemption of the acquired possession, to *the* praise of His glory.

Spiritual Wisdom

[15]Because of this, I also, having heard of the faith in the Lord Jesus among you, and the love toward all the saints, [16]do not cease giving thanks for you, making mention in my prayers, [17]that the God of our Lord Jesus Christ, the Father of glory, may give to you a spirit of wisdom and revelation in *the* knowledge of Him, [18]the eyes your of heart being enlightened, in order for you to know what is the hope of His calling, what *are* the riches of the glory of His inheritance in the saints, [19]and what *is* the surpassing greatness of His power toward us believing according to the working of the power of His might, [20]which He worked in Christ, having raised Him out from *the* dead, and having set *Him* at His right hand in the heavenly realms, [21]above every principality and authority and power and dominion, and every name being named, not only in this age, but also in the *one* coming. [22]And He put all things under His feet and gave Him *to be* head over all things to the church, [23]which is His body, the fullness of the *One* filling all in all.

a 1 Some manuscripts do not include *in Ephesus*

Ephesians 2
Alive with Christ

[1]And you, being dead in your trespasses and sins— [2]in which once you walked according to the age of this world, according to the ruler of the authority of the air, the spirit now working in the sons of disobedience, [3]among whom we all also once lived in the desires of our flesh, doing the things willed of the flesh and of *its* thoughts; and we were by nature children of wrath even as the rest.

[4]But God, being rich in mercy, because of His great love with which He loved us, [5]made *us* alive with Christ even we being dead in trespasses—by grace you are saved— [6]and He raised *us* up together and seated *us* together in the heavenly realms in Christ Jesus, [7]in order that in the coming ages He might show the surpassing riches of His grace in kindness toward us in Christ Jesus.

[8]For by grace you are saved through faith, and this not of yourselves; *it is* the gift of God, [9]not as a result of works, so that no one may boast. [10]For we are His workmanship, having been created in Christ Jesus for good works which God prepared beforehand that we should walk in them.

One in Christ

[11]Therefore remember that formerly you—the Gentiles in *the* flesh, the ones being called *the* uncircumcision by that being called *the* circumcision, made by hands in *the* flesh— [12]that at that time you were separate from Christ, alienated from the commonwealth of Israel, and strangers to the covenants of the promise, not having hope and without God in the world. [13]But now in Christ Jesus you, the *ones* once being far off, have become near by the blood of Christ. [14]For He Himself is our peace, having made both one and having broken down the barrier of the partition of hostility, [15]having annulled in His flesh the law of commandments in ordinances, so that He might create in Himself the two into one new man, making peace, [16]and He might reconcile both to God in one body through the cross, by it having slain the hostility.

[17]And having come, He proclaimed the gospel: peace to you, the *ones* far off, and peace to those near. [18]For through Him we both have access to the Father by one Spirit.

A Temple in the Lord

[19]So then, you are no longer strangers and aliens, but are fellow citizens of the saints and of the household of God, [20]having been built upon the foundation of the apostles and prophets, Christ Jesus Himself being *the* cornerstone, [21]in whom the whole building, being fitted together, is increasing into a holy temple

in *the* Lord, ²²in whom you also are being built together for a habitation of God in *the* Spirit.

Ephesians 3
The Mystery of the Gospel

¹For reason of this, I Paul, the prisoner of Christ Jesus for you Gentiles... ²Surely you have heard of the administration of God's grace, having been given to me toward you, ³that He made known to me the mystery by revelation, just as I have written before in brief, ⁴which, by reading, you are able to understand my insight into the mystery of Christ, ⁵which was not made known to the sons of men in other generations as now it has been revealed in *the* Spirit to His holy apostles and prophets, ⁶that the Gentiles are joint-heirs, and a joint-body, and joint-partakers of the promise in Christ Jesus, through the gospel, ⁷of which I became servant according to the gift of God's grace, having been given to me according to the working of His power.

⁸To me, the very least of all saints, was given this grace: to preach to the Gentiles the unsearchable riches of Christ ⁹and to enlighten all what *is* the administration of the mystery having been hidden from the ages in God, the *One* having created all things, ¹⁰so that now through the church the manifold wisdom of God should be made known to the rulers and authorities in the heavenly realms, ¹¹according to *the* purpose of the ages, which He accomplished in Christ Jesus our Lord, ¹²in whom we have boldness and access in confidence, by faith in Him.

¹³Therefore I implore *you* not to lose heart at my tribulations for you, which is your glory.

Paul's Prayer for the Ephesians

¹⁴... for reason of this I bow my knees to the Father,[a] ¹⁵from whom every family in *the* heavens and on earth is named, ¹⁶that He might give you, according to the riches of His glory, to be strengthened with power by His Spirit in the inner man, ¹⁷*for* Christ to dwell in your hearts through faith, being rooted and being founded in love, ¹⁸so that you may be fully able, with all the saints, to comprehend what *is* the breadth and length and height and depth, ¹⁹and to know the love of Christ surpassing knowledge, so that you may be filled unto all the fullness of God.

²⁰Now to the *One* being able to do exceedingly above all things that we ask or think, according to the power working in us, ²¹to Him *be* the glory in the church and in Christ Jesus to all the generations of the age of the ages. Amen.

a 14 BYZ and TR include *of our Lord Jesus Christ*

Ephesians 4
Unity in the Body

(Psalm 133:1-3; 1 Corinthians 1:10-17)

¹Therefore I, the prisoner in *the* Lord, exhort you to walk worthily of the calling to which you were called, ²with all humility and gentleness; with patience bearing with one another in love; ³being diligent to keep the unity of the Spirit in the bond of peace; ⁴one body and one Spirit, just as also you were called into one hope of your calling; ⁵one Lord, one faith, one baptism; ⁶one God and Father of all, who *is* over all and through all and in all.

⁷Now to each one of us grace has been given according to the measure of the gift of Christ. ⁸Therefore it says:[a]

"Having ascended on high,
    He led captive captivity,
    and gave gifts to men."[b]

⁹Now what is "He ascended," except that He also descended into the lower regions of the earth? ¹⁰The *One* having descended is also the same *one* having ascended above all the heavens, so that He might fill all things.

¹¹And He gave some indeed *to be* apostles, and some prophets, and some evangelists, and some shepherds and teachers, ¹²toward the perfecting of the

saints for *the* work of ministry, for *the* building up of the body of Christ, ¹³until we all may attain to the unity of the faith and of the knowledge of the Son of God, unto a complete man, to *the* measure of *the* stature of the fullness of Christ, ¹⁴so that no longer we might be infants, being tossed by waves and being carried about by every wind of teaching in the cunning, in the craftiness of men with a view to the scheming of deceit. ¹⁵But speaking the truth in love, we should grow up in all things into Him who is the head, Christ, ¹⁶from whom the whole body, being joined together and being held together by every ligament of *its* supply, according to *the* working in *the* measure of each individual part, the increase of the body makes for itself, to *the* building up of itself in love.

New Life in Christ

¹⁷This therefore I say and testify in *the* Lord: You *are* no longer to walk as also the Gentiles are walking, in *the* futility of their mind, ¹⁸being darkened in the understanding, being alienated from the life of God because of the ignorance being in them on account of the hardness of their heart, ¹⁹who, having cast off all feeling, have given themselves up to sensuality for *the* working of all impurity, with greediness *for more*.
²⁰But you have not learned Christ this way, ²¹if indeed you have heard Him and have been taught in Him just as *the* truth is in Jesus. ²²You are to have put off, concerning the former way of life, the old man, which is being corrupted according to *its* desires of deceit, ²³and to be renewed in the spirit of your mind, ²⁴and to have put on the new man, having been created according to God in righteousness and holiness of truth.
²⁵Therefore having put off falsehood, let each one speak truth with his neighbor, because we are members of one another. ²⁶"Be angry, and yet do not sin."ᶜ Let not the sun set upon your anger, ²⁷neither give opportunity to the devil.

²⁸The *one* stealing, let him steal no longer, but rather let him toil, working with the own hands what *is* good, so that he may have *something* to impart to the *one* having need.
²⁹Do not let any unwholesome word go forth out of your mouth, but only good, for edification of the need, so that it may give grace to those hearing.
³⁰And do not grieve the Holy Spirit of God, in whom you were sealed for *the* day of redemption.
³¹Let all bitterness, and rage, and anger, and clamor, and slander, be removed from you, along with all malice. ³²And be kind to one another, tender-hearted, forgiving each other, as also in Christ God forgave you.

a 8 Or *He says*
b 8 Psalm 68:18
c 26 Psalm 4:4

Ephesians 5
Imitators of God

¹Be imitators of God, therefore, as beloved children, ²and walk in love, just as Christ also loved us and gave Himself up for us *as* an offering and a sacrifice to God, into an aroma of a sweet smell.
³But let sexual immorality and all impurity or covetousness not even be named among you, as also is proper to saints, ⁴and filthiness, and foolish talking, or crude joking, which are not fitting, but rather thanksgiving. ⁵For this you know, realizing that any fornicator, or unclean person, or covetous man, who is an idolater, has no inheritance in the kingdom of Christ and of God.
⁶Let no one deceive you with empty words, for because of these things the wrath of God comes upon the sons of disobedience. ⁷Therefore do not be partakers with them.

Children of Light

⁸For you were once darkness, but now *you are* light in *the* Lord. Walk as children of light— ⁹for the fruit of the light *is* in all goodness and righteousness and truth—

¹⁰discerning what is well-pleasing to the Lord.
¹¹And do not have fellowship with the unfruitful works of darkness, but rather even expose *them*. ¹²For it is shameful even to mention the things being done by them in secret. ¹³But everything being exposed by the light is made visible, for everything becoming visible is light. ¹⁴Therefore it says:

> "Awake you, the *one* sleeping,
>   and rise up out from the dead,
>   and Christ will shine upon you."

¹⁵Therefore carefully take heed how you walk, not as unwise but as wise, ¹⁶redeeming the time, because the days are evil. ¹⁷Because of this, do not be foolish, but understand what *is* the Lord's will, ¹⁸and not to be drunk with wine in which is debauchery. Instead be filled with *the* Spirit, ¹⁹speaking to each other in psalms and hymns and spiritual songs, singing and making melody in your heart to the Lord, ²⁰giving thanks at all times for all things in *the* name our Lord Jesus Christ to the God and Father.

Wives and Husbands
(Song of Solomon 1:1-3; 1 Peter 3:1-7)

²¹Be submitting yourselves to one another in reverence of Christ: ²²wives, to the own husbands as to the Lord; ²³for *the* husband is head of the wife as also Christ *is the* head of the church, He Himself Savior of the body. ²⁴But even as the church is subjected to Christ, so also wives to the own husbands in everything. ²⁵Husbands, love the wives just as Christ also loved the church and gave Himself up for her, ²⁶so that He might sanctify her, having cleansed *her* by the washing of water by *the* word, ²⁷so that He might present to Himself the church in glory, not having spot or wrinkle or any of the such things, but that it would be holy and blameless.
²⁸So also husbands ought to love their wives as their own bodies. The *one* loving his wife loves himself. ²⁹For no one at any time hated his flesh. But he nourishes and cherishes it just as Christ also *does* the church. ³⁰For we are members of His body.[a]
³¹"Because of this, a man will leave his father and mother and be joined to his wife, and the two will be into one flesh."[b] ³²This mystery is great; but I speak as to Christ and as to the church. ³³However, you also, every individual, let each so love his wife as himself; and the wife, that she may respect the husband.

a 30 BYZ and TR include *of His flesh and of His bones*
b 31 Genesis 2:24

Ephesians 6
Children and Parents
(Deuteronomy 6:20-25)

¹Children, obey your parents in *the* Lord, for this is right. ²"Honor your Father and mother," which is *the* first commandment with a promise, ³"that it may be well with you and you will be long-lived upon the earth."[a]
⁴And fathers, do not provoke your children, but bring them up in *the* discipline and admonition of *the* Lord.

Slaves and Masters
(1 Timothy 6:1-2)

⁵Slaves, obey the earthly masters with fear and trembling, in sincerity of your heart as to Christ, ⁶not with eye-service as men-pleasers, but as servants of Christ, doing the will of God from *the* heart, ⁷rendering service with good will as to the Lord and not to men, ⁸knowing that each one, whatever good he might have done, this he will receive *back* from *the* Lord, whether *he is* slave or free.
⁹And masters do the same things toward them, giving up threatening, knowing that also their master and yours is in *the* heavens, and there is no partiality with Him.

The Armor of God

¹⁰Henceforth be empowered in *the* Lord and in the strength of His might. ¹¹Put on the complete armor of God, for you to be able to stand against the schemes of the devil, ¹²because to us the wrestling is not against blood and flesh, but against the

rulers, against the authorities, against the cosmic powers of this darkness, against the spiritual *forces* of evil in the heavenly realms.
¹³Because of this, take up the complete armor of God, so that you may be able to withstand in the evil day, and having done all things, to stand. ¹⁴Stand therefore, having girded your loins with truth, and having put on the breastplate of righteousness, ¹⁵and having shod the feet with *the* readiness of the gospel of peace; ¹⁶besides all, having taken up the shield of faith with which you will be able to quench all the flaming arrows of the evil one. ¹⁷And take the helmet of salvation and the sword of the Spirit, which is *the* word of God, ¹⁸through all prayer and supplication, praying in *the* Spirit in every season and unto this very thing, watching with all perseverance and supplication for all saints, ¹⁹and also for me, that in *the* opening of my mouth, divine utterance may be given to me to make known with boldness the mystery of the gospel, ²⁰for which I am an ambassador in a chain, that in it I may be bold, as it behooves me to speak.

Final Greetings
²¹And that you also may know the things concerning me, what I am doing, Tychicus, the beloved brother and faithful servant in *the* Lord, will make known to you all things, ²²whom I have sent to you for this very purpose, that you may know the things concerning us, and he may encourage your hearts.
²³Peace to the brothers and love with faith from God *the* Father and *the* Lord Jesus Christ.
²⁴Grace *be* with all those loving our Lord Jesus Christ in incorruptibility.

a 2-3 Deuteronomy 5:16

Philippians

Philippians 1
Greetings from Paul and Timothy
(2 Samuel 6:12-15; 1 Chronicles 15:1-14; Colossians 1:1-2)

¹Paul and Timothy, servants of Christ Jesus,
To all the saints in Christ Jesus being in Philippi, with *the* overseers and deacons:
²Grace to you and peace from God our Father and *the* Lord Jesus Christ.

Thanksgiving and Prayer
(1 Corinthians 1:4-9; Colossians 1:3-14; 2 Thessalonians 1:3-4)

³I thank my God upon every remembrance of you, ⁴always making the supplication with joy in my every supplication for all of you, ⁵for your partnership in the gospel from the first day until now, ⁶being persuaded of this very thing, that the *One* having begun a good work in you will complete *it* until *the* day of Christ Jesus.
⁷Accordingly, it is right for me to feel this about all of you, since I have you in the heart. Both in my chains and in the defense and confirmation of the gospel, you all are fellow partakers of grace with me. ⁸For God *is* my witness how I long after you all in *the* affection of Christ Jesus.
⁹And this I pray, that your love may abound yet more and more in knowledge and all discernment, ¹⁰for you to approve the things being excellent, so that you may be pure and blameless unto *the* day of Christ, ¹¹being filled with *the* fruit of righteousness that *is* through Jesus Christ, to *the* glory and praise of God.

Paul's Trials Advance the Gospel
(James 1:2-8)

¹²Now I want you to know brothers, that the things concerning me really have turned out to *the* advancement of the gospel, ¹³so as for my chains in Christ to have become clearly known in all the palace guard[a] and to all *the* rest; ¹⁴and

most of the brothers, trusting in *the* Lord by my chains, to dare more abundantly to speak fearlessly the word.[b] ¹⁵For some, even from envy and strife, are proclaiming Christ, but some also from goodwill— ¹⁶the *ones* indeed out of love, knowing that I am appointed for the defense of the gospel; ¹⁷but the *others* are proclaiming Christ out of selfish ambition, not purely, supposing to add tribulation to my chains.

¹⁸What then? Only that in every way, whether in pretext or in truth, Christ is proclaimed. And in this I rejoice. Yes, and I will rejoice, ¹⁹for I know that through your prayer and *the* provision of the Spirit of Jesus Christ, this will turn out for me to deliverance, ²⁰according to my earnest expectation and hope that I will be ashamed in nothing, but in all boldness also now as always, Christ will be magnified in my body, whether by life or by death.

To Live is Christ

²¹For to me, to live *is* Christ and to die *is* gain. ²²But if *I am* to live in flesh, this *is the* fruit of labor for me. And what shall I choose? I do not know. ²³But I am pressed between the two, having the desire to depart and to be with Christ, indeed very much better, ²⁴but to remain in the flesh *is* more necessary for your sake. ²⁵And having been persuaded of this, I know that I will remain and will continue with all of you for your progress and joy of the faith, ²⁶so that through my coming to you again your boasting in me may abound to Christ Jesus.

Worthy of the Gospel

²⁷Only conduct yourselves worthily of the gospel of Christ, so that, whether having come and having seen you, or being absent, I might hear the things concerning you, that you are standing firm in one spirit, striving together with one mind for the faith of the gospel, ²⁸and not being frightened in *anything* by those opposing *you*, which is a demonstration of destruction to them, but of salvation to you—and this from God. ²⁹For it has been granted to you concerning Christ, not only to believe in Him but also to suffer concerning Him, ³⁰having the same conflict such as you saw in me and now hear of in me.

a 13 Or *palace*
b 14 NE and WH *the word of God*

Philippians 2
One in Christ

¹Therefore if *there is* any encouragement in Christ, if any comfort of love, if any fellowship of *the* Spirit, if any affections and compassions, ²fulfill my joy so that you may be of the same mind, having the same love, united in soul, minding the same thing, ³nothing according to self-interest or according to vain conceit, but in humility be esteeming one another surpassing themselves, ⁴each considering not the things of themselves, but each also the things of others.

The Attitude of Christ
(Isaiah 52:13-15)

⁵Let this mind be in you which *was* also in Christ Jesus:

⁶Who, existing in *the* form of God,
did not consider to be equal with God something to be grasped,
⁷but emptied Himself,
having taken *the* form of a servant,
having been made in *the* likeness of men.
⁸And having been found in appearance as a man
He humbled Himself,
having become obedient unto death,
even *the* death of *the* cross.
⁹Therefore God also highly exalted Him,
and granted to Him the name above every name,
¹⁰that at the name of Jesus every knee should bow,
in the heavens and on earth and under the earth,

¹¹and every tongue should confess that Jesus Christ *is* Lord,
>to *the* glory of God *the* Father.

Shining as Stars
(Matthew 5:13-16)

¹²Therefore my beloved, just as always you have obeyed, not only as in my presence, but now much more in my absence, work out your own salvation with fear and trembling. ¹³For God is the *One* working in you both to will and to work according to *His* good pleasure.

¹⁴Do all things without murmurings and disputings, ¹⁵so that you may be blameless and innocent, children of God unblemished in *the* midst of a crooked and perverted generation,ᵃ among whom you shine as lights in *the* world, ¹⁶holding forth *the* word of life unto a boast to me in *the* day of Christ that I did not run in vain nor toil in vain.

¹⁷But even if I am being poured out as a drink offering on the sacrifice and service of your faith, I am glad and rejoice with you all. ¹⁸And likewise you also be glad and rejoice with me.

Timothy and Epaphroditus

¹⁹But I hope in *the* Lord Jesus to send Timothy to you soon, that I also may be encouraged, having known the things concerning you. ²⁰For I have no one like-minded, who genuinely will care for the things relative to you. ²¹For those all are seeking the things of themselves, not the things of Jesus Christ. ²²But you know his proven worth, that as a child *with* a father he has served with me in the gospel. ²³Therefore indeed I hope to send him immediately, when I shall have seen the things concerning me. ²⁴And I am persuaded in *the* Lord that I myself will also come soon.

Epaphroditus Commended

²⁵Now I esteemed *it* necessary to send to you Epaphroditus, my brother and fellow worker and fellow soldier, and your messenger and minister to my need, ²⁶since he was longing after you all and being deeply distressed because you heard that he was ill. ²⁷And indeed he was sick, nearly unto death. But God had mercy on him, and not on him alone but also on me, that I should not have sorrow upon sorrow.

²⁸Therefore I have sent him all the more eagerly, that having seen him again, you may rejoice, and I might be less anxious. ²⁹Therefore, receive him in *the* Lord with all joy, and hold such in honor, ³⁰because for the sake of the work of Christ he came near unto death, having disregarded *his* life so that he might fill up your deficit of service toward me.

a 15 Deuteronomy 32:5

Philippians 3
Righteousness through Faith

¹Finally, my brothers, rejoice in *the* Lord. To write the same things to you indeed *is* not troublesome to me, and *is* safe for you.

²Beware of the dogs! Beware of the evil workers! Beware of the false circumcision! ³For we are the circumcision, those worshiping in *the* Spirit of God, and glorying in Christ Jesus, and not trusting in *the* flesh— ⁴though I have confidence even in *the* flesh.

If any other thinks to trust in *the* flesh, I more: ⁵circumcision on *the* eighth day; of *the* nation of Israel, of *the* tribe of Benjamin; a Hebrew of Hebrews; according to *the* Law, a Pharisee; ⁶according to zeal, persecuting the church; according to righteousness in *the* Law, having become faultless.

Knowing Christ Above All Else

⁷But whatever things were gain to me, these I have esteemed loss because of Christ. ⁸But indeed, therefore, I also count all things to be loss because of the excelling knowledge of Christ Jesus my Lord, because of whom I have lost all things, and esteem *them* rubbish, that I may gain Christ ⁹and be found in Him, not having my own righteousness which *is* of *the* Law, but that which *is* through faith from Christ, the righteousness of God on

the basis of faith, ¹⁰to know Him and the power of His resurrection and the fellowship of His sufferings, being conformed to His death, ¹¹if, by any means, I may attain to the resurrection from out of dead.

Pressing Toward the Goal

¹²Not that already I have obtained *it* or already have been perfected, but I am pursuing, if also I may lay hold of that for which also I was laid hold of by Christ Jesus. ¹³Brothers, I do not consider myself to have taken hold *of it*. But one thing indeed: Forgetting the things behind and reaching forward to the things ahead, ¹⁴I press on toward *the* goal for the prize of the upward calling of God in Christ Jesus.
¹⁵Therefore as many as *are* mature should be of this mind. And if you are minded *in* anything differently, even this God will reveal to you. ¹⁶Nevertheless, to that which we have attained, *we are* to walk by the same.

Citizenship in Heaven

¹⁷Be imitators together of me brothers, and consider those walking thus, as you have us *for* a pattern. ¹⁸For many are walking—*of* whom I have told you often and now I say even weeping—*as* enemies of the cross of Christ, ¹⁹whose end *is* destruction, whose God *is* the belly and glory *is* in their shame, those minding earthly things.
²⁰For our citizenship exists in *the* heavens, from whence also we are awaiting a Savior, *the* Lord Jesus Christ, ²¹who will transform our body of humiliation, conformed to the body of His glory, according to the working enabling Him even to subdue all things to Himself.

Philippians 4
Stand Firm in the Lord

¹Therefore my brothers, beloved and longed for, my joy and crown, in this way stand firm in *the* Lord, beloved.
²I exhort Euodia and I exhort Syntyche to be of the same mind in *the* Lord. ³Yes, and I ask you, true yokefellow, help these *women* who labored together with me in the gospel, with Clement also, and the rest of my fellow workers, whose names *are* in *the* book of life.
⁴Rejoice in *the* Lord always; again I will say, rejoice! ⁵Let your gentleness be known to all men. The Lord *is* near.
⁶Be anxious about nothing, but in everything, by prayer and supplication with thanksgiving, let your requests be made known to God. ⁷And the peace of God, surpassing all understanding, will guard your hearts and your minds in Christ Jesus.

Think on These Things

⁸Finally brothers, whatever is true, whatever *is* venerable, whatever *is* right, whatever *is* pure, whatever *is* lovely, whatever *is* admirable—if any excellence and if any praise—think on these things.
⁹And what you have learned and have received and have heard and have seen in me, practice these things. And the God of peace will be with you.

The Generosity of the Philippians

¹⁰But I rejoiced greatly in *the* Lord that now at last you have revived the caring for me, wherein also you were concerned, but you were lacking opportunity. ¹¹Not that I speak as to destitution, for I have learned to be content in that which I am. ¹²I know also *how* to be brought low, and I know *how* to abound. In everything, and in all things, I have learned the secret also to be full and to hunger, also to abound and to be deficient. ¹³I have strength *for* all things in the *One* strengthening me.
¹⁴But you did well, having fellowship in my affliction. ¹⁵And you Philippians also know that in *the* beginning of the gospel, when I came out from Macedonia, not one church had partnership with me with regard to the matter of giving and receiving, except you alone. ¹⁶For even in Thessalonica, both once and twice, you sent for my needs.

¹⁷Not that I seek after the gift, but I seek after the fruit abounding to your account. ¹⁸But I have all things, and abound. I am full, having received from Epaphroditus the things from you, an odor of a sweet smell, an acceptable sacrifice, well-pleasing to God. ¹⁹And my God will fill up all your needs according to His riches in glory in Christ Jesus. ²⁰Now to our God and Father *be* the glory to the ages of the ages. Amen.

Final Greetings

²¹Greet every saint in Christ Jesus. The brothers with me greet you.
²²All the saints greet you, and especially those of the household of Caesar.
²³The grace of the Lord Jesus Christ *be* with your spirit.[a]

[a] 23 BYZ and TR include *Amen.*

Colossians

Colossians 1
Greetings from Paul and Timothy
(2 Samuel 6:12-15; 1 Chronicles 15:1-14; Philippians 1:1-2)

¹Paul, an apostle of Christ Jesus by *the* will of God, and Timothy the brother,
²To the saints in Colossae and faithful brothers in Christ:
Grace to you and peace from God our Father.[a]

Thanksgiving and Prayer
(1 Corinthians 1:4-9; Philippians 1:3-11; 2 Thessalonians 1:3-4)

³We give thanks to the God *and* Father of our Lord Jesus Christ, praying continually for you, ⁴having heard of your faith in Christ Jesus and the love that you have toward all the saints, ⁵because of the hope being laid up for you in the heavens, which you heard of before in the word of truth, the gospel, ⁶the *one* being present unto you, just as also in all the world it is bearing fruit and increasing, just as also among you from the day you heard and knew the grace of God in truth, ⁷just as you learned from Epaphras, our beloved fellow bond-servant, who is a faithful servant of Christ on behalf of us,[b] ⁸the *one* also having made known to us your love in *the* Spirit.
⁹Because of this also, we from the day we heard, do not cease praying for you and asking that you may be filled with the knowledge of His will in all spiritual wisdom and understanding ¹⁰to walk worthily of the Lord: pleasing in all, bringing forth fruit in every good work, and growing in the knowledge of God, ¹¹being strengthened with all power according to His glorious might, unto all endurance and patience with joy, ¹²giving thanks to the Father, the *One* having qualified you[c] for the share of the inheritance of the saints in light, ¹³who has delivered us from the dominion of darkness and transferred *us* into the kingdom of His beloved Son, ¹⁴in whom we have redemption, the forgiveness of sins.

The Supremacy of Christ
(Hebrews 1:1-14)

¹⁵*He* is *the* image of the invisible God, *the* firstborn over all creation, ¹⁶because in Him were created all things in the heavens and upon the earth, the visible and the invisible, whether thrones or lordships or rulers or authorities; all things have been created through Him and unto Him.
¹⁷And He is before all things, and in Him all things hold together. ¹⁸And He is the head of the body, the church, who is the beginning, firstborn out from the dead, so that He might be holding preeminence in all things, ¹⁹because all the fullness was pleased to dwell in Him, ²⁰and by Him to reconcile all things to Himself, having made peace by the blood of His cross through Him, whether the things on the earth or the things in the heavens.
²¹And you, being once alienated and hostile in mind, in the evil deeds, ²²but now He has reconciled in His body of flesh through death, to present you holy and unblemished and blameless before Him,

²³if indeed you continue in the faith, established and firm, and not being moved away from the hope of the gospel that you have heard, having been proclaimed in all creation[d] under heaven, of which I Paul have become a minister.

Paul's Suffering for the Church
(2 Corinthians 11:16-33)

²⁴Now I rejoice in the sufferings for you, and I am filling up in my flesh that which is lacking of the tribulations of Christ for His body, which is the church, ²⁵of which I became a minister according to the administration of God having been given me toward you, to complete the word of God, ²⁶the mystery having been hidden from the ages and from the generations, but now having been manifested to His saints, ²⁷to whom God has willed to make known what *is* the riches of the glory of this mystery among the Gentiles, which is Christ in you, the hope of glory, ²⁸whom we preach, admonishing every man and teaching every man in all wisdom, so that we may present every man perfect in Christ.

²⁹Unto this also I toil, striving according to His energy, working in me in power.

a 2 BYZ and TR *God our Father and the Lord Jesus Christ*
b 7 NE, NA, BYZ, and TR *your*
c 12 BYZ and TR *us*
d 23 Or *to every creature*

Colossians 2
Absent in Body, Present in Spirit
(Revelation 3:14-22)

¹For I want you to know how great a struggle I am having for you, and those in Laodicea, and as many as have not seen my face in *the* flesh, ²that their hearts may be encouraged, having been knit together in love, and to all *the* riches of the full assurance of understanding, to *the* knowledge of the mystery of God, *which is* Christ, ³in whom are hidden all the treasures of wisdom and of knowledge.

⁴I say this so that no one might delude you by persuasive speech. ⁵Truly indeed, if I am absent in the flesh, yet I am with you in spirit, rejoicing and seeing your good order and the firmness of your faith in Christ.

Alive in Christ

⁶Therefore, just as you have received Christ Jesus the Lord, walk in Him, ⁷having been rooted and being built up in Him, and being strengthened in the faith, just as you were taught, abounding with thanksgiving.

⁸Take heed lest there will be anyone taking you captive through philosophy and empty deceit, according to the tradition of men, according to the principles of the world and not according to Christ. ⁹For in Him all the fullness of the Deity dwells bodily. ¹⁰And you are complete in Him, who is the head of all rule and authority, ¹¹in whom also you were circumcised with *the* circumcision made without hands in the removal of the body of the flesh, in the circumcision of Christ, ¹²having been buried with Him in baptism, in which also you were raised with *Him* through the faith of the working of God, the *One* having raised Him out from the dead.

¹³And you being dead in the trespasses and in the uncircumcision of your flesh, He made alive together with Him, having forgiven us all *our* trespasses, ¹⁴having blotted out the handwriting in the decrees against us, which was adverse to us. And He has taken it out of the way, having nailed it to the cross. ¹⁵Having disarmed the rulers and the authorities, He made a show *of them* in public, having triumphed over them in it.

¹⁶Therefore let no one judge you in regard to food, or in regard to drink, or in regard to a feast, or a New Moon, or Sabbaths, ¹⁷which are a shadow the things coming. But the body *is* of Christ. ¹⁸Let no one disqualify you, delighting in humility and *the* worship of the angels, detailing what he has seen, being puffed up vainly by his mind of the flesh, ¹⁹and not holding fast to the head, from whom the whole body, being supplied and being

knit together by the joints and ligaments, increases with the increase of God.

²⁰If you have died with Christ, away from the principles of the world, why as if living in *the* world do you submit to decrees: ²¹"You should not handle! You should not taste! You should not touch!"?— ²²which are all unto decay with the use, according to the precepts and teachings of men, ²³which having indeed an appearance of wisdom in self-imposed worship and humility and harsh treatment of *the* body, are not of any value against *the* indulgence of the flesh.

Colossians 3
Putting on the New Self

¹If then you have been raised with Christ, seek the things above, where Christ is sitting at *the* right hand of God. ²Set *your* minds on the things above, not the things on the earth. ³For you have died, and your life has been hidden with Christ in God. ⁴When Christ your[a] life may be revealed, then you also will appear with Him in glory.

⁵Therefore put to death the members which *are* upon the earth: sexual immorality, impurity, passion, evil desire, and covetousness, which is idolatry, ⁶because of which things the wrath of God is coming on the sons of disobedience,[b] ⁷in which you also once walked when you were living in them. ⁸But now you also put off all *these* things: anger, rage, malice, slander, foul language out of your mouth.

⁹Do not lie to one another, having put off the old man with his practices, ¹⁰and having put on the new, the *one* being renewed in knowledge according to *the* image of the *one* having created him, ¹¹where there is not Greek and Jew, circumcision and uncircumcision, Barbarian, Scythian, slave, *and* free; but Christ *is* all and in all.

¹²Therefore, as *the* elect of God, holy and beloved, put on hearts of compassion, kindness, humility, gentleness, *and* patience, ¹³bearing with each other and forgiving each other. If anyone should have a complaint against another, even as also the Lord has forgiven you, so also you. ¹⁴And beyond all these, *put on* love, which is *the* bond of perfect unity. ¹⁵And let the peace of Christ rule in your hearts, to which also you were called in one body. And be thankful.

¹⁶Let the word of Christ dwell in you richly, teaching and admonishing each other in all wisdom, singing psalms, hymns, *and* spiritual songs with grace in your hearts to God. ¹⁷And all, whatever you might do in word or in deed, do all in *the* name of *the* Lord Jesus, giving thanks to God *the* Father through Him.

Christian Households

¹⁸Wives, submit yourselves to the husbands, as is fitting in *the* Lord.

¹⁹Husbands, love the wives and do not be harsh toward them.

²⁰Children, obey the parents in all things, for this is well-pleasing in *the* Lord.

²¹Fathers, do not provoke your children lest they might become discouraged.

²²Slaves, obey the earthly masters in all things, not with eye-services as men-pleasers, but in sincerity of heart, fearing the Lord.

²³Whatever you might do, work from *the* soul, as to the Lord and not to men, ²⁴knowing that you will receive from *the* Lord the reward of the inheritance. You serve the Lord Christ! ²⁵For the *one* doing wrong will be repaid *for* what he has done wrong; and there is no partiality.

a 4 NE, WH, BYZ, and TR *our*
b 6 NE, WH, and Tischendorf do not include *on the sons of disobedience*

Colossians 4
Fellow Workers

¹Masters, give to the slaves that which *is* righteous and that which *is* equal, knowing that you also have a Master in heaven.

²Continue steadfastly in prayer, watching in it, with thanksgiving, ³praying at the same time also for us, that God may open

to us a door for the word, to declare the mystery of Christ, on account of which also I have been bound, ⁴so that I should make it clear, as it behooves me to speak. ⁵Walk in wisdom toward those outside, redeeming the time. ⁶Let your speech *be* always in grace, having been seasoned with salt, to know how it behooves you to answer each one.

Final Greetings

⁷All the things concerning me, Tychicus will make known to you, the beloved brother and faithful servant and fellow bond-servant in *the* Lord, ⁸whom I sent to you for this very purpose, that you might know the things concerning us, and he may encourage your hearts, ⁹with Onesimus, the faithful and beloved brother, who is *one* of you. They will make known to you all things here.

¹⁰Aristarchus, my fellow prisoner, greets you, and Mark, the cousin of Barnabas, concerning whom you have received instructions—if he comes to you, welcome him— ¹¹and also Jesus called Justus, these being the only fellow workers for the kingdom of God among *the* circumcision, who have been a comfort to me.

¹²Epaphras greets you, who *is one* of you, a servant of Christ Jesus, always struggling for you in the prayers, so that you may stand mature and fully assured in all *the* will of God. ¹³For I bear witness to him that he has great concern for you and those in Laodicea and those in Hierapolis.

¹⁴Luke, the beloved physician, greets you, and also Demas.

¹⁵Greet the brothers in Laodicea, and also Nympha and the church in her house.

Sharing This Letter

¹⁶And when the letter shall be read among you, cause that it may be read also in the church of *the* Laodiceans, and that you also may read the *one* from Laodicea.

¹⁷And say to Archippus: "Take heed to the ministry that you have received in *the* Lord, that you may fulfill it."

¹⁸The greeting *is* in the own hand—Paul. Remember my chains.

Grace *be* with you.ᵃ

a 18 BYZ and TR include *Amen*.

1 Thessalonians

1 Thessalonians 1
Greetings to the Thessalonians

(2 Thessalonians 1:1-2; Philemon 1:1-3)

¹Paul and Silvanusᵃ and Timothy,
To the church of the Thessalonians in God *the* Father and *the* Lord Jesus Christ:
Grace to you and peace.ᵇ

²We give thanks to God always concerning all of you, making mention in our prayers, ³remembering before our God and Father your work of faith and unceasing labor of love, and the endurance of the hope of our Lord Jesus Christ, ⁴knowing, brothers beloved by God, your election, ⁵because our gospel came to you not in word only, but also in power and in *the* Holy Spirit, and with much full assurance, just as you know what we were among you on account of you.

⁶And you became imitators of us and of the Lord, having received the word in much tribulation, with *the* joy of *the* Holy Spirit, ⁷so as for you to became an example to all the believing *ones* in Macedonia and in Achaia. ⁸For not only has the word of the Lord sounded forth from you in Macedonia and in Achaia, but in every place your faith toward God has gone abroad, so as for us to have no need to say anything. ⁹For they themselves report concerning us what reception we had from you, and how you turned to God from idols, to serve *the* living and true God, ¹⁰and to await His Son from the

heavens, whom He raised out from the dead—Jesus, the *one* delivering us from the coming wrath.

a 1 That is, Silas
b 1 BYZ and TR include *from God our Father and the Lord Jesus Christ*

1 Thessalonians 2
Paul's Ministry

¹For you yourselves know, brothers, that our coming to you has not been in vain. ²But having previously suffered and having been mistreated in Philippi, just as you know, we had boldness in our God to speak to you the gospel of God amid much conflict.

³For our exhortation *was* not of error, nor of impurity, nor in trickery; ⁴but just as we have been approved by God to be entrusted with the gospel, so we speak, not as pleasing men, but God, the *One* examining our hearts. ⁵For never at any time were we with word of flattery, just as you know, nor with a pretext for greed—God *is* witness— ⁶nor seeking glory from men, nor from you, nor from others, *though* having authority with weight to be, as apostles of Christ.

⁷But we were gentle in your midst, as a nursing mother would cherish her own children. ⁸So yearning over you, we were pleased to have imparted to you not only the gospel of God, but also our own lives, because you have become beloved to us. ⁹For you remember, brothers, our labor and hardship: Working night and day in order not to burden any one of you, we proclaimed to you the gospel of God. ¹⁰You *are* witnesses, and God, how holily and righteously and blamelessly we behaved toward you, those believing, ¹¹just as you know how each one of you, as a father his own children, ¹²*we were* exhorting and comforting you and charging unto you to walk worthily of God, who calls you into His kingdom and glory.

¹³And because of this, we also give thanks to God unceasingly that, having received *the* word of God *by your* hearing from us, you accepted not *the* word of men, but even as truly it is, *the* word of God, which also works in you who believe.

¹⁴For you became imitators, brothers, of the churches of God in Judea being in Christ Jesus. For the same as them, you also suffered from the own countrymen as they also *did* from the Jews, ¹⁵who having killed both the Lord Jesus and their own prophets, and having driven us out, and not pleasing God, *are* also set against all men, ¹⁶forbidding us to speak to the Gentiles that they might be saved, so as always to fill up their sins. Now the wrath has come upon them to the utmost.

Paul's Longing to Visit
(Romans 1:8-15)

¹⁷But we, having been bereaved of you, brothers, for *the* time of an hour—in face, not in heart—were more abundantly eager with great desire to see your face. ¹⁸Therefore we wanted to come to you—indeed I Paul, both once and twice—and Satan hindered us. ¹⁹For who *is* our hope or joy or crown of boasting? Or *are* not even you, before our Lord Jesus at His coming? ²⁰For you are our glory and joy.

1 Thessalonians 3
Timothy's Visit

¹Therefore, enduring no longer, we thought it best to be left in Athens alone, ²and we sent Timothy, our brother and fellow worker of God in the gospel of Christ, in order to strengthen and to encourage you concerning your faith, ³that no one be moved in these tribulations. For you yourselves know that we are destined for this. ⁴And indeed, when we were with you, we were telling you beforehand that we are about to suffer affliction, just as also it came to pass, and you know. ⁵Because of this I also, enduring no longer, sent in order to know your faith, lest somehow the *one* tempting had tempted you, and our labor would be in vain.

Timothy's Encouraging Report

⁶But presently, Timothy having come to us from you and having brought good news to us of your faith and love, and that always you have a good remembrance of us, longing to see us just as also we you, ⁷because of this, brothers, we were encouraged as to you in all our distress and tribulation, through your faith. ⁸For now we live, if you are standing firm in *the* Lord.

⁹For what thanksgiving are we able to give to God concerning you in return for all the joy that we rejoice before our God because of you, ¹⁰night and day imploring exceedingly for *us* to see your face and to supply the things lacking of you in faith?

¹¹Now may our God and Father Himself, and our Lord Jesus, direct our way to you. ¹²And may the Lord make you to increase and to abound in love toward one another, and toward all, just as also we toward you, ¹³in order to strengthen your hearts, blameless in holiness before our God and Father at the coming of our Lord Jesus with all His saints. Amen.

1 Thessalonians 4
Living to Please God

¹Finally then, brothers, we implore and exhort you in *the* Lord Jesus, that just as you have received from us in what manner it behooves you to walk and to please God, just as even you walk *now*, so you should abound more. ²For you know what instructions we gave you through the Lord Jesus.

³For this is *the* will of God, your sanctification: You *are* to abstain from sexual immorality; ⁴each of you to know *how* to win mastery over his *own* vessel in holiness and honor, ⁵not in *the* passion of lust, as also the Gentiles, not knowing God; ⁶not to go beyond and to overreach his brother in the matter, because *the* Lord *is* avenging concerning all these things, just as also we told you before and thoroughly warned. ⁷For God has not called us to impurity, but into holiness. ⁸So then, the *one* rejecting *this* does not disregard man but God, the *One* also giving His Holy Spirit to you.

⁹Now concerning brotherly love, you have no need *for me* to write to you, for you yourselves are taught by God in order to love one another. ¹⁰And indeed you are doing this toward all the brothers, the *ones* in all Macedonia. But we exhort you, brothers, to abound more and more, ¹¹and to strive earnestly to live quietly and to attend to your own *matters*, and to work with your own hands, just as we commanded you, ¹²so that you may walk properly toward those outside, and may have need of no one.

The Return of the Lord

¹³But we do not want you to be ignorant, brothers, concerning those having fallen asleep, so that you should not be grieved, just as also the rest, those having no hope. ¹⁴For if we believe that Jesus died and rose again, even so, through Jesus, God will bring with Him those having fallen asleep.

¹⁵For this we declare to you in *the* word of *the* Lord, that we the living, remaining unto the coming of the Lord, shall not precede those having fallen asleep, ¹⁶because the Lord Himself will descend from heaven with a loud command, with the voice of an archangel, and with *the* trumpet of God. And the dead in Christ will rise first. ¹⁷Then we, the living remaining, will be caught away together with them in *the* clouds for *the* meeting of the Lord in *the* air; and so we will be always with *the* Lord.

¹⁸Therefore encourage one another with these words.

1 Thessalonians 5
The Day of the Lord

(Zephaniah 1:7-18; 2 Peter 3:8-13)

¹Now concerning the times and the seasons, brothers, you have no need to be written to you. ²For you yourselves fully know that *the* day of *the* Lord comes

in this manner, as a thief by night. ³For when they might say, "Peace and security," then suddenly destruction comes upon them, as the labor pains to her having in womb; and they shall not escape.
⁴But you, brothers, are not in darkness, so that the day should overtake you like a thief. ⁵For you are all sons of light and sons of day; we are not of night nor of darkness. ⁶So then we should not sleep as the others, but we should watch and we should be sober. ⁷For those sleeping, sleep by night; and those becoming drunk, get drunk by night. ⁸But we being of *the* day should be sober, having put on *the* breastplate of faith and love, and *the* helmet, *the* hope of salvation, ⁹because God has not destined us for wrath, but for obtaining salvation through our Lord Jesus Christ, ¹⁰the *One* having died for us, so that whether we might watch or we might sleep, we may live together with Him. ¹¹Therefore encourage one another and build up one another, just as also you are doing.

Christian Living

¹²But we implore you, brothers, to appreciate those toiling among you, and taking the lead over you in *the* Lord, and admonishing you, ¹³and to esteem them exceedingly in love, because of their work. Be at peace among yourselves.
¹⁴And we exhort you, brothers, to admonish the unruly, encourage the fainthearted, help the weak, be patient toward all.
¹⁵See that no one has repaid to anyone evil for evil, but always pursue the good also toward one another and toward all.
¹⁶Rejoice always. ¹⁷Pray unceasingly. ¹⁸Give thanks in everything, for this *is the* will of God toward you in Christ Jesus.
¹⁹Do not quench the Spirit. ²⁰Do not despise prophecies, ²¹but test all things. Hold fast to the good. ²²Abstain from every form of evil.

Final Blessings

²³Now may the God of peace Himself sanctify you completely, and may your spirit and soul and body be preserved, entirely blameless at the coming of our Lord Jesus Christ. ²⁴The *One* calling you *is* faithful, who also will do *it*.
²⁵Brothers, pray also for us.
²⁶Greet all the brothers with a holy kiss.
²⁷I adjure you *by* the Lord, *this* letter to be read to all the brothers.
²⁸The grace of our Lord Jesus Christ *be* with you.ᵃ

a 28 BYZ and TR include *Amen.*

2 Thessalonians

2 Thessalonians 1
Greetings to the Thessalonians
(1 Thessalonians 1:1-10; Philemon 1:1-3)

¹Paul and Silvanusᵃ and Timothy,
To the church of *the* Thessalonians in God our Father and the Lord Jesus Christ:
²Grace to you and peace from God our Father and the Lord Jesus Christ.
³We ought to thank God always concerning you, brothers, just as it is fitting, because your faith is increasing exceedingly, and the love of each one of you all to one another is abounding, ⁴so as for us ourselves to boast in you in the churches of God about your endurance and faith in all your persecutions, and in the tribulations that you are bearing.

Christ's Coming

⁵*This is* a plain token of the righteous judgment of God, for you to be accounted worthy of the kingdom of God, for which also you suffer. ⁶For indeed *it is* righteous with God to repay those oppressing you with affliction, ⁷and to you being oppressed, repose with us at the revelation of the Lord Jesus from heaven, with His mighty angels, ⁸in a fire of flame, inflicting vengeance on those not

knowing God and on those not obeying the gospel of our Lord Jesus, ⁹who will suffer *the* penalty of eternal destruction away from *the* presence of the Lord and from the glory of His power, ¹⁰when in that day He shall come to be glorified in His saints, and to be marveled at among all those having believed because our testimony to you was believed, ¹¹for which also we pray always for you, that He may count you worthy of the calling of our God, and He may fulfill every good pleasure of goodness and work of faith with power, ¹²so that the name of our Lord Jesus may be glorified in you, and you in Him, according to the grace of our God and of *the* Lord Jesus Christ.

a 1 That is, Silas

2 Thessalonians 2
The Man of Lawlessness

¹Now we implore you, brothers, by the coming of our Lord Jesus Christ and our gathering together unto Him, ²for you not quickly to be shaken in mind, nor to be troubled, neither by spirit, nor by word, nor by letter as if by us, as that day of the Lord is present. ³No one should deceive you in *any* way, because *it is* not until the apostasy shall have come first, and the man of lawlessness shall have been revealed—the son of destruction, ⁴the *one* opposing and exalting himself above every so-called god or object of worship—so as for him to sit down in the temple of God, setting forth that he himself is God. ⁵Do you not remember that, being yet with you, I was saying these things to you? ⁶And now you know that which is restraining for his being revealed in his time. ⁷For the mystery of lawlessness is working already; *there is* only the *one* at present restraining *it*, until he might be *gone* out of *the* midst. ⁸And then the lawless *one* will be revealed, whom the Lord Jesus will consume with the breath of His mouth and will annul by the appearing of His coming, ⁹whose coming is according to *the* working of Satan, in every power, and in signs, and in wonders of falsehood, ¹⁰and in every deception of wickedness unto those perishing, in return for which they did not receive the love of the truth in order for them to be saved. ¹¹And because of this, God will send to them a working of delusion, for them to believe what *is* false, ¹²in order that all those not having believed the truth but having delighted in unrighteousness should be judged.

Stand Firm

¹³But we ought to give thanks to God always concerning you, brothers beloved by *the* Lord, that God has chosen you from *the* beginningᵃ unto salvation in *the* sanctification of *the* Spirit, and *by* faith of *the* truth; ¹⁴to this also He called you through our gospel to *the* obtaining of *the* glory of our Lord Jesus Christ. ¹⁵So then, brothers, stand firm and hold fast to the traditions that you were taught, whether by word, or by letter from us.

¹⁶Now our Lord Jesus Christ Himself, and God our Father, the *One* having loved us and having given *us* eternal comfort and good hope by grace, ¹⁷may He encourage your hearts and may He strengthen *them* in every good work and word.

a 13 Or *God has chosen you as the firstfruits*

2 Thessalonians 3
Request for Prayer

¹Finally, brothers, pray for us, that the word of the Lord may spread quickly and may be glorified, just as also with you, ²and that we may be delivered from perverse and evil men; for not all *are* of the faith. ³But the Lord is faithful, who will strengthen you and will keep *you* from evil. ⁴And we are persuaded in *the* Lord as to you, that both you are doing and you will do the things that we command. ⁵And may the Lord direct your hearts into the love of God and into the steadfastness of Christ.

Warning against Irresponsibility

⁶Now we warn you, brothers, in *the* name of our Lord Jesus Christ, you are to

withdraw from every brother walking idly and not according to the tradition that you received from us. ⁷For you yourselves know how it behooves *you* to imitate us, because we were not idle among you, ⁸nor did we eat bread from anyone without payment, but in labor and toil, working night and day in order not to be burdensome to any of you, ⁹not that we do not have *the* right, but that we may offer ourselves *as* an example to you for you to imitate us. ¹⁰For even when we were with you, we were commanding you this, that "if anyone is not willing to work, neither let him eat."

¹¹For we hear some among you are walking idly, not working at all, but being busybodies. ¹²Now we command and exhort to such by our Lord Jesus Christ so that, working with quietness, they may eat their own bread. ¹³Now you, brothers, shall not grow weary *in* well-doing.

¹⁴And if anyone does not obey our instruction through the letter, take note of this *man*, not to mix with him, so that he may be ashamed. ¹⁵And yet do not esteem *him* as an enemy, but admonish *him* as a brother.

Paul's Final Greetings
(1 Corinthians 16:19-24)

¹⁶Now may the Lord of peace Himself give you peace through all, in every way. The Lord *be* with all of you.

¹⁷The greeting *is* in my own hand—Paul, which is *my* sign in every letter. In this manner I write.

¹⁸The grace of our Lord Jesus Christ *be* with all of you.ᵃ

a 18 BYZ and TR include *Amen.*

1 Timothy

1 Timothy 1
Paul's Greeting to Timothy
(2 Timothy 1:1-2)

¹Paul, an apostle of Christ Jesus, according to *the* command of God our Savior and of Christ Jesus our hope, ²To Timothy, *my* true child in *the* faith: Grace, mercy, *and* peace from God our Father and Christ Jesus our Lord.

Warning against False Teaching

³Just as I urged you to remain in Ephesus *when* I was going to Macedonia, so that you might warn certain men not to teach other doctrines, ⁴nor to give heed to myths and endless genealogies, which bring speculations rather than God's stewardship, which *is* in faith.

⁵Now the goal of *our* instruction is love out of a pure heart, and a good conscience, and a sincere faith, ⁶from which some, having missed the mark, have turned aside to meaningless discourse, ⁷desiring to be teachers of the Law, understanding neither what they are saying nor *that* about which they confidently assert.

⁸Now we know that the Law *is* good, if one uses it lawfully, ⁹knowing this, that law is not enacted for a righteous *one*, but for *the* lawless and insubordinate, for *the* ungodly and sinful, for *the* unholy and profane, for murderers of fathers and murderers of mothers, for slayers of man, ¹⁰for the sexually immoral, homosexuals, enslavers, liars, perjurers, and if anything other is opposed to being sound in the teaching, ¹¹according to the gospel of the glory of the blessed God, with which I have been entrusted.

God's Grace to Paul

¹²I have thankfulness for the *One* having strengthened me, Christ Jesus our Lord, that He esteemed me faithful, having appointed *me* to service, ¹³being formerly a blasphemer, and a persecutor, and insolent; but I was shown mercy, because

I did *it* in unbelief, being ignorant. ¹⁴And the grace of our Lord surpassingly increased with *the* faith and love that *are* in Christ Jesus.

¹⁵Trustworthy *is* the saying, and worthy of full acceptance, that Christ Jesus came into the world to save sinners, of whom I am *the* foremost. ¹⁶But because of this I was shown mercy, that in me, *the* foremost, Christ Jesus might display perfect patience, as a pattern for those being about to believe on Him to eternal life. ¹⁷Now to *the* King of the ages, *the* immortal, invisible, only God, *be* honor and glory to the ages of the ages. Amen. ¹⁸I commit to you this charge, Timothy, *my* child, according to the prophecies going before as to you, that by them you might wage the good warfare, ¹⁹holding faith and a good conscience, which some, having cast away, have caused a shipwreck concerning the faith, ²⁰among whom are Hymenaeus and Alexander, whom I have handed over to Satan, that they may be disciplined not to blaspheme.

1 Timothy 2
A Call to Prayer

¹First of all, therefore, I exhort entreaties, prayers, intercessions, *and* thanksgivings, to be made on behalf of all men ²for kings and all those being in authority, so that we may lead a tranquil and quiet life in all godliness and dignity. ³This *is* good and acceptable before God our Savior, ⁴who desires all men to be saved and to come to *the* knowledge of *the* truth.

⁵For *there is* one God and one mediator between God and men, *the* man Christ Jesus, ⁶the One having given Himself *as* a ransom for all, the testimony in their own proper times, ⁷in regard to which I was appointed a herald and an apostle—I am speaking *the* truth; I do not lie—a teacher of *the* Gentiles in faith and truth. ⁸Therefore I desire the men in every place to pray, lifting up holy hands, apart from anger and dissension.

Instructions to Women

⁹Likewise also women should adorn themselves in respectable apparel, with modesty and self-control, not with braided hair or gold or pearls or costly clothing, ¹⁰but with what is becoming to women, professing *the* fear of God through good works.

¹¹Let a woman[a] learn in quietness, in all submissiveness. ¹²But I do not permit a woman to teach, nor to use authority over a man,[b] but to be in quietness. ¹³For Adam was formed first, then Eve. ¹⁴And Adam was not deceived, but the woman, having been deceived, has come into transgression. ¹⁵But she will be saved through childbearing, if they abide in faith and love and holiness, with self-restraint.

a 11 Or *wife*; also in verse 12
b 12 Or *over her husband*

1 Timothy 3
Qualifications for Overseers

¹Trustworthy *is* the saying: If anyone aspires to overseership, he is desirous of a good work. ²Therefore it behooves the overseer to be above reproach, *the* husband of one wife, sober, self-controlled, respectable, hospitable, able to teach, ³not given to wine, not a striker, but gentle, peaceable, not loving money, ⁴managing the own house well, having children in submission, with all dignity—⁵but if one does not know how to manage the own household, *how* will he care for *the* church of God?— ⁶not a novice, lest having been puffed up, he might fall into *the* judgment of the devil. ⁷And it behooves *him* also to have a good testimony from those outside, so that he might not fall into reproach and *the* snare of the devil.

Qualifications for Deacons
(Acts 6:1-7)

⁸Deacons likewise *must be* dignified, not double-tongued, not being given to much wine, not greedy of dishonest gain, ⁹holding to the mystery of the faith with a clear conscience. ¹⁰And these also, let

them be tested first; then let them serve, being blameless.

¹¹Women[a] likewise *must be* dignified, not slanderers, clear-minded, faithful in all things. ¹²Let deacons be husbands of one wife, managing the children and the own households well. ¹³For those having served well acquire a good standing for themselves and great confidence in *the* faith that *is* in Christ Jesus.

The Mystery of Godliness

¹⁴I am writing these things to you, hoping to come to you in a short time, ¹⁵but if I should delay, so that you may know how it behooves *one* to conduct oneself in *the* household of God, which is *the* church of *the* living God, *the* pillar and base of the truth.

¹⁶And confessedly, great is the mystery of godliness:

>Who was revealed in *the* flesh,
>>was justified in *the* Spirit,[b]
>
>was seen by angels,
>>was proclaimed among *the* nations,
>
>was believed on in *the* world,
>>was taken up in glory.

a 11 Or *their wives*
b 16 Or *justified in spirit*

1 Timothy 4
Warnings against False Teachers

¹But the Spirit expressly states that in later times some will depart from the faith, giving heed to deceitful spirits and teachings of demons, ²in *the* hypocrisy of liars, having been seared in the own conscience, ³forbidding to marry, *commanding* to abstain from foods that God created for reception with thanksgiving by the faithful and *those* knowing the truth. ⁴For every creature of God *is* good, and nothing *is* to be rejected, being received with thanksgiving, ⁵for it is sanctified by *the* word of God and prayer.

A Good Minister of Jesus Christ
(Leviticus 21:1-17)

⁶Laying before the brothers these things, you will be a good servant of Christ Jesus, being nourished in the words of the faith, and of the good teaching that you have closely followed.

⁷But refuse profane and silly fables. Rather, train yourself to godliness. ⁸For bodily exercise is of a little profit, but godliness is profitable for everything, holding *the* promise of the present life and of the *one* coming. ⁹Trustworthy *is* the saying, and worthy of full acceptance. ¹⁰For to this we toil and strive,[a] because we have hope on *the* living God, who is *the* Savior of all men, especially of believers. ¹¹Command and teach these things.

¹²Let no one despise your youth, but be a pattern for the believers in speech, in conduct, in love, in faith, in purity. ¹³Until I come, give heed to the public reading of Scripture, to exhortation, to teaching.

¹⁴Do not be negligent of the gift in you, which was given to you through prophecy, with *the* laying on of the hands of the elderhood. ¹⁵Ponder these things; be absorbed in them, so that your progress may be evident to all. ¹⁶Give heed to yourself and to the teaching. Continue in them; for doing this, you will save both yourself and those hearing you.

a 10 SBL, BYZ, and TR *and suffer reproach*

1 Timothy 5
Guidelines for Reproof

¹Do not rebuke an older man, but exhort *him* as a father; younger *men* as brothers; ²elder *women* as mothers; *and* younger *women* as sisters, in all purity.

Support for Widows
(Ruth 1:1-5)

³Honor widows who *are* truly widows. ⁴But if any widow has children or grandchildren, let them learn to be devout first to the own household and to give recompense to parents; for this is pleasing before God.

⁵Now she who *is* a widow indeed, and being left alone, has hope in God and continues in supplications and prayers night and day. ⁶But she living in self-indulgence is dead *while* living.
⁷Also command these things, so that they should be above reproach. ⁸Now if anyone does not provide for the own, and especially *his* household, he has denied the faith and is worse than an unbeliever.
⁹Let a widow be enrolled, being not less than sixty years *old, the* wife of one man, ¹⁰being borne witness to in good works: if she has brought up children, if she has entertained strangers, if she has washed *the* feet of the saints, if she has imparted relief *to those* being oppressed, if she has followed after every good work.
¹¹But refuse younger widows; for when they might grow wanton against Christ, they desire to marry, ¹²incurring judgment, because they have cast off the first faith. ¹³And at the same time also, going about house to house, they learn *to be* idle; and not only idle, but also gossips and busybodies, speaking things not being proper.
¹⁴Therefore I want *the* younger *ones* to marry, to bear children, to manage their households, to give the *one* opposing no occasion on account of reproach. ¹⁵For already some have turned aside after Satan.
¹⁶If any believing *woman* has *dependent* widows, let her impart relief to them, and let the church not be burdened, so that it may impart relief to those *who are* truly widows.

Honoring Elders

¹⁷Let the elders ruling well be counted worthy of double honor, especially those laboring in *the* word and *the* teaching. ¹⁸For the Scripture says, "You shall not muzzle an ox treading out grain,"[a] and, "The workman *is* worthy of his wages."[b]
¹⁹Do not receive an accusation against an elder, except upon two or three witnesses. ²⁰But those sinning, rebuke before all, so that the rest might have fear as well.

A Charge to Timothy

²¹I earnestly testify before God and Christ Jesus and the elect angels that you should keep these things apart from prejudice, doing nothing out of partiality. ²²Lay hands on no one hastily, nor share in *the* sins of others; keep yourself pure. ²³No longer drink *only* water, but use a little wine, because of the stomach and your frequent ailments.
²⁴The sins of some men are manifest, going before *them* to judgment; but of some also they appear later. ²⁵Likewise also, the good works *are* evident, and even those being otherwise *are* unable to be concealed.

a 18 Deuteronomy 25:4
b 18 Luke 10:7

1 Timothy 6
Instructions to Servants
(Ephesians 6:5-9)

¹As many as are under a yoke *as* slaves, let them esteem the own masters worthy of all honor, so that the name of God and the teaching should not be blasphemed. ²Now those having believing masters, let them not despise *them* because they are brothers; but rather, let them serve *them*, because those being helped by the good service are believing and beloved. Teach and exhort these things.

Reject False Doctrines

³If anyone teaches another doctrine and does not draw near, being sound in *the* words of our Lord Jesus Christ and the teaching according to godliness, ⁴he is puffed up, knowing nothing, but unhealthy about controversies and disputes about words, out of which come envy, strife, slander, evil suspicions, ⁵and constant frictions among men corrupted in mind and destitute of the truth, holding godliness to be a means of gain.[a]

Contentment in Godliness

⁶But godliness with contentment is great gain. ⁷For we brought nothing into the world, because[b] neither are we able to

carry out anything. ⁸But having sustenance and coverings, with these we will be content.

⁹But those desiring to be rich fall into temptation and a snare, and many foolish and harmful desires, which plunge men into ruin and destruction. ¹⁰For the love of money is a root of all kinds of evils, which some, stretching after, have been seduced away from the faith and have pierced themselves with many sorrows.

Fight the Good Fight

¹¹But you, O man of God, flee these things and pursue righteousness, godliness, faith, love, endurance, *and* gentleness. ¹²Fight the good fight of the faith. Lay hold of the eternal life to which you were called, and also did confess the good confession before many witnesses. ¹³I charge you before God, the *One* giving life to all things, and Christ Jesus, the *One* having testified the good confession before Pontius Pilate, ¹⁴for you to keep the commandment, without stain, above reproach, until the appearing of our Lord Jesus Christ, ¹⁵which He will display in the own seasons, blessed and alone Sovereign, the King of those being kings, and *the* Lord of those being lords, ¹⁶alone having immortality, dwelling in unapproachable light, whom no one of men has seen nor is able to see, to whom *be* honor and eternal dominion. Amen.

A Charge to the Rich

¹⁷Instruct the rich in the present age not to be high-minded, nor to have hope in *the* uncertainty of riches, but on God, the *One* richly providing us all things for enjoyment; ¹⁸to do good, to be rich in good works, to be generous in distributing, ready to share, ¹⁹treasuring up for themselves a good foundation for the future, so that they may take hold of that which is indeed life.

Final Guidance

²⁰O Timothy, guard the deposit committed *to you*, avoiding profane, empty babblings, and opposing arguments falsely called knowledge, ²¹which some professing, have gone astray from the faith.

Grace *be* with you all.ᶜ

a 5 BYZ and TR include *Withdraw yourself from such.*
b 7 BYZ and TR *because certainly*
c 21 BYZ and TR include *Amen.*

2 Timothy

2 Timothy 1
Paul's Greeting to Timothy
(1 Timothy 1:1-2)

¹Paul, an apostle of Christ Jesus by *the* will of God, according to *the* promise of life in Christ Jesus,
²To Timothy, *my* beloved child:
Grace, mercy, *and* peace from God *the* Father and Christ Jesus our Lord.

Encouragement to Be Faithful

³I am thankful to God, whom I serve from *my* forefathers with a pure conscience, as I have the remembrance of you unceasingly in my prayers, night and day, ⁴longing to see you, recalling your tears, so that I may be filled with joy, ⁵having taken remembrance of the sincere faith within you, which dwelt first in your grandmother Lois and in your mother Eunice, and I am persuaded that *it is* in you also.

Patience in Persecution
(Matthew 10:16-25)

⁶For this reason I remind you to kindle anew the gift of God, which is in you by the laying on of my hands. ⁷For God has not given us a spirit of cowardice, but of power, and of love, and of self-control. ⁸Therefore you should not be ashamed of the testimony of our Lord, nor of me, His prisoner; but suffer together for the gospel, according to *the* power of God, ⁹the *One* having saved us and having called *us* with a holy calling, not according to our works, but according to His own purpose and grace, having been given us in Christ Jesus before time eternal, ¹⁰and now having been made manifest by the appearing of our Savior Christ Jesus,

having abolished death and having brought to light life and immortality through the gospel, ¹¹to which I was appointed a herald, and an apostle, and a teacher.

¹²For this reason I also suffer these things. But I am not ashamed, for I know whom I have believed, and I am persuaded that He is able to guard my deposit entrusted for that day.

Hold to Sound Teaching

¹³Retain *the* pattern of sound words, which you have heard from me, in *the* faith and love that *are* in Christ Jesus. ¹⁴Keep the good deposit entrusted *to you* by *the* Holy Spirit, the *One* dwelling in us. ¹⁵You know this, that all those in Asia turned away from me, among whom are Phygelus and Hermogenes.

¹⁶May the Lord grant mercy to the household of Onesiphorus, because he refreshed me often, and he was not ashamed of my chain. ¹⁷But having arrived in Rome, he earnestly sought me out and found *me*.

¹⁸May the Lord grant unto him to find mercy from *the* Lord in that day! And you know very well how much he served in Ephesus.

2 Timothy 2
Grace and Perseverance
(Hebrews 12:1-3)

¹You therefore, my son, be strong in the grace that *is* in Christ Jesus. ²And the things that you have heard from me among many witnesses, entrust these to faithful men who will be competent to teach others also.

³Share in suffering as a good soldier of Christ Jesus. ⁴No one serving as a soldier entangles himself in the affairs of this life, that he might please the *one* having enlisted him. ⁵Now also, if anyone competes, he is not crowned unless he shall have competed lawfully. ⁶It is necessary for the hardworking farmer first to partake of the fruits. ⁷Consider the things I am saying, for the Lord will give you understanding in all things.

⁸Remember Jesus Christ, having been raised out from *the* dead, of *the* seed of David, according to my gospel, ⁹in which I suffer hardship even to chains as an evildoer. But the word of God is not bound! ¹⁰Because of this, I endure all things for the sake of the elect, so that they also may obtain *the* salvation that *is* in Christ Jesus, with eternal glory.

¹¹Trustworthy *is* the saying:
> For if we have died together *with Him*,
>> we will also live together *with Him*;
>
> ¹²if we endure,
>> we will also reign together *with Him*;
>
> if we will deny *Him*,
>> He also will deny us;
>
> ¹³if we are faithless,
>> He remains faithful,
>> for He is not able to deny Himself.

The Lord's Approved Workman

¹⁴Remind *them* these things, solemnly charging *them* before God^a not to quarrel about words, for nothing profitable *but* to *the* subversion of those hearing.

¹⁵Hasten to present yourself approved to God, a workman not ashamed, accurately handling the word of truth.

¹⁶But avoid worldly, empty babblings, for they will lead on to more ungodliness, ¹⁷and their talk will have pasture to grow like gangrene, among whom are Hymenaeus and Philetus, ¹⁸who have gone astray concerning the truth, asserting the resurrection already to have taken place; and they are overthrowing the faith of some.

¹⁹Nevertheless, the firm foundation of God stands, having this seal: "*The* Lord knows those being His," and, "Let everyone naming the name of the Lord depart from iniquity."

²⁰Now in a great house, there are not only golden and silver vessels, but also

wooden and earthen; and some indeed unto honor, but some unto dishonor. ²¹Therefore if anyone shall have cleansed himself from these, he will be a vessel for honor, having been sanctified, useful to the Master, having been prepared for every good work.

²²Now flee youthful lusts and pursue righteousness, faith, love, *and* peace, along with those calling on the Lord out of pure a heart.

²³And refuse foolish and ignorant speculations, knowing that they breed quarrels. ²⁴And it behooves *the* bondservant of *the* Lord not to quarrel, but to be gentle toward all, able to teach, forbearing, ²⁵in gentleness disciplining those opposing, lest ever God may give them repentance unto a knowledge of *the* truth, ²⁶and they might come to their senses out of the snare of the devil, having been captured by him for his will.

a 14 SBL, BYZ, and TR *the Lord*

2 Timothy 3
Evil in the Last Days

¹But realize this, that in *the* last days difficult times will be present. ²For men will be lovers of self, lovers of money, boasters, proud, verbally abusive, disobedient to parents, ungrateful, unholy, ³unloving, unforgiving, slanderous, without self-control, savage, haters of good, ⁴betrayers, reckless, puffed up, lovers of pleasure rather than lovers of God, ⁵having a form of godliness but denying its power. And turn away from these.

⁶For out of this sort are those entering into households and taking captive weak women, burdened with sins, being led away by various passions, ⁷always learning and never being able to come to a knowledge of *the* truth. ⁸Now as Jannes and Jambres opposed Moses, so also these oppose the truth, men being depraved in mind, disqualified regarding the faith. ⁹But they will not advance much further, for their folly will be plain to all, as also that of those *two* became.

All Scripture is God-Breathed

¹⁰But you have closely followed my teaching, conduct, purpose, faith, patience, love, endurance, ¹¹persecutions, sufferings such as happened to me in Antioch, in Iconium, in Lystra; what manner of persecutions I endured! And yet the Lord delivered me out of all. ¹²And all also desiring to live piously in Christ Jesus will be persecuted. ¹³But evil men and imposters will advance to worse, deceiving and being deceived.

¹⁴But you, abide in the things you have learned and have been assured of, having known from whom you learned *them*, ¹⁵and that from childhood you have known the sacred writings, being able to make you wise unto salvation through faith in Christ Jesus. ¹⁶Every Scripture *is* God-breathed and profitable for instruction, for conviction, for correction, *and* for training in righteousness, ¹⁷so that the man of God may be complete, having been fully equipped toward every good work.

2 Timothy 4
Preach the Word

¹I earnestly declare before God and Christ Jesus, the *One* being about to judge *the* living and *the* dead, and by His appearing and His kingdom: ²Preach the word; be ready in season *and* out of season; convict, rebuke, *and* exhort, with complete patience and instruction.

³For there will be a time when they will not endure sound teaching, but according to the own desires, having an itching ear, they will gather around *them* teachers to *suit* themselves, ⁴and indeed they will turn away from hearing the truth, and will be turned aside unto myths.

⁵But you, be sober in all things, endure afflictions, do *the* work of an evangelist, fully carry out your ministry. ⁶For already I am being poured out, and the time of

my departure is come. ⁷I have fought the good fight, I have finished the race, I have kept the faith. ⁸From now on the crown of righteousness is laid up for me, which the Lord, the righteous judge, will award to me in that day; but not only to me, but also to all those loving His appearing.

Personal Concerns

⁹Be diligent to come to me quickly, ¹⁰for Demas has deserted me, having loved the present age, and he has gone to Thessalonica, Crescens to Galatia, and Titus to Dalmatia. ¹¹Luke alone is with me. Having taken Mark, bring *him* with you, for he is useful to me for *the* ministry. ¹²But I have sent Tychicus to Ephesus. ¹³*Upon* coming, bring the cloak that I left with Carpus in Troas, and the books, especially the parchments.

¹⁴Alexander the coppersmith did great harm to me. The Lord will render to him according to his deeds, ¹⁵whom you also beware of, for exceedingly he has opposed our message.

The Lord Remains Faithful

¹⁶In my first defense, no one has stood with me, but all deserted me. May it be not charged to them! ¹⁷But the Lord stood by me and strengthened me, so that through me the proclamation would be fully accomplished, and all the Gentiles should hear. And I was delivered out of *the* mouth of the lion. ¹⁸The Lord will deliver me from every evil deed and will bring *me* safely into His heavenly kingdom, to whom *is* the glory unto the ages of the ages. Amen.

Final Greetings

¹⁹Greet Prisca[a] and Aquila, and the house of Onesiphorus.

²⁰Erastus remained in Corinth, but Trophimus I left ailing in Miletus.

²¹Be earnest to come before winter. Eubulus greets you, and Pudens, and Linus, and Claudia, and all the brothers.

²²The Lord *be* with your spirit. Grace *be* with you all.[b]

---

[a] 19 That is, Priscilla
[b] 22 BYZ and TR include *Amen*.

Titus

Titus 1
Paul's Greeting to Titus
(2 Corinthians 8:16-24)

¹Paul, a servant of God and an apostle of Jesus Christ, according to *the* faith of *the* elect of God and *the* knowledge of *the* truth which *is* according to godliness, ²in *the* hope of eternal life, which God, who cannot lie, promised before time eternal ³and *in His* own seasons revealed in His word, in *the* proclamation with which I have been entrusted according to *the* commandment of God our Savior.

⁴To Titus, *my* true child according to *our* common faith:

Grace and peace from God *the* Father and Christ Jesus our Savior.

Appointing Elders on Crete

⁵On account of this I left you in Crete, that you might set in order the things lacking and might appoint elders in every town, as I directed you, ⁶if anyone is blameless, *the* husband of one wife, having believing children, not under accusation of debauchery, or insubordinate.

⁷For it behooves the overseer to be blameless, as God's steward; not self-willed, not quick tempered, not given to wine, not a striker, not greedy of base gain, ⁸but hospitable, a lover of good, self-controlled, upright, holy, *and* disciplined; ⁹holding to the faithful word according to the teaching, that he may be able both to encourage with sound teaching and to convict those contradicting *it*.

Correcting False Teachers

¹⁰For there are also many insubordinate, empty talkers, and deceivers, especially those of the circumcision, ¹¹whom it is necessary to silence, who overthrow whole households, teaching things that

they ought not for *the* sake of base gain. ¹²One of them, a prophet of their own, said, "Cretans *are* always liars, evil beasts, lazy gluttons."ᵃ
¹³This testimony is true, for which cause rebuke them severely, so that they may be sound in the faith, ¹⁴not giving heed to Jewish myths and *the* commandments of men turning away from the truth.
¹⁵To the pure all things *are* pure; but to those being defiled and unbelieving, nothing *is* pure. Instead, both their mind and conscience are defiled. ¹⁶They profess to know God, but in *their* works they deny *Him*, being detestable and disobedient and unfit for any good work.

a 12 This quote has been attributed to the Cretan philosopher Epimenides

Titus 2
Teaching Sound Doctrine

¹But you, speak the things that are consistent with the sound doctrine.
²*The* aged *men* are to be sober-minded, dignified, self-controlled, sound in faith, in love, in endurance; ³*the* aged *women* likewise reverent in behavior, not slanderers, not being enslaved to much wine, teachers of what is good, ⁴so that they may train the young *women* to be lovers of *their* husbands, loving *their* children, ⁵self-controlled, pure, keepers at home, kind, being subject to the own husbands, so that the word of God should not be maligned.
⁶Likewise, exhort the younger *men* to be self-controlled.
⁷In all things be holding forth yourself *as* a pattern of good works, in the teaching, integrity, dignity, ⁸*and* sound speech beyond reproach, so that he who is of the contrary may be ashamed, having nothing evil to say concerning us.
⁹Servants are to be subject to their own masters in everything, to be well-pleasing, not gainsaying, ¹⁰not pilfering, but showing all good fidelity, so that they may adorn the doctrine of God our Savior in all things.

God's Grace Brings Salvation

¹¹For the grace of God has appeared, bringing salvation to all men, ¹²instructing us that, having denied ungodliness and worldly passions, we should live discreetly and righteously and piously in the present age, ¹³awaiting the blessed hope and *the* appearing of the glory of our great God and Savior, Jesus Christ, ¹⁴who gave Himself for us, that He might redeem us from all lawlessness and might purify to Himself a people specially chosen, zealous of good works.
¹⁵Speak these things, and exhort and rebuke with all authority. Let no one despise you.

Titus 3
Obedience to Authorities

¹Remind them to be subject to rulers, to authorities, to be obedient, to be ready for every good work, ²to speak evil of no one, to be peaceable, *to be* gentle, showing all humility toward all men.

God's Mercy to Us

³For we ourselves were also once foolish, disobedient, being deceived, serving various lusts and pleasures, living in malice and envy, hateful, hating one another.
⁴But when the kindness and the love of mankind of God our Savior appeared, ⁵He saved us, not by works in righteousness that we did, but according to His mercy, through *the* washing of regeneration and renewing of *the* Holy Spirit, ⁶whom He poured out on us richly through Jesus Christ our Savior, ⁷so that, having been justified by that grace, we should become heirs according to *the* hope of eternal life.
⁸Trustworthy *is* the saying, and I want you to affirm strongly concerning these things, so that those believing God may take care to be devoted to good works. These things are excellent and profitable to men.

Avoiding Divisions

⁹But avoid foolish controversies and genealogies and arguments and quarrels

about *the* Law; for they are unprofitable and worthless. ¹⁰Reject a factious man after one and a second admonition, ¹¹knowing that such a man is corrupt and is sinning, being self-condemned.

Final Remarks and Greetings

¹²When I shall send Artemas or Tychicus to you, be diligent to come to me into Nicopolis; for I have decided to winter there. ¹³Earnestly equip Zenas the lawyer and Apollos, so that nothing should be lacking to them. ¹⁴And also let our *people* learn to devote themselves to good works for necessary needs, so that they should not be unfruitful.

¹⁵All those with me greet you. Greet those loving us in *the* faith. Grace *be* with all of you.ᵃ

a 15 BYZ and TR include *Amen*.

Philemon

Philemon 1
Greetings from Paul and Timothy
(1 Thessalonians 1:1-10; 2 Thessalonians 1:1-2)

¹Paul, a prisoner of Christ Jesus, and Timothy *our* brother,
To Philemon, our beloved and fellow worker, ²and to Apphia our sister, and to Archippus our fellow soldier, and to the church at your house:
³Grace to you and peace from God our Father and *the* Lord Jesus Christ.

Philemon's Faith and Love

⁴I thank my God always, making mention of you upon my prayers, ⁵hearing of your love and the faith that you have toward the Lord Jesus and toward all the saints, ⁶so that the fellowship of your faith might become effective in *the* acknowledgment of every good *thing* that *is* in you toward Christ. ⁷For I have great joy and encouragement by occasion of your love, because the hearts of the saints have been refreshed by you, brother.

Paul's Appeal for Onesimus

⁸Therefore, having much boldness in Christ to order you what *is* befitting, ⁹rather, I exhort *you* for the sake of love, being such a one as Paul, now aged and also a prisoner of Christ Jesus. ¹⁰I exhort you for my child whom I have begotten in chains, Onesimus,ᵃ ¹¹once useless to you, but now useful both to you and to me, ¹²whom I have sent back to you in person—he who is my very heart— ¹³whom I was wishing to keep with myself, so that on behalf of you he might serve me in the chains of the gospel.

¹⁴But I wanted to do nothing apart from your consent, so that your good may be not as according to necessity, but according to willingness. ¹⁵For perhaps because of this he was separated *from you* for a time, so that you might possess him eternally, ¹⁶no longer as a slave, but above a slave, a beloved brother, especially to me, but how much more to you, both in *the* flesh and in *the* Lord.

¹⁷Therefore, if you consider me a partner, receive him as me. ¹⁸But if in any way he has wronged you or he owes *you*, charge this to me. ¹⁹I Paul did write with my own hand. I will repay *it*, that I may not say to you that you owe also to me even yourself.

²⁰Yes, brother, may I have profit from you in *the* Lord. Refresh my heart in Christ.

²¹Being persuaded of your obedience, I write to you, knowing that you will do even above what I say.

²²Now at the same time, also prepare a lodging for me; for I hope that through your prayers, I will be granted to you.

Additional Greetings

²³Epaphras, my fellow prisoner in Christ Jesus, greets you, ²⁴*as do* Mark, Aristarchus, Demas, *and* Luke, my fellow workers.

²⁵The grace of the Lord Jesus Christ *be* with your spirit.ᵇ

a 10 Onesimus means useful (see verse 11) or beneficial (see verse 20)
b 25 BYZ and TR include *Amen*.

Hebrews

Hebrews 1
The Supremacy of the Son
(Colossians 1:15-23)

¹God, having spoken long ago to *our* fathers in the prophets in many portions and in many ways, ²in these last days has spoken to us in *His* Son, whom He appointed heir of all things, and through whom He made the ages, ³who, being *the* radiance of *His* glory and *the* exact expression of His substance, and upholding all things by the power of His word, through having made *the* purification of sins, sat down at *the* right hand of the Majesty on high, ⁴having become by so much superior to the angels, as much as He has inherited a name more excellent beyond theirs.
⁵For to which of the angels did He ever say:
"You are my Son;
 today I have begotten You"*ᵃ*?
And again:
"I will be to Him for a Father,
 and He will be to Me for a Son"*ᵇ*?
⁶And again, when He brings the Firstborn into the world, He says:
"And let all God's angels worship Him."*ᶜ*
⁷And indeed as to the angels He says:
"The *One* making His angels winds,
 and His ministers a flame of fire."*ᵈ*
⁸But unto the Son:
"Your throne, O God, *is* to the age of the age,
 and the scepter of righteousness *is the* scepter of Your kingdom.
⁹You have loved righteousness and have hated wickedness;
  because of this, God, Your God, has anointed You with *the* oil of exultation
   above Your companions."*ᵉ*
¹⁰And:
"You, Lord, laid the foundation of the earth in *the* beginning,
 and the heavens are works of Your hands.
¹¹They will perish but You remain;
 and all will grow old like a garment;
¹²and like a robe You will roll them up,
 and like a garment*ᶠ* they will be changed;
but You are the same,
 and Your years will never end."*ᵍ*
¹³Now to which of the angels did He ever say:
"Sit at My right hand,
 until I may place Your enemies *as* a footstool for Your feet"*ʰ*?
¹⁴Are they not all ministering spirits, being sent forth for service for the sake of those being about to inherit salvation?

a 5 Psalm 2:7
b 5 2 Samuel 7:14; 1 Chronicles 17:13
c 6 Deuteronomy 32:43
d 7 Psalm 104:4
e 8-9 Psalm 45:6,7
f 12 BYZ and TR do not include *like a garment*
g 10-12 Psalm 102:25-27
h 13 Psalm 110:1

Hebrews 2
Salvation Confirmed

¹Because of this, it behooves us to give heed more abundantly to the things we have heard, lest ever we should drift away. ²For if the word having been spoken by angels was unalterable, and every transgression and disobedience received a just recompense, ³how shall we escape, having neglected such a great salvation, which, having received a commencement declared by the Lord, was confirmed to us by those having heard, ⁴God bearing witness with *them* both by signs and wonders, and by

various miracles and distributions of *the* Holy Spirit, according to His will.

Jesus Like His Brothers

⁵For not to angels did He subject the world that is coming, of which we are speaking, ⁶but someone somewhere has testified, saying,

"What is man, that You are mindful of him,
or *the* son of man, that You care for him?
⁷You made him a little lower*ᵃ* than *the* angels;
You crowned him with glory and honor;*ᵇ*
⁸You have put in subjection all things under his feet.*ᶜ*

For in subjecting all things to him, He left nothing unsubject to him. But at present not yet do we see all things having been subjected to him. ⁹But we see Jesus, who was made a little lower than *the* angels, because of the suffering of death, having been crowned with glory and with honor, so that by *the* grace of God He might taste death for everyone.

¹⁰For it was fitting to Him, for whom *are* all things and by whom *are* all things, having brought many sons to glory, to make perfect the author of their salvation through sufferings. ¹¹For both the *One* sanctifying and those being sanctified *are* all of one, for which reason He is not ashamed to call them brothers, ¹²saying:

"I will declare Your name to My brothers;
in *the* midst of *the* congregation I will sing Your praises."*ᵈ*

¹³And again:
"I will be trusting in Him."*ᵉ*
And again:
"Behold, I and the children whom God has given Me."*ᶠ*

¹⁴Therefore, since the children have partaken of blood and of flesh, He also likewise took part in the same things, so that through *His* death He might destroy the *one* holding the power of death, that is, the devil, ¹⁵and might set free those who all *their time* to live were subject to slavery through fear of death.

¹⁶For surely He helps not *the* angels, but He helps *the* seed of Abraham. ¹⁷Therefore it behooved *Him* to be made like the brothers in all things, so that He might become a merciful and faithful high priest *in* things relating to God, in order to make propitiation for the sins of the people. ¹⁸For in that He Himself has suffered, having been tempted, He is able to help those being tempted.

a 7 Or *a little while lower*, also in verse 9
b 7 WH and TR include *and set him over the works of your hands*
c 6-8 Psalm 8:4-6
d 12 Psalm 22:22
e 13 Isaiah 8:17
f 13 Isaiah 8:18

Hebrews 3
Jesus Our Apostle and High Priest

¹Therefore, holy brothers, partakers of *the* heavenly calling, carefully consider Jesus, the apostle and high priest of our confession, ²being faithful to the *One* having appointed Him, as Moses also in all His house.

³For He has been counted worthy of greater glory than Moses, by so much as the *one* having built it has greater honor than the house *itself*. ⁴For every house is built by someone, but the *One* having built everything *is* God.

⁵And indeed Moses *was* faithful as a servant in all His house,*ᵃ* unto a testimony of the things going to be spoken, ⁶but Christ as *the* Son over His house, whose house we are, if indeed we should hold*ᵇ* our confidence and the boast of *our* hope.

Do Not Harden Your Hearts

⁷Therefore, just as the Holy Spirit says:
"Today if you should hear His voice,
⁸do not harden your hearts,
as in the rebellion,
in the day of testing in the wilderness,
⁹where forty years your fathers tried *Me* by testing

and saw My works.
¹⁰Therefore I was angry with that generation,
and I said,
'Always they go astray in their heart;
and they have not known My ways;'
¹¹so I swore in My wrath,
'They shall not enter into My rest.'"ᶜ

The Peril of Unbelief

¹²Take heed, brothers, lest ever there will be in any of you an evil heart of unbelief, into falling away from *the* living God. ¹³But encourage one another every day, while it is called today, so that not one of you may be hardened by *the* deceitfulness of sin. ¹⁴For we have become partakers of Christ, if indeed we should hold firm unto *the* end the assurance from the beginning. ¹⁵As it is said:
"Today if you should hear His voice,
do not harden your hearts,
as in the rebellion."ᵈ
¹⁶For who *were those* having heard, rebelled, but not all those having come out of Egypt by the leading of Moses? ¹⁷And with whom was He indignant forty years, *if* not with those having sinned, whose bodies fell in the wilderness? ¹⁸And to whom did He swear that they shall not enter into His rest, if not to those having disobeyed? ¹⁹And we see that they were not able to enter in because of unbelief.

a 5 Numbers 12:7
b 6 NE, WH, BYZ, and TR include *firmly to the end*
c 7-11 Psalm 95:7-11
d 15 Psalm 95:7,8

Hebrews 4
The Sabbath Rest

(Genesis 2:1-3; Exodus 16:22-36)

¹Therefore, of the promise to enter into His rest left remaining, we should fear, lest ever any of you should seem to have fallen short. ²And indeed we are *those* having had the gospel preached just as they *did*; but the message of *their* hearing did not profit them, not having been united with the faith of those having heard. ³For those having believed enter into the rest, as He has said:
"So I swore in my wrath,
'they shall not enter into My rest.'"ᵃ
And yet the works have been finished from *the* foundation of *the* world. ⁴For He has spoken somewhere concerning the seventh *day* in this way, "And on the seventh day God rested from all His works."ᵇ ⁵And again in this *passage*. "They shall not enter into My rest."
⁶Therefore, since it remains *for* some to enter into it, and those having received the good news formerly did not enter in because of disobedience, ⁷again He appoints a certain day as "Today," saying through David after so long a time, just as it has been said, "Today, if you shall hear His voice, do not harden your hearts."ᶜ
⁸For if Joshua had given rest to them, He would not have spoken after this about another day. ⁹So then, there remains a Sabbath rest for the people of God. ¹⁰For the *one* having entered into His rest, he also rested from his works, as God *did* from the own. ¹¹Therefore we should be diligent to enter into that rest, so that no one should fall by the same example of disobedience.

God's Word is Living and Active

¹²For the word of God *is* living and active, and sharper than any two-edged sword, penetrating even as far as *the* division of soul and spirit, and of joints and marrows, and able to judge *the* thoughts and intentions of *the* heart. ¹³And there is no creature hidden before Him, but all things *are* uncovered and laid bare to the eyes of Him to whom *is* our reckoning.

Jesus the Great High Priest

¹⁴Therefore having a great high priest having passed through the heavens, Jesus, the Son of God, we should hold firmly to *our* confession. ¹⁵For we do not have a high priest not being able to

sympathize with our weaknesses, but *one* having been tempted in all things by the same way, without sin. ¹⁶Therefore we should come with boldness to the throne of grace, so that we may receive mercy and may find grace for help in time of need.

a 3 Psalm 95:11; also in verse 5
b 4 Genesis 2:2
c 7 Psalm 95:7,8

Hebrews 5
The Perfect High Priest
(Psalm 110:1-7)

¹For every high priest, being taken from among men, is appointed on behalf of men in things relating to God, that he should offer both gifts and sacrifices for sins, ²being able to exercise forbearance with those being ignorant and going astray, since he himself also is encompassed by weakness; ³and because of this, he is obligated to offer sacrifices for sins, so also for himself, just as for the people.
⁴And no one takes upon himself the honor, but rather being called by God, just as Aaron also. ⁵So also Christ did not glorify Himself to become a high priest, but the *One* having said to Him:
 "You are My Son,
  today I have begotten You."ᵃ
⁶Just as He says also in another *place*:
 "You *are* a priest to the age,
  according to the order of Melchizedek."ᵇ
⁷*He* in the days of His flesh, having offered up both prayers and supplications with loud crying and tears to the *One* being able to save Him from death, and having been heard because of reverent submission, ⁸though being a Son, He learned obedience from the things He suffered, ⁹and having been perfected, He became *the* author of eternal salvation to all those obeying Him, ¹⁰having been designated by God a high priest according to the order of Melchizedek.

Warning against Drifting Away
¹¹Concerning this *there is* much speech from us, and difficult in interpretation to speak, since you have become sluggish in the hearings. ¹²For even by the time you ought to be teachers, you have need of *one* to teach you again what *is* the beginning of the principles of the oracles of God; and you have become *those* having need of milk, and not of solid food. ¹³For everyone partaking of milk *is* unskilled in *the* word of righteousness, for he is an infant. ¹⁴But solid food is *for the* mature, the *ones* by constant use having trained the senses for distinguishing both good and evil.

a 5 Psalm 2:7
b 6 Psalm 110:4

Hebrews 6
A Call to Maturity

¹Therefore, having left the beginning teaching of the Christ, we should go on to maturity, not laying again a foundation of repentance from dead works,ᵃ and faith in God, ²instruction about baptisms,ᵇ and of laying on of hands, and of *the* resurrection of *the* dead, and of eternal judgment. ³And this we will do, if God permits.
⁴For *it is* impossible for those once having been enlightened, and having tasted of the heavenly gift, and having become partakers of *the* Holy Spirit, ⁵and having tasted *the* goodness of God's word and *the* power *of the* coming age— ⁶and then having fallen away—to restore *them* again to repentance, crucifying in themselves the Son of God and subjecting *Him* to open shame.
⁷For land having drunk in the rain coming often upon it and producing vegetation useful for those for the sake of whom also it is tilled, partakes of blessing from God. ⁸But *that* bringing forth thorns and thistles *is* worthless and near to a curse, of which the end *is* unto burning.
⁹But even if we speak like this, beloved, we are persuaded of better *things*

concerning you, and *things* accompanying salvation. ¹⁰For God *is* not unjust to forget your work and the love that you have shown toward His name, having ministered to the saints, and *still* ministering.

¹¹And we desire each of you to show the same earnestness, toward the full assurance of the hope unto *the* end, ¹²so that you may not be sluggish, but imitators of those inheriting the promises through faith and patience.

God's Unchangeable Promise

¹³For God, having made His promise to Abraham, since He had no one greater to swear by, swore by Himself, ¹⁴saying, "Surely if blessing, I will bless you; and multiplying, I will multiply you."ᶜ ¹⁵And thus having waited patiently, he obtained the promise.

¹⁶For men swear by *one* greater, and an end of all their disputes, for confirmation, *is* the oath, ¹⁷in which God, desiring to show more abundantly the unchangeableness of His purpose to the heirs of the promise, guaranteed *it* by an oath, ¹⁸so that by two unchangeable things, in which *it is* impossible *for* God to lie, we may have strong encouragement, having fled for refuge, to take hold of the hope being set before *us*, ¹⁹which we have as an anchor of the soul, both sure and unshakable and entering into that within the veil, ²⁰where Jesus, *the* forerunner for us, has entered, having become a high priest to the age, according to the order of Melchizedek.

a 1 Or *from pointless rituals*
b 2 Or *cleansing rites*
c 14 Genesis 22:17

Hebrews 7
Melchizedek and Abraham
(Genesis 14:17-24)

¹For this Melchizedek, king of Salem, priest of God Most High, having met Abraham returning from the slaughter of the kings, and having blessed him, ²*is he* to whom also Abraham apportioned a tenth of all, first indeed being translated, "king of righteousness;" and then also, "king of Salem," which is, "king of peace." ³Without father, without mother, without genealogy, having neither beginning of days nor end of life, but having been made like the Son of God, he remains a priest unto all time.

⁴Now consider how great this one *was*, to whom even Abraham the patriarch gave a tenth out of the best spoils. ⁵And indeed, those out from the sons of Levi receiving the priestly office have a commandment to take a tenth from the people, according to the Law, that is, from their brothers, though having come out of the loin of Abraham. ⁶But the *one* not tracing his ancestry from them has collected a tenth from Abraham and has blessed the *one* having the promises. ⁷And apart from all dispute, the inferior is blessed by the superior.

⁸And indeed here, dying men receive tithes; but in that place, it is testified that he lives on; ⁹and so, to say a word, even Levi, the *one* receiving tithes, has been tithed through Abraham. ¹⁰For he was still in the loin of *his* father when Melchizedek met him.

A Superior Priesthood

¹¹Then indeed, if perfection were by the Levitical priesthood (for upon it the people had received *the* Law) what need *was there* still *for* another priest to arise, according to the order of Melchizedek, and not to be named according to the order of Aaron? ¹²For of the priesthood being changed, from necessity a change of Law also takes place.

¹³For *he* concerning whom these things are said belonged to another tribe, from which no one has served at the altar. ¹⁴For *it is* evident that our Lord has sprung out of Judah, a tribe as to which Moses spoke nothing concerning priests. ¹⁵And it is yet more abundantly evident if another priest according to the likeness of Melchizedek arises, ¹⁶who has been constituted not according to a law of a fleshly commandment, but according to

the power of an indestructible life. ¹⁷For it is testified:

> "You *are* a priest to the age,
>> according to the order of Melchizedek."ᵃ

¹⁸For indeed, there is a putting away of the preceding commandment, because of its weakness and uselessness ¹⁹(for the Law perfected nothing), and *the* introduction of a better hope, by which we draw near to God.

²⁰And inasmuch as *it was* not apart from an oath, for those ones truly are becoming priests without an oath, ²¹He, however, *was* with an oath through the *One* saying to Him:

> "*The* Lord has sworn and will not change His mind,
>> 'You *are* a priest to the age.'"ᵇ

²²By so much also, Jesus has become *the* guarantee of a better covenant.

²³And indeed those having become priests are many, because of being prevented from continuing by death. ²⁴But because of His abiding to the age, He holds the permanent priesthood, ²⁵wherefore also He is able to save to the uttermostᶜ those drawing near to God through Him, always living for to intercede for them.

²⁶For such a high priest indeed was fitting for us, holy, innocent, undefiled, having been separated from sinners, and having become higher than the heavens, ²⁷who has no need every day, as the first high priests, to offer up sacrifices for the own sins, then for those of the people; for He did this once for all, having offered up Himself. ²⁸For the Law appoints as high priests men having weakness; but the word of the oath, which *is* after the Law, a Son having been perfected to the age.

a 17 Psalm 110:4
b 21 Psalm 110:4
c 25 Or *forever*

Hebrews 8
Christ's Eternal Priesthood

¹Now *the* point of the things being spoken of *is that* we have such a high priest, who sat down at *the* right hand of the throne of the Majesty in the heavens, ²a minister in the holy places and in the true tabernacle, which the Lord has pitched, not man.

³For every high priest is appointed in order to offer both gifts and sacrifices; wherefore *it was* necessary *for* this One also to have something that He might offer. ⁴Then certainly if He were on earth, not even would He be a priest, there being those offering the gifts according to Law, ⁵who serve a copy and shadow of the heavenly, as Moses was divinely instructed, being about to complete the tabernacle. For He says, "See that you shall make all things according to the pattern having been shown you in the mountain."ᵃ

The New Covenant

⁶But now He has obtained a more excellent ministry, as much as He is also *the* mediator of a better covenant, which has been enacted upon better promises. ⁷For if what was first had been faultless, no place would have been sought for a second. ⁸For finding fault with them, He says:

> "Behold, *the* days are coming, says *the* Lord,
>> and I will ratify a new covenant with the house of Israel
>> and with the house of Judah,
> ⁹not according to the covenant that I made with their fathers,
>> in *the* day of My having taken hold of their hand,
>> to lead them out of *the* land of Egypt,
> because they did not continue in My covenant,
>> and I disregarded them, says *the* Lord.
> ¹⁰For this *is* the covenant that I will make with the house of Israel
>> after those days, says *the* Lord,
> putting My Laws into their mind,
>> and I will inscribe them upon their hearts;

and I will be to them God,
>   and they will be to Me for a people.
¹¹And they shall not teach, each his neighbor, and each his brother,
>   saying, 'Know the Lord,'
because all will know Me,
>   from *the* least of them to *the* greatest,
¹²because I will be merciful toward their iniquities,
>   and I shall remember their sins no more.[b]

¹³In saying, "new," He has made obsolete the first; and that which is growing old and aging *is* near vanishing.

a 5 Exodus 25:40
b 8-12 Jeremiah 31:31-34

Hebrews 9
The Earthly Tabernacle
(Exodus 25:1-9; Exodus 40:1-33)

¹Therefore also indeed, the first had regulations of worship and an earthly sanctuary. ²For a tabernacle was prepared, the first *room* in which *were* both the lampstand and the table, and the bread of the presentation, which is called *the* Holy *Place*. ³Now behind the second veil *was* a tabernacle, being called *the* Holy of Holies, ⁴having *the* golden altar of incense and the ark of the covenant, having been covered around in every part with gold, in which *was the* golden pot having the manna, and the staff of Aaron having budded, and the tablets of the covenant. ⁵And above it *were the* cherubim of glory, overshadowing the mercy seat; concerning which it is not now *the time* to speak in detail.

⁶Now these things having been prepared thus, indeed the priests enter into the first tabernacle regularly, accomplishing the sacred services. ⁷But only the high priest *enters* into the second, once in the year, not without blood, which he offers for himself and the sins of ignorance of the people.

⁸By this the Holy Spirit was signifying *that* the way into the holy places has not yet been made manifest, the first tabernacle still having a standing, ⁹which *is* a symbol for the present time, in which both gifts and sacrifices are offered, not being able to make perfect in regard to conscience the *one* worshiping, ¹⁰*consisting* only in foods and drinks and various washings—ordinances of *the* flesh being imposed until *the* time of reformation.

Redemption through His Blood

¹¹But Christ, having appeared as high priest of the good things having come,[a] by the greater and more perfect tabernacle not made by hands, that is, not of this creation, ¹²nor by blood of goats and calves, but through the own blood, He entered once for all into the holy places, having obtained eternal redemption.

¹³For if the blood of goats and of bulls and *the* ashes of a heifer sprinkling those having been defiled sanctify *them* for the purification of the flesh, ¹⁴how much more will the blood of Christ, who through *the* eternal Spirit offered Himself unblemished to God, purify our[b] conscience from dead works, in order to serve *the* living God!

¹⁵And because of this, He is *the* mediator of a new covenant, so that, death having taken place for redemption of the transgressions under the first covenant, those having been called might receive the promise of the eternal inheritance.

¹⁶For where *there is* a will, *it is* necessary to establish *the* death of the *one* having made *it*. ¹⁷For a will *is* affirmed after death, since it is not in force at the time when the *one* having made *it* is living, ¹⁸wherefore neither has the first been inaugurated apart from blood. ¹⁹For of every commandment having been spoken by Moses to all the people according to the Law, having taken the blood of calves and of goats, with water and scarlet wool and hyssop, he sprinkled both the book itself and all the people, ²⁰saying, "This *is*

the blood of the covenant, which God commanded unto you."*c*
²¹And likewise he sprinkled also the tabernacle and all the vessels of the ministry with blood. ²²And almost all things are purified with blood according to the Law, and apart from bloodshedding there is no forgiveness.
²³Therefore *it was* necessary indeed *for* the representations of the things in the heavens to be purified with these, but the heavenly things themselves with better sacrifices than these. ²⁴For Christ has entered not into holy places made by hands, copies of the true *ones*, but into heaven itself, now to appear for us in the presence of God, ²⁵nor that He should offer Himself repeatedly, just as the high priest enters into the holy places every year with *the* blood of another.
²⁶Otherwise it was necessary for Him to have suffered repeatedly from *the* foundation of *the* world. But now He has been revealed once in *the* consummation of the ages for *the* putting away of sin by the sacrifice of Himself.
²⁷And inasmuch as it is apportioned to men to die once, and after this, judgment, ²⁸so also Christ, having been offered once in order to bear *the* sins of many, will appear for a second time, apart from sin, to those awaiting Him for salvation.

a 11 BYZ and TR *that are to come*
b 14 BYZ and TR *your*
c 20 Exodus 24:8

Hebrews 10
Christ's Perfect Sacrifice
(Psalm 147:1-20; Romans 3:1-8)

¹For the Law, having a shadow of the good things coming, not the form of the things themselves, never is able each year, with the same sacrifices which they offer continually, to perfect those drawing near. ²Otherwise, would they not have ceased being offered, because of those serving having been cleansed once, no longer having conscience of sins? ³But in these, *there is* a reminder of sins every year. ⁴For *it is* impossible *for the* blood of bulls and of goats to take away sins. ⁵Therefore coming into the world, He says:

"Sacrifice and offering You have not desired,
    but a body You have prepared me.
⁶In burnt offerings and *offerings* for sin
    You have not delighted.
⁷Then I said, 'Behold, I have come—
    in *the* scroll of *the* book it is written of Me—
to do Your will, O God.'"*a*

⁸Saying above, "Sacrifice and offering and burnt offerings and *offerings* for sin, You have not desired, nor have You delighted in" (which are offered according to *the* Law), ⁹then He said, "Behold, I have come to do Your will." He takes away the first that He might establish the second. ¹⁰By that will, we are having been sanctified through the offering of the body of Jesus Christ once for all.
¹¹And indeed every priest stands every day, ministering and offering the same sacrifices repeatedly, which never are able to take away sins. ¹²But this *One*, having offered one sacrifice for sins in perpetuity, sat down at *the* right hand of God, ¹³the henceforth awaiting until His enemies should be placed *as* a footstool for His feet. ¹⁴For by one offering, He has perfected for all time those being sanctified.
¹⁵And the Holy Spirit also bears witness to us; for after having said before:

¹⁶"This *is* the covenant that I will make with them,
    after those days, says *the* Lord,
putting My Laws into their hearts,
    and I will inscribe them into their mind,"*b*
¹⁷and,
"Their sins and their lawless acts,
    I will remember no more."*c*

[18]Now where *there is* forgiveness of these, no longer *is there* an offering for sin.

A Call to Persevere
(Jude 1:17-23)

[19]Therefore brothers, having confidence for entering the holy places by the blood of Jesus, [20]by a new and living way, which He dedicated for us through the veil that is His flesh, [21]and *having* a great priest over the house of God, [22]we should draw near with a sincere heart, in full assurance of faith, *our* hearts having been sprinkled clean from an evil conscience and *our* body having been washed with pure water.

[23]We should hold fast to the confession of *our* hope, unwavering; for the *One* having promised *is* faithful. [24]And we should think toward stirring up one another to love and to good works, [25]not forsaking the assembling together of ourselves as *is the* custom with some, but encouraging *one another*, and so much more as you see the Day drawing near.

[26]For *if* we sin willingly after *we are* to receive the knowledge of the truth, no longer remains a sacrifice for sins, [27]but a certain terrifying expectation of judgment and fury of fire being about to devour the adversaries. [28]Anyone having set aside *the* Law of Moses dies without mercies on the basis of two or three witnesses. [29]How much worse punishment do you think will he deserve, the *one* having trampled upon the Son of God, and having esteemed ordinary the blood of the covenant by which he was sanctified, and having insulted the Spirit of grace?

[30]For we know the *One* having said, "Vengeance *is* Mine; I will repay,"[d] and again, "*The* Lord will judge His people."[e] [31]*it is* a fearful thing to fall into *the* hands of *the* living God.

[32]But remember the former days in which, having been enlightened, you endured a great conflict of sufferings, [33]this indeed, being made a spectacle both by revilings and tribulations; now this, having become partners of those passing through *them* thus. [34]For both you sympathized with the prisoners and you accepted the plundering of your possessions with joy, knowing yourselves to have a better and abiding possession.

[35]Therefore do not throw away your confidence, which has a great reward. [36]For you have need of endurance, so that, having done the will of God, you may receive the promise. [37]For

"Yet in a very while little,
 the *One* coming will come, and
 will not delay.
[38]But My righteous one[f] will live by
 faith;
 and if he might shrink back,
 My soul does not take pleasure
 in him."[g]

[39]But we are not of *those* drawing back to destruction, but of faith to *the* preserving *of the* soul.

a 5-7 Psalm 40:6-8
b 16 Jeremiah 31:33
c 17 Jeremiah 31:34
d 30 Deuteronomy 32:35
e 30 Deuteronomy 32:36; Psalm 135:14
f 38 BYZ and TR *But the righteous*
g 38 Habakkuk 2:3,4

Hebrews 11
Faith and Assurance

[1]Now faith is *the* assurance of *things* hoped for, *the* conviction of things not being seen. [2]For in this the ancients were commended.

[3]By faith we understand the universe to have been formed by *the* word of God, so that the things being seen have not been made from the things being visible.

The Faith of Abel, Enoch, Noah

[4]By faith Abel offered to God a more excellent sacrifice than Cain, through which he was testified to be righteous, God bearing witness to his gifts; and through it, having died, he still speaks.

[5]By faith Enoch was translated not to see death, and he was not found, because God had taken him up.[a] For before the translation, he was commended to have

pleased God. ⁶And without faith, *it is* impossible to please *Him*. For it behooves the one drawing near to God to believe that He exists and *that* He becomes a rewarder to those earnestly seeking Him out.

⁷By faith Noah, having been divinely instructed concerning the things not yet seen, having been moved with fear, prepared an ark for *the* salvation of his household, by which he condemned the world and became heir of the righteousness *that is* according to faith.

The Faith of Abraham and Sarah
(Genesis 15:1-7; Romans 4:1-12; Galatians 3:1-9; James 2:14-26)

⁸By faith Abraham, being called to go out into a place that he was going to receive for an inheritance, obeyed and went out, not knowing where he is going. ⁹By faith he sojourned in *the* land of the promise, as *in* a foreign *country*, having dwelt in tents with Isaac and Jacob, the joint-heirs of the same promise. ¹⁰For he was awaiting the city having foundations, of which *the* architect and builder *is* God. ¹¹By faith also Sarah, herself barren, received power for *the* conception of seed, even beyond the opportune age, since she considered the *One* having promised faithful. ¹²Therefore also were born from one man, and he having been as good as dead, as the stars of heaven in multitude, and countless as the sand by the shore of the sea.

¹³These all died in faith, not having received the promises, but having seen them from afar, and having embraced *them*, and having confessed that they are strangers and sojourners on the earth. ¹⁴For those saying such things make manifest that they are seeking *their* own country. ¹⁵And indeed if they had been remembering that from where they came out, they would have had opportunity to return. ¹⁶But now they stretch forward to a better *one*, that is, a heavenly *one*. Therefore God is not ashamed of them, to be called their God; for He has prepared a city for them.

¹⁷By faith Abraham, being tested, has offered up Isaac. Even the *one* having received the promises was offering up *his* only begotten son, ¹⁸as to whom it was said, "In Isaac your offspring will be reckoned,"ᵇ ¹⁹having reasoned that God *was* able even to raise *him* out from *the* dead, from where he received him also in a simile.

The Faith of Isaac, Jacob, Joseph

²⁰By faith also Isaac blessed Jacob and Esau concerning *the things* coming. ²¹By faith Jacob, dying, blessed each of the sons of Joseph and worshiped on the top of his staff. ²²By faith Joseph, dying, made mention concerning the exodus of the sons of Israel and gave instructions concerning his bones.

The Faith of Moses

²³By faith Moses, having been born, was hidden three months by his parents, because they saw the little child *was* beautiful, and they did not fear the edict of the king. ²⁴By faith Moses, having become grown, refused to be called *the* son of Pharaoh's daughter, ²⁵having chosen to suffer affliction with the people of God, rather than to have *the* fleeting enjoyment of sin, ²⁶having esteemed the reproach of Christ greater wealth than the treasures of Egypt; for he was looking toward the reward. ²⁷By faith he left Egypt, not having feared the anger of the king; for he persevered, as seeing the Invisible *One*. ²⁸By faith he has kept the Passover and the sprinkling of the blood, so that the *one* destroying the firstborn would not touch them. ²⁹By faith they passed through the Red Sea as through dry land, which the Egyptians, an attempt having made, were swallowed up.

The Faith of Many

³⁰By faith the walls of Jericho fell, having been encircled for seven days.

³¹By faith Rahab the prostitute did not perish with those having disobeyed, having received the spies with peace.
³²And what more shall I say? For the time will fail me, telling of Gideon, Barak, Samson, Jephthah, also David, and Samuel, and the prophets, ³³who by faith conquered kingdoms, administered justice, obtained promises; shut *the* mouths of lions, ³⁴quenched *the* power of fire, escaped *the* mouths of *the* sword; acquired strength out of weakness, became mighty in war, put to flight foreign armies.
³⁵Women received back their dead by resurrection; and others were tortured, not having accepted release, so that they might obtain a better resurrection. ³⁶And others received *the* trial of mockings and of scourgings, and in addition, of chains and imprisonment.
³⁷They were stoned, they were sawed in two,ᶜ they were killed by slaughter of *the* sword; they wandered in sheepskins, in goatskins, being destitute, being oppressed, being mistreated; ³⁸of whom the world was not worthy; wandering in deserts, and mountains, and caves, and holes of the earth.
³⁹And these all, having been commended through the faith, did not receive the promise, ⁴⁰God having planned something better for us, so that not apart from us, they should be made perfect.

a 5 Genesis 5:24
b 18 Genesis 21:12
c 37 NE, WH, BYZ, and TR include *they were put to the test,*

Hebrews 12
The Call to Endurance
(2 Timothy 2:1-13)

¹Therefore we also, having such a great cloud of witnesses encompassing us, having laid aside every weight and the sin easily entangling, should run with endurance the race lying before us, ²looking to Jesus, the founder and perfecter of *our* faith, who in view of the joy lying before Him endured *the* cross, having despised *its* shame, and sat down at right hand of the throne of God. ³For consider fully the *One* having endured such great hostility from sinners against Himself, so that you shall not grow weary, fainting in your souls.

God Disciplines His Sons

⁴Not yet have you resisted unto blood, struggling against sin, ⁵and you have forgotten the exhortation that addresses you as to sons:
"My son, do not regard lightly *the* Lord's discipline,
nor faint being reproved by Him.
⁶For *the* Lord disciplines whom He loves,
and He scourges every son whom He receives.ᵃ
⁷If you endure discipline, God is treating you as sons; for what son *is there* whom *his* father does not discipline? ⁸But if you are without discipline, of which they have all become partakers, then you are illegitimate children and not sons. ⁹Furthermore indeed, we have had fathers of our flesh, correctors, and we respected *them*; and shall we not much more be in subjection to the Father of spirits and shall live?
¹⁰For truly they were disciplining *us* for a few days, according to that seeming good to them; but He for *our* benefitting, in order to share His holiness. ¹¹And all discipline indeed for those being present, does not seem to be of joy, but of grief; but afterward it yields *the* peaceable fruit of righteousness to those having been trained by it.
¹²Therefore lift up the drooping hands and enfeebled knees, ¹³and make straight paths for your feet, so that the lame should not be put out of joint, but rather should be healed.

A Call to Holiness
(1 Peter 1:13-21)

¹⁴Pursue peace with all, and holiness, without which no one will see the Lord, ¹⁵observing lest any be failing of the

grace of God, lest any root of bitterness springing up should trouble *you* and by this, the many might be defiled, ¹⁶lest *there be* any fornicator or profane person, as Esau, who for one meal sold his birthright. ¹⁷For you know that even afterward, wishing to inherit the blessing, he was rejected; for he found no place of repentance, although having earnestly sought it with tears.

An Unshakable Kingdom
(Exodus 20:18-21; Deuteronomy 5:22-33)

¹⁸For you have not come to *that* being touched and having been kindled with fire, and to darkness, and to gloom, and to storm, ¹⁹and to *the* sound of a trumpet, and to a voice of words which those having heard excused themselves, *asking the* word not to be addressed to them, ²⁰for they could not bear that being commanded: "If even a beast should touch the mountain, it shall be stoned."[b] ²¹And the thing appearing was so fearful *that* Moses said, "I am greatly afraid and trembling."[c]

²²But you have come to Mount Zion, and *the* city of *the* living God, *the* heavenly Jerusalem, and to myriads of angels, ²³and *to the* assembly, to *the* church of *the* firstborn having been enrolled in *the* heavens, and to God *the* judge of all, and to *the* spirits of *the* righteous having been perfected, ²⁴and to Jesus *the* mediator of a new covenant, and to *the* sprinkling of blood, speaking better things than that of Abel.

²⁵Take heed lest you refuse the *One* speaking. For if they did not escape, having refused the *One* divinely instructing *them* on earth, much less we, turning away from the *One* from *the* heavens, ²⁶whose voice shook the earth at that time; but now He has promised, saying, "Yet once *more* I will shake not only the earth, but also heaven."[d] ²⁷And this, "Yet once *more*," signifies the removing of the *things* being shaken, as having been created, so that the things not being shaken should remain.

²⁸Therefore, receiving a kingdom not to be shaken, we may have grace, by which we may serve God well pleasingly, with fear and reverence. ²⁹For also, our God *is* a consuming fire.[e]

a 5-6 Proverbs 3:11,12
b 20 Exodus 19:12,13
c 21 See Deuteronomy 9:19
d 26 Haggai 2:6
e 29 Deuteronomy 4:24

Hebrews 13
Love for Brothers

¹Let brotherly love abide. ²Do not be forgetful of hospitality, for through this, some have entertained angels unawares. ³Remember prisoners as being bound with *them*; those being mistreated as yourselves also being in *the* body.

⁴*Let* marriage *be* honorable in all, and the marriage bed undefiled; for God will judge the sexually immoral and adulterers.

Christ's Unchanging Nature

⁵*Let your* manner of life *be* without covetousness, being satisfied with the present; for He Himself has said:

"Never will I leave you,
 never will I forsake you."[a]

⁶So we are confident to say:

"*The* Lord *is* my helper, and I will not be afraid;
 what shall man do to me?"[b]

⁷Remember those leading you, who spoke the word of God to you, of whom, considering the outcome of *their* way of life, you are to imitate the faith. ⁸Jesus Christ *is* the same yesterday, and today, and to the ages.

⁹Do not be carried away *by* various and strange teachings; for *it is* good for the heart to be strengthened by grace, not by foods, in which those being devoted were not profited. ¹⁰We have an altar from which those serving in the tabernacle have no authority to eat.

¹¹For the bodies of those animals whose blood is brought for sin into the holy places by the high priest are burned outside the camp. ¹²Therefore Jesus also

suffered outside the gate, so that he might sanctify the people by the own blood. ¹³Therefore we should go forth to Him outside the camp, bearing His reproach. ¹⁴For here we do not have an abiding city, but we are seeking for the coming *one*.

Sacrifice, Obedience, and Prayer

¹⁵Through Him then, we should offer *the* sacrifice of praise continually, everything to God, that is, *the* fruit of *the* lips confessing His name. ¹⁶And do not be forgetful of the good, and of the sharing; for God is well pleased with such sacrifices.

¹⁷Obey you those leading and be submissive—for they watch over your souls, as about to give account—so that they may do this with joy and not groaning, for this *is* unprofitable for you. ¹⁸Pray for us, for we are persuaded that we have a good conscience, desiring to conduct ourselves well in all things. ¹⁹And more abundantly I exhort *you* to do this, so that I may be restored to you more quickly.

Benediction and Farewell

²⁰Now *may* the God of peace, having brought out from *the* dead the great Shepherd of the sheep, our Lord Jesus, by *the* blood of *the* eternal covenant, ²¹equip you in everything good,ᶜ in order to do His will, working in usᵈ that which *is* well pleasing before Him, through Jesus Christ, to whom *be* the glory to the ages of the ages. Amen.

²²Now I exhort you, brothers, bear with the word of exhortation, for I have only written to you in few words.

²³You know our brother Timothy has been released, with whom I will see you if he should come sooner.

²⁴Greet all those leading you and all the saints.

Those from Italy greet you.

²⁵Grace *be* with all of you.ᵉ

a 5 Deuteronomy 31:6
b 6 Psalm 118:6
c 21 BYZ and TR *in every good work*
d 21 BYZ and TR *you*
e 25 BYZ and TR include *Amen*.

James

James 1
Greetings from James
(Jude 1:1-2)

¹James, a servant of God and of *the* Lord Jesus Christ,
To the twelve tribes in the Dispersion:
Greetings.

Rejoicing in Trials
(Philippians 1:12-20)

²Esteem *it* all joy, my brothers, when you might fall into various trials, ³knowing that testing of your faith produces endurance. ⁴And let endurance have *its* perfect work, so that you may be perfect and complete, lacking in nothing.

⁵Now if any of you lacks wisdom, let him ask from God, the *One* giving generously to all and not finding fault, and it will be given to him. ⁶But let him ask in faith, doubting nothing, for the *one* doubting is like a wave of *the* sea, being blown and being tossed by the wind. ⁷For let that man not suppose that he will receive anything from the Lord. ⁸*He is* a double-minded man, unstable in all his ways.

⁹But let the brother of low degree boast in his exaltation, ¹⁰and he who *is* rich, in his humiliation, because he will pass away like a flower of grass. ¹¹For the sun has risen with *its* burning heat and withered the grass, and its flower has fallen, and the beauty of *its* appearance has perished. Thus also the rich *man* will fade away in the midst of his pursuits.

¹²Blessed *is the* man who endures trial, because, having been approved, he will receive the crown of life that He has promised to those loving Him.

Good and Perfect Gifts

¹³Let no one being tempted say, "I am being tempted by God." For God is unable to be tempted by evils, and He Himself tempts no one. ¹⁴But a man is tempted,

being drawn away and being enticed by the own desire. ¹⁵Then desire having conceived, gives birth to sin; and sin having become fully grown, brings forth death.

¹⁶Do not be misled, my beloved brothers. ¹⁷Every good act of giving and every perfect gift is from above, coming down from the Father of lights, with whom there is no variation or shadow of shifting. ¹⁸Having willed *it*, He brought us forth by *the* word of truth, for us to be a kind of firstfruits of His creatures.

Hearing and Doing

¹⁹Know *this*, my beloved brothers. But let every man be swift to hear, slow to speak, slow unto anger; ²⁰for man's anger does not produce *the* righteousness of God. ²¹Therefore, having put aside all filthiness and abounding of wickedness, receive in humility the implanted word, being able to save your souls.

²²But be doers of *the* word, and not hearers only, deceiving yourselves, ²³because if anyone is a hearer of *the* word and not a doer, this one is like a man looking at his natural face in a mirror, ²⁴for he has viewed himself and has gone away, and immediately he has forgotten of what manner he was. ²⁵But the *one* having looked intently into *the* perfect law, that of freedom, and having continued in *it*, not having been a forgetful hearer but a doer of *the* work—this one will be blessed in his work.

²⁶If anyone seems to be religious, not bridling his tongue, but deceiving his heart, the religion of this one *is* worthless. ²⁷Pure and undefiled religion before the God and Father is this: to visit orphans and widows in their tribulation; to keep oneself unstained from the world.

James 2
A Warning against Favoritism

¹My brothers, do not with partiality hold the faith of our Lord Jesus Christ of glory. ²For if a man might come into your assembly in splendid apparel with gold rings, and a poor *man* in shabby apparel also might come in, ³and you should look upon the *one* wearing the splendid apparel and should say, "You sit here honorably," and to the poor should say, "You stand," or, "Sit there under my footstool," ⁴then have you not made a distinction among yourselves and have become judges *with* evil thoughts?

⁵Listen, my beloved brothers: Has not God chosen the poor in this world *to be* rich in faith and heirs of the kingdom that He promised to those loving Him? ⁶But you have dishonored the poor. Are not the rich oppressing you and they dragging you into court? ⁷Are they not blaspheming the good Name having been called upon you?

⁸If indeed you keep *the* royal law according to the Scripture, "You shall love your neighbor as yourself,"ᵃ you are doing well. ⁹But if you show partiality, you are committing sin, being convicted by the law as transgressors.

¹⁰For whoever shall keep the whole Law, but shall stumble in one *point*, he has become guilty of all. ¹¹For the *One* having said, "You shall not commit adultery,"ᵇ also said, "You shall not murder."ᶜ But if you do not commit adultery, but do commit murder, you have become a transgressor of *the* Law.

¹²So speak and so act as being about to be judged by *the* Law of freedom. ¹³For judgment without mercy *will be* to the *one* not having shown mercy. Mercy triumphs over judgment.

Faith and Works
(Genesis 15:1-7; Romans 4:1-12; Galatians 3:1-9; Hebrews 11:8-19)

¹⁴What *is* the profit, my brothers, if anyone says to have faith, but has no works? Is the faith able to save him? ¹⁵Now if a brother or a sister is without clothes and lacking of daily food, ¹⁶and anyone out from you says to them, "Go in peace; be warmed and be filled," but

does not give to them the needful things for the body, what *is* the profit? ¹⁷So also, faith by itself if it has not works, is dead. ¹⁸But someone will say, "You have faith, and I have works." Show me your faith without works, and I will show you faith by my works. ¹⁹You believe that God is one. You are doing well! Even the demons believe *that*, and shudder!

²⁰But do you want to come to know, O foolish man, that faith apart from works is worthless?ᵈ ²¹Was not Abraham our father justified by works, having offered his son Isaac upon the altar? ²²You see that *his* faith was working with his works, and by *his* works, *his* faith was perfected. ²³And the Scripture was fulfilled, saying, "And Abraham believed God, and it was counted to him for righteousness,"ᵉ and he was called a friend of God. ²⁴You see that a man is justified by works, and not by faith alone.

²⁵And likewise was not Rahab the prostitute also justified by works, having received the messengers and having sent *them* forth by another way? ²⁶For just as the body apart from spirit is dead, so also faith apart from works is dead.

a 8 Leviticus 19:18
b 11 Exodus 20:14; Deuteronomy 5:18
c 11 Exodus 20:13; Deuteronomy 5:17
d 20 BYZ and TR *dead*
e 23 Genesis 15:6

James 3
Taming the Tongue

¹Not many *of you* should be teachers my brothers, knowing that we will receive greater judgment. ²For we all stumble in many ways. If anyone does not stumble in what he says, this one *is* a perfect man, able indeed to bridle the whole body.

³Now if we put bits into the mouths of the horses for them to obey us, we turn about even their whole body. ⁴Behold also the ships, being so great and being driven by strong winds, are turned about by a very small rudder wherever the impulse of the *one* steering resolves. ⁵Thus also the tongue is a small member, and boasts exceeding things. Behold a small fire, how great a forest it kindles. ⁶The tongue also *is* a fire, the world of unrighteousness. The tongue is set among our members, defiling all the body, and setting on fire the course of nature, and *itself* being set on fire by Gehenna.

⁷For every species both of beasts and of birds, both of creeping things and things of the sea, is subdued and has been subdued by the human race, ⁸but no one of men is able to subdue the tongue; *it is* an unruly evil, full of deadly poison.

⁹With it we bless our Lord and Father, and with it we curse men, those being made according to *the* likeness of God. ¹⁰Out of the same mouth proceed forth blessing and cursing. My brothers, these things ought not to be so. ¹¹Does the spring pour forth out of the same opening *both* fresh and bitter? ¹²Is a fig tree able, my brothers, to produce olives? Or a vine, figs? Neither *is* a salt *spring able* to produce fresh water.

The Wisdom from Above

¹³Who *is* wise and understanding among you; let him show his works out of the good conduct, in *the* humility of wisdom. ¹⁴But if you have bitter jealousy and self-interest in your heart, do not boast *of it* and lie against the truth. ¹⁵This is not the wisdom coming down from above, but *is* earthly, unspiritual, demonic. ¹⁶For where jealousy and self-interest *exist*, there *will be* disorder and every evil thing. ¹⁷But *the* wisdom from above is indeed first pure, then peaceable, gentle, reasonable, full of mercy and of good fruits, impartial, sincere. ¹⁸And *the* fruit of righteousness is sown in peace by those making peace.

James 4
Warning against Pride

¹From where *come* quarrels and from where conflicts among you? *Is it* not from there, out of your passions warring in

your members? ²You desire and do not have. You kill and covet and are not able to obtain. You fight and quarrel. You do not have, because you do not ask. ³You ask and do not receive, because you ask wrongly, that you may spend *it* in your pleasures.
⁴Adulteresses!ᵃ Do you not know that friendship with the world is hostility *with* God? Therefore whoever has chosen to be a friend of the world is appointed an enemy of God. ⁵Or do you think that the Scripture says in vain, "The Spirit that He has made to dwell in us yearns with envy"? ⁶But He gives greater grace. Therefore it says:

> "God opposes *the* proud,
> but gives grace to *the* humble."ᵇ

Drawing Near to God

⁷Therefore subject yourselves to God. But resist the devil, and he will flee from you. ⁸Draw near to God, and He will draw near to you. Cleanse *your* hands, *you* sinners, and have purified hearts, *you* double-minded. ⁹Be grieved and mourn and weep. Let your laughter be turned to mourning, and the joy to gloom. ¹⁰Humble yourselves in the presence of *the* Lord, and He will exalt you.
¹¹Do not speak against one another, brothers. The *one* speaking against *his* brother or judging his brother speaks against *the* Law and judges *the* Law. But if you judge *the* Law, you are not a doer of *the* Law, but a judge. ¹²There is one Lawgiver and Judge, the *One* being able to save and to destroy. But who are you judging the neighbor?

Do Not Boast of Tomorrow

¹³Come now, those saying, "Today or tomorrow we will go into this city, and will spend a year there, and will trade, and will make a profit," ¹⁴who know not what *is* on the next day. What *is* your life? It is just a vapor, appearing for a little *while*, and then vanishing.
¹⁵Instead you *ought* to say, "If the Lord should will, both we will live and we will do this or that." ¹⁶But now you boast in your arrogance. All such boasting is evil. ¹⁷Therefore to the *one* knowing to do good, and not doing, it is sin.

a 4 See Hosea 3:1
b 6 Proverbs 3:34

James 5
Warning to the Rich

¹Come now, *you* rich, weep, wailing over the miseries that *are* coming upon you. ²Your riches have rotted, and your garments have become moth-eaten. ³Your gold and silver have corroded, and their rust will be for a testimony against you and will eat your flesh like fire.
You have treasured up in *the* last days. ⁴Behold, the wage of the workmen having harvested your fields, having been kept back by you, cries out, and the cries of those having harvested have entered into the ears of *the* Lord of Hosts.
⁵You lived in luxury and lived in self-indulgence upon the earth. You have fattened your hearts in *the* day of slaughter. ⁶You have condemned *and* have put to death the righteous; he does not resist you.

Patience in Suffering
(Job 1:1-5)

⁷Therefore be patient, brothers, until the coming of the Lord. Behold, the farmer awaits the precious fruit of the earth, being patient for it until it receives *the* early and latter *rains*. ⁸You also be patient; strengthen your hearts, because the coming of the Lord has drawn near. ⁹Do not grumble against one another, brothers, so that you may not be condemned. Behold, the Judge is standing before the doors.
¹⁰Brothers *as* an example of suffering evils and of patience, take the prophets who spoke in the name of *the* Lord. ¹¹Behold, we count blessed those having persevered. You have heard of the perseverance of Job, and you have seen the outcome from *the* Lord, that the Lord is full of compassion and *is* merciful.

¹²But before all things, my brothers, do not swear, neither *by* heaven, nor the earth, nor any other oath. But let your "Yes" be yes, and the "No," no, so that you might not fall under judgment.

The Prayer of Faith

¹³Is anyone among you suffering hardships? Let him pray. Is anyone cheerful? Let him sing praises. ¹⁴Is anyone among you sick? Let him call near the elders of the church, and let them pray over him, having anointed him with oil in the name of the Lord. ¹⁵And the prayer of faith will save the one ailing, and the Lord will raise him up, and if he might be *one* having committed sins, it will be forgiven him.

¹⁶Therefore confess the sins to one another and pray for one another, so that you may be healed. *The* prayer of a righteous *man* being made effective prevails much. ¹⁷Elijah was a man of like nature to us, and with fervent prayer he prayed *for it* not to rain, and it did not rain upon the earth three years and six months. ¹⁸And he prayed again, and the heaven gave rain, and the earth produced its fruit.

Restoring a Sinner

¹⁹My brothers, if anyone among you might wander from the truth, and someone should bring him back, ²⁰let him know that the *one* having brought back a sinner from *the* error of his way will save his soul from death, and will cover over a multitude of sins.

1 Peter

1 Peter 1
Greetings from Peter
(2 Peter 1:1-2)

¹Peter, an apostle of Jesus Christ,
To *the* elect sojourners of *the* dispersion of Pontus, Galatia, Cappadocia, Asia, and Bithynia, ²according to *the* foreknowledge of God *the* Father, by *the* sanctification of *the* Spirit unto *the* obedience and sprinkling of *the* blood of Jesus Christ:
May grace and peace be multiplied to you.

A Living Hope

³Blessed *be* the God and Father of our Lord Jesus Christ, the *One* according to His great mercy having begotten us again to a living hope, through *the* resurrection of Jesus Christ out from *the* dead, ⁴to an inheritance imperishable and undefiled and unfading, being reserved in *the* heavens for you, ⁵who *are* being guarded by *the* power of God through faith, for *the* salvation ready to be revealed in *the* last time, ⁶in which you greatly rejoice, at present for a little while if it is being necessary, having been put to grief by various trials, ⁷so that the proven genuineness of your faith, more precious than gold, perishing though being refined by fire, may be discovered to result in praise and glory and honor in *the* revelation of Jesus Christ, ⁸whom not having seen you love, on whom now believing *though* not seeing you also exult with joy inexpressible and filled with glory, ⁹receiving the outcome of your faith, *the* salvation of *your* souls.

¹⁰Concerning this salvation, *the* prophets sought out and searched out diligently, having prophesied of the grace toward you, ¹¹inquiring into what or what manner of time the Spirit of Christ in them was signifying, testifying beforehand of the sufferings of Christ and the glories after these, ¹²to whom it was revealed that they were serving not themselves, but you, in those things which now have been proclaimed to you by those having proclaimed the gospel to you by *the* Holy Spirit having been sent from heaven, into which angels desire to look.

A Call to Holiness
(Hebrews 12:14-17)

¹³Therefore having girded up the loins of your mind, being sober-minded, set *your* hope fully upon the grace being brought to you in *the* revelation of Jesus Christ,

¹⁴as children of obedience, not being conformed to the passions in your former ignorance. ¹⁵But as the *One* having called you *is* holy, be holy yourselves also in all *your* conduct, ¹⁶because it has been written: "You shall be holy, because I am holy."ᵃ

¹⁷And if you call on *as* Father the *One* judging impartially according to the work of each, conduct yourselves in fear during the time of your sojourn, ¹⁸knowing that you were redeemed from your futile manner of life handed down from *your* fathers, not by perishable things—by silver or by gold— ¹⁹but by *the* precious blood of Christ, as of a lamb without blemish and without spot, ²⁰having been foreknown indeed before *the* foundation of *the* world, but having been revealed in the last times for the sake of you, ²¹who by Him believe in God, the *one* having raised Him up out from *the* dead and having given Him glory, so as for your faith and hope to be in God.

The Word of the Lord Stands
(Isaiah 40:6-8)

²²Having purified your souls in obedience to the truth unto sincere brotherly love, love one another fervently, out of a pure heart,ᵇ ²³having been born again, not of perishable seed, but of imperishable, by *the* living and abiding word of God, ²⁴because,

"All flesh *is* like grass,
    and all *the* glory of it like *the* flower of grass.
The grass withers, and the flower falls away,
    ²⁵but the word of *the* Lord abides to the age."ᶜ

And this is the word having been proclaimed to you.

a 16 Leviticus 11:44,45; 19:2; 20:7
b 22 SBL, NE, and WH *from the heart*
c 24-25 Isaiah 40:6-8

1 Peter 2
The Lord is Good

¹Therefore having put aside all malice, and all deceit, and hypocrisy, and envies, and all evil speakings, ²like newborn babies, crave pure reasonable milk, so that by it you may grow up in respect to salvation, ³if indeed you have tasted that the Lord *is* good.

The Living Stone
(Isaiah 28:14-22; 1 Corinthians 3:10-15)

⁴Coming to *Him*, a living stone, indeed rejected by men, but chosen *and* precious in the sight of God, ⁵you yourselves also, as living stones, are being built up as a spiritual house into a holy priesthood, to offer spiritual sacrifices acceptable to God through Jesus Christ. ⁶Therefore it is contained in Scripture:

"Behold, I lay in Zion a stone,
    a chosen precious cornerstone;
and the *one* believing on Him,
    shall not be put to shame."ᵃ

⁷Therefore the preciousness *is* to you believing. But *to those* disobeying,

"*The* stone which those building have rejected,
    this has become into *the* head of *the* corner,"ᵇ

⁸and,

"A stone of stumbling
    and a rock of offense."ᶜ

They stumble at being disobedient to the word, to which also they were appointed. ⁹But you *are* a chosen race, a royal priesthood, a holy nation, a people for *His* possession, so that you may proclaim the excellencies of the *One* having called you out of darkness into His marvelous light, ¹⁰who once *were* not a people, but now *are the* people of God; those not having received mercy, but now having received mercy.

¹¹Beloved, I exhort *you* as aliens and sojourners, to abstain from fleshly desires, which war against the soul, ¹²keeping your conduct among the Gentiles honorable, so that wherein which they speak against you as evildoers, through having witnessed the good deeds, they may glorify God in *the* day of visitation.

Submission to Authorities
(Romans 13:1-7)

¹³Be in subjection to every human institution for the sake of the Lord, whether to *the* king as being supreme, ¹⁴or to governors as being sent by him for vengeance to evildoers and praise to well-doers, ¹⁵because the will of God is this: doing good, to put to silence the ignorance of foolish men, ¹⁶as free, and not having the freedom as a cover-up for evil, but as servants of God.

¹⁷Honor everyone: love the brotherhood, fear God, Honor the king.

¹⁸Servants, be subject to masters with all fear, not only to the good and gentle, but also to the unreasonable. ¹⁹For this *is* acceptable, if for sake of conscience toward God, anyone endures griefs, suffering unjustly. ²⁰For what kind of credit *is it*, if sinning and being struck, you shall endure? But if you shall endure doing good and suffering, this *is* commendable before God.

Christ's Example of Suffering
(Isaiah 53:1-8; Matthew 26:57-68; Mark 14:53-65; John 18:19-24)

²¹For to this hereunto you have been called, because Christ also suffered for you, leaving you an example that you should follow after His steps:

²²"Who committed no sin,
  neither was deceit found in His mouth."[d]

²³Who being reviled
  did not retaliate;
suffering did not threaten,
  but He gave *Himself* over to Him judging justly.

²⁴Who Himself bore our sins in His body on the tree,
  so that, having been dead to sins, we might live to righteousness.
"By whose scourge marks you have been healed."[e]

²⁵For you were like sheep going astray,[f] but now you have returned to the Shepherd and Overseer of your souls.

a 6 Isaiah 28:16
b 7 Psalm 118:22
c 8 Isaiah 8:14
d 22 Isaiah 53:9
e 24 Isaiah 53:5
f 25 Isaiah 53:6

1 Peter 3
Wives and Husbands
(Song of Solomon 1:1-3; Ephesians 5:22-33)

¹Likewise wives, be subject to the own husbands so that, even if any are disobedient to the word, they will be won over without word by the conduct of the wives, ²having witnessed your respectful, pure conduct, ³whose adorning let not be the external, of braiding of hair and putting around of gold, or putting on of garments, ⁴but the hidden man of the heart, in the imperishable of the gentle and quiet spirit, which is of great worth before God.

⁵For in this way formerly, the holy women also hoping in God used to adorn themselves, being subject to the own husbands, ⁶as Sarah obeyed Abraham, calling him lord, of whom you have become children, doing good and not fearing *any* consternation.

⁷Husbands do likewise, dwelling with *them* according to knowledge, as with a weaker vessel, with the female, rendering honor as joint-heirs also of *the* grace of life, so as for your prayers not to be hindered.

Turning from Evil

⁸Now the end: All *be* single-minded, sympathetic, loving as brothers, tender-hearted, humble, ⁹not repaying evil for evil or insult for insult; but on the contrary blessing, because to this you were called, so that you should inherit blessing. ¹⁰For,

"The *one* desiring to love life,
  and to see good days,
let him keep the tongue from evil,
  and lips not to speak deceit.

¹¹Also let him turn away from evil,
  and let him do good.
Let him seek peace and let him pursue it.

¹²Because *the* eyes of *the* Lord *are* on *the* righteous,
    and His ears toward their prayer.
But *the* face of *the* Lord *is* against those doing evil."[a]

¹³And who *is* he who will harm you, if you should be zealous for that which *is* good?

Suffering for Righteousness
(Romans 6:15-23)

¹⁴But even if you should suffer because of righteousness, *you are* blessed. "And you should not be afraid of their threats,[b] neither should you be troubled."[c] ¹⁵But in your hearts sanctify Christ *as* Lord, always ready for a defense to everyone asking you an account concerning the hope in you; yet with gentleness and fear, ¹⁶having a good conscience, so that in the case that they might speak against you, those reviling your good manner of life in Christ, they shall be ashamed.

¹⁷For *it is* better to suffer *for* doing good, if the will of God wills *it*, than doing evil, ¹⁸because Christ also suffered[d] once for sins, *the* righteous for *the* unrighteous, so that He might bring you to God, having been put to death indeed in *the* flesh, but having been made alive in *the* spirit, ¹⁹in which also having gone, He preached to the spirits in prison ²⁰at one time having disobeyed, when the longsuffering of God was waiting in *the* days of Noah, of *the* ark being prepared, in which a few—that is, eight souls—were saved through water, ²¹which also prefigures *the* baptism now saving you, not a putting away of *the* filth of flesh, but *the* demand of a good conscience toward God, through *the* resurrection of Jesus Christ, ²²who is at *the* right hand of God, having gone into heaven, angels and authorities and powers having been subjected to Him.

a 10-12 Psalm 34:12-16
b 14 Or *fear what they fear*
c 14 Isaiah 8:12
d 18 NE and WH *died*

1 Peter 4
Living for God's Glory

¹Therefore Christ having suffered[a] in *the* flesh, you also arm yourselves with the same mind, because the *one* having suffered *in the* flesh is done with sin, ²so as to live the remaining time in *the* flesh no longer to men's desires, but to *the* will of God. ³For the time past *is* sufficient to have carried out the desire of the Gentiles, having walked in sensuality, lusts, drunkenness, orgies, carousing, and abominable idolatries.

⁴With respect to this, they think it strange of you not running with *them* into the same overflow of debauchery, speaking evil *of you*, ⁵who will give account to Him who is ready to judge *the* living and *the* dead. ⁶For to this *end* the gospel was proclaimed even to *the* dead, so that they might be judged indeed according to men in *the* flesh, but they might live in *the* spirit according to God.

⁷Now the end of all has drawn near. Therefore be clear-minded and be sober for the purpose of prayers, ⁸above all things, having fervent love among yourselves, because love covers over a multitude of sins, ⁹hospitable to one another without complaint, ¹⁰as each has received a gift, to them serving each other as good stewards of *the* manifold grace of God: ¹¹if anyone speaks, as oracles of God; if anyone serves, as of strength which God supplies, so that in all things God may be glorified through Jesus Christ, to whom be the glory and the power to the ages of the ages. Amen.

Suffering as Christians

¹²Beloved, do not be surprised at the fire among you taking place for a trial to you, as if a strange thing were happening to you. ¹³But as you have shared in the sufferings of Christ, rejoice, so that also in the revelation of His glory you may rejoice, exulting.

¹⁴If you are insulted in *the* name of Christ, *you are* blessed, because the Spirit

of glory and of God rests upon you.[b] ¹⁵For let not any of you suffer as a murderer, or a thief, or an evildoer, or as a troublesome meddler, ¹⁶but if as a Christian, let him not be ashamed, but let him glorify God in this name.[c] ¹⁷For *it is* the time *for* the judgment to have begun from the house of God; and if from us first, what *will be* the outcome of those disobeying the gospel of God? ¹⁸And,

> "If the righteous *one* is saved with difficulty,
>> where will appear the ungodly and sinner?"[d]

¹⁹Therefore also, those suffering according to the will of God, let them commit their souls to *the* faithful Creator in well-doing.

a 1 BYZ and TR include *for us*
b 14 BYZ and TR include *On their part He is spoken of as evil, but on your part He is glorified.*
c 16 NA *glorify God in this matter*
d 18 Proverbs 11:31

1 Peter 5
Instructions to Elders

¹I exhort[a] *the* elders among you, a fellow elder and witness of the sufferings of Christ, who *am* also a partaker of the glory being about to be revealed: ²Shepherd the flock of God among you, exercising oversight[b] not under compulsion, but willingly according to God;[c] and not for base gain but eagerly, ³not as exercising lordship over those in your charge, but being examples to the flock. ⁴And the Chief Shepherd having been revealed, you will receive the unfading crown of glory.

Cast Your Cares on Him

⁵Likewise, younger *ones*, be subject to *your* elders. And all, gird on humility one to another, because,

> "God opposes *the* proud,
>> but gives grace to *the* humble."[d]

⁶Be humbled therefore under the mighty hand of God, so that He may exalt you in *due* time, ⁷having cast all your anxiety upon Him, because with Him there is care about you.

⁸Be sober-minded; watch. Your adversary the devil prowls about as a roaring lion seeking whom to devour, ⁹whom you should resist, firm in the faith, knowing the same sufferings to be accomplished in your brotherhood throughout the world.

Benediction and Farewell

¹⁰And the God of all grace, the *One* having called you to His eternal glory in Christ,[e] *of you* having suffered a little while, He Himself will perfect, will confirm, will strengthen, *and* will establish *you*. ¹¹To Him *be* the power to the ages of the ages. Amen.

¹²Through Silvanus,[f] the faithful brother as I regard *him*, I have written to you through few *words*, exhorting and testifying this to be *the* true grace of God, in which you stand.

¹³She in Babylon elected with *you* greets you, and my son Mark.

¹⁴Greet one another with a kiss of love. Peace *be* to all of you who *are* in Christ.[g]

a 1 SBL, NE, and WH *Therefore I exhort the elders*
b 2 NE and WH do not include *exercising oversight*
c 2 WH, BYZ, and TR do not include *according to God*
d 5 Proverbs 3:34
e 10 BYZ and TR *in Christ Jesus*
f 12 That is, Silas
g 14 BYZ and TR include *Amen.*

2 Peter

2 Peter 1
Greetings from Peter
(1 Peter 1:1-2)

¹Simon Peter, a servant and apostle of Jesus Christ,
To those having obtained a faith equally precious with ours, through *the* righteousness of our God and Savior Jesus Christ:

²Grace and peace be multiplied to you in *the* knowledge of God and of Jesus our Lord.

Partakers of the Divine Nature

³Accordingly, His divine power has given us all things toward life and godliness, through the knowledge of the *One* having called us *by His* own glory and excellence, ⁴through which He has given to us the precious and magnificent promises, so that through these you might become partakers of *the* divine nature, having escaped the decay in the world in desire. ⁵Now also for this very *reason*, having brought in all earnestness, supplement into your faith virtue, and into virtue knowledge, ⁶and into knowledge self-control, and into self-control endurance, and into endurance godliness, ⁷and into godliness brotherly affection, and into brotherly affection love. ⁸For these things being in you and abounding, make *you* neither idle nor unfruitful as to the knowledge of our Lord Jesus Christ. ⁹For in whomever these things are not present, he is blind, being short sighted, having received forgetfulness of the purification from his former sins.
¹⁰Therefore, brothers, be diligent, rather, to make your calling and election sure. For practicing these things, never at any time shall you stumble. ¹¹For in this way the entrance into the eternal kingdom of our Lord and Savior Jesus Christ will be richly supplied to you.
¹²Therefore I will be ready always to remind you concerning these things, though knowing *them* and having been strengthened in the truth being present *in you*. ¹³Now I esteem it right, as long as I am in this tabernacle, to stir you up by putting *you* in remembrance, ¹⁴knowing that the putting off of my tabernacle is impending, as also our Lord Jesus Christ has made clear to me. ¹⁵And I will be diligent also for you to have at every time after my departure these things, to make a lasting remembrance.

Eyewitnesses of His Majesty
(Matthew 17:1-13; Mark 9:1-13; Luke 9:28-36)

¹⁶For we have not made known to you the power and coming of our Lord Jesus Christ having followed out cleverly devised fables, but having been eyewitnesses of His majesty. ¹⁷For having received honor and glory from God *the* Father, a voice such as follows was brought to Him by the Majestic Glory: "This is My Son, My beloved, in whom I have found delight."[a] ¹⁸And we heard this voice having been brought from heaven, being with Him in the holy mountain.
¹⁹And we have the more certain prophetic word, to which you do well taking heed, as to a lamp shining in a dark place, until this day shall have dawned and *the* morning star shall have arisen in your hearts, ²⁰knowing this first, that any prophecy of Scripture is not of its own interpretation. ²¹For no prophecy at any time was brought by *the* will of man, but men spoke from God, being carried by *the* Holy Spirit.

[a] 17 Matthew 17:5; Mark 9:7; Luke 9:35

2 Peter 2
Deliverance from False Prophets

¹But there were also false prophets among the people, as there will be false teachers among you also, who will stealthily introduce destructive heresies, even denying the Master having bought them, bringing upon themselves swift destruction. ²And many will follow after their sensuality, through whom the way of the truth will be maligned. ³And through covetousness they will exploit you with fabricated words, for whom the judgment of long ago is not idle, and their destruction does not slumber.
⁴For if God did not spare *the* angels having sinned, but having cast *them* down to Tartarus, in chains of gloomy darkness,[a] delivered *them*, being kept for judgment; ⁵and He did not spare *the* ancient world, but preserved Noah, a

herald of righteousness, one of eight, having brought *the* flood upon *the* world of *the* ungodly; ⁶and He condemned *the* cities of Sodom and Gomorrah to destruction,*b* having reduced *them* to ashes, having set an example of what is coming on the ungodly;*c* ⁷and He rescued righteous Lot, being distressed by the conduct in sensuality of the lawless ⁸(for that righteous *man* dwelling, among them, day after day, was tormented in *his* righteous soul, through seeing and hearing *their* lawless deeds)— ⁹*then the* Lord knows to deliver *the* devout out of temptation and to keep *the* unrighteous being punished unto *the* day of judgment, ¹⁰and especially those walking after *the* flesh in *the* passion of defilement and despising authority. Bold, self-willed, they do not tremble blaspheming glorious ones, ¹¹whereas angels, being greater in strength and power, do not bring against them a reviling judgment before *the* Lord. ¹²But these, like irrational animals, having been born as creatures of instinct for capture and destruction, blaspheming in what they are ignorant of, in their destruction also will be destroyed, ¹³suffering wrong *as the* wage of unrighteousness; esteeming carousal in daytime *as* pleasure; blots and blemishes, reveling in their deceptions, feasting with you; ¹⁴having eyes full of adultery, and unceasing from sin; enticing unestablished souls; having a heart having been exercised in craving— children of a curse!
¹⁵Having forsaken *the* straight way, they have gone astray, having followed in the way of Balaam *son* of Bosor, who loved *the* wage of unrighteousness. ¹⁶But he had reproof for his own transgression *by* a mute donkey; having spoken in a man's voice, it restrained the madness of the prophet.
¹⁷These are springs without water and mists being driven by storm, for whom gloom of darkness has been reserved. ¹⁸For speaking arrogant words of vanity, they entice to sensuality with *the* passions of *the* flesh those barely escaping from those living in error, ¹⁹promising them freedom, themselves being slaves of corruption. For by what anyone has been subdued, by that also he is enslaved.
²⁰For if, having escaped the pollutions of the world through *the* knowledge of the Lord and Savior Jesus Christ,*d* now again having been entangled in these they are subdued, the last *state* has become worse to them than the first. ²¹For it would have been better for them not to have known the way of righteousness, than having known *it*, to have turned from the holy commandment having been delivered to them. ²²The thing true of the proverb has happened to them: "A dog having returned to *its* own vomit,"*e* and, "A sow having washed, to *her* rolling place in *the* mire."

a 4 Or *in gloomy dungeons*
b 6 WH *condemned the cities of Sodom and Gomorrah*
c 6 NE, NA, BYZ, and TR *those who were to be ungodly*
d 20 Some manuscripts *our Lord and Savior*
e 22 Proverbs 26:11

2 Peter 3
The Coming Judgment
(Genesis 3:1-7; Genesis 7:1-5; Romans 5:12-21)

¹Beloved, this *is* now *the* second letter I am writing to you, in *both of* which I am stirring up your pure mind in putting *you* in remembrance ²to be mindful of the words having been spoken beforehand by the holy prophets, and of the commandment of the Lord and Savior through your apostles, ³first knowing this, that in the last days scoffers will come with scoffing, following according to their own evil desires, ⁴and saying, "Where is the promise of His coming? For from *the time* that the fathers fell asleep, all things continue as they were from *the* beginning of creation."
⁵For this is concealed from them willingly, that heavens existed long ago and *the* earth, having been composed out of water and through water, by the word of

God, ⁶through which*ᵃ* the world at that time perished, having been deluged with water. ⁷But by the same word now *the* heavens and the earth exist, having been stored up for fire, being kept unto *the* day of judgment and destruction of ungodly men.

The Day of the Lord
(Zephaniah 1:7-18; 1 Thessalonians 5:1-11)

⁸But beloved, do not let *this* one thing be hidden from you, that with *the* Lord one day *is* like a thousand years, and a thousand years like one day. ⁹The Lord does not delay the promise, as some esteem slowness, but is patient toward you, not willing *for* any to perish, but all to come to repentance.

¹⁰But *the* day of *the* Lord will come like a thief, in which the heavens will pass away with a roar, and elements will be dissolved, burning with heat, and *the* earth and the works in it will not be found.*ᵇ*

¹¹All these things being dissolved in this way, what kind ought you to be? In holy conduct and godliness, ¹²expecting and hastening the coming of the day of God, by reason of which *the* heavens will be dissolved, being set on fire, and *the* elements are melting, burning with heat. ¹³But according to His promise, we are awaiting new heavens and a new earth, in which righteousness dwells.

Final Exhortations

¹⁴Therefore, beloved, expecting these things, be diligent to be found by Him in peace, without spot and without blemish. ¹⁵And esteem the patience of our Lord *as* salvation, just as our beloved brother Paul also wrote to you according to the wisdom having been given to him, ¹⁶as also in all the letters,*ᶜ* speaking in them concerning these things, among which some things are difficult to be understood, which the ignorant and unestablished distort*ᵈ* to their own destruction, as also the other Scriptures. ¹⁷Therefore beloved, knowing *this* beforehand, you beware, lest you should fall from the own steadfastness, having been led away by the error of the lawless. ¹⁸But grow in grace and in knowledge of our Lord and Savior Jesus Christ. To Him *be* the glory both now and to *the* day of eternity. Amen.*ᵉ*

a 6 NA *through whom*
b 10 BYZ and TR *will be burned up*; SBL, NE, WH *will be exposed*
c 16 or *in all his letters*
d 16 NA *will distort*
e 18 NE, WH, and NA do not include *Amen.*

1 John

1 John 1
The Word of Life
(Luke 24:36-43; John 20:19-23)

¹That which was from *the* beginning, that which we have heard, that which we have seen with our eyes, that which we have gazed upon, and our hands have handled, concerning the Word of life— ²and the life was made manifest, and we have seen and bear witness, and proclaim to you the eternal life, which was with the Father and was revealed to us— ³that which we have seen and have heard, we proclaim to you also, so that you also may have fellowship with us. And indeed our fellowship *is* with the Father and with His Son, Jesus Christ. ⁴And these things we write, so that our*ᵃ* joy might be complete.

Walking in the Light
(John 8:12-30)

⁵And this is the message that we have heard from Him and we preach to you, that God is light, and in Him is no darkness *at all*. ⁶If we should say that we have fellowship with Him, and yet should walk in the darkness, we lie and do not practice the truth. ⁷But*ᵇ* if we should walk in the light as He is in the light, we have fellowship with one another, and the blood of Jesus His Son cleanses us from all sin.

⁸If we should say that we have no sin, we deceive ourselves, and the truth is not in

us. ⁹If we should confess our sins, He is faithful and just, that He may forgive us *our* sins and might cleanse us from all unrighteousness. ¹⁰If we should say that we have not sinned, we make Him a liar, and His word is not in us.

a 4 BYZ and TR *your*
b 7 NA does not include *But*

1 John 2
Jesus Our Advocate

¹My little children, I am writing these things to you so that you might not sin. And if anyone should sin, we have an advocate with the Father, Jesus Christ *the* Righteous *One*. ²And He is *the* propitiation for our sins, and not only for ours, but also for those of *the* whole world.

³And by this we know that we have come to know Him, if we should keep His commandments. ⁴The *one* saying, "I have known Him," and not keeping His commandments, he is a liar, and the truth is not in him. ⁵But whoever may keep His word, truly in him the love of God has been perfected. By this we know that we are in Him: ⁶The *one* claiming to abide in Him ought also walk just as in the same way that He walked.

A New Commandment

⁷Beloved, I am not writing a new commandment to you, but an old commandment, which you have had from *the* beginning. The old commandment is the word that you have heard. ⁸Again, I am writing a new commandment to you, which is true in Him and in you, because the darkness is passing away and the true light already shines.

⁹The *one* claiming to be in the light and hating his brother is in the darkness even until now. ¹⁰The *one* loving his brother abides in the light, and in him there is no cause for stumbling. ¹¹But the *one* hating his brother is in the darkness, and walks in the darkness; and he knows not where he is going, because the darkness has blinded his eyes.

¹²I am writing to you, little children, because the sins have been forgiven you for the sake of His name.

¹³I am writing to you, fathers because you have known Him who *is* from *the* beginning.
I am writing to you, young men, because you have overcome the evil *one*.
I have written to you, little children, because you know the Father.

¹⁴I have written to you, fathers, because you know Him who *is* from *the* beginning.
I have written to you, young men, because you are strong, and the word of God abides in you, and you have overcome the evil *one*.

Do Not Love the World

¹⁵Do not love the world nor the things in the world. If anyone should love the world, the love of the Father is not in him, ¹⁶because all that *is* in the world, the desire of the flesh and the desire of the eyes and the vaunting of life, is not from the Father, but is from the world. ¹⁷And the world is passing away, and its desire; but the *one* doing the will of God abides to the age.

Beware of Antichrists

¹⁸Little children, it is *the* last hour, and as you have heard that antichrist is coming, even now many antichrists have arisen, whereby we know that it is *the* last hour. ¹⁹They went out from among us, but they were not of us; for if they had been of us, they would have remained with us. But *it is* so that it might be made manifest that they are not all of us.

²⁰And you have *the* anointing from the Holy One, and all *of* you know.ᵃ ²¹I have not written to you because you do not know the truth, but because you know it, and because any lie is not of the truth. ²²Who is the liar, except the *one* denying that Jesus is the Christ? This is the antichrist, the *one* denying the Father and the Son. ²³Everyone denying the Son does not have the Father. The *one* confessing the Son has the Father also.

Continue in Him

[24] You, let what you have heard from *the* beginning abide in you. If what you have heard from *the* beginning should abide in you, you also will abide in the Son and in the Father. [25] And this is the promise that He promised us: eternal life.

[26] I have written these things to you concerning those leading you astray. [27] And you, the anointing that you received from Him abides in you, and you have no need that anyone should teach you. But just as the same anointing teaches you concerning all things and is true and is no lie, and just as it has taught you, you shall abide in Him.

[28] And now, little children, abide in Him, so that when He appears we might have boldness and not shrink away from Him in shame at His coming.

[29] If you know that He is righteous, you know also that everyone practicing righteousness has been begotten of Him.

a 20 BYZ and TR *and you know all things*

1 John 3
Children of God

[1] Behold what love the Father has given to us, that we should be called children of God—and we are! Because of this, the world does not know us, because it did not know Him. [2] Beloved, now we are children of God, and what we will be has not yet been revealed. We know that when He appears,[a] we will be like Him, for we will see Him as He is. [3] And everyone having this hope in Him purifies himself, just as He is pure.

[4] Everyone committing sin also commits lawlessness; and sin is lawlessness. [5] And you know that He appeared, so that He might take away sins; and in Him there is no sin. [6] Anyone abiding in Him does not sin; anyone sinning has not seen Him, nor has he known Him.

[7] Little children,[b] let no one lead you astray; the *one* practicing righteousness is righteous, just as He is righteous. [8] The *one* practicing sin is of the devil, because the devil has been sinning from *the* beginning. For this *reason* the Son of God was revealed, so that He might destroy the works of the devil.

[9] Anyone having been born of God does not practice sin, because His seed abides in him, and he is not able to continue sinning, because he has been born of God. [10] Through this, the children of God and the children of the devil are manifest: anyone not practicing righteousness is not of God, and also the *one* not loving his brother.

Love One Another
(John 13:31-35; Romans 12:9-13)

[11] For this is the message that you have heard from *the* beginning, that we should love one another, [12] not as Cain, *who* was of the evil *one* and slew his brother. And why did he slay him? Because his works were evil, but those of his brother, righteous. [13] And do not be surprised, brothers, if the world hates you.

[14] We know that we have passed from death to life, because we love *our* brothers. The *one* not loving abides in death. [15] Everyone hating his brother is a murderer; and you know that any murderer does not have eternal life abiding in him.

[16] By this we have known love, because He laid down His life for us; and we ought to lay down *our* lives for *our* brothers. [17] Now whoever might have the world's goods, and might see his brother having need, and might close up his heart from him, how does the love of God abide in him?

[18] Little children, we should love not in word, nor in tongue, but in action and in truth. [19] And by this we will know that we are of the truth, and we will assure our heart before Him, [20] that if our heart should condemn *us*, that God is greater than our heart, and He knows all things. [21] Beloved, if our heart should not condemn *us*, we have confidence toward God, [22] and whatever we might ask, we receive from Him, because we keep His

commandments and we do the things pleasing before Him. ²³And this is His commandment, that we should believe in the name of His Son, Jesus Christ, and we should love one another, just as He gave *the* commandment to us. ²⁴And the *one* keeping His commandments abides in Him, and He in him. And by this we know that He abides in us: by the Spirit whom He has given to us.

a 2 Or *when it appears*
b 7 NA *little children* or *little children in training*

1 John 4
Testing the Spirits

¹Beloved, do not believe every spirit, but test the spirits, whether they are of God, because many false prophets have gone out into the world. ²By this you know the Spirit of God: Every spirit that confesses Jesus Christ having come in *the* flesh is of God, ³and every spirit that does not confess Jesus[a] is not of God, and this is that of the antichrist, which you heard that is coming, and now is already in the world.
⁴You are of God, little children, and have overcome them, because the *One* in you is greater than the *one* in the world. ⁵They are of the world; because of this they speak from out of the world, and the world listens to them. ⁶We are of God. The *one* knowing God listens to us. He who is not of God does not listen to us. By this we know the Spirit[b] of truth and the spirit of falsehood.

Love Comes from God

⁷Beloved, we should love one another, because love is from God; and everyone loving has been born from God and knows God. ⁸The *one* not loving has not known God, because God is love.
⁹In this the love of God has been revealed among us, that God has sent His only begotten Son into the world, so that we might live through Him. ¹⁰In this is love, not that we loved God, but that He loved us, and sent His Son *as* a propitiation for our sins.

¹¹Beloved, if God so loved us, we also ought to love one another. ¹²No one has seen God at any time; if we should love one another, God abides in us, and His love is having been perfected in us. ¹³By this we know that we abide in Him and He in us: because He has given to us from out of His Spirit. ¹⁴And we have seen and testify that the Father has sent the Son *as* Savior of the world.
¹⁵Whoever shall confess that Jesus is the Son of God, God abides in him, and he in God. ¹⁶And we have come to know and have come to believe the love that God has as to us. God is love, and the *one* abiding in love abides in God, and God abides in him. ¹⁷In this, love has been perfected with us, so that we may have confidence in the day of judgment that, just as He is, also are we in this world.
¹⁸There is no fear in love, but perfect love casts out fear, because fear has punishment; and the *one* fearing has not been perfected in love. ¹⁹We love because He first loved us.
²⁰If anyone should say, "I love God," and should hate his brother, he is a liar. For the *one* not loving his brother, whom he has seen, is not able to love God, whom he has not seen. ²¹And this commandment we have from Him, that the *one* loving God should love his brother also.

a 3 BYZ and TR *that Jesus Christ has come in the flesh*
b 6 Or *spirit*

1 John 5
Overcoming the World

¹Everyone believing that Jesus is the Christ has been born of God, and everyone loving the *One* having begotten *Him* also loves the *one* having been begotten from Him. ²By this we know that we love the children of God, when we love God and keep His commandments. ³For this is the love of God, that we should keep His commandments; and His commandments are not burdensome. ⁴For everyone having been born of God

overcomes the world; and this is the victory having overcome the world: our faith.

⁵Now who is the *one* overcoming the world, except the *one* believing that Jesus is the Son of God? ⁶This is the *One* having come by water and blood, Jesus Christ; not by water only, but by water and by blood. And the Spirit is the *One* testifying, because the Spirit is the truth. ⁷For there are three bearing testimony:ᵃ ⁸the Spirit and the water and the blood—and these are three in one.

God's Testimony about His Son

⁹If we receive the testimony of men, the testimony of God is greater. For this is the testimony of God that He has testified concerning His Son. ¹⁰The *one* believing in the Son of God has the testimony in himself; the *one* not believing God has made Him a liar, because he has not believed in the testimony that God has testified concerning His Son.

¹¹And this is the testimony: that God has given to us eternal life, and this life is in His Son. ¹²The *one* having the Son has life; the *one* not having the Son of God does not have life.

Effective Prayer

¹³I have written these things to you, the ones believing in the name of the Son of God, so that you may know that you have eternal life.ᵇ ¹⁴And this is the confidence that we have toward Him, that if we might ask anything according to His will, He hears us. ¹⁵And if we know that He hears us, whatever we might ask, we know that we have the requests that we have asked from Him.

¹⁶If anyone should see his brother sinning a sin not unto death, he shall ask, and He will give him life, to those sinning not unto death. There is a sin unto death; I do not say that he should implore concerning that. ¹⁷All unrighteousness is sin, and there is sin not unto death.

Concluding Remarks

¹⁸We know that everyone having been born of God does not continue to sin, but the *One* having been begotten of God protects him,ᶜ and the evil *one* does not touch him. ¹⁹We know that we are of God, and the whole world lies in the evil *one*. ²⁰Now we know that the Son of God is come and has given us understanding, so that we may know Him who *is* true; and we are in Him who *is* true, in His Son Jesus Christ. He is the true God and eternal life.

²¹Little children, keep yourselves from idols.ᵈ

a 7 TR and GOC include *testify in heaven: the Father, the Word and the Holy Spirit, and these three are one. 8 And there are three that testify on earth:*
b 13 BYZ and TR include *and that you may believe on the name of the Son of God*
c 18 Or *the one who was born of God protects himself*, or *God protects the one born of Him*
d 21 BYZ and TR include *Amen.*

2 John

2 John 1
Greeting from the Elder
(3 John 1:1-4)

¹The elder,

To *the* elect lady and her children, whom I love in truth, and not only I, but also all those having known the truth— ²because of the truth abiding in us and that will be with us to the age:

³Grace, mercy, *and* peace will be with us from God *the* Father and from Jesus Christ, the Son of the Father, in truth and love.

Walking in the Truth
(John 8:30-41)

⁴I rejoiced exceedingly that I have found *some* of your children walking in truth, just as we have received a commandment from the Father. ⁵And now I implore you, lady, not as though I am writing to you a new commandment, but that which we have had from *the* beginning, that we should love one another. ⁶And this is love, that we should walk according to His commandments. This is the commandment, just as you have heard

from *the* beginning, so that you should walk in it.

Beware of Deceivers

⁷For many deceivers have entered into the world, those not confessing Jesus Christ coming in flesh. This is the deceiver and the antichrist. ⁸Watch yourselves, so that you should not lose what things we have worked for,ᵃ but you may receive a full reward. ⁹Anyone going on ahead, and not abiding in the teaching of Christ, does not have God. The *one* abiding in the teaching, this *one* has both the Father and the Son.

¹⁰If anyone comes to you and does not bring this teaching, do not receive him into *the* house, and do not tell him to rejoice. ¹¹For the *one* telling him to rejoice partakes in his evil works.

Final Greetings

¹²Having many things to write to you, I purposed not with paper and ink, but I hope to come to you and to speak mouth to mouth, so that our joy may be having been completed.

¹³The children of your elect sister greet you.ᵇ

a 8 NE and WH *what you have worked for*
b 13 BYZ and TR include *Amen.*

3 John

3 John 1
Greeting to Gaius from the Elder
(2 John 1:1-3)

¹The elder,
To Gaius the beloved, whom I love in truth.
²Beloved, I pray you to prosper concerning all things and to be in good health, just as your soul prospers. ³For I rejoiced exceedingly of *the* brothers coming and bearing witness of your truth, just as you are walking in truth. ⁴I have no greater joy than these things, that I should hear of my children walking in the truth.

Gaius Commended for His Hospitality

⁵Beloved, you are doing faithfully whatever you might have done toward the brothers, and they are strangers, ⁶who testified of your love before *the* church, whom you will do well having set forward worthily of God. ⁷For they went forth on behalf of the name, accepting nothing from the Gentiles. ⁸Therefore we ought to receive such *men*, so that we may be fellow workers in the truth.

Diotrephes and Demetrius

⁹I have written something to the church; but Diotrephes, the *one* loving to be first among them, does not welcome us. ¹⁰Because of this, if I might come, I will bring to remembrance his works which he is doing, speaking against us with evil words; and not being satisfied with these, neither he receives the brothers himself, and he forbids those purposing, and he casts *them* out from the church.

¹¹Beloved, do not imitate what *is* evil, but what *is* good. The *one* doing good is of God; the *one* doing evil has not seen God. ¹²Witness has been given to Demetrius by all, and by the truth itself; and we also bear witness, and you know that our testimony is true.

Conclusion

¹³I had many things to write to you, but I do not desire to write to you with ink and pen; ¹⁴but I hope to see you soon, and we will speak mouth to mouth.
Peace to you.
The friends greet you.
Greet the friends by name.

Jude

Jude 1
Greetings from Jude
(James 1:1-1)

¹Jude, a servant of Jesus Christ, and brother of James,

To those called, having been loved in God the Father and having been kept in Jesus Christ.
²Mercy and peace and love be multiplied to you.

God's Judgment on the Ungodly
(Genesis 4:1-7; Romans 2:1-16)

³Beloved, using all diligence to write to you concerning our common salvation, I had necessity to write to you, exhorting *you* to contend earnestly for the faith having been delivered once for all to the saints. ⁴For certain men came in stealthily, those having been designated long ago unto this condemnation, ungodly *ones* changing the grace of our God into sensuality and denying our only master and Lord, Jesus Christ.

⁵Now I want to remind you, you having known all this, that Jesus,ᵃ having saved at one time a people out of *the* land of Egypt, afterward He destroyed those not having believed. ⁶And *the* angels not having kept their *own* domain, but having abandoned the own dwelling, He keeps in eternal chains under darkness, unto *the* judgment of *the* great day; ⁷just as Sodom and Gomorrah and the cities around them, having indulged in sexual immorality and having gone after strange flesh, in like manner with them are set forth as an example, undergoing *the* penalty of eternal fire.

⁸Yet likewise also these dreaming *ones* indeed defile *the* flesh, and set aside authority, and blaspheme glorious *ones*. ⁹But Michael the archangel, when he was reasoning with the devil, disputing about the body of Moses, did not dare to bring against *him* a blasphemous judgment, but he said "*The* Lord rebuke you."ᵇ ¹⁰But these indeed speak evil of whatever things they have not seen; and whatever things they understand naturally, as the irrational animals, in these things they corrupt themselves. ¹¹Woe to them, because they have gone in the way of Cain, and rushed for profit to the error of Balaam, and perished in the rebellion of Korah.

¹²These are the hidden reefs,ᶜ feasting together *with you* fearlessly in your love feasts; shepherding themselves; clouds without water, being carried about by winds; autumnal trees without fruit, twice having died, having been uprooted; ¹³wild waves of *the* sea, foaming out of their *own* shame; wandering stars, to whom the gloom of darkness has been reserved to *the* age.

¹⁴And Enoch, *the* seventh from Adam, also prophesied as to these, saying: "Behold, *the* Lord has come amidst myriads of His holy *ones*, ¹⁵to execute judgment against all, and to convict all the ungodly concerning all the works of ungodliness which they have done in an ungodly way, and concerning all the harsh *things* that ungodly sinners have spoken against Him."ᵈ

¹⁶These are grumblers, discontented, following after the own lusts; and their mouth speaks great swelling *words*, flattering faces for the sake of profit.

A Call to Persevere
(Hebrews 10:19-39)

¹⁷But you, beloved, remember the words having been spoken beforehand by the apostles of our Lord Jesus Christ, ¹⁸that they were saying to you, "In *the* last time there will be scoffers, following after their own passions of ungodlinesses." ¹⁹These are those causing divisions, worldly-minded, not having *the* Spirit.

²⁰But you, beloved, building up yourselves in your most holy faith, praying in *the* Holy Spirit, ²¹keep yourselves in *the* love of God, awaiting the mercy of our Lord Jesus Christ unto eternal life.

²²And indeed have mercy on those who are doubting; ²³and save others, snatching *them* out of *the* fire; and show mercy to others with fear, hating even the clothing having been stained by the flesh.

Doxology
(Romans 11:33-36; Romans 16:25-27)

²⁴Now to Him being able to keep you from stumbling and to present *you* blameless in the presence of His glory, with exultation— ²⁵to *the* only God our Savior, through Jesus Christ our Lord, *be* glory, majesty, dominion, and authority, before all time and now and to all the ages. Amen.

a 5 NE, WH, BYZ, and TR *the Lord*
b 9 See the Testament of Moses
c 12 Or *blemishes*
d 15 See the First Book of Enoch

Revelation

Revelation 1
Prologue
(Daniel 12:1-13)

¹*The* revelation of Jesus Christ, which God gave Him to show to His bondservants what things it behooves to take place in quickness. And He signified *it* through having sent His angel to His servant, John, ²who testified to the word of God and to the testimony of Jesus Christ, as much as he saw.

³Blessed *is* the *one* reading, and those hearing the words of the prophecy, and keeping the things having been written in it; for the time *is* near.

John Greets the Seven Churches

⁴John,
To the seven churches in Asia:
Grace to you and peace from Him being and who was and who is coming, and from the seven Spirits*ᵃ* before His throne, ⁵and from Jesus Christ, the faithful witness, the firstborn of the dead, and the ruler of the kings of the earth.
To the *One* loving us and releasing us from our sins through His blood, ⁶and He has made us a kingdom, priests to His God and Father—to Him *be* the glory and the dominion to the ages of the ages. Amen.

⁷Behold, He is coming with the clouds, and every eye will see Him, and those who pierced Him, and all the tribes of the earth will wail because of Him. Yes! Amen!

⁸"I am the Alpha and the Omega,"*ᵇ* says Lord God, the *One* being, and who was, and who is coming, the Almighty.

John's Vision on Patmos

⁹I John, your brother and fellow-partaker in the tribulation and kingdom and perseverance in Jesus, was in the island called Patmos on account of the word of God and the testimony of Jesus. ¹⁰I was in *the* Spirit on the Lord's day, and I heard behind me a loud voice, like that of a trumpet, ¹¹saying,*ᶜ* "What you see, write in a book and send to the seven churches: to Ephesus, and to Smyrna, and to Pergamum, and to Thyatira, and to Sardis, and to Philadelphia, and to Laodicea."

¹²And I turned to see the voice that was speaking with me. And having turned, I saw seven golden lampstands, ¹³and in *the* midst of the lampstands, *One* like *the* Son of Man,*ᵈ* having been clothed to the feet, and having been girded about at the breasts with a golden sash. ¹⁴Now His head and *His* hairs *are* white like wool, white as snow; and His eyes *are* like a flame of fire; ¹⁵and His feet *are* like fine bronze, as having been refined in a furnace; and His voice *is* like *the* voice of many waters; ¹⁶and He is holding in His right hand seven stars, and a sharp two-edged sword is going forth out of His mouth; and His face *is* like the sun shining in its full strength.

¹⁷And when I saw Him, I fell at His feet as though dead. And He placed His right hand upon me, saying, "Fear not. I am the First and the Last, ¹⁸and the Living *One*. And I was dead, and behold I am living to the ages of the ages, and I have the keys of Death and of Hades. ¹⁹Therefore write the things that you have seen, and the things that are, and the things that are about to take place

after these, ²⁰the mystery of the seven stars, which you saw on My right hand, and the seven golden lampstands: The seven stars are *the* angels of the seven churches, and the seven lampstands are *the* seven churches.

a 4 Or *sevenfold Spirit*; also in chapters 3, 4, and 5
b 8 TR includes *the Beginning and the End*
c 11 TR includes *I am Alpha and Omega, the First and the Last, and*
d 13 See Daniel 7:13

Revelation 2
To the Church in Ephesus
(Acts 19:8-12)

¹To the messenger of the church in Ephesus write:

These things says the *One* holding the seven stars in His right hand, walking in *the* midst of the seven golden lampstands.

²I know your works and your labor and endurance, and that you are not able to tolerate evil *ones*. And you have tested those claiming to be apostles and are not, and you have found them false. ³And you have perseverance, and have endured for the sake of My name, and have not grown weary.

⁴But I have against you that you have abandoned your first love. ⁵Remember therefore from where you have fallen, and repent, and do the first works. But if not, I am coming to you, and I will remove your lampstand out of its place, unless you should repent.

⁶But you have this, that you hate the works of the Nicolaitans, which I also hate.

⁷The *one* having an ear, let him hear what the Spirit says to the churches. To the *one* overcoming, I will give to him to eat of the tree of life, which is in the paradise of God.

To the Church in Smyrna

⁸And to the messenger of the church in Smyrna write:

These things says the First and the Last, who became dead and came to life.

⁹I know your tribulation and poverty—but you are rich—and the blasphemy of those claiming themselves to be Jews and are not, but *are* a synagogue of Satan.

¹⁰Do not fear what you are about to suffer. Behold, the devil is about to cast *some* of you into prison, so that you might be tested; and you shall have tribulation ten days. Be faithful unto death, and I will give to you the crown of life.

¹¹The *one* having an ear, let him hear what the Spirit says to the churches. The *one* overcoming shall not be injured by the second death.

To the Church in Pergamum

¹²And to *the* messenger of the church in Pergamum write:

These things says the *One* having the sharp two-edged sword.

¹³I know where you dwell, where the throne of Satan *is*; and you hold fast to My name, and you have not denied My faith, even in the days of Antipas My witness, My faithful *one*, who was killed among you, where Satan dwells.

¹⁴But I have a few things against you, because you have *some* there holding the teaching of Balaam, who would teach Balak to cast a snare before the sons of Israel, to eat things sacrificed to idols, and to commit sexual immorality. ¹⁵So likewise you also have *some* holding the teaching of the Nicolaitans. ¹⁶Therefore repent! But if not, I am coming to you quickly, and I will make war against them with the sword of My mouth.

¹⁷The *one* having an ear, let him hear what the Spirit says to the churches. The *one* overcoming, I will give to him the manna having been hidden, and I will give to him a white stone, and on the stone new a name having been written, which no one has known, except the *one* receiving *it*.

To the Church in Thyatira
(Acts 16:11-15)

¹⁸And to *the* messenger of the church in Thyatira write:

These things says the Son of God, the *One* having His eyes like a flame of fire, and His feet like burnished bronze.
¹⁹I know your works, and your love and faith and service and perseverance; and your latter works *are* greater than the first.
²⁰But I have against you that you tolerate the woman Jezebel, the *one* calling herself a prophetess and teaching and misleading My servants to commit sexual immorality and to eat things sacrificed to idols. ²¹And I have given her time that she might repent, and she is not willing to repent of her sexual immorality.
²²Behold, I will cast her into a sickbed, and those committing adultery with her into great tribulation, unless they shall repent of her deeds. ²³And I will kill her children with death, and all the churches will know that I am the *One* searching affections and hearts; and I will give to each of you according to your works.
²⁴But I say to you, to *the* rest of those in Thyatira, as many as do not have this teaching, who have not known the depths of Satan, as they say: I will not cast upon you any other burden. ²⁵But hold fast to what you have until which *time* I might come. ²⁶And the *one* overcoming and keeping My works until *the* end, I will give to him authority over the nations, ²⁷and he will shepherd them with a rod of iron, as the vessels *of* the potter are broken in pieces^a—just as I also have received from My Father. ²⁸And I will give to him the morning star.
²⁹The *one* having an ear, let him hear what the Spirit says to the churches.

a 26-27 **Psalm 2:8,9**

Revelation 3
To the Church in Sardis

¹And to the messenger of the church in Sardis write:
These things says the *One* having the seven Spirits of God and the seven stars. I know your deeds, that you have *the* characterization that you are alive, and yet you are dead. ²Be watching, and strengthen the things that remain, which are about to die; for I have not found your works having been completed in the sight of My God. ³Remember, therefore, what you have received and heard—and keep *it* and repent. If therefore you shall not watch, I will come like a thief, and you shall not know at what hour I will come upon you.
⁴But you have a few people in Sardis who have not soiled their garments, and they will walk with Me in white, because they are worthy. ⁵The *one* overcoming thus will be clothed in white garments. And I will never blot out his name from the book of life, and I will confess his name before My Father and before His angels.
⁶The *one* having an ear, let him hear what the Spirit says to the churches.

To the Church in Philadelphia

⁷And to *the* messenger of the church in Philadelphia write:
These things says the Holy *One*, the True *One*, having the key of David, the *One* opening and no one will shut, and shutting and no one opens.
⁸I know your deeds. Behold, I have set before you a door having been opened, which no one is able to shut it, because you have little power, and yet you have kept My word and have not denied My name. ⁹Behold, I give *those* from the synagogue of Satan—those declaring themselves to be Jews, and are not, but they lie—behold, I will cause them that they will come and will worship before your feet, and they shall know that I have loved you.
¹⁰Because you have kept the word of My patient endurance, I also will keep you out of the hour of the trial being about to come upon the whole inhabited world, to try those dwelling upon the earth. ¹¹I am coming quickly. Hold fast to what you have, so that no one may take your crown. ¹²The *one* overcoming, I will make him a pillar in the temple of My God, and he shall not go out anymore.

And I will write upon him the name of My God, and the name of the city of My God, the new Jerusalem coming down out of heaven from My God, and My new name. ¹³The *one* having an ear, let him hear what the Spirit says to the churches.

To the Church in Laodicea
(Colossians 2:1-5)

¹⁴And to the messenger of the church in Laodicea write:

These things says the Amen, the faithful and true Witness, the Beginning of God's creation. ¹⁵I know your works, that you are neither cold nor hot. I wish you would be cold or hot. ¹⁶So because you are lukewarm, and neither hot nor cold, I am about to spit you out of My mouth. ¹⁷For you say, 'I am rich, and I have grown rich, and I have need of nothing.' And you do not realize that you are wretched, and miserable, and poor, and blind, and naked. ¹⁸I counsel you to buy from Me gold having been refined by fire so that you may be rich, and white garments so that you may be clothed and the shame your of nakedness might not be made manifest, and eye-salve to anoint your eyes so that you may see. ¹⁹As many as I might love, I rebuke and discipline; therefore be zealous and repent. ²⁰Behold, I stand at the door and knock. If anyone should hear My voice and open the door, then I will come in to him and will dine with him, and he with Me. ²¹The *one* overcoming, I will give to him to sit with Me on My throne, as I also overcame and sat down with My Father on His throne. ²²The *one* having an ear, let him hear what the Spirit says to the churches."

Revelation 4
The Throne in Heaven

¹After these things I looked, and behold, a door was standing open in heaven, and the first voice that I heard like a trumpet was speaking with me, saying, "Come up here, and I will show to you what it behooves to take place after these things." ²Immediately I was in *the* Spirit, and behold, a throne was set in heaven, and *One* sitting upon the throne, ³and the *One* sitting, in appearance *was* like jasper and carnelian stone. And a rainbow *was* around the throne, in appearance like an emerald. ⁴And around the throne *were* twenty-four thrones; and sitting on the thrones twenty-four elders, having been clothed in white garments; and on their heads, golden crowns.

Worship of the Creator

⁵And out of the throne come flashes of lightning, and voices, and thunderings. And *there were* seven lamps of fire burning before the throne, which are the seven Spirits of God. ⁶And before the throne *was something* like a sea of glass, like crystal. And in *the* midst of the throne and around the throne *were* four living creatures, being full of eyes in front and behind. ⁷And the first living creature *was* like a lion, and the second living creature like a calf, and the third living creature having the face as of a man, and the fourth living creature like an eagle flying. ⁸And the four living creatures, each of them had six wings respectively, full of eyes all around and within; and they did not have rest day and night, saying:

"Holy, Holy, Holy,
Lord God Almighty,
the *One* having been, and the *One* being, and the *One* coming."

⁹And whenever the living creatures will give glory and honor and thanksgiving to the *One* sitting upon the throne, the *One* living to the ages of the ages, ¹⁰the twenty-four elders will fall before the *One* sitting upon the throne, and they will worship the *One* living to the ages of the ages, and they will cast their crowns before the throne, saying:

¹¹"Worthy are You, our Lord and God,
to receive glory and honor and power;

for You created all things,
>   and because of Your will, they existed and were created."

Revelation 5
The Scroll with Seven Seals

¹And I saw on the right hand of the *One* sitting upon the throne a scroll, having been written inside and on *the* back, having been sealed with seven seals. ²And I saw a strong angel proclaiming in a loud voice, "Who is worthy to open the scroll, and to break its seals?" ³And no one in heaven, nor upon the earth, nor under the earth, was able to open the scroll, nor to see it. ⁴And I was weeping loudly, because no one was found worthy to open the scroll, nor to see it.

The Lamb is Worthy

⁵And one of the elders says to me, "Do not weep. Behold, the Lion of the tribe of Judah, the root of David, has overcome to open the scroll and its seven seals." ⁶And I saw in *the* midst of the throne and of the four living creatures, and in *the* midst of the elders, a Lamb standing as having been slain, having seven horns and seven eyes, which are the seven Spirits of God having been sent out into all the earth. ⁷And He came and took *it* out of the right hand of the *One* sitting on the throne.

⁸And when He had taken the scroll, the four living creatures and the twenty-four elders fell down before the Lamb, each having a harp, and golden bowls being full of incenses, which are the prayers of the saints. ⁹And they are singing a new song, saying,

> "Worthy are You to take the scroll
>   and to open its seals,
>   because You were slain,
>   and You purchased to God by Your blood,
>   out of every tribe and tongue
>   and people and nation,

¹⁰and You have made them a kingdom and priests to our God;
>   and they will reign*ᵃ* upon the earth."

The Lamb Exalted

¹¹And I looked, and I heard *the* voice of many angels around the throne, and of the living creatures, and of the elders; and their number was myriads of myriads and thousands of thousands, ¹²saying in a loud voice:

> "Worthy is the Lamb having been slain,
>   to receive the power and riches
>   and wisdom and strength
>   and honor and glory and blessing!"

¹³And I heard every creature which is in heaven, and upon the earth, and under the earth, and on the sea, and everything in them, saying:

> "To the *One* sitting on the throne,
>   and to the Lamb,
> blessing and honor and glory and might
>   to the ages of the ages."

¹⁴And the four living creatures kept saying, "Amen." And the elders fell down and worshiped.*ᵇ*

a 10 WH *they reign*
b 14 TR includes *Him who lives for ever and ever*

Revelation 6
The First Seal: The White Horse

¹And I watched when the Lamb opened one of the seven seals, and I heard one of the four living creatures saying, as a voice of thunder, "Come!" ²And I looked, and behold, a white horse, and the *one* sitting on it having a bow; and a crown was given to him, and he went forth overcoming, and that he might conquer.

The Second Seal: War

³And when He opened the second seal, I heard the second living creature saying, "Come!" ⁴And another horse went forth, bright red; and to the *one* sitting on it, to him was granted to take the peace from the

earth, and that they will slay one another; and a great sword was given to him.

The Third Seal: Famine

⁵And when He opened the third seal, I heard the third living creature saying, "Come!"

And I looked, and behold, a black horse, and the *one* sitting on it having a pair of scales in his hand. ⁶And I heard *something* like a voice in *the* midst of the four living creatures, saying, "A choenix of wheat for a denarius,ᵃ and three choenixes of barley for a denarius; and you should not injure the oil and the wine."

The Fourth Seal: Death

⁷And when He opened the fourth seal, I heard *the* voice of the fourth living creature saying, "Come!"

⁸And I looked, and behold, a pale horse, and the *one* sitting on it, *the* name of him *was* Death, and Hades was following with him; and authority was given to them over the fourth of the earth, to kill with sword, and with famine, and with plague, and by the beasts of the earth.

The Fifth Seal: The Martyrs

⁹And when He opened the fifth seal, I saw under the altar the souls of those having been slain because of the word of God, and because of the testimony which they had upheld. ¹⁰And they were crying in a loud voice, saying, "Until when, O Lord, holy and true, do You not judge and avenge our blood from those dwelling upon the earth?"

¹¹And to each of them were given white robes, and it was said to them that they shall rest yet a little time, until their fellow servants would also be complete, and their brothers, those being about to be killed as they also *had been*.

The Sixth Seal: Terror

¹²And I saw when He opened the sixth seal, and there was a great earthquake, and the sun became black as sackcloth of hair, and the whole moon became like blood, ¹³and the stars of heaven fell to the earth, as a fig tree casts its unripe figs, being shaken by a great wind. ¹⁴And heaven departed like a scroll being rolled up, and every mountain and island were moved out of their places.

¹⁵And the kings of the earth, and the great ones, and the commanders, and the rich, and the powerful, and every slave and free, hid themselves in the caves, and among the rocks of the mountains. ¹⁶And they say to the mountains and to the rocks, "Fall on us and hide usᵇ from *the* face of the *One* sitting on the throne, and from the wrath of the Lamb, ¹⁷because the great day of Theirᶜ wrath has come, and who is able to stand?"

a 6 A choenix was a Greek dry measure, equivalent to 1.92 pints. A denarius was customarily a day's wage for a laborer (see Matthew 20:2)
b 16 See Hosea 10:8
c 17 BYZ and TR *His*

Revelation 7
144,000 Sealed

¹After these things I saw four angels standing upon the four corners of the earth, holding the four winds of the earth, so that no wind would blow on the earth, nor on the sea, nor on any tree. ²And I saw another angel, having ascended from *the* rising of *the* sun, having *the* seal of *the* living God. And he cried in a loud voice to the four angels to whom it had been given to them to harm the earth and the sea, ³saying, "Do not harm the earth, nor the sea, nor the trees, until we shall have sealed the servants of our God on their foreheads."

⁴And I heard the number of those having been sealed, one hundred forty-four thousand, having been sealed out of every tribe of *the* sons of Israel:

⁵Out of *the* tribe of Judah twelve thousand having been sealed,
out of *the* tribe of Reuben twelve thousand,
out of *the* tribe of Gad twelve thousand,
⁶out of *the* tribe of Asher twelve thousand,

out of *the* tribe of Naphtali twelve thousand,
out of *the* tribe of Manasseh twelve thousand,
⁷out of *the* tribe of Simeon twelve thousand,
out of *the* tribe of Levi twelve thousand,
out of *the* tribe of Isaachar twelve thousand,
⁸out of *the* tribe of Zebulun twelve thousand,
out of *the* tribe of Joseph twelve thousand,
out of *the* tribe of Benjamin twelve thousand having been sealed.

Praise from the Great Multitude

⁹After these things I looked, and behold, a great multitude, which no one was able to number it, out of every nation, and tribes, and peoples, and tongues, standing before the throne and before the Lamb, having been clothed with white robes, and palm branches in their hands. ¹⁰And they were crying out in a loud voice, saying:

"Salvation to our God,
  the *One* sitting on the throne,
 and to the Lamb!"

¹¹And all the angels stood around the throne, and the elders, and the four living creatures, and they fell upon their faces before the throne and worshiped God, ¹²saying, "Amen! Blessing, and glory, and wisdom, and thanksgiving, and honor, and power, and strength, to our God, to the ages of the ages! Amen."

¹³And one of the elders answered, saying to me, "These having been clothed with the white robes, who are they, and from where have they come?"

¹⁴And I said to him, "My lord, you know." And he said to me, "These are the *ones* coming out of the great tribulation, and they have washed their robes and made them white in the blood of the Lamb. ¹⁵Because of this,

 'They are before the throne of God,
 and serve Him day and night in His temple;
 and the *One* sitting on the throne
  will tabernacle over them.
 ¹⁶they will not hunger any more,
  neither will they thirst anymore,
 nor shall the sun at all fall upon them,
  nor any scorching heat;ᵃ
 ¹⁷because the Lamb in *the* center of the throne
  will shepherd them,ᵇ
 and He will lead them to fountains living of waters,ᶜ
  and God will wipe away every tear from their eyes.'ᵈ"

a 16 Isaiah 49:10
b 17 Psalm 23:1
c 17 Psalm 23:2
d 17 Isaiah 25:8

Revelation 8
The Seventh Seal

¹And when He opened the seventh seal, there was silence in heaven for about half an hour. ²And I saw the seven angels who stand before God, and seven trumpets were given to them.

³And another angel having a golden censer came and stood at the altar, and much incense was given to him, that he will offer *it* with the prayers of all the saints upon the golden altar before the throne. ⁴And the smoke of the incense went up before God, with the prayers of the saints, out of *the* hand of the angel. ⁵And the angel took the censer, and filled it from the fire of the altar, and cast *it* to the earth; and there were thunders, and rumblings, and flashes of lightning, and an earthquake.

The First Four Trumpets

⁶And the seven angels having the seven trumpets prepared themselves, that they might sound the trumpets.

⁷And the first sounded *his* trumpet, and there was hail and fire having been mixed with blood, and it was cast upon the earth. And a third of the earth was burned

up, and a third of the trees were burned up, and all *the* green grass was burned up.

⁸And the second angel sounded *his* trumpet, and *something* like a great mountain burning with fire was cast into the sea. And a third of the sea became blood, ⁹and a third of the creatures having life in the sea died, and a third of the ships were destroyed.

¹⁰And the third angel sounded *his* trumpet, and a great star fell out of heaven, burning like a torch. And it fell upon a third of the rivers, and upon the springs of waters. ¹¹And the name of the star is called Wormwood. And a third of the waters became wormwood, and many of the men died from the waters, because they were made bitter.

¹²And the fourth angel sounded *his* trumpet, and a third of the sun was struck, and a third of the moon, and a third of the stars, so that a third of them should be darkened, and the day should not appear *for* a third of it, and the night likewise.

¹³And I looked, and I heard one eagle flying in mid-heaven, saying in a loud voice, "Woe! Woe! Woe to those dwelling on the earth, because of the remaining voices of the trumpet of the three angels being about to sound *their* trumpets!"

Revelation 9
The Fifth Trumpet

¹And the fifth angel sounded *his* trumpet, and I saw a star having fallen out of heaven to the earth, and the key of the pit of the abyss was given to it. ²And he opened the pit of the abyss, and smoke went up out of the pit, like *the* smoke of a great furnace, and the sun and the air were darkened by the smoke of the pit.

³And out of the smoke, locusts came forth unto the earth, and power was given to them, like the scorpions of the earth have power. ⁴And it was said to them that they shall not harm the grass of the earth, nor any green thing, nor any tree, but only the men not having the seal of God on the foreheads. ⁵And it was granted to them that they should not kill them, but that they shall torment *them* five months. And their torment *was* like *the* torment of a scorpion when it might strike a man. ⁶And in those days, men will seek death, and will not find it; and they will long to die, and death shall flee from them.

⁷And the appearance of the locusts *was* like horses having been prepared for battle, and upon their heads *were something* like crowns, like gold; and their faces like *the* faces of men. ⁸And they had hair like hair of women, and their teeth were like *those* of lions. ⁹And they had breastplates like breastplates of iron, and the sound of their wings *was* like *the* sound of many chariots of horses rushing into battle. ¹⁰And they have tails and stingers like scorpions, and their power to injure men for five months *is* in their tails. ¹¹They have a king over them, the angel of the abyss. His name in Hebrew *is* Abaddon,ᵃ and in the Greek, he has *the* name Apollyon.ᵇ

¹²The first woe has passed. Behold, two woes still are coming after these things.

The Sixth Trumpet

¹³And the sixth angel sounded *his* trumpet, and I heard one voice from the four horns of the golden altar before God, ¹⁴saying to the sixth angel, the *one* having the trumpet, "Release the four angels, those having been bound at the great river Euphrates." ¹⁵And the four angels having been prepared for the hour and day and month and year were released, so that they might kill a third of mankind. ¹⁶And the number of the armies of the cavalry *was* twice ten thousand ten thousands; I heard the number of them.

¹⁷And thus I saw the horses in the vision, and those sitting on them, having fiery and hyacinthine and brimstone breastplates. And the heads of the horses *were* like heads of lions, and out of their mouths proceed fire and smoke and

brimstone. ¹⁸By these three plagues, a third of mankind was killed, by the fire, and by the smoke, and by the brimstone proceeding out of their mouths. ¹⁹For the powers of the horses are in their mouths and in their tails; for their tails *are* like serpents having heads, and with them they injure.

²⁰And the rest of the men who were not killed by these plagues did not even repent of the works of their hands so that they will not worship the demons, and the golden and silver and bronze and stone and wooden idols, which are able neither to see, nor to hear, nor to walk. ²¹And they did not repent of their murders, nor of their sorceries, nor of their sexual immorality, nor of their thefts.

a 11 Abaddon means destruction
b 11 Apollyon means destroyer

Revelation 10
The Angel and the Small Scroll

¹And I saw another mighty angel coming down out of heaven, clothed with a cloud, and a rainbow upon his head, and his face *was* like the sun, and his feet like pillars of fire, ²and having in his hand a little scroll being open. And he placed his right foot upon the sea, and the left upon the earth. ³And he cried out in a loud voice as a lion roars. And when he cried out, the seven thunders sounded their voice.

⁴And when the seven thunders had spoken, I was about to write. But I heard a voice out of heaven, saying, "Seal what the seven thunders have spoken, and do not write them."

⁵And the angel whom I saw standing on the sea and on the land lifted up his right hand to heaven, ⁶and he swore by the *One* living to the ages of the ages, who created heaven and the things in it, and the earth and the things in it, and the sea and the things in it, "There will be no more delay! ⁷But in the days of the voice of the seventh angel, when he is about to sound *the* trumpet, then the mystery of God would be completed, as proclaimed to His servants, the prophets."

⁸And the voice that I heard out of heaven was speaking with me again and saying, "Go, take the little scroll having been opened in the hand of the angel standing upon the sea and upon the land."

⁹And I went to the angel, saying to him, "Give me the little scroll."

And he says to me, "Take and eat it; and your stomach it will make bitter, but in your mouth it will be sweet as honey."ᵃ

¹⁰And I took the little scroll out of the hand of the angel, and I ate it; and it was sweet as honey in my mouth; and when I had eaten it, my stomach was made bitter.

¹¹And they say to me, "It is necessary for you to prophesy again concerning many peoples, and nations, and tongues, and kings."

a 9 Numbers 5:24; Ezekiel 3:3

Revelation 11
The Two Witnesses

¹And a measuring rod like a staff was given to me, saying, "Rise and measure the temple of God, and the altar, and those worshiping in it. ²And leave out the courtyard outside the temple, and do not measure it, because it has been given *up* to the nations, and they will trample upon the holy city forty and two months. ³And I will grant to my two witnesses, and they will prophesy a thousand two hundred sixty days, clothed in sackcloth."

⁴These are the two olive trees and the two lampstands standing before the Lord of the earth.ᵃ ⁵And if anyone should desire to harm them, fire goes out of their mouth and devours their enemies. And if anyone should desire to harm them, thus it is necessary for him to be killed. ⁶These have the power to shut the sky, so that no rain shall fall in the days of their prophecy; and they have power over the waters, to turn them into blood, and to strike the earth with every plague, as often as they might desire.

The Witnesses Killed and Raised

⁷And when they shall have completed their testimony, the beast coming up out of the abyss will make war with them, and will overcome them, and will kill them. ⁸And their body *will be* upon the street of the great city, which is called spiritually Sodom and Egypt, where also their Lord was crucified. ⁹And *those* of the peoples and tribes and tongues and nations gaze upon their bodies three and a half days, and they will not allow their bodies to be put into a tomb. ¹⁰And those dwelling on the earth rejoice over them and make merry, and will send gifts to one another, because these two prophets have tormented those dwelling upon the earth. ¹¹And after the three and a half days, *the* spirit of life from God entered into them, and they stood upon their feet; and great fear fell upon those beholding them. ¹²And they heard a great voice out of heaven, saying to them, "Come up here." And they went up to heaven in the cloud, and their enemies beheld them.

¹³And in that hour there was a great earthquake, and a tenth of the city fell, and seven thousand names of men were killed in the earthquake. And the rest became terrified and gave glory to the God of heaven.

¹⁴The second woe has passed. Behold, the third woe is coming quickly.

The Seventh Trumpet

¹⁵And the seventh angel sounded *his* trumpet, and there were great voices in heaven, saying:

"The kingdom of the world has become *that* of our Lord
and of His Christ,
and He will reign to the ages of the ages."

¹⁶And the twenty-four elders sitting on their thrones before God fell upon their faces and worshiped God, ¹⁷saying:

"We give thanks to You, Lord God Almighty,
the *One* being and who was,[b]
that You have taken Your great power
and have begun to reign.
¹⁸And the nations were enraged,
and Your wrath came,
and the time for the dead to be judged,
and to give the reward to Your servants, the prophets,
and to the saints,
and to those fearing Your name,
the small and the great,
and to destroy those who are destroying the earth."

¹⁹And the temple of God in heaven was opened, and the ark of His covenant was seen in His temple. And there were flashes of lightning, and voices, and thunders, and an earthquake, and great hail.

a 4 Zechariah 4:3,11,14.
b 17 TR includes *and who is to come*

Revelation 12
The Woman and the Dragon

¹And a great sign was seen in heaven: a woman clothed with the sun, and the moon under her feet, and on her head a crown of twelve stars, ²and having in womb. And she cries out, being in travail, and being in pain to bring forth. ³And another sign was seen in heaven, and behold, a great red dragon having seven heads and ten horns, and upon his heads, seven diadems. ⁴And his tail drags a third of the stars of heaven, and he cast them to the earth. And the dragon stands before the woman being about to bring forth, so that when she should bring forth, he might devour her child. ⁵And she brought forth a male son, who is about to shepherd all the nations with a rod of iron;[a] and her child was caught up to God, and to His throne. ⁶And the woman fled into the wilderness, where she has a place having been prepared there by God, so that they should nourish her there one thousand two hundred sixty days.

The War in Heaven

⁷And there was war in heaven: Michael and his angels warred against the dragon, and the dragon and his angels warred *back*. ⁸And he did not have strength, nor was found a place for them any longer in heaven. ⁹And the great dragon was thrown *out*, the ancient serpent, who is called *the* devil and Satan, deceiving the whole inhabited *world*. He was thrown down to the earth, and his angels were thrown down with him.

¹⁰And I heard a great voice in heaven, saying:

> "Now the salvation, and the power,
> and the kingdom of our God,
> and the authority of His Christ have come,
> because the accuser of our brothers has been thrown down,
> the *one* accusing them before our God day and night.
> ¹¹And they have overcome him by reason of the blood of the Lamb,
> and by reason of the word of their testimony;
> and they have not loved their life unto death.
> ¹²Because of this, rejoice O heavens,
> and those dwelling in them!
> Woe to the earth and the sea,
> because the devil has come down to you, having great fury,
> knowing that he has a short time."

The Woman Persecuted

¹³And when the dragon saw that he had been thrown down to the earth, he persecuted the woman who had brought forth the male *child*. ¹⁴And the two wings of the great eagle were given to the woman, so that she could fly from *the* face of the serpent into the wilderness, into her place, where she is nourished there a time, and times, and half a time. ¹⁵And out of his mouth the serpent cast water as a river after the woman, so that he might cause her to be carried away by a flood. ¹⁶And the earth helped the woman, and the earth opened its mouth and swallowed up the river, which the dragon had cast out of his mouth. ¹⁷And the dragon was angry with the woman, and he went to make to war with the rest of her children keeping the commandments of God and holding the testimony of Jesus.

And he stood upon the sand of the sea.[b]

a 5 Psalm 2:9
b 17 BYZ and TR *And I stood on the sand of the sea.* Some texts number this sentence as verse 18, and others include it with 13:1.

Revelation 13
The Beast from the Sea

¹And I saw rising out of the sea a beast, having ten horns, and seven heads, and on its horns, ten diadems, and upon its heads, names of blasphemy. ²And the beast that I saw was like a leopard, and its feet like a bear's, and its mouth like *the* mouth of a lion. And the dragon gave to it his power, and his throne, and great authority.

³And one of its heads *was* as having been slain to death. And its wound of death was healed, and the whole earth marveled after the beast. ⁴And they worshiped the dragon, who had given authority to the beast; and they worshiped the beast, saying, "Who *is* like the beast? And who is able to make war against it?"

⁵And a mouth was given to it, speaking great things and blasphemy, and it was given authority to act forty and two months. ⁶And it opened its mouth unto blasphemies against God, to blaspheme His name and His tabernacle, those dwelling in heaven.

⁷And there was given to it to make war with the saints, and to overcome them. And authority was given to it over every tribe and people and tongue and nation. ⁸And all dwelling on the earth will worship it, of whom their names have not been written from *the* founding of *the* world in

the book of life of the Lamb having been slain.

⁹If anyone has an ear, let him hear.

> ¹⁰"If anyone *is to go* into captivity,
> into captivity he goes;
> If anyone is to be killed[a] with *the* sword,
> by *the* sword it is necessary for him to be killed."[b]

Here is the endurance and the faith of the saints.

The Beast from the Earth

¹¹And I saw another beast rising out of the earth, and it had two horns like a lamb, and it was speaking like a dragon. ¹²And it exercises all the authority of the first beast in the presence of it, and causes the earth and those dwelling in it, that they will worship the first beast, of whom its fatal wound had been healed. ¹³And it works great signs, so that it should even cause fire out of heaven to come down to the earth in the presence of men. ¹⁴And it deceives those dwelling on the earth, by reason of the signs that were given to it to perform before the beast, telling those dwelling on the earth to make an image to the beast that has the wound of the sword and has lived. ¹⁵And there was given to it to give breath to the image of the beast, so that image of the beast also should speak, and should cause that as many as would not worship the image of the beast would be killed.

The Mark of the Beast

¹⁶And it causes all the small and the great, and the rich and the poor, and the free and the servants, that it should give them a mark on their right hand or on their forehead, ¹⁷and that no one should be able to buy or to sell, if not the *one* having the mark—the name of the beast, or the number of its name.

¹⁸Here is the wisdom. The *one* having understanding, let him count the number of the beast, for it is a man's number, and its number *is* six hundred sixty-six.[c]

---

a 10 NE, WH, and BYZ *if anyone kills*
b 10 Jeremiah 15:2
c 18 Some manuscripts *six hundred sixteen*

Revelation 14
The Lamb and the 144,000

¹And I looked, and behold, the Lamb was standing upon Mount Zion, and with Him one hundred forty-four thousand having His name and the name of His Father having been written on their foreheads. ²And I heard a voice out of heaven like *the* sound of many waters, and like *the* sound of loud thunder. And the voice that I heard *was* like that of harpists harping with their harps.

³And they are singing as a new song before the throne, and before the four living creatures, and the elders. And no one was able to learn the song, except the one hundred forty-four thousand having been redeemed from the earth. ⁴These are they who have not been defiled with women; for they are pure, these following the Lamb wherever He shall go. These have been redeemed out from men *as* firstfruits to God and to the Lamb. ⁵And in their mouth no lie was not found; they are blameless.[a]

The Three Angels and Babylon's Fall

⁶And I saw another angel flying in midheaven, having *the* everlasting glad tidings to preach upon those dwelling on the earth, and upon every nation and tribe and tongue and people, ⁷saying in a loud voice, "Fear God and give Him glory, because the hour of His judgment has come. And worship the *One* having made heaven, and the earth, and sea, and springs of waters."

⁸And another, a second angel, followed, saying, "Fallen, Fallen is Babylon the great,[b] who has given all the Gentiles to drink of the wine of the passion of her immorality."

⁹And another, a third angel, followed them, saying in loud a voice, "If anyone worships the beast and its image, and receives a mark on his forehead or upon his hand, ¹⁰he also will drink of the wine

of the anger of God, having been mixed undiluted in the cup of His wrath; and he will be tormented in fire and brimstone before *the* holy angels and before the Lamb. [11]And the smoke of their torment goes up to ages of ages; and those worshiping the beast and its image have no rest day and night, and if anyone receives the mark of its name."

[12]Here is the endurance of the saints, those keeping the commandments of God, and the faith of Jesus.

[13]And I heard a voice out of heaven, saying "Write, 'Blessed *are* the dead dying in *the* Lord from now on.'"

"Yes," says the Spirit, "so that they will rest from their labors; for their works follow with them."

The Harvest of the Earth

[14]And I looked, and behold, a white cloud, and upon the cloud is sitting *One* like *the* Son of Man,[c] having on His head a golden crown, and in His hand a sharp sickle.

[15]And another angel came out of the temple, crying in a loud voice to the *One* sitting on the cloud, "Put forth Your sickle and reap, because the hour to reap has come, because the harvest of the earth has ripened." [16]And the *One* sitting upon the cloud put forth His sickle upon the earth, and the earth was harvested.

[17]And another angel came out of the temple in heaven, he also having a sharp sickle. [18]And another angel having authority over the fire came out of the altar, and he called in a loud cry to the *one* having the sharp sickle, saying, "Put forth your sharp sickle, and gather the clusters from the vine of the earth, because its grapes have fully ripened."

[19]And the angel put forth his sickle to the earth and gathered the vine of the earth, and cast *them* into the great winepress of the wrath of God. [20]And the winepress was trodden outside the city, and blood flowed out of the winepress, as high as the bridles of the horses, to the distance of one thousand six hundred stadia.[d]

a 5 BYZ and TR include *before the throne of God*
b 8 Isaiah 21:9; Daniel 4:30
c 14 See Daniel 7:13
d 20 About 183 miles or 29 kilometers

Revelation 15
The Song of Moses and the Lamb

[1]And I saw another great and wonderful sign in heaven: seven angels, having seven plagues—the last, because in them the wrath of God was completed.

[2]And I saw *something* like a sea of glass mingled with fire, and those conquering over the beast, and over its image, and over the number of its name, standing upon the sea of glass, having harps of God. [3]And they are singing the song of Moses, the servant of God, and the song of the Lamb, saying,

> "Great and wonderful *are* Your works,
> Lord God the Almighty!
> Righteous and true *are* Your ways,
> O King of the nations![a]
> [4]Who should not fear *You*, O Lord,
> and will glorify Your name?
> For *You* alone *are* holy.
> For all the nations will come and will worship before You,
> because Your righteous acts have been revealed."

Preparation for Judgment

[5]And after these things I looked, and the temple of the tabernacle of the testimony in heaven was opened. [6]And the seven angels having the seven plagues came forth out of the temple, having been clothed in pure, bright linen, and having been girded with golden sashes around the chests.

[7]And one of the four living creatures gave to the seven angels seven golden bowls full of the wrath of God, the *One* living to the ages of the ages. [8]And the temple was filled with smoke from the glory of God, and from His power; and no one was able to enter into the temple until the seven plagues of the seven angels were completed.

a 3 SBL and WH *ages*; TR *saints*

Revelation 16
The First Six Bowls of Wrath

¹And I heard a loud voice from the temple saying to the seven angels, "Go and pour out into the earth the seven bowls of the wrath of God."
²And the first departed and poured out his bowl into the earth, and an evil and grievous sore came upon the men having the mark of the beast and those worshiping its image.
³And the second poured out his bowl into the sea, and it became blood, as of *one* dead; and every living soul that was in the sea died.
⁴And the third poured out his bowl into the rivers and the springs of the waters, and they became blood. ⁵And I heard the angel of the waters saying:

"Righteous are You
    the *One* being, and having been, O holy One,
    because You have judged these things,
⁶because they have poured out *the* blood of saints and of prophets,
    and You have given to them blood to drink,
    they are worthy."

⁷And I heard the altar saying:
"Yes, Lord God Almighty,
    true and righteous *are* Your judgments."

⁸And the fourth poured out his bowl upon the sun, and there was given to it to scorch men with fire. ⁹And the men were scorched with great heat, and they blasphemed the name of God, the *One* having authority over these plagues; and they did not repent to give Him glory.
¹⁰And the fifth poured out his bowl upon the throne of the beast, and its kingdom became darkened, and they were gnawing their tongues for the distress, ¹¹and they blasphemed the God of heaven on account of their distresses, and on account of their sores; and they did not repent of their deeds.

¹²And the sixth poured out his bowl upon the great river Euphrates, and its water was dried up, so that the way might be prepared of the kings of the rising of the sun.
¹³And I saw *coming* out of the mouth of the dragon, and out of the mouth of the beast, and out of the mouth of the false prophet, three unclean spirits, like frogs; ¹⁴for they are spirits of demons, performing signs, which go forth to the kings of the whole inhabited *world*, to gather them together unto the battle of the great day of God the Almighty.
¹⁵"Behold, I am coming like a thief. Blessed *is* the *one* watching and keeping his garments, so that he should not walk naked and they might see his shame."
¹⁶And he gathered them together unto the place called in Hebrew Armageddon.

The Seventh Bowl of Wrath

¹⁷And the seventh poured out his bowl upon the air, and a loud voice came out from the temple, from the throne, saying, "It is done!"
¹⁸And there were flashes of lightning, and voices, and thunders; and there was a great earthquake, such as there had not been since men were upon the earth—so great *was the* earthquake, so mighty, ¹⁹and the great city was *split* into three parts, and the cities of the nations fell, and Babylon the great was remembered before God, to give her the cup of the wine of the fury of His wrath.
²⁰And every island fled, and mountains were not to be found. ²¹And a great hail, about a talent weight,[a] comes down out of heaven upon the men. And the men blasphemed God on account of the plague of the hail, for the plague of it is exceedingly severe.

a 21 About 100 pounds or 45 kilograms

Revelation 17
The Woman on the Beast

¹And one of the seven angels having the seven bowls came and spoke with me, saying, "Come here, I will show you the

punishment of the great prostitute, the *one* sitting upon many waters, ²with whom the kings of the earth have committed sexual immorality, and those dwelling on the earth have been made drunk with the wine of her sexual immorality."

³And he carried me away in *the* Spirit into a wilderness, and I saw a woman sitting upon a scarlet beast being full of names of blasphemy, having seven heads and ten horns. ⁴And the woman was clothed in purple and scarlet, and adorned with gold and precious stone and pearls, holding a golden cup in her hand, being full of abominations and the impurity of her sexual immorality. ⁵And upon her forehead a name was written, a mystery:
BABYLON THE GREAT,
THE MOTHER OF THE PROSTITUTES,
AND OF THE ABOMINATIONS OF THE EARTH.

The Mystery Explained

⁶And I saw the woman being drunk with the blood of the saints, and with the blood of the witnesses of Jesus. And having seen her, I marveled with great wonder.

⁷And the angel said to me, "Why did you marvel? I will tell you the mystery of the woman, and of the beast carrying her, having the seven heads and the ten horns.

⁸The beast that you saw was, and is not, and is about to come up out of the abyss and go into destruction; and those dwelling on the earth whose names are not written in the book of life from *the* foundation of *the* world will wonder, seeing the beast which was, and is not, and yet will be.

⁹Here *is* the mind having wisdom: The seven heads are seven mountains, where the woman sits on them; ¹⁰and there are seven kings. The five are fallen, the one is, the other has not yet come; and when he shall have come, it behooves him to remain a little while.

¹¹And the beast which was, and is not, is also himself an eighth, and is of the seven, and goes into destruction. ¹²And the ten horns which you saw are ten kings who have not yet received a kingdom, but receive authority as kings one hour, along with the beast. ¹³These have one mind, and they shall give up their power and authority to the beast.

The Victory of the Lamb

¹⁴These will make war with the Lamb, and the Lamb will overcome them, because He is Lord of lords and King of kings; and those with Him *are* called and chosen and faithful."

¹⁵And he says to me, "The waters that you saw where the prostitute sits are peoples and multitudes and nations and tongues. ¹⁶And the ten horns that you saw, and the beast, these will hate the prostitute, and will make her desolate and naked, and will eat her flesh, and will burn her with fire. ¹⁷For God has put into their hearts to accomplish His purpose, and to do one purpose, and to give their kingdom to the beast, until the words of God will be fulfilled. ¹⁸And the woman whom you saw is the great city, having kingship over the kings of the earth."

Revelation 18
Babylon is Fallen

¹After these things I saw another angel descending out of heaven, having great authority; and the earth was illuminated from his glory. ²And he cried out in a mighty voice, saying:

"Fallen, Fallen is Babylon the great!ᵃ
And she has become a habitation of demons,
and a prison of every unclean spirit,
and a prison of every unclean bird,
and a prison of every unclean creatureᵇ also having been hated.

³For all the nations have drunk
ofᶜ the wine of the wrath of her sexual immorality;

and the kings of the earth have committed sexual immorality with her;
> and the merchants of the earth have been enriched
> through the power of her luxury."

⁴And I heard another voice from heaven, saying:
> "Come out of her, my people,ᵈ
> > so that you may not have fellowship in her sins,
> > and so that you may not receive of her plagues.

⁵For her sins have been heaped as high as heaven,
> and God has remembered her iniquities.

⁶Give back to her as she also has rendered;
> and pay back double to her,
> twofold according to her works.

In the cup which she has mixed,
> mix double to her.

⁷So much as she has glorified herself and lived in luxury,
> give to her as much torment and misery,

because in her heart she says, 'I sit *as* a queen,
> and I am never a widow,
> and never shall I see mourning.'

⁸Because of this, her plagues will come in one day,
> death and misery and famine,

and she will be burned up with fire,
> because mighty *is the* Lord God, the *One* having judged her."

Lament over Babylon

⁹And the kings of the earth, the *ones* having committed sexual immorality and having lived luxuriously with her, will weep and will wail for her when they see the smoke of her burning, ¹⁰standing from afar because of the fear of her torment, saying:
> "Woe, woe, the great city, Babylon, the strong city!
> For *in* one hour
> > your judgment has come."

¹¹And the merchants of the earth weep and mourn for her, because no one buys their cargo *any* longer— ¹²cargo of gold, and of silver, and of precious stone, and of pearls; and of fine linen, and of purple, and of silk, and of scarlet; and all thyine wood and of every article of ivory and every article of most precious wood; and of bronze, and of iron, and of marble; ¹³and cinnamon, and spice, and incense, and myrrh, and frankincense; and wine, and oil, and finest flour, and wheat; and cattle, and sheep, and of horses, and of chariots; and of slaves and souls of men.

¹⁴"And the ripe fruits of the desire of your soul
> are departed from you,
> and all the sumptuous things and the splendid things have departed from you,
> and they will not find them *any* longer."

¹⁵The merchants of these things having been enriched from her will stand from afar, weeping and mourning because of the fear of her torment, ¹⁶saying:
> "Woe, woe, the great city,
> > having been clothed with fine linen and purple and scarlet,
> > and having been adorned with gold and precious stone and pearl!

¹⁷For *in* one hour
> > such great wealth has been brought to desolation."

And every shipmaster, and all those sailing to a place, and sailors, and as many as trade by the sea, stood at a distance, ¹⁸and were crying out, seeing the smoke of her burning, saying, 'What *is* like the great city?' ¹⁹And they cast dust upon their heads, and they were crying out, weeping and mourning, saying:
> "Woe, woe, the great city,

in which all those having ships in the sea
>were enriched through her wealth!

For in one hour she has been brought to desolation."

²⁰"Rejoice over her, O heaven,
>and *you* saints and apostles and prophets,

because God has judged for you
>the judgment against her."

The Doom of Babylon

²¹And one mighty angel took up a stone like a great millstone and cast *it* into the sea, saying:

"Thus Babylon will be cast down with violence,
>the great city,
>and shall never be found any longer.

²²And *the* sound of harpists and musicians,
>and flute players and trumpeters,
>shall never be heard in you any longer.

And any craftsmen of any craft
>shall never be found in you any longer,

and *the* sound of a millstone
>shall never be heard in you any longer.

²³And *the* light of lamp
>shall never shine in you any longer,

and *the* voice of a bridegroom and a bride
>shall never be heard in you any longer.

For your merchants were the great ones of the earth,
>because by your sorcery all the nations were deceived."

²⁴And in her was found *the* blood of prophets and of saints and of all those having been slain on the earth.

a 2 Isaiah 21:9; Daniel 4:30
b 2 NE, WH, BYZ, and TR do not include *and a prison of every unclean creature*
c 3 SBL and WH *have fallen by*
d 4 Jeremiah 51:45

Revelation 19
Rejoicing in Heaven

¹After these things I heard *something* like a loud voice of a great multitude in heaven, crying out:

"Hallelujah!
The salvation and the glory and the power to our God!

²For His judgments *are* true and righteous,

because He has judged the great prostitute,
>who had corrupted the earth with her sexual immorality,

and He has avenged the blood of His servants,
>out of her hand."

³And a second time they said:
"Hallelujah!
And her smoke goes up to the ages of the ages."

⁴And the twenty-four elders and the four living creatures fell down and worshiped God, the *One* sitting on the throne, saying:

"Amen, Hallelujah!"

⁵And a voice came forth from the throne, saying:

"Praise our God,
>all *you* His servants,
and those fearing Him,
>the small and the great!"

The Marriage of the Lamb

⁶And I heard *something* like *the* voice of a great multitude, and like *the* sound of many waters, and like a sound of mighty thunders, saying:

"Hallelujah!
>For the Lord God our Almighty has reigned.

⁷We should rejoice and should exult
>and will give to Him the glory,

because the marriage of the Lamb has come,
>and His bride has made herself ready.

⁸And it was given to her
> that she should be clothed in bright, pure, fine linen."

For the fine linen is the righteous acts of the saints.

⁹And he says to me, "Write, 'Blessed *are* those having been invited to the supper of the marriage of the Lamb.'" And he says to me, "These are the true words of God."

¹⁰And I fell before his feet to worship to him. And he says to me, "See that you not *do this*. I am a fellow servant with you and your brothers, holding the testimony of Jesus. Worship God! For the testimony of Jesus is the spirit of prophecy."

The Rider on the White Horse

¹¹And I saw heaven having been opened, and behold, a white horse, and the *One* sitting upon it called Faithful and True, and in righteousness He judges and makes war. ¹²Now His eyes *are* like a flame of fire, and upon His head many diadems, having a name having been written, which no one except He Himself knows, ¹³and having been clothed with a garment having been dipped in blood.ᵃ And His name is called The Word of God. ¹⁴And the armies who were in heaven, having been clothed in pure, white, fine linen were following Him upon white horses. ¹⁵And out of His mouth goes forth a sharp sword, so that with it He may strike down the nations; and He will shepherd them with a rod of iron.ᵇ And He treads the press of the wine of the fury of the wrath of God the Almighty. ¹⁶And He has a name having been written upon the robe and upon His thigh:

KING OF KINGS AND LORD OF LORDS.

Defeat of the Beast and False Prophet

¹⁷And I saw one angel standing in the sun, and he cried out in loud a voice, saying to all the birds flying in mid-heaven, "Come, gather yourselves unto the great supper of God, ¹⁸so that you may eat *the* flesh of kings, and *the* flesh of commanders, and *the* flesh of captains, and *the* flesh of horses and of those sitting on them, and *the* flesh of all, both free and slaves, and small and great."

¹⁹And I saw the beast, and the kings of the earth, and their armies, having been gathered together to make war with the *One* sitting on the horse and with His army. ²⁰And the beast was captured, and with him the false prophet, the *one* having done the signs before him, by which he deceived those having received the mark of the beast and those worshiping its image. The two were cast living into the lake of fire burning with brimstone. ²¹And the rest were killed with the sword of the *One* sitting on the horse having gone forth out of his mouth. And all the birds were filled with their flesh.

a 13 WH *sprinkled with blood*
b 15 Psalm 2:9

Revelation 20
Satan Bound

¹And I saw an angel descending out of heaven, holding in his hand the key of the Abyss, and a great chain. ²And he seized the dragon, the ancient serpent, who is *the* devil and Satan, and bound him for a thousand years. ³And he cast him into the Abyss, and shut and sealed *it* over him, so that he should not deceive the nations any longer, until the thousand years were completed. After these things it is necessary for him to be released for a little time.

⁴And I saw thrones, and they sat upon them, and judgment was given to them, and the souls of those having been beheaded because of the testimony of Jesus and because of the word of God, and those who did not worship the beast, nor his image, and did not take the mark upon the forehead, and upon their hand. And they lived and reigned with Christ a thousand years.

⁵The rest of the dead did not live again until the thousand years shall have been completed. This *is* the first resurrection.

⁶Blessed and holy *is* the *one* having a part in the first resurrection! Over these the second death has no authority, but they will be priests of God and of Christ, and will reign with Him a thousand years.

Satan Cast into the Lake of Fire

⁷And when the thousand years shall have been completed, Satan will be released out of his prison, ⁸and will go out to deceive the nations in the four corners of the earth, Gog and Magog, to gather them together unto the war, of whom *is* the number of them like the sand of the sea.
⁹And they marched up over the breadth of the earth and encircled the camp of the saints and the city having been beloved. But fire came down out of heaven[a] and devoured them. ¹⁰And the devil, the *one* deceiving them, was cast into the lake of fire and of sulfur, where the beast and the false prophet also *are*; and they will be tormented day and night to the ages of the ages.

The Final Judgment

¹¹And I saw a great white throne and the *One* sitting on it, from whose face the earth and heaven fled, and no place was found for them. ¹²And I saw the dead, great and small, standing before the throne, and books were opened.
And another book was opened, which is the *one* of life. And the dead were judged out of the things having been written in the books, according to their deeds. ¹³And the sea gave up the dead who were in it; and death and Hades gave up the dead who were in them; and each *of them* were judged according to their works.
¹⁴And death and Hades were cast into the lake of fire. This is the second death, the lake of fire. ¹⁵And if anyone was not found having been written in the book of life, he was cast into the lake of fire.

a 9 BYZ and TR include *from God*

Revelation 21
A New Heaven and a New Earth

¹And I saw a new heaven and a new earth,[a] for the first heaven and the first earth had passed away, and the sea is no more. ²And I saw the holy city, *the* new Jerusalem, coming down out of heaven from God, having been prepared as a bride having been adorned for her husband.
³And I heard a great voice out of heaven, saying:

"Behold, the tabernacle of God *is* with men,
and He will tabernacle with them,
and they will be His peoples,
and God Himself will be with them *as* their God.[b]

⁴And He will wipe away every tear from their eyes,[c]
and death will be no more
nor mourning nor crying nor pain;
they will be no more,
because the former things have passed away."

⁵And the *One* sitting on the throne said, "Behold, I make all things new." And He says, "Write *this*, because these words are faithful and true." ⁶And He said to me, "It is done! I am the Alpha and the Omega, the beginning and the end. To the *one* thirsting I will give of the spring of the water of life freely. ⁷The *one* overcoming will inherit all things, and I will be his God, and he will be My son. ⁸But to *the* cowardly and unbelieving and having become abominable and murderers and the sexually immoral and sorcerers and idolaters and all liars, their portion *is* in the lake burning with fire and brimstone, which is the second death."

The New Jerusalem

⁹And one of the seven angels having the seven bowls being full of the seven last plagues came and spoke with me, saying, "Come here, I will show you the bride, the wife of the Lamb."

¹⁰And he carried me away in *the* Spirit to a great and high mountain, and he showed me the holy city Jerusalem, descending out of heaven from God, ¹¹having the glory of God. Its radiance *was* like a most precious stone, like a jasper stone being clear as crystal, ¹²having a great and high wall, having twelve gates, and at the gates twelve angels, and names having been inscribed which are the names of the twelve tribes of *the* sons of Israel. ¹³On *the* east *were* three gates, and on *the* north three gates, and on *the* south three gates, and on *the* west three gates. ¹⁴And the wall of the city had twelve foundations, and in them *the* twelve names of the twelve apostles of the Lamb.

¹⁵And the *one* speaking with me had a golden measuring reed, so that he could measure the city, and its gates, and its wall. ¹⁶And the city lies foursquare, and its length the same as also the width. And he measured the city with the reed at twelve thousand stadia.[d] The length and the breadth and the height of it are equal. ¹⁷And he measured its wall, one hundred forty-four cubits,[e] *the* measure of man, that is of the angel.

¹⁸And the structure of its wall *was* jasper, and the city pure gold, like clear glass, ¹⁹the foundations of the wall of the city having been adorned with every precious stone: the first foundation jasper, the second sapphire, the third chalcedony, the fourth emerald, ²⁰the fifth sardonyx, the sixth sardius, the seventh chrysolite, the eighth beryl, the ninth topaz, the tenth chrysoprase, the eleventh jacinth, the twelfth amethyst.

²¹And the twelve gates *were* twelve pearls; each one of the gates respectively was of one pearl, and the street of the city pure gold, transparent as glass.

²²And I saw no temple in it, for the Lord God Almighty is its temple, and the Lamb. ²³And the city has no need of the sun, nor of the moon, that they should shine in it; for the glory of God enlightened it, and its lamp *is* the Lamb. ²⁴And the nations will walk by its light, and the kings of the earth bring their glory[f] into it. ²⁵And its gates shall not be shut by day, for there will be no night there.

²⁶And they will bring the glory and the honor of the nations into it. ²⁷And anything defiling, and those practicing abomination and a lie, never shall enter into it; only those having been written in the Lamb's book of life.

a 1 Isaiah 65:17; 66:22
b 3 SBL, NE, WH, and BYZ do not include *as their God*
c 4 Isaiah 25:8
d 16 About 1,370 miles or 2,200 kilometers
e 17 That is, about 200 feet or 65 meters. The measure could indicate either height or thickness.
f 24 BYZ and TR include *and honor*

Revelation 22
The River of Life

¹And he showed me a river of water of life, clear as crystal, flowing out of the throne of God and of the Lamb. ²In the middle of its street and of the river, on this side and on that side, *was a* tree of life, producing twelve fruits, yielding its fruit according to each month; and the leaves of the tree *are* for *the* healing of the nations.

³And there will not be any curse any longer. And the throne of God and of the Lamb will be in it, and His servants will serve Him. ⁴And they will see His face, and His name *will be* on their foreheads. ⁵And there will be no night there, and they have no need of *the* light of a lamp and of *the* light of *the* sun, because *the* Lord God will enlighten upon them, and they will reign to the ages of the ages.

Jesus is Coming

⁶And he said to me, "These words *are* faithful and true. And the Lord, the God of the spirits of the prophets, sent His angel to show His servants the things that must come to pass in quickness."

⁷"And behold, I am coming quickly. Blessed *is* the *one* keeping the words of the prophecy of this book."

⁸And I, John, *am* the *one* hearing and seeing these things. And when I heard

and saw, I fell down to worship before the feet of the angel showing these things me. ⁹And he says to me, "See that you not *do this*. I am your fellow servant, and with your brothers the prophets, and with those keeping the words of this book. Worship God!"

¹⁰And he says to me, "Do not seal the words of the prophecy of this book; for the time is near. ¹¹The *one* being unrighteous, let him be unrighteous still; and he who is filthy, let him be filthy still; and he who *is* righteous, let him practice righteousness still; and he who *is* holy, let him be holy still."

¹²"Behold, I am coming quickly, and My reward *is* with Me, to give to each as is his work. ¹³I *am* the Alpha and the Omega, the First and the Last, the Beginning and the End."

¹⁴Blessed *are* those washing their robes,[a] that their right will be to the tree of life, and they shall enter into the city by the gates. ¹⁵Outside *are* the dogs, and the sorcerers, and the sexually immoral, and the murderers, and the idolaters, and everyone loving and practicing falsehood.

¹⁶"I, Jesus, have sent My angel to testify to all of you these things in the churches. I am the root and the offspring of David, the bright morning star."

¹⁷And the Spirit and the bride say, "Come!" And the *one* hearing, let him say, "Come!" And the *one* thirsting let him come; the *one* desiring, let him take freely *the* water of life.

Nothing May Be Added

¹⁸I testify to everyone hearing the words of the prophecy of this book: If anyone should add to these things, God will add unto him the plagues having been written in this book. ¹⁹And if anyone should take away from the words of the book of this prophecy, God will take away his part from the tree of life, and out of the holy city, of those having been written in this book.

²⁰The *One* testifying these things says, "Yes, I am coming quickly." Amen. Come, Lord Jesus!

²¹The grace of the Lord Jesus[b] *be* with all the saints.[c]

Amen.[d]

a 14 BYZ and TR *doing his commandments*
b 21 WH and BYZ *the Lord Jesus Christ*; TR *our Lord Jesus Christ*
c 21 SBL, WH, NE, and TR do not include *the saints*
d 21 SBL, WH, NE, and NA do not include *Amen*.